KB100592

1학기 전과정

적중 100 plus

영어 기출문제집

중3

시사 | 송미정

Best Collection

구성과 특징

교과서의 주요 학습 내용을 중심으로 학습 영역별 특성에 맞춰 단계별로 다양한 학습 기회를 제공하여
단원별 학습능력 평가는 물론 중간 및 기말고사 시험 등에 완벽하게 대비할 수 있도록 내용을 구성

Words & Expressions

Step1　Key Words 단원별 핵심 단어 설명 및 풀이
　　　　　Key Expression 단원별 핵심 숙어 및 관용어 설명
　　　　　Word Power 반대 또는 비슷한 뜻 단어 배우기
　　　　　English Dictionary 영어로 배우는 영어 단어

Step2　실력평가 단원별 수시평가 대비 주관식, 객관식 문제풀이

Step3　서술형 대비 학업성취도 및 수행능력평가 대비 서술형 문제풀이

Conversation

Step1　핵심 의사소통 소통에 필요한 주요 표현 방법 요약
　　　　　핵심 Check 기본적인 표현 방법 및 활용능력 확인

Step2　대화문 익히기 교과서 대화문 심층 분석 및 확인

Step3　교과서 확인학습 빈칸 채우기를 통한 문장 완성 능력 확인

Step4　기본평가 시험대비 기초 학습 능력 평가

Step5　실력평가 단원별 수시평가 대비 주관식, 객관식 문제풀이

Step6　서술형 대비 학업성취도 및 수행능력평가 대비 서술형 문제풀이

Grammar

Step1　주요 문법 단원별 주요 문법 사항과 예문을 알기 쉽게 설명
　　　　　핵심 Check 기본 문법사항에 대한 이해 여부 확인

Step2　기본평가 시험대비 기초 학습 능력 평가

Step3　실력평가 단원별 수시평가 대비 주관식, 객관식 문제풀이

Step4　서술형 대비 학업성취도 및 수행능력평가 대비 서술형 문제풀이

Reading

Step1　구문 분석 단원별로 제시된 문장에 대한 구문별 분석과 내용 설명
　　　　　확인문제 문장에 대한 기본적인 이해와 인지능력 확인

Step2　확인학습A 빈칸 채우기를 통한 문장 완성 능력 확인

Step3　확인학습B 제시된 우리말을 영어로 완성하여 작문 능력 키우기

Step4　실력평가 단원별 수시평가 대비 주관식, 객관식 문제풀이

Step5　서술형 대비 학업성취도 및 수행능력평가 대비 서술형 문제풀이
　　　　　교과서 구석구석 교과서에 나오는 기타 문장까지 완벽 학습

Composition

|영역별 핵심문제|

단어 및 어휘, 대화문, 문법, 독해 등 각 영역별 기출문제의 출제 유형을 분석하여 실전에 대비하고 연습할 수 있도록 문제를 배열

|단원별 예상문제|

기출문제를 분석한 후 새로운 시험 출제 경향을 더하여 새롭게 출제될 수 있는 문제를 포함하여 시험에 완벽하게 대비할 수 있도록 준비

|서술형 실전 및 창의사고력 문제|

학교 시험에서 점차 늘어나는 서술형 시험에 집중 대비하고 고득점을 취득하는데 만전을 기하기 위한 학습 코너

|단원별 모의고사|

영역별, 단계별 학습을 모두 마친 후 실전 연습을 위한 모의고사

교과서 파헤치기

- **단어Test1~3** 영어 단어 우리말 쓰기, 우리말을 영어 단어로 쓰기, 영영풀이에 해당하는 단어와 우리말 쓰기

- **대화문Test1~2** 대화문 빈칸 완성 및 전체 대화문 쓰기

- **본문Test1~5** 빈칸 완성, 우리말 쓰기, 문장 배열연습, 영어 작문하기 복습 등 단계별 반복 학습을 통해 교과서 지문에 대한 완벽한 습득

- **구석구석지문Test1~2** 지문 빈칸 완성 및 전문 영어로 쓰기

Contents

Passion for Life

 의사소통 기능

- 정보 묻고 답하기
  A: How was he able to become a famous reporter?
  B: He practiced speaking with people in public.

- 알고 있는지 묻기
  A: Have you heard of Mia, the guitar player?
  B: Yes, I have. I heard that she taught herself to play.

 언어 형식

- too ... to부정사
  You knew that you were **too** far behind **to** win a medal.

- to부정사의 부정형
  For me and my country, it was important **not to** give up.

Words & Expressions

Key Words

- **accept** [æksépt] 동 받다
- **accident** [ǽksidənt] 명 사고
- **admire** [ædmáiər] 동 존중하다
- **athlete** [ǽθliːt] 명 운동선수
- **author** [ɔ́ːθər] 명 작가
- **cartoon** [kɑːrtúːn] 명 만화
- **celebrate** [séləbrèit] 동 축하하다, 기념하다
- **celebration** [sèləbréiʃən] 명 축하
- **ceremony** [sérəmòuni] 명 식, 의식
- **cheer** [tʃiər] 동 환호성을 지르다, 환호하다
- **competition** [kàmpətíʃən] 명 시합
- **congratulate** [kəngrǽtʃulèit] 동 축하하다
- **contest** [kántest] 명 경연
- **decide** [disáid] 동 결정하다
- **developer** [divéləpər] 명 개발자
- **draw** [drɔː] 동 그리다
- **enter** [éntər] 동 들어가다
- **especially** [ispéʃəli] 부 특별히
- **experiment** [ikspérəmənt] 동 실험하다
- **famous** [féiməs] 형 유명한
- **finish line** 결승선
- **happen** [hǽpən] 동 일어나다
- **hurt** [həːrt] 동 다치다
- **injure** [índʒər] 동 부상을 입히다
- **injury** [índʒəri] 명 부상
- **invent** [invént] 동 발명하다
- **knock** [nɑk] 동 두드리다
- **leave** [liːv] 동 떠나다
- **lie** [lai] 명 거짓말
- **marathon** [mǽrəθɑ̀n] 명 마라톤
- **movie** [múːvi] 명 영화
- **nearby** [nìərbái] 형 부근의 부 부근에
- **official** [əfíʃəl] 명 관료, 공무원, 경기 임원
- **passion** [pǽʃən] 명 열정
- **photographer** [fətágrəfər] 명 사진사
- **plan** [plæn] 동 계획을 세우다
- **practice** [prǽktis] 명 연습
- **preparation** [prèpəréiʃən] 명 준비
- **prepare** [pripɛ́ər] 동 준비하다
- **proud** [praud] 형 자랑스러운
- **public** [pʌ́blik] 명 대중
- **realize** [ríːəlàiz] 동 깨닫다
- **remove** [rimúːv] 동 제거하다
- **reporter** [ripɔ́ːrtər] 명 기자, 리포터
- **represent** [rèprizént] 동 대표하다
- **respect** [rispékt] 동 존경하다
- **shout** [ʃaut] 동 외치다
- **stadium** [stéidiəm] 명 경기장
- **suddenly** [sʌ́dnli] 부 갑자기
- **toward** [tɔːrd] 전 ~ 쪽으로, ~을 향하여
- **training** [tréiniŋ] 명 훈련
- **try** [trai] 명 시도
- **volunteer** [vɑləntíər] 명 자원봉사자
- **whenever** [hwenévər] 접 ~할 때마다
- **winner** [wínər] 명 우승자, 수상자

Key Expressions

- **as a result** 결과적으로
- **at war** 전쟁 중인
- **be done with** ~을 끝내다
- **be good at** ~을 잘하다
- **be into** ~에 관심이 많다
- **be proud of** ~을 자랑스러워하다
- **come up to** ~에 다가가다
- **fall to the ground** 땅에 넘어지다
- **far behind** 멀리 뒤쳐진
- **give up** 포기하다
- **in public** 공개적으로, 사람들이 있는 데서
- **keep -ing** 계속 ~하다
- **more than** ~ 이상
- **stand for** ~을 나타내다, 상징하다
- **take a picture** 사진을 찍다
- **teach oneself** 독학하다
- **that's why** 그것이 ~하는 이유다, 그런 이유로 ~
- **Why not?** 왜 아니겠어?

Word Power

※ 서로 비슷한 뜻을 가진 어휘

- admire 존경하다 : respect 존경하다
- cheer 환호하다 : encourage 격려하다
- happen 일어나다 : take place 발생하다
- passion 열정 : enthusiasm 열정
- remove 제거하다 : eliminate 제거하다

- author 작가 : writer 작가
- competition 시합 : contest 경연
- leave 떠나다 : depart 떠나다
- realize 깨닫다 : understand 이해하다

※ 서로 반대되는 뜻을 가진 어휘

- accept 받다 ↔ refuse 거절하다
- famous 유명한 ↔ infamous 악명이 높은
- public 대중적인 ↔ private 사적인

- praise 칭찬하다 ↔ blame 비난하다
- far 먼 ↔ near 가까운
- suddenly 갑자기 ↔ expectedly 예상대로

※ 동사+-ation = 명사

- prepare 준비하다 – preparation 준비
- invite 초대하다 – invitation 초대
- recommend 추천하다 – recommendation 추천
- organize 조직하다 – organization 조직
- celebrate 축하하다 – celebration 축하
- experiment 실험하다 – experimentation 실험

- inform 알리다, 정보를 주다 – information 정보
- transport 수송하다 – transportation 수송
- found 설립하다 – foundation 설립
- admire 존중하다 – admiration 존중
- congratulate 축하하다 – congratulation 축하
- realize 깨닫다 – realization 깨달음

English Dictionary

- accept 받다
  → to take something that someone offers
    어떤 사람이 제안하는 것을 받아들이다

- athlete 운동선수
  → a person who plays sports well 운동을 잘하는 사람

- author 작가
  → the writer of a book 책의 저자

- congratulate 축하하다
  → to tell someone that you are happy when something pleasant has happened to them
    어떤 좋은 일이 일어난 사람에게 기쁘다고 말하다

- far 먼
  → used to talk about a great distance
    매우 먼 거리에 관하여 말할 때 사용되는

- give up 포기하다
  → to stop doing something that you have tried hard to do 열심히 애쓰던 일을 중단하다

- injury 부상

  → harm or damage to a person's or an animal's body
    사람이나 동물의 신체에 가해지는 손상

- marathon 마라톤
  → a race where people run a distance of 42.195 kilometers 42.195킬로미터 거리를 달리는 시합

- passion 열정
  → a strong emotion or feeling 강렬한 정서나 감정

- realize 깨닫다
  → to become aware of something 어떤 것을 인식하게 되다

- remove 없애다
  → to take something away 무엇인가를 치우다

- represent 대표하다
  → to officially speak or take action for people in a group
    집단에 속한 사람들을 위하여 공식적으로 대신 말하거나 행동을 취하다

- toward ~을 향해서
  → in the direction of someone or something
    어떤 사람 또는 사물이 있는 방향으로

Words & Expressions 시험대비 실력평가 **Step2**

서답형

01 〈보기〉와 같은 관계가 되도록 빈칸에 알맞은 말을 쓰시오.

┤ 보기 ├

invite : invitation

(1) _____ : celebration
(2) _____ : information

02 다음 빈칸에 들어가기에 적절한 단어를 써서 문장을 완성했을 때 자연스러운 것은?

The last runner finished the race more than an hour before. "There will be no more runners coming," the _____ decided.

① Kelly represented our _____ at the quiz show.
② Running a _____ is challenging.
③ This area is only for the _____.
④ Harry prepares _____ every Sunday for his family.
⑤ The student was proud of himself when he got a good _____ on the math exam.

03 다음 중 밑줄 친 부분의 뜻풀이가 바르지 <u>않은</u> 것은?

① Finally, the <u>athlete</u> was able to take part in the Olympic games. (운동선수)
② Eric's passing the exam called for a big <u>celebration</u>. (축하)
③ They <u>cheered</u> when the soccer player scored the first goal. (환호했다)
④ My sister is busy preparing for her wedding <u>ceremony</u>. (의식, 기념식)
⑤ I <u>gave up</u> trying to solve the problem because it was difficult. (나누어주었다)

04 다음 중 〈보기〉에 있는 단어를 사용하여 자연스러운 문장을 만들 수 <u>없는</u> 것은?

┤ 보기 ├

cheered marathon remove ceremony

① There will be a graduation _____ in the auditorium.
② My classmates _____ for me and shouted my name.
③ Kee-chung Sohn was a _____ runner who won a gold medal at the 1936 Berlin Olympics.
④ The players are _____ for the final match.
⑤ I boiled the meat to _____ the fat.

05 다음 밑줄 친 부분과 의미가 가장 가까운 것을 고르시오.

He became an <u>author</u> late in life.

① competitor   ② athlete
③ creator   ④ writer
⑤ developer

06 다음 빈칸에 공통으로 들어가기에 알맞은 것은?

• She must be very proud _____ herself.
• How was Hyeon Chung able to be one _____ the final four players in the tennis competition?

① to   ② of   ③ in
④ on   ⑤ with

01 주어진 단어를 이용해 빈칸을 완성하시오.

> Careful _____ for the exam is essential.

➡ _____ (prepare)

02 다음 짝지어진 단어의 관계가 같도록 빈칸에 알맞은 말을 쓰시오.

> congratulate : congratulation
> = experiment : _____

[03-04] 빈칸에 공통으로 들어갈 단어를 쓰시오.

03

> • She shut her eyes and wished for him to _____ better.
> • Left alone, the problem could _____ worse.

04

> • There is no bus service. That's _____ I usually take a taxi.
> • "Let's eat out." "_____ not?"

05 밑줄 친 부분과 의미가 가장 가까운 단어를 주어진 철자로 시작하여 쓰시오.

> His father noticed his <u>passion</u> for football.

➡ e_____

06 빈칸에 알맞은 단어를 〈보기〉에서 골라 쓰시오.

> ┤ 보기 ├
> up   done   good   result

(1) Skiing is not easy. Not many people are _____ at skiing.

(2) When I'm _____ with the pencil case, I'm planning to make my own desk.

(3) Reporters came _____ to Wasiqi and started asking him questions.

(4) Finally I won a marathon in Germany. As a _____, I was able to come to Atlanta.

07 다음 우리말에 맞게 빈칸에 알맞은 말을 쓰시오.

(1) 네가 만화 클럽에 가입했다고 들었어. 만화 그리기에 관심 있니?

➡ I heard that you joined the cartoon club. Are you _____ in drawing cartoons?

(2) 경기 중에 제 상처는 점점 더 심각해졌지만, 저는 포기할 수 없었습니다.

➡ The injury got worse during the race, but I couldn't _____ up.

(3) 그는 대중 앞에서 사람들과 말하는 것을 연습했다.

➡ He practiced speaking with people in _____.

(4) 그러나 그는 계속 결승선을 향해 움직였다.

➡ Still, he kept going _____ the finish line.

Conversation

교과서

1 정보 묻고 답하기

> **A** How was he able to become a famous reporter? 그가 어떻게 유명한 기자가 될 수 있었지?
> **B** He practiced speaking with people in public.
> 그는 대중 앞에서 사람들과 말하는 것을 연습했어.

■ 상대에게 방법 등의 정보를 요청할 때는 "How 동사+주어 ~?"(어떻게 ~?)로 물어볼 수 있다. "How was she/he able to ~?" 또는 "How were you able to ~?"는 "어떻게 ~할 수 있게 되었는가?"라는 뜻으로 어떻게 된 일인지에 대하여 묻는 말이다. 자신이 원하는 정보에 따라 시간, 장소, 이유, 방법 등 적절한 의문사로 물을 수 있다. 각각의 의문사는 when(언제), where(어디서), who(누가), what(무엇을), how(어떻게), why(왜)의 의미를 가진다.

■ 의문사를 사용하지 않고 원하는 정보를 묻고자 할 때 사용하는 표현으로는 "Can/Could you tell me ~?", "Would/Will you please tell me ~?" 등이 있다. 동사 know를 사용하여 "Do you know ~?", "Do you know 의문사절?", "Do you happen to know 의문사 ~?" 등도 상대에게 정보를 요청하는 표현이고, "Would you like to show me ~?"(~에 대해서 알려주시겠습니까?)와 같은 표현으로도 상대에게 정보를 요청할 수 있다.

■ 상대에게 정보를 요청하는 표현은 평서문의 형태로 "I wonder/am wondering ~."(나는 ~가 궁금하다) 처럼 말할 수도 있다. wonder를 사용할 때 어순은 「I wonder+의문사+주어+동사~.」, 「I wonder+if/whether+주어+동사 ~.」이다. 또한 궁금한 내용을 "I want to know ~.", "I don't know why ~."로 표현할 수 있다.

정보 묻고 답하기

• How was she/he able to ~?	그녀가/그가 어떻게 ~할 수 있게 되었니?
• Could/Can you tell me ~?	~에 대해 말해 줄 수 있니?
• Can I ask you + 의문사절?	~에 대하여 물어봐도 되니?
• Do you know ~?	~을 알고 있니?
• I want to know 명사구/명사절.	~을 알고 싶다.
• I'm wondering + if/whether 주어+동사/의문사절.	~인지 궁금하다.

핵심 Check

1. 다음 우리말에 해당하는 영어 문장을 주어진 단어를 포함하여 완성하시오.

B: _____? (able / so well)

(어떻게 그녀가 영어를 그렇게 잘 말할 수 있게 되었지?)

G: She learned English by watching many Hollywood movies.

② 알고 있는지 묻기

> **A** Have you heard of Mia, the guitar player? 미아라는 기타 연주자에 대하여 들어 본 적이 있니?
>
> **B** Yes, I have. I heard that she taught herself to play.
> 응, 들어 봤어. 그녀가 연주를 독학으로 배웠다고 들었어.

- "Have you heard of/about ~?"는 "~대하여 들어 본 적이 있니?"라는 의미로 상대방이 지금 이야기하는 것에 대해 알고 있는지의 여부를 물어보는 말이다. 접속사 that을 사용하여 "Have you heard that 주어+동사 ~?" 형태로 말할 수도 있다.

- 어떤 사실을 상대방이 알고 있는지 물어보는 말은 know를 사용하여 "Do you know about ~?"(~을 아십니까?) 또는 "You know about ~, don't you?", "Did you know that ~?", "Do you know (about) ~?"라고 물어볼 수도 있다. "You know ~, don't you?"는 "너는 ~을 알고 있지?"라는 뜻으로 상대방이 이미 알고 있을 법한 소재의 이야기를 꺼낼 때 사용한다. hear를 사용하여 "Have you (ever) heard about ~?"(~을 들어본 적이 있니?) 또는 "Did you hear about ~?"라고 하면 know를 사용하여 직접적으로 물어보는 것보다는 완화된 느낌을 준다.

- "Have you heard ~?"는 현재완료를 사용하여 어떤 일에 대하여 과거에 들어 본 적이 있어서 현재에 그것을 알고 있는지 물어보는 것으로, 현재완료의 용법 중에서 '경험'에 해당한다. "Have you heard ~?"에 대한 대답은 "Yes, I have.", "No, I haven't."라고 하여야 하지만 경우에 따라서는 "Have you heard ~?"로 질문하는 경우에 그 의도가 새로운 정보를 전달하는 것일 때도 있기 때문에 "Really?" "I didn't know that." 등으로 대답하기도 한다.

알고 있는지 묻기

- Have you (ever) heard (about) ~? (한번이라도) ~을(에 대해서) 들어 본 적이 있습니까?

- Have you been told about ~? ~에 대하여 들어 본 적이 있지?

- You know that ~, don't you? 너 ~을 알지, 그렇지 않니? • Do you know about/that ~? ~을 아십니까?

- Are you aware of/that ~? ~을 알고 있니? • Do you realize that ~? ~을 알고 있니?

핵심 Check

2. 다음 밑줄 친 말 대신 쓰기에 적절한 것은?

B: <u>Have you heard of</u> the winner of the singing contest?

G: No, I haven't. Who won?

B: The winner is Vintop, who wrote all of his own songs.

① Why did you know ② Have you been told about

③ What have you told ④ Have you talked about

⑤ How did you realize

Conversation 교과서 대화문 익히기

 Real-Life Zone

G: ❶Have you heard of Eui Hyun Sin, the skier?

B: No. Who is he?

G: He's a Paralympian skier. He won the first gold medal for Korea in the 2018 Winter Paralympics.

B: Wow! That's great.

G: ❷He was in a car accident in his early twenties and hurt his legs.

B: How was he able to become a skier?

G: After his accident, he tried several different sports to get better. Then he became especially interested in skiing.

B: Skiing is not easy. Not many people are good at skiing.

G: ❸That's why he's so respected.

G: 신의현이라는 스키 선수에 대해 들어 본 적 있니?
B: 아니, 그가 누구야?
G: 그는 페럴림픽의 스키 선수야. 그는 2018 동계 페럴림픽에서 한국의 첫 금메달을 땄어.
B: 와! 훌륭하다.
G: 그는 20대 초반에 차 사고를 당하고 다리를 다쳤어.
B: 어떻게 그가 스키 선수가 될 수 있었니?
G: 사고 후에 그는 회복하기 위해 여러 가지 운동들을 시도했어. 그때 그는 특히 스키 타는 것에 관심을 가지게 됐어.
B: 스키를 타는 것은 쉽지 않잖아. 스키를 잘 타는 사람들은 많지 않아.
G: 그것이 그가 그렇게 존경받는 이유야.

❶ "Have you heard of ~?"는 "~에 대하여 들어 본 적이 있니?"라고 상대에게 알고 있는지를 묻는 질문이다.
❷ "in his early twenties"는 "이십대 초반에"라는 뜻으로 "~십대"는 "~ties"라고 한다.
❸ "That's why"는 "그런 이유로 ~하다/그것이 ~한 이유이다"의 뜻으로 관계부사의 선행사 the reason이 생략된 표현이다.

Check(√) True or False

(1) Eui Hyun Sin won the first gold medal for Korea in the 2018 Winter Paralympics.   T ☐ F ☐

(2) He was in a car accident in his early thirties and hurt his legs.   T ☐ F ☐

(3) After his accident, he tried several different sports to get better.   T ☐ F ☐

 Wrap Up

B: Sora, ❶have you heard about the fire last night?

G: Yes, I heard that there was a big fire in a building nearby. Was anybody hurt?

B: No, one man saved ten people ❷who were in the building.

G: Oh, really? How was he able to save so many people?

B: He knocked on every door to tell people to leave the building.

G: Wow, that's amazing!

B: 소라야, 지난밤 화재에 대해 들었니?
G: 응, 이 근처 건물에서 큰 화재가 있었다고 들었어. 다친 사람이 있어?
B: 아니, 한 남자가 건물 안에 있던 열 명의 사람들을 구했어.
G: 오, 진짜? 어떻게 그는 그 많은 사람들을 구할 수 있었니?
B: 그는 사람들에게 건물을 떠나라고 말하기 위해서 모든 문을 두드렸어.
G: 와, 정말 놀랍구나!

❶ "last night"은 명사 "the fire"를 수식한다. last night이 동사를 수식할 때는 현재완료를 쓸 수 없다.
❷ who는 주격 관계대명사로 ten people을 선행사로 하고 있다.

Check(√) True or False

(4) Sora didn't hear about the fire last night.   T ☐ F ☐

(5) One man knocked on every door to tell people to leave the building.   T ☐ F ☐

Listen & Speak 1 Listen

1. B: How was she able to become a great runner?
   G: She ran 3 kilometers every day.
2. G: How was he able to become a basketball player?
   B: He was short, but he ❶practiced shooting three-point shots a lot.
3. B: How was she able to speak English so well?
   G: She learned English ❷by watching many Hollywood movies.
4. G: How was he able to become a famous reporter?
   B: He practiced speaking with people in public.

❶ practiced의 목적어로 동명사 shooting이 사용되었다.
❷ 전치사 by의 목적어로 동명사가 쓰였다.

 Listen & Speak 1 A-1

B: How was Thomas Edison able to invent so many things?
G: Many people think that he invented things on his first try, but that's not true.
B: Oh, really?
G: Yes. Whenever he invented something, he experimented many times.
B: Maybe ❶that's why so many people admire him.

❶ "that's why ~."는 "that's the reason why ~"에서 선행사 the reason을 생략한 형태로 "그런 이유로 ~하다."로 해석한다.

 Listen & Speak 1 A-2

G: How was Hyeon Chung able to be one of the final four players in the tennis competition?
B: He could do it only after years of hard training.
G: I see. ❶When did he start playing tennis?
B: He started to play tennis when he was seven.

❶ "When ~?"은 시점을 묻는 말이므로 현재완료와는 같이 쓰지 않는다.

 Listen & Speak 2 Listen

1. B: Have you heard of the winner of the singing contest?
   G: No, I haven't. Who won?
   B: The winner is Vintop, ❶who wrote all of his own songs.
2. G: Have you heard of Mia, the guitar player?
   B: Yes, I have. ❷I heard that she taught herself to play.
3. B: Have you heard about BTG, the world famous dance group?
   G: Yes, I have. I have watched their video many times on the Internet.
4. G: Have you heard of Jiho, the photographer?
   B: No, I haven't. What kind of pictures does he take?
   G: He usually takes pictures of street artists.

❶ who는 계속 용법으로 쓰인 주격 관계대명사이다.
❷ "teach oneself to ~"는 "~을 독학하다"의 뜻이다.

 Listen & Speak 2 A-1

B: Have you heard about the cartoon club, Edutoon?
G: Yes, I have. ❶Are you interested in drawing cartoons?
B: Yes, I want to be a famous cartoon writer, so I want to join that club.
G: Oh, I didn't know ❷that you're interested in drawing cartoons.

❶ "be interested in"은 "~에 관심을 가지다"의 뜻이다.
❷ that은 접속사로 사용되어 know의 목적어가 되는 명사절을 유도한다.

 Listen & Speak 2 A-2

G: Have you heard of D.I.Y.?
B: No, what is D.I.Y.?
G: D.I.Y. ❶stands for 'do-it-yourself.' I'm really into it. Right now, I'm making a pencil case.
B: What are you going to make after you finish that?
G: ❷When I'm done with the pencil case, I'm planning to make my own desk.

❶ "stand for ~"는 "~을 나타내다, 상징하다"의 뜻이다.
❷ "be done with ~"는 "~을 끝내다"라는 뜻이다.

● 다음 우리말과 일치하도록 빈칸에 알맞은 말을 쓰시오.

Listen & Speak 1 Listen

1. **B:** _____ was she _____ to become a great _____?
   G: She _____ 3 kilometers _____ day.

2. **G:** How was he _____ to become a _____ player?
   B: He was _____, but he _____ shooting three-point shots a lot.

3. **B:** _____ was she _____ to _____ English so _____?
   G: She _____ English by _____ many Hollywood movies.

4. **G:** _____ was he able to _____ a famous _____?
   B: He _____ speaking with people in _____.

Listen & Speak 1-A

1. **B:** _____ was Thomas Edison _____ to invent so many things?
   G: Many people _____ that he _____ things on his _____ try, but that's not _____.
   B: Oh, _____?
   G: Yes. _____ he invented something, he _____ many times.
   B: Maybe that's _____ so many people _____ him.

2. **G:** _____ was Hyeon Chung able to be one of the _____ four _____ in the tennis competition?
   B: He _____ do it _____ years of hard training.
   G: I see. When did he start _____ _____?
   B: He _____ to play tennis when he was _____.

Listen & Speak 2 Listen

1. **B:** _____ you heard of the _____ of the singing _____?
   G: No, I _____. Who won?
   B: The _____ is Vintop, who wrote all of his _____ songs.

2. **G:** Have you _____ of Mia, the _____ _____?
   B: Yes, I have. I heard that she _____ herself to play.

3. **B:** Have you _____ about BTG, the world famous _____ group?
   G: Yes, I have. I have _____ their video many _____ on the Internet.

4. **G:** Have you _____ of Jiho, the _____?
   B: No, I _____. What kind of _____ does he _____?
   G: He usually _____ pictures of _____ artists.

해석

1. **B:** 어떻게 그녀는 훌륭한 달리기 선수가 될 수 있었니?
   G: 그녀는 매일 3킬로미터를 달렸어.
2. **G:** 어떻게 그는 농구 선수가 될 수 있었니?
   B: 그는 작았지만 3점 슛을 많이 연습했어.
3. **B:** 어떻게 그녀는 영어를 잘할 수 있었니?
   G: 그는 많은 할리우드 영화를 보면서 영어를 배웠어.
4. **G:** 어떻게 그는 유명한 기자가 될 수 있었니?
   B: 그는 대중 앞에서 사람들과 말하는 것을 연습했어.

1. **B:** 어떻게 토머스 에디슨은 그렇게 많은 것들을 발명할 수 있었을까?
   G: 많은 사람들은 그가 그것들을 첫 시도에 발명했다고 생각하지만 그것은 사실이 아니야.
   B: 오, 진짜?
   G: 응. 그는 무언가를 발명할 때마다 여러 번 실험했어.
   B: 아마 그것이 그렇게 많은 사람들이 그를 존경하는 이유일 거야.
2. **G:** 정현이 어떻게 테니스 경기에서 마지막 네 선수 중 한 명이 될 수 있었을까?
   B: 그는 혹독한 훈련을 몇 년 거친 뒤에야 그것을 할 수 있었어.
   G: 그렇구나. 그는 언제 테니스 치는 것을 시작했니?
   B: 그는 일곱 살 때 테니스 치는 것을 시작했어.

1. **B:** 노래 대회 우승자에 대해 들어 본 적 있니?
   G: 아니, 못 들어 봤어. 누가 이겼어?
   B: 우승자는 빈탑인데, 그는 자신의 모든 노래를 작곡했어.
2. **G:** 미아라는 기타 연주자에 대해 들어 본 적 있니?
   B: 응, 들어 봤어. 나는 그녀가 연주를 독학했다고 들었어.
3. **B:** BTG라는 세계적으로 유명한 댄스 그룹에 대해 들어 본 적 있니?
   G: 응, 들어 봤어. 나는 인터넷에서 그들의 영상을 여러 번 본 적이 있어.
4. **G:** 지호라는 사진작가에 대해 들어 본 적 있니?
   B: 아니, 못 들어 봤어. 그는 어떤 종류의 사진을 찍니?
   G: 그는 보통 거리 예술가들의 사진을 찍어.

Listen & Speak 2-A

1. B: _____ you _____ about the _____ club, Edutoon?

   G: Yes, I have. Are you _____ in _____ _____?

   B: Yes, I _____ _____ _____ a famous cartoon writer, so I want to _____ that club.

   G: Oh, I didn't _____ that you're _____ in _____ cartoons.

2. G: Have you _____ of D.I.Y.?

   B: No, _____ is D.I.Y.?

   G: D.I.Y. _____ for 'do-it-yourself.' I'm really _____ it. Right now, I'm _____ a pencil _____.

   B: _____ are you going to make _____ you _____ that?

   G: When I'm _____ with the _____ case, I'm _____ to make my own _____.

Real-Life Zone

G: _____ you heard of Eui Hyun Sin, the _____?

B: No. _____ is _____?

G: He's a Paralympian _____. He won the first gold _____ for Korea in the 2018 Winter Paralympics.

B: Wow! That's _____.

G: He _____ in a car _____ in his early _____ and hurt his legs.

B: How was he able to _____ a skier?

G: After his _____, he tried _____ different sports to _____ better. Then he became _____ interested in _____.

B: _____ is not easy. Not many people _____ _____ at skiing.

G: That's _____ he's so _____.

Wrap Up

B: Sora, have you _____ about the _____ last night?

G: Yes, I _____ that there _____ a big fire in a building _____. Was anybody _____?

B: No, _____ man _____ ten people who _____ in the building.

G: Oh, really? _____ was he able to _____ so many people?

B: He _____ on every door to _____ people to _____ the building.

G: Wow, that's _____!

1. B: 에듀툰이라는 만화 동아리에 대해 들어 본 적 있니?
   G: 응, 있어. 만화 그리는 것에 관심이 있니?
   B: 나는 유명한 만화 작가가 되고 싶어서 그 동아리에 가입하고 싶어.
   G: 오, 나는 네가 만화 그리기에 관심이 있는 줄 몰랐어.
2. G: D.I.Y에 대해 들어 본 적 있니?
   B: 아니, D.I.Y가 뭐야?
   G: D.I.Y는 '너 스스로 해라'를 의미해. 나는 그것에 푹 빠졌어. 지금 나는 필통을 만들고 있어.
   B: 그것을 완성하고 나면 무엇을 만들 거니?
   G: 필통을 완성하면, 나는 내 책상을 만들 계획이야.

G: 신의현이라는 스키 선수에 대해 들어 본 적 있니?
B: 아니, 그가 누구야?
G: 그는 패럴림픽의 스키 선수야. 그는 2018 동계 패럴림픽에서 한국의 첫 금메달을 땄어.
B: 와! 훌륭하다.
G: 그는 20대 초반에 차 사고를 당하고 다리를 다쳤어.
B: 어떻게 그가 스키 선수가 될 수 있었니?
G: 사고 후에 그는 회복하기 위해 여러 가지 운동들을 시도했어. 그때 그는 특히 스키 타는 것에 관심을 가지게 됐어.
B: 스키를 타는 것은 쉽지 않잖아. 스키를 잘 타는 사람들은 많지 않아.
G: 그것이 그가 그렇게 존경받는 이유야.

B: 소라야, 지난밤 화재에 대해 들었니?
G: 응, 이 근처 건물에서 큰 화재가 있었다고 들었어. 다친 사람이 있어?
B: 아니, 한 남자가 건물 안에 있던 열 명의 사람들을 구했어.
G: 오, 진짜? 어떻게 그는 그 많은 사람들을 구할 수 있었니?
B: 그는 사람들에게 건물을 떠나라고 말하기 위해서 모든 문을 두드렸어.
G: 와, 정말 놀랍구나!

[01~02] 다음 대화의 빈칸에 들어갈 말로 알맞은 것은?

01

> G: ___(A)___ was Hyeon Chung able to be one of the final four players in the tennis competition?
> B: He could do it only after years of hard training.
> G: I see. ___(B)___ did he start playing tennis?
> B: He started to play tennis when he was seven.

① How – When ② Where – When ③ Why – How
④ What – How ⑤ When – How

02

> G: _____
> B: No, what is D.I.Y.?
> G: D.I.Y. stands for 'do-it-yourself.' I'm really into it. Right now, I'm making a pencil case.
> B: What are you going to make after you finish that?
> G: When I'm done with the pencil case, I'm planning to make my own desk.

① How about hearing D.I.Y.? ② Where did you hear of it?
③ What did you hear of? ④ Have you heard of D.I.Y.?
⑤ Have you done with D.I.Y.?

03 대화에 이어지기에 적절하게 배열된 순서를 고르시오.

> B: Sora, have you heard about the fire last night?
> G: Yes, I heard that there was a big fire in a building nearby. Was anybody hurt?
> (A) He knocked on every door to tell people to leave the building.
> (B) No, one man saved ten people who were in the building.
> (C) Oh, really? How was he able to save so many people?
> G: Wow, that's amazing!

① (A) – (C) – (B) ② (B) – (A) – (C) ③ (B) – (C) – (A)
④ (C) – (A) – (B) ⑤ (C) – (B) – (A)

01 다음 대화의 빈칸에 적절한 것은?

> B: How was she able to become a great runner?
>
> G: _____

① She practiced speaking in public.
② She ran 3 kilometers every day.
③ She didn't skip any meals of the day.
④ She learned English by watching many Hollywood movies.
⑤ She practiced shooting shots a lot.

[02~03] 다음 대화를 읽고 물음에 답하시오.

> B: How was Thomas Edison able to invent so many things?
>
> G: Many people think that he invented things on his first try, but that's not true.
>
> B: Oh, really?
>
> G: Yes. _____ he invented something, he experimented many times.
>
> B: Maybe that's why so many people admire him.

02 위 대화의 빈칸에 들어가기에 적절한 것은?

① Whenever   ② However
③ Wherever   ④ Whoever
⑤ Whatever

03 위 대화의 내용과 일치하지 <u>않는</u> 것은?

① Thomas Edison invented many things.
② The boy didn't know about Edison.
③ Edison experimented many times when he invented something.
④ Edison didn't usually invent something on his first try.
⑤ Many people admire Edison.

[04~05] 다음 대화를 읽고 물음에 답하시오.

> B: (A)Have you heard about the cartoon club, Edutoon?
>
> G: Yes, I have. Are you interested in drawing cartoons?
>
> B: Yes, I want to be a famous cartoon writer, so I want to join that club.
>
> G: Oh, I didn't know that you're interested in drawing cartoons.

04 위 대화의 밑줄 친 (A)가 의도하는 것은?

① 소개하기   ② 정보 교환하기
③ 알고 있는지 묻기   ④ 광고하기
⑤ 충고하기

05 위 대화의 내용과 일치하지 <u>않는</u> 것은?

① The boy asks the girl if she knows about the cartoon club.
② The girl has heard about the cartoon club.
③ The girl wants to be a cartoon writer.
④ The boy will join the cartoon club.
⑤ The boy is interested in drawing cartoons.

06 다음 대화의 빈칸에 적절한 것은?

> B: Have you heard of the winner of the singing contest?
>
> G: No, I haven't. _____
>
> B: The winner is Vintop, who wrote all of his own songs.

① Who won?   ② What's that?
③ I know that.   ④ She is the winner.
⑤ Are you busy?

[07~09] 다음 대화를 읽고 물음에 답하시오.

G: Have you heard of Eui Hyun Sin, the skier?

B: No. ___(가)___ is he? (A)

G: He's a Paralympian skier. He won the first gold medal for Korea in the 2018 Winter Paralympics. (B)

B: Wow! That's great.

G: He was in a car accident in his early twenties and hurt his legs. (C)

B: ___(나)___ was he able to become a skier?

G: After his accident, he tried several different sports to get better. (D)

B: Skiing is not easy. Not many people are good at skiing. (E)

G: That's why he's so respected.

07 대화의 내용으로 보아, 빈칸 (가), (나)에 들어가기에 가장 적절한 것은?

① When – Who　　② Who – Why

③ Who – How　　④ How – Why

⑤ What – When

08 (A)～(E) 중에서 다음 문장이 들어가기에 가장 적절한 곳은?

> Then he became especially interested in skiing.

① (A)　② (B)　③ (C)　④ (D)　⑤ (E)

09 위 대화를 읽고 대답할 수 없는 것은?

① Does the boy know about Eui Hyun Sin?

② When did Eui Hyun Sin win the gold medal?

③ Why did Eui Hyun Sin become a skier?

④ Who told Eui Hyun Sin to be a skier?

⑤ Why do people respect Eui Hyun Sin?

[10~11] 다음 대화를 읽고 물음에 답하시오.

B: Sora, _____(A)_____ the fire last night?

G: Yes, I heard that there was a big fire in a building nearby. Was anybody hurt?

B: No, one man saved ten people ___(B)___ were in the building.

G: Oh, really? How was he able to save so many people?

B: He knocked on every door to tell people to leave the building.

G: Wow, that's amazing!

10 빈칸 (A)에 들어가기에 적절한 것은?

① have you been to　　② have you seen

③ have you saved　　④ have you gone to

⑤ have you heard about

11 다음 중 (B)에 들어갈 말과 같은 말이 들어갈 수 있는 것은?

① I read the book _____ he had written.

② This is the house _____ he designed.

③ Do you know the man _____ helped her?

④ Would you tell me _____ you were late for class?

⑤ I know _____ he lives.

[01~03] 다음 대화를 읽고 물음에 답하시오.

B: _____(A)_____ to invent so many things? (어떻게 Thomas Edison은 그렇게 많은 것을 발명할 수 있었니?)

G: ⓐMany people think that ⓑhe invented things on his first try, but ⓒthat's true.

B: Oh, really?

G: Yes. Whenever ⓓhe invented something, he experimented many times.

B: Maybe that's ___(B)___ so many people ⓔ admire him.

01 빈칸 (A)를 주어진 우리말에 어울리는 영어 표현을 넣어 문장을 완성하시오. (able을 포함할 것)

➡ _____

02 빈칸 (B)에 알맞은 단어를 쓰시오.

➡ (B) _____

03 ⓐ~ⓔ 중에서 대화의 흐름상 어색한 것을 찾아 쓰고 적절한 것으로 바꾸어 쓰시오.

어색한 것의 기호 → 적절한 표현

_____ ➡ _____

04 밑줄 친 (가)의 우리말을 영어로 옮기시오. (주어진 단어를 포함하고, 필요한 단어를 추가할 것)

> G: Have you heard of Mia, the guitar player?
> B: Yes, I have. (가)나는 그녀가 독학으로 연주하는 것을 배웠다고 들었어. (herself) (8 words)

➡ _____

[05~06] 다음 대화를 읽고 물음에 답하시오.

G: Have you heard of D.I.Y.?

B: No, what is D.I.Y.?

G: D.I.Y. stands for 'do-it-yourself.' (가)나는 그것에 정말로 관심이 많아.(into) Right now, I'm making a pencil case.

B: What are you going to make after you finish that?

G: When ___(나)___ with the pencil case, I'm planning to make my own desk.

05 밑줄 친 (가)의 우리말을 영작하시오. (주어진 단어를 포함할 것)

➡ _____

06 내용상 (나)에 들어가기에 적절한 두 단어를 쓰시오. (축약형은 한 단어 취급)

➡ _____

07 다음 대화의 내용에 어울리도록 아래 빈칸에 적절한 말을 쓰시오.

> B: Sora, have you heard about the fire last night?
> G: Yes, I heard that there was a big fire in a building nearby. Was anybody hurt?
> B: No, one man saved ten people who were in the building.
> G: Oh, really? How was he able to save so many people?
> B: He knocked on every door to tell people to leave the building.
> G: Wow, that's amazing!

> There was a big fire last night. But no one was hurt because a man (A)_____ on every door to tell people to (B)_____ the building.

Grammar

1 too ... to부정사

> - You knew that you were **too** far behind **to** win a medal.
>   당신은 메달을 따기에 너무도 멀리 뒤떨어져 있었다는 것을 알고 있었잖아요.
> - It was **too** hot **to** go out. 날씨가 너무 더워서 밖에 나갈 수가 없었다.

- 'too ~ to부정사'는 '너무 ~해서 …할 수 없다[…하기에는 너무 ~하다]'라는 의미이다.
  - I was **too** nervous **to eat**. 나는 너무 불안해서 먹을 수가 없었다.
  - It's **too** late **to save** her now. 이제 그녀를 구하기에는 너무 늦다.

- 'too … to부정사'는 'so … that + 주어 + can't[couldn't] + 동사원형'으로 바꾸어 쓸 수 있다.
  - She was **too** weak **to stand**. 그녀는 너무 힘이 없어서 서 있을 수가 없었다.
    = She was **so** weak **that** she couldn't stand.
  - He's **too** young **to go** on his own. 그는 혼자 가기에는 너무 어리다.
    = He's **so** young **that** he can't go on his own.

- 'enough + to부정사'는 '~하기에 충분한'이라는 의미를 나타내며, 'so … that + 주어 + can[could] + 동사원형'으로 바꾸어 쓸 수 있다.
  - I was stupid **enough to** believe him. 내가 그를 믿을 만큼 어리석었다.
    = I was **so** stupid **that** I could believe him.
  - It's warm **enough to** eat outside. 밖에서 식사를 해도 될 정도로 날이 따뜻하다.
    = It's **so** warm **that** we[I] can eat outside.

핵심 Check

1. 다음 괄호 안에서 알맞은 말을 고르시오.

(1) Is it (so / too) late to cancel my order?

(2) He is (so / too) strong that he can bend almost any metal.

(3) He's (old enough / enough old) to take care of himself.

② to부정사의 부정형

- For me and my country, it was important **not to give** up.
  저와 제 조국을 위해서는. 포기하지 않는 것이 중요했어요.
- Try **not to get** your shoes wet. 네 신발이 젖지 않도록 해라.

■ to부정사의 부정은 to부정사 바로 앞에 'not'이나 'never'를 쓴다. 보통, 'never'는 부정의 의미를 더 강조하고 싶을 때 사용한다.

- She decided **not to go** through with the operation. 그녀는 그 수술을 받지 않기로 했다.
- He makes it a rule **never to borrow** money. 그는 절대 돈을 빌리지 않는 것을 원칙으로 삼고 있다.

■ **to부정사 부정의 의미**

to부정사의 내용과 반대되는 말을 할 때

to부정사의 해석	to부정사 부정의 해석
~하는 것 (명사적 용법)	~하지 않는 것 (명사적 용법)
~하는 (형용사적 용법)	~하지 않는 (형용사적 용법)
~하기 위해서 (부사적 용법)	~하기 않기 위해서 (부사적 용법)

- He decided **not to go** there. 그는 그곳에 안 가기로 결정했다.
- You are **not to leave** your station without permission. 허락 없이 자기 위치를 떠나서는 안 된다.
- Be careful **not to cross** the line. 선을 넘어가지 않도록 조심하라.

■ **to부정사 부정의 형태**

to부정사 바로 앞에 'not'이나 'never'를 쓴다.

- It was an opportunity **not[never] to be** missed. 그것은 놓쳐서는 안 될 기회였다.

핵심 Check

2. 다음 괄호 안에서 알맞은 말을 고르시오.

(1) Try (to not / not to) wake the baby up.

(2) He pretended (not to / to never) notice that she was there.

(3) I tried hard (don't to / never to) laugh.

01 다음 중 어법상 바르지 <u>않은</u> 것은?

① This light is too dim to read a book by.
② The joke is too rude to repeat.
③ The computer in the classroom is too slow to use.
④ Is it so late to cancel my order?
⑤ He was so tired that he could not walk straight.

02 다음 중 어법상 바른 것을 <u>두 개</u> 고르시오.

① Be careful to not wake the baby.
② She begged him not to go.
③ To not smile was hard.
④ I was resolved to see not him.
⑤ He warned me not to be late.

03 다음 주어진 단어를 어법에 맞게 빈칸에 쓰시오.

(1) The gloves were too small _____. (wear)
(2) We were all too polite _____. (object)
(3) I'm so busy that I can't _____ to the meeting. (come)

04 괄호 안에 주어진 어휘를 이용하여 우리말을 영어로 옮기시오.

(1) 그녀는 뽑히지 못해서 실망했다.
   (disappointed, chosen, 7 단어)
   ➡ _____

(2) 그것은 너무 오래전이라 기억할 수 없어요.
   (it, long, ago, so, 9 단어)
   ➡ _____

(3) 그녀는 항상 너무 바빠 들어 줄 시간이 없었다.
   (busy, listen, to, 7 단어)
   ➡ _____

(4) 그녀가 친절하게도 우리에게 밥을 사 주었다.
   (buy, kind, a meal, to, 9 단어)
   ➡ _____

01 다음 대화의 빈칸에 들어갈 말로 가장 적절한 것은?

> A: Let's go swimming.
> B: Sorry, but I can't. I am _____ to go swimming.

① busy   ② really busy
③ very busy   ④ so busy
⑤ too busy

02 다음 중 어법상 자연스러운 것은?

① Anne asked me not waited for her.
② She studied hard to fail not the math exam.
③ The teacher warned us not use our cell phone in class.
④ A lot of young people in the country choose not to marry.
⑤ The doctor told me not smoking.

03 주어진 문장과 같은 의미의 문장은?

> She was so lucky that she could be chosen for the team.

① She was too lucky to be chosen for the team.
② She was too lucky for being chosen for the team.
③ She was lucky enough to be chosen for the team.
④ She was lucky and she was chosen for the team.
⑤ She was very lucky being chosen for the team.

서답형
04 다음 괄호 안에서 알맞은 말을 고르시오.

(1) Eddie was too sick (to go / going) to school yesterday.
(2) The desk was (too / so) heavy for me to move alone.
(3) Micky begged his mom (not to / to not) punish him.
(4) Can you promise (never to / to never) repeat that?

05 다음 우리말을 영어로 바르게 옮긴 것을 <u>모두</u> 고르시오.

> 그 아이들은 콘서트 내내 앉아 있기에는 너무 어리다.

① The children are too young to sit through a concert.
② The children are so young that they can't sit through a concert.
③ The children are so young that they can sit through a concert.
④ The children are too young that they can't sit through a concert.
⑤ The children are young enough to sit through a concert.

06 다음 중 'not'이 들어갈 위치로 알맞은 것은?

> In the library, ① we ② need ③ to be careful ④ to make ⑤ any noise.

①   ②   ③   ④   ⑤

서답형

07 다음 문장에서 어법상 <u>어색한</u> 부분을 바르게 고치시오.

(1) The sea was too rough for us to sailing that night.

_____ ➡ _____

(2) I was too excited that I couldn't even eat my dinner.

_____ ➡ _____

(3) I was foolish enough believe what Jeff told me.

_____ ➡ _____

(4) I told him to never be late for meetings again.

_____ ➡ _____

(5) We have decided to pursue not the matter.

_____ ➡ _____

서답형

08 다음 문장과 같은 의미의 문장을 쓰시오.

I am too shy to sing in front of many people.

➡ _____

_____ .

09 다음 우리말을 영어로 바르게 옮긴 것을 고르시오.

Brian은 버스를 놓치지 않기 위해서 빠르게 달렸다.

① Brian ran fast to miss the bus.
② Brian ran fast to not miss the bus.
③ Brian ran fast not to miss the bus.
④ Brian didn't run fast to miss the bus.
⑤ Brian didn't run fast not to miss the bus.

10 다음 빈칸에 들어갈 말로 가장 적절한 것은?

My brother was too young _____ that horror movie.

① seeing   ② to see
③ to seeing   ④ that he could see
⑤ that he couldn't see

중요

11 다음 두 문장이 같은 의미가 되도록 빈칸에 들어갈 말로 알맞은 것은?

The man is holding the umbrella not to get wet.
= The man is holding the umbrella _____ get wet.

① enough not to   ② too to not
③ so not to   ④ as to not
⑤ so as not to

서답형

12 다음 문장을 같은 의미의 문장으로 바꿔 쓰시오.

(1) The cellphone was too expensive for me to buy.

➡ _____

_____

(2) The ice is too thin to bear your weight.

➡ _____

_____

(3) The rope was long enough to reach the ground.

➡ _____

_____

(4) She is healthy enough to travel.

➡ _____

_____

13 다음 빈칸에 알맞은 것을 고르시오.

> We talked quietly so as _____ wake the baby.

① not to   ② to not
③ to   ④ not
⑤ at

14 다음 중 빈칸에 들어갈 말이 바르게 짝지어진 것은?

> • You knew that you were _____ far behind to win a medal.
> • From now on, _____ let it happen again, I will always check what day it is.

① enough – to not
② too – not to
③ so – to
④ too – not to
⑤ enough – to not

서답형

15 그림을 보고 주어진 문장의 빈칸을 괄호 안의 어휘를 이용하여 알맞게 채우시오.

(1) He drove _____ with the car coming toward him. (fast, avoid, collide, to)

(2) When driving, be careful _____ a car accident. (cause)

중요
16 다음 문장의 빈칸에 들어갈 말로 어법상 올바른 것을 고르시오.

> I told him a big secret and asked _____.

① him not tell anybody
② him telling not anybody
③ him not telling anybody
④ him to not tell anybody
⑤ him not to tell anybody

17 다음 우리말을 10 단어의 영어로 옮길 때, 4 번째와 7 번째로 오는 단어를 바르게 묶은 것은?

> 내 동생은 너무 어려서 음식을 스스로 먹을 수 없다.

① too – to   ② too – eat
③ enough – to   ④ enough – eat
⑤ enough – food

서답형

18 다음 밑줄 친 부분을 부정하여 문장을 다시 쓰시오.

> My sister went to Japan to open a restaurant, to study Japanese.

➡ _____

_____

중요
19 다음 빈칸에 알맞은 말을 고르시오.

> The text is too long for me to read.
> = The text is _____ _____ _____ _____ _____ read it.

① too long that I can't
② too long that I can
③ so long that I can't
④ so long that I can
⑤ such long that I can

01 다음 문장을 that을 이용하여 바꿔 쓰시오.

(1) This computer is too slow to surf the web.

➡ _____

(2) Boris was too nervous to give a speech.

➡ _____

(3) The woman was kind enough to help the old lady.

➡ _____

(4) The cable is long enough to reach the socket.

➡ _____

(5) Your computer is too slow to use.

➡ _____

02 괄호 안에 주어진 어휘를 이용하여 우리말을 영어로 옮기시오.

(1) 이 TV는 너무 커서 나 혼자서는 들 수 없다.
(big, carry, this TV, on my own, to)

➡ _____

(2) Susie는 너무 느려서 Mike를 따라잡을 수 없었다. (slow, catch up with, to)

➡ _____

(3) 그 가방은 너무 작아서 그 책들을 담을 수 없다.
(small, the bag, put, so, in)

➡ _____

03 다음 두 문장을 해석하고 그 차이를 서술하시오.

(1) I didn't tell him to go.
(2) I told him not to go.

➡ 해석: (1) _____
　　　　(2) _____

　　차이: _____

_____

04 다음 우리말을, (a) to를 이용하여 (b) that을 이용하여 영작하시오.

(1) 그 닭튀김은 너무 매워서 먹을 수가 없다. (eat, the fried chicken, spicy)

(a) _____
(b) _____

(2) 그 질문들은 답하기에 너무 어렵다. (answer, the questions, difficult)

(a) _____
(b) _____

(3) 그는 자동차 한 대도 충분히 들어올릴 정도로 힘이 세요. (a car, strong, lift)

(a) _____
(b) _____

(4) 인쇄물이 충분히 선명해서 읽을 수 있었어. (read, the print, clear)

(a) _____
(b) _____

05 빈칸을 채워 다음 표지판이 의미하는 바를 완성하시오.

We ask you _____ your mobile phone here.

➡ _____

06 to부정사를 이용하여 주어진 두 문장을 한 문장으로 연결하시오.

(1) • I run very slowly.
 • I can't finish the race within the limited amount of time given.
  ➡ _____
  _____

(2) • This coat is too big.
 • So it can't fit you.
  ➡ _____

(3) • I can't read the text.
 • It's because the text is so long.
  ➡ _____

(4) • The man is very strong.
 • So he can move the rock.
  ➡ _____

(5) • She can make a good decision.
 • It's because she is very wise.
  ➡ _____

(6) • The dress is so beautiful.
 • You can wear it at the party.
  ➡ _____
  _____

07 다음 두 문장이 같은 뜻을 갖도록 빈칸을 알맞게 채우시오.

(1) She said to me, "Please don't make a noise."
 = She asked me _____.

(2) The officer told us, "Do not run."
 = The officer ordered us _____.

08 주어진 형용사와 to부정사를 활용하여 빈칸을 알맞게 채우시오.

smart / young / weak / good

(1) The girl is _____ ride a roller coaster.

(2) I think you are _____ carry those bags at a time.

(3) Don is not _____ be our leader.

(4) Consumers are _____ to know that.

09 다음 문장과 같은 의미의 문장을 쓰시오.

(1) Henry was too busy to answer the phone.
  ➡ _____
  _____

(2) The car is too old for me to drive.
  ➡ _____
  _____

(3) A boy under 15 is too young to watch the movie.
  ➡ _____
  _____

(4) The film was interesting enough for me to watch again.
  ➡ _____
  _____

Reading

The Last Runner

The last runner finished the race more than an hour before. "There
= over. ~ 이상
will be no more runners coming," the officials decided. They removed
앞에 '관계대명사+be동사(who are)'를 생략
the tape at the finish line and started to prepare for the closing
to부정사의 명사적 용법, 동사 'started'의 목적어로 쓰였다.
ceremony for the 1996 Atlanta Summer Olympics in the United States.

Someone shouted, "Look! There comes another runner!" A runner
부사 There를 강조하기 위해 문두로 이동시키고, 주어 'another runner'와 동사 'comes'가 도치
was just entering the stadium, but there was something wrong with
'-thing'으로 끝나는 대명사는 형용사가 뒤에서 수식
his legs. Still, he kept going toward the finish line. The band and
그래도, 그럼에도 불구하고(부사)   keep ~ing: 계속 ~하다
the volunteers stopped their preparations for the closing ceremony.
All eyes were on the runner.
All eyes were on ~: 모든 눈이 ~을 주시했다(~에게 머물렀다)
Suddenly, the band started playing celebration music, and the
= All at once. All of a sudden
volunteers cheered. "Go! Go! Go for it!" Two volunteers ran to the
finish line with a tape. Finally, the runner ran through the tape and then
~을 가지고   ~을 통해, ~을 관통하여(전치사)
fell to the ground. His name was Abdul Baser Wasiqi. He was from
Afghanistan.

official 관료, 공무원, 경기 임원
remove 제거하다
prepare 준비하다
ceremony 식, 의식
stadium 경기장
toward ~ 쪽으로, ~을 향하여
celebration 축하
cheer 환호성을 지르다, 환호하다

확인문제

• 다음 문장이 본문의 내용과 일치하면 T, 일치하지 <u>않으면</u> F를 쓰시오.

1 People thought the last runner finished the race over an hour before. ☐

2 The officials started to prepare for the opening ceremony for the 1996 Atlanta
   Summer Olympics in the United States. ☐

3 A runner was just entering the stadium, but there was something wrong with his
   legs. ☐

4 The band and the volunteers kept preparing for the closing ceremony. ☐

5 Two volunteers ran to the finish line with a tape. ☐

6 The runner fell to the ground, so he couldn't run through the tape. ☐

Reporters came up to Wasiqi and started asking him questions.
= approached

Reporter: What happened to you?
happen to ~ ((일·사건 등이) 일어나다, 생기다)

Wasiqi: I injured my leg during a practice run. The injury got worse
(사고로) 부상을 입히다(타동사)   get/become/grow+비교급: 더 ~해지다
during the race, but I couldn't give up.
= abandon: 포기하다

Reporter: Why not? You knew that you were too far behind to win a
too … to부정사: 너무 …해서 ~할 수 없다
medal.

Wasiqi: I am the only athlete here representing Afghanistan. There was
현재분사: 대표하는
no way I could give up.

Reporter: Afghanistan is still at war, isn't it?
= That's the reason that

Wasiqi: Yes, we have been at war for 16 years. That's why we were not
현재완료 계속적 용법   That's why: 그래서 ~하게 된 것이다. why 뒤에는 어떤 행동의 결과가 되는 내용이 옴.
able to send athletes to the Barcelona Olympics four years ago.
I was sad for my country back then when I could see no Afghan
athletes in the opening ceremony.

Reporter: Were you running marathons then?
과거진행형 시제: 과거 특정 시점에 진행되고 있던 일을 묻고 있음.

Wasiqi: No. I started running after Barcelona. I ran in lots of races.
Finally I won a marathon in Germany. As a result, I was able to
win: ~에서 이기다(타동사), 전치사 없이 바로 목적어를 취한다.   그 결과
come to Atlanta.

Reporter: How do you feel now?

Wasiqi: I am proud of myself and proud to be from Afghanistan. For me
to부정사의 부사적 용법(감정의 원인)
and my country, it was important not to give up. I didn't come
to부정사의 부정은 to 앞에 not을 쓴다.
here to win. For me, it was enough to be here and to finish the
to부정사의 부사적 용법(목적)
race.

reporter 기자, 리포터
injure 부상을 입히다
athlete 운동선수
represent 대표하다
give up 포기하다
at war 전쟁 중인
marathon 마라톤
be proud of ~을 자랑스러워하다

확인문제

● 다음 문장이 본문의 내용과 일치하면 T, 일치하지 않으면 F를 쓰시오.

1 Wasiqi injured his leg during a practice run. ☐

2 Wasiqi didn't know that he was too far behind to win a medal. ☐

3 Wasiqi was the only athlete there representing Afghanistan. ☐

4 Afghanistan was not able to send athletes to the Atlanta Olympics. ☐

5 Wasiqi won a marathon in Germany. ☐

6 For Wasiqi and his country, winning was very important. ☐

● 우리말을 참고하여 빈칸에 알맞은 말을 쓰시오.

1 The _____ Runner

2 The last runner finished the race _____ _____ an hour before.

3 "There will be _____ _____ runners _____," the officials decided.

4 They removed the tape at the finish line and started to _____ _____ the _____ _____ for the 1996 Atlanta Summer Olympics in the United States.

5 Someone shouted, "Look! _____ _____ _____ runner!"

6 A runner was just entering the stadium, but there was _____ _____ with his legs.

7 _____, he _____ _____ toward the finish line.

8 The band and the volunteers _____ _____ _____ for the closing ceremony.

9 _____ _____ _____ _____ the runner.

10 Suddenly, the band started playing _____ _____, and the volunteers _____.

11 "Go! Go! _____ _____ _____!"

12 Two volunteers ran to the finish line _____ _____ _____.

13 _____, the runner _____ _____ the tape and then _____ _____ the ground.

14 _____ _____ was Abdul Baser Wasiqi.

15 He _____ _____ Afghanistan.

16 Reporters _____ _____ _____ Wasiqi and started asking him questions.

17 **Reporter:** What _____ _____ you?

18 **Wasiqi:** I injured my leg _____ _____ _____.

1	마지막 주자
2	마지막 주자가 한 시간도 더 전에 경주를 끝냈다.
3	"더 들어오는 선수는 없을 겁니다."라고 경기 임원들은 결론을 내렸다.
4	그들은 결승선에서 테이프를 걷어내고 1996년 미국 애틀랜타 하계 올림픽의 폐막식을 준비하기 시작했다.
5	누군가가 외쳤다. "봐! 저기 또 다른 선수가 온다!"
6	한 선수가 경기장으로 막 들어오고 있었는데, 그의 다리에 이상이 있었다.
7	그러나 그는 계속 결승선을 향해 움직였다.
8	밴드와 자원봉사자들이 폐막식을 위한 준비를 멈추었다.
9	모든 눈들이 그 선수에게 머물렀다.
10	갑자기 밴드가 축하 음악을 연주하기 시작했고, 자원봉사자들이 환호했다.
11	"달려! 달려! 잘해라!"
12	두 명의 자원봉사자가 테이프를 가지고 결승선으로 달려갔다.
13	결국, 그 주자는 테이프를 통해 달렸고, 바닥에 쓰러졌다.
14	그의 이름은 압둘 베사르 와시키였다.
15	그는 아프가니스탄 출신이었다.
16	기자들은 와시키에게 가서 그에게 질문을 하기 시작했다.
17	리포터: 당신에게 무슨 일이 있었나요?
18	와시키: 저는 연습 경기를 하던 중 다리를 다쳤습니다.

19 The injury _____ _____ during the race, but I couldn't give up.

20 Reporter: _____ _____ ?

21 You knew that you were too _____ _____ to win a medal.

22 Wasiqi: I am the only athlete here _____ _____ .

23 There was _____ _____ I could give up.

24 Reporter: Afghanistan is still _____ _____ , _____ _____ ?

25 Wasiqi: Yes, we _____ _____ at war for 16 years.

26 _____ _____ we were not able to send athletes to the Barcelona Olympics four years ago.

27 I _____ _____ _____ my country _____ _____ when I could see no Afghan athletes in the opening ceremony.

28 Reporter: _____ you _____ marathons then?

29 Wasiqi: No. I _____ _____ after Barcelona.

30 I ran in _____ _____ races.

31 Finally I _____ _____ in Germany.

32 _____ _____ _____ , I was able to come to Atlanta.

33 Reporter: _____ do you feel now?

34 Wasiqi: I am proud of _____ and proud _____ _____ _____ Afghanistan.

35 For me and my country, it was important _____ _____ _____ _____ .

36 I didn't come here _____ _____ .

37 For me, _____ _____ to be here and to finish the race.

경기 중에 제 상처는 점점 더 심각해졌지만, 저는 포기할 수 없었습니다.

20 리포터: 왜 포기할 수 없었죠?

21 당신은 메달을 얻기에 너무도 크게 뒤떨어져 있었다는 것을 알고 있었잖아요.

22 와시키: 저는 아프가니스탄을 대표하는 유일한 선수입니다.

23 제가 포기할 수 있는 방법은 없었습니다.

24 리포터: 아프가니스탄은 여전히 전쟁 중입니다. 맞나요?

25 와시키: 네. 우리나라는 16년째 전쟁 중입니다.

26 그것이 우리가 4년 전 바르셀로나 올림픽에 선수들을 보낼 수 없었던 이유입니다.

27 저는 개회식에서 아프가니스탄 선수를 볼 수 없었던 그 당시, 제 나라에 대해 매우 슬펐습니다.

28 리포터: 그 당시 마라톤을 뛰고 있었나요?

29 와시키: 아니요. 저는 바르셀로나 올림픽 이후에 달리기를 시작했습니다.

30 저는 많은 경주에서 뛰었어요.

31 마침내 독일 마라톤에서 우승했지요.

32 그 결과 애틀랜타에 올 수 있었어요.

33 리포터: 지금은 기분이 어떠신가요?

34 와시키: 저는 제 자신이, 그리고 제가 아프가니스탄 출신인 것이 자랑스러워요.

35 저와 제 조국을 위해서는, 포기하지 않는 것이 중요했어요.

36 저는 이곳에 이기러 온 것이 아닙니다.

37 제가 여기에 있고 경주를 끝마친 것으로 충분합니다.

● 우리말을 참고하여 본문을 영작하시오.

1 마지막 주자
➡ _____

2 마지막 주자가 한 시간도 더 전에 경주를 끝냈다.
➡ _____

3 "더 들어오는 선수는 없을 겁니다."라고 경기 임원들은 결론을 내렸다.
➡ _____

4 그들은 결승선에서 테이프를 걷어내고 1996년 미국 애틀랜타 하계 올림픽의 폐막식을 준비하기 시작했다.
➡ _____
_____

5 누군가가 외쳤다. "봐! 저기 또 다른 선수가 온다!"
➡ _____

6 한 선수가 경기장으로 막 들어오고 있었는데, 그의 다리에 이상이 있었다.
➡ _____

7 그러나 그는 계속 결승선을 향해 움직였다.
➡ _____

8 밴드와 자원봉사자들이 폐막식을 위한 준비를 멈추었다.
➡ _____

9 모든 눈들이 그 선수에게 머물렀다.
➡ _____

10 갑자기 밴드가 축하 음악을 연주하기 시작했고, 자원봉사자들이 환호했다.

11 "달려! 달려! 잘해라!"
➡ _____

12 두 명의 자원봉사자가 테이프를 가지고 결승선으로 달려갔다.
➡ _____

13 결국, 그 주자는 테이프를 통과해 달렸고, 바닥에 쓰러졌다.
➡ _____

14 그의 이름은 압둘 베사르 와시키였다.
➡ _____

15 그는 아프가니스탄 출신이었다.
➡ _____

16 기자들은 와시키에게 가서 그에게 질문을 하기 시작했다.
➡ _____

17 리포터: 당신에게 무슨 일이 있었나요?
➡ _____

18 와시키: 저는 연습 경기를 하던 중 다리를 다쳤습니다.
➡ _____

19 경기 중에 제 상처는 점점 더 심각해졌지만, 저는 포기할 수 없었습니다.

➡ _____

20 리포터: 왜 포기할 수 없었죠?

➡ _____

21 당신은 메달을 얻기에 너무도 크게 뒤떨어져 있었다는 것을 알고 있었잖아요.

➡ _____

22 와시키: 저는 아프가니스탄을 대표하는 유일한 선수입니다.

➡ _____

23 제가 포기할 수 있는 방법은 없었습니다.

➡ _____

24 리포터: 아프가니스탄은 여전히 전쟁 중입니다, 맞나요?

➡ _____

25 와시키: 네, 우리나라는 16년째 전쟁 중입니다.

➡ _____

26 그것이 우리가 4년 전 바르셀로나 올림픽에 선수들을 보낼 수 없었던 이유입니다.

➡ _____

27 저는 개회식에서 아프가니스탄 선수를 볼 수 없었던 그 당시, 제 나라에 대해 매우 슬펐습니다.

➡ _____

28 리포터: 그 당시 마라톤을 뛰고 있었나요?

➡ _____

29 와시키: 아니요. 저는 바르셀로나 올림픽 이후에 달리기를 시작했습니다.

➡ _____

30 저는 많은 경주에서 뛰었어요.

➡ _____

31 마침내 독일 마라톤에서 우승했지요.

➡ _____

32 그 결과 애틀랜타에 올 수 있었어요.

➡ _____

33 리포터: 지금은 기분이 어떠신가요?

➡ _____

34 와시키: 저는 제 자신이, 그리고 제가 아프가니스탄 출신인 것이 자랑스러워요.

➡ _____

35 저와 제 조국을 위해서는, 포기하지 않는 것이 중요했어요.

➡ _____

36 저는 이곳에 이기러 온 것이 아닙니다.

➡ _____

37 제가 여기에 있고 경주를 끝마친 것으로 충분합니다.

➡ _____

[01~03] 다음 글을 읽고 물음에 답하시오.

The last runner finished the race more than an hour before. "(A)There will be no more runners coming," the officials decided. They removed the tape at the finish line and started to prepare ____ⓐ____ the closing ceremony ____ⓑ____ the 1996 Atlanta Summer Olympics in the United States.

01 위 글의 빈칸 ⓐ와 ⓑ에 공통으로 들어갈 전치사를 고르시오.

① to ② at
③ with ④ for
⑤ on

서답형

02 위 글의 밑줄 친 문장 (A)에서 coming 앞에 생략된 두 단어를 쓰시오.

➡ _____

서답형

03 Why did the officials decide that there would be no more runners coming? Answer in English beginning with "Because".

➡ _____
_____

[04~06] 다음 글을 읽고 물음에 답하시오.

Reporters came up to Wasiqi and started asking him questions.

Reporter: What ⓐhappened to you?

Wasiqi: I injured my leg during a practice run. The injury got worse during the race, but I couldn't give up.

Reporter: Why not? You knew that you were too far behind to win a medal.

Wasiqi: I am the only athlete here representing Afghanistan. There was no way I could give up.

Reporter: Afghanistan is still at war, isn't it?

Wasiqi: Yes, we have been at war for 16 years. ⓑThat's because we were not able to send athletes to the Barcelona Olympics four years ago. I was sad for my country back then when I could see no Afghan athletes in the opening ceremony.

중요

04 위 글의 밑줄 친 ⓐhappened to와 같은 의미로 쓰인 것을 모두 고르시오.

① She happened to be out when we called.
② Something must have happened to him.
③ I happened to see him on the street.
④ He happened to hear it.
⑤ Yesterday something strange happened to her.

서답형

05 위 글의 밑줄 친 ⓑ에서 어법상 틀린 부분을 찾아 고치시오.

_____ ➡ _____

서답형

06 다음 문장에서 위 글의 내용과 다른 부분을 찾아서 고치시오.

Wasiqi injured his leg during the race.

_____ ➡ _____ 또는
_____ ➡ _____

[07~09] 다음 글을 읽고 물음에 답하시오.

Someone shouted, "Look! There comes another runner!" A runner was just entering the stadium, but there was something wrong with his legs. Still, he kept going toward the finish line. The band and the volunteers stopped their preparations for the closing ceremony. All eyes were on the runner.

ⓐSuddenly, the band started playing celebration music, and the volunteers cheered. "Go! Go! Go for it!" Two volunteers ran to the finish line with a tape. Finally, the runner ran through the tape and then fell to the ground. His name was Abdul Baser Wasiqi. He was from Afghanistan.

07 다음 중 위 글의 분위기로 가장 알맞은 것을 모두 고르시오.

① shameful   ② touching
③ moving   ④ embarrassing
⑤ disappointing

서답형

08 위 글의 밑줄 친 ⓐSuddenly와 바꿔 쓸 수 있는 말을 쓰시오.

➡ _____

09 According to the passage, which is NOT true?

① There was something wrong with Wasiqi's legs.
② The band and the volunteers stopped preparing for the closing ceremony.
③ All the people in the stadium watched Wasiqi.
④ Wasiqi ran toward the finish line but fell to the ground before it.
⑤ Abdul Baser Wasiqi was from Afghanistan.

[10~13] 다음 글을 읽고 물음에 답하시오.

Finally, the runner ran through the tape and then fell to the ground. His name was Abdul Baser Wasiqi. He was from Afghanistan.

Reporters came up to Wasiqi and (A)started asking him questions.

Reporter: What happened to you?

Wasiqi: I injured my leg during a practice run. The injury got worse during the race, but I couldn't give up.

Reporter: Why not? You knew that you were too far behind to win a medal.

Wasiqi: I am the only athlete here ___ⓐ___ Afghanistan. There was no way I could give up.

Reporter: Afghanistan is still at war, isn't it?

Wasiqi: Yes, we (B)have been at war for 16 years. That's why we were not able to send athletes to the Barcelona Olympics four years ago. I was sad for my country back then when I could see no Afghan athletes in the opening ceremony.

서답형

10 위 글의 빈칸 ⓐ에 represent를 알맞은 형태로 쓰시오.

서답형 ➡ _____

11 위 글의 밑줄 친 (A)와 같은 뜻이 되도록 빈칸을 채우시오.

➡ started asking questions _____ him

12 위 글의 밑줄 친 (B)have been과 현재완료의 용법이 같은 것을 모두 고르시오.

① Have you ever been to Japan?
② She has been sick since last Friday.
③ I have been to the station to see my friend off.
④ I have been to Jeju Island three times.
⑤ He has been in his room for hours.

서답형

13 본문을 참조하여 다음 빈칸 (A)와 (B)에 알맞은 단어를 쓰시오. 단, (A)에는 interview를 알맞은 형태로 쓰시오.

> The reporters are having an interview with an (A)_____. He was Wasiqi, a marathon runner from Afghanistan. It can be said that he showed the spirit of Olympics by finishing the race without (B)_____ _____ in spite of the severe injury.

[14~15] 다음 글을 읽고 물음에 답하시오.

> Reporter: How do you feel now?
>
> Wasiqi: I am proud of myself and proud to be from Afghanistan. For me and my country, ⓐ포기하지 않는 것이 중요했어요. I didn't come here to win. For me, it was enough ⓑto be here and to finish the race.

서답형

14 위 글의 밑줄 친 ⓐ의 우리말에 맞게 가주어를 사용하여 7 단어로 영작하시오.

➡ _____

15 아래 〈보기〉에서 위 글의 밑줄 친 ⓑto be와 to부정사의 용법이 같은 것의 개수를 고르시오.

> ┤ 보기 ├
> ① It is warm enough to be outside.
> ② It was good enough to be present at the party.
> ③ He was wise enough to be satisfied with the present.
> ④ It is strong enough to be used here.
> ⑤ I practiced hard enough to be far ahead of others.

① 1개 ② 2개 ③ 3개 ④ 4개 ⑤ 5개

[16~18] 다음 글을 읽고 물음에 답하시오.

> Someone shouted, "Look! There comes another runner!" A runner was just entering the stadium, but there was something wrong with his legs. ⓐStill, he kept going toward the finish line. The band and the volunteers stopped their preparations for the closing ceremony. All eyes were on the runner.
>
> Suddenly, the band started playing celebration music, and the volunteers cheered. "Go! Go! Go for it!" Two volunteers ran to the finish line with a tape. Finally, the runner ran through the tape and then fell to the ground. His name was Abdul Baser Wasiqi. He was from Afghanistan.

16 위 글의 밑줄 친 ⓐStill과 같은 의미로 쓰인 것을 고르시오.

① Do you still live at the same address?
② The next day was still warmer.
③ Keep still while I brush your hair.
④ The weather was cold and wet. Still, we had a great time.
⑤ I wrote to them last month and I'm still waiting for a reply.

17 위 글의 제목으로 알맞은 것을 고르시오.

① The Last but the Most Impressive Runner
② Preparations for the Closing Ceremony
③ The Consideration of the Volunteers
④ The Band Playing Celebration Music
⑤ Alas! The Runner Fell to the Ground

18 Which question CANNOT be answered after reading the passage?

① What was wrong with Wasiqi when he was entering the stadium?

② Did the band and the volunteers keep preparing for the closing ceremony after Wasiqi entered the stadium?

③ What did the band and the volunteers do when they were watching Wasiqi?

④ What happened right after Wasiqi ran through the tape at the finish line?

⑤ How long did Wasiqi run?

[19~20] 다음 글을 읽고 물음에 답하시오.

Reporter: Were you running marathons then?

Wasiqi: No. I started running after Barcelona. I ran in lots of races. Finally I won a marathon in Germany. ____ⓐ____, I was able to come to Atlanta.

Reporter: How do you feel now?

Wasiqi: I am proud of myself and proud to be from Afghanistan. For me and my country, it was important not to give up. I didn't come here to win. For me, it was enough to be here and to finish the race.

19 위 글의 빈칸 ⓐ에 들어갈 알맞은 말을 고르시오.

① As a result   ② However

③ Still   ④ Whereas

⑤ For example

20 Which question CANNOT be answered after reading the passage?

① When did Wasiqi start running?

② How many races did Wasiqi participate in before he won a marathon in Germany?

③ How did Wasiqi feel at the time of the interview?

④ What was important for Wasiqi and his country?

⑤ Did Wasiqi come to Atlanta to win?

[21~23] 다음 글을 읽고 물음에 답하시오.

Someone shouted, "Look! (A)There comes the other runner!" A runner was just entering the stadium, but there was something wrong with his legs. Still, he kept going toward the finish line. The band and the volunteers stopped their preparations ____ⓐ____ the closing ceremony. (B)모든 눈들이 그 선수에게 머물렀다. Suddenly, the band started playing celebration music, and the volunteers cheered. "Go! Go! Go for it!" Two volunteers ran to the finish line with a tape. Finally, the runner ran ____ⓑ____ the tape and then fell to the ground. His name was Abdul Baser Wasiqi. He was from Afghanistan.

21 위 글의 빈칸 ⓐ와 ⓑ에 들어갈 전치사가 바르게 짝지어진 것은?

ⓐ　　ⓑ　　　　　ⓐ　　ⓑ

① for – from   ② at – through

③ for – through   ④ at – to

⑤ on – to

서답형

22 위 글의 밑줄 친 (A)에서 어법상 틀린 부분을 찾아 고치시오.

_____ ➡ _____

서답형

23 위 글의 밑줄 친 (B)의 우리말에 맞게 주어진 어휘를 이용하여 6 단어로 영작하시오.

all eyes

➡ _____

[01~03] 다음 글을 읽고 물음에 답하시오.

The (A)[last / latest] runner finished the race ⓐmore than an hour before. "ⓑ더 들어오는 선수는 없을 겁니다," the officials decided. They (B)[installed / removed] the tape at the finish line and started to prepare for the (C)[closing / opening] ceremony for the 1996 Atlanta Summer Olympics in the United States.

01 위 글의 괄호 (A)~(C)에서 문맥상 알맞은 낱말을 골라 쓰시오.

➡ (A) _____ (B) _____ (C) _____

02 위 글의 밑줄 친 ⓐmore than과 바꿔 쓸 수 있는 한 단어를 쓰시오.

➡ _____

03 위 글의 밑줄 친 ⓑ의 우리말에 맞게 주어진 어휘를 이용하여 7 단어로 영작하시오.

> there, no, coming

➡ _____

[04~06] 다음 글을 읽고 물음에 답하시오.

Someone shouted, "Look! There comes another runner!" A runner was just entering the stadium, but there was something wrong with his legs. Still, he kept ___ⓐ___ toward the finish line. The band and the volunteers stopped their preparations for the closing ceremony. All eyes were on the runner.

Suddenly, the band started playing celebration music, and the volunteers cheered. "Go! Go! ___ⓑ___!" Two volunteers ran to the finish line with a tape. Finally, the runner ran through the tape and then fell to the ground. His name was Abdul Baser Wasiqi. He was from Afghanistan.

04 위 글의 빈칸 ⓐ에 go를 알맞은 형태로 쓰시오.

➡ _____

05 위 글의 빈칸 ⓑ에 go를 포함하는 격려와 응원의 구호를 쓰시오. (세 단어)

➡ _____

06 다음 문장에서 위 글의 내용과 다른 부분을 찾아서 고치시오.

> When Wasiqi entered the stadium, the band and the volunteers stopped to prepare for the closing ceremony.

_____ ➡ _____

[07~10] 다음 글을 읽고 물음에 답하시오.

Reporters came up to Wasiqi and started asking him questions.

Reporter: What happened to you?

Wasiqi: I injured my leg during a practice run. The injury got worse during the race, but I couldn't give up.

Reporter: Why not? You knew that (A)you were too far behind to win a medal.

Wasiqi: I am the only athlete here representing Afghanistan. There was no way I could give up.

Reporter: Afghanistan is still at war, ___ⓐ___?

Wasiqi: Yes, we have been at war for 16 years. That's why we were not able to send athletes to the Barcelona Olympics four years ago. I was sad for my country back then when I could see no Afghan athletes in the opening ceremony.

07 위 글의 빈칸 ⓐ에 들어갈 알맞은 부가의문문을 쓰시오.

➡ _____

중요

08 위 글의 밑줄 친 (A)를 복문으로 고치시오.

➡ _____
_____

09 Why couldn't Afghanistan send athletes to the Barcelona Olympics? Fill in the blanks with suitable words.

> Because Afghanistan had been _____ _____ for 12 years at that time.

10 본문의 내용과 일치하도록 다음 빈칸 (A)와 (B)에 알맞은 단어를 쓰시오.

> Even though Wasiqi knew it was impossible for him to win a medal, he couldn't (A)_____ _____ because he was the only athlete there (B)_____ _____.

[11~14] 다음 글을 읽고 물음에 답하시오.

Reporter: Were you running marathons then?
Wasiqi: No. I started running after Barcelona. I ran in lots of races. ⓐFinally I won a marathon in Germany. As a result, I was able to come to Atlanta.

Reporter: How do you feel now?
Wasiqi: ⓑI am proud of myself and proud to be from Afghanistan. For me and my country, it was important not to give up. I didn't come here to win. For me, it was enough to be here and to finish the race.

11 위 글의 밑줄 친 ⓐFinally와 바꿔 쓸 수 있는 말을 쓰시오.

➡ _____

중요

12 위 글의 밑줄 친 ⓑ를 다음과 같이 바꿔 쓸 때 빈칸에 공통으로 들어갈 알맞은 단어를 쓰시오.

➡ I take _____ in myself and _____ in being from Afghanistan.

13 How was Wasiqi able to come to Atlanta? Fill in the blanks (A) and (B) with suitable words.

> After Wasiqi started running, he ran in (A)_____ races and finally won a marathon in (B)_____, which led him to come to Atlanta.

14 본문의 내용과 일치하도록 다음 빈칸 (A)와 (B)에 알맞은 단어를 쓰시오.

> Wasiqi was proud of himself and proud to be an Afghan athlete. For him and his country, not (A)_____ _____ was important. He didn't come to Atlanta (B)_____ _____, and it was sufficient for him to take part in the Atlanta Olympics and finish the race.

해석

Communication Task

A: Have you heard of Jain Kim?
"~에 대하여 들어 본 적이 있니?"(경험을 나타내는 현재완료)

B: Yes, I have. She's a famous rock climber.
현재완료에 대한 대답은 have/has를 사용하여 대답한다.

A: How was she able to become a famous rock climber?

B: She trained hard for five hours every day.
시간을 포함하는 일반적인 기간은 전치사 for를 사용한다.

구문해설 • rock climber: 암벽 등반가 • train: 훈련하다

A: 너는 김자인에 대하여 들어본 적이 있니?

B: 그래. 그녀는 유명한 암벽 등반가야.

A: 어떻게 그녀가 유명한 암벽 등반가가 될 수 있었지?

B: 그녀는 5년 동안 매일 열심히 훈련했어.

Language in Use B

Last night, I set my clock for 8 o'clock not to be late for school today.
to부정사의 부정

Because it is a long way to my school, it is important not to miss the bus.
비인칭주어   가주어   to부정사의 부정

Without having breakfast, I quickly left the house and went to the bus stop.
전치사 다음에 나온 동명사

Surprisingly, there was nobody. Then, I remembered that today was Saturday.
nobody가 주어이므로 단수 동사   명사절을 이끄는 접속사

From now on, not to let it happen again, I will always check what day it is.
to부정사의 부정   사역동사 let의 목적격보어(동사원형)   간접의문문

구문해설 • set: (시계를) 맞추다 • surprisingly: 놀랄 정도로, 놀랍게도, 의외로

어젯밤에 나는 오늘 학교에 늦지 않으려고 시계를 8시에 맞춰 놓았다. 학교까지는 길이 멀기 때문에, 버스를 놓치지 않는 것이 중요하다. 아침도 먹지 않고 나는 빠르게 집을 떠나 버스 정거장으로 갔다. 놀랍게도 아무도 없었다. 그때, 나는 오늘이 토요일임을 기억했다. 이제부터 그런 일이 다시 일어나지 않도록, 나는 항상 무슨 요일인지 확인하겠다.

Writing Workshop Step 3

I Have a Goal to Win the Singing Contest

I want to win the school singing contest. I love singing, and I think I
winning(×)   = to sing

have a good voice. However, I am too shy to sing in front of many people.
= I am so shy that I can't sing in front of many people

Not to be nervous during the contest, I will practice singing in front of my
= In order that I may not be nervous   to sing(×)

class first.

구문해설 • goal: 목표 • singing contest: 노래 대회 • shy: 수줍어[부끄러워]하는
• nervous: 불안해[초조해/두려워] 하는 • practice: 연습하다

나는 노래 대회에서 이기려는 목표를 가지고 있다

나는 학교 노래 대회에서 이기고 싶다. 나는 노래 부르는 것을 좋아하고 목소리가 좋다고 생각한다. 그러나, 나는 너무 수줍어서 많은 사람들 앞에서 노래를 부를 수 없다. 대회 도중에 불안해하지 않기 위해서 먼저 학급 친구들 앞에서 노래 부르기를 연습할 것이다.

영역별 핵심문제

01 다음 두 문장에 공통으로 알맞은 것을 고르시오.

> • Come _____ to the front when I call your names.
> • He chose not to give _____ hope.

① at　　　　② on　　　　③ up
④ by　　　　⑤ in

02 다음 빈칸에 들어가기에 적절한 단어의 형태를 고르시오.

> All the _____ will be done soon.

① prepare　　　② prepared
③ prepares　　　④ to prepare
⑤ preparation

03 다음 영영풀이에 해당하는 단어를 고르시오.

> a person who plays sports well

① athlete　　　② driver
③ trainer　　　④ developer
⑤ scientist

04 다음 밑줄 친 부분의 우리말 뜻이 알맞지 <u>않은</u> 것은?

① Why did the woman <u>injure</u> her knee? (부상을 입다)
② This must not <u>happen</u> again. (일어나다)
③ Will you <u>join</u> us? (보호하다)
④ I will <u>invent</u> a robot. (발명하다)
⑤ Don't <u>knock</u> the door. (두드리다)

[05~06] 다음 우리말과 일치하도록 빈칸에 알맞은 말을 쓰시오.

05
> B: _____ (노래 대회 우승자에 대해 들어 본 적 있니?) (hear of, singing contest, 10 words)
> G: No, I haven't. Who won?
> B: The winner is Vintop, who wrote all of his own songs.

➡ _____

06
> B: _____ (어떻게 그녀가 영어를 잘할 수 있었니?) (able, speak, so, 9 words)
> G: She learned English by watching many Hollywood movies.

➡ _____

07 다음 대화의 빈칸 (가)에 들어가기에 적절한 것은?

> B: How was Thomas Edison able to invent so many things?
> G: Many people think that he invented things on his first try, but that's not true.
> B: Oh, really?
> G: Yes. Whenever he invented something, he experimented many times.
> B: Maybe _____ (가) _____ so many people admire him.

① that's the way　　② this is the place
③ that's why　　　④ that's where
⑤ this is because

[08~10] 다음 대화를 읽고 물음에 답하시오.

G: Have you heard of Eui Hyun Sin, the skier?

B: No. Who is he?

G: He's a Paralympian skier. He won the first gold medal for Korea in the 2018 Winter Paralympics.

B: Wow! That's great.

G: (A)그는 20대 초반에 차 사고를 당하고 다리를 다쳤어.

B: How was he able to become a skier?

G: After his accident, he tried several different sports to get better. Then he became especially __(B)__ in skiing.

B: Skiing is not easy. Many people are good at skiing.

G: That's why he's so respected.

08 (A)의 우리말에 해당하는 영어 문장으로 적절한 것은?

① He hurt his legs in his early twenties and in a car accident.

② He was and hurt his legs in a car accident in his early twenties.

③ He was his legs and hurt in a car accident in his early twenties

④ He in a car accident was in his early twenties hurt and his legs.

⑤ He was in a car accident in his early twenties and hurt his legs.

09 빈칸 (B)에 들어가기에 적절한 것은?

① surprised   ② frightened

③ interested   ④ amazed

⑤ increased

10 위 대화에서 내용상 어색한 부분이 있는 문장을 찾아 자연스러운 문장으로 고쳐 쓰시오.

➡ _____

_____

[11~13] 다음 대화를 읽고 물음에 답하시오.

B: Sora, (A)have you heard about the fire last night?

G: Yes, I heard that there was a big fire in a building nearby. Was anybody hurt?

B: No, one man saved ten people who were in the building.

G: Oh, really? How was he able to save so many people?

B: He __(B)__ on every door to tell people to leave the building.

G: Wow, that's amazing!

11 (A)와 같은 의미의 문장으로 적절하지 <u>않은</u> 것은? (2개)

① have you told about the fire last night?

② have you been told about the fire last night?

③ do you know about the fire last night?

④ are you aware of the fire last night?

⑤ are you heard about the fire last night?

12 빈칸 (B)에 들어가기에 적절한 것은?

① painted   ② fixed

③ locked   ④ drew

⑤ knocked

13 위 대화를 통해서 알 수 있는 것이 <u>아닌</u> 것은?

① There was a big fire last night.

② The boy has heard about the big fire.

③ The girl didn't know how many people were saved.

④ The man told people to leave the building.

⑤ One fireman saved ten people.

Grammar

14 다음 중 나머지 넷과 의미가 <u>다른</u> 문장은?

① I was too slow to win the race.

② I was so slow but I could win the race.

③ I was so slow that I couldn't win the race.

④ I couldn't win the race because I was so slow.

⑤ I was very slow, so I couldn't win the race.

15 다음 중 어법상 옳은 문장은?

① Some people told her to become not a professional.

② I read the newspaper every morning in not order to get behind the times.

③ The teacher asked us to not make any sounds during the class.

④ I hurried not so as to be late for the meeting.

⑤ The weather is getting colder, so you need to be careful not to catch a cold.

16 주어진 단어를 활용하여 다음 우리말을 영어로 쓰시오.

> 나는 나의 학급 친구들을 방해하지 않기 위해 조용히 책을 읽었다. (quietly, disturb, 10 words)

➡ _____

17 다음 중 <u>어색한</u> 것을 고르시오.

① The smartphone was cheap enough to buy.
  → The smartphone was very cheap, so I could buy it.

② The puppy was very small, so she could hold it in one hand.
  → The puppy was so small that she could hold it in one hand.

③ The box was too heavy for me to carry.
  → The box was so heavy that I couldn't carry.

④ Jim is so rich that he can buy the luxurious car.
  → Jim is rich enough to buy the luxurious car.

⑤ Mike is very poor. He can't buy the ring for his wife.
  → Mike is too poor to buy the ring for his wife.

18 다음 밑줄 친 부분을 부정하여 문장을 다시 쓰시오.

> They tried hard so as <u>to fail</u> the entrance exam.

➡ _____
  _____

19 다음 문장의 빈칸에 들어갈 알맞은 것은?

> It's too hot for us to take a long walk.
> = It's _____ we can't take a long walk.

① very hot that   ② hot enough that

③ so hot that   ④ not hot enough to

⑤ too hot that

20 다음 두 문장을 지시에 맞게 하나의 문장으로 쓰시오.

> • We were very late.
> • We couldn't catch the last train.

(1) to부정사를 활용하여

➡ _____

(2) that을 활용하여

➡ _____

21 다음 문장의 빈칸에 들어갈 올바른 것을 고르시오.

> Linda got a terrible cold, so she asked her husband _____.

① not opening the window
② not to opening the window
③ to not open the window
④ never to open the window
⑤ never opening the window

22 주어진 단어를 활용하여 다음 우리말을 영어로 쓰시오.

> 그 남자는 너무 피곤해서 테니스를 칠 수 없었다.
> (tired, play tennis, so)

➡ _____

23 다음 우리말에 맞게 괄호 안의 단어를 배열할 때, 6번째 올 어휘를 고르시오.

> 학생들은 다시는 소란을 피우지 않겠다고 약속했다. (not, any, the, make, noise, to, again, students, promised)

① promised   ② not   ③ noise
④ make   ⑤ to

24 to부정사를 이용하여 주어진 두 문장을 한 문장으로 연결하시오.

(1) • I can't focus on the test.
  • It's because I was very tired.

  ➡ _____

(2) • The presenter was really nervous.
  • So, he couldn't eat dinner.

  ➡ _____

(3) • The evidence is detailed.
  • So, it can support his argument.

  ➡ _____

25 주어진 문장을 that을 이용하여 바꿔 쓰시오.

> The cellphone was too expensive for me to buy.

➡ _____

_____

Reading

[26~27] 다음 글을 읽고 물음에 답하시오.

Reporters came up to Wasiqi and started asking him questions.
Reporter: What happened to you?
Wasiqi: I injured my leg during a practice run. The injury got worse during the race, but I couldn't give up.
Reporter: Why not? You knew that you were too far behind to win a medal.
Wasiqi: I am the only athlete here representing Afghanistan. There was no way I could give up.

Reporter: ⓐ아프가니스탄은 여전히 전쟁 중입니다, isn't it?

Wasiqi: Yes, we have been at war for 16 years. That's why we were not able to send athletes to the Barcelona Olympics four years ago. I was sad for my country back then when I could see no Afghan athletes in the opening ceremony.

26 위 글의 밑줄 친 ⓐ의 우리말에 맞게 5 단어로 영작하시오.

➡ _____

27 According to the passage, which is NOT true?

① Wasiqi injured his leg during a practice run.
② Wasiqi's injury got worse during the race.
③ Wasiqi was too far behind to win a medal.
④ Wasiqi couldn't give up because he was the only athlete there representing Afghanistan.
⑤ Wasiqi was sad when he was the only Afghan athlete in the opening ceremony.

[28~29] 다음 글을 읽고 물음에 답하시오.

A Little Big Hero from Afghanistan

There was a marathon race at the end of the 1996 Atlanta Summer Olympics. When most runners finished ___ⓐ___, and the officials started to prepare for the closing ceremony, a runner entered the stadium. The runner finally ran through the tape and then fell to the ground. His name was Abdul Baser Wasiqi, and he was the only athlete representing Afghanistan. He did not give up running the race for his country.

28 위 글의 빈칸 ⓐ에 race를 알맞은 형태로 쓰시오.

➡ _____

29 위 글의 종류로 알맞은 것을 고르시오.

① diary
② article
③ biography
④ book report
⑤ review

[30~32] 다음 글을 읽고 물음에 답하시오.

I Have a Goal to Win the Singing Contest

I want to win the school singing contest. I love singing, and I think I have a good voice. ___ⓐ___, ⓑI am too shy to sing in front of many people. Not to be nervous during the contest, I will practice singing in front of my class first.

30 위 글의 빈칸 ⓐ에 들어갈 알맞은 말을 고르시오.

① For example
② Therefore
③ However
④ That is
⑤ Moreover

31 위 글의 밑줄 친 ⓑ를 복문으로 고치시오.

➡ _____
_____

32 위 글을 읽고 글쓴이의 목표를 달성하는 데에 있어 (1) 강점과 약점 (2) 약점 때문에 하기 어려운 것 (3) 이를 극복하기 위한 계획을 우리말로 쓰시오.

➡ (1) 강점: _____
   약점: _____
   (2) _____
   (3) _____
   _____

출제율 95%

01 짝지어진 단어의 관계가 같도록 빈칸에 알맞은 말을 쓰시오.

> author : writer = a_____ : respect

출제율 90%

02 다음 빈칸에 들어갈 말로 적절한 것은?

> What does this picture _____?

① represent   ② reduce

③ take   ④ save

⑤ realize

출제율 95%

03 다음 빈칸에 들어갈 말이 바르게 짝지어진 것은?

> • She must be very _____ of herself.
> • I'm not very _____ at tennis.

① proud – aware   ② aware – poor

③ poor – aware   ④ proud – good

⑤ careful – proud

출제율 100%

04 다음 제시된 단어로 자연스러운 문장을 만들 수 <u>없는</u> 것은?

> ┤ 보기 ├
> public removed officials preparation

① I think _____ for the party started early.

② They _____ the tape at the finish line.

③ He was educated at a _____ school when he was a child.

④ Someday, she will be _____ for her acting.

⑤ The ship was boarded by customs _____.

[05~07] 다음 대화를 읽고 물음에 답하시오.

G: Have you   (A)   of Eui Hyun Sin, the skier?

B: No. Who is he?

G: He's a Paralympian skier. He won the first gold medal for Korea in the 2018 Winter Paralympics.

B: Wow! That's great.

G: He was in a car accident in his early twenties and hurt his legs.

B: (가)How was he able to become a skier?

G: After his accident, he tried several different sports to   (B)   better. Then he became especially interested in skiing.

B: Skiing is not easy. Not many people are good at skiing.

G: That's why he's so respected.

출제율 90%

05 밑줄 친 (가) 대신 쓰기에 적절한 것은?

① Do you know he was a skier?

② Do you know why he was able to become a skier?

③ Could you tell me how he was able to become a skier?

④ Did you realize how to become a skier?

⑤ Do you know that he was a skier?

출제율 95%

06 빈칸 (A)와 (B)에 들어가기에 알맞은 것으로 짝지어진 것은?

	(A)	(B)
①	taken	stay
②	made	look
③	heard	take
④	heard	get
⑤	taken	make

07 Which one of the following is NOT true according to the text above?

① Eui Hyun Sin is a Paralympian skier.
② The boy didn't hear of Eui Hyun Sin.
③ The skier hurt his legs in a car accident.
④ Eui Hyun Sin won the first gold medal for Korea in the 2018 Winter Paralympics.
⑤ The boy tried several different kinds of sports.

[08~10] 다음 대화를 읽고 물음에 답하시오.

G: ①Have you heard of D.I.Y.?
B: No, what is D.I.Y.?
G: ②D.I.Y. stands for 'do-it-yourself.' (A)I'm really into it. ③Right now, I'm buying a pencil case.
B: ④What are you going to make after you finish that?
G: When I'm done with the pencil case, ⑤I'm planning to make my own desk.

08 밑줄 친 (A)에 대신 쓸 수 있는 것은?

① I'm running for it.
② I'm doing it myself.
③ I have talked about it.
④ I'm really interested in it.
⑤ I really don't like it.

09 위 대화의 흐름상 어색한 문장은?

①　　②　　③　　④　　⑤

10 Which one CANNOT be answered from the dialogue above?

① Does the girl know about D.I.Y.?
② What does D.I.Y. stand for?
③ What is the girl interested in?
④ Where did the girl hear about D.I.Y.?
⑤ What will the girl make after she finishes a pencil case?

11 다음 빈칸에 들어갈 말로 가장 적절한 것은?

> No one is too old to learn.
> = No one is ＿＿＿＿＿＿＿＿＿＿.

① very old to learn
② old enough to learn
③ very old that he can learn
④ so old that he can't learn
⑤ so old that he can learn

12 괄호 안의 어휘를 이용하여 다음 우리말을 영어로 옮길 때 8번째로 오는 단어는?

> 그 노인은 화를 내지 않기 위해 심호흡을 했다.
> (a deep breath, took, upset)

① took　　② breath　　③ not
④ upset　　⑤ deep

13 다음 중 어법상 바르지 않은 것은?

① The noodles were so delicious that I can't help overeating.
② He was so poor that he couldn't buy bread.
③ He was simple enough to believe that.
④ I was too short to reach the top shelf.
⑤ I'm so hungry that I can eat anything.

14 다음 중 어법상 적절한 것은?

① To not be nervous during the contest, I will practice singing in front of my class first.

② Because it is a long way to my school, it is important not to miss the bus.

③ The player practiced hard to be proud of himself, not win a gold medal.

④ I was taught from the cradle never cry.

⑤ For me and my country, it was important not to giving up.

15 다음 문장을 that을 이용하여 바꿔 쓰시오.

(1) I'm too sick to go out to eat.

➡ _____

(2) She is old enough to do what she wants.

➡ _____

[16~17] 다음 글을 읽고 물음에 답하시오.

Someone shouted, "Look! There comes another runner!" A runner was just entering the stadium, but there was something wrong ____ⓐ____ his legs. Still, he kept going toward the finish line. The band and the volunteers stopped their preparations for the closing ceremony. All eyes were ____ⓑ____ the runner.

Suddenly, the band started playing celebration music, and the volunteers cheered. "Go! Go! Go for it!" Two volunteers ran to the finish line with a tape. Finally, the runner ran through the tape and then fell to the ground. His name was Abdul Baser Wasiqi. He was from Afghanistan.

16 위 글의 빈칸 ⓐ와 ⓑ에 들어갈 전치사가 바르게 짝지어진 것은?

	ⓐ	ⓑ		ⓐ	ⓑ
①	with – on		②	about – by	
③	about – to		④	with – by	
⑤	to – on				

17 위 글에서 알 수 있는 Wasiqi의 성격으로 가장 알맞은 것을 고르시오.

① generous   ② outgoing
③ passive   ④ strong-willed
⑤ aggressive

[18~20] 다음 글을 읽고 물음에 답하시오.

Reporters came up to Wasiqi and started asking him questions.

Reporter: What happened to you?

Wasiqi: I injured my leg during a practice run. The injury got worse during the race, but I couldn't give up.

Reporter: ⓐWhy not? You knew that you were too far behind to win a medal.

Wasiqi: I am the only athlete here representing Afghanistan. There was no way I could give up.

Reporter: Afghanistan is still at war, isn't it?

Wasiqi: Yes, we have been at war for 16 years. ⓑ그것이 우리가 4년 전 바르셀로나 올림픽에 선수들을 보낼 수 없었던 이유입니다. I was sad for my country back then when I could see no Afghan athletes in the opening ceremony.

18 위 글의 밑줄 친 ⓐWhy not?에 생략된 말을 넣어 문장을 다시 쓰시오.

➡ _____

19 위 글의 밑줄 친 ⓑ의 우리말에 맞게 한 단어를 보충하여, 주어진 어휘를 알맞게 배열하시오.

> were not able to / four years / to / we / ago / athletes / that's / the Barcelona Olympics / send

➡ _____

_____

20 위 글의 제목으로 알맞은 것을 고르시오.

① How Embarrassing! Injury During the Race!
② Too Far Behind to Win a Medal!
③ Finishing a Marathon? It's Full of Pain!
④ What I Must Give Up Is to Give Up!
⑤ No Afghan Athletes? How Sad It Is!

[21~22] 다음 글을 읽고 물음에 답하시오.

Reporter: Were you running marathons then?
Wasiqi: No. I started running after Barcelona. I ran in lots of races. Finally I won a marathon in Germany. As a result, I was able to come to Atlanta.
Reporter: How do you feel now?
Wasiqi: ⓐI am proud of me and proud to be from Afghanistan. For me and my country, it was important not to give up. I didn't come here to win. For me, it was enough to be here and to finish the race.

21 위 글의 밑줄 친 ⓐ에서 어법상 틀린 부분을 찾아 고치시오.

_____ ➡ _____

22 According to the passage, which is NOT true?

① Wasiqi started running after the Barcelona Olympics.
② Wasiqi participated in a lot of races before he won a marathon in Germany.
③ After the marathon ended, Wasiqi was proud of himself and proud to be from Afghanistan.
④ To win in the Atlanta Olympics was important for Wasiqi and his country.
⑤ Wasiqi didn't come to Atlanta to win.

[23~24] 다음 글을 읽고 물음에 답하시오.

I Have a Goal to Run a 5 Kilometer Marathon

I want to take part in and complete a 5 (A)[kilometer / kilometers] marathon. I have a lot of time to exercise and a strong will to do my best in every activity. However, I run too slowly to finish the race within the limited amount of time (B)[giving / given]. ⓐNot to fall behind the other runners, I will practice (C)[running / to run] faster every morning.

23 위 글의 괄호 (A)~(C)에서 문맥이나 어법상 알맞은 낱말을 골라 쓰시오.

➡ (A) _____ (B) _____ (C) _____

24 위 글의 밑줄 친 ⓐ를 In order that을 사용하여 고치시오.

➡ _____

[01~03] 다음 대화를 읽고 물음에 답하시오.

> B: How was Thomas Edison able to invent so many things?
>
> G: Many people think that he ___(A)___ things on his first try, but that's not true.
>
> B: Oh, really?
>
> G: Yes. ___(B)___ (~할 때마다) he invented something, he experimented many times.
>
> B: (C)아마 그것이 그토록 많은 사람들이 그를 존경하는 이유일 것이다. (maybe, admire)

01 빈칸 (A)에 들어가기에 적절한 단어를 쓰시오.

➡ _____

02 (B)에 주어진 뜻에 어울리는 단어를 쓰시오. (한 단어)

➡ _____

03 밑줄 친 (C)의 우리말에 해당하는 영어 문장을 주어진 단어를 이용하여 쓰시오. (8 words)

➡ _____

04 다음 우리말을 괄호 안에 주어진 어휘를 이용하여 영작하시오.

(1) 우리는 너무 바빠서 산책하러 나갈 수가 없다. (go out, busy, too)

➡ _____

(2) Jin은 너무 늦어서 9시 기차를 탈 수 없다. (take the 9 o'clock train, that)

➡ _____

(3) 사과들이 따야 할 만큼 익었다. (be picked, the apples, ripe, to)

➡ _____

(4) 이 경기장은 천 명의 사람들을 수용할 만큼 크다. (this stadium, people, hold, large, so, that)

➡ _____

(5) Ellen은 체중이 늘지 않기 위해서 매일 운동한다. (exercises, gain weight)

➡ _____

(6) 그 소녀는 한 단어도 놓치지 않기 위해서 주의 깊게 수업을 들었다. (listened, miss, carefully, in class)

➡ _____

05 다음 문장에서 어법상 어색한 것을 바르게 고치시오.

(1) Andrew promised me to be late never for the meeting again.

➡ _____

(2) In order to not forget certain events with my dog, I always take pictures with her.

➡ _____

(3) I will practice running every morning not so as to fall behind the other runners.

➡ _____

(4) I was too busy going to bed before midnight.

➡ _____

(5) No wonder my grade was so low for me to pass the exam.

➡ _____

Someone shouted, "Look! ⓐAnother runner comes there!" A runner was just entering the stadium, but there was something wrong with his legs. Still, he kept going toward the finish line. The band and the volunteers stopped their preparations for the closing ceremony. All eyes were on the runner.

Suddenly, the band started playing celebration music, and the volunteers cheered. "Go! Go! Go for it!" Two volunteers ran to the finish line with a tape. Finally, the runner ran through the tape and then fell to the ground. His name was Abdul Baser Wasiqi. He was from Afghanistan.

06 위 글의 밑줄 친 ⓐ의 there를 문두로 이동시켜 강조하는 문장을 쓰시오.

➡ _____

07 본문의 내용과 일치하도록 다음 빈칸 (A)와 (B)에 알맞은 단어를 쓰시오.

> Though there was (A)_____ _____ with his legs, Wasiqi didn't give up racing and kept running for so long that when he entered the stadium, the band and the volunteers were preparing for the (B)_____ _____.

08 Why did two volunteers run to the finish line with a tape? Fill in the blanks with suitable words.

> Because they wanted to hold the tape for Wasiqi to _____ _____ it.

Reporters came up to Wasiqi and started asking him questions.

Reporter: What happened to you?

Wasiqi: I injured my leg (A)[during / while] a practice run. The injury got worse during the race, but I couldn't give up.

Reporter: Why not? You knew that you were too far (B)[ahead / behind] to win a medal.

Wasiqi: I am the only athlete here representing Afghanistan. There was no way I could give up.

Reporter: Afghanistan is still at war, isn't it?

Wasiqi: Yes, we have been at war (C)[during / for] 16 years. ⓐThat's why we were not able to send athletes to the Barcelona Olympics four years ago. I was sad for my country back then when I could see no Afghan athletes in the opening ceremony.

09 위 글의 괄호 (A)~(C)에서 문맥이나 어법상 알맞은 낱말을 골라 쓰시오.

➡ (A) _____ (B) _____ (C) _____

10 위 글의 밑줄 친 ⓐ를 다음과 같이 바꿔 쓸 때 빈칸에 들어갈 알맞은 한 단어를 쓰시오.

➡ For that _____, we were not able to send athletes to the Barcelona Olympics four years ago.

창의사고력 서술형 문제

01 리포터가 인터뷰한 후에 작성한 기사를 완성해 봅시다.

A Little Big Hero from Afghanistan

There was a _____ race at the end of the 1996 Atlanta Summer Olympics. When most runners _____ racing, and the officials started to prepare for the _____ ceremony, a runner entered the stadium. The runner finally _____ the tape and then fell to the ground. His name was Abdul Baser Wasiqi, and he was the only athlete _____ Afghanistan. He did not give up running the race for his country.

---

finished	closing	marathon	representing	ran through

---

02 다음 그림을 참고하여 대화의 빈칸을 알맞게 채우시오.

A: I heard that there was a big fire in a building nearby.
B: Was it (A)_____ to hurt a lot of people? (dangerous)
A: Fortunately, no one was hurt. A man knocked every door to tell people (B)_____ inside the building. (be)
B: Wow, that's amazing!

03 다음 내용을 바탕으로 기억 상자에 넣을 다짐의 글을 쓰시오.

My Goal   I want to run a 5 km marathon
Strength   a lot of time to exercise, a strong will
Weakness   run slowly
• I run too slowly to finish the race within the limited amount of time given.
→ I will practice running faster every morning.

I Have a Goal to Run a 5 Kilometer Marathon

I want to take part in and complete a (A)_____. I have (B)_____ and a strong will to do my best in every activity. However, I run (C)_____ to finish the race (D)_____. Not to fall behind the other runners, I will practice (E)_____.

단원별 모의고사

01 다음 짝지어진 두 단어의 관계가 같도록 빈칸에 알맞은 말을 쓰시오.

invite : invitation – transport : _____

02 다음 영영풀이에 해당하는 단어로 적절한 것은?

a strong emotion or feeling

① author
② passion
③ information
④ foundation
⑤ cheer

03 다음 〈보기〉에서 알맞은 말을 골라 써 넣어 문장을 완성하시오.

┌─ 보기 ─┐
stadium   cheered   celebration   war
└────────┘

(1) The two countries have been at _____ for many years.
(2) The Olympic _____ was filled with people.
(3) We had a big _____ for his son's first birthday.
(4) My classmates _____ for me and shouted my name.

04 다음 빈칸에 들어갈 말로 적절한 것은?

It wasn't easy to sing in _____.

① public
② mind
③ plan
④ officials
⑤ place

[05~07] 다음 대화를 읽고 물음에 답하시오.

G: How was Hyeon Chung _____(A)_____ one of the final four players in the tennis competition?

B: (B)He could do it only after years of hard training.

G: I see. When did he start playing tennis?

B: He started to play tennis when he was seven.

05 빈칸 (A)에 적절한 것은?

① can do
② able to be
③ would like to
④ become to
⑤ aware of

06 밑줄 친 (B)를 다음과 같이 바꾸어 쓸 때 빈칸에 적절한 단어를 쓰시오.

➡ He had trained hard for years _____ he could do it.

07 위 대화의 내용과 일치하지 <u>않는</u> 것은?

① Hyeon Chung was a tennis player.
② Hyeon Chung trained hard for years.
③ Hyeon Chung was the winner of the tennis competition.
④ Hyeon Chung started to play tennis at seven.
⑤ The girl wanted to know about Hyeon Chung.

[08~10] 다음 대화를 읽고 물음에 답하시오.

G: Have you heard of Eui Hyun Sin, the skier?

B: No. Who is he?

G: He's a Paralympian skier. (A) He won the first gold medal for Korea in the 2018 Winter Paralympics. (B)

B: Wow! That's great. (C)

G: He was in a car accident in his early twenties and hurt his legs. (D)

B: How was he able to become a skier?

G: (E) Then he became especially interested in skiing.

B: Skiing is not easy. (가)많은 사람들이 스키를 잘 타는 것은 아니다.

G: That's why he's so respected.

08 (A)~(E) 중에서 다음 문장이 들어가기에 적절한 곳은?

> After his accident, he tried several different sports to get better.

① (A)   ② (B)   ③ (C)   ④ (D)   ⑤ (E)

09 밑줄 친 (가)의 우리말과 같은 뜻이 되도록 빈칸에 알맞은 말을 쓰시오.

➡ _____ many people are _____ _____ skiing.

10 Which one is TRUE according to the dialogue?

① Eui Hyun Sin won the first gold medal for Korea for the first time.

② Eui Hyun Sin participated in the 2018 Winter Olympics.

③ Eui Hyun Sin hurt his legs in a car accident.

④ He was interested in skiing before he tried several different sports.

⑤ Skiing is not easy, so he respects many skiers.

[11~12] 다음 대화를 읽고 물음에 답하시오.

B: Sora, have you heard about the fire last night? (A)

G: Yes, I heard that there was a big fire in a building nearby. (B)

B: No, one man saved ten people who were in the building. (C)

G: Oh, really? How was he able to save so many people? (D)

B: He knocked on every door to tell people to leave the building. (E)

G: Wow, that's amazing!

11 다음 문장이 들어가기에 적절한 곳은?

> Was anybody hurt?

① (A)   ② (B)   ③ (C)   ④ (D)   ⑤ (E)

12 위 대화의 내용과 일치하는 것은?

① Sora didn't hear about the fire.

② The boy didn't know who was hurt.

③ No one saved people in the building.

④ A man knocked on every door.

⑤ There weren't any people in the building.

13 다음 문장과 같은 의미로 쓰인 것은?

> The subway I was going to take was too crowded to get on.

① The subway I was going to take was so crowded that I can get on.

② The subway I was going to take was so crowded that I can't get on.

③ The subway I was going to take was so crowded that I could get on it.

④ The subway I was going to take was so crowded that I could get on it.

⑤ The subway I was going to take was so crowded that I couldn't get on it.

14 다음 중 어법상 바르지 <u>않은</u> 것은?

① The last runner ran as fast as possible not to fall behind.

② I always try hard not to wake up late.

③ I told him to never tell a lie again.

④ We booked the concert tickets in advance not to miss the chance to see the idol.

⑤ The boy told a lie to his mom not to disappoint her.

15 두 문장의 의미가 같도록 빈칸을 완성하시오. (6 단어)

> I couldn't solve the problem because it was very difficult.
> = The problem was _____.

➡ _____

16 우리말과 같은 의미가 되도록 괄호 안의 단어를 바르게 배열하시오.

(1) Sally는 감기에 걸리지 않기 위해서 따뜻한 옷을 입었다. (Sally, clothes, not, a, wore, catch, warm, cold, to)

➡ _____

_____

(2) 사람들은 공공장소에서 다른 사람들을 방해하지 않기 위해 조용히 있어야 한다. (people, places, others, disturb, should, not, stay, quiet, public, to, in)

➡ _____

_____

(3) Amy는 너무 아파서 친구들과 놀 수 없었다. (her, Amy, friends, sick, too, play, was, to, with)

➡ _____

_____

17 다음 중 어법상 바른 문장은?

① The song is too difficult to singing.

② The question was enough easy to answer.

③ My mother was too busy to pick me up.

④ You must remember to not make a loud noise.

⑤ She is intelligent enough to not miss a trick.

[18~19] 다음 글을 읽고 물음에 답하시오.

Someone shouted, "Look! There comes another runner!" A runner was just entering the stadium, but there was something wrong with his legs. Still, he kept going toward the finish line. The band and the volunteers stopped their _____ⓐ_____ for the closing ceremony. All eyes were on the runner.

Suddenly, the band started playing celebration music, and the volunteers cheered. "Go! Go! Go for it!" Two volunteers ran to the finish line with a tape. Finally, the runner ran through the tape and then fell to the ground. His name was Abdul Baser Wasiqi. He was from Afghanistan.

18 위 글의 빈칸 ⓐ에 prepare를 알맞은 형태로 쓰시오.

➡ _____

19 위 글의 주제로 알맞은 것을 고르시오.

① something wrong with a marathon runner

② the true sportsmanship which never gives in to hardship

③ the surprise that the band and the volunteers felt

④ hot cheering of the band and the volunteers

⑤ a hard day of an exhausted marathon runner

[20~22] 다음 글을 읽고 물음에 답하시오.

Reporters came up to Wasiqi and started asking him questions.

Reporter: What happened to you?

Wasiqi: (①) I injured my leg during a practice run. The injury got worse during the race, but I couldn't give up.

Reporter: (②) You knew that you were too far behind to win a medal.

Wasiqi: (③) I am the only athlete here representing Afghanistan. (④) There was no way I could give up.

Reporter: (⑤) Afghanistan is still at war, isn't it?

Wasiqi: Yes, we have been at war for 16 years. That's why we were not able to send athletes to the Barcelona Olympics four years ago. I was sad for my country back then when I could see no ____ⓐ____ athletes in the opening ceremony.

20 위 글의 빈칸 ⓐ에 Afghanistan을 알맞은 형태로 쓰시오.

➡ _____

21 위 글의 흐름으로 보아, 주어진 문장이 들어가기에 가장 적절한 곳은?

Why not?

①   ②   ③   ④   ⑤

22 Why was Wasiqi sad for his country at the time when the Barcelona Olympics were held? Fill in the blanks (A) and (B) with suitable words.

Because at that time Afghanistan was not able to (A)_____ _____ to the Barcelona Olympics because of the war, so there were no athletes representing Afghanistan in the (B)_____ ceremony.

[23~25] 다음 글을 읽고 물음에 답하시오.

A Little Big Hero from Afghanistan

There was a marathon race at the end of the 1996 Atlanta Summer Olympics. When most runners finished racing, and the officials started to prepare for the closing ceremony, a runner entered the stadium. The runner finally ran through the tape and then fell to the ground. His name was Abdul Baser Wasiqi, and he was the only athlete representing Afghanistan. He did not give up ____ⓐ____ the race for his country.

23 위 글의 빈칸 ⓐ에 run을 알맞은 형태로 쓰시오.

➡ _____

24 주어진 영영풀이에 해당하는 단어를 본문에서 찾아 쓰시오.

people who hold a position of authority in an organization

➡ _____

25 위 글을 읽고 답할 수 없는 질문을 고르시오.

① When did Wasiqi enter the stadium?
② Did Wasiqi run through the tape?
③ Were there any other athletes representing Afghanistan except Wasiqi?
④ For what did Wasiqi keep running the race?
⑤ How long did Wasiqi run?

Lesson 2

Teens' Worries

 의사소통 기능

- 동의나 이의 여부 표현하기
  A: I think listening to music helps you relax.
  B: I agree.

- 안심시키기
  A: I'm worried about making friends at my new school.
  B: Don't worry. I'm sure you'll make a lot of friends there.

 언어 형식

- 분사구문
  Daeho, **thinking that new things will make him more popular**, often wants new things just because his friends have them.

- 명사절을 이끄는 접속사 'if'
  You should just ask her **if** there is something wrong.

Words & Expressions

Key Words

- **advise**[ədváiz] 동 충고하다
- **afraid**[əfréid] 형 걱정하는, 불안한
- **agree**[əgríː] 동 동의하다
- **avoid**[əvɔ́id] 동 피하다
- **counselor**[káunsələr] 명 카운슬러, 상담역
- **decide**[disáid] 동 결정하다
- **disagree**[dìsəgríː] 동 동의하지 않다
- **else**[els] 형 다른
- **experiment**[ikspérəmənt] 명 실험
- **festival**[féstəvəl] 명 축제
- **final**[fáinl] 명 결승, 기말고사 형 마지막의
- **fun**[fʌn] 명 재미
- **guy**[gai] 명 (비격식) 녀석, 남자
- **hate**[heit] 동 매우 싫어하다
- **helpful**[hélpfəl] 형 도움이 되는
- **hurt**[həːrt] 동 다치다
- **if**[if] 접 ~인지 아닌지
- **latest**[léitist] 형 최신의
- **management**[mǽnidʒmənt] 명 관리
- **match**[mætʃ] 명 시합
- **matter**[mǽtər] 명 문제
- **mistake**[mistéik] 명 실수
- **misunderstand**[misəndərstǽnd] 동 오해하다
- **number**[nʌ́mbər] 동 번호를 매기다
- **P.E. teacher** 체육 교사
- **part**[pɑːrt] 명 부분, 배역, 역할
- **popular**[pɑ́pjulər] 형 인기 있는
- **project**[prɑ́dʒekt] 명 과제
- **protein**[próutiːn] 명 단백질
- **prove**[pruːv] 동 증명하다, 입증하다
- **recently**[ríːsntli] 부 최근에
- **relax**[rilǽks] 동 쉬다
- **snap**[snæp] 명 찰칵하는 소리를 내며 움직이는 것
- **sneakers**[sníːkərz] 명 운동화
- **speech contest** 웅변대회
- **still**[stil] 부 아직도
- **stress**[stress] 명 스트레스
- **strict**[strikt] 형 엄격한
- **teenager**[tíːnèidʒər] 명 청소년
- **try**[trai] 동 시도하다
- **upset**[ʌ́pset] 형 기분이 상한
- **vocabulary**[voukǽbjulèri] 명 어휘
- **worry**[wɔ́ːri] 명 걱정 동 걱정하다

Key Expressions

- **a couple of** 두서너 개의, 몇 개의, 몇 사람의
- **a lot of** 많은
- **ask A for B** A에게 B를 요청하다
- **ask somebody out** ~에게 데이트를 신청하다
- **be asked out** 데이트 신청을 받다
- **be nervous about** ~에 대하여 불안하다
- **be ready for** ~에 준비가 되다
- **be worried about** ~에 대해 걱정하다
- **do one's job** ~의 일을 하다
- **do one's part** ~의 역할을 하다
- **end up -ing** 결국 ~하게 되다
- **focus on** 집중하다
- **for a long time** 오랫동안
- **for now** 당분간은, 현재로는
- **get started** 시작하다
- **get together** 모이다
- **get 목적어 to 동사원형** ~에게 … 하도록 하다
- **have a hard time -ing** ~하는 데 어려움이 있다
- **in style** 유행하는, 유행되는
- **Is something wrong?** 뭐가 잘못되었나요?
- **look worried** 걱정스러워 보이다
- **make friends** 친구를 사귀다
- **no longer** 더 이상 ~가 아닌
- **not ~ anymore** 더 이상 ~가 아닌
- **not yet** 아직 ~가 아닌
- **take time** 시간이 걸리다
- **without -ing** ~하지 않고, ~ 없이
- **write down** 기록하다

Word Power

※ 서로 비슷한 뜻을 가진 어휘

- □ **afraid** 걱정하는, 불안한 : **nervous** 불안한
- □ **decide** 결정하다 : **determine** 결정하다
- □ **hurt** 다치다 : **injure** 부상을 입다
- □ **project** 과제 : **task** 과제

- □ **avoid** 피하다 : **evade** 피하다
- □ **hate** 매우 싫어하다 : **detest** 몹시 싫어하다
- □ **part** 배역, 역할 : **role** 역할
- □ **strict** 엄격한 : **rigid** 엄격한

※ 서로 반대되는 뜻을 가진 어휘

- □ **afraid** 걱정하는 ↔ **unafraid** 걱정하지 않는
- □ **avoid** 피하다 ↔ **face** 마주하다

- □ **agree** 동의하다 ↔ **disagree** 동의하지 않다
- □ **hate** 매우 싫어하다 ↔ **like** 좋아하다

※ 같은 형태로 동사와 명사로 쓰이는 낱말

- □ **worry** 동 걱정하다 명 걱정
- □ **need** 동 필요하다 명 필요
- □ **act** 동 행동하다 명 행동
- □ **design** 동 디자인하다 명 디자인
- □ **rain** 동 비 내리다 명 비

- □ **answer** 동 대답하다 명 대답
- □ **raise** 동 인상하다 명 인상
- □ **address** 동 주소를 쓰다 명 주소
- □ **fight** 동 싸우다 명 싸움
- □ **use** 동 사용하다 명 사용

- □ **hope** 동 희망하다 명 희망
- □ **taste** 동 맛보다 명 맛
- □ **care** 동 돌보다 명 돌봄
- □ **help** 동 돕다 명 도움
- □ **visit** 동 방문하다 명 방문

※ 동사 - 명사

- □ **relax** 쉬다 - **relaxation** 휴식
- □ **agree** 동의하다 - **agreement** 동의, 일치

- □ **prove** 입증하다 - **proof** 증거
- □ **manage** 관리하다 - **management** 관리

English Dictionary

- □ **a couple of** 두서너 개의, 몇 개의, 몇 사람의
  → two people or things of the same category
  같은 유형의 두 사람 또는 두 개
- □ **agree** 동의하다
  → to have the same opinion as someone about a topic
  어떤 주제에 대하여 다른 사람과 같은 의견을 가지다
- □ **counselor** 카운슬러, 상담역
  → someone whose job is to provide help and advice to people with problems
  문제가 있는 사람에게 도움이나 조언을 제공하는 직업을 가진 사람
- □ **disagree** 동의하지 않다
  → to have a different opinion 다른 의견을 가지다
- □ **hate** 매우 싫어하다
  → to dislike something strongly 어떤 것을 강하게 싫어하다
- □ **latest** 최신의
  → most recent and newest 가장 새롭고 가장 최근의

- □ **mistake** 실수
  → something that you do wrong without wanting to
  원치 않으면서 저지르는 잘못
- □ **prove** 증명하다, 입증하다
  → to show that something is true
  어떤 것이 사실이라는 것을 보여주다
- □ **recently** 최근에
  → not long ago 얼마 전에
- □ **sneakers** 운동화
  → soft sided sports shoes 부드러운 소재의 운동화
- □ **teenager** 청소년
  → a person who is between the ages of 13 and 19
  13세에서 19세 사이의 사람
- □ **vocabulary** 어휘
  → words that are used in a language
  어떤 언어에서 사용되는 단어

서답형

01 〈보기〉와 같은 관계가 되도록 빈칸에 알맞은 말을 쓰시오. (주어진 철자로 시작할 것)

> ┌ 보기 ┐
>
> decide : determine

(1) hate : d_____
(2) afraid : n_____

02 다음 주어진 문장의 빈칸에 들어갈 단어를 사용하여 자연스러운 문장을 만들 수 있는 것은?

> Ella _____ to the judge that she hadn't stolen the money.

① I _____ with you about our field trip.
② Clair _____ Mason out, and they went to a movie.
③ Many people _____ with Mr. Smith.
④ He _____ that he hadn't made the mistake.
⑤ The two boys _____ each other.

03 다음 중 밑줄 친 부분의 뜻풀이가 바르지 <u>않은</u> 것은?

① Daniel is <u>afraid</u> of going to the dentist. (두려운)
② The <u>counselor</u> advised me to get more sleep. (상담역)
③ Jack bought the <u>latest</u> model of the car. (마지막의)
④ Lucas got a C on the math test because he made too many <u>mistakes</u>. (실수)
⑤ Ryan <u>misunderstood</u> what I said. (오해했다)

중요

04 다음 중 〈보기〉에 있는 단어를 사용하여 자연스러운 문장을 만들 수 <u>없는</u> 것은?

> ┌ 보기 ┐
>
> hate   guy   end   a couple of

① I saw _____ boys playing catch ball.
② If you do not leave now, you will _____ up being late.
③ Lucas is a nice _____ because he has good manners.
④ I _____ jelly because of its texture.
⑤ Luna wants to buy a dress that is _____ style.

05 다음 밑줄 친 부분과 의미가 가장 가까운 것을 고르시오.

> I think he will <u>decide</u> to travel with us.

① avoid   ② act
③ design   ④ answer
⑤ determine

중요

06 다음 빈칸에 공통으로 들어가기에 알맞은 것은?

> • You have to _____ started by the count of 10.
> • I hope that you _____ better soon.

① take   ② get   ③ hold
④ make   ⑤ grow

01 주어진 단어를 이용해 빈칸을 완성하시오.

Time _____ is an important skill for them to learn.

➡ _____ (manage)

02 다음 짝지어진 단어의 관계가 같도록 빈칸에 알맞은 말을 쓰시오.

relax : relaxation = prove : _____

중요

[03~04] 빈칸에 공통으로 들어갈 단어를 쓰시오.

03
• The house stood empty _____ a long time.
• The plane is ready _____ take-off.

04
• I was asked _____ to dinner.
• She went _____ of the room.

05 빈칸에 알맞은 단어를 〈보기〉에서 골라 쓰시오.

┌ 보기 ┐
style   end   about   now

(1) I'm worried _____ the safety of the project.
(2) I always _____ up eating too much during the holidays.
(3) The project of the team has been stopped for _____.
(4) Short skirts are in _____ these days.

06 다음 우리말에 맞게 빈칸에 알맞은 말을 쓰시오.

(1) 영어 수업의 팀 프로젝트는 시간이 많이 걸리고 있다.
➡ The team project for English class is _____ a lot of time.

(2) 나는 새로운 영어 단어를 배우느라 어려움을 겪고 있어.
➡ I'm _____ a hard time learning new English words.

(3) 그는 일어나서 아무에게도 말하지 않고 떠났다.
➡ He stood up and left _____ telling anyone.

(4) 가족과 친구들이 모여 그의 생일을 축하해 주었다.
➡ His family and friends got _____ and celebrated his birthday.

Conversation

1 동의나 이의 여부 표현하기

> **A** I think listening to music helps you relax.
> 나는 음악을 듣는 것이 긴장을 푸는 데 도움이 된다고 생각해.
>
> **B** I agree. 동의해.

- 상대방의 말이나 의견에 동의할 때는 "I agree with you." 또는 "You can say that again."이라고 한다. 상대방의 말에 동의하지 않을 때는 "I don't agree."라고 한다.

- 상대방에게 자신의 말에 대하여 동의를 구할 때 간단하게는 부가의문문을 덧붙여서 나타낼 수 있지만, 다른 영어 표현으로 "Don't you agree (with me)?"가 있다. "(제 생각에) 동의하지 않으세요?"의 의미로 "Don't you think so?"라고 할 수도 있다.

- 상대방의 의견에 동의할 때는 '나도 그래.'의 의미로 "Me, too." 또는 "So+동사+주어."의 형태를 쓴다. 이때 사용하는 동사는 be동사, do, does, did를 포함하는 조동사들이다. 부정문에 이어지는 경우에는 so 대신 neither를 사용하여 "Neither+동사+주어."라고 하거나, "Me neither."라고 할 수 있다. 동의하지 않는 것을 좀 더 공손하게 표현할 때 "I'm afraid."를 덧붙여 말할 수도 있다.

동의나 이의 여부를 나타내는 표현

〈동의하기〉

- I agree (with you). 동의해.
- So am/do I. / Me, too. / Me, neither. 나도 마찬가지야.
- Same here. 나도 마찬가지야.
- You can say that again. 네 말이 맞아.
- That's a neat/good/great idea. 그거 좋은 생각이야.

〈이의 제기하기〉

- I don't agree. 저는 동의하지 않아요.
- I don't believe so. 그렇게 생각하지 않습니다.
- I don't think so. 그렇게 생각하지 않아요.
- I disagree with you. 저는 동의하지 않습니다.

동의하는지 묻는 표현

- Don't you agree (with me)? 동의하지 않으세요?
- Don't you think so? 그렇게 생각하지 않으세요?

핵심 Check

1. 다음 빈칸에 들어갈 말로 적절하지 <u>않은</u> 것을 고르시오.

   G: I think reading history comic books is helpful.

   B: _____ I learn a lot from them.

   ① I agree.　　　　② Same here.　　　　③ So do I.
   ④ I think so too.　　⑤ Don't you think so?

② 안심시키기

> **A** I'm worried about making friends at my new school.
> 난 새로운 학교에서 친구를 사귀는 것이 걱정이 돼.
>
> **B** Don't worry. I'm sure you'll make a lot of friends there.
> 걱정하지 마. 네가 거기에서 많은 친구를 사귈 것이라고 확신해.

■ 상대방이 걱정스러워 보이거나 불안해 보일 때 상대를 안심시키는 말은 "Don't worry."(걱정하지 마.), "It's all right. Don't worry."(괜찮아, 걱정하지 마.) 등이다. 보통 시험이나 시합 또는 새로운 일을 앞두고 불안해 할 때 걱정하지 말라고 안심시키는 말을 하거나, "잘할 거라고 확신한다."는 의미로 "I'm sure you will fine.", "I'm sure it will be okay." 또는 "I'm sure you'll do better." 등의 표현을 사용한다.

■ worry를 사용하는 표현 이외에 안심시키는 표현은 "That's/It's all right.", "That's/It's okay.", "Everything will be okay." 등으로 상대의 마음을 편하게 해주는 표현이다. 보통 상대가 불안하다는 의사 표현을 했을 때 거기에 대하여 적절한 해결책을 제시하고 "Everything will be all right.", "Everything will be okay." 등의 표현을 사용한다.

■ 걱정하는 내용에 따라서 상대가 잘할 거니까 걱정하지 말라고 안심을 시키는 경우에는 "Cheer up. I'm sure that you will do better next time.", "I'm confident that you will succeed.", "I'm sure that you'll pass the exam." 등으로 나타낼 수 있다.

안심시키기

- Everything will be okay. 모든 게 잘 될 거야.
- Take it easy. Everything will be all right. 마음 편히 가져. 모든 일이 좋아질 거야.
- Don't sweat it. Nothing to worry about. 괜찮아. 걱정할 것 하나도 없어.
- Never mind, it'll be all right. 신경쓰지 마. 괜찮을 거야.
- Cheer up. I'm sure that you will do better next time. 힘내. 너는 다음 번에는 더 잘할 거라고 확신해.
- I'm confident that you will succeed. 네가 성공할 거라고 확신해.

핵심 Check

2. 다음 밑줄 친 말과 바꿔 쓸 수 있는 것은?

B: I have a big soccer match tomorrow. I'm nervous.
G: Don't worry. <u>I'm sure you'll play very well.</u>

① I'm all right.
② Everything will be all right.
③ I don't think so.
④ Have you ever played soccer?
⑤ You have heard of it.

Real-Life Zone

B: The team project for English class is ❶taking a lot of time.

G: I agree. I have a problem. One of the people on our team isn't ❷doing his part.

B: That's not good. Everybody on the team has to do their job.

G: I know, but I don't know how to get him to do his part.

B: Maybe he doesn't know how to get started or doesn't like his part.

G: Then what should I do?

B: Talk to him. Ask him ❸why he's not doing his part. Then tell him you'll help him if he wants.

G: Okay. I'll try that.

B: I'm sure he'll do better after you talk to him. Good luck with your project.

G: Thanks.

B: 영어 수업의 팀 프로젝트는 시간이 많이 걸려.

G: 나도 동의해. 나 문제가 있어. 우리 팀의 한 사람이 자기 역할을 다하지 않아.

B: 좋지 않네. 팀의 모든 사람들은 자신들의 일을 해야 해.

G: 알아. 하지만 어떻게 그가 그의 역할을 하게 할지 모르겠어.

B: 어쩌면 그는 시작하는 법을 모르거나 자기 역할을 좋아하지 않을 수도 있어.

G: 그러면 나는 무엇을 해야 할까?

B: 그에게 말해. 그에게 왜 자신의 역할을 안 하는지 물어봐. 그러고 나서 원한다면 네가 도와주겠다고 말해.

G: 그래. 한번 해 볼게.

B: 나는 네가 말하고 나면 그가 더 잘할 거라고 확신해. 네 프로젝트가 잘 되길 바랄게.

G: 고마워.

❶ take a lot of time = 많은 시간이 걸리다
❷ do one's part = 자신의 역할을 하다
❸ "why he's not doing his part"는 ask의 직접목적어로 쓰인 간접의문문이다.

Check(√) True or False

(1) Some of the members on the girl's team aren't doing their part. T ☐ F ☐

(2) The girl will ask the student why he isn't doing his part. T ☐ F ☐

 Wrap Up

G: What's the matter, Dongha? You look worried.

B: I'm not ready for the finals. I sit at my desk to study but ❶end up doing something else.

G: Well, time management is not easy.

B: I agree. What should I do?

G: ❷Number the things you have to do. Then write down how much time you need to finish each one.

B: Thank you, Emily. I'll try your idea.

G: I'm sure that will be helpful for you. Good luck with your finals.

G: 동하야, 무슨 일이야? 걱정스러워 보여.

B: 기말고사 준비가 안 됐어. 나는 공부하기 위해 책상에 앉지만 결국 다른 것을 하게 돼.

G: 음, 시간 관리가 쉽지 않지.

B: 나도 동의해. 내가 어떻게 해야 할까?

G: 해야 할 일에 번호를 매겨. 그러고 나서 각 항목을 끝내는 데 필요한 시간을 적어봐.

B: 고마워, 에밀리. 네 방안을 한번 해 볼게.

G: 나는 그것이 너에게 도움이 될 거라고 확신해. 기말고사 잘 보길 바랄게.

❶ end up -ing = 결국 ~하게 되다
❷ 이 문장의 "Number"는 동사로 쓰여서 "번호를 매기다"의 뜻이다.

Check(√) True or False

(3) Dongha sits at the desk to study but ends up doing something else. T ☐ F ☐

(4) Dongha disagrees that time management is not easy. T ☐ F ☐

Listen & Speak 1 Listen

1. G: ❶I think listening to music helps you relax.
   B: I agree.
2. G: I think ❷reading history comic books is helpful.
   B: I agree. I learn a lot from them.
3. G: Our school festival is going to be a lot of fun.
   B: I agree.
4. B: Our P.E. teacher is too strict. ❸Don't you agree?
   G: No, I don't agree. ❹I don't think he's too strict.

❶ helps의 목적격보어로 원형부정사 relax가 쓰였다. to relax라고도 할 수 있다.
❷ 종속절의 주어 "reading history comic books"는 단수 취급해서 동사 is가 쓰였다.
❸ "Don't you agree?"는 상대에게 동의 여부를 묻는 말이다.
❹ "I don't think ~."는 "~라고 생각하지 않는다."의 뜻으로 이의를 나타낸다.

Listen & Speak 1 A-1

G: Mom told me ❶I could use the computer for only one hour a day. She thinks that's enough time.
M: I agree with her.
G: Sometimes, ❷when doing my homework, I need to use it for a long time.
M: Hmm. Then maybe we should all get together and talk about it.
G: Thanks for your understanding, Dad.

❶ 동사 told의 직접목적어로 쓰인 명사절의 접속사 that이 생략되었다.
❷ "when doing my homework"는 시간의 부사절에 "주어+be동사"가 생략된 형태이다.

Listen & Speak 1 A-2

B: I just talked about the science project with Jinho and Mina.
G: ❶Has your team decided what you will do?
B: No, not yet. Jinho wants to visit a science museum, but Mina wants to do an experiment.
G: ❷Who do you agree with, Jinho or Mina?
B: ❸I agree with Mina because I think the experiment would be more interesting.

❶ 완료를 나타내는 현재완료이며, "what you will do"는 간접의문문이다.
❷ 의문사 Who는 전치사 with의 목적어에 해당한다. Whom을 써도 좋다.
❸ "agree with+사람", "agree to+의견"이다.

Listen & Speak 2 Listen

1. B: I have a big soccer match tomorrow. I'm nervous.
   G: Don't worry. ❶I'm sure you'll play very well.
2. G: ❷I'm nervous about tomorrow's speech contest.
   B: I'm sure you'll do fine. Don't worry.
3. G: I'm worried about making friends at my new school.
   M: Don't worry. I'm sure you'll make a lot of friends there.

❶ "I'm sure ~"는 상대를 안심시키기 위해서 확신을 주는 말이다.
❷ "be nervous about ~"는 "be worried about ~"처럼 불안, 염려를 나타낸다.

Listen & Speak 2 A-1

B: You look worried. ❶Is something wrong?
G: Yes, ❷my sister is upset with me.
B: Why? What did you do?
G: I wore one of her shirts without asking.
B: Tell her you're sorry. I'm sure she'll understand.

❶ "Is something wrong?"은 "What's the matter?"처럼 상대가 안 좋아 보일 때 무슨 문제가 있는지 묻는 말이다.
❷ "be upset with"는 "~에게 화내다"의 뜻이다.

Listen & Speak 2 A-2

B: ❶I'm having a hard time learning new English words.
G: I had the same problem, ❷so I asked my English teacher for advice.
B: What did he say?
G: ❸He advised me to use an English vocabulary app. It has helped me a lot. I'm sure it would work for you, too.

❶ "have a hard time -ing"는 "have trouble -ing" 또는 "have a difficult time -ing"처럼 "~하는 데 어려움을 겪다"라는 의미이다.
❷ so는 원인에 이어서 결과를 유도하는 등위 접속사이다.
❸ "~에게 … 하도록 충고하다"는 "advise+목적어+to부정사"이다.

● 다음 우리말과 일치하도록 빈칸에 알맞은 말을 쓰시오.

Listen & Speak 1 Listen

1. **B**: I think _____ to music _____ you _____.
   G: I _____.

2. **G**: I think _____ history comic books is _____.
   B: I agree. I _____ a lot _____ them.

3. **G**: Our school _____ is going to be a lot of _____.
   B: I agree.

4. **B**: Our P.E. _____ is too _____. Don't you _____?
   G: No, I _____ agree. I don't think he's too _____.

Listen & Speak 1 A

1. **G**: Mom _____ me I could _____ the computer _____ only one hour a _____. She thinks that's _____ time.
   M: I _____ _____ her.
   G: Sometimes, when _____ my homework, I _____ to use it _____ a long time.
   M: Hmm. Then maybe we should all _____ together and _____ about it.
   G: Thanks _____ your understanding, Dad.

2. **B**: I _____ talked _____ the science _____ with Jinho and Mina.
   G: Has your team _____ what you will _____?
   B: No, _____ yet. Jinho wants to _____ a science museum, but Mina _____ to do an _____.
   G: Who do you agree _____, Jinho or Mina?
   B: I agree _____ Mina because I think the _____ would be more _____.

Listen & Speak 2 Listen

1. **B**: I _____ a big soccer _____ tomorrow. I'm _____.
   G: Don't _____. I'm _____ you'll _____ very well.

2. **G**: I'm _____ about tomorrow's _____ contest.
   B: I'm sure you'll _____ fine. Don't _____.

3. **G**: I'm _____ about making _____ at my new _____.
   M: Don't worry. I'm _____ you'll _____ a lot of _____ there.

해석

1. B: 나는 음악을 듣는 것이 긴장을 푸는 데 도움이 된다고 생각해.
   G: 나도 동의해.
2. G: 나는 역사 만화책을 읽는 것이 도움이 된다고 생각해.
   B: 나도 동의해. 나는 그것들로부터 많은 것을 배워.
3. G: 우리 학교 축제는 아주 재미있을 거야.
   B: 나도 동의해.
4. B: 우리 체육 선생님은 너무 엄격하셔. 너도 동의하지 않니?
   G: 응, 난 동의하지 않아. 나는 그가 너무 엄격하다고 생각하지 않아.

1. G: 엄마는 제가 하루에 한 시간만 컴퓨터를 사용할 수 있다고 말씀하셨어요. 그녀는 그게 충분한 시간이라고 생각하세요.
   M: 나도 그녀의 말에 동의한단다.
   G: 숙제를 할 때 그것을 오래 사용할 필요가 있어요.
   M: 음. 그러면 아마 우리는 다 같이 모여 그것에 대해 이야기를 해야 할 것 같구나.
   G: 이해해 줘서 고마워요. 아빠.
2. B: 나는 진호랑 미나랑 과학 프로젝트에 대해 방금 이야기했어.
   G: 너희 팀은 무엇을 할지 결정했니?
   B: 아니, 아직. 진호는 과학 박물관을 방문하고 싶어하지만, 미나는 실험을 하고 싶어해.
   G: 너는 진호나 미나 중에 누구에게 동의해?
   B: 나는 실험이 더 흥미로울 거라고 생각해서 미나의 말에 동의해.

1. B: 내일 큰 축구 경기가 있어. 긴장돼.
   G: 걱정하지 마. 난 네가 아주 잘 경기할 거라고 확신해.
2. G: 내일 있을 말하기 대회 때문에 긴장돼.
   B: 난 네가 잘할 거라고 확신해. 걱정하지 마.
3. G: 새 학교에서 친구를 사귀는 게 걱정돼요.
   M: 걱정하지 마. 난 네가 그곳에서 많은 친구들을 사귈 거라고 확신해.

Listen & Speak 2 A

1. **B:** You look _____. Is something _____?

   G: Yes, my sister is _____ with me.

   B: _____? What did you _____?

   G: I _____ one of her shirts _____ asking.

   B: Tell her you're _____. I'm sure she'll _____.

2. **B:** I'm _____ a hard time _____ new English words.

   G: I _____ the same problem, so I _____ my English _____ for advice.

   B: _____ did he say?

   G: He _____ me to _____ an English _____ app. It has helped me a lot. I'm _____ it would work for you, too.

Real-Life Zone

B: The team _____ for English class is _____ a lot of time.

G: I _____. I have a problem. _____ of the _____ on our team isn't _____ his part.

B: _____ not good. Everybody on the _____ has to do their job.

G: I _____, but I don't _____ how to _____ him _____ do his part.

B: Maybe he _____ know how to get _____ or doesn't _____ his _____.

G: Then _____ should I _____?

B: Talk _____ him. Ask him _____ he's not _____ his part. _____ tell him _____ help him _____ he _____.

G: Okay. I'll _____ that.

B: I'm _____ he'll do _____ after you _____ to him. Good luck with your _____.

G: Thanks.

Wrap Up

G: What's the _____, Dongha? You _____ worried.

B: I'm not _____ for the _____. I sit at my _____ to _____ but end _____ doing _____ else.

G: Well, time _____ is not _____.

B: I _____. What _____ I do?

G: _____ the things you _____ to do. _____ write how _____ time _____ need to _____ each one.

B: Thank you, Emily. I'll _____ your idea.

G: I'm sure _____ will be helpful for you. Good luck _____ your finals.

해석

1. B: 걱정스러워 보여. 무슨 일 있니?
   G: 응, 우리 언니가 나한테 화가 났어.
   B: 왜? 무엇을 했니?
   G: 내가 묻지도 않고 언니의 셔츠 중에 하나를 입었어.
   B: 그녀에게 미안하다고 말해. 나는 그녀가 이해해 줄 거라고 확신해.
2. B: 나는 새로운 영어 단어를 배우는 데 어려움을 겪고 있어.
   G: 나도 같은 문제가 있어서 영어 선생님께 조언을 구했어.
   B: 그가 뭐라고 하셨어?
   G: 그는 나에게 영어 어휘 앱을 사용하라고 조언해 주셨어. 그것은 나에게 큰 도움이 됐어. 나는 그것이 너에게도 효과가 있을 거라고 확신해.

B: 영어 수업의 팀 프로젝트는 시간이 많이 걸려.
G: 나도 동의해. 나 문제가 있어. 우리 팀의 한 사람이 자기 역할을 다하지 않아.
B: 좋지 않네. 팀의 모든 사람들은 자신들의 일을 해야 해.
G: 알아. 하지만 어떻게 그가 그의 역할을 하게 할지 모르겠어.
B: 어쩌면 그는 시작하는 법을 모르거나 자기 역할을 좋아하지 않을 수도 있어.
G: 그러면 나는 무엇을 해야 할까?
B: 그에게 말해. 그에게 왜 자신의 역할을 안 하는지 물어봐. 그러고 나서 원한다면 네가 도와주겠다고 말해.
G: 그래. 한번 해 볼게.
B: 나는 네가 말하고 나면 그가 더 잘할 거라고 확신해. 네 프로젝트가 잘 되길 바랄게.
G: 고마워.

G: 동하야, 무슨 일이야? 걱정스러워 보여.
B: 기말고사 준비가 안 됐어. 나는 공부하기 위해 책상에 앉지만 결국 다른 것을 하게 돼.
G: 음, 시간 관리가 쉽지 않지.
B: 나도 동의해. 내가 어떻게 해야 할까?
G: 해야 할 일에 번호를 매겨. 그러고 나서 각 항목을 끝내는 데 필요한 시간을 적어 봐.
B: 고마워, 에밀리. 네 방안을 한번 해 볼게.
G: 나는 그것이 너에게 도움이 될 거라고 확신해. 기말고사 잘 보길 바랄게.

[01~02] 다음 대화의 빈칸에 들어갈 말로 알맞은 것은?

01

G: Mom told me I could use the computer for only one hour a day. She thinks that's enough time.

M: I _____ her.

G: Sometimes, when doing my homework, I need to use it for a long time.

M: Hmm. Then maybe we should all get together and talk about it.

G: Thanks for your understanding, Dad.

① agree with   ② approve   ③ am anxious about

④ am worried about   ⑤ am ready for

02

B: You look worried. Is something wrong?

G: Yes, my sister is upset with me.

B: Why? What did you do?

G: I wore one of her shirts without asking.

B: Tell her you're sorry. _____

① You don't worry about her.

② I don't know why you were worried.

③ I will make her not be upset with you.

④ I'm sure she'll understand.

⑤ I'm pleased with her shirt.

03 대화에 이어지기에 적절하게 배열된 순서를 고르시오.

B: I just talked about the science project with Jinho and Mina.

G: Has your team decided what you will do?

(A) I agree with Mina because I think the experiment would be more interesting.

(B) Who do you agree with, Jinho or Mina?

(C) No, not yet. Jinho wants to visit a science museum, but Mina wants to do an experiment.

① (A) – (C) – (B)   ② (B) – (A) – (C)   ③ (B) – (C) – (A)

④ (C) – (A) – (B)   ⑤ (C) – (B) – (A)

01 다음 빈칸에 적절한 말은?

> G: I think reading history comic books is helpful.
>
> B: I agree. _____

① I learn a lot from them.
② I don't like reading comic books.
③ Reading comic books is wasting time.
④ Why do you like reading comic books?
⑤ I won't read comic books any more.

[02~03] 다음 대화를 읽고 물음에 답하시오.

> B: I ___(가)___ learning new English words.
>
> G: I had the same problem, so I asked my English teacher for advice.
>
> B: What did he say?
>
> G: He advised me to use an English vocabulary app. It has helped me a lot. I'm sure it would work for you, too.

02 빈칸 (가)에 들어가기에 적절한 것은?

① have always enjoyed
② didn't really mind
③ wouldn't like
④ look forward to
⑤ am having a hard time

03 위 대화의 내용과 일치하지 <u>않는</u> 것은?

① The boy wants to improve his English.
② The girl has a hard time learning new English words.
③ The girl had the same problem.
④ The girl asked her teacher for advice.
⑤ The girl thinks using an English vocabulary app helped her.

[04~06] 다음 대화를 읽고 물음에 답하시오.

> G: What's the matter, Dongha? ___(가)___.
>
> B: I'm not ready for the finals. I sit at my desk to study but end up doing something else. (A)
>
> G: Well, time management is not easy.
>
> B: I agree. What should I do? (B)
>
> G: Number the things you have to do. (C)
>
> B: Thank you, Emily. (D) I'll try your idea.
>
> G: I'm sure that will be helpful for you. (E) Good luck with your finals.

04 다음 중 빈칸 (가)에 들어가기에 적절한 것은?

① You look delighted.
② You look worried.
③ Didn't you know about the finals?
④ Are you aware of the finals?
⑤ You have too much work to do.

05 (A)~(E) 중에서 다음 문장이 들어가기에 가장 적절한 곳은?

> Then write down how much time you need to finish each one.

① (A) ② (B) ③ (C) ④ (D) ⑤ (E)

06 Which one CANNOT be answered from the dialogue above?

① Who is preparing for the finals?
② What is the problem Dongha has?
③ Why is time management important?
④ What does Emily advise Dongha to do?
⑤ What will Dongha do for his time management?

[07~09] 다음 대화를 읽고 물음에 답하시오.

B: The team project for English class is taking a lot of time.

G: I agree. I have a problem. One of the people on our team isn't doing his part.

B: That's not good. Everybody on the team has to do their job.

G: I know, but I don't know how to ___(A)___ him to do his part.

B: Maybe he doesn't know how to ___(B)___ started or doesn't like his part.

G: Then what should I do?

B: Talk to him. Ask him why he's not doing his part. Then tell him you'll help him if he wants.

G: Okay. I'll try that.

B: I'm sure he'll do better after you talk to him. Good luck with your project.

G: Thanks.

서답형

07 위 대화에서 다음 영어 설명에 해당하는 단어를 찾아 쓰시오.

> to have the same opinion as someone about a topic

➡ _____

08 위 대화의 빈칸 (A), (B)에 공통으로 들어가기에 적절한 것은?

① grow   ② make

③ get   ④ have

⑤ help

09 위 대화의 내용과 일치하지 <u>않는</u> 것은?

① 영어 조별 과제는 시간이 많이 걸린다.

② 소녀의 조원 중 한 명에게 문제가 있다.

③ 소녀의 조원은 모두 자기 역할을 다하고 있다.

④ 소년은 소녀에게 충고를 하고 있다.

⑤ 소녀는 문제가 있는 조원과 이야기를 할 것이다.

[10~12] 다음 대화를 읽고 물음에 답하시오.

B: You look ___(가)___ . Is something wrong?

G: Yes, my sister is upset with me.

B: Why? ___(나)___ did you do?

G: I wore one of her shirts without ___(A)___ .

B: Tell her you're sorry. (B)<u>I'm sure she'll understand.</u>

10 위 대화의 빈칸 (가), (나)에 들어가기에 가장 적절한 것은?

① surprised – Who   ② fun – How

③ worried – What   ④ tired – Why

⑤ pleased – How

11 다음 중 빈칸 (A)에 들어가기에 가장 적절한 것은?

① asked   ② asks   ③ ask

④ to ask   ⑤ asking

12 밑줄 친 문장 (B)가 의도하는 것은?

① 방법 묻기   ② 동의하기

③ 걱정 표현하기   ④ 설명 요청하기

⑤ 안심시키기

01 다음 우리말에 어울리는 영어 문장을 완성하시오.

> B: I have a big soccer match tomorrow. I'm nervous.
> G: Don't worry. 나는 네가 시합을 매우 잘할 거라고 확신해. (play, very well, 6 words)

➡ _____

02 다음 주어진 대화의 빈칸에 들어가기에 적절한 한 단어를 쓰시오.

> B: Our P.E. teacher is too strict. Don't you _____?
> G: No, I don't _____. I don't think he's too strict.

➡ _____

[03~05] 다음 대화를 읽고 물음에 답하시오.

> B: (A)나는 새로운 영어 단어를 배우는 데 어려움을 겪고 있어. (a hard time)
> G: I had the same problem, so I asked my English teacher for advice.
> B: What did he say?
> G: He advised me to use an English vocabulary app. It has helped me a lot. I'm sure it would work against you, too.

03 위 대화에서 밑줄 친 (A)의 우리말을 적절한 영어 문장으로 옮기시오. (주어진 단어를 포함할 것)

➡ _____

_____

04 위 대화에서 다음 설명에 해당하는 단어를 찾아 쓰시오.

> words that are used in a language

➡ _____

05 위 대화에서 흐름상 어색한 한 단어를 찾아 쓰고 적절한 단어로 바꾸시오.

_____ ➡ _____

[06~07] 다음 대화를 읽고 물음에 답하시오.

> B: The team project for English class is taking a lot of time.
> G: I agree. I have a problem. One of the people on our team isn't doing his (A)part.
> B: That's not good. Everybody on the team has to do their job.
> G: I know, but I don't know how to get him to do his part.
> B: Maybe he doesn't know how to get started or doesn't like his part.
> G: Then what should I do?
> B: Talk to him. Ask him why he's not doing his part. Then tell him you'll help him if he wants.
> G: Okay. I'll try that.
> B: (B)나는 네가 그와 이야기한 이후로 그가 더 잘할 것이라고 확신해. Good luck with your project.
> G: Thanks.

06 밑줄 친 (A)와 같은 의미로 바꾸어 쓸 수 있는 단어를 본문에서 찾아 쓰시오.

➡ _____

07 밑줄 친 (B)의 우리말을 적절한 영어 문장으로 옮기시오. (better, talk to 포함) (10 words)

➡ _____

Grammar

① 분사구문

> • Daeho, **thinking that new things will make him more popular**, often wants new things just because his friends have them. 대호는 새 물건이 그를 더 인기 있게 만들어 줄 것이라고 생각해서 단지 친구들이 그것을 가지고 있다는 이유로 종종 새 물건을 사기를 원합니다.

■ 분사가 이끄는 구를 분사구문이라고 하며, 이유, 조건, 시간, 동시동작, 양보 등의 뜻을 나타낸다. 분사구문은 '접속사+주어+동사'로 이루어진 부사절의 주어가 주절의 주어와 일치할 때 접속사와 주어를 생략하고 동사를 분사(동사원형+-ing)로 만든 구문이다. 이때 생략되는 접속사에 따라 뜻이 달라진다.

　• He was lying in an armchair, as he watched TV. → He was lying in an armchair, **watching TV**.
　(시간) 그는 TV를 보며 안락의자에 누워 있었다.

■ 부사절과 주절의 주어가 다를 때는 부사절의 주어를 생략하지 않고 사용하며 이것을 독립분사구문이라고 한다.

　• As it was fine, I went for a walk in the park. → **It being fine**, I went for a walk in the park.
　날씨가 좋아서 나는 공원으로 산책하러 갔다.

■ 분사구문에서 Being이나 Having been은 보통 생략한다.

　• I broke a tooth when I was eating something hard. → I broke a tooth (**being**) **eating something hard**. 나는 딱딱한 것을 먹고 있을 때 이가 부러졌습니다.

■ 분사구문의 부정은 분사 앞에 'not'이나 'never'를 쓴다.

　• As he didn't prepare for the exam, he got a bad grade. → **Not preparing for the exam**, he got a bad grade. 그가 시험을 위해 준비하지 않았기 때문에 나쁜 성적을 얻었다.

■ 분사구문의 뜻을 명확히 하기 위해 접속사를 생략하지 않기도 한다.

　• **After taking a quick shower**, I make my own bed. 재빨리 샤워를 한 후에, 저는 잠자리를 준비합니다.

■ 과거분사로 시작되는 분사구문은 being이 생략된 것으로 수동의 의미를 갖는다.

　• **Disappointed with the news**, she went to him and explained her difficulty.
　그 소식에 실망해서 그녀는 그에게 가서 자신의 어려움을 설명했다.

핵심 Check

1. 다음 괄호 안에서 알맞은 말을 고르시오.

　(1) He had some chips, (watch / watching) the TV.

　(2) (Listening / listened) to the music, he was reading a comic book.

② 명사절을 이끄는 접속사 if

* You should just ask her **if** there is something wrong.

  뭔가 잘못된 것이 있는지 그녀에게 물어봐.

* Do you know **if** he's married? 그가 결혼을 했는지 아니?

■ if나 whether는 '~인지 (아닌지)'라는 의미의 접속사로 어떠한 사실의 여부를 확인하거나 불확실함을 나타낼 때 쓰이며, 주로 ask, be not sure, find out, know, see, tell, wonder 등의 동사의 목적어 역할을 하는 명사절을 이끈다. if[whether] 뒤에 오는 절은 의문사가 없는 간접의문문으로 'if[whether]+주어+동사'의 어순으로 쓴다. if는 주어나 보어가 되는 명사절을 이끌 수 없다.

* I'm not sure **if[whether]** he's coming. 그가 올지 확실히 모르겠어. 〈목적어〉

* **Whether** he will come (or not) is not certain. 그가 올지 안 올지 확실치 않다. 〈주어〉

* The most important thing is **whether** you answered appropriately or not. 가장 중요한 것은 네가 적절하게 대답을 했는지 안 했는지이다. 〈보어〉

* I wonder. + He is at home.

  → I wonder **if** he is at home. 그가 집에 있을지 모르겠다.

■ if가 명사절을 이끄는 접속사로 그 명사절이 문장 내에서 동사의 목적어로 쓰일 때는 whether로 바꿔 쓸 수 있다. whether 다음에는 or not을 바로 붙여 쓸 수 있지만, if는 바로 붙여 쓸 수 없다.

* I'll ask **if** it's all right to park here. 여기에 주차를 해도 괜찮은지 물어 볼게.

  = I'll ask **whether** it's all right to park here.

* I don't know **whether** or not it was true. 전 그게 사실이었는지 아닌지 몰라요.

  = I don't know **if** or not it was true. (×)

cf. 보통 if가 조건의 부사절을 이끌 때는 '만약 ~라면'이라는 의미로 쓰이며, whether가 부사절을 이끌 경우에는 '~이든 (아니든)'이라는 '양보'의 의미로 쓰인다.

* **If** metal gets hot, it expands. 금속은 열을 받으면 팽창한다. 〈조건〉

* **Whether** you agree or not, I will help them. 네가 동의하든 말든 그들을 돕겠다. 〈양보〉

핵심 Check

2. 다음 빈칸에 들어갈 말을 〈보기〉에서 골라 쓰시오.

┌── 보기 ──┐

whether   if   that

(1) When they asked me _____ I wanted the job, I said yes.

(2) I'm not sure _____ I can do it.

(3) They have never decided _____ or not he was murdered.

01 다음 빈칸에 들어갈 말로 알맞은 것은?

> _____ me, he smiled brightly.

① Seeing   ② Seen   ③ Sees

④ Saw   ⑤ See

02 다음 괄호 안에서 알맞은 말을 고르시오.

(1) Lisa listens to music, (walk / walking) around the park.

(2) (Knowing not / Not knowing) her, I kept silent.

(3) He asked me (if / that) I could solve the puzzle.

(4) I am not sure (if / whether) or not he is going to the dance on Friday night.

03 다음 우리말에 맞게 빈칸에 알맞은 것은?

> 다른 선택이 있는지 모르겠어요.
> = I don't know _____ I have another choice.

① which   ② that   ③ what

④ unless   ⑤ if

04 다음 우리말에 맞게 주어진 어휘를 바르게 배열하시오.

(1) 나를 바라보면서, 그녀는 환하게 미소를 지었다.

(she, me, looking, smiled, brightly, at)

➡ _____

(2) 회사에서 집으로 걸어오는 중에 이 근사한 빵집을 발견했어.

(work, this, home, while, bakery, I, walking, found, great, from)

➡ _____

(3) 소문이 사실인지 확인해 볼 필요가 있다

(the rumor, we, need, is, find, true, if, out, to)

➡ _____

01 다음 중 어법상 어색한 것은?

① Feeling tired, she went to bed early.

② Aaron danced with great joy, singing in the rain.

③ Mike was standing outside the house, wait for her.

④ While working together in the field, they became friends.

⑤ Turning left there, you will find the building.

02 다음 중 어법상 어색한 것은?

① I want to ask her if she likes chocolate cake.

② I'm not sure whether I can go to the concert or not.

③ He couldn't tell if she was laughing or crying.

④ I just wanted to know that everything was all right.

⑤ I'm wondering whether you could help me.

03 다음 빈칸에 알맞은 말이 바르게 짝지어진 것은?

- I'd like to know _____ Sora likes spicy food.
- _____ his homework, the boy played computer games.

① if – Finishing

② that – Finishing

③ if – Finished

④ that – Finished

⑤ whether – Finish

04 다음 괄호 안에서 알맞은 말을 고르시오.

(1) Do you know (that / if) Kate will come back soon?

(2) A number of factors decide (whether / that) a movie will be successful or not.

(3) You can find out online (whether / if) or not they have the book.

(4) (Neglect / Neglecting) his duty, he was fired.

(5) You need to watch your tongue when (talk / talking) to your boss.

(6) (Getting not / Not getting) a message from her, he just waited there.

05 주어진 두 문장을 한 문장으로 바꿀 때 옳지 않은 것은?

- He came back from the trip.
- He looked like a beggar.

① When he came back from the trip, he looked like a beggar.

② As he came back from the trip, he looked like a beggar.

③ Coming back from the trip, he looked like a beggar.

④ When coming back from the trip, he looked like a beggar.

⑤ When came back from the trip, he looked like a beggar.

06 빈칸 (A)와 (B)에 알맞은 것으로 짝지어진 것은?

> • You did not tell me ___(A)___ you would come to the party.
> • ___(B)___ or not this company will succeed depends on the outcome of the project.

	(A)	(B)
①	whether	If
②	which	If
③	if	Whether
④	which	Whether
⑤	if	While

07 다음 문장의 밑줄 친 부분 중 어법상 어색한 것은?

> Daeho, ⓐthinks that new things ⓑwill make him more popular, often ⓒwants new things just ⓓbecause his friends have ⓔthem.

① ⓐ   ② ⓑ   ③ ⓒ
④ ⓓ   ⑤ ⓔ

08 다음 밑줄 친 부분과 바꿔 쓸 수 있는 것은?

> I don't know if Bora has the key.

① unless   ② that   ③ what
④ which   ⑤ whether

09 다음 두 문장을 한 문장으로 바꿔 쓸 때 빈칸에 알맞은 말을 쓰시오.

> • I was lonely.
> • I decided to make some friends.
> = _____ lonely, I decided to make some friends.

10 다음 우리말을 바르게 영작한 것을 고르시오.

> Justine은 내가 영어 시험에서 좋은 점수를 받았는지 물어본다.

① Justine asks me if I get a good grade in the English test.
② Justine asks me if I got a good grade in the English test.
③ Justine asks me that I got a good grade in the English test.
④ Justine asks me because I got a good grade in the English test.
⑤ Justine asks me if or not I got a good grade in the English test.

11 밑줄 친 부분의 쓰임이 주어진 문장과 같은 것은?

> Getting hot, metal expands.

① You should not blink your eyes when taking pictures.
② Turning to the right, you will find the post office.
③ Having nothing to do, I went to see a film.
④ He kept on reading, while eating snacks.
⑤ Being nervous, she said it was a good experience.

12 다음 문장에서 생략할 수 있는 것을 찾아 쓰시오.

(1) Though I was sleepy, I forced myself to stay awake.
   ➡ _____

(2) He got interested in politics when he was in college.
   ➡ _____

13 주어진 문장의 틀린 부분을 찾아 바르게 고치지 <u>않은</u> 것을 고르시오.

> I wonder that our flight will leave today or not.

① I wonder whether our flight will leave today.

② I wonder whether our flight will leave today or not.

③ I wonder whether or not our flight will leave today.

④ I wonder if or not our flight will leave today.

⑤ I wonder if our flight will leave today or not.

서답형
14 다음 문장에서 어법상 어색한 것을 바르게 고쳐 다시 쓰시오.

(1) We don't know if Mark succeeds.

➡ _____

_____

(2) If I believe you or not is not important now.

➡ _____

_____

(3) Ridden a bike, he always wears his helmet.

➡ _____

_____

(4) Feeling not good about it, he wrote a letter to her.

➡ _____

_____

(5) Disappointing with the result, she walked out of her room.

➡ _____

_____

15 다음 우리말을 바르게 영작한 것을 고르시오.

> 좋은 점수를 받고 싶어서, 그는 공부를 열심히 하기로 결심했다.

① Wanted to get good grades, he decides to study hard.

② Wants to get good grades, he decides to study hard.

③ Want to get good grades, he decided to study hard.

④ Wanted to get good grades, he decided to study hard.

⑤ Wanting to get good grades, he decided to study hard.

16 다음 중 어법상 <u>어색한</u> 것을 <u>모두</u> 고르시오.

① I want to know if you can help me with my math homework.

② That depends on if you send it by air or ship.

③ He didn't decide if to go or stay.

④ Try these tips, and then let me know if they work for you.

⑤ Why don't you ask her if there is anything wrong?

서답형
17 다음 두 문장을 한 문장으로 바꿔 쓰시오.

> • She advises Sohui to ask Hayeon.
> • Is there something wrong?

➡ _____

_____

01 주어진 문장을 분사구문으로 바꿔 쓰시오.

(1) As he was so upset, he went out without saying anything.

➡ _____

_____

(2) If you cancel the order, you will lose your money.

➡ _____

_____

(3) Although I am tired of a lot of homework, I won't give up.

➡ _____

_____

(4) Because I didn't feel good, I stayed in bed all morning.

➡ _____

_____

(5) If it is fine, I will start tomorrow.

➡ _____

_____

02 if를 이용하여 다음 두 문장을 한 문장으로 바꿔 쓰시오.

(1) • He couldn't tell.

• Was she laughing or crying?

➡ _____

_____

(2) • I'm not sure.

• Did he explain everything about your compensation?

➡ _____

_____

03 다음 우리말에 맞게 주어진 단어를 바르게 배열하시오.

(1) 이 기차를 탄다면, 너는 오후 1시에 부산에 도착할 거야. (you'll, this train, 1 p.m., Busan, get, taking, at, to)

➡ _____

(2) 바쁠지라도, Amy는 항상 기꺼이 나를 도와주려 한다. (Amy, me, always, busy, is, being, help, willing, to)

➡ _____

(3) 나는 그가 이 근처에 사는지 궁금하다. (I, he, here, wonder, lives, near, if)

➡ _____

(4) 나는 그가 아직도 나를 기억하고 있는지 잘 모르겠어. (I, me, he, sure, am, remembers, not, still, if)

➡ _____

04 다음 문장에서 잘못된 것을 알맞게 고쳐 다시 쓰시오.

(1) If he will continue to be successful in future is open to doubt.

➡ _____

_____

(2) Some friends asked me if or not I had an accident.

➡ _____

_____

(3) I was debating in my mind if to go or not.

➡ _____

_____

05 그림을 보고 주어진 어휘를 이용하여 빈칸을 알맞게 채우시오.

(1) Mina wonders _____ at her new school. (can, she, make friends)

(2) John is not sure _____ well at the soccer match. (can, he, play)

(3) Suzie worries about _____ fine at the speech contest. (can, do, she)

06 그림을 보고 접속사 없이 주어진 어휘를 이용하여 빈칸을 알맞게 채우시오.

(1) _____, Minho dropped his bag and it opened. (do, check-in)

(2) Jane checked her schedule, _____ with Tom. (have a talk)

(3) _____ of the airport, Don felt very cold. (come, out)

07 다음 우리말을 괄호 안의 지시대로 영작하시오.

(1) 그는 아파서 하루 종일 집에 있었다.

➡ _____

(분사구문을 써서)

➡ _____

(접속사를 써서)

(2) 길을 걸으면서 너의 전화기를 보지 마라.

➡ _____

(분사구문을 써서)

➡ _____

(접속사를 써서)

(3) 표를 가지고 계신지 여쭤봐도 될까요?

➡ _____

(접속사를 써서)

(4) 나는 그가 그 시험을 합격할 수 있을지 궁금하다.

➡ _____

(접속사를 써서)

08 다음 문장에서 어법상 어색한 것을 분사구문을 이용하여 바르게 고쳐 다시 쓰시오.

(1) Writing in haste, this book has a lot of mistakes.

➡ _____

_____

(2) There was no train left, he had to stay at a hotel.

➡ _____

_____

Reading

What Should I Do?

Everyone has worries. When you have things you worry about, what
do you do? Here are some things that three teenagers worry about.

Sohui thought Hayeon was her best friend, but now, Sohui feels that

Hayeon has changed and she is avoiding her.

Sohui: (To her older sister) You know my friend Hayeon, don't you?

Sister: Yeah. Why? What about her?

Sohui: I feel she's avoiding me. When I see her at school, she turns

around and walks away from me.

Sister: I'm sorry to hear that. Do you have any idea why she does that?

Sohui: No. I don't think I've done anything wrong. It just feels like

she doesn't like me anymore.

Sister: Maybe you should just ask her if there is something wrong.

Sohui: Maybe I should. I still want to be friends with her.

---

everyone 모든 사람

worry 걱정거리, 걱정(되는 일); 걱정하다

teenager 청소년(나이가 13–19세인 사람)

avoid 피하다

turn around 돌아서다

not ~ anymore 더 이상 ~ 않다

avoid 피하다

if ~인지 아닌지

maybe 아마도

still 아직도

확인문제

● 다음 문장이 본문의 내용과 일치하면 T, 일치하지 않으면 F를 쓰시오.

1 Sohui thought Hayeon was her best friend. ☐

2 Now, Hayeon feels that Sohui has changed and she is avoiding her. ☐

3 When Sohui sees Hayeon at school, Hayeon turns around and walks away from Sohui. ☐

4 Sohui thinks she has done something wrong. ☐

5 Sohui's sister advises Sohui to ask Hayeon if there is something wrong. ☐

6 Sohui doesn't want to be friends with Hayeon anymore. ☐

Daeho, thinking that new things will make him more popular, often
wants new things just because his friends have them.

Daeho: Seongjin, look at my new sneakers. What do you think?

Seongjin: They're nice, but didn't you just buy new sneakers a couple of months ago?

Daeho: Yeah, but they're no longer in style. I look cooler in these, right?

Seongjin: Daeho, wearing the latest fashion doesn't make you cooler or more popular. People like you because you're you, not because of your clothes.

Daeho: Yeah?

Seongjin: Listen, you're a great guy. You don't need new sneakers to prove it.

Recently, Minkyeong was asked out by a boy in her class. She wants to say no but does not want to hurt his feelings.

Minkyeong: I need your advice. A boy in my class asked me out. I like him, but for now I don't want to go out with him. I need to focus on my studies. What should I do?

Counselor: Why don't you tell him why you can't go?

Minkyeong: I'm afraid I might hurt his feelings.

Counselor: If you don't tell him soon, he will misunderstand your feelings, and you may end up hurting him even more.

Minkyeong: Maybe you're right. Thanks for the advice.

sneakers 운동화

latest 최신의

guy (비격식) 녀석, 남자

prove 증명하다, 입증하다

a couple of 두서너 개의, 몇 개의, 몇 사람의

in style 유행하는, 유행되는

recently 최근에

afraid 걱정하는, 불안한

counselor 카운슬러, 상담역

misunderstand 오해하다

ask somebody out ~에게 데이트를 신청하다

end up 결국 ~하게 되다

확인문제

● 다음 문장이 본문의 내용과 일치하면 T, 일치하지 않으면 F를 쓰시오.

1 Daeho thinks that new things will make him more popular. ☐

2 Seongjin doesn't like Daeho's new sneakers. ☐

3 Seongjin says wearing the latest fashion doesn't make Daeho cooler or more popular. ☐

4 Daeho needs new sneakers to prove he is a great guy. ☐

5 Recently, a boy in Minkyeong's class asked Minkyeong out. ☐

6 Minkyeong doesn't want to go out with him because she doesn't like him. ☐

● 우리말을 참고하여 빈칸에 알맞은 말을 쓰시오.

1 What _____ I Do?

2 Everyone _____ worries.

3 When you have things you worry about, _____ _____ _____ _____?

4 _____ _____ _____ _____ that three teenagers worry about.

5 Sohui thought Hayeon was _____ _____ _____, but now, Sohui feels that Hayeon _____ _____ and she _____ _____ her.

6 Sohui: (To her older sister) You know my friend Hayeon, _____ _____?

7 Sister: Yeah. Why? _____ _____ her?

8 Sohui: _____ _____ she's avoiding me.

9 When I see her at school, she _____ _____ and _____ _____ me.

10 Sister: I'm sorry _____ _____ _____.

11 Do you have any idea _____ _____ _____ _____?

12 Sohui: No. I don't think _____ _____ _____ _____.

13 It just _____ _____ she doesn't like me anymore.

14 Sister: Maybe you _____ just ask her _____ there is _____ _____.

15 Sohui: Maybe I should. I _____ want to be friends _____ her.

16 Daeho, _____ that new things will make him more popular, often wants new things _____ _____ his friends have them.

17 Daeho: Seongjin, look at my _____ _____.

18 _____ do you think?

---

1 제가 어떻게 해야 할까요?

2 누구나 고민은 있습니다.

3 여러분은 걱정되는 것이 있을 때 무엇을 하나요?

4 여기 세 명의 청소년이 걱정하는 것들이 있습니다.

5 소희는 하연이가 그녀의 가장 친한 친구라고 생각했지만, 지금은 하연이가 변했고 그녀를 피한다고 느낍니다.

6 소희: (그녀의 언니에게) 내 친구 하연이 알지, 그렇지?

7 언니: 응. 왜? 그녀가 어떤데?

8 소희: 나는 그녀가 나를 피하고 있다고 느껴.

9 학교에서 내가 그녀를 볼 때 그녀는 돌아서서 나로부터 멀리 걸어가.

10 언니: 그거 참 안타깝구나.

11 너는 그녀가 왜 그렇게 하는지 아니?

12 소희: 아니. 나는 내가 잘못한 것이 있다고 생각하지 않아.

13 단지 그녀가 더 이상 나를 좋아하지 않는다고 느껴져.

14 언니: 혹시 모르니 뭔가 잘못된 것이 있는지 그녀에게 물어봐.

15 소희: 아마 그래야겠어. 나는 여전히 그녀와 친구로 지내고 싶거든.

16 대호는 새 물건이 그를 더 인기 있게 만들어 줄 것이라고 생각해서 단지 친구들이 그것을 가지고 있다는 이유로 종종 새 물건을 사기를 원합니다.

17 대호: 성진아, 내 새 운동화 봐.

18 어떠니?

19 **Seongjin:** They're nice, but _____ _____ just buy new sneakers a _____ _____ months ago?

20 **Daeho:** Yeah, but they're no longer _____ _____.

21 I look cooler _____ _____, right?

22 **Seongjin:** Daeho, _____ the latest fashion doesn't make you _____ or _____ _____.

23 People like you _____ _____ _____, not because of your clothes.

24 **Daeho:** Yeah?

25 **Seongjin:** Listen, you're _____ _____ _____.

26 You don't need new sneakers _____ _____ _____.

27 Recently, Minkyeong _____ _____ by a boy in her class.

28 She wants to say no but does not want _____ _____ _____ _____.

29 **Minkyeong:** I need your _____.

30 A boy in my class _____ _____ _____.

31 I like him, but _____ _____ I don't want to _____ _____ him.

32 I need to _____ _____ my studies.

33 What _____ I do?

34 **Counselor:** _____ _____ _____ tell him why you can't go?

35 **Minkyeong:** _____ I might hurt his feelings.

36 **Counselor:** _____ _____ _____ _____ him soon, he will misunderstand your feelings, and you may _____ _____ _____ him even more.

37 **Minkyeong:** Maybe _____.

38 _____ _____ the advice.

---

19 성진: 멋지다. 그런데 너 겨우 몇 달 전에 새 운동화 사지 않았니?

20 대호: 응, 하지만 그건 더 이상 유행이 아니야.

21 이걸 신으니까 더 멋져 보이지, 그렇지?

22 성진: 대호야, 최신 유행하는 것을 입는 것이 너를 더 멋지고 더 인기 있게 만들어 주지는 않아.

23 사람들은 네가 너이기 때문에 너를 좋아하는 것이지, 네 옷 때문이 아니야.

24 대호: 그래?

25 성진: 들어봐. 너는 멋진 사람이야.

26 그것을 증명하기 위해 새 운동화가 필요하지 않아.

27 최근에 민경이는 그녀의 반 남자아이에게 데이트 신청을 받았습니다.

28 그녀는 거절하고 싶지만 그의 감정을 상하게 하고 싶지는 않습니다.

29 민경: 저는 선생님의 조언이 필요해요.

30 같은 반 남자아이가 저에게 데이트 신청을 했어요.

31 저는 그를 좋아하지만 당분간은 그와 데이트하고 싶지 않아요.

32 저는 공부에 집중해야 해요.

33 제가 어떻게 해야 할까요?

34 상담 선생님: 왜 네가 데이트를 할 수 없는지 그에게 말하는 것은 어떨까?

35 민경: 제가 그의 감정을 상하게 할까 봐 걱정돼요.

36 상담 선생님: 네가 그에게 빨리 말하지 않으면, 그는 네 감정을 오해할 것이고, 너는 그를 더 아프게 할 수도 있단다.

37 민경: 선생님 말씀이 맞는 것 같아요.

38 조언 감사합니다.

● 우리말을 참고하여 본문을 영작하시오.

1 제가 어떻게 해야 할까요?
➡ _____

2 누구나 고민은 있습니다.
➡ _____

3 여러분은 걱정되는 것이 있을 때 무엇을 하나요?
➡ _____

4 여기 세 명의 청소년이 걱정하는 것들이 있습니다.
➡ _____

5 소희는 하연이가 그녀의 가장 친한 친구라고 생각했지만, 지금은 하연이가 변했고 그녀를 피한다고 느낍니다.
➡ _____
_____

6 소희: (그녀의 언니에게) 내 친구 하연이 알지, 그렇지?
➡ _____

7 언니: 응. 왜? 그녀가 어떤데?
➡ _____

8 소희: 나는 그녀가 나를 피하고 있다고 느껴.
➡ _____

9 학교에서 내가 그녀를 볼 때 그녀는 돌아서서 나로부터 멀리 걸어가.
➡ _____

10 언니: 그거 참 안타깝구나.
➡ _____

11 너는 그녀가 왜 그렇게 하는지 아니?
➡ _____

12 소희: 아니. 나는 내가 잘못한 것이 있다고 생각하지 않아.
➡ _____

13 단지 그녀가 더 이상 나를 좋아하지 않는다고 느껴져.
➡ _____

14 언니: 혹시 모르니 뭔가 잘못된 것이 있는지 그녀에게 물어봐.
➡ _____

15 소희: 아마 그래야겠어. 나는 여전히 그녀와 친구로 지내고 싶거든.
➡ _____

16 대호는 새 물건이 그를 더 인기 있게 만들어 줄 것이라고 생각해서 단지 친구들이 그것을 가지고 있다는 이유로 종종 새 물건을 사기를 원합니다.
➡ _____
_____

17 대호: 성진아, 내 새 운동화 봐.
➡ _____

18 어떠니?
➡ _____

19 성진: 멋지다, 그런데 너 겨우 몇 달 전에 새 운동화 사지 않았니?
➡ _____

20 대호: 응, 하지만 그건 더 이상 유행이 아니야.
➡ _____

21 이걸 신으니까 더 멋져 보이지, 그렇지?
➡ _____

22 성진: 대호야, 최신 유행하는 것을 입는 것이 너를 더 멋지고 더 인기 있게 만들어 주지는 않아.
➡ _____

23 사람들은 네가 너이기 때문에 너를 좋아하는 것이지, 네 옷 때문이 아니야.
➡ _____

24 대호: 그래?
➡ _____

25 성진: 들어봐. 너는 멋진 사람이야.
➡ _____

26 그것을 증명하기 위해 새 운동화가 필요하지 않아.
➡ _____

27 최근에 민경이는 그녀의 반 남자아이에게 데이트 신청을 받았습니다.
➡ _____

28 그녀는 거절하고 싶지만 그의 감정을 상하게 하고 싶지는 않습니다.
➡ _____

29 민경: 저는 선생님의 조언이 필요해요.
➡ _____

30 같은 반 남자아이가 저에게 데이트 신청을 했어요.
➡ _____

31 저는 그를 좋아하지만 당분간은 그와 데이트하고 싶지 않아요.
➡ _____

32 저는 공부에 집중해야 해요.
➡ _____

33 제가 어떻게 해야 할까요?
➡ _____

34 상담 선생님: 왜 네가 데이트를 할 수 없는지 그에게 말하는 것은 어떨까?
➡ _____

35 민경: 제가 그의 감정을 상하게 할까 봐 걱정돼요
➡ _____

36 상담 선생님: 네가 그에게 빨리 말하지 않으면, 그는 네 감정을 오해할 것이고, 너는 그를 더 아프게 할 수도 있단다.
➡ _____
_____

37 민경: 선생님 말씀이 맞는 것 같아요.
➡ _____

38 조언 감사합니다.
➡ _____

[01~03] 다음 글을 읽고 물음에 답하시오.

Daeho, (A)thinking that new things will make him more popular, often wants new things just because his friends have them.

Daeho: Seongjin, look at my new sneakers. What do you think?

Seongjin: They're nice, but didn't you just buy new sneakers a couple of months ago?

Daeho: Yeah, but they're no longer ⓐ style. I look cooler ⓑ these, right?

Seongjin: Daeho, wearing the latest fashion doesn't make you cooler or more popular. People like you because you're you, not because of your clothes.

Daeho: Yeah?

Seongjin: Listen, you're a great guy. You don't need new sneakers to prove (B)it.

서답형

01 위 글의 빈칸 ⓐ와 ⓑ에 공통으로 들어갈 알맞은 전치사를 쓰시오.

➡ _____

02 위 글의 밑줄 친 (A)thinking과 문법적 쓰임이 같은 것을 모두 고르시오.

① Just thinking about her makes me happy.

② She answered the questions thinking carefully.

③ I turned left without thinking anything.

④ We need to start thinking globally.

⑤ I didn't lose hope thinking positively.

서답형

03 위 글의 밑줄 친 (B)it이 가리키는 것을 본문에서 찾아 쓰시오.

➡ _____

[04~05] 다음 글을 읽고 물음에 답하시오.

Recently, Minkyeong was asked out by a boy in her class. She wants to say no but does not want to hurt his feelings.

Minkyeong: I need your advice. A boy in my class asked me out. I like him, but for now I don't want to go out with him. I need to focus on my studies. What should I do?

Counselor: ⓐWhy don't you tell him why you can't go?

Minkyeong: I'm afraid I might hurt his feelings.

Counselor: If you don't tell him soon, he will misunderstand your feelings, and you may end up hurting him even more.

Minkyeong: Maybe you're right. Thanks for the advice.

서답형

04 위 글의 밑줄 친 ⓐ를 다음과 같이 바꿔 쓸 때 빈칸에 들어갈 알맞은 말을 두 단어로 쓰시오.

➡ _____ telling him why you can't go?

05 위 글의 제목으로 알맞은 것을 고르시오.

① Wow! Minkyeong Is Very Popular!

② Sorry, But You're Not My Type!

③ Sorry! For Now I Need to Focus on My Studies!

④ How about Telling Him You Like Him, Too?

⑤ Time to Say Hello and Goodbye

[06~07] 다음 글을 읽고 물음에 답하시오.

Everyone has worries. When you have things you worry ___ⓐ___, what do you do? Here are some things that three teenagers worry ___ⓑ___.

서답형

06 위 글의 빈칸 ⓐ와 ⓑ에 공통으로 들어갈 알맞은 전치사를 쓰시오.

➡ _____

07 위 글의 뒤에 올 내용으로 가장 알맞은 것을 고르시오.

① the most common concerns of people
② the way to give effective advice
③ the importance of friendship
④ the worries of three teenagers
⑤ the routine of most teenagers

[08~10] 다음 글을 읽고 물음에 답하시오.

Sohui thought Hayeon was ①her best friend, but now, Sohui feels that Hayeon has changed and she is avoiding ②her.

Sohui: (To ③her older sister) You know ④my friend Hayeon, don't you?

Sister: Yeah. Why? What about ⑤her?

Sohui: I feel she's avoiding me. When I see her at school, she turns around and walks away from me.

Sister: I'm sorry ⓐto hear that. Do you have any idea why she does that?

Sohui: No. I don't think I've done anything wrong. It just feels like she doesn't like me anymore.

Sister: Maybe you should just ask her if there is something wrong.

Sohui: Maybe I should. I still want to be friends with her.

중요

08 밑줄 친 ①~⑤ 중에서 가리키는 대상이 나머지 넷과 다른 것은?

①   ②   ③   ④   ⑤

09 다음 부사적 용법의 to부정사들 중에서 위 글의 밑줄 친 ⓐ to hear와 쓰임이 같은 것을 고르시오.

① He grew up to be a scientist.
② She must be smart to say so.
③ She was surprised to hear the news.
④ He is rich enough to buy a car of his own.
⑤ I got up early to catch the first train.

10 According to the passage, which is NOT true?

① Sohui feels Hayeon is avoiding her.
② When Sohui sees Hayeon at school, Sohui turns around and walks away from Hayeon.
③ Sohui doesn't think she has done anything wrong.
④ Sohui's sister advises Sohui to ask Hayeon if there is something wrong.
⑤ Sohui still wants to be friends with Hayeon.

[11~12] 다음 글을 읽고 물음에 답하시오.

Daeho, thinking that new things will make him more popular, often wants new things just because his friends have them.

Daeho: Seongjin, look at my new sneakers. What do you think?

Seongjin: They're nice, but didn't you just buy new sneakers a couple of months ago?

Daeho: Yeah, but ⓐthey're no longer in style. I look cooler in these, right?

Seongjin: Daeho, wearing the latest fashion doesn't make you cooler or more popular. People like you because you're you, not because of your clothes.

Daeho: Yeah?

Seongjin: Listen, you're a great guy. You don't need new sneakers to prove it.

서답형

11 다음 빈칸에 알맞은 단어를 넣어 위 글의 밑줄 친 ⓐthey가 가리키는 것을 완성하시오.

> the _____ _____ that Daeho bought a couple of months ago

중요

12 위 글의 '대호'를 설명할 수 있는 말로 가장 알맞은 것을 고르시오.

① old-fashioned ② sociable

③ modest ④ trendy

⑤ frugal

[13~15] 다음 글을 읽고 물음에 답하시오.

(A)Recently, Minkyeong was asked out by a boy in her class. She wants to say no but does not want to hurt his feelings.

Minkyeong: I need your advice. A boy in my class asked me out. I like him, but ____ⓐ____ now I don't want to go out with him. I need to focus ____ⓑ____ my studies. What should I do?

Counselor: Why don't you tell him why you can't go?

Minkyeong: I'm afraid I might hurt his feelings.

Counselor: If you don't tell him soon, he will misunderstand your feelings, and you may end up hurting him (B)even more.

Minkyeong: Maybe you're right. Thanks for the advice.

13 위 글의 빈칸 ⓐ와 ⓑ에 들어갈 전치사가 바르게 짝지어진 것은?

	ⓐ	ⓑ		ⓐ	ⓑ
①	for	about	②	in	to
③	at	on	④	for	on
⑤	at	to			

서답형

14 위 글의 밑줄 친 (A)를 능동태로 고치시오.

➡ _____

_____

중요

15 위 글의 밑줄 친 (B)even과 같은 의미로 쓰인 것을 고르시오.

① He never even opened the letter.

② You know even less about it than I do.

③ You need an even surface to work on.

④ Even a child can understand it.

⑤ Our scores are now even.

[16~18] 다음 글을 읽고 물음에 답하시오.

Daeho, thinking that new things will make him more popular, often wants new things just because his friends have ⓐthem.

Daeho: Seongjin, look at my new sneakers. What do you think?

Seongjin: They're nice, but didn't you just buy new sneakers a couple of months ago?

Daeho: Yeah, but they're no longer in style. I look cooler ____ⓑ____ these, right?

Seongjin: Daeho, wearing the latest fashion doesn't make you cooler or more popular. ⓒ사람들은 네가 너이기 때문에 너를 좋아하는 것이지, 네 옷 때문이 아니야.

Daeho: Yeah?

Seongjin: Listen, you're a great guy. You don't need new sneakers to prove it.

16 위 글의 밑줄 친 ⓐthem이 가리키는 것을 본문에서 찾아 쓰시오.

➡ _____

17 위 글의 빈칸 ⓑ에 알맞은 것을 고르시오.

① on ② to ③ in
④ for ⑤ with

18 위 글의 밑줄 친 ⓒ의 우리말에 맞게 한 단어를 보충하여, 주어진 어휘를 알맞게 배열하시오.

> your clothes / like / because / not / you / you / because / people / you're / ,

➡ _____

_____

[19~21] 다음 글을 읽고 물음에 답하시오.

Sohui thought Hayeon was her best friend, but now, Sohui feels that Hayeon ⓐhas changed and she is avoiding her.

Sohui: (To her older sister) You know my friend Hayeon, don't you?

Sister: Yeah. Why? What about her? (①)

Sohui: (②) I feel she's avoiding me. (③) When I see her at school, she turns around and walks away from me.

Sister: (④) Do you have any idea why she does that?

Sohui: (⑤) No. I don't think I've done anything wrong. It just feels like she doesn't like me anymore.

Sister: Maybe you should just ask her if there is something wrong.

Sohui: Maybe I should. I still want to be friends with her.

19 위 글의 흐름으로 보아, 주어진 문장이 들어가기에 가장 적절한 곳은?

> I'm sorry to hear that.

① ② ③ ④ ⑤

20 위 글의 밑줄 친 ⓐhas changed와 현재완료의 용법이 같은 것을 모두 고르시오.

① I have spent all the money, so I have no money.
② I have known her for 5 years.
③ How many times have you seen it?
④ She has gone to Paris.
⑤ How long have you been in Korea?

21 위 글의 제목으로 알맞은 것을 고르시오.

① Yes, I Mean It. A Friend in Need Is a Friend Indeed.
② That's Enough! She Is No More My Best Friend!
③ Don't Worry Too Much! Every Dog Has His Day!
④ You've Changed. I Wonder If There's Something Wrong.
⑤ Why Don't You Also Ignore Her?

[01~03] 다음 글을 읽고 물음에 답하시오.

Recently, Minkyeong was asked out by a boy in her class. She wants to say no but does not want to hurt his feelings.

Minkyeong: I need your advice. A boy in my class asked me out. I like him, but for now I don't want to go out with him. I need to focus on my studies. What should I do?

Counselor: Why don't you tell him why you can't go?

Minkyeong: I'm afraid I might hurt his feelings.

Counselor: (A)If you don't tell him soon, he will misunderstand your feelings, and you may end up ⓐ him even more.

Minkyeong: Maybe you're right. Thanks for the advice.

01 위 글의 빈칸 ⓐ에 hurt를 알맞은 형태로 쓰시오.

➡ _____

02 위 글의 밑줄 친 (A)를 다음과 같이 바꿔 쓸 때 빈칸에 들어갈 알맞은 말을 두 단어로 쓰시오.

➡ _____ _____ tell him soon, he will misunderstand your feelings.

03 본문의 내용과 일치하도록 다음 빈칸 (A)와 (B)에 알맞은 단어를 쓰시오.

> A boy in Minkyeong's class asked her (A)_____, but she wants to turn him down without (B)_____ _____.

[04~06] 다음 글을 읽고 물음에 답하시오.

Daeho, ⓐthinking that new things will make him more popular, often wants new things just because his friends have them.

Daeho: Seongjin, look at my new sneakers. What do you think?

Seongjin: They're nice, but didn't you just buy new sneakers a couple of months ago?

Daeho: Yeah, but they're no longer in style. I look cooler in these, right?

Seongjin: Daeho, wearing the latest fashion doesn't make you cooler or more popular. ⓑPeople like you because you're you, not because your clothes.

Daeho: Yeah?

Seongjin: Listen, you're a great guy. You don't need new sneakers to prove it.

04 위 글의 밑줄 친 ⓐ를 부사절로 고치시오.

➡ _____
_____

05 위 글의 밑줄 친 ⓑ에서 어법상 틀린 부분을 찾아 고치시오.

_____ ➡ _____

06 본문의 내용과 일치하도록 다음 빈칸 (A)와 (B)에 알맞은 단어를 쓰시오.

> Daeho often wants new things just because (A)_____ _____ have them, and he bought new sneakers again, thinking the sneakers that he bought a couple of months ago are no longer (B)_____ _____.

[07~09] 다음 글을 읽고 물음에 답하시오.

Daeho, thinking that new things will make him more popular, often wants new things just because his friends have them.

Daeho: Seongjin, look at my new sneakers. (A)[How / What] do you think?

Seongjin: They're nice, but didn't you just buy new sneakers a couple of months ago?

Daeho: Yeah, but they're no longer in style. I look cooler in ⓐthese, right?

Seongjin: Daeho, wearing the (B)[last / latest] fashion doesn't make you cooler or more popular. People like you because you're you, not because of your (C)[cloths / clothes].

Daeho: Yeah?

Seongjin: Listen, you're a great guy. You don't need new sneakers to prove it.

07 위 글의 괄호 (A)~(C)에서 문맥이나 어법상 알맞은 낱말을 골라 쓰시오.

➡ (A) _____ (B) _____ (C) _____

08 위 글의 밑줄 친 ⓐthese가 가리키는 것을 본문에서 찾아 쓰시오.

➡ _____

09 Does Seongjin think wearing the latest fashion makes Daeho cooler or more popular? Answer in English in a full sentence. (3 words)

➡ _____

[10~12] 다음 글을 읽고 물음에 답하시오.

Sohui thought Hayeon was her best friend, but now, Sohui feels that Hayeon has changed and she is avoiding her.

Sohui: (To her older sister) You know my friend Hayeon, don't you?

Sister: Yeah. Why? What about her?

Sohui: I feel she's avoiding me. When I see her at school, she turns around and walks away from me.

Sister: I'm sorry to hear that. Do you have any idea _____ⓐ_____?

Sohui: No. I don't think I've done anything wrong. It just feels like she doesn't like me anymore.

Sister: Maybe you should just ask her if there is something wrong.

Sohui: Maybe I should. I still want to be friends with her.

10 위 글의 빈칸 ⓐ에 다음 문장을 알맞은 형태로 쓰시오.

| Why does she do that? |

➡ _____

11 다음 문장에서 위 글의 내용과 <u>다른</u> 부분을 찾아서 고치시오. (두 군데)

| Sohui thinks she has done something wrong. |

➡ _____ , _____

12 다음 빈칸 (A)~(C)에 알맞은 단어를 넣어 소희의 고민과 그에 알맞은 조언을 완성하시오.

- **Sohui's worry:** I feel like my best friend Hayeon (A)_____ _____ and she (B)_____ _____ me.
- **Advice:** Why don't you ask her if there is anything (C)_____?

교과서

구석구석

Communication Task

A: I think school should start later in the morning.
동사 think 뒤에는 접속사 that이 생략되었다.

B: I agree with you. We can get more sleep if school starts later.
조건을 나타내는 if절에서는 미래시제를 쓰지 않고 현재시제를 쓴다.

A: I think school should start later in the morning.

B: I don't agree with you. School will finish later if it starts later.
"agree with+사람"이다.

구문해설 · **later**: 더 늦게 · **get sleep**: 잠을 자다

Writing Workshop

Hena's World

I want to grow taller. I do not feel good being the shortest in the group. I'd like
분사구문(= as[because] I am)

to know how I can get taller.
간접의문문(의문사+주어+동사)

tallboy1201

I heard you are wondering if you can get taller. I suggest you eat foods
명사절을 이끄는 접속사(~인지 아닌지)   = should eat(suggest that+주어+(should)+동사원형)

like eggs, milk, and beans. These foods, having lots of protein and calcium,
like(전치사: ~와 같은) = such as   분사구문(= as they have)

can help you grow taller. Also, you should sleep at least eight hours every
help의 목적격보어(= to grow)

night. I hope these tips will be helpful to you.
= advice

구문해설 · **at least**: 적어도

After You Read B

· I feel like my best friend avoids me.

Why don't you ask her if there is anything wrong?
Why don't you 동사원형 ~?: ~하는 게 어때? if: ~인지 아닌지

· I need new clothes. They'll make me more popular.
= new clothes

People like you because you're you, not because of your clothes.
because+주어와 동사로 이루어진 절. because of+명사(구)

· How can I say no without hurting his feelings?
전치사 without+동명사

Why don't you tell him why you can't go?
의문사가 이끄는 명사절로 'tell'의 목적어. 간접의문문(why+주어+동사)

구문해설 · **avoid**: ~을 피하다 · **if**: ~인지 아닌지 · **clothes**: 옷, 의복 · **hurt**: 다치게[아프게] 하다

해석

A: 나는 학교가 아침에 더 늦게 시작해야 한다고 생각해.

B: 나도 네 말에 동의해. 학교가 늦게 시작하면 우리는 더 많이 잠을 잘 수 있어.

A: 나는 학교가 아침에 더 늦게 시작해야 한다고 생각해.

B: 나는 동의하지 않아. 학교가 늦게 시작하면 더 늦게 끝날 거야.

Hena의 세계

나는 키가 더 크고 싶어. 나는 그룹에서 키가 가장 작아서 기분이 안 좋아. 나는 내가 키가 더 클 수 있는 방법을 알고 싶어.

tallboy1201

나는 네가 키가 더 클 수 있는지 궁금해한다고 들었어. 나는 네가 달걀. 우유. 콩 같은 음식을 먹을 것을 제안해. 이 음식들은 많은 단백질과 칼슘을 갖고 있어서 네가 키가 더 크는 것을 도와줄 수 있어. 또한 너는 매일 밤 적어도 8시간을 자야 해. 이 조언들이 네게 도움이 되기를 바라.

· 내 가장 친한 친구가 나를 피하고 있다고 느껴.
뭔가 잘못된 것이 있는지 그녀에게 물어보는 게 어때?

· 나는 새 옷이 필요해. 그것들은 나를 더 인기 있게 만들어 줄 거야.
사람들은 네가 너이기 때문에 너를 좋아하는 것이지. 네 옷 때문이 아니야.

· 어떻게 그의 감정을 상하게 하지 않으면서 거절할 수 있을까?
왜 네가 데이트를 할 수 없는지 그에게 말하는 것은 어떨까?

01 다음 빈칸에 들어가기에 적절한 단어를 고르시오.

> Daeho, thinking that new things will make him more _____, often wants new things just because his friends have them.

① inventive   ② careful   ③ healthy

④ recent   ⑤ popular

02 다음 영영풀이에 해당하는 단어를 고르시오.

> someone whose job is to provide help and advice to people with problems

① counselor   ② scientist   ③ lawyer

④ teenager   ⑤ designer

03 다음 두 문장에 공통으로 알맞은 것을 고르시오.

> • Can I ask you _____ some help?
> • I am not ready _____ the audition.

① with   ② by   ③ for

④ about   ⑤ on

04 다음 밑줄 친 부분과 같은 뜻으로 쓰인 것은?

> One of the people on our team isn't doing his part.

① Which part of the movie is good?

② I have a small part in the play.

③ This part of the song is easy.

④ I like this part of the game.

⑤ In part, his success is by luck.

[05~06] 다음 우리말과 일치하도록 빈칸에 알맞은 말을 쓰시오.

05

> G: Mom told me I could use the computer for only one hour a day. She thinks that's enough time.
> M: I agree with her.
> G: Sometimes, _____.
> (숙제할 때 나는 그것을 오랫동안 사용할 필요가 있어요.) (doing, for 포함, 13단어)
> M: Hmm. Then maybe we should all get together and talk about it.
> G: Thanks for your understanding, Dad.

➡ _____

_____

06

> G: I'm worried about making friends at my new school.
> M: Don't worry. _____.
> (나는 네가 거기에서 많은 친구를 사귈 것이라고 확신해.) (sure, a lot of 포함, 9단어)

➡ _____

_____

07 다음 대화의 빈칸에 들어가기에 적절하지 <u>않은</u> 것은?

> G: I think our school festival is going to be a lot of fun.
> B: _____

① I agree.

② So do I.

③ That's your idea.

④ Same here.

⑤ You can say that again.

[08~10] 다음 대화를 읽고 물음에 답하시오.

B: The team project for English class is taking a lot of time.

G: I agree. I have a problem. ⓐOne of the people on our team isn't doing his part.

B: That's not good. (A)팀의 모든 사람들은 자신들의 역할을 해야 해.

G: ⓑI know, but I don't know how to get him to do his part.

B: ⓒMaybe he doesn't know how to get started or doesn't like his part.

G: Then _____ (B) _____?

B: Talk to him. ⓓAsk him why he's doing his part. Then tell him you'll help him if he wants.

G: Okay. I'll try that.

B: ⓔI'm sure he'll do better after you talk to him. Good luck with your project.

G: Thanks.

08 밑줄 친 (A)의 우리말에 해당하는 것으로 적절한 것은?

① Everybody have to do our job on the team.

② Somebody on the team has to do their job.

③ Everybody on the team have to do their job.

④ Everybody on the team has to do their job.

⑤ Every job on the team has to do their part.

09 빈칸 (B)에 들어가기에 적절한 것은?

① where is he now

② who is not doing his part

③ why is he doing his best

④ what would you do

⑤ what should I do

10 위 대화의 밑줄 친 ⓐ~ⓔ 중에서 내용상 어색한 부분이 있는 문장을 찾아 번호를 쓰고 자연스러운 문장으로 고치시오.

➡ _____

[11~13] 다음 대화를 읽고 물음에 답하시오.

G: What's the matter, Dongha? You look ⓐworried.

B: I'm not ready ____(A)____ the finals. I sit at my desk ⓑto study but end ____(B)____ doing something else.

G: Well, time management is not easy.

B: I agree. ⓒWhat should I do?

G: ⓓNumber the things you have to do. Then write down how much time you need to finish each ⓔones.

B: Thank you, Emily. I'll try your idea.

G: I'm sure that will be helpful ____(C)____ you. Good luck with your finals

11 빈칸 (A), (B), (C)에 들어가기에 알맞은 것을 〈보기〉에서 골라 쓰시오. (중복 가능)

┌─ 보기 ─┐

about   with   up   on   for

➡ (A) _____ (B) _____ (C) _____

12 위 대화의 ⓐ~ⓔ 중에서 어법상 어색한 것을 고르시오.

① ⓐ   ② ⓑ   ③ ⓒ   ④ ⓓ   ⑤ ⓔ

13 위 대화의 내용과 일치하지 않는 것은?

① Emily thinks Dongha looks worried.

② Dongha doesn't sit at the desk to study for the finals.

③ Dongha is going to take the finals.

④ Dongha is not good at time management.

⑤ Dongha agrees with Emily.

14 다음 문장을 바꾸어 쓸 때 가장 적절한 것은?

> Finishing my homework, I will go to Amy's house.

① Though I finish my homework, I will go to Amy's house.
② After I finish my homework, I will go to Amy's house.
③ Before I will finish my homework, I will go to Amy's house.
④ If I will finish my homework, I will go to Amy's house.
⑤ I finish my homework, after I will go to Amy's house.

15 다음 밑줄 친 부분과 바꿔 쓸 수 있는 것은?

> Maybe you should ask her <u>if</u> there is something wrong.

① whether   ② unless   ③ what
④ that   ⑤ which

16 다음 문장 중에서 어법상 <u>어색한</u> 문장을 고르시오.

① Not arriving on time, we could not enter the theater.
② She does not feel good being the shortest in the group.
③ Becoming more tired, she made more errors in her work.
④ He broke down and wept hearing the news.
⑤ Making a name for himself, he became arrogant.

17 다음 그림을 보고 주어진 어휘를 활용하여 빈칸을 알맞게 채우시오.

Tom asked her _____ the race. (she, give up, will)

18 다음 문장을 바꿔 쓸 때 빈칸에 알맞은 말을 쓰시오.

(1) Listening to music, Minji walked into the classroom.
　➡ _____, Minji walked into the classroom.

(2) He was smiling broadly being so happy.
　➡ He was smiling broadly _____ so happy.

19 다음 중 밑줄 친 부분의 의미가 나머지와 <u>다른</u> 것은?

① <u>If</u> Wendy comes back, say I've got a headache.
② <u>If</u> he thinks it's easy to get a job, he's living in a dream world.
③ I doubt <u>if</u> she will like my present.
④ A fortune will come to you <u>if</u> you take this offer.
⑤ You will have to work hard <u>if</u> you are to succeed.

20 다음 ⓐ~ⓖ 중 어법상 옳은 것을 모두 고르시오.

> ⓐ Chloe watched a movie, ate some popcorn.
> ⓑ Knowing not what to do, he asked for my advice.
> ⓒ Seeing from a distance, the rock looks like a rabbit.
> ⓓ Being a Sunday, Mr. Edgar and all the servants went to church.
> ⓔ Helping us see far, telescopes are still limited.
> ⓕ I wonder that the rumor is true.
> ⓖ I'd like to know if you use social networking sites.

➡ _____

21 다음 문장을 같은 의미의 문장으로 바르게 바꾼 것은?

> If you turn to the right, you will find a white building on the left.

① Turn to the right, you will find a white building on the left.
② Turned to the right, you will find a white building on the left.
③ You turn to the right, you will find a white building on the left.
④ Turning to the right, you will find a white building on the left.
⑤ You turning to the right, you will find a white building on the left.

22 다음 중 어법상 잘못된 문장을 고르시오.

① I will see whether we can come up with a better solution.
② Check whether you agree or disagree.
③ Many people wonder if he resigns before the election.
④ I know you are wondering if you can get taller.
⑤ I don't know if he will follow my advice or not.

23 다음 문장을 바르게 영작한 것은?

> 나는 돈이 부족해서 스마트폰을 살 수 없다.

① Having not enough money, I cannot buy the smartphone.
② Not having enough money, I cannot buy the smartphone.
③ Have not enough money, I cannot buy the smartphone.
④ I do not have enough money, I cannot buy the smartphone.
⑤ Though I don't have enough money, I cannot buy the smartphone.

Reading

[24~26] 다음 글을 읽고 물음에 답하시오.

> Sohui thought Hayeon was her best friend, but now, Sohui feels that Hayeon has changed and she is avoiding her.
> Sohui: (To her older sister) You know my friend Hayeon, don't you?
> Sister: Yeah. Why? What about her?
> Sohui: I feel she's avoiding me. When I see her at school, she turns around and walks away from me.

Sister: I'm sorry to hear ⓐ<u>that</u>. Do you have any idea why she does that?

Sohui: No. I don't think I've done anything wrong. It just feels ⓑ<u>like</u> she doesn't ⓒ<u>like</u> me anymore.

Sister: Maybe you should just ask her if there is something wrong.

Sohui: Maybe I should. I still want to be friends with her.

24 위 글의 밑줄 친 ⓐthat이 가리키는 것을 본문에서 찾아 쓰시오.

➡ _____

_____

25 위 글의 밑줄 친 ⓑlike, ⓒlike와 문법적 쓰임이 같은 것을 각각 고르시오.

① Do you <u>like</u> vegetables?

② No one sings the blues <u>like</u> she did.

③ It didn't turn out <u>like</u> I intended.

④ I <u>like</u> playing tennis.

⑤ <u>Like</u> I said, you're always welcome to stay.

➡ ⓑ와 같은 것: _____, ⓒ와 같은 것: _____

26 위 글을 읽고 대답할 수 <u>없는</u> 질문은?

① Why does Sohui feel that Hayeon has changed and she is avoiding her?

② Does Sohui's sister know Hayeon?

③ Does Sohui have any idea why Hayeon avoids her?

④ What does Sohui's sister advise Sohui to do?

⑤ Why does Hayeon no more like Sohui?

[27~28] 다음 글을 읽고 물음에 답하시오.

Daeho, thinking that new things will make him more popular, often wants new things just because his friends have them.

Daeho: Seongjin, look at my new sneakers. (①) What do you think?

Seongjin: (②) They're nice, but didn't you just buy new sneakers a couple of months ago?

Daeho: (③) I look cooler in these, right?

Seongjin: (④) Daeho, wearing the latest fashion doesn't make you cooler or more popular. (⑤) People like you because you're you, not because of your clothes.

Daeho: Yeah?

Seongjin: Listen, you're a great guy. You don't need new sneakers to prove it.

27 위 글의 흐름으로 보아, 주어진 문장이 들어가기에 가장 적절한 곳은?

> Yeah, but they're no longer in style.

①　　②　　③　　④　　⑤

28 위 글의 제목으로 알맞은 것을 고르시오.

① Be More Popular by Buying New Things!

② Can New Things Really Make You More Popular?

③ Hey, These Look Cooler, Don't They?

④ No! People Like Me Because of My Clothes!

⑤ How to Prove You're a Great Guy

[29~30] 다음 글을 읽고 물음에 답하시오.

Recently, Minkyeong was asked out by a boy in her class. She wants to say no but does not want to hurt his feelings.

Minkyeong: I need your advice. A boy in my class asked me out. I like him, but for now I don't want to go out with him. I need to focus on my studies. What should I do?

Counselor: Why don't you tell him why you can't go?

Minkyeong: I'm afraid I might hurt his feelings.

Counselor: If you don't tell him soon, he will misunderstand your feelings, and you may end up hurting him even more.

Minkyeong: Maybe you're right. Thanks for the advice.

29 위 글에서 알 수 있는 '민경이'의 성격으로 알맞은 말을 <u>모두</u> 고르시오.

① selfish   ② thoughtful
③ outgoing   ④ talkative
⑤ considerate

30 Why does Minkyeong want to refuse to go out with the boy who asked her out? Answer in English beginning with "Because". (10 words)

➡ _____

_____

[31~33] 다음 글을 읽고 물음에 답하시오.

▽ Hena's World

I want to grow taller. I do not feel good being the shortest in the group. I'd like to know how I can get taller.

↳ **tallboy1201**

I heard you are wondering if you can get taller. I suggest you eat foods like eggs, milk, and beans. These foods, ⓐ<u>having lots of protein and calcium</u>, can help you grow taller. Also, you should sleep at least eight hours every night. I hope ⓑ<u>these tips</u> will be helpful to you.

31 What is Hena's worry? Fill in the blanks (A) and (B) with suitable words.

Hena wants to (A)_____ _____. She does not feel good being the (B)_____ in the group.

32 위 글의 밑줄 친 ⓐ를 부사절로 고치시오.

➡ _____

_____

33 위 글의 밑줄 친 ⓑ의 내용을 본문에서 찾아 우리말로 쓰시오.

➡ (1) _____

(2) _____

단원별 예상문제

01 출제율 95%

짝지어진 단어의 관계가 같도록 빈칸에 알맞은 말을 쓰시오. (주어진 철자로 시작할 것.)

> strict : rigid = p_____ : task

02 출제율 90%

다음 빈칸에 들어갈 말로 적절한 것은?

> He's too shy to _____ her out.

① try ② prove
③ inform ④ hurt
⑤ ask

03 출제율 95%

다음 빈칸에 들어가기에 적절한 말이 바르게 짝지어진 것은?

> • Your skirt is in _____ these days.
> • What did you _____ up doing last night?

① pride – try ② part – upset
③ relax – look ④ style – end
⑤ prove – get

04 출제율 100%

다음 〈보기〉의 단어로 자연스러운 문장을 만들 수 없는 것은?

> ┤ 보기 ├
> teenagers   sneakers   strict   snap

① She closed her purse with a _____.
② He wore old jeans and _____.
③ They were always very _____ with their children.
④ His _____ was due to inexperience.
⑤ Here are some things that three _____ worry about.

[05~07] 다음 대화를 읽고 물음에 답하시오.

> B: You look worried. _____ (가) _____
> G: Yes, my sister is upset with me.
> B: Why? What did you do?
> G: I wore one of her shirts ___(A)___ asking.
> B: Tell her you're sorry. I'm ___(B)___ she'll understand.
> G: OK. I will.

05 출제율 100%

빈칸 (가)에 들어가기에 적절하지 않은 것은?

① Is something wrong?
② What's the matter?
③ What's the occasion?
④ What's wrong with you?
⑤ What happened?

06 출제율 95%

빈칸 (A)와 (B)에 들어가기에 알맞은 것으로 짝지어진 것은?

	(A)	(B)
①	with	sure
②	about	aware
③	for	worried
④	without	sure
⑤	by	confident

07 출제율 100%

Which one of the following is NOT true according to the dialogue above?

① The boy looks worried.
② The girl's sister is upset.
③ The boy wants the girl not to worry.
④ The girl wore her sister's shirt.
⑤ The girl will say sorry to her sister.

[08~10] 다음 대화를 읽고 물음에 답하시오.

G: What's the matter, Dongha? ①You look worried.

B: I'm not ready for the finals. I sit at my desk to study but end up doing something else.

G: ②Well, time management is not easy.

B: (A)I agree. What should I do?

G: ③Number the things you have to do. Then write down how much time you need to finish each one.

B: Thank you, Emily. ④I'll try your idea.

G: ⑤I'm sure that will be useless for you. Good luck with your finals.

08 밑줄 친 (A) 대신 쓸 수 있는 것은?

① Why did you say that?

② Neither do I.

③ So do I.

④ You can say that again.

⑤ Don't you agree?

09 위 대화의 밑줄 친 ①~⑤ 중 흐름상 어색한 문장은?

①　　②　　③　　④　　⑤

10 Which one CANNOT be answered from the dialogue above?

① Does Dongha have a problem?

② Why does Dongha look worried?

③ What will Dongha be ready for?

④ When will Dongha sit at the desk?

⑤ What will Dongha try?

[11~12] 다음 대화를 읽고 물음에 답하시오.

B: I just talked about the science project with Jinho and Mina.

G: (A)너희 팀은 무엇을 할지 결정했니?

B: No, not yet. Jinho wants to visit a science museum, but Mina wants to do an experiment.

G: Who do you agree with, Jinho or Mina?

B: I agree with Mina because I think the experiment would be more interesting.

11 밑줄 친 (A)의 우리말에 해당하는 영어 문장으로 적절한 것은?

① Did your team know what will you do?

② Has your team decided what you will do?

③ Will your team decide what you will do?

④ Has your team decided what are you going to do?

⑤ What has your team decided you are going to do?

12 위 대화의 내용과 일치하는 것은?

① The boy will do the science project with the girl.

② The girl wants to do an experiment for the science project.

③ The boy wants to do an experiment for the science project.

④ Jinho and Mina both want to visit a science museum.

⑤ Jinho will ask why Mina wants to do an experiment.

13 다음 문장에서 어법상 어색한 것을 바르게 고쳐 다시 쓰시오.

(1) My concern is if or not they are alive.

➡ _____

_____

(2) I'll check if he sees this painting.

➡ _____

_____

(3) Win the game, Ben is very happy.

➡ _____

_____

(4) Properly conducting, this business is not a public danger.

➡ _____

_____

14 다음 문장의 빈칸에 알맞은 말은?

> I'd like to know _____ Jongmin is good at soccer.

① if   ② as   ③ what
④ that   ⑤ which

15 다음 문장을 분사구문을 이용한 문장으로 바꿔 쓰시오.

(1) As he felt tired, he took a warm bath.

➡ _____

(2) I make delicious food with a dream to be a cook.

➡ _____

(3) Although it was raining, 75 people were waiting for her.

➡ _____

16 다음 그림을 보고 주어진 어휘를 이용하여 빈칸을 알맞게 채우시오.

Do you know _____
for school today or not? (Minji, late)

17 다음 중 어법상 적절한 문장은?

① These foods, have lots of protein and calcium, can help you grow taller.
② Mason listened to the music, to take a shower.
③ When served in the army, he felt a strong tie with his colleagues.
④ Not having any money, I can't buy a car.
⑤ Being disappointing, I kept writing and now I'm a writer.

[18~20] 다음 글을 읽고 물음에 답하시오.

Sohui thought Hayeon was her best friend, but now, Sohui feels that Hayeon has changed and she is avoiding her.

Sohui: (To her older sister) You know my friend Hayeon, don't you?

Sister: Yeah. Why? What about her?

Sohui: I feel she's avoiding me. When I see her at school, she turns around and walks away from me.

Sister: I'm sorry to hear that. Do you have any idea why she does that?

Sohui: No. I don't think I've done anything wrong. ⓐIt just feels like she doesn't like me anymore.

Sister: Maybe you should just ask her ⓑif there is something wrong.

Sohui: Maybe I should. I still want to be friends with her.

✎ 출제율 90%

18 위 글의 밑줄 친 ⓐ를 다음과 같이 바꿔 쓸 때 빈칸에 들어갈 알맞은 말을 두 단어로 쓰시오.

➡ It just feels like she _____ _____ likes me.

✎ 출제율 95%

19 위 글의 밑줄 친 ⓑif와 문법적 쓰임이 같은 것을 모두 고르시오.

① He couldn't tell if she was laughing or crying.
② You can stay here for the weekend if you like.
③ I'll buy the car if you offer me more money.
④ Do you know if he's married?
⑤ I wonder if I should wear a coat.

✎ 출제율 100%

20 위 글에서 알 수 있는 '소희'의 심경으로 가장 알맞은 것을 고르시오.

① ashamed   ② relieved
③ upset   ④ frightened
⑤ bored

[21~23] 다음 글을 읽고 물음에 답하시오.

Daeho, thinking that new things will make him more popular, often wants new things just because his friends have them.

Daeho: Seongjin, look at my new sneakers. What do you think?

Seongjin: They're nice, but didn't you just buy new sneakers a couple of months ago?

Daeho: ⓐYeah, but they're no longer out of style. I look cooler in these, right?

Seongjin: Daeho, ⓑwearing the latest fashion doesn't make you cooler or more popular. People like you because you're you, not because of your clothes.

Daeho: Yeah?

Seongjin: Listen, you're a great guy. You don't need new sneakers to prove it.

✎ 출제율 90%

21 위 글의 밑줄 친 ⓐ에서 흐름상 어색한 부분을 찾아 고치시오.

_____ ➡ _____

✎ 출제율 95%

22 아래 〈보기〉에서 위 글의 밑줄 친 ⓑwearing과 문법적 쓰임이 다른 것의 개수를 고르시오.

┌─── 보기 ───┐
① She was wearing a cap.
② Do you know the man wearing a cap?
③ It is no use wearing a cap.
④ She is fond of wearing a cap.
⑤ I saw her wearing a cap.
└─────────┘

① 1개   ② 2개   ③ 3개   ④ 4개   ⑤ 5개

23 Why does Seongjin think people like Daeho? Fill in the blanks (A) and (B) with suitable words.

출제율 90%

> He thinks people like Daeho because (A)_____ _____, not because of (B)_____ _____.

[24~26] 다음 글을 읽고 물음에 답하시오.

> Recently, Minkyeong was asked out by a boy in her class. She wants to say no but does not want to hurt his feelings.
>
> Minkyeong: I need your advice. A boy in my class asked me out. I like him, but for now I don't want to go out with him. I need to focus on my studies. What should I do?
>
> Counselor: ⓐ왜 네가 데이트를 할 수 없는지 그에게 말하는 것은 어떨까?
>
> Minkyeong: I'm afraid I might hurt his feelings.
>
> Counselor: ⓑIf you won't tell him soon, he will misunderstand your feelings, and you may end up hurting him even more.
>
> Minkyeong: Maybe you're right. Thanks for the advice.

출제율 90%

24 위 글의 밑줄 친 ⓐ의 우리말에 맞게 주어진 어휘를 이용하여 9 단어로 영작하시오.

> don't, why, can't go

➡ _____

출제율 95%

25 위 글의 밑줄 친 ⓑ에서 어법상 틀린 부분을 찾아 고치시오.

_____ ➡ _____

출제율 100%

26 According to the passage, which is NOT true?

① Recently, a boy in Minkyeong's class asked Minkyeong out.

② Minkyeong wants to refuse to go out with the boy because she doesn't like him.

③ Minkyeong does not want to hurt his feelings.

④ The counselor advises Minkyeong to tell the boy why she can't go.

⑤ The counselor says unless Minkyeong tells him soon, he will misunderstand her feelings.

[27~28] 다음 글을 읽고 물음에 답하시오.

> Don't worry. If you follow my advice, you will grow taller. I suggest you try not to get too stressed out. Too much stress can cause a decrease in growth hormone production. Also, you should try to get some exercise every day like swimming, jumping rope, or playing basketball. (A)These types of exercises can stimulate your growth plates, helping you to grow taller. Try these tips, and then let me know ___ⓐ___ they work for you. I hope these tips will be helpful.

출제율 90%

27 위 글의 빈칸 ⓐ에 들어갈 알맞은 말을 모두 고르시오.

① that   ② if

③ what   ④ which

⑤ whether

출제율 95%

28 위 글의 밑줄 친 (A)These types of exercises에 해당하지 않는 것을 모두 고르시오.

① 수영   ② 줄다리기

③ 줄넘기   ④ 농구

⑤ 야구

[01~03] 다음 대화를 읽고 물음에 답하시오.

B: The team project for English class is taking a lot of time.

G: I agree. I have a problem. One of the people on our team isn't doing his part.

B: That's not good. Everybody on the team ___(A)___ to do their job.

G: I know, but I don't know how to ___(B)___ him to do his part. (자기의 역할을 하도록 하다)

B: Maybe he doesn't know how to get started or doesn't like his part.

G: Then what should I do?

B: Talk to him. (가)그에게 왜 자신의 역할을 하지 않는지 물어봐.(doing, part) Then tell him you'll help him if he wants.

G: Okay. I'll try that.

B: I'm sure he'll do better after you talk to him. Good luck with your project.

G: Thanks.

01 빈칸 (A)에 들어가기에 적절한 한 단어를 쓰시오.

➡ _____

02 빈칸 (B)에 괄호 안의 우리말 뜻에 어울리는 한 단어를 쓰시오.

➡ _____

03 밑줄 친 (가)의 우리말에 해당하는 영어 문장을 쓰시오. (주어진 단어 포함, 8 words)

➡ _____

04 분사구문은 부사절로, 부사절은 분사구문으로 바꿔 쓰시오.

(1) Being interested in soccer, I joined a soccer club.

➡ _____
_____

(2) Emily opened her birthday present, smiling happily.

➡ _____
_____

(3) When she heard about the accident, she was shocked.

➡ _____
_____

(4) If it is cold tomorrow, I won't go there.

➡ _____
_____

05 다음 문장에서 어법상 어색한 것을 바르게 고쳐 다시 쓰시오.

(1) He can't decide if to buy it.

➡ _____
_____

(2) I don't know if she comes tomorrow.

➡ _____
_____

(3) Jane watched a baseball game on TV, had dinner.

➡ _____
_____

(4) Put eggs on the bread, Yena made the sandwiches more delicious.

➡ _____
_____

Sohui thought Hayeon was her best friend, but now, Sohui feels that Hayeon has changed and she is avoiding her.

Sohui: (To her older sister) You know my friend Hayeon, ____ⓐ____?

Sister: Yeah. Why? What about her?

Sohui: I feel she's avoiding me. When I see her at school, she turns around and walks away from me.

Sister: I'm sorry to hear that. Do you have any idea why she does ⓑthat?

Sohui: No. I don't think I've done anything wrong. It just feels like she doesn't like me anymore.

Sister: Maybe you should just ask her if there is something wrong.

Sohui: Maybe I should. I still want to be friends with her.

06 위 글의 빈칸 ⓐ에 들어갈 알맞은 부가의문문을 쓰시오.

➡ _____

07 위 글의 밑줄 친 ⓑthat이 가리키는 것을 우리말로 쓰시오.

➡ _____
_____

08 위 글의 내용을 다음과 같이 정리하고자 한다. 빈칸 (A)와 (B)에 들어갈 알맞은 단어를 쓰시오. (A)에는 철자 w로, (B)에는 철자 a로 시작하는 단어를 쓰시오.

Sohui is (A)_____ that her best friend Hayeon has changed and she is avoiding her, and then her sister (B)_____ her to ask Hayeon if there is something wrong.

Daeho, thinking that new things will make him more popular, often wants new things just because his friends have them.

Daeho: Seongjin, look at my new sneakers. What do you think?

Seongjin: They're nice, but didn't you just buy new sneakers ⓐ몇 달 전에?

Daeho: Yeah, but they're no longer in style. I look cooler in these, right?

Seongjin: Daeho, wearing the latest fashion doesn't make you cooler or more popular. People like you because you're you, not because of your clothes.

Daeho: Yeah?

Seongjin: Listen, you're a great guy. You don't need new sneakers to prove it.

09 위 글의 밑줄 친 ⓐ의 우리말에 맞게 5 단어로 영작하시오.

➡ _____

10 다음 문장에서 위 글의 내용과 다른 부분을 찾아서 고치시오.

Seongjin says Daeho needs new sneakers to prove he's a great guy.

_____ ➡ _____

11 다음 빈칸 (A)~(D)에 알맞은 단어를 넣어 대호의 고민과 그에 알맞은 조언을 완성하시오.

• **Daeho's worry:** I need (A)_____ clothes. They'll make me (B)_____
_____.

• **Advice:** People like you not (C)_____
_____ your clothes but (D)_____
you're you.

창의사고력 서술형 문제

01 주어진 그림과 다음 표현을 보고 if를 이용하여 다음 문장의 빈칸을 알맞게 채우시오.

- Does listening to music help you relax?
- Is reading history comic books helpful?
- Is our P.E. teacher too strict?
- Will our school festival be a lot of fun?

(1) I'd like to know _____ .

(2) I'd like to know _____ .

(3) I'd like to know _____ .

(4) I'd like to know _____ .

02 다음 내용을 바탕으로 헤나의 SNS에 고민 상담 댓글을 쓰시오.

Worry: Hena wants to grow taller. She does not feel good being the shortest in the group.
- Eat foods that help you grow taller, like eggs, milk, and beans.
- Sleep at least eight hours every night.

⊽ Hena's World

I want to (A)_____. I do not feel good (B)_____ in the group. I'd like to know how I can get taller.

↳ 🧑 **tallboy1201**

I heard you are wondering if you can get taller. I suggest you eat foods like (C)_____. These foods, having lots of protein and calcium, can help you grow taller. Also, you should sleep at least (D)_____ every night. I hope these tips will be helpful to you.

단원별 모의고사

01 다음 짝지어진 두 단어의 관계가 같도록 빈칸에 알맞은 말을 쓰시오. (주어진 철자로 시작할 것.)

> avoid : face = agree : d_____

02 다음 영영풀이에 해당하는 단어로 적절한 것은?

> a person who is between the ages of 13 and 19

① counselor   ② manager
③ athlete   ④ teenager
⑤ author

03 다음 문장의 빈칸에 알맞은 것을 〈보기〉에서 찾아 쓰시오.

> ┌─ 보기 ─┐
> relax   worry   avoid   agree

(1) I entirely _____ with you.
(2) I left early to _____ the rush hour.
(3) Just _____ and enjoy the movie.
(4) Don't _____ about the exam – just do your best.

04 다음 빈칸에 들어갈 말로 적절하지 <u>않은</u> 것은?

> You will have _____ solving the problem.

① thought   ② difficulty
③ a difficult time   ④ trouble
⑤ a hard time

[05~07] 다음 대화를 읽고 물음에 답하시오.

B: The team project for English class is taking a lot of time.
G: I agree. I have a problem. (A) One of the people on our team isn't doing his part.
B: _____(가)_____ Everybody on the team has to do their job.
G: I know, but I don't know how to get him to do his part. (B)
B: Maybe he doesn't know how to get started or doesn't like his part.
G: Then what should I do? (C)
B: Talk to him. Ask him why he's not doing his part. (D)
G: Okay. I'll try that. (E)
B: I'm sure he'll do better after you talk to him. Good luck with your project.
G: Thanks.

05 빈칸 (가)에 들어가기에 적절한 것은?

① That's what I thought.
② That's a good idea.
③ That's not good.
④ I said it many times.
⑤ Is it your idea?

06 (A)~(E) 중에서 다음 문장이 들어가기에 적절한 곳은?

> Then tell him you'll help him if he wants.

① (A)   ② (B)   ③ (C)   ④ (D)   ⑤ (E)

07 Which one is TRUE according to the dialogue?

① The boy thinks the team project is easy.
② One of the people on the girl's team isn't doing his part.
③ The girl doesn't like her part in the team project.
④ The girl doesn't know how to get started.
⑤ The boy will ask why he's not doing his part.

[08~10] 다음 대화를 읽고 물음에 답하시오.

G: What's the matter, Dongha? You look worried.
B: I'm not ⓐready for the finals. I sit at my desk to study but ___(A)___ doing something else.
G: Well, time ⓑmanagement is not easy.
B: I agree. What should I do?
G: ⓒNumber the things you have to do. Then write down how much time ⓓdo you need to finish each one.
B: Thank you, Emily. I'll try your idea.
G: I'm sure ⓔthat will be helpful for you. Good luck with your finals.

08 빈칸 (A)에 적절한 것은?

① enjoy
② dislike
③ end up
④ mind
⑤ finish

09 밑줄 친 ⓐ~ⓔ 중에서 어법상 어색한 것은?

① ⓐ
② ⓑ
③ ⓒ
④ ⓓ
⑤ ⓔ

10 Which one of the following is NOT true according to the dialogue above?

① Emily thinks Dongha looks worried.
② Dongha didn't study hard for the finals.
③ Emily doesn't know how to manage her time.
④ Dongha agrees that time management is not easy.
⑤ Emily is sure that her idea will be helpful for Dongha.

11 다음 우리말을 주어진 어휘를 이용하여 영작하시오.

(1) 그 소식을 들었을 때, 그는 충격으로 바닥에 주저앉았다. (from, drop down on the floor, 11 단어)

➡ _____

_____

(2) 아버지께 말씀드리고 난 후, 나는 기분이 훨씬 나아졌다. (my dad, felt, talk, much, to, 9 단어)

➡ _____

_____

(3) 나는 네가 나를 기억하는지 확신하지 못한다. (sure, remember, not, 8 단어)

➡ _____

_____

(4) 집을 나갈 때 스토브가 꺼졌는지 확인해야 해. (the house, the stove, check, leave, should, if, off, 12 단어)

➡ _____

_____

12 Which is grammatically WRONG?

① Could you check if everything is correct?

② Hansu is not sure if he closed all the windows.

③ The question is if or not I have the patience to read it through.

④ I wonder if Sue knows my secret.

⑤ Jay asked me if I could join his club.

13 다음 두 문장을 한 문장으로 바꿔 쓸 때 빈칸에 알맞은 말을 쓰시오.

(1) • Do you know?

　• Will he come to the party tonight?

　→ Do you know _____

　_____?

(2) • I wonder.

　• Does he like playing baseball?

　→ I wonder _____

　_____.

(3) • Please check.

　• Is dinner ready?

　→ Please check _____.

14 다음 중 어법상 옳은 문장을 모두 고르시오.

① Ms. Brown asked me if I knew the answer.

② Do you know if she comes back soon?

③ My mom always checks if I finish my homework.

④ It being Sunday, most shops were closed.

⑤ Writing too quickly, the letter had many mistakes.

⑥ Feeling not well, I came home early.

⑦ Listening to music, he drinks tea.

[15~17] 다음 글을 읽고 물음에 답하시오.

Sohui thought Hayeon was her best friend, but now, Sohui feels that Hayeon has changed and she is avoiding her.

Sohui: (To her older sister) You know my friend Hayeon, don't you?

Sister: Yeah. Why? What about her?

Sohui: I feel she's avoiding me. When I see her at school, she turns around and walks away from me.

Sister: I'm sorry to hear that. Do you have any idea why she does that?

Sohui: No. ⓐ나는 내가 잘못한 것이 있다고 생각하지 않아. It just feels like she doesn't like me anymore.

Sister: ⓑMaybe you should just ask her that there is something wrong.

Sohui: Maybe I should. I still want to be friends with her.

15 위 글의 주제로 알맞은 것을 고르시오.

① the way to give effective advice

② worry about friendship and advice

③ the common concerns of teenagers

④ the importance of friendship

⑤ worry about the school life and solution

16 위 글의 밑줄 친 ⓐ의 우리말에 맞게 주어진 어휘를 알맞게 배열하시오.

done / wrong / I / think / I've / anything / don't

➡ _____

17 위 글의 밑줄 친 ⓑ에서 어법상 틀린 부분을 찾아 고치시오.

_____ ➡ _____

[18~20] 다음 글을 읽고 물음에 답하시오.

Daeho, thinking that new things will make ①him more popular, often wants new things just because his friends have them.

Daeho: Seongjin, look at ②my new sneakers. What do ③you think?

Seongjin: They're nice, but didn't ④you just buy new sneakers a couple of months ago?

Daeho: Yeah, but they're no longer in style. ⑤I look cooler in these, right?

Seongjin: Daeho, wearing the latest fashion doesn't make you cooler or more popular. People like you because you're you, not because of your clothes.

Daeho: Yeah?

Seongjin: Listen, you're a great guy. You don't need new sneakers ⓐto prove it.

18 밑줄 친 ①~⑤ 중에서 가리키는 대상이 나머지 넷과 다른 것은?

①   ②   ③   ④   ⑤

19 아래 <보기>에서 위 글의 밑줄 친 ⓐto prove와 to부정사의 용법이 같은 것의 개수를 고르시오.

┌─── 보기 ├───
① She was pleased to prove it.
② He tried to prove it.
③ Tell me the way to prove it.
④ He was clever enough to prove it.
⑤ Was it easy to prove it?
└──────────────

① 1개   ② 2개   ③ 3개   ④ 4개   ⑤ 5개

20 According to the passage, which is NOT true?

① Daeho thinks that new things will make him more popular.

② Seongjin says Daeho's new sneakers are nice.

③ Daeho says the sneakers he bought a couple of months ago are out of style.

④ Seongjin says wearing the latest fashion makes Daeho cooler or more popular.

⑤ Seongjin says Daeho is a great guy.

[21~22] 다음 글을 읽고 물음에 답하시오.

Recently, Minkyeong was asked out by a boy in her class. She wants to say no but does not want to hurt his feelings. (①)

Minkyeong: I need your advice. (②) A boy in my class asked me out. (③) I like him, but for now I don't want to go out with him. (④) I need to focus on my studies. (⑤)

Counselor: Why don't you tell him why you can't go?

Minkyeong: I'm afraid I might hurt his feelings.

Counselor: If you don't tell him soon, he will misunderstand your feelings, and you may end up hurting him even more.

Minkyeong: Maybe you're right. Thanks for the advice.

21 위 글의 흐름으로 보아, 주어진 문장이 들어가기에 가장 적절한 곳은?

┌─────────────────────────┐
│   What should I do?   │
└─────────────────────────┘

①   ②   ③   ④   ⑤

22 다음 빈칸 (A)와 (B)에 알맞은 단어를 넣어 민경이의 고민과 그에 알맞은 조언을 완성하시오.

- **Minkyeong's worry:** How can I (A) _____ _____ without hurting his feelings?
- **Advice:** How about telling him why you (B)_____ _____?

Lesson

3

Healthy Living, a Happy Life

 의사소통 기능

- 강조하기
  A: I think it's important to eat a good breakfast.
  B: I think so, too.

- 안타까움, 후회 표현하기
  A: Your bag is too small.
  B: Yes. I should have brought a bigger one.

언어 형식

- 'the 비교급, the 비교급'
  The more sun you get, **the more** "happy hormone"
  the brain produces.

- It is ... that 강조 구문
  It is calcium **that** builds strong bones and teeth.

Words & Expressions

Key Words

- **already** [ɔːlrédi] 부 이미, 벌써
- **arrive** [əráiv] 동 도착하다
- **avoid** [əvɔ́id] 동 피하다
- **benefit** [bénəfit] 명 이득 동 이득을 보다
- **blanket** [blǽŋkit] 명 이불, 담요
- **bone** [boun] 명 뼈
- **brain** [brein] 명 뇌
- **calcium** [kǽlsiəm] 명 칼슘
- **calming** [kɑːmiŋ] 형 진정시키는
- **check** [tʃek] 동 점검하다
- **clearly** [klíərli] 부 또렷하게
- **create** [kriéit] 동 만들어 내다, 창조하다
- **decide** [disáid] 동 결심하다, 결정하다
- **direct** [dirékt] 형 직접적인, (열기나 빛이) 직접 닿는
- **effect** [ifékt] 명 효과
- **exercise** [éksərsàiz] 동 운동하다
- **finally** [fáinəli] 부 마침내
- **flight** [flait] 명 항공편, 비행
- **fortunately** [fɔ́ːrtʃənətli] 부 다행스럽게도
- **grade** [greid] 명 성적
- **hang** [hæŋ] 동 걸다
- **healthy** [hélθi] 형 건강한
- **hormone** [hɔ́ːrmòun] 명 호르몬
- **interestingly** [íntərəstiŋli] 부 흥미롭게도
- **journal** [dʒə́ːrnl] 명 일지, 일기
- **leave** [liːv] 동 떠나다
- **level** [lévəl] 명 수준, 수치
- **mood** [muːd] 명 기분, 감정
- **moreover** [mɔːróuvər] 부 게다가
- **nature-friendly** 형 자연친화적인
- **outdoors** [áutdɔrz] 부 야외에서
- **peak** [piːk] 형 절정의, 최고조의 명 절정, 최고조
- **produce** [prədjúːs] 동 만들어 내다
- **properly** [prɑ́pərli] 부 제대로
- **protect** [prətékt] 동 보호하다
- **reach** [riːtʃ] 동 도달하다
- **regret** [rigrét] 동 후회하다
- **regularly** [régjulərli] 부 규칙적으로
- **review** [rivjúː] 동 복습하다
- **role** [roul] 명 역할
- **safely** [séifli] 부 안전하게
- **serotonin** [serətóunin] 명 세로토닌
- **shine** [ʃain] 동 빛나다
- **skin** [skin] 명 피부
- **sunlight** [sʌ́nlait] 명 햇살
- **sunscreen** [sʌ́nskriːn] 명 자외선 차단제
- **sunshine** [sʌ́nʃain] 명 햇볕, 햇빛
- **vitamin** [váitəmin] 명 비타민
- **weather** [wéðər] 명 날씨
- **wet** [wet] 형 젖은

Key Expressions

- **be good for** ~에 유익하다
- **both A and B** A와 B 둘 다
- **full of** ~로 가득 찬
- **get sleep** 잠자다
- **go up** 높아지다
- **have a snack** 간식을 먹다
- **keep ~ in mind** ~을 명심하다
- **make a world of difference** 큰 차이를 만들다
- **on time** 제시간에
- **play an important role in** ~에 중요한 역할을 하다
- **put on** 착용하다, 바르다
- **put out** 내놓다
- **should have p.p.** ~했어야 했는데
- **stay healthy** 건강을 유지하다
- **stay up** 깨어 있다
- **surf the Internet** 인터넷 검색을 하다
- **too ~ to ...** 너무 ~해서 …할 수 없다

Word Power

※ 서로 비슷한 뜻을 가진 어휘

- □ **arrive** 도착하다 : **reach** 도착하다
- □ **exercise** 운동하다 : **work out** 운동하다
- □ **fortunately** 다행스럽게도 : **luckily** 운 좋게도
- □ **leave** 떠나다 : **depart** 떠나다
- □ **protect** 보호하다 : **cover** 보호하다

- □ **benefit** 이점 : **advantage** 이점, 장점
- □ **finally** 마침내 : **ultimately** 결국
- □ **grade** 성적 : **degree** 점수
- □ **properly** 제대로 : **suitably** 적절하게
- □ **role** 역할 : **part** 배역

※ 서로 반대되는 뜻을 가진 어휘

- □ **avoid** 피하다 ↔ **face** 마주하다
- □ **direct** 직접적인 ↔ **indirect** 간접적인
- □ **wet** 젖은 ↔ **dry** 건조한

- □ **clearly** 또렷하게 ↔ **vaguely** 모호하게
- □ **healthy** 건강한 ↔ **unhealthy** 건강하지 못한
- □ **regularly** 규칙적으로 ↔ **irregularly** 불규칙하게

※ 동사 – 명사

- □ **arrive** 도착하다 – **arrival** 도착
- □ **decide** 결심하다 – **decision** 결심
- □ **protect** 보호하다 – **protection** 보호

- □ **avoid** 피하다 – **avoidance** 회피
- □ **produce** 만들어 내다 – **production** 생산

English Dictionary

- □ **benefit** 이득을 보다
  → to take advantages from something
  무엇인가로부터 이득을 얻다

- □ **blanket** 이불, 담요
  → a large piece of cloth used as a covering for warmth
  따뜻하도록 덮개로 사용되는 큰 천

- □ **bone** 뼈
  → the hard part of the body that forms a framework inside people or animals
  사람이나 동물의 내부에서 골격을 형성하는 신체의 단단한 부분

- □ **brain** 뇌
  → the organ inside the head that control movements and feelings
  움직임과 감정을 조절하는 머리 속에 있는 기관

- □ **go up** 올라가다
  → to become higher or greater 더 높거나 크게 되다

- □ **journal** 일지, 일기
  → a book in which people regularly write about what has happened to them
  자신들에게 일어난 일을 규칙적으로 기록하는 책

- □ **mood** 기분, 감정
  → a temporary state of mind 일시적인 마음의 상태

- □ **peak** 절정, 최고조
  → the highest level or degree of excellence, quantity, activity, etc. 탁월함, 수량, 활동 등의 가장 높은 수준이나 정도

- □ **regularly** 규칙적으로
  → at the same time every day, week, month, or year
  매일, 매주, 매달, 매년 똑같은 시간에

- □ **role** 역할
  → the part assumed to be played by a person
  사람에 의해 수행되도록 떠맡겨지는 배역

- □ **skin** 피부
  → the outer layer of a person's or animal's body
  사람이나 동물 신체의 가장 바깥 층

- □ **sunshine** 햇빛
  → light and heat from the sun 태양으로부터의 빛과 열

- □ **wet** 젖은
  → covered or touched with water or another liquid
  물이나 다른 액체로 덮여 있거나 접촉한

01 다음 밑줄 친 부분과 의미가 가장 가까운 것을 고르시오.

> As you can see, sunshine has many benefits, but how can you enjoy its benefits safely?

① impacts ② favors ③ joys
④ events ⑤ advantages

02 다음 문장의 빈칸에 들어갈 단어를 사용하여 문장을 자연스럽게 완성할 수 있는 것은?

> What are the positive and negative _____ of social networking sites?

① A letter _____ for you this morning.
② He tends to _____ all physical contact.
③ He has cracked a _____ in his arm.
④ The drug has some bad side _____.
⑤ People need _____ to have strong bones.

03 다음 빈칸에 공통으로 들어가기에 알맞은 것은?

> • Look at my face. I should have _____ on some sunscreen.
> • I _____ the blanket out in the sun this morning.

① got ② had ③ put
④ let ⑤ left

04 〈보기〉와 같은 관계가 되도록 빈칸에 알맞은 말을 쓰시오.

> ┤ 보기 ├
> avoid : face

(1) wet : _____
(2) regular : _____

05 다음 중 밑줄 친 부분의 뜻풀이가 바르지 <u>않은</u> 것은?

① One of the <u>benefits</u> of a smartphone is that you can reach someone quickly in an emergency. (이점)
② This exercise helps increase growth <u>hormone</u>. (호르몬)
③ Some research has shown us that our sports ability is also related to our <u>brains</u>. (뇌)
④ This steak was cooked with <u>direct</u> heat. (즉각적인)
⑤ The house has a reasonable price. <u>Moreover</u>, the location is very good. (게다가)

06 다음 중 〈보기〉에 있는 단어를 사용하여 자연스러운 문장을 만들 수 <u>없는</u> 것은? (대·소문자 무시)

> ┤ 보기 ├
> difference mood outdoors fortunately

① _____, the typhoon weakened before getting to my town.
② When you are cold, wearing a muffler will make a world of _____.
③ This book talks about how to get out of a bad _____.
④ Children enjoy playing _____.
⑤ When is the _____ hour for electricity use?

[01~02] 빈칸에 공통으로 들어갈 단어를 쓰시오.

01

> • A walk in the sun is good _____ both your mind and your body.
> • I have decided to exercise on the weekend _____ my health.

02 중요

> • It's important to arrive at school _____ time.
> • Serotonin helps you focus better _____ what you are doing.

03 밑줄 친 부분과 의미가 가장 가까운 단어를 주어진 철자로 시작하여 쓰시오.

> I am not really <u>suitably</u> dressed for a party.

➡ p_____

04 중요 주어진 단어를 이용해 빈칸을 완성하시오.

> We apologize for the late _____ of the train.

➡ _____ (arrive)

05 다음 짝지어진 단어의 관계가 같도록 빈칸에 알맞은 말을 쓰시오.

> healthy : unhealthy = direct : _____

06 중요 빈칸에 알맞은 단어를 〈보기〉에서 골라 쓰시오. (어형 변화 가능)

> ┤ 보기 ├
> skin   produce   role   properly

(1) This factory _____ car parts.
(2) Managing your time _____ is the key to success.
(3) Sue has an important _____ in our group.
(4) I need to buy a facial cream for dry _____.

07 다음 우리말에 맞게 빈칸에 알맞은 말을 쓰시오.

(1) Davis 박사는 햇살이 피부에 끼치는 영향을 연구 중이다.
   ➡ Dr. Davis is studying the action of _____ on the skin.
(2) 그는 아시아 횡단 여행에 대해 일기를 썼다.
   ➡ He kept a _____ of his travels across Asia.
(3) 75점 이상의 점수에 대해서는 A 학점을 받는다.
   ➡ You get an A _____ for scores of 75 and over.
(4) 제가 한 말을 유의하시기 바랍니다.
   ➡ I hope you'll keep in _____ what I've told you.

Conversation

교과서

① 강조하기

> **A** I think it's important to eat a good breakfast. 아침을 잘 먹는 것이 중요하다고 생각해.
> **B** I think so, too. 나도 역시 그렇게 생각해.

- 전달하고자 하는 내용을 강조하는 표현은 다양하다. to부정사를 사용하여 부정사 부분을 강조할 때는 "It's important to V" 구문으로 나타내고, 절을 강조할 때에는 "It's important that S+V"의 형태를 취하고, "I think it's important to ~" 또는 "I think it's important that S+V"의 형태가 되기도 한다.

- "It's important to + 동사원형~"은 "~하는 것은 중요하다"라는 의미이고, 이 표현에서 it은 가주어이고 "to부정사"가 진주어이다. 이 표현은 to부정사 부분을 강조하는 표현이다. "It's important that S+V"의 형태에서는 that절이 강조되는 내용이다.

- to부정사를 강조할 때는 "important" 대신 necessary(필요한), essential(필수적인), crucial(중요한, 치명적인) 등을 이용하여 "It is necessary/important/essential/crucial to ~" 또는 "It is important/essential/crucial that S+V ~"라고 할 수도 있다.

- 그 외에 강조하는 표현으로는 강조할 내용에 따라, 동사를 강조할 때는 강조의 조동사 do, does, did를 사용하고, 문장의 어느 한 성분을 강조할 때는 "It is ~ that" 강조구문을 사용할 수 있다.

강조를 나타내는 표현

- It is important[necessary] to/that ~. ~하는 것이 중요/필요하다
- I want to stress that ~. ~을 강조하고 싶다
- It is essential to V ~. ~하는 것이 필수적이다
- It's crucial[critical] to V ~. ~하는 것이 중요하다
- It's significant to V ~. ~하는 것이 중요하다

핵심 Check

1. 다음 밑줄 친 우리말에 해당하는 표현으로 적절하지 <u>않은</u> 것은?

G: How can we stay healthy?

B: Well, <u>아침을 잘 먹는 것이 중요해.</u>

① I think it's important to eat a good breakfast
② it's important that you should eat a good breakfast
③ I want to stress that you eat a good breakfast
④ I think I will have a good breakfast, too
⑤ it's significant to have a good breakfast

안타까움, 후회 표현하기

> **A** Your bag is too small. 네 가방이 너무 작아.
>
> **B** Yes. I should have brought a bigger one. 맞아. 나는 더 큰 것을 가지고 왔어야 했는데.

■ 과거의 행위에 대한 안타까움, 후회 또는 유감을 나타낼 때는 "should have+과거분사"의 표현을 사용한다. "should have+과거분사"는 "~했어야 했는데(하지 못해 유감이다)"의 의미로 과거와 반대되는 상황을 나타내기 위하여 사용할 수 있다.

■ 이 표현에서는 "should"를 "ought to"로 바꾸어 "ought to have+과거분사"로 표현할 수 있다. "~하지 말았어야 했는데 (했다)"의 의미는 "should not have+과거분사" 또는 "ought not to have+과거분사"로 나타낸다.

■ 안타까움, 후회를 나타내는 비슷한 표현으로 "I had to ~, but I didn't.", "I (really) regret ~." 등이 있고, sorry를 사용하여 "I'm sorry that 주어+과거동사 ~"로 나타내기도 한다. "should have+과거분사"는 과거 사실에 대한 가정의 표현으로 "~했어야 했는데 (하지 않았다)"의 의미를 나타내어 과거에 하지 않은 일에 대해 후회하는 표현이다. should 대신 could를 사용하여 "could have+과거분사"가 되면 "~할 수 있었는데"의 의미가 될 수 있다.

■ "should have p.p."는 과거에 했어야 하는 일이나 하지 못한 일에 대한 후회, 유감, 안타까움을 표현하며 "~했어야 했는데 (못했다)"의 의미로 사용되고, "could/would have p.p."는 과거의 일에 대한 유감을 의미하여 "~할 수 있었는데(못했다), ~했어야 했는데(못했다)"의 의미로 가정법에 주로 사용된다. "must have p.p."는 과거에 대한 강한 추측을 나타내어 "~이었음에 틀림없다"의 의미로 사용되고, 그에 반해, "may have p.p."는 과거에 대한 약한 추측을 나타내어 "~했을지도 모른다"의 의미로 사용된다.

안타까움, 후회 표현하기

• 주어+should[shouldn't] have+과거분사 ~	~했어야[하지 말았어야] 했는데
• 주어+ought[ought not] to have+과거분사 ~	~했어야[하지 말았어야] 했는데
• I (really) regret (that) 주어+과거동사 ~	~한 것이 유감이다/후회한다
• I'm sorry that 주어+과거동사 ~	~한 것이 유감이다

핵심 Check

2. 다음 밑줄 친 말 대신 쓰기에 적절한 것은?

G: Aren't you cold?

B: Yes. <u>I should have worn a jacket.</u>

① Everything will be all right.　② You ought to wear a jacket.

③ I must have worn a jacket.　④ I am sorry that you wear a jacket.

⑤ I regret that I didn't wear a jacket.

Real-Life Zone

G: Ben, you look full of energy today!

B: Do I? Maybe ❶that's because I finally got a good night's sleep last night.

G: Why? Don't you usually get enough sleep?

B: No, ❷I know it's really important to get a good night's sleep, but I always stay up late surfing the Internet or playing with my phone.

G: That sometimes happens to me too.

B: After I do that, I regret it the next morning and say, "I should have gone to bed earlier last night."

G: How was yesterday different?

B: Well, yesterday afternoon I climbed the mountain with my dad. I was really tired when I got home. I went to sleep right after I went to bed.

G: Outdoor activities are a great way ❸to help you get a good night's sleep.

G: 벤, 너 오늘 기운 차 보여!

B: 내가 그래? 그건 아마 내가 지난밤 마침내 잠을 잘 잤기 때문일 거야.

G: 왜? 평소에 충분한 잠을 자지 못하니?

B: 응, 잠을 잘 자는 것이 정말 중요하다는 것은 알지만 나는 언제나 인터넷 검색을 하거나 휴대폰을 가지고 놀면서 늦게까지 깨어 있어.

G: 그건 나에게도 가끔 일어나는 일이야.

B: 그러고 난 뒤에, 나는 다음 날 아침 후회하고 "지난밤에 더 일찍 잠들었어야 했는데."라고 말해.

G: 어제는 어떻게 달랐니?

B: 음, 어제 오후에 나는 아빠와 등산을 했어. 집에 왔을 때 나는 매우 피곤했어. 나는 침대에 가자마자 바로 잠들었어.

G: 야외 활동은 네가 잠을 잘 자도록 돕는 훌륭한 방법이구나.

❶ "that's because ~"는 "그것은 ~이기 때문이다"라는 뜻으로 이어지는 내용이 앞에 나온 것에 대한 이유가 된다.
❷ "I know" 뒤에는 명사절을 유도하는 접속사 that이 생략되어 있다.
❸ "to help"는 명사 way를 수식하는 형용사적 용법의 to부정사이다.

Check(√) True or False

(1) The boy didn't get a good night's sleep last night. T ☐ F ☐

(2) Yesterday afternoon the boy climbed the mountain with his dad. T ☐ F ☐

Wrap Up 1

W: Oh, your blanket is wet from the rain! I should have checked the weather.

B: Did you wash it?

W: No. ❶I just put it out in the sun this morning.

B: Why didn't you wash it?

W: Hanging a blanket in the sun is ❷a nature-friendly way to keep the blanket clean.

B: Oh, I didn't know that. I'll remember that.

W: And it's also important to remember to do it regularly.

W: 오, 네 이불이 비에 젖었어! 내가 날씨를 확인했어야 했는데.

B: 그것을 빨았어요?

W: 아니. 오늘 아침에 그냥 햇볕에 널어놓았어.

B: 왜 빨지 않았어요?

W: 햇볕에 이불을 널어놓는 것은 이불을 깨끗하게 유지하는 친환경적인 방법이야.

B: 오, 저는 그것을 몰랐어요. 기억해 둘게요.

W: 그리고 정기적으로 그렇게 하는 것을 기억하는 것 또한 중요해.

❶ "put ~ out"은 "~을 밖에 내놓다"의 의미를 가진다.
❷ "a nature-friendly way to keep the blanket clean"에서 to keep은 way를 수식하는 형용사적 용법이다.

Check(√) True or False

(3) The woman regrets that she didn't wash the blanket. T ☐ F ☐

(4) It is important to remember to wash a blanket regularly. T ☐ F ☐

Listen & Speak 1 Listen

1. **G:** How can we stay healthy?
   B: Well, ❶it's important to eat a good breakfast.
2. **B:** What can we do to get good grades?
   G: It's important to review every day.
3. **G:** ❷I think it's important to write a journal after reading.
   B: I agree.
4. **B:** It's important to write down ❸what you spend your money on.
   G: I think so, too.

❶ "it's important to ~"에서 it은 가주어이고, to ~는 진주어이다.
❷ 강조하는 의미의 "It's important to ~"는 "I think it's important to ~"라고 할 수 있다.
❸ "what you spend ~"는 "무엇에 돈을 쓰는지"의 의미로 간접의문문이다.

 Listen & Speak 1 A-1

B: What did you do on the weekend?
G: I played tennis. ❶I have decided to exercise on the weekend for my health.
B: Good for you. It's important to exercise regularly.
G: Right. ❷How about playing tennis with me?
B: Why not?

❶ 동사 decided의 목적어는 to부정사이다.
❷ "How about ~ing ?"는 "~하는 것이 어때?"의 의미로 상대에게 제안하는 표현이다.

 Listen & Speak 1 A-2

M: John, you are late again.
B: I'm sorry. ❶I took the wrong bus.
M: ❷I think you need to leave home a little earlier.
B: I think so, too. Next time I won't be late.
M: It's important to arrive at school on time.

❶ take the wrong bus = 버스를 잘못 타다
❷ 동사 think의 목적어 역할을 하는 명사절에서 접속사 that이 생략되어 있다.

 Listen & Speak 2 Listen

1. **G:** Your bag is too small.
   B: Yes. I should have brought a bigger one.

2. **G:** Aren't you cold?
   B: ❶Yes. I should have worn a jacket.
3. **B:** We ❷missed our flight.
   G: Oh, no. We should have come earlier.
4. **G:** Look at my face. I should have put on some sunscreen.
   B: Yes. You're right.

❶ "Aren't you ~?"에 해당하는 부정의 질문에 대한 대답은 대답이 긍정이면 Yes, 부정이면 No이다.
❷ miss flight = 항공편을 놓치다

 Listen & Speak 2 A-1

B: Mina, ❶how was the movie?
G: I didn't enjoy it. It was boring.
B: What was bad about it?
G: I already knew the ending. I ❷shouldn't have read about it before seeing it.
B: Oh, I'm sorry you didn't like it.

❶ "how was the movie?"는 영화가 만족스러운지를 묻는 질문이다.
❷ "shouldn't have+과거분사"는 "~하지 말았어야 했는데"의 의미로 과거 사실에 대한 유감이나 후회를 나타낸다.

 Listen & Speak 2 A-2

B: We still have 30 minutes ❶to go before we reach the top of the mountain. Let's sit down over there and have a snack.
G: Oh, I brought only water. I should have brought some snacks.
B: That's okay. I brought a lot. We can share.
G: I'll keep ❷it in mind to bring some snacks next time.

❶ "to go ~"는 minutes를 수식하는 형용사적 용법이다.
❷ it은 가목적어이고, to bring이 진목적어이다.

 Wrap Up 2

G: Ryan, ❶are you okay? You look tired.
B: I couldn't sleep well last night.
G: Why is that? Did you have too much homework?
G: No. I ❷watched a movie on TV, and it didn't end until after 2:00.
G: Oh, you should have gone to bed earlier.

❶ "are you okay?"는 상대의 안부를 묻는 말이다.
❷ "watch a movie on TV"는 "TV로 영화를 보다"의 뜻이다.

다음 우리말과 일치하도록 빈칸에 알맞은 말을 쓰시오.

Listen & Speak 1 Listen

1. **G:** How _____ we _____ healthy?
   B: _____, it's _____ to eat a good _____.
2. **B:** _____ can we _____ to get good _____?
   G: It's _____ to review every day.
3. **G:** I _____ it's important to _____ a _____ after reading.
   B: I agree.
4. **B:** It's important to _____ _____ what you _____ your money _____.
   G: I _____ so, too.

Listen & Speak 1 A

1. **B:** _____ did you _____ on the _____?
   G: I _____ tennis. I have _____ to _____ on the weekend _____ my health.
   B: Good for _____. It's _____ to exercise _____.
   G: _____. How _____ playing tennis _____ me?
   B: Why not?
2. **M:** John, you are _____ again.
   B: I'm sorry. I _____ the wrong _____.
   M: I _____ you need to _____ home a little _____.
   B: I think so, _____. Next time I _____ be late.
   M: It's important to _____ at school _____ time.

Listen & Speak 2

1. **G:** Your bag is _____ small.
   B: Yes. I _____ have _____ a bigger _____.
2. **G:** Aren't you _____?
   B: Yes. I should _____ worn a jacket.
3. **B:** We _____ our flight.
   G: Oh, no. We should _____ come _____.
4. **G:** _____ at my face. I _____ have _____ _____ some sunscreen.
   B: Yes. You're _____.

해석

1. G: 우리는 어떻게 건강을 유지할 수 있을까?
   B: 음, 든든한 아침 식사를 하는 것이 중요해.
2. B: 좋은 점수를 받기 위해 우리는 무엇을 할 수 있을까?
   G: 매일 복습하는 것이 중요해.
3. G: 나는 독서 후에 일기를 쓰는 것이 중요하다고 생각해.
   B: 나도 동의해.
4. B: 네가 돈을 어디에 썼는지 적는 것은 중요해.
   G: 나도 그렇게 생각해.

1. B: 주말에 뭐 했니?
   G: 나는 테니스를 쳤어. 나는 건강을 위해 주말에 운동을 하기로 결정했어.
   B: 잘했어. 규칙적으로 운동하는 것은 중요해.
   G: 맞아. 나와 테니스 치는 것은 어때?
   B: 왜 안 되겠어?
2. M: 존, 또 지각이구나!
   B: 죄송해요. 버스를 잘못 탔어요.
   M: 나는 네가 집에서 좀 더 빨리 출발할 필요가 있다고 생각한단다.
   B: 저도 그렇게 생각해요. 다음번에는 늦지 않을 게요.
   M: 학교에 제시간에 오는 것은 중요하단다.

1. G: 네 가방은 정말 작아.
   B: 응. 난 더 큰 것을 가져왔어야 했어.
2. G: 춥지 않니?
   B: 응. 나는 재킷을 입었어야 했어.
3. B: 우리 비행기를 놓쳤어.
   G: 오, 안 돼. 우리는 더 빨리 왔어야 했어.
4. G: 내 얼굴 좀 봐. 나는 자외선 차단제를 발랐어야 했어.
   B: 그래. 네 말이 맞아.

Listen & Speak 2 A

1. **B:** Mina, _____ was the _____?
   G: I didn't _____ it. It _____ boring.
   B: _____ was bad _____ it?
   G: I already _____ the ending. I shouldn't _____ read about it _____ seeing it.
   B: Oh, I'm _____ you didn't _____ it.
2. **B:** We _____ have 30 _____ to go _____ we reach the _____ of the mountain. Let's sit _____ over there _____ have a _____.
   G: Oh, I _____ only water. I should have _____ some snacks.
   B: That's _____. I brought a lot. We can _____.
   G: I'll _____ it in _____ to bring _____ snacks next _____.

Real-Life Zone

G: Ben, you _____ full of _____ today!
B: Do I? Maybe that's _____ I finally _____ a good night's sleep _____ night.
G: Why? Don't you _____ get _____ sleep?
B: No, I _____ it's really _____ to get a good _____ sleep, but I _____ stay _____ late _____ the Internet or _____ with my _____.
G: That _____ happens to _____ too.
B: _____ I do that, I _____ it the next _____ and say, "I should _____ gone to bed _____ last night."
G: How was yesterday _____?
B: Well, yesterday afternoon I _____ the mountain with my _____. I was really _____ when I got _____. I went to _____ right _____ I went to bed.
G: _____ activities _____ a great _____ to help you _____ a good night's sleep.

Wrap Up 1

W: Oh, your _____ is _____ from the rain! I should have _____ the weather.
B: Did you _____ it?
W: No. I just _____ it out in the _____ this morning.
B: _____ didn't you _____ it?
W: Hanging a _____ in the sun is a nature-friendly _____ to _____ the blanket _____.
B: Oh, I didn't _____ that. I'll _____ that.
W: And it's also _____ to _____ to do it _____.

해석

1. **B:** 미나야, 영화 어땠니?
   G: 나는 그것을 즐기지 못했어. 지루했어.
   B: 무엇이 별로였니?
   G: 나는 이미 결말을 알고 있었어. 보기 전에 그것에 대해 읽지 말았어야 했는데.
   B: 오, 네가 좋아하지 않다니 유감이야.
2. **B:** 우리는 산 정상에 도착하기까지 아직 30분은 더 가야 해. 저기서 앉아서 간식 먹고 가자.
   G: 오, 난 물만 가져왔어. 간식을 가져왔어야 했는데.
   B: 괜찮아. 내가 많이 가져왔어. 우리는 같이 먹을 수 있어.
   G: 다음번에는 간식을 가져올 것을 명심할게.

G: 벤, 너 오늘 기운 차 보여!
B: 내가 그래? 그건 아마 내가 지난밤 마침내 잠을 잘 잤기 때문일 거야.
G: 왜? 평소에 충분한 잠을 자지 못하니?
B: 응, 잠을 잘 자는 것이 정말 중요하다는 것은 알지만 나는 언제나 인터넷 검색을 하거나 휴대폰을 가지고 놀면서 늦게까지 깨어 있어.
G: 그건 나에게도 가끔 일어나는 일이야.
B: 그러고 난 뒤에, 나는 다음 날 아침 후회하고 "지난밤에 더 일찍 잠들었어야 했는데."라고 말해.
G: 어제는 어떻게 달랐니?
B: 음, 어제 오후에 나는 아빠와 등산을 했어. 집에 왔을 때 나는 매우 피곤했어. 나는 침대에 가자마자 바로 잠들었어.
G: 야외 활동은 네가 잠을 잘 자도록 돕는 훌륭한 방법이구나.

W: 오, 네 이불이 비에 젖었어! 내가 날씨를 확인했어야 했는데.
B: 그것을 빨았어요?
W: 아니. 오늘 아침에 그냥 햇볕에 널어 놓았어.
B: 왜 빨지 않았어요?
W: 햇볕에 이불을 널어놓는 것은 이불을 깨끗하게 유지하는 친환경적인 방법이야.
B: 오, 저는 그것을 몰랐어요. 기억해 둘게요.
W: 그리고 정기적으로 그렇게 하는 것을 기억하는 것 또한 중요해.

[01~02] 다음 대화의 빈칸에 들어갈 말로 알맞은 것은?

01

> B: What did you do on the weekend?
> G: I played tennis. I have decided to exercise on the weekend for my health.
> B: Good for you. It's important to exercise regularly.
> G: Right. _____ playing tennis with me?
> B: Why not?

① How about ② Will you avoid ③ Do you like
④ Are you ⑤ Why do you enjoy

02

> M: John, you are late again.
> B: I'm sorry. _____
> M: I think you need to leave home a little earlier.
> B: I think so, too. Next time I won't be late.
> M: It's important to arrive at school on time.

① I won't leave home early.
② Will you say that again?
③ I'm sure you will be all right.
④ I can drive a car myself.
⑤ I took the wrong bus.

03 다음 대화에 이어지기에 적절하게 배열된 순서를 고르시오.

> B: Mina, how was the movie?
> G: I didn't enjoy it. It was boring.
>
> (A) I already knew the ending. I shouldn't have read about it before seeing it.
> (B) Oh, I'm sorry you didn't like it.
> (C) What was bad about it?

① (A) – (C) – (B) ② (B) – (A) – (C) ③ (B) – (C) – (A)
④ (C) – (A) – (B) ⑤ (C) – (B) – (A)

01 다음 빈칸에 적절한 말은?

> B: It's important to write down what you
>   spend your money on.
> G: _____, too.

① You heard it   ② I don't know

③ I think so   ④ We will do it

⑤ They are ready

[02~03] 다음 대화를 읽고 물음에 답하시오.

> B: What did you do on the weekend?
> G: I played tennis. I have decided to
>   _____(A)_____ for my health.
> B: Good for you. It's important to exercise
>   regularly.
> G: Right. How about playing tennis with me?
> B: Why not?

02 빈칸 (A)에 들어가기에 적절한 것은?

① be ready for my finals

② invite you to my house

③ watch a tennis match

④ exercise on the weekend

⑤ write down how much I spend

03 위 대화를 읽고 알 수 없는 것은?

① The boy asked the girl what she did on the weekend.

② The girl played tennis on the weekday.

③ The girl decided to play tennis for the health.

④ The boy thinks it's important to exercise regularly.

⑤ The boy will play tennis with the girl.

[04~06] 다음 대화를 읽고 물음에 답하시오.

> G: Ben, you look full of energy today!
> B: Do I? Maybe that's because I finally got a
>   good night's sleep last night.
> G: Why? Don't you usually get enough sleep?
> B: No, I know it's really important to
>   get a good night's sleep, but I always
>   _____ late surfing the Internet or
>   playing with my phone. (A)
> G: That sometimes happens to me too.
> B: After I do that, I regret it the next morning
>   and say, "I should have gone to bed earlier
>   last night." (B)
> G: How was yesterday different? (C)
> B: Well, yesterday afternoon I climbed the
>   mountain with my dad. (D) I went to
>   sleep right after I went to bed.
> G: Outdoor activities are a great way to help
>   you get a good night's sleep. (E)

04 위 대화의 빈칸에 들어가기에 가장 적절한 것은?

① make bed   ② wake up

③ stay up   ④ call you

⑤ work out

05 (A)~(E) 중에서 다음 주어진 문장이 들어가기에 적절한 곳은?

> I was really tired when I got home.

① (A)   ② (B)   ③ (C)   ④ (D)   ⑤ (E)

06 위 대화의 내용과 일치하지 <u>않는</u> 것은?

① Ben feels very good today.
② Ben slept well last night.
③ Ben will surf the Internet late at night.
④ Yesterday Ben climbed the mountain with his father.
⑤ Ben slept early last night.

[07~09] 다음 대화를 읽고 물음에 답하시오.

> B: ⓐ<u>Mina, how was the movie?</u>
> G: _____(A)_____ ⓑ<u>It was boring.</u>
> B: ⓒ<u>What was bad about it?</u>
> G: I already knew the ending. ⓓ<u>I should have read about it before seeing it.</u>
> B: ⓔ<u>Oh, I'm sorry you didn't like it.</u>

07 다음 중 빈칸 (A)에 들어가기에 적절한 것은?

① I didn't enjoy it.
② Do you like it?
③ How was the ending?
④ The story was very good.
⑤ Did you like it?

08 ⓐ~ⓔ 중에서 대화의 내용상 <u>어색한</u> 것은?

① ⓐ   ② ⓑ   ③ ⓒ   ④ ⓓ   ⑤ ⓔ

09 Which one CANNOT be answered from the dialogue above?

① What are they talking about right now?
② How did the girl think about the movie?
③ Did the girl know the ending of the movie?
④ Did the girl read about the movie?
⑤ Why didn't the boy like the movie?

[10~12] 다음 대화를 읽고 물음에 답하시오.

> B: We still have 30 minutes to go before we reach the top of the mountain. Let's sit down over there and have a snack.
> G: Oh, I brought only water. (A)<u>I should bring some snacks.</u>
> B: That's okay. I brought a lot. We can ___(B)___.
> G: I'll ___(C)___ it in mind to bring some snacks next time.

10 위 대화의 밑줄 친 (A)를 흐름상 알맞은 문장으로 고치시오.

➡ _____

11 위 대화의 빈칸 (B), (C)에 들어가기에 적절한 것은?

	(B)		(C)
①	share	–	keep
②	take	–	make
③	keep	–	get
④	share	–	have
⑤	help	–	keep

12 위 대화의 내용과 일치하지 <u>않는</u> 것은?

① They are going up the mountain.
② They are going to take some rest.
③ They don't have enough snacks.
④ The girl didn't bring any snacks.
⑤ The girl says she will bring some snacks next time.

01 다음 우리말을 영어로 쓰시오.

> G: Aren't you cold?
> B: Yes. 나는 재킷을 입었어야 했어.

➡ _____

02 다음 대화의 순서를 올바르게 배열하시오.

> G: Ryan, are you okay? You look tired.
> B: I couldn't sleep well last night.
> (A) Oh, you should have gone to bed earlier.
> (B) Why is that? Did you have too much homework?
> (C) No. I watched a movie on TV, and it didn't end until after 2:00.

➡ _____

[03~05] 다음 대화를 읽고 물음에 답하시오.

> B: What did you do on the weekend?
> G: I played tennis. I have decided to ___(A)___ on the weekend for my health.
> B: Good for you. (B)규칙적으로 운동하는 것은 중요해.
> G: Right. How about (C)(play) tennis with me?
> B: Why not?

03 주어진 영영풀이를 참고하여 빈칸 (A)에 철자 e로 시작하는 단어를 쓰시오.

> to do physical activities in order to make yourself stronger and healthier

➡ _____

04 (B)에 주어진 우리말에 해당하는 영어 문장을 쓰시오.

➡ _____

05 (C)에 주어진 단어의 올바른 형태를 쓰시오.

➡ _____

[06~08] 다음 대화를 읽고 물음에 답하시오.

> B: Mina, how was the movie?
> G: I didn't enjoy it. It was boring.
> B: What was good about it?
> G: I already knew the ending. (A)(read, it, I shouldn't, before, have, seeing, about, it.)
> B: Oh, _____(B)_____ you didn't like it.

06 위 대화에서 (A)의 괄호 안에 주어진 단어를 적절하게 배열하시오.

➡ _____

07 내용상 빈칸 (B)에 들어가기에 적절한 표현을 쓰시오. (2 words)

➡ _____

08 위 대화에서 흐름상 어색한 한 단어를 찾아 쓰고 적절한 단어로 바꾸시오.

➡ _____ ➡ _____

Grammar

교과서

1. the 비교급, the 비교급

- **The more** sun you get, **the more** "happy hormone" the brain produces.
  여러분이 햇빛을 많이 쬐면 쬘수록 뇌는 행복 호르몬을 더 만들어 냅니다.

- **The stronger** will you have, **the more** you will learn.
  의지가 더 강하면 강할수록 더 많이 배울 것이다.

■ the 비교급+주어+동사 ～, the 비교급+주어+동사 …

- 의미: ～하면 할수록 더 …하다

- 형태: 'the 비교급+주어+동사 ～, the 비교급+주어+동사 …'

■ 'the 비교급+주어+동사 ～, the 비교급+주어+동사 …' 구문은 정도가 점점 더해지거나 덜해지는 것을 표현할 때 사용한다.

- **The more, the better**. 많으면 많을수록 더 좋다.

■ 최상급이 아닌 비교급임에도 the를 쓰는 것에 주의해야 하며, be동사나 반복되는 어구는 종종 생략된다. 이 구문에 쓰이는 'the'는 정관사가 아니라 부사이다.

- **The harder** you work, **the more** you get. 더 열심히 일할수록 더 많이 얻는다.
- **The less** my hope, **the hotter** my love. 내 희망이 적을수록 내 사랑은 더 뜨겁다.

■ 'the 비교급+주어+동사 ～, the 비교급+주어+동사 …' 구문은 'As+주어+동사+비교급 ～, 주어+동사+비교급 …'으로 바꿔 쓸 수 있다.

- **The higher** we go up, **the colder** the air becomes.

  = **As** we go up **higher**, the air becomes **colder**. 높이 올라가면 올라갈수록 공기가 더욱 더 차가워진다.

cf. '비교급 and 비교급'은 '점점 더 …하다'의 뜻이다

- It is getting **colder and colder**. 날씨가 점점 더 추워지고 있다.

핵심 Check

1. 다음 괄호 안에서 알맞은 말을 고르시오.

(1) The (long / longer) the soup is cooked, the thicker it gets.

(2) The more I want to get something done, the (less / least) I call it work.

2 It is[was] ... that 강조 구문

- **It** is calcium **that** builds strong bones and teeth. 튼튼한 뼈와 치아를 만드는 것은 칼슘입니다.
- **It** was his family **that** Sam wanted to meet before he died.
  샘이 죽기 전에 만나보고 싶은 것은 바로 그의 가족이었다.

■ 'It + is/was + 강조어(구) + that ...'의 형태로 특정 부분을 강조하여 나타낼 때 사용한다. 강조하고자 하는 부분을 'It is/was'와 'that' 사이에 쓰고, 나머지 부분을 that 뒤에 써서 주어, 목적어인 명사, 부사 (구/절) 등을 강조한다. 'be'동사는 문장의 시제에 맞춰 'is'나 'was'를 사용한다.

- His laughter broke the silence in the room.
  → **It was** his laughter **that** broke the silence in the room. (주어 강조)
  → **It was** the silence **that** his laughter broke in the room. (목적어인 명사 강조)
  → **It was** in the room **that** his laughter broke the silence. (부사구 강조)

■ 'It is[was] ~ that ...' 강조 구문에서 강조하는 대상이 명사일 경우, that 대신에 관계대명사 who[whom](사람일 경우) 또는 which(사물이나 동물일 경우)로 바꿔 쓸 수 있으며, 시간 또는 장소 의 부사(구/절)일 경우, when(시간) 또는 where(장소)로 바꿔 쓸 수 있다.

- I bought the brush at the shop yesterday. 나는 어제 그 가게에서 빗을 샀다.
  → **It was** I **that[who]** bought the brush at the shop yesterday.
  → **It was** the brush **that[which]** I bought at the shop yesterday.
  → **It was** yesterday **that[when]** I bought the brush at the shop.
  → **It was** at the shop **that[where]** I bought the brush yesterday.

■ 'It is[was] ~ that ...' 강조 구문에서 강조하는 대상이 부사(구/절)일 경우 that 다음에 완전한 절이 나오지만 그 외의 경우에는 불완전한 절이 나오는 것에 유의한다. 또한 강조되는 부분에 형용사나 동사는 올 수 없다.

- **It was** a new smartphone **that[which]** I wanted to buy. 내가 사고 싶었던 것은 바로 새 스마트폰이었다. (that 다음에 buy의 목적어가 없는 불완전한 절)
- **It was** at the library **that[where]** I studied math. 내가 수학을 공부한 곳은 바로 그 도서실에서였다. (that 다음 에 완전한 절)
- It is beautiful that she is. (형용사 강조 ×)
- It was bought that I the books yesterday. (동사 강조 ×)

핵심 Check

2. 다음 괄호 안에서 알맞은 말을 고르시오.

(1) It is Minjun (that / what) is playing basketball.

(2) (It / That) was in the morning that I got a call from Samuel.

(3) It was Dean (whom / which) they wanted for a king.

01 다음 각 문장의 빈칸에 공통으로 들어갈 말로 알맞은 것은?

> • It is California _____ Layla comes from.
> • It was her wallet _____ Linda lost in the subway yesterday.

① where   ② when   ③ who
④ that   ⑤ what

02 다음 빈칸에 들어갈 말로 알맞은 것은?

> • The _____ you laugh, the happier you become!

① much   ② many   ③ more
④ few   ⑤ fewer

03 다음 중 어법상 바르지 <u>않은</u> 것은?

① It was Mike that stole the wallet.
② It was John which loved her.
③ It was Clair whom he met again.
④ It was in the library that we studied together.
⑤ It was on Friday when we had dinner together.

04 다음 우리말에 맞게 주어진 어휘를 바르게 배열하시오.

(1) 내가 사랑하는 건 바로 너야.
   (that, I, it, you, is, love)
   ➡ _____

(2) 튼튼한 뼈와 치아를 만드는 것은 칼슘입니다.
   (calcium, bones, teeth, that, it, builds, strong, is, and)
   ➡ _____

(3) 운동을 하면 할수록 나는 더 강해진다.
   (I, I, get, exercise, the, the, more, stronger)
   ➡ _____

(4) 많으면 많을수록 더 좋다.
   (the, the, better, more)
   ➡ _____

01 다음 중 어법상 어색한 것은?

① The more I read, the more I learn.

② The hot it gets, the hard it is to work.

③ The colder it gets, the more clothes you need.

④ It is the baby that she should take care of.

⑤ It was some flowers which he bought for her.

02 다음 중 어법상 옳은 것은?

① It was the shoes which Ted bought last Sunday.

② It was James which went to the shop to buy some bread.

③ It is on Sundays where Daniel and I meet.

④ The much I play, the much I want to play.

⑤ The older he gets, the wise he becomes.

03 다음 문장과 같은 뜻의 문장은?

> As I study harder, I learn more.

① Because I studied harder, I learned the more.

② I have studied the harder, so I have learned the more.

③ The hard I study, the much I learn.

④ The harder I study, the more I learn.

⑤ The hardest I study, the most I learn.

04 다음 밑줄 친 부분과 바꿔 쓸 수 있는 것은?

> It was James <u>that</u> went to Amy's birthday party last Friday.

① whether   ② what

③ it   ④ which

⑤ who

[05~06] 다음 우리말을 알맞게 영작한 것을 모두 고르시오.

05

> 여러분이 햇볕을 더 많이 쬘수록 뇌는 행복 호르몬을 더 만들어 냅니다.

① More sun you get, more "happy hormone" the brain produces.

② The most sun you get, the most "happy hormone" the brain produces.

③ The more sun you get, the more "happy hormone" the brain produces.

④ Because you get more sun, the brain produces the more "happy hormone".

⑤ As you get more sun, the brain produces more "happy hormone".

06

> Tom이 매일 먹는 것은 바로 사과이다.

① It is an apple what Tom eats every day.

② It is an apple who Tom eats every day.

③ It is an apple which Tom eats every day.

④ It is an apple when Tom eats every day.

⑤ It is an apple where Tom eats every day.

07 다음 우리말과 일치하는 문장을 쓸 때, 빈칸에 알맞은 말은?

> 어두워질수록 우리의 두려움은 더 커졌다.
> = _____ it grew, the bigger our fear became.

① Dark
② Darker
③ Darkest
④ The darker
⑤ The darkest

08 다음 〈보기〉의 밑줄 친 that과 쓰임이 같은 것은?

> ┤ 보기 ├
> It was in the library that Ryan met Suho yesterday.

① He isn't that rich.
② It was the cookies that Amy made for me yesterday.
③ That's the nice tie I bought.
④ That the earth is round is common knowledge today.
⑤ That fifty dollars helped me greatly.

09 다음 문장의 빈칸 (A), (B)에 들어갈 말로 가장 적절한 것은?

> ____(A)____ she grows, ____(B)____ she becomes.

	(A)	(B)
①	The older	the prettier
②	The older	prettier
③	The old	the pretty
④	Older	the prettier
⑤	Older	prettier

10 다음 문장의 빈칸에 알맞은 말을 모두 고르시오.

> It was a book _____ Eric lent me in the library yesterday.

① that
② what
③ when
④ which
⑤ where

11 다음 문장과 비슷한 뜻이 되도록 비교급을 사용하여 바꿔 쓰시오.

(1) As I went up higher, the air was fresher.
➡ _____

(2) If you walk much, you will get tired.
➡ _____

12 다음 중 It ~ that 쓰임이 나머지와 다른 하나는?

① It was in the park that I played soccer with my friends.
② It is essential that you have some experience.
③ It was yesterday that I met him in the park.
④ It was math that I studied at the library.
⑤ It was when Kate came into the room that the phone rang.

13 다음 문장을 어법에 맞게 고쳐 쓰시오.

(1) This red dress looks prettier of the two.
➡ _____
_____

(2) More water we use, drier our well will become.
➡ _____
_____

(3) Much stress I get, much emotional I become.
➡ _____
_____

[14~15] 다음 중 어법상 올바른 문장을 고르시오.

14 ① That was a new smartphone which I wanted to buy.
② It is meet that Daniel and I on Sundays.
③ It was comfortable that you felt.
④ It is he who make decisions on the matter.
⑤ It is the blue shirt that Jay wants to buy.

15 중요
① The older the queen got, the ugly she got.
② The more slowly you drive, the more safe you are.
③ I believe the more often we laugh, the happier we will be.
④ My English is getting good and good.
⑤ My new computer was nicer of the two.

서답형
16 다음 문장에서 어법상 <u>어색한</u> 부분을 바르게 고치시오.

(1) It was because he was sick why we decided to return.

_____ ➡ _____

(2) It is a good breakfast who helps the brain work properly.

_____ ➡ _____

(3) It was July 26 when Gustav Jung was born.

_____ ➡ _____

서답형
17 괄호 안에서 알맞은 것을 고르시오.

(1) (The spicier / The spicy) the food is, (the more / the much) Kevin likes it.
(2) (The more / Much) Andy worked, (the more / much) money he earned.
(3) It was last Friday (which / when) James went to Amy's birthday party.
(4) It was under the bed (which / where) Tina found the wallet yesterday.
(5) It was William (whom / which) she wanted to see.

중요
18 주어진 문장을 'the movie'를 강조하는 문장으로 바르게 고친 것은?

James watched the movie with his girl friend last night.

① It is the movie what James watched with his girl friend last night.
② It was the movie which James watched with his girl friend last night.
③ It is the movie whom James watched with his girl friend last night.
④ It is the movie when James watched with his girl friend last night.
⑤ It was the movie who James watched with his girl friend last night.

19 다음 빈칸에 들어갈 수 <u>없는</u> 것은?

The finer the weather is, _____ I become.

① the more gloomy   ② the happier
③ the brighter   ④ the merrier
⑤ the more excited

01 다음 두 문장을 〈보기〉와 같이 한 문장으로 완성하시오.

> 보기
> • You get much sunlight.
> • You feel happy and strong.
> → The more sunlight you get, the happier and stronger you feel.

(1) • A bird flies high.
   • It can see far.
   ➡ _____

(2) • They have much.
   • They want much.
   ➡ _____

02 다음 문장에서 어법상 어색한 것을 바르게 고쳐 다시 쓰시오.

(1) More stress I get, more emotional I become.
   ➡ _____
   _____

(2) Ryan thinks the much slowly he eats, the full he gets.
   ➡ _____
   _____

(3) Youngest you are, easiest it is to learn.
   ➡ _____
   _____

(4) This country is better of the two.
   ➡ _____
   _____

(5) It was Hamin which played basketball with Eric last Saturday.
   ➡ _____
   _____

(6) It is on Saturdays which there are lots of weddings.
   ➡ _____
   _____

(7) It was Hangang Park which Ms. Jones was at 2 p.m. last Saturday.
   ➡ _____
   _____

(8) It was Amy's house where James visited last Friday.
   ➡ _____
   _____

03 다음 그림을 보고 각 질문에 'It ~ that' 강조 구문을 사용하여 답하시오.

Jenny's family

(1) Who went to the beach last summer?
   ➡ _____
   _____

(2) Where did Jenny's family go last summer?
   ➡ _____
   _____

(3) When did Jenny's family go to the beach?
   ➡ _____
   _____

04 다음 문장과 비슷한 뜻이 되도록 비교급을 사용하여 바꿔 쓰시오.

(1) If I like her much, I will miss her much.

➡ _____

_____

(2) If you leave early, you will arrive there early.

➡ _____

_____

(3) As you study harder for the exam, you will do better.

➡ _____

_____

(4) As you are more careful, you will make fewer mistakes.

➡ _____

_____

05 다음 문장을 주어진 단어를 강조하는 문장으로 고쳐 쓰시오. that은 사용하지 말 것.

> Anna bought the dress on the Internet last Sunday.

(1) Anna

➡ _____

_____

(2) bought

➡ _____

_____

(3) the dress

➡ _____

_____

(4) on the Internet

➡ _____

_____

(5) last Sunday

➡ _____

_____

06 괄호 안에 주어진 어휘를 이용하여 빈칸에 알맞은 말을 쓰시오.

(1) The more you walk, _____ _____. (healthy, will, feel)

(2) The hotter the weather is, _____ _____. (hard, doing outdoor activities)

(3) The faster you drive, _____ _____. (dangerous, will, be)

07 다음 우리말과 일치하도록 괄호 안에 주어진 어휘를 이용하여 영작하시오.

(1) 공부를 많이 할수록, 너는 더 똑똑해질 것이다. (much, smart, become)

➡ _____

_____

(2) 당신이 돈을 덜 쓸수록, 당신은 당신의 계좌에 더 많은 돈을 갖게 될 것이다. (little, spend, have in your account)

➡ _____

_____

(3) Mr. Smith가 우리 아파트로 이사 온 것은 바로 5년 전이었다. (move to, apartment)

➡ _____

_____

(4) 내가 이 조리법을 배운 곳은 바로 그 이탈리아 식당이었다. (learned, this recipe)

➡ _____

_____

(5) Jack이 시장에서 잃어버린 것은 바로 그의 책이었다. (lost, at the market)

➡ _____

_____

Reading

Enjoy the Sunshine

How much time do you spend every day out in the sun? Not much, right? Most people are too busy at school or at work to spend much time
= Most people are so busy at school or at work that they cannot spend much time outdoors.
too ~ to부정사 = so ~ that 주어 cannot

outdoors. However, the sun plays an important role in your health. It
play an important role in: ~에서 중요한 역할을 하다   = the sun

helps you stay healthy.
help+목적어+목적격보어(to부정사 또는 동사원형)

Everyone feels happier when the sun shines. This is because of
Everyone: 단수 취급, 단수 동사

serotonin, the body's happy hormone. The more sun you get, the more
동격의 콤마. the body's happy hormone = serotonin   the 비교급 ~, the 비교급 …: ~할수록 …하다

"happy hormone" the brain produces. When your serotonin level goes

up, you feel happier and stronger. This helps you fight everyday stress.
비교급 and 비교급   = to fight

Serotonin also has a calming effect, helping you focus better on what
분사구문. and it helps you   = the thing(s) which[that]

you are doing. Moreover, serotonin helps you get a good night's sleep
= to get

because it helps the brain produce a sleep hormone.
= serotonin   = to produce

sunshine 햇빛

outdoors 야외에서

role 역할

hormone 호르몬

brain 뇌

produce 만들어 내다, 생산하다

effect 효과

moreover 게다가

go up 올라가다

확인문제

● 다음 문장이 본문의 내용과 일치하면 T, 일치하지 않으면 F를 쓰시오.

1 Most people are so busy at school or at work that they cannot spend much time outdoors. ☐

2 The sun plays an insignificant role in your health. ☐

3 Everyone feels happier when the sun shines. ☐

4 As you get more sun, the brain produces less "happy hormone". ☐

5 Serotonin has a calming effect. ☐

6 Serotonin helps you get a good night's sleep because it helps the brain produce a calming hormone. ☐

Sunshine does not just make you feel and sleep better. It also
make(사역동사)+목적어+목적격보어(동사원형): ~에게 ···하게 하다

helps build strong bones. As you all know, it is calcium that builds
help가 준사역동사로 사용된   as: ~한 것처럼, ~하다시피(접속사)   'it ... that' 강조 구문: 강조하고자 하는 부분을 it과 that 사이에 쓰고,
문장으로, 목적어가 생략됨.   it 뒤에 오는 be동사는 문장의 시제에 맞춰 is나 was를 사용한다.

strong bones and teeth. However, for the body to use calcium properly,
for+목적격: to부정사의 의미상의 주어

it needs vitamin D. Interestingly, the skin creates vitamin D when

sunlight shines on it. The easiest way to make strong bones is to go
to부정사의 형용사적 용법   to부정사의 명사적 용법(보어)

outside and enjoy the sun.
enjoy 앞에 to가 생략된 것임.

As you can see, sunshine has many benefits, but how can you enjoy

its benefits safely? Fortunately, getting direct sunlight on your skin for
동명사 주어

10 to 20 minutes a day is enough to benefit from it. Try to go out into
하루에   enough+to부정사: ~하기에 충분한

the sun between classes or during lunch breaks and get sunshine on

your arms and hands. A walk in the sun, for just a few minutes every
= only

day, is good for both your mind and your body. However, avoid the
both A and B: 'A와 B 둘 다'. A와 B는 문법적으로 성격과 형식이 같은 요소가 와야 한다.

sun during peak summer hours, between 11 and 3, and use sunscreen

to protect your face and neck. Enjoy the sun safely and see how a little
to부정사의 부사적 용법(목적: ~하기 위해)

sunshine can make a world of difference in your health and your mood.
간접의문문(의문사+주어+동사), see의 목적어   a[the] world of: 산더미 같은, 막대한

bone 뼈

properly 제대로, 적절하게

vitamin 비타민

skin 피부

sunlight 햇빛, 햇살

benefit 이득; 이득을 보다

fortunately 다행스럽게도

direct (열기나 빛이) 직접 닿는

peak 절정의, 최고조의

sunscreen 자외선 차단제

mood 기분, 감정

📎 확인문제

• 다음 문장이 본문의 내용과 일치하면 T, 일치하지 않으면 F를 쓰시오.

1 Sunshine helps build strong bones as well as makes you feel and sleep better. ☐

2 For the body to use vitamin D properly, it needs calcium. ☐

3 The easiest way to make strong bones is to go outside and enjoy the sun. ☐

4 Getting direct sunlight on your skin for 10 to 20 minutes a day isn't enough to benefit from it. ☐

5 A walk in the sun, for just a few minutes every day, is good for both your mind and your body. ☐

6 A little sunshine can make a little difference in your health and your mood. ☐

● 우리말을 참고하여 빈칸에 알맞은 말을 쓰시오.

1 Enjoy the _____

2 How much time do you spend every day _____ _____ _____ _____?

3 _____ _____, right?

4 Most people are _____ _____ at school or at work _____ _____ much time _____.

5 However, the sun _____ _____ _____ _____ in your health.

6 It helps you _____ _____.

7 Everyone _____ _____ when the sun shines.

8 This is because of serotonin, _____ _____ _____ _____.

9 _____ _____ _____ you get, _____ _____ "_____ _____" the brain produces.

10 When your serotonin level _____ _____, you feel happier and stronger.

11 This helps you _____ _____ _____.

12 Serotonin also has a _____ _____, helping you focus better on _____ _____ _____ _____.

13 _____, serotonin helps you get _____ _____ _____ _____ because it helps the brain produce a sleep hormone.

14 Sunshine does _____ _____ make you feel and sleep better.

1 햇빛을 즐기세요

2 여러분은 매일 햇빛 속에서 얼마나 많은 시간을 보내나요?

3 많지 않죠, 그렇죠?

4 대부분의 사람들은 학교와 직장에서 너무 바빠서 많은 시간을 야외에서 보내지 못합니다.

5 그러나 햇빛은 여러분의 건강에 중요한 역할을 합니다.

6 그것은 여러분이 건강을 유지하는 데 도움을 줍니다.

7 모든 사람들은 해가 비칠 때 더 행복하게 느낍니다.

8 이것은 몸의 행복 호르몬인 세로토닌 때문입니다.

9 여러분이 햇빛을 쬘수록 뇌는 행복 호르몬을 더 만들어 냅니다.

10 여러분의 세로토닌 수치가 높아지면, 여러분은 더 행복하고 더 건강하게 느낍니다.

11 이것은 여러분이 매일의 스트레스를 이겨 내는 데 도움을 줍니다.

12 세로토닌은 또한 진정 효과가 있고, 여러분이 하는 일에 더 잘 집중할 수 있도록 도와줍니다.

13 게다가, 세로토닌은 뇌가 수면 호르몬을 생성하도록 도와주기 때문에 여러분이 숙면을 취하도록 해 줍니다.

14 햇빛은 단지 여러분이 더 기분 좋게 느끼고 잠을 더 잘 자게 하는 것만은 아닙니다.

15 It _____ helps _____ _____ _____ .

16 _____ _____ _____ _____ , it is calcium that builds strong bones and teeth.

17 However, _____ _____ _____ _____ _____ calcium properly, it needs vitamin D.

18 Interestingly, the skin creates vitamin D _____ _____ _____ on it.

19 The easiest way to make strong bones is _____ _____ _____ and enjoy the sun.

20 _____ _____ _____ _____ , sunshine has many benefits, but how can you _____ _____ _____ _____ ?

21 Fortunately, _____ _____ _____ on your skin for 10 to 20 minutes a day is enough _____ _____ _____ _____ .

22 _____ _____ _____ _____ the sun between classes or during lunch breaks and _____ _____ _____ your arms and hands.

23 A walk in the sun, _____ _____ _____ , is good for both your mind and your body.

24 However, avoid the sun during peak summer hours, between 11 and 3, and use sunscreen _____ _____ _____ _____ _____ _____ .

25 Enjoy the sun safely and see how _____ _____ _____ can _____ _____ _____ _____ in your health and your mood.

15 그것은 또한 튼튼한 뼈를 만드는 것을 돕습니다.

16 여러분 모두가 알다시피, 튼튼한 뼈와 치아를 만드는 것은 칼슘입니다.

17 그러나 몸이 칼슘을 적절하게 사용하기 위해서는 비타민 D가 필요합니다.

18 흥미롭게도, 피부는 햇빛이 피부에 비칠 때 비타민 D를 만들어 냅니다.

19 튼튼한 뼈를 만드는 가장 쉬운 방법은 밖으로 나가서 햇빛을 즐기는 겁니다.

20 보시다시피, 햇빛은 많은 이점이 있지만, 어떻게 그것의 이점을 안전하게 즐길 수 있을까요?

21 다행히도, 하루에 10분에서 20분 동안 피부에 직사광선을 쬐이는 것은 햇빛으로부터 이점을 얻는 데 충분합니다.

22 수업 시간 사이나 점심시간에 햇빛을 쬐러 밖으로 나가서 팔과 손에 햇빛을 쬐어 보세요.

23 매일 단 몇 분 동안 햇살을 쬐며 걷는 것은 여러분의 마음과 몸 모두에 좋습니다.

24 그러나 여름 절정 시간인 11시에서 3시 사이에는 햇빛을 피하고, 얼굴과 목을 보호하기 위해 자외선 차단제를 사용하세요.

25 태양을 안전하게 즐기고 적은 양의 햇빛이 여러분의 건강과 기분에 얼마나 큰 차이를 만들어 내는지 보세요.

● 우리말을 참고하여 본문을 영작하시오.

1 햇빛을 즐기세요

➡ _____

2 여러분은 매일 햇빛 속에서 얼마나 많은 시간을 보내나요?

➡ _____

3 많지 않죠, 그렇죠?

➡ _____

4 대부분의 사람들은 학교와 직장에서 너무 바빠서 많은 시간을 야외에서 보내지 못합니다.

➡ _____

5 그러나 햇빛은 여러분의 건강에 중요한 역할을 합니다.

➡ _____

6 그것은 여러분이 건강을 유지하는 데 도움을 줍니다.

➡ _____

7 모든 사람들은 해가 비칠 때 더 행복하게 느낍니다.

➡ _____

8 이것은 몸의 행복 호르몬인 세로토닌 때문입니다.

➡ _____

9 여러분이 햇빛을 쬘수록 뇌는 행복 호르몬을 더 만들어 냅니다.

➡ _____

10 여러분의 세로토닌 수치가 높아지면, 여러분은 더 행복하고 더 건강하게 느낍니다.

➡ _____

11 이것은 여러분이 매일의 스트레스를 이겨 내는 데 도움을 줍니다.

➡ _____

12 세로토닌은 또한 진정 효과가 있고, 여러분이 하는 일에 더 잘 집중할 수 있도록 도와줍니다.

➡ _____

13 게다가, 세로토닌은 뇌가 수면 호르몬을 생성하도록 도와주기 때문에 여러분이 숙면을 취하도록
해 줍니다.

➡ _____

14 햇빛은 단지 여러분이 더 기분 좋게 느끼고 잠을 더 잘 자게 하는 것만은 아닙니다.

➡ _____

15 그것은 또한 튼튼한 뼈를 만드는 것을 돕습니다.

➡ _____

16 여러분 모두가 알다시피, 튼튼한 뼈와 치아를 만드는 것은 칼슘입니다.

➡ _____

17 그러나 몸이 칼슘을 적절하게 사용하기 위해서는 비타민 D가 필요합니다.

➡ _____

18 흥미롭게도, 피부는 햇빛이 피부에 비칠 때 비타민 D를 만들어 냅니다.

➡ _____

19 튼튼한 뼈를 만드는 가장 쉬운 방법은 밖으로 나가서 햇빛을 즐기는 겁니다.

➡ _____

20 보시다시피, 햇빛은 많은 이점이 있지만, 어떻게 그것의 이점을 안전하게 즐길 수 있을까요?

➡ _____

21 다행히도, 하루에 10분에서 20분 동안 피부에 직사광선을 쪼이는 것은 햇빛으로부터 이점을 얻는 데 충분합니다.

➡ _____

_____

22 수업 시간 사이나 점심시간에 햇빛을 쬐러 밖으로 나가서 팔과 손에 햇빛을 쬐어 보세요.

➡ _____

_____

23 매일 단 몇 분 동안 햇살을 쬐며 걷는 것은 여러분의 마음과 몸 모두에 좋습니다.

➡ _____

24 그러나 여름 절정 시간인 11시에서 3시 사이에는 햇빛을 피하고, 얼굴과 목을 보호하기 위해 자외선 차단제를 사용하세요.

➡ _____

_____

25 태양을 안전하게 즐기고 적은 양의 햇빛이 여러분의 건강과 기분에 얼마나 큰 차이를 만들어 내는지 보세요.

➡ _____

_____

[01~04] 다음 글을 읽고 물음에 답하시오.

How much time do you spend every day out in the sun? Not much, right? (A)[Almost / Most] people are too busy at school or at work to spend much time (B)[outdoor / outdoors]. ⓐ , the sun plays an important ⓑrole in your health. It helps you stay (C)[healthy / healthily].

01 위 글의 빈칸 ⓐ에 들어갈 알맞은 말을 고르시오.

① Thus
② Moreover
③ For example
④ In other words
⑤ However

서답형
02 위 글의 괄호 (A)~(C)에서 문맥이나 어법상 알맞은 낱말을 골라 쓰시오.

➡ (A) _____ (B) _____ (C) _____

서답형
03 위 글의 밑줄 친 ⓑrole과 바꿔 쓸 수 있는 말을 쓰시오.

➡ _____

서답형
04 다음 문장에서 위 글의 내용과 <u>다른</u> 부분을 찾아서 고치시오.

Almost all the people spend much time outside a building or in the open air.

_____ ➡ _____

[05~06] 다음 글을 읽고 물음에 답하시오.

As you can see, sunshine has many benefits, but how can you enjoy its benefits safely? Fortunately, getting direct sunlight on your skin for 10 to 20 minutes a day is enough to benefit from it. Try to go out into the sun between classes or during lunch breaks and get sunshine on your arms and hands. A walk in the sun, for just a few minutes every day, is good for both your mind and your body. However, avoid the sun during peak summer hours, between 11 and 3, and use ⓐ to protect your face and neck. Enjoy the sun safely and see how a little sunshine can make a world of difference in your health and your mood.

중요
05 위 글의 제목으로 알맞은 것을 고르시오.

① Sunshine and Our Everyday Activity
② How to Enjoy Many Benefits of Sunshine Safely
③ How to Get Direct Sunlight
④ Take Advantage of Spare Time to Enjoy the Sun
⑤ Make a Difference in Your Health and Your Mood!

서답형
06 주어진 영영풀이를 참고하여 빈칸 ⓐ에 철자 s로 시작하는 단어를 쓰시오.

a cream that protects your skin from the sun's rays, especially in hot weather

➡ _____

[07~10] 다음 글을 읽고 물음에 답하시오.

Sunshine does not just make you feel and sleep better. It also helps build strong bones. As you all know, ⓐ튼튼한 뼈와 치아를 만드는 것은 칼슘입니다. However, for the body ⓑ to use calcium properly, it needs vitamin D. Interestingly, the skin creates vitamin D when sunlight shines on it. The easiest way to make strong bones is to go outside and enjoy the sun.

서답형

07 위 글의 밑줄 친 ⓐ의 우리말에 맞게 주어진 어휘를 이용하여 9 단어로 영작하시오.

> it, that, builds

➡ _____

08 아래 〈보기〉에서 위 글의 밑줄 친 ⓑto use와 to부정사의 용법이 다른 것의 개수를 고르시오.

┌─── 보기 ───┐
① I don't know how to use this machine.
② This machine is very simple to use.
③ Can you show me the way to use this machine?
④ It is easy to use this machine.
⑤ He is too old to use this machine.
└──────────┘

① 1개　② 2개　③ 3개　④ 4개　⑤ 5개

중요

09 위 글의 주제로 알맞은 것을 고르시오.

① Sufficient calcium intake is very important to build strong bones.
② What's the nutritional value of vitamin D?
③ Are there any side effects caused by strong sunshine?
④ How much calcium is needed to build strong bones?

⑤ Sunshine is the easiest way to make strong bones.

서답형

10 What is necessary for the body to use calcium properly? Fill in the blanks with suitable words.

➡ _____ _____ is necessary.

[11~13] 다음 글을 읽고 물음에 답하시오.

As you can see, sunshine has many benefits, but how can you enjoy its benefits safely? (①) Fortunately, getting direct sunlight on your skin ___ⓐ___ 10 to 20 minutes a day is enough to benefit from it. (②) Try to go out into the sun between classes or during lunch (A)breaks and get sunshine on your arms and hands. (③) A walk ___ⓑ___ the sun, for just a few minutes every day, is good for both your mind and your body. (④) Enjoy the sun safely and see how a little sunshine can make a world of difference in your health and your mood. (⑤)

11 위 글의 빈칸 ⓐ와 ⓑ에 들어갈 전치사가 바르게 짝지어진 것은?

　　ⓐ　　　ⓑ　　　　　　ⓐ　　　ⓑ
① for　－ to　　　② on　－ in
③ for　－ in　　　④ from － to
⑤ from － for

중요

12 위 글의 흐름으로 보아, 다음 문장이 들어가기에 가장 적절한 곳은?

> However, avoid the sun during peak summer hours, between 11 and 3, and use sunscreen to protect your face and neck.

①　　　②　　　③　　　④　　　⑤

13 위 글의 밑줄 친 (A)breaks와 같은 의미로 쓰인 것을 고르시오.

① He breaks the chocolate in two.
② We could see the moon through breaks in the clouds.
③ He always breaks the speed limit.
④ Can you take coffee breaks whenever you want?
⑤ She breaks the silence by coughing.

[14~17] 다음 글을 읽고 물음에 답하시오.

Everyone feels happier when the sun shines. This is because of serotonin, the body's happy hormone. The more sun you get, the more "happy hormone" the brain produces. When your serotonin level goes up, you feel happier and stronger. This helps you fight everyday stress. Serotonin also has a calming effect, ⓐhelping you focus better on what you are doing. Moreover, serotonin helps you get a good night's sleep because ⓑit helps the brain produce a sleep hormone.

14 위 글의 밑줄 친 ⓐhelping과 문법적 쓰임이 같은 것을 모두 고르시오.

① Do you have a mentor helping you in your life?
② I will take pleasure in helping you.
③ I don't mind helping you if you can't find anyone else.
④ Jack listened to music, helping her sister do her homework.
⑤ Helping you has made my life meaningful.

서답형
15 위 글의 밑줄 친 ⓑit이 가리키는 것을 본문에서 찾아 쓰시오.

➡ _____

16 According to the passage, which is NOT true?

① Serotonin is the body's happy hormone.
② The brain produces more "happy hormone" as you get more sun.
③ If you want to feel happier and stronger, you had better lower your serotonin level.
④ Serotonin's calming effect helps you focus better on what you are doing.
⑤ Serotonin helps the brain produce a sleep hormone.

서답형
17 본문의 내용과 일치하도록 다음 빈칸 (A)와 (B)에 알맞은 단어를 쓰시오.

Thanks to (A)_____, you can have a good night's sleep. That's because it helps the brain produce a (B)_____ _____.

[18~20] 다음 글을 읽고 물음에 답하시오.

ⓐSunshine does not just make you feel and sleep better. ⓑIt also helps build strong bones. As you all know, it is calcium ⓒthat builds strong bones and teeth. However, for the body to use calcium properly, ⓓit needs vitamin D. Interestingly, the skin creates vitamin D when sunlight shines on it. The easiest way to make strong bones is to go outside and enjoy the sun.

서답형
18 위 글의 밑줄 친 ⓐ와 ⓑ를 as well as를 사용하여 한 문장으로 바꿔 쓰시오.

➡ _____

_____

19 위 글의 밑줄 친 ⓒthat과 문법적 쓰임이 같지 <u>않은</u> 것을 <u>모두</u> 고르시오.

① She was so tired <u>that</u> she couldn't think straight.
② It is you <u>that</u> are to blame.
③ What kind of work is it <u>that</u> you want?
④ It's possible <u>that</u> he has not received the letter.
⑤ It was an accident <u>that</u> changed my mind.

서답형

20 위 글의 밑줄 친 ⓓit이 가리키는 것을 본문에서 찾아 쓰시오.

➡ _____

[21~22] 다음 글을 읽고 물음에 답하시오.

ⓐ보시다시피, sunshine has many benefits, but how can you enjoy its benefits safely? Fortunately, getting direct sunlight on your skin for 10 to 20 minutes a day is enough to benefit from it. Try to go out into the sun between classes or during lunch breaks and get sunshine on your arms and hands. A walk in the sun, for just a few minutes every day, is good for both your mind and your body. However, avoid the sun during peak summer hours, between 11 and 3, and use sunscreen to protect your face and neck. Enjoy the sun safely and see how a little sunshine can make a world of difference in your health and your mood.

서답형

21 위 글의 밑줄 친 ⓐ의 우리말에 맞게 4 단어로 영작하시오.

➡ _____

22 다음 중 위 글의 내용을 바르게 이해하지 <u>못한</u> 사람을 고르시오.

① 진수: 햇빛의 이점들을 안전하게 즐길 수 있는 방법은 찾기 어려워.
② 영혜: 매일 단 몇 분 동안 햇빛을 쬐며 걷는 것은 우리의 마음과 몸 모두에 좋아.
③ 경호: 그러나 여름에 절정 시간인 11시에서 3시 사이에는 햇빛을 피해야 해.
④ 기철: 응, 그리고 얼굴과 목을 보호하기 위해 자외선 차단제를 사용해야 해.
⑤ 성미: 적은 양의 햇빛도 우리의 건강과 기분에 큰 차이를 만들어 낼 수 있어.

[23~24] 다음 글을 읽고 물음에 답하시오.

Everyone feels happier when the sun shines. This is because of serotonin, the body's happy hormone. The more sun you get, the more "happy hormone" the brain produces. When your serotonin level goes up, you feel happier and stronger. This helps you fight everyday stress. Serotonin also has a calming effect, ⓐ<u>helping you focus better on what you are doing</u>. Moreover, serotonin helps you get a good night's sleep because it helps the brain produce a sleep hormone.

서답형

23 위 글의 밑줄 친 ⓐhelping을 접속사를 사용하여 고쳐 쓰시오.

➡ _____

중요

24 위 글의 제목으로 알맞은 것을 고르시오.

① What Makes You Feel Happy?
② The Difficulty of Increasing the Level of Serotonin
③ How to Fight Everyday Stress by Serotonin
④ Various Benefits of Serotonin
⑤ The Effect of Serotonin on Your Sleep Pattern

[01~03] 다음 글을 읽고 물음에 답하시오.

How much time do you spend every day out in the sun? Not much, right? ⓐMost people are too busy at school or at work to spend much time outdoors. However, the sun plays an important role in your health. ⓑIt helps you stay healthy.

중요
01 위 글의 밑줄 친 ⓐ를 복문으로 고치시오.

➡ _____

_____

02 위 글의 밑줄 친 ⓑIt이 가리키는 것을 본문에서 찾아 쓰시오.

➡ _____

중요
03 본문의 내용과 일치하도록 다음 빈칸 (A)와 (B)에 알맞은 단어를 쓰시오.

The sun has an important effect on your (A)_____, helping you to stay (B)_____.

[04~06] 다음 글을 읽고 물음에 답하시오.

Everyone feels happier when the sun shines. This is because of serotonin, the body's happy hormone. ⓐThe more sun you get, the more "happy hormone" the brain produces. When your serotonin level goes up, you feel happier and stronger. This helps you fight everyday stress. Serotonin also has a calming effect, ⓑ여러분이 하는 일에 더 잘 집중할 수 있도록 도와줍니다. Moreover, serotonin helps you get a good night's sleep because it helps the brain produce a sleep hormone.

중요
04 위 글의 밑줄 친 ⓐ를 접속사 As를 사용하여, 고쳐 쓰시오.

➡ _____

_____

05 위 글의 밑줄 친 ⓑ의 우리말에 맞게 한 단어를 보충하여, 주어진 어휘를 알맞게 배열하시오.

better / helping / what / doing / are / you / focus / you

➡ _____

고난이도
06 본문의 내용과 일치하도록 다음 빈칸 (A)와 (B)에 알맞은 단어를 쓰시오.

When you are in the sun, (A)_____ _____ produces serotonin, and in proportion to its level, you can feel happier. So, you can call serotonin the body's (B)_____ _____.

*in proportion to: …에 비례하여

[07~09] 다음 글을 읽고 물음에 답하시오.

Sunshine does not just make you feel and sleep better. It also helps build strong bones. As you all know, it is calcium that builds strong bones and teeth. ⓐTherefore, for the body to use calcium properly, it needs vitamin D. Interestingly, the skin creates vitamin D when sunlight shines on ⓑit. The easiest way to make strong bones is to go outside and enjoy the sun.

07 Write the three benefits of sunshine in English.

➡ (1) _____

(2) _____

(3) _____

08 위 글의 밑줄 친 ⓐ에서 흐름상 어색한 부분을 찾아 고치시오.

_____ ➡ _____

09 위 글의 밑줄 친 ⓑit이 가리키는 것을 본문에서 찾아 쓰시오.

➡ _____

[10~11] 다음 글을 읽고 물음에 답하시오.

Sunshine does not just make you feel and sleep better. It also helps build strong bones. As you all know, it is calcium that builds strong bones and teeth. However, for the body to use calcium properly, it needs vitamin D. Interestingly, the skin creates vitamin D when sunlight shines on it. The easiest way to make strong bones is to go outside and enjoy the sun.

10 위 글의 내용을 다음과 같이 정리하고자 한다. 빈칸 (A)~(C)에 들어갈 알맞은 단어를 본문에서 찾아 쓰시오.

The body needs (A)_____ _____ to use calcium properly, which builds strong bones. The skin creates vitamin D when (B)_____ shines on it, so the easiest way to make strong bones is to go outside and (C)_____ _____ _____ .

11 다음 문장에서 위 글의 내용과 다른 부분을 찾아서 고치시오.

Sunshine does not make you feel and sleep better.

_____ ➡ _____

[12~13] 다음 글을 읽고 물음에 답하시오.

As you can see, sunshine has many benefits, but how can you enjoy its benefits safely? Fortunately, getting direct sunlight on your skin for 10 to 20 minutes a day is enough to benefit from it. Try to go out into the sun between classes or during lunch breaks and get sunshine on your arms and hands. A walk in the sun, for just a few minutes every day, is good for both your mind and your body. However, avoid the sun (A)[during / for] peak summer hours, between 11 and 3, and use sunscreen to (B)[prevent / protect] your face and neck. Enjoy the sun safely and see how a little sunshine can make (C)[a number of / a world of] difference in your health and your mood.

12 위 글의 괄호 (A)~(C)에서 문맥이나 어법상 알맞은 낱말을 골라 쓰시오.

➡ (A) _____ (B) _____ (C) _____

13 In order to benefit from sunlight, how long do you need to get direct sunlight? Fill in the blanks with suitable words.

We need to get direct sunlight on our skin for _____ _____ _____ minutes a day to benefit from it.

Communication Task

A: I think it's important to exercise every day. Do you exercise every day?

B: Yes, I do.

B: No, I don't. But I'll try.
"시도하다. 노력하다"

A: Good for you.
잘했다

A: Okay.

해석

A: 나는 매일 운동하는 것이 중요하다고 생각해. 너는 매일 운동하니?

B: 네. 그렇습니다.

A: 잘했다.

B: 아니요, 하지만 노력하겠습니다.

A: 알았어.

After You Read A

The Benefits of Sunshine

1. Sunshine helps you deal with stress and feel happier.
= treat. handle

2. Sunshine helps you focus better on what you are doing.
= the thing(s) which

3. If you get enough sunshine, you will sleep better at night.
조건의 부사절에서 현재시제가 미래시제를 대신함.

4. When the sun shines on your skin, your skin produces vitamin D, which is
that(×)

needed for strong bones.

구문해설 • benefit: 혜택, 이득, 좋은 점 • deal with: 다루다 • focus on: ～에 주력하다, 초점을 맞추다
• produce: 생산하다

햇빛의 좋은 점

1. 햇빛은 여러분이 스트레스를 다루고 더 행복하게 느끼도록 돕는다.

2. 햇빛은 여러분이 하는 일에 더 잘 집중할 수 있도록 도와준다.

3. 햇빛을 충분히 쬐면 밤에 잠을 더 잘 잘 것이다.

4. 해가 여러분의 피부에 비칠 때, 여러분의 피부는 비타민 D를 만드는데, 그것은 튼튼한 뼈를 만드는 데 필요하다.

Writing Workshop

Health Comes First!

1. Wash your hands after going out. You will not catch a cold easily if you
명령문   동명사(전치사 뒤)   조건의 접속사
wash your hands well.

2. Get direct sunlight for 10 to 20 minutes every day. The more sunlight you
～동안
get, the happier and stronger you feel.
the 비교급+주어+동사 ～. the 비교급+주어+동사 …: ～할수록 …하다

3. It is a good breakfast that helps the brain work properly. When you eat a
It is[was] ～ that … 강조 구문   = which   = to work   ～하면(= If)
good breakfast, you can focus more clearly on your work and remember

things better.

구문해설 • direct sunlight: 직사광선 • focus on: ～에 집중하다

건강이 먼저야!

1. 외출 후에는 손을 씻어라. 손을 잘 씻으면 쉽게 감기에 걸리지 않을 것이다.

2. 매일 직사광선을 10~20분간 받아라. 햇빛을 더 많이 받을수록 더 행복하고 더 강하게 느낄 것이다.

3. 두뇌가 적절히 작동하도록 돕는 것은 좋은 아침식사이다. 아침을 잘 먹으면, 일에 분명히 집중하고 더 잘 기억할 수 있다.

Words & Expressions

01 다음 빈칸에 들어가기에 적절한 단어를 고르시오.

> It was the most difficult _____ of her life.

① decision　　② decide　　③ decided
④ decisive　　⑤ deciding

02 다음 영영풀이에 해당하는 단어를 고르시오.

> the outer layer of a person's or animal's body

① knee　　　　② mood
③ cloth　　　　④ skin
⑤ production

03 다음 두 문장에 공통으로 알맞은 것을 고르시오.

> • The bus came right _____ time.
> • You'd better put _____ your coat in this cold weather.

① about　　② by　　③ for
④ with　　⑤ on

04 다음 밑줄 친 부분과 같은 뜻으로 쓰인 것은?

> What do you do to <u>stay</u> healthy?

① Where will you <u>stay</u> tomorrow?
② He will <u>stay</u> here for a month.
③ Will you <u>stay</u> there till he comes?
④ Remember to <u>stay</u> calm.
⑤ We enjoyed every minute of our <u>stay</u>.

Conversation

[05~06] 다음 우리말과 일치하도록 빈칸에 알맞은 말을 쓰시오.

05
> M: John, you are late again.
> B: I'm sorry. I took the wrong bus.
> M: I think you need to leave home a little earlier.
> B: I think so, too. Next time I won't be late.
> M: _____
> (학교에 제시간에 도착하는 것이 중요하다.)
> (arrive, on time) (8 words)

➡ _____

06
> B: Mina, how was the movie?
> G: I didn't enjoy it. It was boring.
> B: What was bad about it?
> G: I already knew the ending. _____
> _____ before seeing it. (나는 영화를 보기 전에 그것에 관하여 읽지 말았어야 했는데.) (should) (6 words)
> B: Oh, I'm sorry you didn't like it.

➡ _____

07 다음 대화의 빈칸에 들어가기에 적절하지 <u>않은</u> 것은?

> B: We missed our flight.
> G: Oh, no. _____

① We ought to have come earlier.
② We should have come earlier.
③ I am sorry that we didn't come earlier.
④ I regret that we didn't come earlier.
⑤ We have to come earlier.

[08~10] 다음 대화를 읽고 물음에 답하시오.

B: Mina, ⓐ<u>how</u> was the movie?
G: I didn't ⓑ<u>enjoy</u> it. It was ___(A)___.
B: ⓒ<u>What was bad about it?</u>
G: I already knew the ending. I ⓓ<u>shouldn't have read</u> about it before ⓔ<u>seen</u> it.
B: Oh, I'm sorry you didn't ___(B)___ it.

08 빈칸 (A), (B)에 들어가기에 알맞은 것을 〈보기〉에서 골라 쓰시오.

┌─── 보기 ───┐
exciting   boring   like   see   read
└───────────┘

➡ (A) _____   (B) _____

09 위 대화의 밑줄 친 ⓐ~ⓔ 중에서 어법상 어색한 것을 고르시오.

① ⓐ   ② ⓑ   ③ ⓒ   ④ ⓓ   ⑤ ⓔ

10 위 대화를 통해서 알 수 있는 것은?

① Mina likes watching movies in her free time.
② The boy enjoyed the movie.
③ Mina has already read about the movie.
④ Mina thought the movie would be exciting.
⑤ The boy wants to read about the movie.

Grammar

11 다음 밑줄 친 부분과 바꿔 쓸 수 있는 것은?

It was last week <u>that</u> Mr. Miller asked me to attend the meeting.

① what   ② when   ③ who
④ where   ⑤ which

12 주어진 단어가 알맞은 형태로 바르게 짝지어진 것은?

- _____ we got to the fire, the warmer we felt. (close)
- _____ you ride a mountain bike, the more you will enjoy it. (much)

① Close – Much
② Closer – Much
③ Closer – The more
④ The close – The much
⑤ The closer – The more

13 다음 중 어법상 올바른 것은?

① Which one is the bigger of the two?
② The high the top of a mountain, the good the view.
③ More I got to know her, more I liked her.
④ The more angrier she got, the more loudly she yelled.
⑤ The older David gets, the wiser becomes.

14 다음 문장을 각각의 주어진 단어를 강조하는 문장으로 바꿔 쓰시오.

Tina bought a camera at the shop yesterday.

(1) Tina
➡ _____
_____

(2) bought
➡ _____
_____

(3) a camera

➡ _____

_____

(4) at the shop

➡ _____

_____

(5) yesterday

➡ _____

_____

15 다음 중 어법상 올바른 문장을 고르시오.

① It was my uncle what bought this smartphone for me on my birthday.

② It is Brian where broke the door.

③ It was his room which Kevin cleaned this morning.

④ It is the new car that my son wants to buy it.

⑤ It was on the day where I met her.

16 다음 밑줄 친 부분의 쓰임이 적절한 것은?

① <u>More</u> we exercise, <u>the healthier</u> we will get.

② <u>More</u> you study, <u>better</u> scores you will get in the test.

③ <u>Much</u> she gets to know him, <u>the more</u> she will like him.

④ <u>The higher</u> the bird flied up, <u>the more</u> it could see.

⑤ <u>The old</u> Ronald grew, <u>the wise</u> he became.

17 다음 괄호 안에서 어법상 알맞은 것을 고르시오.

(1) (The healthier / Healthier) one's mind is, (the healthier / healthier) one's body will be.

(2) I think (the much / the more) time I spend without her, (the sad / the sadder) I will become.

(3) It was getting (the darker and the darker / darker and darker), so we hurried to the shore.

(4) It was in the park (which / where) he left his car.

(5) It is the phone (which / when) I am looking for.

18 밑줄 친 말을 강조할 때, 빈칸에 알맞은 말을 쓰시오.

He had to reserve many seats <u>at the restaurant</u>.

→ _____ _____ at the restaurant _____ he had to reserve many seats.

Reading

[19~20] 다음 글을 읽고 물음에 답하시오.

Everyone feels happier when the sun shines. This is because of serotonin, the body's happy hormone. The more sun you get, the more "happy hormone" the brain produces. When your serotonin level goes up, you feel happier and stronger. This helps you fight everyday stress. Serotonin also has a calming effect, helping you focus better on what you are doing. ____ⓐ____, serotonin helps you get a good night's sleep because it helps the brain produce a sleep hormone.

19 위 글의 빈칸 ⓐ에 들어갈 알맞은 말을 고르시오.

① For example   ② That is
③ Therefore   ④ Moreover
⑤ However

20 According to the passage, which is NOT true about serotonin?

① Because of it, everyone feels happier when the sun shines.
② You can feel happier and stronger by raising your serotonin level.
③ Raising your serotonin level can help you fight everyday stress.
④ Its calming effect helps us focus better on what we are doing.
⑤ Serotonin has nothing to do with a good night's sleep.

[21~22] 다음 글을 읽고 물음에 답하시오.

Sunshine does not just make you feel and sleep better. It also helps build strong bones. As you all know, it is calcium that builds strong bones and teeth. However, for the body to use calcium properly, it needs vitamin D. Interestingly, the skin creates vitamin D when sunlight shines on it. The easiest way to make strong bones is ⓐto go outside and enjoy the sun.

21 위 글의 밑줄 친 ⓐto go와 to부정사의 용법이 같은 것을 모두 고르시오.

① Why do you want to go outside?
② He likes to go outside.
③ She was pleased to go outside.
④ It's time for you to go outside.
⑤ You must be joking to go outside in this weather.

22 위 글의 제목으로 알맞은 것을 고르시오.

① Enjoying the Sun, the Easiest Way to Make Strong Bones!
② Various Usages of Vitamin D
③ How to Use Calcium Properly for Your Teeth
④ The Nutritional Value of Calcium
⑤ Too Much Sunshine and Your Skin Health

[23~25] 다음 글을 읽고 물음에 답하시오.

As you can see, sunshine has many benefits, but how can you enjoy its benefits safely? Fortunately, getting direct sunlight on your skin ⓐ하루에 10분에서 20분 동안 is enough to benefit from it. Try to go out into the sun between classes or during lunch breaks and get sunshine on your arms and hands. A walk in the sun, for just a few minutes every day, is good for both your mind and your body. However, avoid the sun during peak summer hours, ____ⓑ____ 11 and 3, and use sunscreen to protect your face and neck. Enjoy the sun safely and see how a little sunshine can make a world of difference in your health and your mood.

23 위 글의 밑줄 친 ⓐ의 우리말에 맞게 7 단어로 영작하시오.

➡ _____

24 위 글의 빈칸 ⓑ에 알맞은 말을 쓰시오.

➡ _____

25 Which question CANNOT be answered after reading the passage?

① Is there any way to enjoy the benefits of sunshine safely?

② On what ground is getting direct sunlight on your skin for 10 to 20 minutes a day enough to benefit from it?

③ When is it that the writer advises you to go out into the sun?

④ When is it that you need to avoid the sun?

⑤ How can you protect your face and neck during peak summer hours?

[26~29] 다음 글을 읽고 물음에 답하시오.

Health Comes First!

1. Wash your hands after going out. You will not catch a cold easily if you wash your hands well.

2. Get direct sunlight for 10 to 20 minutes every day. ⓐThe more sunlight you get, the happier and stronger you feel.

3. It is a good breakfast that helps the brain work properly. When you eat a good breakfast, you can focus more clearly on your work and remember things better.

26 위 글의 밑줄 친 ⓐ를 접속사 As를 사용하여, 고쳐 쓰시오.

➡ _____

_____

27 According to the passage above, in order not to have a cold easily, what will be helpful? Fill in the blanks with suitable words.

If you _____ _____ _____ well after going out, you won't have a cold easily.

28 위 건강 홍보물의 내용과 일치하지 <u>않는</u> 것은?

① 외출한 다음에는 손을 씻어야 한다.

② 매일 10분에서 20분 동안 피부에 직사광선을 쬐는 것이 좋다.

③ 햇빛을 쬘수록 여러분은 더 행복하고 더 건강하게 느낀다.

④ 좋은 아침 식사는 뇌가 올바르게 작동하는 데 도움이 된다.

⑤ 아침 식사를 거르면 당신의 일에 더 잘 집중할 수 있고 사물들을 더 잘 기억할 수 있다.

29 본문의 내용과 일치하도록 다음 빈칸에 알맞은 단어를 쓰시오.

A _____ _____ helps you focus more clearly on your work and remember things better.

01 짝지어진 단어의 관계가 같도록 빈칸에 알맞은 말을 쓰시오.
출제율 95%

> wet : dry = regularly : _____

02 다음 빈칸에 들어갈 말로 적절한 것은?
출제율 90%

> Enjoy the sun safely and see how a little sunshine can make a _____ of difference in your health and your mood.

① word　　　② sky　　　③ world
④ light　　　⑤ sunshine

03 다음 빈칸에 들어가기에 적절한 것은?
출제율 95%

> • When I have spare time, I usually _____ the Internet.
> • The sun _____ an important role in your health.

① play – tries　　　② play – grows
③ surf – relaxes　　④ surf – plays
⑤ keep – gets

04 다음 제시된 단어로 자연스러운 문장을 만들 수 없는 것은?
출제율 100%

> ┤ 보기 ├
> flight　effect　journal　grade

① You will see the positive _____ of the advice.
② My _____ was an hour late because of bad weather.
③ He got the best _____ on the midterm exam.
④ He kept a _____ of his travels across Asia.
⑤ I came to _____ my rude remarks.

[05~07] 다음 대화를 읽고 물음에 답하시오.

> B: We still have 30 minutes to go before we _____ (A) the top of the mountain. Let's sit down over there and have a snack.
> G: Oh, I brought only water. (B)내가 간식을 좀 가지고 왔어야 했는데.
> B: That's okay. I brought a lot. We can share.
> G: I'll keep it in mind to bring some snacks next time.

05 빈칸 (A)에 들어가기에 알맞은 것은?
출제율 90%

① go　　　② work　　　③ reach
④ arrive　　⑤ walk

06 밑줄 친 (B)에 우리말을 바르게 영작한 것은?
출제율 90%

① I will have to bring some snacks.
② I should have brought some snacks.
③ I ought to have some snacks to bring.
④ I must have brought some snacks.
⑤ I should have to bring some snacks.

07 Which one of the following is NOT true according to the dialogue above?
출제율 95%

① They have been climbing the mountain for 30 minutes.
② They will reach the top of the mountain in half an hour.
③ The girl has brought no snacks.
④ The boy has brought enough snacks for the two.
⑤ The girl will bring enough snacks next time.

[08~09] 다음 대화를 읽고 물음에 답하시오.

G: Ben, you look full of energy today!

B: Do I? Maybe that's because I finally got a good night's sleep last night.

G: Why? Don't you usually get enough sleep?

B: No, I know it's really important to get a good night's sleep, but I always stay ___(A)___ late surfing the Internet or playing with my phone.

G: That sometimes happens to me too.

B: After I do that, I regret it the next morning and say, "I ___(B)___ to bed earlier last night."

G: How was yesterday different?

B: Well, yesterday afternoon I climbed the mountain with my dad. I was really tired when I got home. I went to sleep right after I went to bed.

G: Outdoor activities are a great way to help you get a good night's sleep.

출제율 90%

08 위 대화의 빈칸 (A)에 알맞은 것은?

① up   ② on   ③ to

④ with   ⑤ from

출제율 95%

09 빈칸 (B)에 알맞은 것은?

① must go   ② will go

③ should go   ④ must have gone

⑤ should have gone

출제율 90%

10 밑줄 친 부분을 강조하는 문장으로 고쳐 쓰시오.

(1) We are pretty much unsure about <u>the whole thing</u>.

➡ _____

_____

(2) She went to the movies <u>with her friends</u> last Sunday.

➡ _____

_____

(3) <u>A friend of mine</u> bought a luxurious car yesterday.

➡ _____

_____

출제율 95%

11 다음 중 어법상 어색한 것은?

① The more things I have to do, the more tired I feel.

② The smarter the journalists are, the better off our society is.

③ I think the more you know a musical, the more you will enjoy it.

④ The red the apples are, the sweet they taste.

⑤ The more, the merrier.

출제율 100%

12 다음 중 어법상 올바른 문장을 모두 고르시오. (정답 2개)

① The high I went up, the foggy it became.

② Of the two boys, Simon is taller.

③ The lower the grade is, the worse Noah feels.

④ It is too costly that buying new furniture may prove.

⑤ It was my dad that suggested I do mountain biking.

⑥ It was played that he basketball at the playground.

⑦ It was last Friday where Bill lost his smartphone.

13 괄호 안에 주어진 어휘를 활용하여 글자 수에 맞게 다음 우리말을 영작하시오.

(1) 우리는 주의할수록, 실수를 더 적게 한다. (few, much, make, careful, mistakes, 10단어)

➡ _____

_____

(2) 외출 전에 네가 발라야 하는 것은 자외선 차단제이다. (put on, should, that, go out, sunscreen, 12단어)

➡ _____

_____

[14~16] 다음 글을 읽고 물음에 답하시오.

Everyone feels happier when the sun shines. ⓐThis is because of serotonin, the body's happy hormone. (①) The more sun you get, the more "happy hormone" the brain produces. (②) This helps you fight everyday stress. (③) Serotonin also has a calming effect, helping you focus better on what you are doing. (④) Moreover, serotonin helps you get a good night's sleep because it helps the brain produce a sleep hormone. (⑤)

14 위 글의 흐름으로 보아, 주어진 문장이 들어가기에 가장 적절한 곳은?

> When your serotonin level goes up, you feel happier and stronger.

① ② ③ ④ ⑤

15 위 글의 밑줄 친 ⓐThis가 가리키는 것을 본문에서 찾아 쓰시오.

➡ _____

16 위 글의 주제로 알맞은 것을 고르시오.

① the kinds of happy hormones in our body
② the influence of sunlight on our stress
③ the roles of the beneficial hormone, serotonin
④ the way to focus on what you're doing
⑤ the happy hormone versus the sleep hormone

[17~18] 다음 글을 읽고 물음에 답하시오.

Sunshine does not just make you feel and sleep better. It also helps build strong bones. ⓐAs you all know, it is calcium that builds strong bones and teeth. However, for the body to use calcium properly, it needs vitamin D. Interestingly, the skin creates vitamin D when sunlight shines on it. The easiest way to make strong bones is to go outside and enjoy the sun.

17 위 글의 밑줄 친 ⓐAs와 같은 의미로 쓰인 것을 고르시오.

① Sumi is not as pretty as Mary.
② As spring comes, the birds move northward.
③ As rust eats iron, so care eats the heart.
④ As she was tired, she didn't go there.
⑤ His anger grew as he talked.

18 According to the passage, which is NOT true?

① Sunshine makes you feel and sleep better.
② Sunshine helps build strong bones.
③ Calcium builds strong bones and teeth.

④ The body needs calcium to use vitamin D properly.

⑤ When sunlight shines on the skin, it creates vitamin D.

[19~21] 다음 글을 읽고 물음에 답하시오.

ⓐ<u>As you can see, sunshine has many benefits, but how can you enjoy its benefits safe?</u> Fortunately, getting direct sunlight on your skin for 10 to 20 minutes a day is enough to benefit from it. Try to go out into the sun between classes or during lunch breaks and get sunshine on your arms and hands. A walk in the sun, for just a few minutes every day, is good for both your mind and your body. However, avoid the sun during peak summer hours, between 11 and 3, and use sunscreen to protect your face and neck. Enjoy the sun safely and see how a little sunshine can make a world of difference in your health and your mood.

🖉 출제율 95%

19 위 글의 밑줄 친 ⓐ에서 어법상 틀린 부분을 찾아 고치시오.

_____ ➡ _____

🖉 출제율 90%

20 When do you need to avoid the sun? Fill in the blanks with suitable words.

> We need to avoid the sun during (A)_____ _____ _____ between 11 and 3.

🖉 출제율 100%

21 다음 중 본문에 소개된 '햇빛의 많은 이점을 즐길 수 있는 방법'에 해당하지 **않는** 것을 고르시오.

① 하루에 10분에서 20분 동안 피부에 직사광선을 쬔다.

② 수업 시간 사이나 점심시간에 햇빛을 쬐러 밖으로 나가서 팔과 손에 햇빛을 쬔다.

③ 매일 단 몇 분 동안 햇살을 쬐며 걷는다.

④ 얼굴과 목을 보호하기 위해 자외선 차단제를 사용한다.

⑤ 매일 많은 양의 햇빛을 쬐어 자신의 건강과 기분에 큰 차이를 만들어 낸다.

[22~24] 다음 글을 읽고 물음에 답하시오.

Good morning. Welcome to the ___ⓐ___. I'm Hana Kim. Here's today's weather for three cities in different parts of the world. The sun is shining and it's warm in Seoul. In the afternoon, there may be a shower. In New York, the rain stopped early this morning. It's cloudy now. In Paris, it'll be cloudy today with a chance of showers. ⓑ<u>If you're in Seoul or Paris, take your sunscreen.</u> Have a wonderful day.

🖉 출제율 95%

22 위 글의 빈칸 ⓐ에 들어갈 알맞은 말을 고르시오.

① Book Report   ② Today's Article

③ Weather Report   ④ Movie Review

⑤ Cool Travel Essay

🖉 출제율 90%

23 위 글의 밑줄 친 ⓑ에서 흐름상 어색한 부분을 찾아 고치시오.

_____ ➡ _____

🖉 출제율 100%

24 위 글의 내용과 일치하지 **않는** 것은?

① 서울은 현재 화창하고 따뜻하다.

② 오후에 서울에는 비가 내릴 수 있다.

③ 뉴욕은 오늘 아침 일찍 비가 그쳤다.

④ 뉴욕은 현재 날씨가 화창하다.

⑤ 파리는 오후에 흐리고 비가 내릴 가능성이 있다.

[01~03] 다음 대화를 읽고 물음에 답하시오.

G: Ben, ①you look full of energy today!

B: Do I? Maybe that's because (A)마침내 나는 지난밤에 잠을 잘 잤다. (got, good)

G: Why? ②Don't you usually get enough sleep?

B: No, I know it's really important to get a good night's sleep, but I always stay up late surfing the Internet or playing with my phone.

G: ③That sometimes happens to me too.

B: After I do that, I regret it the next morning and say, "I should have gone to bed earlier last night."

G: ④How was yesterday the same?

B: Well, yesterday afternoon I climbed the mountain with my dad. ⑤I was really tired when I got home. I went to sleep right after I went to bed.

G: _____(B)_____ activities are a great way to help you get a good night's sleep.

01 밑줄 친 ①~⑤ 중에서 내용상 어색한 문장을 찾아 번호를 쓰고 적절한 내용으로 바꾸어 다시 쓰시오.

➡ _____, _____

02 밑줄 친 (A)의 우리말에 해당하는 영어 문장을 쓰시오. (9 words)

➡ _____

03 빈칸 (B)에 적절한 한 단어를 쓰시오.

➡ _____

04 어법상 어색한 것을 찾아 바르게 고쳐 문장을 다시 쓰시오.

(1) I think the old Sue gets, the wise she becomes.

➡ _____
_____

(2) Few the words, the good the prayer.

➡ _____
_____

(3) It was the library that he lent me the book yesterday.

➡ _____
_____

(4) It was last year where my family traveled to Busan.

➡ _____
_____

(5) It was because she lost her mother who the girl was confused.

➡ _____
_____

05 다음 그림을 보고, 'It ~ that …' 강조 구문과 주어진 어휘를 활용하여 빈칸에 알맞게 쓰시오.

➡ _____ is the bus that _____
_____ to go to the theater. (be, wait, in the rain)

Everyone feels happier when the sun shines. This is because of serotonin, the body's happy hormone. The more sun you get, the more "happy hormone" the brain produces. When your serotonin level goes (A)[down / up], you feel happier and stronger. This helps you fight everyday stress. Serotonin also has a (B)[calming / calmed] effect, (C)[helps / helping] you focus better on what you are doing. Moreover, serotonin helps you get a good night's sleep because it helps the brain produce a sleep hormone.

06 위 글의 괄호 (A)~(C)에서 문맥이나 어법상 알맞은 낱말을 골라 쓰시오.

➡ (A) _____ (B) _____ (C) _____

07 본문의 내용과 일치하도록 다음 빈칸 (A)와 (B)에 알맞은 단어를 쓰시오.

> If you need to fight (A)_____ _____, you may as well raise your (B)_____ _____, because it can help you feel happier and stronger.

[08~10] 다음 글을 읽고 물음에 답하시오.

As you can see, sunshine has many benefits, but how can you enjoy its benefits safely? Fortunately, getting direct sunlight on your skin for 10 to 20 minutes a day is enough to

benefit from ⓐit. Try to go out into the sun between classes or during lunch breaks and get sunshine on your arms and hands. A walk in the sun, for just a few minutes every day, is good for both your mind and your body. However, avoid the sun during peak summer hours, between 11 and 3, and use sunscreen to protect your face and neck. Enjoy the sun safely and ⓑ적은 양의 햇빛이 여러분의 건강과 기분에 얼마나 큰 차이를 만들어 내는지 보세요.

08 위 글의 밑줄 친 ⓐit이 가리키는 것을 본문에서 찾아 쓰시오. (1 word)

➡ _____

09 위 글의 밑줄 친 ⓑ의 우리말에 맞게 주어진 어휘를 알맞게 배열하시오.

> your mood / your health / how / difference / can / see / and / in / a little sunshine / a world of / make

➡ _____
_____

10 본문의 내용과 일치하도록 다음 빈칸 (A)~(C)에 알맞은 단어를 쓰시오.

> You can enjoy (A)_____ _____ of sunshine in a (B)_____ way by getting direct sunlight on your skin for 10 to 20 minutes a day. You must also avoid the sun during peak summer hours, between 11 and 3, and use (C)_____ to protect your face and neck.

창의사고력 서술형 문제

01 빈칸에 알맞은 낱말을 골라 햇빛의 좋은 점을 완성해 봅시다.

> **The Benefits of Sunshine**
> 1. Sunshine helps you deal with _____ and feel _____.
> 2. Sunshine helps you _____ better on what you are doing.
> 3. If you get enough sunshine, you will _____ better at night.
> 4. When the sun shines on your skin, your skin produces _____, which is needed for strong _____.

> stress   vitamin D   focus   bones   happier   sleep

02 다음 그림을 보고, 'It ~ that ...' 강조 구문을 활용하여 자유롭게 영작하시오.

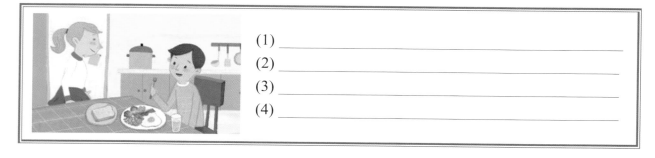

(1) _____

(2) _____

(3) _____

(4) _____

03 다음 내용을 바탕으로 나만의 건강 홍보물을 만드시오.

> 건강을 위한 습관 중 실천하지 못하고 있는 것
> • Washing your hands after going out
> • Getting direct sunlight for 10 to 20 minutes a day
> • Eating a good breakfast

> **Health Comes First!**
> 1. Wash your hands (A)_____. You will not catch a cold easily if you (B)_____ well.
> 2. Get (C)_____ for (D)_____ every day. The more sunlight you get, the happier and stronger you feel.
> 3. It is a good breakfast that helps the brain work properly. When you eat (E)_____, you can focus more clearly on your work and remember things better.

단원별 모의고사

01 다음 짝지어진 두 단어의 관계가 같도록 빈칸에 알맞은 말을 쓰시오.

> wide : narrow = healthy : _____

02 다음 영영풀이에 해당하는 단어로 적절한 것은?

> a book in which people regularly write about what has happened to them

① novel   ② comic book
③ journal   ④ poem
⑤ newspaper

03 다음 빈칸에 들어갈 말로 적절한 것은?

> Layla always applies _____ before she goes outside.

① sunlight   ② sunshine
③ sunset   ④ sunrise
⑤ sunscreen

04 다음 문장의 빈칸에 알맞은 것을 〈보기〉에서 찾아 쓰시오.

> ┌─ 보기 ─┐
> properly   outdoors   mood   peak

(1) He's always in a bad _____.
(2) The rain prevented them from eating _____.
(3) The hotels are always full during the _____ season.
(4) The television isn't working _____.

[05~07] 다음 대화를 읽고 물음에 답하시오.

W: Oh, your blanket is wet from the rain! I should _____(가)_____.
B: Did you wash it? (A)
W: No. I just put it out in the sun this morning. (B)
B: Why didn't you wash it? (C)
W: Hanging a blanket in the sun is a nature-friendly way to keep the blanket clean.
B: Oh, I didn't know that. (D)
W: And it's also important to remember to do it regularly. (E)

05 빈칸 (가)에 들어가기에 적절한 것은?

① watch weather report
② have checked the weather
③ call the weather reporter
④ have known about the blanket
⑤ expect the sun

06 (A)~(E) 중에서 다음 문장이 들어가기에 적절한 곳은?

> I'll remember that.

① (A)   ② (B)   ③ (C)   ④ (D)   ⑤ (E)

07 Which one is NOT true according to the dialogue?

① The boy's blanket is wet from the rain.
② The woman didn't check the weather.
③ The woman washed the blanket this morning.
④ The woman hung the blanket in the sun.
⑤ The boy didn't know the nature-friendly way to keep the blanket clean.

[08~10] 다음 대화를 읽고 물음에 답하시오.

G: Ben, you look full of energy today!

B: Do I? Maybe that's ⓐbecause I finally got _____(A)_____ last night.

G: Why? Don't you usually get enough sleep?

B: No, I know it's really important to get a good night's sleep, but I always stay up late surfing the Internet or ⓑplay with my phone.

G: That sometimes happens to me too.

B: After I do that, I regret it the next morning and say, "I ⓒshould have gone to bed earlier last night."

G: How was yesterday different?

B: Well, yesterday afternoon I ⓓclimbed the mountain with my dad. I was really tired when I ⓔgot home. I went to sleep right after I went to bed.

G: Outdoor activities are a great way to help you get a good night's sleep.

08 빈칸 (A)에 적절한 것은?

① a good night's sleep
② a long sleeping
③ a poor sleeping condition
④ a quiet room
⑤ a full stomach

09 밑줄 친 ⓐ~ⓔ 중에서 어법상 어색한 것은?

① ⓐ ② ⓑ ③ ⓒ ④ ⓓ ⑤ ⓔ

10 Which one of the following CANNOT be answered according to the dialogue above?

① Does Ben look full of energy today?
② What does Ben usually do before going to bed?
③ Does Ben usually get enough sleep?
④ With whom did Ben climb the mountain yesterday?
⑤ What outdoor activities does Ben like most?

11 빈칸을 채워 주어진 문장과 같은 의미의 문장을 쓰시오.

(1) I do not think that the richer I become, the happier I am.

= I do not think that as _____

_____.

(2) The bigger the magnet is, the stronger it is.

= As _____.

(3) The more you practice, the better your English speaking skills are.

= As _____

_____.

12 다음 문장의 밑줄 친 부분을 강조하는 문장으로 바꿔 쓰시오.

(1) You should put away your smartphone.

➡ _____

_____

(2) I did not learn Hangeul until I came to Korea.

➡ _____

_____

(3) Jina had a chocolate cake for dessert.

➡ _____

_____

(4) Minji and Jian want to join the art club.

➡ _____

_____

13 다음 문장의 빈칸에 들어갈 수 <u>없는</u> 말을 고르시오.

> The _____, the better.

① sooner ② faster ③ less
④ bitter ⑤ more

14 다음 중 어법상 <u>어색한</u> 것을 <u>모두</u> 고르시오.

① The more Dan practices, the more skillful he is.
② The fast you go, the early you will reach your grandma's house.
③ It is on Sundays when Daniel and I meet.
④ It was the window what John broke.
⑤ The more Jay read this book, the more interested he is in it.
⑥ It was played that Harry the violin yesterday.
⑦ It was thoughtfully that I walked towards the train.

15 다음 우리말을 주어진 어휘를 이용하여 영작하시오.

(1) 국물을 오래 끓일수록 맛이 좋아진다. (I, taste, boil, long, good, it)

➡ _____

(2) 날씨가 좋을수록, 나는 기분이 더 좋다. (good, the weather, feel)

➡ _____

(3) Layla가 Jinho를 만난 곳은 바로 학교였다. (at)

➡ _____

(4) Ella가 가장 존경하는 사람은 바로 그녀의 아버지이다. (respect, the most)

➡ _____

[16~18] 다음 글을 읽고 물음에 답하시오.

Everyone feels happier when the sun shines. This is because of serotonin, the body's happy hormone. (A)여러분이 햇빛을 더 많이 쬘수록 뇌는 행복 호르몬을 더 만들어 냅니다. When your serotonin level goes up, you feel happier and stronger. (B)This helps you fight everyday stress. Serotonin also has a calming effect, helping you focus better on ____ⓐ____ you are doing. Moreover, serotonin helps you get a good night's sleep because it helps the brain produce a sleep hormone.

16 위 글의 빈칸 ⓐ에 들어갈 알맞은 말을 고르시오.

① that ② what ③ when
④ which ⑤ where

17 위 글의 밑줄 친 (A)의 우리말에 맞게 주어진 어휘를 이용하여 12 단어로 영작하시오.

> sun, get, happy, produce

➡ _____

18 위 글의 밑줄 친 (B)가 가리키는 것을 본문에서 찾아 쓰시오.

➡ _____

[19~21] 다음 글을 읽고 물음에 답하시오.

As you can see, sunshine has many benefits, but how can you enjoy its benefits safely? Fortunately, ⓐgetting direct sunlight on your skin for 10 to 20 minutes a day is enough to benefit from it. Try to go out into the sun between classes or during lunch breaks and get sunshine on your arms and hands. A walk in the sun, for just a few minutes every day, is good for both your mind and your body. However, avoid the sun during peak summer hours, between 11 and 3, and use sunscreen to protect your face and neck. Enjoy the sun safely and see how a little sunshine can make a world of difference in your health and your mood.

19 위 글의 밑줄 친 ⓐgetting과 문법적 쓰임이 같은 것을 모두 고르시오.

① My dream is getting ahead of him.
② Did she give up getting the job?
③ It's getting warmer and warmer.
④ Is there any advantage in getting there early?
⑤ The nights are getting longer.

20 위 글의 주제로 알맞은 것을 고르시오.

① many benefits of walking
② the proper amount of getting direct sunlight on your skin
③ the way to enjoy many benefits of sunshine safely
④ the time to avoid the sun
⑤ the right way to use sunscreen to protect your face and neck

21 According to the passage, which is NOT true?

① Sunshine has many benefits.
② To get direct sunlight on your skin for 10 to 20 minutes a day isn't enough to benefit from it.
③ A walk in the sun, for just a few minutes every day, is good for both your mind and your body.

④ It's necessary to avoid the sun during peak summer hours, between 11 and 3.
⑤ It's possible to enjoy the sun safely and see how a little sunshine can make lots of difference in your health and your mood.

[22~23] 다음 글을 읽고 물음에 답하시오.

The   ⓐ   of Sunshine
1. Sunshine helps you deal with stress and feel happier.
2. Sunshine helps you focus better on what you are doing.
3. If you get enough sunshine, you will sleep better at night.
4. When the sun shines on your skin, your skin produces vitamin D, which is needed for strong bones.

22 주어진 영영풀이를 참고하여 빈칸 ⓐ에 철자 B로 시작하는 단어를 쓰시오.

the helps that you get from something or the advantages that results from something

➡ _____

23 다음 중 햇빛의 좋은 점에 해당하지 <u>않는</u> 것을 고르시오.

① 여러분이 스트레스를 다루고 더 행복하게 느끼도록 돕는다.
② 여러분이 하는 일에 더 잘 집중할 수 있도록 도와준다.
③ 햇빛을 충분히 쬐면 밤에 잠을 잘 잘 수 없다.
④ 해가 여러분의 피부에 비칠 때, 여러분의 피부는 비타민 D를 만든다.
⑤ 비타민 D는 튼튼한 뼈를 만드는 데 필요하다.

Lesson 4

Safety First

 의사소통 기능

- 의무 표현하기
  A: You have to watch out for bees.
  B: Okay, I will.

- 가능성 정도 표현하기
  A: You should do some warm-up exercises.
  B: Why?
  A: Jumping into cold water can be dangerous.

 언어 형식

- 접속사 'although'
  Although camping trips can create sweet memories for many people, they can also be occasions when bad things happen.

- seem to
  They **seem to** know what to do to make their camping trip safe and fun.

Words & Expressions

교과서

Key Words

- **accident** [æksidənt] 명 사고
- **although** [ɔ:lðóu] 접 비록 ~이긴 하지만
- **apply** [əplái] 동 (크림 등을) 바르다
- **attention** [əténʃən] 명 주의, 집중
- **avoid** [əvɔ́id] 동 피하다
- **burn** [bə́:rn] 동 (불이) 타다
- **burner** [bə́:rnər] 명 (취사용) 버너, 가열 기구
- **by** [bai] 전 ~ 옆에
- **cause** [kɔ:z] 동 ~을 야기하다
- **clear** [kliər] 형 (하늘이) 맑은, 청명한
- **create** [kriéit] 동 창조하다
- **deep** [di:p] 형 깊은
- **earthquake** [ə́:rθkweik] 명 지진
- **electricity** [ilekrísəti] 명 전기
- **enough** [ináf] 형 충분한
- **entrance** [éntrəns] 명 (출)입구, 문
- **explode** [iksplóud] 동 폭발하다
- **fall** [fɔ:l] 동 넘어지다
- **feed** [fi:d] 동 먹이를 주다
- **flat** [flæt] 형 평평한
- **flooding** [flʌ́diŋ] 명 홍수, 범람
- **fit** [fit] 동 ~에 맞다
- **garlic** [gá:rlik] 명 마늘
- **guess** [ges] 동 추측하다, 짐작하다
- **hang** [hæŋ] 동 걸다, 매달다
- **inform** [infɔ́:rm] 동 알리다, 통지하다
- **lightning** [láitniŋ] 명 번개
- **location** [loukéiʃən] 명 장소
- **memory** [méməri] 명 기억, 추억
- **mosquito** [məskí:tou] 명 모기
- **nature-friendly** [néitʃərfréndli] 형 자연 친화적인
- **occasion** [əkéiʒən] 명 (특정한) 때, 경우
- **overeat** [òuvərí:t] 동 과식하다
- **overflow** [òuvərflóu] 동 흘러넘치다, 범람하다
- **overuse** [òuvərjú:z] 동 남용하다, 너무 많이 사용하다
- **overwork** [òuvərwə́rk] 동 과로하다, 혹사하다
- **oxygen** [áksidʒən] 명 산소
- **pack** [pæk] 동 (짐을) 꾸리다
- **pan** [pæn] 명 (손잡이가 달린 얕은) 냄비, 팬
- **path** [pæθ] 명 길, 통로
- **peel** [pi:l] 명 (과일 또는 채소의) 껍질
- **place** [pleis] 동 놓다, 두다
- **prepare** [pripɛ́ər] 동 준비하다, 대비하다
- **protect** [prətékt] 동 보호하다
- **reach** [ri:tʃ] 동 ~에 이르다, 도달하다
- **regularly** [régjulərli] 부 규칙적으로
- **report** [ripɔ́:rt] 명 보도, 기사
- **rub** [rʌb] 동 문지르다, 비비다
- **safety** [séifti] 명 안전, 안전성
- **seem** [si:m] 동 ~인 것 같다
- **several** [sévərəl] 형 몇몇의, 각각의
- **sink** [siŋk] 명 싱크대
- **spill** [spil] 동 흘리다
- **strike** [straik] 동 (세게) 치다
- **sunscreen** [sʌ́nskri:n] 명 자외선 차단제, 선크림
- **traffic** [træfik] 명 교통
- **trip** [trip] 동 걸려 넘어지다, (발이) 걸리다
- **uncomfortable** [ənkʌ́mfərtəbəl] 형 불편한
- **warm-up** [wɔ́rmʌp] 명 몸 풀기, 준비
- **wet** [wet] 형 젖은
- **weather** [wéðər] 명 날씨

Key Expressions

- **by -ing** ~함으로써
- **close to** ~에 가까운
- **do one's best** 최선을 다하다
- **hang out** 어울리다
- **instead of** ~ 대신에
- **keep away** ~을 접근하지 못하게 하다
- **keep ~ in mind** ~을 명심하다
- **keep -ing** 계속 ~하다
- **pass out** 의식을 잃다, 기절하다
- **put on** ~을 바르다
- **put up** 설치하다, 세우다
- **stay up** 안 자다, 깨어 있다
- **try to부정사** ~하려고 노력하다, ~하려고 애쓰다
- **use up** ~을 다 써버리다

Word Power

※ 서로 반대되는 뜻을 가진 어휘

- □ **popular**(인기 있는) ↔ **unpopular**(인기 없는)
- □ **available**(구할 수 있는) ↔ **unavailable**(구할 수 없는)
- □ **healthy**(건강한) ↔ **unhealthy**(건강하지 않은)

- □ **whole**(전체의) ↔ **partial**(일부분의)
- □ **nervous**(초조한) ↔ **calm**(차분한)
- □ **top**(맨 위의) ↔ **bottom**(밑바닥의)

※ 동사 – 명사

- □ **avoid**(피하다) – **avoidance**(회피)
- □ **attend**(주의를 기울이다) – **attention**(주의)
- □ **prepare**(준비하다) – **preparation**(준비)
- □ **create**(창조하다) – **creation**(창조)

- □ **explode**(폭발하다) – **explosion**(폭발)
- □ **inform**(알리다, 통지하다) – **information**(전달, 통지)
- □ **protect**(보호하다) – **protection**(보호)
- □ **memorize**(기억하다) – **memory**(기억)

※ 동사 – over+동사

- □ **act** (행동하다) → **overact** (과장된 행동을 하다)
- □ **cook** (요리하다) → **overcook** (너무 오래 익히다)
- □ **do** (하다) → **overdo** (지나치게 하다)
- □ **flow** (흐르다) → **overflow** (흘러넘치다, 범람하다)

- □ **eat** (먹다) → **overeat** (과식하다)
- □ **use** (사용하다) → **overuse** (남용하다)
- □ **work** (일하다) → **overwork** (과로하다, 혹사하다)
- □ **sleep** (잠자다) → **oversleep** (늦잠 자다)

English Dictionary

- □ **apply** (크림 등을) 바르다
  → to put or spread something such as paint, cream, etc. onto a surface
  페인트, 크림 등과 같은 것을 표면에 바르거나 펴 바르다

- □ **earthquake** 지진
  → a sudden, violent shaking of the earth's surface
  지구 표면의 갑작스럽고 격렬한 흔들림

- □ **entrance** (출)입구, 문
  → a door, gate, passage, etc. used for entering a room, building, or place
  방, 건물 또는 장소에 들어갈 때 사용하는 문, 대문, 통로 등

- □ **explode** 폭발하다
  → to burst, or to make something burst, loudly and violently, causing damage
  폭발하거나 무언가를 터지게 하여, 크고 격렬하게 피해를 입히다

- □ **flooding** 홍수, 범람
  → a situation in which water from a river or from rain covers large areas of land
  강물이나 빗물이 넓은 지역의 땅을 덮고 있는 상황

- □ **lightning** 번개
  → the bright flashes of light that you see in the sky during a storm
  폭풍우가 칠 때 여러분이 하늘에서 보는 밝은 빛

- □ **memory** 기억, 추억
  → something that you remember
  기억하고 있는 것

- □ **mosquito** 모기
  → a small flying insect that bites the skin of people and animals and sucks their blood
  사람과 동물의 피부를 물고 피를 빨아먹는 작은 날벌레

- □ **peel** (과일 또는 채소의) 껍질
  → the skin of a fruit
  과일의 껍질

- □ **rub** 문지르다, 비비다
  → to press and move your hands or an object over a surface
  손이나 물체를 어떤 표면 위로 누르고 움직이다

- □ **strike** (세게) 치다
  → to hit someone or something hard or with force
  누군가나 뭔가를 세게 때리거나 힘을 가해서 때리다

- □ **sunscreen** 자외선 차단제, 선크림
  → a cream that you can rub onto your skin to stop it from being burned by the sun
  햇빛에 타는 것을 막기 위해 피부에 비벼도 되는 크림

서답형

01 다음 짝지어진 단어의 관계가 같도록 빈칸에 알맞은 말을 쓰시오.

> wet : dry = entrance : _____

02 다음 영영풀이가 가리키는 것은?

> a situation in which water from a river or from rain covers large areas of land

① path　　　　② accident
③ weather　　　④ earthquake
⑤ flooding

서답형

03 다음 우리말과 같도록 빈칸에 알맞은 말을 쓰시오.

> 내일 정원 주위에 울타리를 설치하자.

➡ Let's _____ _____ a fence around the garden tomorrow.

중요

04 다음 문장에 공통으로 들어갈 알맞은 것은?

> • He finished in third _____.
> • Please _____ the book on my desk.

① set　　　　② place
③ lay　　　　④ feed
⑤ prize

중요

05 다음 중 밑줄 친 부분의 뜻풀이가 바르지 않은 것은?

① This river flows in the East Sea. (흐르다)
② You should apply the cream to the sunburned area. (신청하다)
③ I will pack my things for a trip to Vietnam. (꾸리다)
④ His eyes got red after he rubbed them. (문지르다)
⑤ He walks a path through the forest every week. (길)

06 다음 빈칸에 알맞은 말이 바르게 짝지어진 것은?

> • When I was hit on the head, I almost _____ out.
> • Jiho has _____ up my phone's battery playing games.

① took – used　　② took – put
③ passed – used　　④ passed – put
⑤ passed – needed

서답형

07 다음 우리말에 맞게 빈칸에 알맞은 말을 쓰시오.

(1) 너는 과식하지 않는 편이 좋겠다.
　➡ You had better not _____.
(2) 그 폭탄은 큰 소음을 내며 폭발했다.
　➡ The tomb _____ with a loud noise.
(3) 너는 연설에 집중해야 한다.
　➡ You should pay _____ to the speech.

01 다음 짝지어진 단어의 관계가 같도록 빈칸에 알맞은 말을 쓰시오.

> comfortable : uncomfortable
> = regularly : _____

02 다음 영영풀이에 해당하는 단어를 〈보기〉에서 찾아 쓰시오.

┌─ 보기 ┐
> lightning   earthquake   memory

(1) a sudden, violent shaking of the earth's surface: _____
(2) something that you remember: _____
(3) the bright flashes of light that you see in the sky during a storm: _____

03 다음 빈칸에 알맞은 말을 〈보기〉에서 골라 쓰시오.

┌─ 보기 ┐
> safety   entrance   overflow   apply

(1) We should _____ sunscreen on our skin before we go out.
(2) We must put _____ before anything else.
(3) As it is raining a lot, the river can _____.
(4) Lots of people were waiting at the _____ to the baseball park.

04 다음 우리말에 맞게 주어진 단어를 바르게 배열하시오.

> 내가 말했던 것을 명심하세요.
> (what / you / keep / told / in / I / mind)

➡ _____

05 다음 문장의 빈칸에 다음 영어 설명에 해당하는 단어를 써 넣으시오.

> Do not _____ your eyes with dirty hands.

> <영어 설명> to press and move your hands or an object over a surface

➡ _____

06 다음 우리말에 맞게 빈칸에 알맞은 말을 쓰시오.

(1) 집에 거미가 접근하지 못하게 하는 방법을 알고 있니?
➡ Do you know how to _____ spiders _____ from your home?
(2) 그녀는 출산 후 기절했다.
➡ She _____ _____ after giving birth.
(3) 이 크림을 바르는 것이 도움이 될 것이다.
➡ It will be helpful to _____ _____ this cream.
(4) 내가 실수로 내 가방 대신에 네 가방을 가져갔어.
➡ I took your bag _____ _____ mine by mistake.

Conversation

① 의무 표현하기

> A: You have to watch out for bees. 너는 벌들을 조심해야 해.
> B: Okay, I will. 알았어, 그럴게.

- '~해야 한다'라는 의미로 의무를 나타낼 때는 'have to+동사원형'을 쓴다. 비슷한 표현으로는 'must', 'should', 'need to(~할 필요가 있다)' 등이 있다.

  - We must watch out for bees. 우리는 벌들을 조심해야만 해.
  - We should watch out for bees. 우리는 벌들을 조심해야만 해.
  - We need to watch out for bees. 우리는 벌들을 조심할 필요가 있어.

- 'must(~해야 한다)'는 'have to'보다 의미가 강하고, should는 'have to'보다 약한 의미로 도덕적 의무나 비강제적 의무를 나타낼 때 쓸 수 있다.

- '~해서는 안 된다'는 'must not'이나 'should not'으로 표현할 수 있다. 'do not have[need] to'는 '~할 필요가 없다'는 뜻임에 주의한다.

  - You must[should] not run from here. 너는 여기서부터 뛰면 안 된다.
  - You don't have[need] to run from here. 너는 여기서부터 뛰지 않아도 된다.

핵심 Check

1. 다음 우리말과 일치하도록 빈칸에 알맞은 말을 쓰시오.

   A: Can we go this way? It looks nice.

   B: No. We _____ _____ go straight if we want to get to the top.
   (정상에 가기를 원한다면 우리는 똑바로 가야 해.)

2. 다음 주어진 어구를 사용하여 대화를 완성하시오.

   A: Oh, the stairs are wet.

   B: Then _____.

   (the stairs / walk / to / we / slowly / down / have)

2 가능성 정도 표현하기

A: You should do some warm-up exercises. 너는 준비 운동을 해야 해.

B: Why? 왜?

A: Jumping into cold water can be dangerous. 차가운 물에 뛰어드는 것은 위험할 수 있어.

- ■ 'can[may]+동사원형'은 '~할 수도 있다'라는 뜻으로 어떤 일이 발생할 수 있다는 가능성을 나타낸다.

  • The trip can be canceled because of the earthquake. 지진 때문에 여행이 취소될 수 있다.

  • It's cloudy. You may need your umbrella in the afternoon. 날씨가 흐려. 너는 오후에 우산이 필요할 수도 있어.

- ■ can이 일반적이고 이론적인 가능성을 나타낸다면 'may', 'could', 'might'는 그보다 가능성의 정도가 적은 경우에 사용할 수 있다.

- ■ 'can'은 '~할 수 있다(능력)', '~해도 된다(허가, 허락)' 등의 의미로도 쓸 수 있다.

  • Sumi can play the guitar. 수미는 기타를 연주할 수 있다.

  • Can I use this table? 제가 이 탁자를 사용해도 될까요?

핵심 Check

3. 다음 주어진 말을 사용하여 대화를 완성하시오.

   A: Can I swim right after eating?

   B: Swimming with a full stomach _____ _____ _____.
      (uncomfortable, be)

4. 다음 대화의 순서를 바르게 배열하시오.

   (A) If we don't leave now, we may not get to the concert in time.

   (B) Not, not yet. I have to check if I turned off the gas.

   (C) Mina, are you ready to leave?

   ➡ _____

Real-Life Zone

B: Uncle John, look at my new bike. What do you think?

M: It's really nice. Where are you going?

B: ❶To the park to meet a friend.

M: Where's your helmet?

B: ❷I don't have one. It's just a short ride.

M: Put on your helmet. ❸You may hurt yourself.

B: ❹But I see a lot of people riding bikes without helmets.

M: ❺You have to wear a helmet. It protects your head in an accident.

B: Okay. I'll get my dad's helmet.

M: No. You have to wear a helmet that fits you. ❻If not, it cannot protect your head.

B: I guess I'll have to buy one for myself.

B: 존 삼촌. 제 새로운 자전거 좀 보세요. 어떻게 생각하세요?
M: 아주 멋지구나. 어디를 가고 있니?
B: 친구 만나러 공원에요.
M: 네 헬멧이 어디 있니?
B: 저는 헬멧이 없어요. 그냥 잠 깐 타는 거예요.
M: 헬멧을 쓰렴. 다칠 수 있단다.
B: 하지만 저는 헬멧 없이 자전거 를 타는 많은 사람들을 봐요.
M: 너는 헬멧을 써야만 한다. 그것은 사고가 났을 때 네 머 리를 보호해 줘.
B: 알았어요. 아빠의 헬멧을 가 져올게요.
M: 아니. 너는 네게 맞는 헬멧을 써야 해. 그렇지 않으면 그것 은 네 머리를 보호해 줄 수 없어.
B: 저를 위한 헬멧을 사야겠어요.

❶ 'to meet'은 to부정사의 부사적 용법 중 목적(~하기 위해)으로 쓰였다.
❷ one은 부정대명사로 'a helmet'을 대신하여 쓰였다.
❸ may는 '~할 수도 있다, ~일 수도 있다'라는 뜻으로 'could'나 'might'로 바꿔 쓸 수 있다.
❹ see+목적어+목적격 보어: ~가 …하는 것을 보다
❺ have to는 '~해야 한다, ~할 필요가 있다'라는 뜻으로 must, should, need to 등으로 바꿔 쓸 수 있다.
❻ If not은 If you don't wear a helmet that fits you를 대신하는 말이다.

Check(√) True or False

(1) The boy is riding a bicycle with his uncle. T ☐ F ☐

(2) The boy will buy a helmet for himself. T ☐ F ☐

 Listen & Speak 1 A-1

G: Mom, can I play outside this afternoon?

W: Sure. ❶Don't forget to put on sunscreen before you go out.

G: But it's cloudy today. ❷Do I have to put on sunscreen?

W: Yes, you have to wear sunscreen every day.

G: Okay. ❸Then I'll put some on now.

G: 엄마, 오후에 밖에서 놀아도 될까요?
W: 물론이지. 나가기 전에 선크 림 바르는 것을 잊지 말아라.
G: 그렇지만 오늘은 흐려요. 선 크림을 발라야 하나요?
W: 그럼, 매일 선크림을 발라야 한단다.
G: 알겠어요. 그러면 지금 바를 게요.

❶ Don't forget to ~.: ~할 것을 잊지 마라. / put on: ~을 바르다
❷ have to: ~해야 한다
❸ some은 부정대명사로 some sunscreen을 가리킨다. 구동사의 목적어로 대명사가 쓰이는 경우 대명사는 부사 사이에 위치한다.

Check(√) True or False

(3) The girl will not put on sunscreen before going outside. T ☐ F ☐

(4) The weather is cloudy today. T ☐ F ☐

Listen & Speak 1 Listen

1. **B:** ❶We have to watch out for bees.
   G: Oh, there are bees. Run!
2. **G:** Can we go this way? ❷It looks nice.
   B: No. ❸We have to go straight if we want to get to the top.
3. **B:** Oh, the stairs are wet.
   G: Then we have to walk down the stairs slowly.
4. **G:** Let's climb some more. I want to reach the top of the mountain.
   B: First we have to check the weather. ❹Oh, it says it's going to rain. We should go down.

❶ have to=must, should, need to
❷ look+형용사: ~하게 보이다
❸ get to: ~에 도착하다, ~에 이르다
❹ It says ~.: ~라고 한다.

Listen & Speak 1 A-2

B: ❶Let's go bowling.
G: I'm sorry, I can't. ❷I have to go see a doctor.
B: ❸Oh, what's wrong?
G: I don't know, but my stomach hurts.

❶ go -ing: ~하러 가다
❷ go see a doctor: 병원에 가다
❸ What's wrong?은 What's the matter?, What's the problem? 등으로 바꿔 쓸 수 있다.

Listen & Speak 2 Listen

1. **M:** Don't run. ❶You may fall.
   B: Okay, I won't run.
2. **B:** ❷Jumping into cold water without warming up can be dangerous.
   G: Oh, okay. I will warm up.
3. **G:** Mom, I want to swim here.
   W: ❸Okay, but first you should check how deep the water is. It may be deeper than you think.
4. **B:** ❹Can I swim right after eating?
   G: Swimming with a full stomach can be uncomfortable.

❶ may는 '~할 수도 있다, ~일 수도 있다'는 의미로 가능성을 나타낸다.
❷ without -ing: ~하지 않고, ~하지 않은 채로
❸ should는 '~해야 한다, ~하는 게 좋겠다'는 의미로 충고를 나타낸다.
❹ can은 '~해도 된다'는 뜻의 허가의 의미로 쓰였다.

Listen & Speak 2 A-1

M: Flooding can cause big problems. ❶However, you may not know what to do when it happens. There are several things you have to do. First, you have to turn off the water and the electricity. Second, pack water and food when you leave the house. ❷Finally, you have to move to a high and safe place and keep listening to the weather report.

❶ may not: ~하지 않을 수도 있다 / what to do: 무엇을 해야 할지
❷ keep -ing: 계속 ~하다

Listen & Speak 2 A-2

B: Mina, are you ready to leave?
G: No, not yet. ❶I have to check if I turned off the gas.
B: ❷If we don't leave now, we may not get to the concert in time.
G: Okay, but I have to check the gas first. ❸It will only take a minute.

❶ if: ~인지 아닌지
❷ in time: 제 시간에, 늦지 않게
❸ take: 시간이 걸리다

Wrap Up

B: Here comes the bus!
G: ❶Oh, but first I have to finish drinking my tea.
B: ❷Why don't you just take it with you? ❸I'm sure that it will be okay if you are careful.
G: No. If the bus stops suddenly. I may spill it.
B: ❹Okay, then I can just wait for you to finish your drink. I'm sure another bus will come soon.
G: Thanks.

❶ finish는 동명사를 목적어로 취한다.
❷ Why don't you ~?: ~하는 게 어때?
❸ I'm sure that ~.: 나는 ~라고 확신한다.
❹ wait for+목적어+to부정사: …가 ~하는 것을 기다리다

● 다음 우리말과 일치하도록 빈칸에 알맞은 말을 쓰시오.

Listen & Speak 1 Listen

1. **B:** We _____ _____ _____ _____ for bees.
   G: Oh, there are bees. Run!
2. **G:** Can we go this way? It _____ _____.
   B: No. We have to go straight if we want _____ _____ the top.
3. **B:** Oh, the stairs are _____.
   G: Then we _____ _____ _____ _____ the stairs slowly.
4. **G:** _____ _____ some more. I want to reach the _____ of the mountain.
   B: First we _____ _____ _____ the weather. Oh, it says it's _____ _____ _____. We _____ go down.

Listen & Speak 1 A

1. **G:** Mom, can I _____ _____ this afternoon?
   W: Sure. _____ _____ _____ put on sunscreen before you go out.
   G: But it's _____ today. Do I _____ _____ _____ _____ sunscreen?
   W: Yes, you have to _____ sunscreen _____ _____.
   G: Okay. Then I'll _____ some _____ now.
2. **B:** Let's _____ _____.
   G: I'm sorry, I can't. I have to _____ _____ _____ _____.
   B: Oh, what's _____?
   G: I don't know, but my stomach _____.

Listen & Speak 2 Listen

1. **M:** Don't run. You _____ _____.
   B: Okay, I _____ _____.
2. **B:** Jumping _____ cold water _____ _____ _____ can be dangerous.
   G: Oh, okay. I will warm up.
3. **G:** Mom, I want _____ _____ here.
   W: Okay, but first you should check _____ _____ _____ _____ _____. It may be _____ _____ you think.
4. **B:** Can I swim _____ after eating?
   G: Swimming _____ a full stomach can be _____.

해석

1. **B:** 우리는 벌들을 조심해야만 해.
   G: 오, 벌들이다. 뛰어!
2. **G:** 이쪽으로 갈 수 있을까? 좋아 보여.
   B: 아니. 정상에 가기를 원한다면 우리는 똑바로 가야 해.
3. **B:** 오, 계단이 젖었어.
   G: 그러면 우리는 계단을 천천히 내려가야 해.
4. **G:** 조금 더 올라가 보자. 나는 산 정상에 닿고 싶어.
   B: 우리는 먼저 날씨를 확인해야 해. 오, 비가 내릴 예정이래. 우리는 내려가야 해.

1. **G:** 엄마, 오후에 밖에서 놀아도 될까요?
   W: 물론이지. 나가기 전에 선크림 바르는 것을 잊지 말아라.
   G: 그렇지만 오늘은 흐려요. 선크림을 발라야 하나요?
   W: 그럼, 매일 선크림을 발라야 한단다.
   G: 알겠어요. 그러면 지금 바를게요.

2. **B:** 볼링 치러 가자.
   G: 미안해. 갈 수 없어. 병원에 가야 하거든.
   B: 오, 무슨 문제 있니?
   G: 몰라, 하지만 배가 아파.

1. **M:** 뛰지 마. 넘어질 수도 있단다.
   B: 알겠어요, 뛰지 않을게요.
2. **B:** 준비 운동을 하지 않고 차가운 물로 뛰어드는 것은 위험할 수 있어.
   G: 오, 알았어. 준비 운동할게.
3. **G:** 엄마, 여기에서 수영하고 싶어요.
   W: 그래, 하지만 우선 물이 얼마나 깊은지 확인해야 한단다. 네가 생각하는 것보다 물이 깊을 수 있어.
4. **B:** 먹고 난 후에 바로 수영해도 될까?
   G: 배가 부른 채로 수영하는 것은 불편할 수 있어.

Listen & Speak 2 A

1. **M:** Flooding _____ _____ big problems. However, you may not know _____ _____ _____ when it happens. There are several things you _____ _____ _____. First, you _____ _____ _____ _____ the water and the electricity. Second, _____ water and food when you leave the house. _____, you have to move to a high and _____ _____ and _____ _____ _____ the weather report.

2. **B:** Mina, are you _____ _____ leave?

   G: No, not _____. I have to check _____ I _____ _____ _____ the gas.

   B: If we don't leave now, we _____ _____ _____ _____ the concert _____ _____.

   G: Okay, but I _____ _____ _____ the gas first. It will only take a minute.

Real-Life Zone

B: Uncle John, _____ _____ my new bike. _____ do you _____?

M: It's really nice. Where _____ you _____?

B: To the park _____ _____ a friend.

M: Where's your helmet?

B: I don't have _____. It's just a _____ _____.

M: _____ _____ your helmet. You may hurt _____.

B: But I see a lot of people _____ bikes _____ helmets.

M: You _____ _____ _____ a helmet. It _____ your head in an accident.

B: Okay. I'll get my dad's helmet.

M: No. You have to wear a helmet that _____ you. If _____, it cannot protect your head.

B: I guess I'll _____ _____ _____ one for myself.

Wrap Up

B: Here comes the bus!

G: Oh, but first I have to _____ _____ my tea.

B: _____ _____ you just take it with you? I'm _____ _____ it will be okay if you are careful.

G: No. If the bus stops _____, I _____ _____ _____ it.

B: Okay, then I can just _____ _____ you to finish your drink. I'm sure _____ _____ will come soon.

G: Thanks.

해석

1. **M:** 홍수는 큰 문제들을 일으킬 수 있습니다. 그러나, 당신은 홍수가 발생할 때 무엇을 해야 하는지 모를 수도 있습니다. 당신이 해야 하는 몇 가지 것들이 있습니다. 첫째, 수도와 전기를 꺼야 합니다. 둘째, 집을 떠날 때 물과 음식을 꾸려야 합니다. 마지막으로, 높고 안전한 곳으로 이동하여 일기 예보를 계속 들어야 합니다.

2. **B:** 미나야, 떠날 준비됐어?
   G: 아니, 아직. 가스를 껐는지 확인해야 해.
   B: 만약 우리가 지금 떠나지 않으면, 제 시간에 콘서트에 도착하지 못할 수도 있어.
   G: 알았어. 하지만 나는 우선 가스를 확인해야 해. 잠깐이면 될 거야.

B: 존 삼촌, 제 새로운 자전거 좀 보세요. 어떻게 생각하세요?
M: 아주 멋지구나. 어디를 가고 있니?
B: 친구 만나러 공원에요.
M: 네 헬멧이 어디 있니?
B: 저는 헬멧이 없어요. 그냥 잠깐 타는 거예요.
M: 헬멧을 쓰렴. 다칠 수 있단다.
B: 하지만 저는 헬멧 없이 자전거를 타는 많은 사람들을 봐요.
M: 너는 헬멧을 써야만 한단다. 그것은 사고가 났을 때 네 머리를 보호해 줘.
B: 알았어요. 아빠의 헬멧을 가져올게요.
M: 아니. 너는 네게 맞는 헬멧을 써야 해. 그렇지 않으면 그것은 네 머리를 보호해 줄 수 없어.
B: 저를 위한 헬멧을 사야겠어요.

B: 버스가 온다!
G: 오, 그렇지만 나는 우선 차 마시는 것을 끝내야 해.
B: 그냥 그것을 가지고 타는 것은 어때? 네가 조심한다면 괜찮을 거라고 확신해.
G: 아니, 만약 버스가 갑자기 멈춘다면, 나는 차를 흘릴 수도 있어.
B: 알았어, 그러면 난 네가 음료를 다 마실 때까지 기다릴 수 있어. 곧 다른 버스가 올 것이라고 확신해.
G: 고마워.

01 다음 대화의 밑줄 친 말의 의도로 알맞은 것은?

> A: Oh, the stairs are wet.
> B: <u>Then we have to walk down the stairs slowly.</u>

① 강조하기　　　② 요청하기　　　③ 의무 표현하기

④ 오해 지적하기　　⑤ 가능성 표현하기

02 다음 대화가 자연스럽게 이어지도록 순서대로 배열하시오.

> (A) Oh, what's wrong?
> (B) Let's go bowling.
> (C) I don't know, but my stomach hurts.
> (D) I'm sorry, I can't. I have to go see a doctor.

➡ _____

[03~04] 다음 대화를 읽고, 물음에 답하시오.

> B: Mina, are you ready to leave?
> G: No, not yet. I have to check ___(A)___ I turned off the gas.
> B: If we don't leave now, (B)우리는 제 시간에 콘서트에 도착하지 못할 수도 있어.(in, may, to)
> G: Okay, but I have to check the gas first. It will only take a minute.

03 위 대화의 빈칸 (A)에 알맞은 것은?

① that　　　② if　　　③ which

④ what　　　⑤ who

04 위 대화의 밑줄 친 (B)의 우리말을 주어진 단어를 이용하여 영어로 쓰시오.

➡ _____

[01~04] 다음 대화를 읽고 물음에 답하시오.

B: Uncle John, look at my new bike. What do you think?
M: It's really nice. Where are you going?
B: To the park to meet a friend. (①)
M: Where's your helmet?
B: I don't have one. It's just a short ride. (②)
M: ___(A)___ your helmet. You may hurt yourself.
B: But I see a lot of people riding bikes without helmets. (③)
M: You have to wear a helmet. (④)
B: Okay. I'll get my dad's helmet. (⑤)
M: No. You ___(B)___ wear a helmet that fits you. If not, it cannot protect your head.
B: I guess I'll have to buy one for myself.

01 위 대화의 ①~⑤ 중 주어진 문장이 들어갈 알맞은 것은?

> It protects your head in an accident.

①   ②   ③   ④   ⑤

서답형
02 위 대화의 빈칸 (A)에 알맞은 말을 두 단어로 쓰시오.

➡ _____

03 위 대화의 빈칸 (B)에 알맞은 말을 모두 고르시오.

① can   ② should
③ might   ④ need to
⑤ have to

04 위 대화를 읽고 답할 수 없는 질문은?

① What does Uncle John think about the boy's new bike?
② Where is the boy going?
③ Does the boy have his own helmet?
④ Why is the boy going to the park?
⑤ When will the boy buy his helmet?

[05~07] 다음 대화를 읽고 물음에 답하시오.

G: Mom, can I play outside this afternoon?
B: Sure. ___(A)___ sunscreen before you go out.
G: But it's cloudy today. (B)제가 선크림을 발라야 하나요? (have, put)
W: Yes, you have to wear sunscreen every day.
G: Okay. Then I'll put (C)some on now.

05 위 대화의 빈칸 (A)에 들어갈 말로 알맞은 것은?

① Remember to remove
② Make sure that you bring
③ Don't forget to put on
④ Be careful not to wear
⑤ Don't forget wearing

서답형
06 위 대화의 밑줄 친 (B)의 우리말을 주어진 단어를 이용하여 영어로 쓰시오.

➡ _____

서답형
07 위 대화의 밑줄 친 (C)가 가리키는 것을 쓰시오.

➡ _____

[08~10] 다음 대화를 읽고 물음에 답하시오.

B: Here comes the bus!

G: Oh, but first I have to finish drinking my tea.

B: Why don't you just take it with you? I'm sure that it will be okay if you are careful.

G: No. If the bus stops suddenly, I __(A)__ spill it.

B: Okay, then I can just wait for you to finish your drink. I'm sure another bus will come soon.

G: Thanks.

08 위 대화의 빈칸 (A)에 알맞은 것은?

① may   ② will
③ must   ④ should
⑤ have to

서답형

09 위 대화에서 다음 영영풀이에 해당하는 단어를 찾아 쓰시오

> to cause or allow something to fall, flow, or run over the edge of a container usually in an accidental way

➡ _____

중요

10 위 대화의 내용과 일치하지 <u>않는</u> 것은?

① They are waiting for the bus.
② The girl is drinking tea.
③ The girl will get on the bus with her tea.
④ The girl thinks she may spill her tea in the bus.
⑤ They decided to take the next bus.

11 다음 짝지어진 대화 중 <u>어색한</u> 것은?

① A: You have to check the weather.
   B: Okay, I will.
② A: Can I swim right after eating?
   B: Swimming with a full stomach can be comfortable.
③ A: Don't run. You may fall.
   B: Okay, I won't run.
④ A: Jumping into cold water without warming up can be dangerous.
   B: Oh, okay. I will warm up.
⑤ A: Do we have to close the windows before leaving?
   B: Yes, we have. The rain may start to pour.

[12~14] 다음 대화를 읽고 물음에 답하시오.

B: (A)Let's go bowling.

G: I'm sorry, I can't. (B)<u>나는 병원에 가야 하거든</u>.(see, have, doctor)

B: Oh, what's wrong?

G: I don't know, but my stomach hurts.

서답형

12 위 대화의 밑줄 친 (A)를 다음과 같이 바꿔 쓸 때 빈칸에 알맞은 말을 쓰시오.

> _____ _____ _____ go bowling?

서답형

13 위 대화의 밑줄 친 (B)의 우리말을 주어진 단어를 이용하여 영어로 쓰시오. (7 words)

➡ _____

서답형

14 Why does the girl have to go to the hospital? Answer in English. (4 words)

➡ _____

다음 대화가 자연스럽게 이어지도록 순서대로 배열하시오.

(A) Mina, are you ready to leave?

(B) If we don't leave now, we may not get to the concert in time.

(C) Okay, but I have to check the gas first. It will only take a minute.

(D) No, not yet. I have to check if I turned off the gas.

➡ _____

[02~04] 다음 대화를 읽고 물음에 답하시오.

B: Here comes the bus!

G: Oh, but first 나는 내 차 마시는 것을 끝내야 해.

B: Why don't you just take it with you? I'm sure that it will be okay (A)[if / that] you are careful.

G: No. If the bus (B)[stops / will stop] suddenly, I may spill it.

B: Okay, then I can just wait for you to finish your drink. I'm sure (C)[other / another] bus will come soon.

G: Thanks.

02 위 대화의 밑줄 친 우리말을 주어진 단어를 이용하여 영어로 쓰시오. (7 words)

(to / my / I / drink / tea / finish)

➡ _____

03 위 대화의 괄호 (A)~(C)에서 알맞은 것을 골라 쓰시오.

(A) _____ (B) _____ (C) _____

04 위 대화의 내용에 맞게 다음 빈칸에 알맞은 말을 쓰시오.

After the talk, the boy will _____ until the girl _____ her tea.

[05~07] 다음 대화를 읽고 물음에 답하시오.

B: Uncle John, look at my new bike. What do you think?

M: It's really nice. Where are you going?

B: __(A)__ the park to meet a friend.

M: Where's your helmet?

B: I don't have one. It's just a short ride.

M: Put __(B)__ your helmet. You may hurt yourself.

B: But I see a lot of people riding bikes without helmets.

M: You have to wear a helmet. It protects your head in an accident.

B: Okay. I'll get my dad's helmet.

M: No. (C)너는 네게 맞는 헬멧을 써야 해. If not, it cannot protect your head.

B: I guess I'll have to buy (D)one for myself.

05 위 대화의 빈칸 (A)와 (B)에 알맞은 말을 쓰시오.

(A) _____ (B) _____

06 위 대화의 밑줄 친 (C)의 우리말을 주어진 단어를 모두 배열하여 영작하시오.

(a / you / that / you / helmet / to / fits / wear / have)

➡ _____

07 위 대화의 밑줄 친 (D)가 가리키는 것을 쓰시오.

➡ _____

Grammar

교과서

① 접속사 although

> • **Although** camping trips can create sweet memories for many people, they can also be occasions when bad things happen.
> 캠핑 여행은 많은 사람들에게 좋은 추억을 만들어 주기도 하지만, 나쁜 일이 일어나는 때가 될 수도 있습니다.

- although는 '비록 ~이지만'의 뜻으로 종속절을 이끈다.
  - **Although** I am not good at English, I love studying it.
    나는 영어를 잘 못하지만, 영어 공부하는 것을 아주 좋아한다.
    = I love studying English **although** I am not good at it.

- although 대신 though, even though, even if를 쓸 수 있다.
  - **Even though** dinosaurs were large, no dinosaur was over 165 feet long.
    비록 공룡은 거대했지만, 어떤 공룡도 165피트 이상으로 길지는 않았다.
  - **Though** the teacher was patient, he was hurt by the student's behavior.
    그 교사는 참을성이 있었지만, 그 학생의 행동에 상처받았다.
  - **Even if** you don't like cheesecake, try a piece of this.
    설령 네가 치즈케이크를 싫어한다 하더라도, 이것을 한 조각 먹어 봐라.

- 부사절을 이끄는 although, though, even though, even if는 접속사를 중심으로 앞뒤 내용이 대조적 의미를 갖는다.
  - **Although** Annie is not tall, she wants to be a model.
    비록 Annie는 키가 크지 않지만, 모델이 되고 싶어 한다.

- even though 뒤에는 이미 일어난 일이나 현실에 대한 사실을 말하는 문장이 오고, even if 뒤에는 명확한 사실이 아니거나 아직 일어나지 않은 일을 가정하는 문장이 온다.
  - I like her, **even though** she can be annoying at times. 그녀는 가끔 짜증낼 수도 있지만 난 그녀를 좋아해.
  - I've got to get home **even if** it means flying the plane myself.
    내가 직접 비행기를 조종하게 되더라도 난 집에 가야 한다.

- although와 같은 뜻을 지닌 전치사로 despite(~임에도 불구하고)가 있다. despite은 전치사이므로 바로 뒤에 명사가 이어진다.
  - **Despite** the opposition, the policy was changed. 반대에도 불구하고 정책이 바뀌었습니다.

핵심 Check

1. 다음 괄호 안에서 알맞은 것을 고르시오.
   (1) I wasn't late for school (because / although) I got up late.
   (2) Even though Samantha (to eat / eats) almost all vegetables, she doesn't eat cucumbers.

② seem to

> • They **seem to** know what to do to make their camping trip safe and fun.
> 그들은 그들의 캠핑 여행을 안전하고 재미있게 만들기 위해 무엇을 해야 하는지 알고 있는 것 같습니다.
>
> • You **seem to** be a little busy these days. 요즘 너는 약간 바빠 보이는구나.

■ '주어+seem+to부정사'의 형태로 쓰인다.
  • Two friends **seem to** like each other. 두 친구들은 서로를 좋아하는 것처럼 보인다.

■ 부정은 '주어 don't/didn't seem to부정사'이다.
  • She doesn't **seem to** be OK. 그녀는 괜찮아 보이지 않아.
  • They didn't **seem to** have a good idea. 그들은 좋은 생각을 갖고 있는 것 같지 않았다.

■ it을 써서 'It seems/seemed that+주어+동사' 구문으로 바꿔 쓸 수 있다. 이 때 seem to의 동사 시제가 현재인지 과거인지에 따라 'It seems/seemed that절' 구문으로 변환 시 that절 안의 동사의 시제를 일치시켜 주어야 한다.
  • The teacher **seems to** understand me. 선생님은 나를 이해하는 것처럼 보인다.
    = **It seems that** the teacher understands me.
  • The teacher **seemed to** understand me. 선생님은 나를 이해하는 것처럼 보였다.
    = **It seemed that** the teacher understood me.

■ '주어+seem/seems/seemed+완료부정사(to have+과거분사)'는 that절 안의 동사의 시제가 앞설 경우이다.
  • He **seems to have been** rich when he was young.
    = **It seems that he was** rich when he was young.
    그는 젊었을 때 부자였던 것처럼 보인다. (지금 그가 과거에 부자였던 것처럼 보이는 것을 의미한다.)
  • He **seemed to have been** rich.
    = **It seemed that he had been** rich.
    그는 부자였던 것처럼 보였었다. (예전에 그가 부자였던 것처럼 과거에 그렇게 보였던 것을 의미한다.)

핵심 Check

2. 다음 문장을 it을 이용하여 바꿔 쓰시오.
  (1) You <u>seem</u> to dance very well.
    ➡ _____
  (2) Sara <u>seems</u> to like you
    ➡ _____
  (3) You <u>seem</u> to be angry.
    ➡ _____

01 다음 문장에서 어법상 <u>어색한</u> 부분을 바르게 고쳐 쓰시오.

(1) Besides Yumin is famous in Korea, many Americans do not know her.

_____ ➡ _____

(2) Although Maria is almost 50, she seems to is 30 years old.

_____ ➡ _____

(3) You seem to enjoying playing computer games.

_____ ➡ _____

(4) It seems to Mina disagrees with the suggestion.

➡ _____

02 두 문장을 한 문장으로 쓰시오. (접속사 even though를 사용할 것)

> • I have a lot to do.
> • I am doing nothing.

➡ _____

➡ _____

03 be가 들어갈 곳으로 적절한 곳을 고르시오.

> • That car ① seems ② to ③ new because ④ there ⑤ are no scratches on it.

04 다음 우리말에 맞게 주어진 단어를 활용하여 영작하시오.

(1) 이 컵은 아름답지만 옆에 금이 가 있다. (even though, beautiful, crack)

➡ _____

➡ _____

(2) Rose는 잠자리에 늦게 든 것처럼 보였다. (seem)

➡ _____

➡ _____

(3) Alex는 요즘 우울한 것처럼 보인다. (seem, depressed)

➡ _____

➡ _____

서답형

01 다음 문장에서 어법상 틀린 부분을 찾아 바르게 고쳐 쓰시오.

> Despite it was pretty cold, the girl wasn't wearing a jacket.

_____ ➡ _____

02 다음 빈칸에 공통으로 들어갈 말로 알맞은 것을 고르시오.

> • It seems _____ Jay knows the answer.
> • It seems _____ he is leaving soon.

① with   ② at
③ to   ④ in
⑤ that

서답형

03 괄호 안의 단어와 조건을 참고하여 우리말에 맞게 영작하시오.

(1) 그는 외로워 보인다. (lonely)
   ➡ (to부정사 사용) _____
   ➡ (It seems/seemed that 사용)
   _____

(2) 그녀는 행복해 보인다. (happy)
   ➡ (to부정사 사용) _____
   ➡ (It seems/seemed that 사용)
   _____

(3) Sally는 바쁜 것 같아 보인다. (in a hurry)
   ➡ (to부정사 사용) _____
   ➡ (It seems/seemed that 사용)
   _____

(4) 컴퓨터가 전혀 작동하지 않는 것처럼 보였다.
   (work, at)
   ➡ (It seems/seemed that 사용)

중요

04 다음 중 어색한 문장을 고르시오.

① My father seems to be angry.
② It seems that they will get back soon.
③ Kidson doesn't seem like her new hairstyle.
④ He doesn't seem to have any plans.
⑤ It seems that she misses her family.

05 다음 문장을 뜻이 같은 문장으로 바르게 고쳐 쓴 것을 고르시오.

> It seems that he was busy.

① He seems to have been busy.
② He doesn't seem to be busy.
③ He didn't seem to be busy.
④ He seemed to be busy.
⑤ It seemed that he wasn't busy.

06 다음 빈칸에 들어갈 말로 적절한 것은?

> _____ he's ninety, his mental faculties remain unimpaired.
> *faculty: 기능, *unimpaired: 손상되지 않은

① Although   ② Because
③ Due to   ④ However
⑤ Despite

07 다음 중 빈칸에 공통으로 들어갈 단어로 알맞은 것을 고르시오. (대·소문자 무시)

> • Even _____ you run, you'll still be late.
> • _____ it may sound strange, I was pleased the game was over.

① though   ② although   ③ so
④ if   ⑤ that

서답형

08 although로 시작하고, 괄호 안의 단어를 활용하여 영작하시오.

(1) 많이 시끄러웠지만 아기는 깨지 않았다.
   (a loud noise, wake up)

   ➡ _____

   _____

(2) 그는 영화를 싫어하지만 여자 친구를 즐겁게 해 주기 위해 그녀와 함께 영화를 보러 갔다.
   (dislike, go, movies, please)

   ➡ _____

   _____

중요

09 다음 두 문장의 의미가 같지 <u>않은</u> 것은?

① They seem to know what to do to make their camping trip safe.
   = It seems that they know what to do to make their camping trip safe.
② They seem to have known what to do to make their camping trip safe.
   = It seems that they knew what to do to make their camping trip safe.
③ They seemed to know what to do to make their camping trip safe.
   = It seemed that they knew what to do to make their camping trip safe.
④ They seemed to have known what to do to make their camping trip safe.

= It seemed that they have known what to do to make their camping trip safe.
⑤ They seem to be a little busy these days.
   = It seems that they are a little busy these days.

서답형

10 다음 괄호 안에서 알맞은 것을 고르시오.

(1) They seem (to be / being) close friends.
(2) It seems (that / to be) she likes him.

11 다음 문장의 빈칸에 알맞은 말은?

> Harry and Catherine _____ to love each other.

① seem like   ② seems
③ seem   ④ look
⑤ looks

서답형

12 종속절과 주절 간에 대조적 의미를 담고 있는 부분을 찾으시오.

(1) Although she is three years old, she can read and write.
   ➡ 종속절: _____
   ➡ 주절: _____
(2) I think they're fantastic, even though they haven't won any games this season.
   ➡ 종속절: _____
   ➡ 주절: _____
(3) You're still going to be cold even if you put on two or three jumpers.
   ➡ 종속절: _____
   ➡ 주절: _____

13 다음 빈칸에 들어갈 말로 알맞은 것은?

> He seems to _____ an honest man.

① be   ② is

③ been   ④ was

⑤ being

14 다음 우리말을 옮긴 것으로 알맞은 것을 <u>모두</u> 고르시오.

> 돈이 많았지만 나는 행복하지 않았다.

① Although I had much money, I was not happy.

② Though I had much money, I was not happy.

③ I had much money although I was not happy.

④ I had much money though I was not happy.

⑤ Although I hadn't much money, I am happy.

15 다음 빈칸에 들어갈 말로 바르게 짝지어진 것을 고르시오.

> • _____ seems that she worries about everything.
> • Kevin seems _____ like his new school.
> • The children seemed to _____ hungry.

① She – that – was   ② She – that – be

③ It – to – be   ④ It – that – be

⑤ It – to – was

16 다음 문장을 같은 뜻으로 바꿔 쓸 때 어색한 것을 <u>모두</u> 고르시오.

① The jacket seems to have a hidden pocket.

= It seems that the jacket had a hidden pocket.

② You seem to have a fever.

= It seems that you have a fever

③ I seem to have picked up the wrong set of keys.

= It seemed that I had picked up the wrong set of keys.

④ You seem to know a lot of these rumors.

= It seems that you know a lot of these rumors.

⑤ He doesn't seem to agree with this suggestion.

= It doesn't seem that he agrees with this suggestion.

서답형

17 우리말에 맞게 괄호 안의 어휘들을 배열하여 영작할 때, 주어진 조건에 맞게 쓰시오.

(1) 5번째, 8번째 단어를 쓰시오.

• 그는 부자라 하더라도, 나는 그와 결혼하지 않을 거야. (he, rich, is, though, even, him, not, I will, marry)

➡ _____

(2) 4번째 단어를 쓰시오.

• 난 감기에 걸린 것 같아. (have, seem, I, to, cold, a)

➡ _____

(3) 4번째 단어를 쓰시오.

• 난 무언가 잊어버린 것 같아. (something, have, I, forgotten, to, seem)

➡ _____

(4) 8번째 단어를 쓰시오

• 악천후에도 불구하고 그들은 동물원에서 즐거운 하루를 보냈다. (enjoyed, day, their, they, the, despite, at, zoo, weather, the, bad)

➡ _____

01 우리말에 맞게 괄호 안의 단어를 활용하여 빈칸을 채우시오.

(1) 그들은 항상 우는 것 같아. (cry all the time)
➡ They _____.
➡ It _____.

(2) 그녀가 나쁜 남자들하고 어울려 다니는 것 같아.
(get along with, guys)
➡ She _____.
➡ It _____.

(3) 너는 그 영화를 재미있게 보는 것 같지 않았다.
(enjoy)
➡ You _____.

(4) 올해에는 아무것도 그 팀을 멈추지 못할 듯이
보였다. (nothing, this year)
➡ It _____
_____.

(5) 그녀는 실망한 것처럼 보였다.
➡ It _____.

02 괄호 안의 단어와 조건을 보고 문장을 완성하시오.

(1) 그는 아픈 것 같다. (ill)
➡ (to부정사 사용) _____
➡ (It seems/seemed that 사용)
_____

(2) 그들은 무엇이든지 알고 있는 것 같다.
(know everything)
➡ (to부정사 사용) _____
➡ (It seems/seemed that 사용)
_____

(3) 그는 거기에 없었던 것 같다. (there)
➡ (It seems/seemed that 사용)
_____

(4) 그는 독살된 것 같다. (poison)
➡ (It seems/seemed that 사용)
_____

03 그림을 참고하여 우리말과 같도록 괄호 안의 단어를 활용하여 영작하시오.

차량 충돌 사고가 있었지만, 인명 피해는 없었다.
(although, crash, be lost)

➡ _____
_____

04 다음 그림을 참고하고 괄호 안의 단어를 사용하여 문장을
완성하시오.

(seem, enjoy themselves)

➡ They _____.

05 to부정사를 활용하여 문장을 완성하시오.

(1) 그녀는 피곤해 보여.

➡ She _____ tired.

(2) 그들은 좋은 아이디어가 있는 것 같아.

➡ They _____ a good idea.

(3) 너는 경제학에 대해 많이 알고 있는 것 같다.

➡ You _____ a lot about economics.

(4) 난 선글라스를 제자리에 두지 않은 것 같아.

➡ I _____ misplaced my sunglasses.

06 'It seems/seemed that'을 활용하여 문장을 완성하시오.

(1) 나는 그녀에게 친절하지 못했던 것 같다.

➡ _____ I was unkind to her.

(2) 이것은 큰 문제인 것 같다.

➡ _____ this is a big problem.

07 다음 문장을 같은 뜻으로 바꿔 쓰시오.

(1) She seems to have been angry last night.

➡ _____

(2) It seems that he fell in love with the girl.

➡ _____

08 그림에 맞게 괄호 안의 단어를 활용하여 5 단어로 영작하시오.

(seem, cold)

➡ It _____ .

09 괄호 안의 단어를 활용하여 우리말에 맞게 영작하시오.

(1) 비가 내렸지만 그들은 밖에서 축구를 했다.
(although, rain, it, soccer)

➡ _____
_____

(2) 내 남동생은 음식을 먹었지만 여전히 배가 고팠다.
(eat, younger, be)

➡ _____
_____
_____

(3) 어젯밤 잠을 많이 못 잤는데도 피곤하지 않다.
(although, sleep, be)

➡ _____
_____
_____

(4) 그녀는 바빴지만, 절대 도움을 요청하려고 하지 않았다. (although, would, ask for)

➡ _____
_____
_____

10 though와 괄호 안의 단어를 활용하여 우리말에 맞게 빈칸을 채우시오.

나는 그를 좋아하지 않지만, 그가 좋은 매너를 가졌다는 건 인정해. (like, agree)

➡ _____ I _____ _____ him, I
_____ that he has good manners. 또
는 I _____ that he has good manners
_____ I _____ _____ him.

Safe Camping

Although camping trips can create sweet memories for many people,
they can also be occasions when bad things happen. If you plan to go
camping with family or friends this summer, you need to keep several
things in mind for your safety.

Listen to Yumin's family talk about their camping trip. They seem to
know what to do to make their camping trip safe and fun.

Yumin: Dad, why don't we put up our tent over here by this river?

Dad: I don't think that's a good idea. If it starts to rain, the river might

overflow.

Yumin: I know, but the sky is clear. I really like the sound of the water!

Dad: The weather can change quickly in the mountains. You never

know when it might start to rain.

Yumin: Okay. Safety first! Let's find another place.

When you set up a tent, choose a flat, sunny area. Avoid places too
close to big trees that might be struck by lightning.

Hajun: Mom, I'm hungry. What's for lunch?

Mom: I'm cooking Samgyepsal.

---

safe 안전한

create 만들다, 창조하다

memory 추억

occasion 때, 경우

happen (사건 등이) 일어나다

keep ~ in mind ~을 명심하다

safety 안전

fun 재미있는

put up (텐트 등을) 치다, 세우다

overflow 범람하다

sound 소리, 음

weather 날씨

flat 평평한

sunny 햇볕이 잘 드는

avoid 피하다

strike 치다

lightning 번개

확인문제

● 다음 문장이 본문의 내용과 일치하면 T, 일치하지 않으면 F를 쓰시오.

1　Bad things cannot happen when we go camping. ☐

2　There are several things to remember when you go camping. ☐

3　Yumin wants to put up a tent by the river. ☐

4　It is a good idea to put up a tent by the river. ☐

5　When we set up a tent, we should choose a flat, sunny area. ☐

Hajun: Mom, that's not enough for all of us. Can we cook <u>more</u> in a bigger pan?
much의 비교급

Mom: I'm going to cook more, but we <u>have to</u> use this small pan.
= must

Hajun: Why do we have to use a small pan?

Mom: Because the pan should not be bigger than the burner. If you use a big pan, it <u>sends the heat back</u> to the burner, and the gas <u>can</u> explode!
send+목적어(명사)+부사
~할 수 있다(가능성)

Hajun: Oh, I didn't know <u>that</u>.
앞 문장의 내용을 받는 지시대명사

Here is one more tip about fire when you go camping. Never use a gas heater or burner inside a tent. Your tent may catch fire, or you <u>might</u> pass out because the fire will use up the oxygen in the tent as <u>it</u> burns.
= may(추측의 조동사)
~하면서

Yumin: Ouch! Mosquitoes!

Mom: Oh, I <u>forgot to</u> tell you to apply some bug spray. Here.
forget+to부정사: ~할 것을 잊다

Yumin: Thanks, Mom. Oh, <u>you know what?</u> We can rub orange peels on our skin instead of <u>applying</u> bug spray. It is a nature-friendly way <u>to keep</u> mosquitoes away.
그거 아세요?
동명사(전치사의 목적어)
to부정사의 형용사적 용법

Mom: That's interesting!

Garlic can also keep bugs away. You can place <u>pieces of</u> garlic at the entrance to the tent, <u>and</u> bugs will not come inside.
물질명사를 세는 단위
그러면

글자 pick 고르기, 선택
enough 충분한
pan 팬, 냄비
burner 버너
send back ~을 다시 돌려보내다
explode 폭발하다
tip 팁, 조언
inside ~ 안에서
catch fire 불이 붙다
pass out 의식을 잃다
use up ~을 다 쓰다
oxygen 산소
burn 타다
ouch 앗
mosquito 모기
apply 바르다, 뿌리다
bug 벌레, 곤충
spary 스프레이
nature-friendly 자연 친화적인
keep away ~을 접근하지 못하게 하다
garlic 마늘
entrance 입구

📎 **확인문제**

● 다음 문장이 본문의 내용과 일치하면 T, 일치하지 <u>않으면</u> F를 쓰시오.

1 Hajun wanted his mom to cook more in a bigger pan. ☐

2 Hajun's mom will cook more in a bigger pan. ☐

3 The pan should not be bigger than the burner. ☐

4 It is dangerous to use a gas heater or burner inside a tent. ☐

5 We must not apply some bug spray. ☐

6 We can rub orange peels on our skin to keep mosquitoes away. ☐

● 우리말을 참고하여 빈칸에 알맞은 말을 쓰시오.

Safe Camping

1 Although camping trips can _____ sweet _____ for many people, they can also be occasions _____ bad things _____.

2 If you _____ _____ go camping with family or friends this summer, you _____ to keep several things _____ _____ for your safety.

3 Listen to Yumin's family _____ about their _____ _____.

4 They _____ to know _____ _____ do to make their camping trip _____ and fun.

5 Yumin: Dad, _____ _____ we _____ _____ our tent over here _____ this river?

6 Dad: I don't _____ that's a good _____.

7 If it _____ _____ rain, the river _____ overflow.

8 Yumin: I know, _____ the sky is _____.

9 I really like the _____ of the water!

10 Dad: The _____ can _____ quickly in the mountains.

11 You _____ know _____ it _____ start to rain.

12 Yumin: Okay. _____ first! Let's find _____ place.

13 When you _____ a tent, _____ a flat, sunny area.

14 _____ places too _____ to big trees that might _____ _____ by lightning.

15 Hajun: Mom, I'm _____. What's _____ lunch?

16 Mom: I'm _____ Samgyepsal.

17 Hajun: Mom, that's not _____ for _____ of us. Can we cook _____ in a bigger pan?

안전한 캠핑

1 캠핑 여행이 많은 사람들에게 좋은 추억을 만들어 주기도 하지만, 나쁜 일이 일어나는 때가 될 수도 있습니다.

2 여러분이 이번 여름에 가족이나 친구들과 함께 캠핑을 하려고 계획하고 있다면, 여러분은 여러분의 안전을 위해서 몇 가지 사항을 명심해야 합니다.

3 유민이의 가족이 그들의 캠핑 여행에 대해 이야기하는 것을 들어 보세요.

4 그들은 그들의 캠핑 여행이 안전하고 재미있게 하기 위해 무엇을 해야 하는지 알고 있는 것 같습니다.

5 유민: 아빠, 이 강 근처 이쪽에 텐트를 치면 어때요?

6 아빠: 그건 좋은 생각 같지 않구나.

7 만약 비가 내리기 시작하면, 강이 범람할지도 몰라.

8 유민: 저도 알아요. 하지만 하늘이 맑잖아요.

9 저는 물소리를 정말 좋아한단 말이에요!

10 아빠: 산속의 날씨는 곧 바뀔 수 있어.

11 언제 비가 올지 절대 알 수 없는 일이지.

12 유민: 알겠어요. 안전이 우선이지요! 다른 곳을 찾아봐요.

13 텐트를 칠 때는 평평하고 햇볕이 잘 드는 장소를 고르세요.

14 번개를 맞을지도 모르는 키 큰 나무에 너무 가까운 장소는 피해야 합니다.

15 하준: 엄마, 저 배고파요. 점심이 뭐예요?

16 엄마: 삼겹살을 요리하고 있단다.

17 하준: 엄마, 그건 우리 모두가 먹기에 충분하지 않아요. 우리 더 큰 팬에 더 많이 요리하면 안 돼요?

18 Mom: I'm _____ _____ cook more, but we _____ _____ use this small pan.

19 Hajun: _____ do we _____ to use a small pan?

20 Mom: _____ the pan _____ _____ be bigger than the burner.

21 _____ you use a big pan, it _____ the heat _____ to the burner, and the gas can _____!

22 Hajun: Oh, I didn't _____ that.

23 _____ is one more _____ about fire _____ you go camping.

24 _____ use a gas heater or burner _____ a tent.

25 Your tent _____ catch fire, _____ you might _____ out because the fire will _____ up the _____ in the tent as it burns.

26 Yumin: Ouch! Mosquitoes!

27 Mom: Oh, I _____ _____ tell you to _____ some bug spray. Here.

28 Yumin: Thanks, Mom. Oh, you know _____?

29 We can _____ orange peels _____ our skin _____ of _____ bug spray.

30 It is a nature-friendly way _____ _____ mosquitoes _____.

31 Mom: That's _____!

32 Garlic can also _____ bugs _____.

33 You can place _____ _____ garlic at the _____ to the tent, and bugs will not _____ _____.

18 엄마: 더 굽긴 할 거야. 하지만 우리는 이 작은 팬을 써야 해.

19 하준: 왜 우리는 작은 팬을 써야 하죠?

20 엄마: 왜냐하면 팬이 버너보다 더 크면 안 되기 때문이야.

21 만약 큰 팬을 사용하면, 팬이 열을 버너로 다시 돌려보내서, 가스가 폭발할 수 있어!

22 하준: 오, 그것은 몰랐어요.

23 캠핑할 때 불을 사용하는 것에 대한 또 하나의 팁이 있습니다.

24 텐트 안에서 가스난로나 버너를 절대 쓰지 마세요.

25 여러분의 텐트에 불이 붙거나, 불이 타면서 텐트 내 산소를 다 써 버려서 여러분이 의식을 잃을 수도 있습니다.

26 유민: 앗! 모기!

27 엄마: 아, 벌레 퇴치 스프레이를 뿌리라고 네게 말하는 걸 잊었구나. 여기 있단다.

28 유민: 고마워요, 엄마. 아, 그거 아세요?

29 벌레 퇴치 스프레이를 뿌리는 것 대신에 오렌지 껍질을 피부에 문질러도 돼요.

30 모기가 접근하지 못하게 하는 자연 친화적인 방법이에요.

31 엄마: 그거 재미있구나!

32 마늘 또한 벌레가 접근하지 못하게 막을 수 있습니다.

33 마늘 조각을 텐트 입구에 놓아두면, 벌레가 안으로 들어오지 않을 것입니다.

● 우리말을 참고하여 본문을 영작하시오.

Safe Camping

1 캠핑 여행이 많은 사람들에게 좋은 추억을 만들어 주기도 하지만, 나쁜 일이 일어나는 때가 될 수도 있습니다.
➡ _____
_____

2 여러분이 이번 여름에 가족이나 친구들과 함께 캠핑을 하려고 계획하고 있다면, 여러분은 여러분의 안전을 위해서 몇 가지 사항을 명심해야 합니다.
➡ _____
_____

3 유민이의 가족이 그들의 캠핑 여행에 대해 이야기하는 것을 들어 보세요.
➡ _____

4 그들은 그들의 캠핑 여행이 안전하고 재미있게 하기 위해 무엇을 해야 하는지 알고 있는 것 같습니다.
➡ _____

5 유민: 아빠, 이 강 근처 이쪽에 텐트를 치면 어때요?
➡ _____

6 아빠: 그건 좋은 생각 같지 않구나.
➡ _____

7 만약 비가 내리기 시작하면, 강이 범람할지도 몰라.
➡ _____

8 유민: 저도 알아요. 하지만 하늘이 맑잖아요.
➡ _____

9 저는 물소리를 정말 좋아한단 말이에요!
➡ _____

10 아빠: 산속의 날씨는 곧 바뀔 수 있어.
➡ _____

11 언제 비가 올지 절대 알 수 없는 일이지.
➡ _____

12 유민: 알겠어요. 안전이 우선이지요! 다른 곳을 찾아봐요.
➡ _____

13 텐트를 칠 때는 평평하고 햇볕이 잘 드는 장소를 고르세요.
➡ _____

14 번개를 맞을지도 모르는 키 큰 나무에 너무 가까운 장소는 피해야 합니다.
➡ _____

15 하준: 엄마, 저 배고파요. 점심이 뭐예요?
➡ _____

16 엄마: 삼겹살을 요리하고 있단다.
➡ _____

17 하준: 엄마, 그건 우리 모두가 먹기에 충분하지 않아요. 우리 더 큰 팬에 더 많이 요리하면 안 돼요?
➡ _____

18 엄마: 더 굽긴 할 거야. 하지만 우리는 이 작은 팬을 써야 해.

➡ _____

19 하준: 왜 우리는 작은 팬을 써야 하죠?

➡ _____

20 엄마: 왜냐하면 팬이 버너보다 더 크면 안 되기 때문이야.

➡ _____

21 만약 큰 팬을 사용하면, 팬이 열을 버너로 다시 돌려보내서, 가스가 폭발할 수 있어!

➡ _____

22 하준: 오, 그것은 몰랐어요.

➡ _____

23 캠핑할 때 불을 사용하는 것에 대한 또 하나의 팁이 있습니다.

➡ _____

24 텐트 안에서 가스난로나 버너를 절대 쓰지 마세요.

➡ _____

25 여러분의 텐트에 불이 붙거나, 불이 타면서 텐트 내 산소를 다 써 버려서 여러분이 의식을 잃을 수도 있습니다.

➡ _____

➡ _____

26 유민: 앗! 모기!

➡ _____

27 엄마: 아, 벌레 퇴치 스프레이를 뿌리라고 네게 말하는 걸 잊었구나. 여기 있단다.

➡ _____

28 유민: 고마워요, 엄마. 아, 그거 아세요?

➡ _____

29 벌레 퇴치 스프레이를 뿌리는 것 대신에 오렌지 껍질을 피부에 문질러도 돼요.

➡ _____

30 모기가 접근하지 못하게 하는 자연 친화적인 방법이에요.

➡ _____

31 엄마: 그거 재미있구나!

➡ _____

32 마늘 또한 벌레가 접근하지 못하게 막을 수 있습니다.

➡ _____

33 마늘 조각을 텐트 입구에 놓아두면, 벌레가 안으로 들어오지 않을 것입니다.

➡ _____

[01~03] 다음 글을 읽고 물음에 답하시오.

Although camping trips can create sweet memories for many people, they can also be occasions __(A)__ bad things happen. If you plan to go camping with family or friends this summer, you need to keep several things __(B)__ mind for your safety.

Listen to Yumin's family talk about their camping trip. They seem to know what to do to make their camping trip safe and fun.

01 빈칸 (A)에 들어갈 말로 적절한 것은?

① why   ② who
③ what   ④ when
⑤ which

02 위 글의 빈칸 (B)에 적절한 전치사를 쓰시오.

➡ _____

03 다음 중 위 글의 내용으로 보아 알 수 <u>없는</u> 것은?

① 캠핑 여행은 많은 사람들에게 즐거운 추억을 남긴다.
② 캠핑을 갈 때는 위험한 일이 일어날 수 있다.
③ 캠핑을 갈 때는 안전에 유의해야 한다.
④ 유민의 가족은 자주 캠핑을 간다.
⑤ 유민의 가족은 캠핑 여행이 어떻게 하면 안전하고 즐거울 수 있는 지 아는 것 같다.

[04~06] 다음 글을 읽고 물음에 답하시오.

Yumin: Dad, why don't we put up our tent over here by this river? (①)

Dad: (②) I don't think (A)that's a good idea. If it starts to rain, the river might overflow.

Yumin: I know, but the sky is clear. I really like the sound of the water! (③)

Dad: (④) You never know when it might start to rain.

Yumin: Okay. _____(B)_____ Let's find another place. (⑤)

04 위 문장의 ①~⑤ 중 다음 주어진 문장이 들어갈 알맞은 곳은?

> The weather can change quickly in the mountains.

①   ②   ③   ④   ⑤

05 밑줄 친 (A)That이 가리키는 것을 우리말로 쓰시오.

➡ _____

06 빈칸 (B)에 들어갈 말로 가장 적절한 것은?

① Time is money!
② Hurry up.
③ Safety first!
④ Charity begins at home.
⑤ Health is above wealth!

[07~10] 다음 글을 읽고 물음에 답하시오.

Hajun: Mom, I'm hungry. What's for lunch?

Mom: I'm cooking Samgyepsal.

Hajun: Mom, that's not enough ___ⓐ___ all of us. Can we cook more in a bigger pan?

Mom: I'm going to cook more, (A)(so, but) we have to use this small pan.

Hajun: Why do we have to use a (B)(big, small) pan?

Mom: Because the pan should not be bigger than the burner. (C)(If, Though) you use a big pan, it sends the heat back to the burner, and the gas can ___ⓑ___!

Hajun: Oh, I didn't know that.

07 빈칸 ⓐ에 들어갈 말로 적절한 것은?

① at
② for
③ on
④ with
⑤ from

서답형

08 다음과 같이 풀이되는 말을 위 글의 빈칸 ⓑ에 쓰시오.

> something bursts loudly and with great force, often causing damage or injury

➡ _____

09 (A)~(C)에서 글의 흐름상 올바른 것으로 짝지어진 것은?

① but – small – If
② so – big – If
③ but – big – If
④ so – small – Though
⑤ but – small – Though

중요

10 다음 중 위 글의 내용으로 보아 질문에 답할 수 <u>없는</u> 것은?

① Why is Hajun hungry?
② What is Hajun's mom cooking?
③ Why is Hajun's mom using a small pan?
④ Is Hajun's mom going to cook more?
⑤ Why should the burner be bigger than the pan?

[11~13] 다음 글을 읽고 물음에 답하시오.

Here is one more tip about fire when you go ⓐcamp. Never use a gas heater or burner inside a tent. Your tent may catch fire, or you ⓑmight pass out because the fire will use ___ⓒ___ the oxygen in the tent as it burns.

서답형

11 밑줄 친 ⓐcamp를 알맞은 형으로 고치시오.

➡ _____

12 밑줄 친 ⓑmight와 의미가 <u>다른</u> 것을 <u>모두</u> 고르시오.

① I <u>might</u> be wrong.
② <u>Might</u> I leave now?
③ I thought that she <u>might</u> be angry.
④ She said that I <u>might</u> go home.
⑤ Ted said that it <u>might</u> rain.

서답형

13 빈칸 ⓒ에 알맞은 말을 쓰시오.

➡ _____

[14~18] 다음 글을 읽고 물음에 답하시오.

> **Yumin:** Ouch! Mosquitoes!
>
> **Mom:** Oh, I forgot (A)(to tell, telling) you to apply some bug spray. Here.
>
> **Yumin:** Thanks, Mom. Oh, you know __(B)__ ? We can rub orange peels on our skin instead of applying bug spray. It is a nature-friendly way ⓐto keep mosquitoes away.
>
> **Mom:** That's interesting!
>
> Garlic can also keep bugs away. You can place pieces of garlic at the entrance to the tent, and bugs will not come inside.

서답형

14 괄호 (A)에서 알맞은 것을 고르시오.

➡ _____

15 빈칸 (B)에 들어갈 말로 적절한 것은?

① it   ② this

③ that   ④ what

⑤ which

16 밑줄 친 ⓐto keep과 to부정사의 용법이 같은 것을 고르시오.

① They want to be friends with us.

② There is nothing to worry about.

③ Kathy came to Korea to be a K-pop singer.

④ She was pleased to hear of my success.

⑤ It is our duty to obey laws.

중요
17 다음 중 위 글의 내용으로 보아 알 수 없는 것은?

① There were some mosquitoes.

② Yumin's mom applied some bug spray.

③ We can rub orange peels on our skin to keep mosquitoes away.

④ Garlic can keep bugs away.

⑤ Bugs don't like garlic.

서답형
18 Where can you place pieces of garlic? Answer in Korean.

➡ _____

[19~23] 다음 글을 읽고 물음에 답하시오.

> __(A)__ camping trips can create sweet memories for many people, they can also be occasions when bad things happen. If you plan to go camping with family or friends this summer, you need to keep several things __(B)__ mind for your (C)safe.
>
> Listen to Yumin's family talk about their camping trip. (D)They seem to know what to do to make their camping trip safe and fun.

19 다음 중 위 글의 빈칸 (A)에 들어갈 말과 다른 것이 들어가는 것은?

① _____ he's nearly 90, he is still very active.

② _____ the sun was shinning, it wasn't very warm.

③ _____ it was very cold, the boy wasn't wearing a coat.

④ _____ it smells bad, it's probably not safe to eat.

⑤ _____ it rained a lot, they played soccer outside.

20 빈칸 (B)에 들어갈 말로 적절한 것은?

① in ② at
③ to ④ for
⑤ with

서답형

21 밑줄 친 (C)safe를 알맞은 형으로 고치시오.

➡ _____

서답형

22 밑줄 친 (D)와 같은 뜻이 되도록 빈칸에 알맞은 말을 쓰시오.

They seem to know what _____ _____ _____ to make their camping trip safe and fun.

중요

23 다음 중 위 글의 내용을 잘못 이해한 사람은?

① Amelia: Camping trips can create sweet memories for many people.
② Brian: When you go on camping trips, bad things may happen.
③ Chris: When we go on camping trips, we should take care of our safety.
④ David: I think Yumin's family will go on a camping trip.
⑤ Eden: I'm afraid Yumin's family may have an accident while camping.

[24~26] 다음 글을 읽고 물음에 답하시오.

Yumin: (①) Dad, why ⓐdon't we put up our tent over here by this river?

Dad: (②) If it starts to rain, the river ⓑmight overflow.

Yumin: I know, ⓒbut the sky is clear. I really like the sound of the water! (③)

Dad: The weather can change quickly in the mountains. (④) You never know when it might start to rain.

Yumin: (⑤) Okay. Safety first! Let's find ⓓother place.

When you set up a tent, choose a flat, sunny area. Avoid places too close to big trees that ⓔmight be struck by lightning.

24 위 글의 ①~⑤ 중 다음 주어진 문장이 들어갈 알맞은 곳은?

I don't think that's a good idea.

① ② ③ ④ ⑤

25 밑줄 친 ⓐ~ⓔ 중 어법상 올바르지 않은 것은?

① ⓐ ② ⓑ ③ ⓒ ④ ⓓ ⑤ ⓔ

중요

26 다음 중 위 글을 읽고 답할 수 없는 것은?

① Why does Yumin want to put up their tent by this river?
② Does Yumin's dad agree to her idea?
③ Does Yumin like the sound of the water?
④ Why can the weather change quickly in the mountains?
⑤ Why should we avoid places too close to big trees?

[01~04] 다음 글을 읽고 물음에 답하시오.

Hajun: Mom, I'm ___(A)___ . What's for lunch?

Mom: I'm cooking Samgyepsal.

Hajun: Mom, that's not enough for all of us. Can we cook more in a bigger pan?

Mom: (B)나는 더 요리할 거야, 하지만 우리는 이 작은 팬을 사용해야 해.

Hajun: Why do we have to use a small pan?

Mom: ___(C)___ the pan should not be bigger than the burner. If you use a big pan, it sends the heat back to the burner, and the gas can explode!

Hajun: Oh, I didn't know (D)that.

01 빈칸 (A)에 다음 영영풀이에 해당하는 단어를 쓰시오.

> wanting some food because you have not eaten for some time and have an uncomfortable or painful feeling in your stomach

➡ _____

02 주어진 단어를 활용하여 밑줄 친 우리말 (B)를 영어로 쓰시오.

> (go / much / have / pan)

➡ _____
_____

03 빈칸 (C)에 알맞은 접속사를 쓰시오.

➡ _____

04 밑줄 친 (D)that이 구체적으로 가리키는 것을 우리말로 쓰시오.

➡ _____
_____

[05~06] 다음 글을 읽고 물음에 답하시오.

(A)여기 캠핑을 갈 때 불에 관한 조언이 하나 더 있다. Never use a gas heater or burner inside a tent. Your tent may ___(B)___ fire, or you might pass out because the fire will use up the oxygen in the tent as it burns.

05 주어진 단어를 활용하여 밑줄 친 우리말 (A)를 영어로 쓰시오.

> (here / much / tip / when / go)

➡ _____

06 빈칸 (B)에 문맥상 알맞은 단어를 쓰시오.

➡ _____

[07~09] 다음 글을 읽고 물음에 답하시오.

Yumin: Ouch! Mosquitoes!

Mom: Oh, I forgot to tell you to apply some bug spray. Here.

Yumin: Thanks, Mom. Oh, you know what? We can rub orange peels on our skin instead ___(A)___ applying bug spray. It is a nature-friendly way to keep mosquitoes away.

Mom: (B)That is interesting!

Garlic can also keep bugs away. You can place pieces ___(C)___ garlic at the entrance to the tent, and bugs will not come inside.

07 빈칸 (A)와 (C)에 공통으로 들어갈 말을 쓰시오.

➡ _____

08 밑줄 친 (B)That이 가리키는 것을 우리말로 쓰시오.

➡ _____
_____

09 What did Yumin's mom forget to do? Answer in English with a full sentence.

➡ _____

[10~13] 다음 글을 읽고 물음에 답하시오.

Although camping trips can create sweet ___(A)___ for many people, (B)they can also be occasions when bad things happen. If you plan to go camping with family or friends this summer, you need to keep several things in mind for your safety.

Listen to Yumin's family talk about their camping trip. (C)They seem to know what to do to make their camping trip safe and fun.

10 빈칸 (A)에 다음 영영풀이에 해당하는 단어를 알맞은 형으로 쓰시오.

something that you remember from the past

➡ _____

11 밑줄 친 (B)와 같은 의미가 되도록 빈칸을 완성하시오.

they can also be occasions _____ _____ bad things happen

12 밑줄 친 (C)와 같은 의미가 되도록 빈칸을 완성하시오.

It _____ _____ they _____ what to do to make their camping trip safe and fun.

13 What do Yumin's family seem to know? Answer in Korean.

➡ _____
_____

구석구석

Before You Read

Welcome to Our Sky Camping Trip!

We have prepared many activities for the two-day camping trip. Because we
현재완료 용법 중 완료   숫자+단위명사는 단수형으로 쓴다.
always think about your safety first, we do our best to prepare for anything
do one's best: 최선을 다하다 to부정사의 부사적 용법 중 목적(~하기 위하여)
bad that may happen. We help people have a comfortable stay by placing a
help+목적어+(to) 동사원형: ~가 …하도록 돕다   by -ing: ~함으로써
can of bug spray in each tent so you can avoid getting bitten by mosquitoes.
avoid+동명사
We hope everyone takes home good memories of the trip!

구문해설 • **prepare**: 준비하다 • **safety**: 안전 • **happen**: 발생하다 • **comfortable**: 편안한
• **bite**: 물다 • **mosquito**: 모기 • **memory**: 추억, 기억

스카이 캠핑 여행에 오신 것을 환영합니다! 저희는 이틀간의 캠핑 여행을 위해 많은 활동들을 준비했습니다. 저희는 항상 여러분의 안전을 우선으로 생각하기 때문에, 발생할 수 있는 나쁜 일에 대비하기 위해 최선을 다합니다. 저희는 여러분이 모기에 물리는 것을 피할 수 있도록 각각의 텐트에 벌레 퇴치 스프레이를 한 통씩 비치해 둠으로써 여러분이 편안하게 머물도록 돕습니다. 저희는 모든 분들이 여행의 좋은 추억을 집으로 가져가시기를 바랍니다.

Writing Workshop

Although you would think that you are free from an earthquake, that is not
although+주어+동사, 주어+동사(부사절과 주절이 대조를 이룸)
true. Then, what should you do when it strikes? There are several things you
= an earthquake   목적격 관계대명사 that 생략
need to keep in mind. First, stay inside and keep informed until the shaking
stops. It seems to be safe to go outside, but something might fall on you.
= It seems that to go outside is safe. It: 가주어, to go outside: 진주어   = may
Second, turn off the gas and the electricity. Third, get under the table and
cover your head with your arms. It is important to protect your head. Finally,
get과 병렬 관계   가주어   진주어
if you are outside, try to get as far away from buildings, trees, and streetlights
as possible. By following these tips, you can be safe from the earthquake.
by -ing: ~함으로써

구문해설 • **keep in mind**: 명심하다 • **until**: ~할 때까지

비록 여러분이 지진으로부터 자유롭다고 생각할 수 있지만, 사실은 그렇지 않습니다. 그러면 지진이 발생하면 여러분은 무엇을 해야 할까요? 여러분이 명심해야 할 것이 몇 가지 있습니다. 첫째, 흔들림이 멈출 때까지 안에서 머물며 계속 정보를 받아야 합니다. 밖으로 나가는 게 안전해 보이지만 무언가가 여러분에게 떨어질 수도 있습니다. 둘째, 가스와 전기를 끄십시오. 셋째, 테이블 아래로 들어가서 팔로 머리를 감싸세요. 여러분의 머리를 보호하는 것이 중요합니다. 마지막으로, 만일 여러분이 밖에 있다면, 가능한 한 건물이나 나무, 가로등으로부터 멀리 떨어지세요. 이 팁을 따름으로써 여러분은 지진으로부터 안전할 수 있습니다.

Wrap Up

My Camping Trip Diary

Location: Yeongwol   Date: September 12

Traveled with: my family

I went to Yeongwol with my family on September 12.
날짜 앞에는 전치사 on
During the trip, we enjoyed rafting and hiking. Although I was afraid of doing
during+기간을 나타내는 명사
rafting at first, it was really fun and exciting. I'll go rafting again if I have a
chance.

구문해설 • **diary**: 일기 • **location**: 위치, 장소 • **date**: 날짜 • **rafting**: 급류 타기
• **be afraid of**: ~을 무서워하다 • **at first**: 처음에 • **chance**: 기회

나의 캠핑 여행 일기
위치: 영월   날짜: 9월 12일
함께 여행한 사람: 나의 가족
나는 9월 12일에 나의 가족과 함께 영월에 갔다. 여행 중에 우리는 급류 타기와 하이킹을 즐겼다. 나는 처음에 급류 타기를 무서워했지만, 그것은 정말 재미있고 신났다. 기회가 있다면 나는 다시 급류 타기를 하러 갈 것이다.

영역별 핵심문제

01 다음 문장의 빈칸에 알맞은 것은?

> I called the police when I heard a bomb
> _____.

① avoid   ② rub   ③ apply
④ explode   ⑤ happen

02 다음 영영풀이에 해당하는 단어를 쓰시오.

> a plant like a small onion that is used in cooking to give a strong taste

➡ _____

03 다음 빈칸에 공통으로 들어갈 단어를 쓰시오.

> • Kate, _____ this lesson in mind.
> • She told him to do the dishes, so he couldn't _____ watching TV.

➡ _____

04 다음 빈칸에 알맞은 말을 <보기>에서 골라 쓰시오.

> 보기
> up   on   away   out

(1) I often hang _____ with my friends after school.
(2) The fire will use _____ the oxygen in the tent as it burns.
(3) He warned Billy to keep _____ from his daughter.
(4) Before you go out, don't forget to put _____ sunscreen.

05 다음 빈칸에 들어갈 단어를 <보기>에서 골라 쓰시오.

> 보기
> overeat   overuse   overwork

(1) It is not good to _____ computers.
(2) Think of your health and don't _____ yourself.
(3) If you skip breakfast, you tend to _____ at lunch.

[06~08] 다음 대화를 읽고 물음에 답하시오.

> G: Mom, can I play outside this afternoon?
> W: Sure. (A)Don't forget to put on sunscreen before you go out.
> G: But it's cloudy today. _____(B)_____
> W: Yes, you have to __(C)__ sunscreen every day.
> G: Okay. Then I'll put some on now.

06 위 대화의 밑줄 친 (A)를 다음과 같이 바꿔 쓸 때 빈칸에 알맞은 말을 쓰시오.

> _____ to put on sunscreen before you go out.

07 위 대화의 빈칸 (B)에 들어갈 말로 나머지 넷과 의도가 다른 것은?

① Do I have to put on sunscreen?
② Must I put on sunscreen?
③ Should I put on sunscreen?
④ Do I need to put on sunscreen?
⑤ May I put on sunscreen?

08 위 대화의 빈칸 (C)에 위 대화에 나오는 어구와 같은 의미의 단어를 한 단어로 쓰시오.

➡ _____

[09~12] 다음 대화를 읽고 물음에 답하시오.

B: Uncle John, look at my new bike. What do you think?

M: It's really nice. Where are you going?

B: To the park to meet a friend. (①)

M: Where's your helmet?

B: I don't have (A)one. It's just a short ride.

M: Put on your helmet. You may hurt (a)yourself. (②)

B: But I see (b)a lot of people (c)riding bikes without helmets. (③)

M: You have to wear a helmet. It protects your head in an accident. (④)

B: Okay. I'll get my dad's helmet.

M: No. You have to wear a helmet that (d)fits you. (⑤)

B: I guess I'll have to buy one for (e)me.

09 위 대화의 밑줄 친 (A)one이 가리키는 것을 영어로 쓰시오.

➡ _____

10 위 대화의 ①~⑤ 중 주어진 문장이 들어갈 위치로 알맞은 것은?

If not, it cannot protect your head.

①　　　②　　　③　　　④　　　⑤

11 위 대화의 밑줄 친 (a)~(e) 중 어법상 틀린 것은?

① (a)　② (b)　③ (c)　④ (d)　⑤ (e)

12 위 대화의 내용과 일치하지 않는 것은?

① The boy is going to the park to meet a friend.

② The boy doesn't have a helmet.

③ The boy sees many people riding bikes without helmets.

④ The boy got hurt while riding a bike.

⑤ The boy will buy a helmet for himself.

Grammar

13 다음 문장에서 어법상 어색한 부분을 찾아 올바른 문장으로 고쳐 쓰시오.

(1) The tickets seemed to had got lost.

➡ _____

(2) Despite the sun was shining, it wasn't very warm.

➡ _____
_____

(3) The children always seem to are hungry.

➡ _____

(4) Because he's nearly 80, he is still very active.

➡ _____
_____

14 다음 중 어법상 올바른 문장을 고르시오.

① He's the best teacher, even though he has the least experience.

② She never took a taxi, even she could afford to.

③ Because I'm sad, I can't cry in front of them.

④ Even it were free, I wouldn't take it.

⑤ I wouldn't go if I could.

15 우리말과 같은 뜻이 되도록 괄호 안의 단어를 배열하여 영작하시오.

> 저는 그녀가 안 와도 상관없어요. (I로 시작할 것)
> (mind, if, don't, I, even, doesn't, she, come)

➡ _____

16 우리말에 맞게 괄호 안의 단어를 활용하여 영작하시오.

> 부엌이 작긴 하지만 설계가 잘 되어 있다.
> (although로 시작할 것)
> (although, small, well designed)

➡ _____

_____

17 괄호 안의 단어를 활용하여 우리말에 맞게 빈칸을 채우시오.

(1) 그녀는 그런 척하긴 했지만 그를 사랑하지 않았다. (though, love)

➡ She _____ she pretended to.   *pretend to: ~인 척하다

(2) Karen이 올지 확실히 알지 못하지만 Mike는 다음 주에 머무르러 올 것이다. (although, come)

➡ Mike _____ I'm not sure Karen is coming.

18 종속절과 주절 간에 대조적인 의미를 담고 있는 부분을 찾으시오.

> Although he is very young, he acts like an old man.

➡ 종속절: _____
➡ 주절: _____

19 그림을 보고 괄호 안의 단어를 활용하여 다음 빈칸을 채우시오.

> • The turtle _____ to win the race. (happy)
> • The rabbit _____ to lose the race. (sad)

20 괄호 안의 단어를 활용하여 우리말에 맞게 빈칸을 채우시오.

(1) 그는 백만장자임에도 불구하고, 아주 작은 집에서 산다. (millionaire, live in)

➡ Even though he is a _____, he _____ _____ a very small house.

(2) 비가 오고 있기는 하지만 우리는 외출을 했다. (go out, be)

➡ We _____ _____ although it _____ _____.

21 다음 우리말에 맞게 빈칸에 알맞은 말을 〈보기〉에서 고르시오.

> ┤ 보기 ├
> despite   although

> 그는 엉겁결에 웃어버렸다.
> ➡ He had to laugh _____ himself.

[22~25] 다음 글을 읽고 물음에 답하시오.

Yumin: Dad, (A)why don't we put up our tent over here by this river?

Dad: I don't think that's a good idea. If it starts to rain, the river (B)might overflow.

Yumin: I know, but the sky is clear. I really like the sound of the water!

Dad: The weather can change quickly in the mountains. You never know when it might start to rain.

Yumin: Okay. Safety first! Let's find another place.

22 위 글의 밑줄 친 (A)와 같은 뜻이 되도록 다음 문장의 빈칸에 알맞은 말을 쓰시오.

_____ put up our tent over here by this river.

23 위 글의 밑줄 친 ⓑmight와 의미가 다른 것을 모두 고르시오.

① The rumor might be false.

② Might I use your camera?

③ I think that Kathy might be wrong.

④ Jake said that she might use her cell phone.

⑤ Amy said that Ted might be innocent.

24 다음 중 위 글의 내용과 일치하지 않는 것은?

① Yumin wants to put up their tent by this river.

② Yumin's dad agrees to Yumin's idea.

③ Yumin likes the sound of the water.

④ The weather can change quickly in the mountains.

⑤ They will find another place to put up their tent.

25 Why doesn't Yumin's dad think Yumin's idea is good? Answer in Korean.

➡ _____

[26~29] 다음 글을 읽고 물음에 답하시오.

Although you would think that you are free ①from an earthquake, (A)that is not true. Then, what should you do when it strikes? There are several things you need ②to keep in mind. First, stay inside and keep informed __(B)__ the shaking stops. It seems to be safe to go outside, but something might fall on you. Second, turn ③on the gas and the electricity. Third, get ④under the table and cover your head with your arms. It is important to protect your head. Finally, if you are outside, try to get as far away from buildings, trees, and streetlights as possible. By ⑤following these tips, you can be safe from the earthquake.

26 위 글의 밑줄 친 (A)가 구체적으로 가리키는 것을 우리말로 쓰시오.

➡ _____

27 다음 중 빈칸 (B)에 들어갈 말로 가장 적절한 것은?

① if   ② when
③ until   ④ though
⑤ while

28 밑줄 친 ①~⑤ 중 어법상 또는 문맥상 올바르지 <u>않은</u> 것은?

①   ②   ③   ④   ⑤

29 다음 중 지진이 일어날 때 해야 할 행동으로 알맞지 <u>않은</u> 것은?

① 흔들림이 멈출 때까지 집안에 머물며 지진에 대한 정보를 들어야 한다.
② 즉시 집밖으로 나가야 한다.
③ 가스와 전기를 꺼야 한다.
④ 테이블 밑으로 들어가 팔로 머리를 감싸야 한다.
⑤ 밖에 있을 때는 건물들이나 나무들 또는 가로등으로부터 가급적 멀리 떨어져 있어야 한다.

[30~33] 다음 글을 읽고 물음에 답하시오.

> My Camping Trip Diary
> ___(A)___ : Yeongwol
> Date: September 12
> Traveled with: my family
> I went to Yeongwol with my family on September 12. During the trip, we enjoyed rafting and hiking. Although I was afraid of doing rafting ___(B)___, it was really fun and (C)excite. I'll go rafting again if I have a chance.
>
> I=Yumi

30 위 글의 빈칸 (A)에 다음 영영풀이에 해당하는 단어를 쓰시오.

> the place where something happens or is situated

➡ _____

31 다음 중 빈칸 (B)에 들어갈 말로 가장 적절한 것은?

① at first   ② at last
③ above all   ④ in the end
⑤ on the contrary

32 위 글의 밑줄 친 (C)를 알맞은 형으로 고치시오.

➡ _____

33 다음 중 위 글의 내용과 일치하지 <u>않는</u> 것은?

① 유미의 가족은 영월로 캠핑 여행을 갔다.
② 유미의 가족은 9월 12일에 여행을 갔다.
③ 유미는 여행 중에 하이킹을 했다.
④ 급류 타기는 처음에는 무서웠지만, 정말 재미있었다.
⑤ 유미의 가족은 곧 다시 캠핑 여행을 갈 것이다.

출제율 90%

01 다음 짝지어진 단어의 관계가 같도록 빈칸에 알맞은 말을 쓰시오.

> safety : danger = deep : _____

출제율 95%

02 다음 빈칸에 공통으로 들어갈 말을 쓰시오.

(1)

> - They also use _____ our natural resources.
> - They put _____ a tent in the backyard and slept there.

(2)

> - I will _____ in mind your favorite saying, "Think big."
> - Parents should _____ hot pans away from children.

출제율 90%

03 다음 영영풀이에 해당하는 단어를 쓰시오.

> to flow over the edge or top of something

➡ _____

출제율 95%

04 다음 빈칸 (A)와 (B)에 들어갈 말로 알맞은 것끼리 짝지어진 것을 고르시오.

> - I drank coffee (A)_____ tea this morning.
> - (B)_____ she has lots of money, she isn't happy.

① except for – In spite of
② except for – Despite
③ instead of – Although
④ instead of – Despite
⑤ instead of – In spite of

출제율 95%

05 다음 빈칸에 알맞은 단어를 〈보기〉에서 골라 쓰시오.

> ┌── 보기 ──┐
> put   stay   close   try

(1) Always _____ to do your best.
(2) Can I _____ up late tonight?
(3) I'll _____ on sunscreen now.
(4) I went to an aquarium _____ to my house.

출제율 100%

06 다음 중 밑줄 친 부분의 뜻풀이가 바르지 <u>않은</u> 것은?

① My mother washes the dishes in the <u>sink</u>. (싱크대)
② Do not swim here. The water is too <u>deep</u>. (깊은)
③ You have to dress properly for the <u>occasion</u>.(경우, 때)
④ A <u>flooding</u> often destroys animals' shelters. (가뭄)
⑤ I <u>spilled</u> some of the tea when going up the stairs. (흘렸다)

[07~08] 다음 대화를 읽고 물음에 답하시오.

> B: Mina, are you ready to leave?
> G: No, not yet. I have to check if I __(A)__ the gas.
> B: If we don't leave now, we may not __(B)__ to the concert in time.
> G: Okay, but I have to check the gas first. It will only take a minute.

출제율 95%

07 위 대화의 빈칸 (A)에 들어갈 말로 적절한 것은?

① pick up   ② put off
③ turn on   ④ turn down
⑤ turn off

08 위 대화의 빈칸 (B)에 알맞은 것은?

① get   ② make   ③ do

④ have   ⑤ take

[09~11] 다음 대화를 읽고 물음에 답하시오.

B: Here comes the bus!

G: Oh, but first I have to finish (A)drink my tea.

B: Why don't you just take it with you? I'm sure that it will be okay if you are ___(B)___ .

G: No. If the bus stops suddenly, I may spill it.

B: Okay, then I can just wait for you to finish your drink. (C)곧 다른 버스가 올 것이라고 확신해.

G: Thanks.

출제율 90%

09 위 대화의 밑줄 친 (A)를 알맞은 형태로 고쳐 쓰시오.

➡ _____

출제율 95%

10 위 대화의 빈칸 (B)에 들어갈 말로 적절한 것은?

① terrible   ② serious

③ careful   ④ strange

⑤ wonderful

출제율 95%

11 위 대화의 밑줄 친 (C)의 우리말을 주어진 단어를 이용하여 영작하시오. (8 words)

(soon, sure)

➡ _____

[12~14] 다음 글을 읽고 물음에 답하시오.

M: ___(A)___ can ①cause big problems. However, you may not know what to do when it happens. (B)당신이 해야 할 몇 가지 것들이 있습니다. First, you have to ②turn off the water and the electricity. Second, ③unpack water and food when you leave the house. Finally, you have to move to a ④high and safe place and keep listening to the ⑤weather report.

출제율 90%

12 위 글은 어떤 상황에 관한 행동 요령인지 빈칸 (A)에 알맞은 말을 주어진 철자로 시작하여 쓰시오.

➡ F_____

출제율 95%

13 위 글의 밑줄 친 ①~⑤ 중 문맥상 어울리지 않는 것은?

①   ②   ③   ④   ⑤

출제율 95%

14 위 글의 밑줄 친 (B)의 우리말을 주어진 단어를 이용하여 영어로 쓰시오. (8 words)

(several, there, have)

➡ _____

15 보기에서 알맞은 단어를 골라 빈칸을 채우시오.

보기

although   despite

(1) _____ I studied hard, I failed to pass the exam.

(2) _____ the bad weather, we decided to carry out the plan to go on a picnic.

(3) _____ Jay got up early, he left home later than usual.

(4) _____ Jay brought an umbrella, he still got wet.

(5) _____ our worries, everything turned out well.

(6) _____ his cries, no one came to his assistance.

16 괄호 안의 단어를 사용하여 우리말에 맞게 영작하시오.

Jamin은 열심히 공부했지만 시험을 잘 치지 못했다. (study, do well) (although로 시작할 것)

➡ _____

_____

17 다음 중 어색한 문장을 고르시오.

① Although it is cheap, I will really buy it.

② Although I failed the test, I will never give up.

③ Despite hot weather, you are wearing a coat.

④ Although he lost everything, I still love him.

⑤ Despite the recession, demand is growing.

*recession: 불경기

18 괄호 안의 조건과 단어를 활용하여 우리말에 맞게 영작하시오.

(1) 그는 그 시험 결과를 아는 듯이 보인다. (know, test, to부정사 사용)

➡ _____

(2) 그들은 그 시험 결과에 만족하는 듯이 보인다. (satisfied with, it 사용)

➡ _____

(3) 모두 내 얼굴을 보고 있는 듯이 보인다. (everyone, be, it 사용)

➡ _____

(4) Suji는 매일 아침 식사를 하는 것처럼 보인다. (have, to부정사 사용)

➡ _____

[19~22] 다음 글을 읽고 물음에 답하시오.

Hajun: Mom, I'm hungry. (①) What's for lunch?

Mom: I'm cooking Samgyepsal.

Hajun: Mom, that's not enough for all of us. (②)

Mom: I'm going to cook ___(A)___, but we have to use this small pan. (③)

Hajun: Why do we have to use a small pan? (④)

Mom: (⑤) Because the pan should not be ___(B)___ than the burner. If you use a big pan, it sends the heat back to the burner, and the gas can explode!

Hajun: Oh, I didn't know (C)that.

19 위 글의 ①~⑤ 중 다음 주어진 문장이 들어갈 알맞은 곳은?

Can we cook more in a bigger pan?

①　②　③　④　⑤

20 빈칸 (A)에 much, (B)에 big를 어법에 맞게 쓰시오.

(A) _____ (B) _____

21 밑줄 친 (C)that이 가리키는 것을 우리말로 구체적으로 쓰시오.

➡ _____

_____

22 다음 중 위 글의 내용과 일치하지 <u>않는</u> 것은?

① Hajun is hungry now.

② Hajun's mom is cooking Samgyepsal.

③ Hajun's mom has to use a small pan.

④ Hajun's mom isn't going to cook more.

⑤ The burner should be bigger than the pan.

[23~26] 다음 글을 읽고 물음에 답하시오.

_____(A)_____ you would think that you are free from an earthquake, that is not true. Then, what should you do when ⓐit strikes? There are several things you need to keep in mind. First, stay inside and keep informed until the shaking stops. It seems to be safe to go outside, _____(B)_____ something might fall on you. Second, turn off the gas and the electricity. Third, get under the table and cover your head with your arms. It is important to protect your head. Finally, if you are outside, ⓑtry to get as far away from buildings, trees, and streetlights as possible. By following these tips, you can be _____(C)_____ from the earthquake.

23 위 글의 빈칸 (A)와 (B)에 들어갈 말이 알맞게 짝지어진 것은?

① While – or

② If – and

③ Although – but

④ Unless – and

⑤ Because – for

24 다음 중 빈칸 (C)에 들어갈 말로 가장 적절한 것은?

① hurt   ② sick

③ safe   ④ healthy

⑤ dangerous

25 밑줄 친 ⓐit이 가리키는 것을 영어로 쓰시오.

➡ _____

26 밑줄 친 ⓑ와 같은 뜻이 되도록 다음 문장의 빈칸에 알맞은 말을 쓰시오.

> try to get as far away from buildings, trees, and streetlights as _____ _____

[01~04] 다음 대화를 읽고 물음에 답하시오.

B: Uncle John, look at my new bike. What do you think?

M: It's really nice. Where are you going?

B: To the park to meet a friend.

M: Where's your helmet?

B: I don't have one. It's just a short ride.

M: _____ (A) _____ your helmet. You may hurt yourself.

B: But (B)저는 헬멧 없이 자전거 타는 많은 사람들을 봐요.

M: You have to wear a helmet. It protects your head in an accident.

01 위 대화의 빈칸 (A)에 다음 영영풀이에 해당하는 말을 두 단어로 쓰시오.

> to have something on your body as clothing, decoration, or protection

➡ _____

02 위 대화의 밑줄 친 (B)의 우리말과 같도록 주어진 어구를 바르게 배열하시오.

> bikes / see / people / without / a lot of / helmets / I / riding

➡ _____

03 Why is the boy going to the park?

➡ _____

04 Write the reason why you have to wear a helmet when riding a bike. Answer in English

➡ _____

05 seem과 괄호 안의 단어를 활용하여 문장을 완성하시오.

(1) 그들은 서로를 사랑하는 것 같다. (love)

➡ _____

➡ _____

(2) 그들은 서로를 사랑했던 것 같다. (loved)

➡ _____

➡ _____

(3) Reina는 집에 고양이 한 마리를 키우는 것처럼 보인다. (raise)

➡ _____

➡ _____

(4) Reina는 집에 고양이 한 마리를 키웠던 것처럼 보인다. (raised)

➡ _____

➡ _____

06 그림을 보고 〈보기〉의 단어를 활용하여 빈칸을 채우시오.

(1)

> ┌ 보기 ┐
> although   headache

• _____ he slept well last night, he _____ _____ _____.

• He _____ _____ _____ he slept well last night.

(2)

보기
seem   prepare

- They _____ the food.
- It _____ the food.

[07~10] 다음 글을 읽고 물음에 답하시오.

My Camping Trip Diary

Location: Yangpyeong
Date: May 10
Traveled with: middle school friends
I went to Yangpyeong with my friends on May 10. (A)(During, While) the trip, we baked potatoes, and played a board game. Although we tried to stay ___(B)___ all night, we were not able to do it. (C)나는 우리가 얼마나 즐겁게 지냈는지 결코 잊지 못할 것이다.

I=Yumin

07 괄호 (A)에서 알맞은 것을 고르시오.

➡ _____

08 빈칸 (B)에 알맞은 부사를 쓰시오.

➡ _____

09 밑줄 친 우리말 (C)를 주어진 어구를 이용해서 영어로 옮기시오.

never, how, fun, have

➡ _____

10 According to the passage, what did they bake? Answer in English with a full sentence.

➡ _____

[11~13] 다음 글을 읽고 물음에 답하시오.

Yumin: Ouch! Mosquitoes!
Mom: Oh, I forgot (A)(telling, to tell) you to apply some bug spray. Here.
Yumin: Thanks, Mom. Oh, you know what? We can rub orange peels on our skin instead of (B)apply bug spray. It is a nature-friendly way to keep mosquitoes away.
Mom: That's interesting!
  Garlic can also keep bugs away. You can place pieces of garlic at the ___(C)___ to the tent, and bugs will not come inside.

11 괄호 (A)에서 알맞은 것을 고르시오.

➡ _____

12 밑줄 친 (B)apply를 알맞은 형으로 고치시오.

➡ _____

13 빈칸 (C)에 다음 영영풀이에 해당하는 단어를 쓰시오.

the way into a place, for example a door or gate

➡ _____

01 다음 표를 참고하여 구매 후기를 완성하시오.

What I bought	a pair of running shoes
What I like about the product	They are very comfortable, so I wear them often.
What I don't like about the product	The color is white, so they get dirty easily.
Stars	( ) not satisfied (✓) satisfied ★★★★☆

A Pair of Running Shoes

This is what I bought. I'd like to begin with ＿＿＿＿＿＿＿＿＿＿. ＿＿＿＿＿＿＿

＿＿＿＿＿＿＿＿＿＿＿＿＿＿＿. Now, let me write ＿＿＿＿＿＿＿＿＿＿＿＿ .

＿＿＿＿＿＿＿＿＿＿＿＿＿＿＿＿＿. All in all, I'm ＿＿＿＿＿＿ the shoes,

and I give the product ＿＿＿＿＿＿＿ .

02 다음은 학교에서 지켜야 할 규칙에 대해 열거되어 있다. 그림을 참고하여 순서에 맞게 문장을 배열하시오.

(1) First, do not just leave your bag on the floor.

(2) Here are three safety rules you should follow at school.

(3) You might fall and hurt yourself.

(4) Someone can trip over it.

(5) You might bump into someone.

(6) Second, do not run in the hallway.

(7) Third, do not jump on desks or chairs.

(8) Keep these rules in mind so that everyone can be safe.

단원별 모의고사

01 다음 빈칸에 공통으로 들어갈 말을 쓰시오.

> • They _____ up hidden cameras.
> • She _____ sunscreen on her face.

➡ _____

[02~03] 다음 주어진 영어 설명에 해당하는 어휘를 빈칸에 쓰시오.

02

> Try not to _____ the medication.

> <영어 설명> to use something too much or too often

03

> I slipped and fell on a banana _____.

> <영어 설명> the skin of a fruit

04 다음 중 <보기>에 있는 단어를 사용하여 자연스러운 문장을 만들 수 없는 것은?

> ┤ 보기 ├
> avoid   pan   memory   flat

① The earth is not _____.
② Pour milk into the _____ and boil it.
③ As it is raining a lot, the river can _____.
④ Tell me about one happy _____ you have.
⑤ We have to hurry up to _____ rush hour.

05 다음 주어진 문장 다음에 이어질 대화의 순서를 바르게 배열하시오.

> Mom, can I play outside this afternoon?

(A) Okay. Then I'll put some on now.
(B) But it's cloudy today. Do I have to put on sunscreen?
(C) Sure. Don't forget to put on sunscreen before you go out.
(D) Yes, you have to wear sunscreen every day.

➡ _____

[06~08] 다음 글을 읽고 물음에 답하시오.

> M: Flooding can _____(A)_____ big problems. However, you may not know what to do when it happens. There are several things you have to do. First, you have to turn off the water and the electricity. Second, pack water and food when you leave the house. Finally, you have to move to a high and safe place and keep (B)listen to the weather report.

06 위 글의 빈칸 (A)에 다음 영영풀이에 해당하는 단어를 쓰시오.(주어진 철자로 시작할 것)

> to make something happen or exist

➡ c_____

07 위 글의 밑줄 친 (B)listen을 알맞은 형태로 고쳐 쓰시오.

➡ _____

08 홍수가 발생했을 때, 행동 요령 세 가지를 우리말로 쓰시오.

➡ _____

_____

_____

09 다음 빈칸에 공통으로 들어갈 단어를 고르시오. (대·소문자 무시)

> • I'll get there _____ if I have to walk.
> • _____ though he lied to me, I still trust him.

① as ② although ③ despite

④ even ⑤ in

10 다음 빈칸에 들어갈 알맞은 것을 고르시오.

> Even though I _____ in the USA, I'm having a hard time speaking English.

① live ② lived

③ doesn't live ④ have lived

⑤ had lived

11 다음 우리말에 맞게 빈칸에 알맞은 말을 쓰시오.

(1) 나는 바가지를 쓴 것 같아요.

➡ I _____ _____ be overcharged.

(2) 네 방은 더러워 보인다.

➡ Your room _____ _____ be dirty.

(3) 비록 여행은 짧았지만 나는 잊을 수 없는 많은 추억을 만들었다.

➡ _____ it was a short trip, I made many unforgettable memories.

(4) 우리는 밤을 꼬박 새려고 했지만 그렇게 할 수 없었다.

➡ _____ we tried to stay up all night, we were not able to do it.

12 even if를 사용하여 (A)와 (B)의 문장을 연결해 문장을 완성하시오.

> (A)
> • He gets accepted to Harvard.
> • You should always exercise.
> • The government survives this crisis.
> • He's going to buy the farm.

> (B)
> • He won't be able to afford the tuition.
> • It's only 10 minutes a day.
> • They still face big problems.
> • The government raises the price.
>
> *tuition: 수업료

➡ _____

➡ _____

➡ _____

➡ _____

13 다음 중 어법상 어색한 것은?

① Even if he lies again, I'll forgive him.

② Even though she lied to me, we are still good friends.

③ His grades were up despite his bad behavior.

④ Despite she is beautiful, she lacks intellectual beauty.

⑤ I still look fat, even though I've been exercising regularly.

14 우리말에 맞게 괄호 안의 단어를 배열하시오.

> 미국에서 태어났지만 그는 대한민국의 아들이다.
> (he, he, even though, born, was, America, in, is, son, Korean, a) (even though로 시작할 것)

➡ _____

_____

15 다음 그림을 보고 괄호 안의 단어를 활용하여 빈칸을 채우시오.

> Although my mom _____ _____ (try) iron, it didn't work well. The iron seems _____ _____ _____ (be) broken.

[16~19] 다음 글을 읽고 물음에 답하시오.

> Listen to Yumin's family ①talk about their camping trip. They seem to know __(A)__ to do to make their camping trip ②safely and fun.
>
> **Yumin:** Dad, __(B)__ don't we put up our tent over here by this river?
>
> **Dad:** I don't think that's a good idea. If it starts ③to rain, the river might overflow.
>
> **Yumin:** I know, but the sky is clear. I really like the sound of the water!
>
> **Dad:** The weather can change ④quickly in the mountains. You never know when it might start to rain.

> **Yumin:** Okay. Safety first! Let's find ⑤another place.
>
> When you set up a tent, choose a flat, (C)sun area. Avoid places too close to big trees that might be struck by lightning.

16 밑줄 친 ①~⑤ 중 어법상 어색한 것은?

①   ②   ③   ④   ⑤

17 다음 중 빈칸 (A)와 (B)에 알맞은 것으로 짝지어진 것은?

① what – why   ② when – how

③ when – why   ④ which – what

⑤ what – how

18 밑줄 친 (C)를 알맞은 형으로 고치시오.

➡ _____

19 According to the passage, why should we avoid places too close to big trees? Answer in English by beginning with 'because'. (7 words)

➡ _____

[20~23] 다음 글을 읽고 물음에 답하시오.

> **Yumin:** Ouch! Mosquitoes! (①)
> **Mom:** (②) Oh, I forgot to tell you to apply some bug spray. Here.
> **Yumin:** Thanks, Mom. (③) We can rub orange peels on our skin instead ___(A)___ applying bug spray. It is a nature-friendly way ⓐto keep mosquitoes away. (④)
> **Mom:** (⑤) ⓑThat's interesting!
>
> Garlic can also keep bugs away. You can place pieces ___(B)___ garlic at the entrance to the tent, and bugs will not come inside.

20 위 글의 ①~⑤ 중 다음 주어진 문장이 들어갈 알맞은 곳은?

> Oh, you know what?

①   ②   ③   ④   ⑤

21 위 글의 빈칸 (A)와 (B)에 공통으로 알맞은 전치사를 쓰시오.

➡ _____

22 밑줄 친 ⓐto keep과 용법이 같은 것은?

① I want to learn Chinese culture.
② Is there anything to eat in the fridge?
③ Were you glad to hear the news?
④ Love is to trust each other.
⑤ Her daughter grew up to be an actress.

23 밑줄 친 ⓑThat이 가리키는 것을 우리말로 쓰시오.

➡ _____
_____

[24~26] 다음 글을 읽고 물음에 답하시오.

> **Welcome to Our Sky Camping Trip!**
> We have prepared many activities for the ① two-days camping trip. Because we always think about your safety first, we do our best to prepare for ②anything bad that (A)may happen. We help people have a comfortable stay by ③placing a can of bug spray in each tent ___(B)___ you can avoid ④getting bitten by mosquitoes. We hope everyone takes ⑤home good memories of the trip!

24 밑줄 친 ①~⑤ 중 어법상 어색한 것은?

①   ②   ③   ④   ⑤

25 다음 중 밑줄 친 (A)may와 같은 용법으로 쓰인 것은?

① You may come in if you wish.
② May she rest in peace!
③ The rumor may be false.
④ May I take a picture here?
⑤ You may stay at this hotel for a week.

26 빈칸 (B)에 알맞은 것은?

① in   ② to
③ with   ④ so
⑤ for

Special

Coach Carter

교과서

Words & Expressions

Key Words

- **accept** [əksépt] 동 받아들이다
- **actually** [ǽktʃuəli] 부 실제로, 정말로
- **allow** [əláu] 동 허락하다
- **attend** [əténd] 동 참석하다
- **bonus** [bóunəs] 명 보너스, 상여금
- **care** [kɛər] 동 마음을 쓰다, 걱정하다
- **championship** [tʃǽmpiənʃip] 명 선수권 대회, 챔피언전
- **coach** [koutʃ] 명 (스포츠 팀의) 코치
- **college** [kálidʒ] 명 대학
- **contract** [kántrækt] 명 계약, 계약서
- **decide** [disáid] 동 결정하다
- **decision** [disíʒən] 명 결정, 판단
- **demand** [dimǽnd] 명 요구
- **disappointed** [dìsəpɔ́intid] 형 실망한, 낙담한
- **either** [íːðər] 부 (부정문에서) 역시, 또한
- **eventually** [ivéntʃuəli] 부 결국, 마침내
- **exactly** [igzǽktli] 부 정확히
- **except** [iksépt] 전 ~을 제외하고
- **famous** [féiməs] 형 유명한
- **follow** [fálou] 동 (충고·지시 등을) 따르다
- **future** [fjúːtʃər] 명 미래
- **grade** [greid] 명 성적
- **gym** [dʒim] 명 체육관

- **happen** [hǽpən] 동 일어나다, 발생하다
- **hard** [hɑːrd] 부 열심히 형 힘든, 어려운
- **imagine** [imǽdʒin] 동 상상하다
- **improve** [imprúːv] 동 향상하다, 향상시키다
- **life** [laif] 명 인생, 삶
- **lock** [lɑk] 동 잠그다
- **lose** [luːz] 동 지다, 패하다
- **order** [ɔ́ːrdər] 동 명령하다
- **pack** [pækt] 동 (짐을) 싸다, 꾸리다
- **part** [pɑːrt] 명 역할, 부분
- **plan** [plæn] 명 계획 동 계획하다
- **practice** [prǽktis] 동 연습하다
- **principal** [prínsəpəl] 명 교장
- **promise** [prámis] 동 약속하다
- **realize** [ríːəlàiz] 동 깨닫다, 알아차리다
- **refuse** [rifjúːz] 동 거절하다
- **reopen** [ríóupən] 동 다시 문을 열다, 다시 시작하다
- **rule** [ruːl] 명 규칙
- **send** [send] 동 보내다, 발송하다
- **seriously** [síəriəsli] 부 심각하게
- **sign** [sain] 동 서명하다
- **win** [win] 동 이기다, 얻다
- **winner** [wínər] 명 승리자

Key Expressions

- **A as well as B** B뿐만 아니라 A도
- **become used to -ing** ~하는 데 익숙해지다
- **by -ing** ~함으로써
- **carry out** 이행하다, 수행하다
- **find out** ~을 찾아보다
- **for the first time** 처음으로
- **from that point on** 그때 이후로

- **game after game** 경기마다
- **how+to부정사** ~하는 방법
- **in addition to** 게다가, ~에 더하여
- **one after another** 잇따라서
- **pay attention to** ~에 유의하다, ~에 관심을 가지다
- **take action** 조치를 취하다
- **to make matters worse** 설상가상으로

Word Power

※ 서로 반대되는 뜻을 가진 어휘

- □ **win** (이기다) ↔ **lose** (지다)
- □ **future** (미래) ↔ **past** (과거)

- □ **pack** ((짐을) 꾸리다) ↔ **unpack** ((짐을) 풀다)
- □ **lock** (잠그다) ↔ **unlock** (열다)

※ 서로 비슷한 뜻을 가진 어휘

- □ **famous** (유명한) – **well-known** (유명한, 잘 알려진)
- □ **refuse** (거절하다) – **reject** (거절하다)
- □ **actually** (정말로) – **really** (정말로)
- □ **exactly** (정확히) – **correctly** (정확하게)

- □ **hard** (어려운) – **difficult** (어려운)
- □ **allow** (허락하다) – **permit** (허락하다)
- □ **eventually** (결국, 마침내) – **finally** (결국, 마침내)
- □ **order** (명령하다) – **command** (명령하다)

English Dictionary

- □ **attend** 참석하다
  → to go to and be present at an event, meeting, etc.
  행사, 모임 등에 참석하다

- □ **bonus** 상여금, 보너스
  → an extra amount of money that is given to an employee
  고용인에게 주는 가외의 돈

- □ **coach** (스포츠 팀의) 코치
  → a person who teaches and trains an athlete
  운동선수를 가르치고 훈련시키는 사람

- □ **contract** 계약서
  → a document on which the words of a contract are written
  계약의 내용을 적은 서류

- □ **demand** 요구
  → a forceful statement in which you say that something must be done or given to you
  어떤 것을 해야 한다거나 받아야 한다는 강력한 주장

- □ **gym** 체육관
  → a room or hall with equipment for doing physical exercise, for example in a school
  예를 들어 학교에서 운동할 수 있는 장비가 있는 방이나 홀

- □ **improve** 향상시키다
  → to make something better
  어떤 것을 더 나아지게 하다

- □ **order** 명령하다
  → to use your authority to tell someone to do something
  권위를 사용하여 누군가에게 어떤 일을 하라고 시키다

- □ **pack** (짐을) 꾸리다, 싸다
  → to put something into a bag, suitcase, etc., so that you can take it with you
  어떤 것을 가져갈 수 있도록 가방, 여행 가방 등에 넣다

- □ **principal** 교장
  → the person in charge of a school or college
  학교나 대학의 책임자

- □ **refuse** 거절하다
  → to say that you will not do something that someone has asked you to do
  누군가가 부탁한 일을 하지 않겠다고 말하다

- □ **rule** 규칙
  → a statement that tells you what is or is not allowed in a particular game, situation, etc.
  특정한 게임, 상황 등에서 할 수 있는 일과 할 수 없는 일을 알려 주는 말

- □ **sign** 서명하다
  → to write your name on something
  어떤 것에 이름을 쓰다

- □ **win** 이기다
  → to achieve victory in a fight, contest, game, etc.
  싸움, 시합, 경기 등에서 승리를 거두다

Reading

Coach Carter

Welcome to *Movie Trip*. Today we're going to talk about the movie *Coach Carter*. Can you imagine a basketball coach who doesn't allow his players to practice? That's exactly what Coach Carter does. This moive is about a coach who cares more about his students than about winning games.

The basketball team at Richmond High School in Richmond, California, was having one losing season after another. The players became used to losing. To make matters worse, they had no plans for the future; they went to school only to play baskeball, and they did not do that very well. Then they got a new coach, Kenny Carter. Coach Carter wanted to change things. He wanted to teach kids how to play basketball well and win. But more than that, he wanted to give the players a future by sending them to college.

To carry out his plan, Coach Carter had the players sign a contract. They had to promise to study hard in addition to playing basketball. At first, students did not take his idea for a contract seriously.

coach (스포츠 팀의) 코치
allow 허락하다
exactly 정확하게
care 마음을 쓰다. 걱정하다
send 보내다. 발송하다
college 대학
sign 서명하다
contract 계약서
promise 약속하다
seriously 심각하게

확인문제

● 다음 문장이 본문의 내용과 일치하면 T, 일치하지 <u>않으면</u> F를 쓰시오.

1 The name of the movie program is *Movie Trip*. ☐

2 The basketball team at Richmond High School kept winning. ☐

3 Before the new coach came, the players were used to losing. ☐

4 The players went to school to study hard for their future. ☐

5 Coach Carter had the players sign a contract to carry out his plan. ☐

6 The players took Carter's idea for a contract seriously. ☐

Carter: I'm going to give you a contract.

Cruz: "Attend all classes," "Get a C⁺ or higher," "Don't be late...."
부정명령문: Don't[Never]+동사원형 ~
What are all these rules about? Do I get a signing bonus for
전치사+동명사
signing this contract?

Carter: Yes. You will get a big bonus because you will become a
접속사: ~ 때문에
winner in the game of basketball as well as in the game of life.
A as well as B: B뿐만 아니라 A도
With hard work and a new game plan, the team began to win for
~으로 인해
the first time in many years. From that point on, they won game
그때 이후로   경기마다
after game. Everybody, except Coach Carter, was happy. The players
did not do the "study" part of their contract. Few of them actually
부정의 의미
believed∧they could go to college, so they paid little attention to their
접속사 that 생략   pay attention to: ~에 관심을 가지다
grades. Carter decided to take stronger action.
조치를 취하다
He locked the gym and refused to let them play basketball until their
사역동사+목적어+동사원형: ~가 …하도록 허락하다
grades improved, as promised in the contract. The players did not like
~한 대로
it. They told him that his actions were just for him, not for them.
명사절을 이끄는 접속사 that   = Carter   = the players

attend 참석하다

rule 규칙

bonus 상여금, 보너스

except ~을 제외하고

actually 실제로, 정말로

grade 성적

lock 잠그다

gym 체육관

refuse 거절하다

until ~할 때까지

improve 향상하다

📎 **확인문제**

● 다음 문장이 본문의 내용과 일치하면 T, 일치하지 <u>않으면</u> F를 쓰시오.

1 Coach Carter was not happy when the team won game after game. ☐

2 Most of the players believed they could go to college. ☐

3 The players paid much attention to their grades. ☐

4 Coach Carter didn't allow the players to play basketball until their grades improved. ☐

5 The players complained when Coach Carter locked the gym. ☐

Worm: We're the basketball team. All∧we see is you on TV, getting famous.

Carter: If you think so, go home and ask yourself, "Do I want a better life?" If the answer is yes, I will do everything in my power to help you. But you have to do your part.

The players' parents did not like Carter's decision either. At the parents' demand, the principal ordered Carter to reopen the gym. Disappointed, Carter decided to leave Richmond High. When he entered the gym to pack his things, however, all of his players were there.

We want you to enjoy the movie, so we won't tell you what happens next. Find out for yourself by watching the movie *Coach Carter*.

---

famous 유명한
part 역할
decision 결정. 판단
demand 요구
principal 교장
order 명령하다
gym 체육관
pack (짐을) 싸다

확인문제

● 다음 문장이 본문의 내용과 일치하면 T, 일치하지 <u>않으면</u> F를 쓰시오.

1   Carter required the players to do their part. ☐

2   Both the players and their parents did not like Carter's decision. ☐

3   At the parents' demand, the principal forced the players to take more classes. ☐

4   Satisfied with the result, Carter decided to leave Richmond High. ☐

5   When Carter entered the gym to pack his things, only the parents were there. ☐

● 우리말을 참고하여 빈칸에 알맞은 말을 쓰시오.

1 ＿＿＿＿＿＿ ＿＿＿＿＿ *Movie Trip.*

2 Today we're ＿＿＿＿＿ ＿＿＿＿＿ ＿＿＿＿＿ about the movie *Coach Carter.*

3 Can you ＿＿＿＿＿ a basketball coach who doesn't ＿＿＿＿＿ his players ＿＿＿＿＿ ＿＿＿＿＿?

4 That's exactly ＿＿＿＿＿ Coach Carter ＿＿＿＿＿.

5 This movie is about a coach who ＿＿＿＿＿ more ＿＿＿＿＿ his students than ＿＿＿＿＿ ＿＿＿＿＿ ＿＿＿＿＿.

6 The basketball team at Richmond High School in Richmond, California, was having ＿＿＿＿＿ losing season ＿＿＿＿＿ ＿＿＿＿＿.

7 The players ＿＿＿＿＿ ＿＿＿＿＿ ＿＿＿＿＿ ＿＿＿＿＿.

8 ＿＿＿＿＿ ＿＿＿＿＿ matters ＿＿＿＿＿, they had no plans for the future; they went to school ＿＿＿＿＿ ＿＿＿＿＿ ＿＿＿＿＿ basketball, and they did not do that very well.

9 Then they got a ＿＿＿＿＿ ＿＿＿＿＿, Kenny Carter.

10 Coach Carter wanted ＿＿＿＿＿ ＿＿＿＿＿ things.

11 He wanted to teach kids ＿＿＿＿＿ ＿＿＿＿＿ ＿＿＿＿＿ basketball well and win.

12 But ＿＿＿＿＿ ＿＿＿＿＿ that, he wanted to give the players a future ＿＿＿＿＿ ＿＿＿＿＿ them to college.

13 ＿＿＿＿＿ ＿＿＿＿＿ ＿＿＿＿＿ his plan, Coach Carter had the players sign a ＿＿＿＿＿.

1 「영화 여행」에 오신 것을 환영합니다.

2 오늘 우리는 영화 「코치 카터」에 대해 이야기할 것입니다.

3 선수들이 연습하는 것을 허락하지 않는 농구 코치를 상상할 수 있나요?

4 그것이 바로 카터 코치가 한 것입니다.

5 이 영화는 경기에서 이기는 것보다 학생들을 더 걱정하는 코치에 대한 영화입니다.

6 캘리포니아 리치몬드 지역의 리치몬드 고등학교 농구 팀은 연속해서 경기에서 지고 있었습니다.

7 선수들도 지는 것에 익숙하게 되었습니다.

8 설상가상으로 그들은 미래에 대한 계획도 없었습니다. 즉, 그들은 단지 농구하기 위해 학교에 갔고, 그것마저도 잘하지 못했습니다.

9 그때 그들은 케니 카터라는 새로운 코치를 선임했습니다.

10 카터 코치는 몇 가지를 바꾸고자 했습니다.

11 그는 아이들에게 어떻게 농구를 잘하고 이기는지를 가르치기를 원했습니다.

12 그러나 그것보다도, 그는 그들을 대학에 보냄으로써 선수들에게 미래를 주기를 원했습니다.

13 그의 계획을 실행하기 위해서, 카터 코치는 선수들에게 계약서에 서명하게 했습니다.

14 They _____ _____ promise to study hard _____ _____ _____ playing basketball.

15 _____ _____, students did not take his idea for a contract _____.

16 Carter: I'm going to _____ _____ _____ _____.

17 Cruz: "_____ all classes," "Get a C⁺ or higher," "Don't _____ _____…."

18 What are _____ _____ _____ about?

19 Do I get a _____ _____ for signing this contract?

20 Carter: Yes. You will get a big bonus _____ you will become a winner in the game of basketball _____ _____ _____ in the game of life.

21 _____ hard work and a new game plan, the team began to win for the first time _____ _____ _____.

22 _____ that _____ _____, they won game _____ game.

23 Everybody, _____ Coach Carter, was happy.

24 The players did not do the "study" _____ _____ their contract.

25 _____ _____ them actually believed they could go to college, so they _____ _____ _____ _____ their grades.

26 Carter decided to _____ stronger _____.

27 He locked the gym and refused to _____ them _____ basketball _____ their grades _____, _____ promised in the contract.

---

14 그들은 농구를 하는 것뿐만 아니라 열심히 공부할 것도 약속해야만 했습니다.

15 처음에는 학생들이 계약서에 대한 그의 생각을 심각하게 받아들이지 않았습니다.

16 카터: 내가 너희들에게 계약서를 줄 것이다.

17 크루즈: "모든 수업에 출석하라." "C 플러스 또는 그 이상 받아라." "지각하지 말아라."

18 이 모든 규칙들은 무엇이죠?

19 제가 이 계약서에 사인하면 사이닝 보너스를 받나요?

20 카터: 그래. 너는 큰 보너스를 받게 될 거야. 왜냐하면 인생의 게임에서뿐 아니라 농구 경기에서도 승리자가 될 것이기 때문이지.

21 맹연습과 새로운 경기 전략으로 그 팀은 몇 년 만에 처음으로 이기기 시작했습니다.

22 그때 이후로 경기마다 이겼습니다.

23 카터 코치를 제외한 모든 이들이 행복했습니다.

24 선수들은 그들 계약의 '학습' 부분을 하지 않았습니다.

25 그들 중 정말 그들이 대학을 갈 수 있다고 믿는 사람들은 거의 없었습니다. 그래서 그들은 성적에는 거의 관심을 두지 않았습니다.

26 카터는 더 강력한 조치를 취하기로 결심했습니다.

27 그는 체육관 문을 잠그고 계약서에서 약속한 대로 그들의 성적이 좋아질 때까지 농구를 못하게 했습니다.

28 The players did not like _____.

29 They told him _____ his actions were _____ for him, _____ for them.

30 Worm: We're the _____ _____.

31 _____ _____ _____ is you on TV, getting famous.

32 Carter: _____ you think so, go home and ask _____, "Do I want a _____ _____?"

33 If the answer is yes, I will do everything in my power _____ _____ you.

34 But you _____ _____ do your part.

35 The players' parents did not like Carter's decision _____.

36 At the parents' _____, the principal _____ Carter _____ _____ the gym.

37 _____, Carter _____ _____ leave Richmond High.

38 _____ he entered the gym _____ _____ his things, however, all of his players _____ there.

39 We want you to enjoy the movie, so we won't tell you _____ _____ _____.

40 _____ _____ for yourself _____ _____ the movie *Coach Carter*.

28 선수들은 그것을 좋아하지 않았습니다.

29 그들은 그에게 그의 행동들이 그들을 위한 것이 아닌 단지 카터 자신을 위한 것이라고 말했습니다.

30 웜: 우리는 농구 팀이에요.

31 우리가 보는 모든 것은 유명세를 타며 TV에 있는 당신이에요.

32 카터: 네가 그렇게 생각한다면, 집으로 가서 너 자신에게 물어봐. "나는 더 나은 삶을 원하는가?"

33 대답이 '맞다'라면, 나는 너를 돕기 위해 내 힘이 닿는 한 모든 것을 할 거야.

34 그러나 너는 네 역할을 해야만 해.

35 선수들의 부모들 역시 카터의 결정을 좋아하지 않았습니다.

36 부모들의 요구에 따라 교장은 카터에게 체육관을 다시 열도록 했습니다.

37 실망한 카터는 리치몬드 고등학교를 떠나기로 결심했습니다.

38 그가 짐을 싸기 위해 체육관으로 들어섰을 때, 그의 선수들 모두가 그곳에 있었습니다.

39 우리는 여러분이 이 영화를 즐기기 원합니다. 그래서 당신에게 다음에 무슨 일이 일어나는지 이야기하지 않을 것입니다.

40 영화 「코치 카터」를 보고 스스로 찾아보세요.

● 우리말을 참고하여 본문을 영작하시오.

1 「영화 여행」에 오신 것을 환영합니다.

➡ _____

2 오늘 우리는 영화 「코치 카터」에 대해 이야기할 것입니다.

➡ _____

3 선수들이 연습하는 것을 허락하지 않는 농구 코치를 상상할 수 있나요?

➡ _____

4 그것이 바로 카터 코치가 한 것입니다.

➡ _____

5 이 영화는 경기에서 이기는 것보다 학생들을 더 걱정하는 코치에 대한 영화입니다.

➡ _____

6 캘리포니아 리치몬드 지역의 리치몬드 고등학교 농구 팀은 연속해서 경기에서 지고 있었습니다.

➡ _____

_____

7 선수들도 지는 것에 익숙하게 되었습니다.

➡ _____

8 설상가상으로 그들은 미래에 대한 계획도 없었습니다. 즉, 그들은 단지 농구하기 위해 학교에 갔고, 그것마저도 잘하지 못했습니다.

➡ _____

_____

9 그때 그들은 케니 카터라는 새로운 코치를 선임했습니다.

➡ _____

10 카터 코치는 몇 가지를 바꾸고자 했습니다.

➡ _____

11 그는 아이들에게 어떻게 농구를 잘하고 이기는지를 가르치기를 원했습니다.

➡ _____

12 그러나 그것보다도, 그는 그들을 대학에 보냄으로써 선수들에게 미래를 주기를 원했습니다.

➡ _____

13 그의 계획을 실행하기 위해서, 카터 코치는 선수들에게 계약서에 서명하게 했습니다.

➡ _____

14 그들은 농구를 하는 것뿐만 아니라 열심히 공부할 것도 약속해야만 했습니다.

➡ _____

15 처음에는 학생들이 계약서에 대한 그의 생각을 심각하게 받아들이지 않았습니다.

➡ _____

16 카터: 내가 너희들에게 계약서를 줄 것이다.

➡ _____

17 크루즈: "모든 수업에 출석하라," "C 플러스 또는 그 이상 받아라," "지각하지 말아라."

➡ _____

18 이 모든 규칙들은 무엇이죠?

➡ _____

19 제가 이 계약서에 사인하면 사이닝 보너스를 받나요?

➡ _____

20 카터: 그래. 너는 큰 보너스를 받게 될 거야. 왜냐하면 인생의 게임에서뿐 아니라 농구 경기에서도 승리자가 될 것이기 때문이지.

➡ _____

_____

21 맹연습과 새로운 경기 전략으로 그 팀은 몇 년 만에 처음으로 이기기 시작했습니다.

➡ _____

22 그때 이후로 경기마다 이겼습니다.

➡ _____

23 카터 코치를 제외한 모든 이들이 행복했습니다.

➡ _____

24 선수들은 그들 계약의 '학습' 부분을 하지 않았습니다.

➡ _____

25 그들 중 정말 그들이 대학을 갈 수 있다고 믿는 사람들은 거의 없었습니다. 그래서 그들은 성적에는 거의 관심을 두지 않았습니다.

➡ _____

_____

26 카터는 더 강력한 조치를 취하기로 결심했습니다.

➡ _____

27 그는 체육관 문을 잠그고 계약서에서 약속한 대로 그들의 성적이 좋아질 때까지 농구를 못하게 했습니다.

➡ _____

_____

28 선수들은 그것을 좋아하지 않았습니다.

➡ _____

29 그들은 그에게 그의 행동들이 그들을 위한 것이 아닌 단지 카터 자신을 위한 것이라고 말했습니다.

➡ _____

30 윔: 우리는 농구 팀이에요.

➡ _____

31 우리가 보는 모든 것은 유명세를 타며 TV에 있는 당신이에요.

➡ _____

32 카터: 네가 그렇게 생각한다면, 집으로 가서 너 자신에게 물어봐. "나는 더 나은 삶을 원하는가?"

➡ _____

33 대답이 '맞다'라면, 나는 너를 돕기 위해 내 힘이 닿는 한 모든 것을 할 거야.

➡ _____

34 그러나 너는 네 역할을 해야만 해.

➡ _____

35 선수들의 부모들 역시 카터의 결정을 좋아하지 않았습니다.

➡ _____

36 부모들의 요구에 따라 교장은 카터에게 체육관을 다시 열도록 했습니다.

➡ _____

37 실망한 카터는 리치몬드 고등학교를 떠나기로 결심했습니다.

➡ _____

38 그가 짐을 싸기 위해 체육관으로 들어섰을 때, 그의 선수들 모두가 그곳에 있었습니다.

➡ _____

39 우리는 여러분이 이 영화를 즐기기 원합니다. 그래서 당신에게 다음에 무슨 일이 일어나는지 이야기하지 않을 것입니다.

➡ _____

40 영화 「코치 카터」를 보고 스스로 찾아보세요.

➡ _____

01 다음 짝지어진 단어의 관계가 같도록 빈칸에 알맞은 말을 쓰시오.

win : lose = lock : _____

02 다음 문장의 빈칸에 들어갈 말을 〈보기〉에서 골라 쓰시오.

┌─ 보기 ─┐
take action / one after another /
carry out / for the first time

(1) Jane visited Korea _____.
(2) We should _____ his plans immediately.
(3) The company will _____ to prevent further damage.
(4) Many animals died _____.

03 다음 우리말에 맞게 빈칸에 알맞은 말을 쓰시오.

(1) 그는 즉시 그 문서에 서명해야 한다.
➡ He has to _____ the document immediately.
(2) 당신은 계약서에서 세부사항을 확인할 수 있다.
➡ You can see the details in the _____.
(3) 그 식당은 일요일을 제외하고 매일 영업한다.
➡ The restaurant is open every day _____ Sundays.

04 다음 영영풀이에 알맞은 어휘를 〈보기〉에서 찾아 쓰시오.

┌─ 보기 ─┐
order   pack   improve   attend

(1) to make something better: _____
(2) to go to and be present at an event, meeting, etc.: _____
(3) to use your authority to tell someone to do something: _____
(4) to put something into a bag, suitcase, etc., so that you can take it with you: _____

05 다음 문장의 괄호 안에서 알맞은 것을 고르시오.

(1) Do you know (what, when, where) to come here again?
➡ _____
(2) She ordered me (wash, washing, to wash) the dishes.
➡ _____
(3) We were (too, so, enough) tired to walk anymore.
➡ _____

06 다음 우리말에 맞게 주어진 어휘를 바르게 배열하시오.

(1) Brown 씨는 그의 아들이 파티에 가게 허락했다.
(Mr. Brown, the party, his son, go, let, to)
➡ _____
(2) 프로젝트 책임자는 우리를 오전 9시에 만나게 했다.
(the project manager, us, had, meet, 9 a.m., at)
➡ _____

(3) 그들은 내게 그 이야기 전체를 반복하게 만들었다.

(me, they, story, repeat, whole, made, the)

➡ _____

(4) 그녀는 내가 이 숙제를 끝낼 수 있도록 도와주었다.

(this assignment, she, me, complete, helped, to)

➡ _____

07 관계대명사 what을 사용하여 주어진 두 문장을 한 문장으로 바꾸시오.

(1) • I want to do something for the community.
    • It is to pick up trash.

➡ _____

    _____

(2) • I liked the thing.
    • Yuna gave it to me last month.

➡ _____

(3) • Did you enjoy the movie?
    • We saw it at the movie theater last night.

➡ _____

_____

08 다음 두 문장을 괄호 안의 조건대로 한 문장으로 쓰시오.

> • He has knowledge. (well을 이용하여)
> • He has experience, too.

➡ _____

_____

[09~10] 다음 글을 읽고, 물음에 답하시오.

To carry ____ⓐ____ his plan, Coach Carter had the players sign a contract. They had to promise to study hard in addition ____ⓑ____ playing basketball. At first, students did not take his idea for a contract ⓒserious.

09 위 글의 빈칸 ⓐ와 ⓑ에 알맞은 단어를 쓰시오.

ⓐ _____ ⓑ _____

10 위 글의 밑줄 친 ⓒ를 알맞은 형으로 고치시오.

➡ _____

[11~12] 다음 글을 읽고, 물음에 답하시오.

Welcome to *Movie Trip*. Today we're going to talk about the movie *Coach Carter*. Can you imagine a basketball coach who doesn't allow his players to practice? That's exactly ____ⓐ____ Coach Carter does. This movie is about a coach who cares more about his students than about ⓑwin games.

11 위 글의 빈칸 ⓐ에 알맞은 말을 쓰시오.

➡ _____

12 위 글의 밑줄 친 ⓑwin을 알맞은 형으로 고치시오.

➡ _____

The basketball team at Richmond High School in Richmond, California, was having one losing season after another. The players became used to losing. ⓐ설상가상으로, they had no plans for the future; they went to school only to play basketball, and ⓑthey did not do that very well. Then they got a new coach, Kenny Carter. Coach Carter wanted to change things. He wanted to teach kids _____ⓒ_____ to play basketball well and win. But more than that, he wanted to give the players a future by sending them to college.

13 위 글의 밑줄 친 ⓐ를 주어진 단어를 써서 영어로 옮기시오.

(make, worse)

➡ _____

14 위 글의 밑줄 친 ⓑ가 do that의 의미가 구체적으로 들어나도록 우리말로 옮기시오.

➡ _____

15 위 글의 빈칸 ⓒ에 알맞은 의문사를 쓰시오.

➡ _____

16 Carter가 어떤 변화를 원했는지 우리말로 쓰시오.

(1) _____

(2) _____

With hard work and a new game plan, the team began to win for the first time in many years. From that point on, they won game _____ⓐ_____ game. Everybody, except Coach Carter, was happy. The players did not do the "study" part of their contract. Few of them actually believed they could go to college, so they paid ⓑ(little / a little) attention to their grades. Carter decided to take stronger action. He locked the gym and refused to let them play basketball until their grades improved, as promised in the contract. The players did not like it. They told him that his actions were just for him, not for them.

17 위 글의 빈칸 ⓐ에 알맞은 단어를 쓰시오.

➡ _____

18 위 글의 괄호 ⓑ에서 알맞은 것을 고르시오.

➡ _____

19 Why wasn't Coach Carter happy? Answer in English by beginning with 'Because'. (12 words)

➡ _____

_____

20 Carter가 취한 더 강한 조치가 구체적으로 무엇인지 우리말로 쓰시오.

➡ _____

_____

01 다음 문장의 빈칸에 들어갈 말을 〈보기〉에서 골라 쓰시오.

| 보기 |
| coach / exactly / imagine / lock / college |

(1) Please describe _____ what you saw.

(2) If you shut the door, it will _____ automatically.

(3) She will graduate from _____ this year.

(4) The _____ is teaching him how to jump.

(5) Close your eyes and _____ that you are in a forest.

02 다음 영영풀이에 해당하는 단어는?

| a document on which the words of a contract are written |

① grade   ② data
③ diagram   ④ contract
⑤ evidence

03 다음 중 밑줄 친 부분의 뜻풀이가 바르지 <u>않은</u> 것은?

① Jack runs every day to <u>improve</u> his health. (향상시키다)

② They're waiting to <u>sign</u> the contract. (서명하다)

③ My mom will <u>allow</u> me to keep a dog. (허락하다)

④ I work every day <u>except</u> Monday. (~을 포함하여)

⑤ The store will <u>reopen</u> at 9 a.m. on 2 January. (다시 문을 열다)

04 다음 짝지어진 두 단어의 관계가 같도록 빈칸에 알맞은 말을 쓰시오.

| decide : decision = refuse : _____ |

05 다음 문장의 빈칸에 공통으로 들어갈 알맞은 것은?

| • I'd like to _____ Chinese food.
• I _____ you to leave here immediately! |

① sign   ② pack
③ order   ④ allow
⑤ care

06 다음 빈칸을 〈보기〉에 있는 어휘를 이용하여 채우시오.

| 보기 |
| take   make   pay   carry |

(1) She didn't _____ out her promise.

(2) My car broke down, and to _____ matters worse, it began to rain.

(3) Why don't you _____ attention to me when I speak to you?

(4) I asked him to _____ appropriate action.

07 다음 영영풀이에 해당하는 단어를 쓰시오. (d로 시작할 것)

| a forceful statement in which you say that something must be done or given to you |

➡ _____

08 다음 중 어법상 어색한 것은?

① He is the man who taught me how to ski.
② This is the pen which I bought yesterday.
③ That he says is not important.
④ The letter that came this morning is from my father.
⑤ You are the only person that can help me.

09 다음 중 어법상 어색한 것은?

① He felt the house shake.
② She made us to work all night.
③ Did you notice anyone leave?
④ He told me to hold my tongue.
⑤ Dave let the children play in his yard.

10 다음 중 어법상 바르게 쓰인 문장은?

① This is one of the toy cars what are displayed at a toy exhibition.
② That seems easy to the teacher often seems difficult to the students.
③ She likes the things what he gave to her.
④ Is the new position what he is looking for in the company?
⑤ The report showed that I wanted to know.

11 다음 우리말을 주어진 어휘를 활용하여 영작하시오.

(1) 나는 네가 돌아올 때까지 여기서 기다리겠다.
(until, back)

➡ _____

(2) 그는 우리가 그의 말을 잘 들을 수 있도록 명확히 말했다. (clearly, so, may)

➡ _____

(3) 나는 그녀가 이 시끄러운 곳에서 잘 수 있을지 알고 싶다. (know, this noisy place)

➡ _____

_____

(4) 그는 지난 금요일 이후로 춤 연습을 하지 않고 있다. (since, be, practice, dance)

➡ _____

_____

(5) 그녀는 너무 배가 고파서 계속 걸을 수 없었다.
(feel, keep, to)

➡ _____

(6) 그는 춤을 아주 잘 춰서 1등상을 받았다.
(well, win, so, prize)

➡ _____

[12~13] 다음 두 문장이 같은 뜻이 되도록 빈칸에 알맞은 것은?

12

> I had the mechanic examine the car brakes.
> = I got the mechanic _____ the car brakes.

① examine   ② examined
③ examining   ④ to examine
⑤ to examining

13

출제율 100%

> Tom let me use his computer.
> = Tom allowed me _____ his computer.

① used   ② using   ③ to use
④ to using   ⑤ for use

14

출제율 85%

다음 두 문장이 같은 뜻이 되도록 빈칸에 알맞은 말을 쓰시오.

(1) I don't know what to do next.
    = I don't know what _____ _____ _____ next.

(2) He showed me how to open the safe.
    = He showed me how _____ _____ _____ the safe.

(3) Please tell him where to get it.
    = Please tell him where _____ _____ _____ it.

15

출제율 95%

다음 빈칸에 들어갈 말이 바르게 짝지어진 것을 고르시오.

> • I heard the car _____.
> • He allowed her _____ as she pleased.

① stop – do   ② stop – doing
③ stop – to do   ④ to stop – doing
⑤ to stop – to do

[16~19] 다음 글을 읽고, 물음에 답하시오.

The basketball team at Richmond High School in Richmond, California, was having one losing season after another. The players became used to ⓐlose. To make matters worse, they had no plans for the future; they went to school only to play basketball, and they did not ⓑdo that very well. Then they got a new coach, Kenny Carter. Coach Carter wanted to change things. He wanted to teach kids ____ⓒ____ to play basketball well and win. But more than that, he wanted to give the players a future by sending them to college.

16

출제율 95%

위 글의 밑줄 친 ⓐ를 알맞게 고치시오.

➡ _____

17

출제율 90%

위 글의 밑줄 친 ⓑdo that이 가리키는 것을 영어로 쓰시오.

➡ _____

18

출제율 90%

위 글의 빈칸 ⓒ에 알맞은 것은?

① what   ② how
③ why   ④ when
⑤ which

19

출제율 100%

위 글의 내용으로 보아 대답할 수 없는 것은?

① Why did the team lose games in a row?
② Did the players of the team have plans for the future?
③ Why did the players of the team go to school?
④ Did the new coach want to change things?
⑤ Why did the new coach want the players of the team to go to college?

[20~22] 다음 글을 읽고 물음에 답하시오.

Carter: I'm going to give you a contract.

Cruz: "ⓐAttend at all classes," "Get a C⁺ or higher," "Don't be late...." What are all these ___ⓑ___ about? Do I get a signing bonus for signing this contract?

Carter: Yes. You will get a big bonus ___ⓒ___ you will become a winner in the game of basketball as well as in the game of life.

출제율 85%

20 위 글의 밑줄 친 ⓐ에서 어법상 어색한 것을 고르시오.

➡ _____ ➡ _____

출제율 90%

21 위 글의 빈칸 ⓑ에 다음 정의에 해당하는 영어 단어를 쓰시오.

> instructions that tell you what you are allowed to do and what you are not allowed to do

➡ _____

출제율 95%

22 위 글의 빈칸 ⓒ에 알맞은 것은?

① if ② though ③ unless
④ because ⑤ while

[23~27] 다음 글을 읽고 물음에 답하시오.

With hard work and a new game plan, the team began ①to win for the first time in many years. ⓐFrom that point on, they won a game after a game. Everybody, ②except Coach Carter, was happy. The players did not do the "study" part of their contract. Few of them actually believed they could go to college, ___ⓑ___ they paid little attention to their grades. Carter decided ③to take stronger action. He locked the gym and refused to let them ④to play basketball until their grades improved, as ⑤promised in the contract. The players did not like ⓒit. They told him that his actions were just for him, not for them.

출제율 90%

23 위 글의 밑줄 친 ①~⑤ 중 어법상 어색한 것은?

① ② ③ ④ ⑤

출제율 95%

24 위 글의 밑줄 친 ⓐ를 어법상 어색한 것을 고쳐 다시 쓰시오.

➡ _____

출제율 90%

25 위 글의 빈칸 ⓑ에 알맞은 것은?

① or ② but ③ so
④ for ⑤ because

출제율 95%

26 위 글의 밑줄 친 ⓒ가 가리키는 것을 우리말로 쓰시오.

➡ _____

_____

출제율 100%

27 위 글의 내용과 일치하지 <u>않는</u> 것은?

① The team won for the first time in many years.
② Both Coach Carter and the players were happy.
③ The players didn't study hard.
④ Many of the players didn't believe they could go to college.
⑤ Coach Carter didn't allow the players to play basketball as their grades didn't improve.

[28~30] 다음 글을 읽고 물음에 답하시오.

> Worm: We're the basketball team. All we see is you on TV, ⓐget famous.
>
> Carter: If you think ⓑso, go home and ask yourself, "Do I want a better life?" If the answer is yes, I will do everything in my power ⓒto help you. But you have to do your part.

출제율 90%

28 위 글의 밑줄 친 ⓐ를 알맞은 형으로 고치시오.

➡ _____

출제율 95%

29 위 글의 밑줄 친 ⓑso가 가리키는 것을 우리말로 쓰시오.

➡ _____

출제율 95%

30 위 글의 밑줄 친 ⓒto help와 용법이 같은 것을 고르시오.

① I have a baseball cap to wear.
② Love is to trust each other.
③ To live without air is impossible.
④ I went to a shopping mall to buy clothes.
⑤ I have some homework to do today.

[31~34] 다음 글을 읽고 물음에 답하시오.

> The players' parents did not like Carter's ⓐ decide either. At the parents' demand, the principal ordered Carter (A)[reopen / to reopen] the gym. ⓑDisappoint, Carter decided to leave Richmond High. When he (B)[entered / entered into] the gym to pack his things, however, all of his players were there.
>
> We want you to enjoy the movie, so we won't tell you what happens next. Find out for (C) [you / yourself] by watching the movie *Coach Carter*.

출제율 95%

31 위 글의 밑줄 친 ⓐ를 알맞은 형으로 고치시오.

➡ _____

출제율 90%

32 위 글의 밑줄 친 ⓑ를 알맞은 형으로 고치시오.

➡ _____

출제율 95%

33 위 글의 괄호 (A)~(C)에서 어법상 알맞은 낱말을 골라 쓰시오.

(A) _____
(B) _____
(C) _____

출제율 100%

34 위 글의 내용으로 보아 알 수 없는 것은?

① 선수들의 부모는 Carter의 결정을 좋아하지 않았다.
② 교장 선생은 Carter에게 체육관을 다시 열라고 명령했다.
③ Carter는 리치몬드 고등학교를 떠나기로 결심했다.
④ 선수들은 Carter가 리치몬드 고등학교를 떠나는 것을 환영했다.
⑤ 영화 Coach Carer의 결말은 알 수 없다.

MEMO

MEMO

INSIGHT
on the textbook

교과서 파헤치기

※ 다음 영어를 우리말로 쓰시오.

01 athlete	
02 celebrate	
03 whenever	
04 competition	
05 respect	
06 decide	
07 famous	
08 happen	
09 passion	
10 injure	
11 accident	
12 represent	
13 public	
14 realize	
15 admire	
16 injury	
17 accept	
18 hurt	
19 lie	
20 practice	
21 suddenly	

22 nearby	
23 official	
24 ceremony	
25 developer	
26 especially	
27 training	
28 experiment	
29 preparation	
30 author	
31 cheer	
32 remove	
33 shout	
34 toward	
35 be into	
36 give up	
37 teach oneself	
38 be proud of	
39 as a result	
40 be done with	
41 stand for	
42 come up to	
43 far behind	

※ 다음 우리말을 영어로 쓰시오.

01 깨닫다	
02 시합	
03 결정하다	
04 연습	
05 개발자	
06 제거하다	
07 다치다	
08 사고	
09 식, 의식	
10 대표하다	
11 환호성을 지르다, 환호하다	
12 결승선	
13 존중하다	
14 부상	
15 운동선수	
16 작가	
17 부상을 입히다	
18 축하	
19 실험하다	
20 대중	
21 일어나다	

22 부근의; 부근에	
23 두드리다	
24 갑자기	
25 ~쪽으로, ~을 향하여	
26 관료, 공무원, 경기 임원	
27 열정	
28 받다	
29 준비	
30 ~할 때마다	
31 준비하다	
32 특별히	
33 우승자, 수상자	
34 훈련	
35 나타내다, 상징하다	
36 포기하다	
37 멀리 뒤쳐진	
38 ~에 관심이 많다	
39 ~을 끝내다	
40 ~에 다가가다	
41 독학하다	
42 결과적으로	
43 ~을 자랑스러워하다	

※ 다음 영영풀이에 알맞은 단어를 <보기>에서 골라 쓴 후, 우리말 뜻을 쓰시오.

1 _____ : the writer of a book: _____

2 _____ : used to talk about a great distance: _____

3 _____ : to take something that someone offers: _____

4 _____ : a person who plays sports well: _____

5 _____ : a strong emotion or feeling: _____

6 _____ : to become aware of something: _____

7 _____ : to take something away: _____

8 _____ : in the direction of someone or something: _____

9 _____ : stop doing something that you have tried hard to do: _____

10 _____ : harm or damage to a person's or an animal's body: _____

11 _____ : the process of learning the skills that you need to do a job: _____

12 _____ : a race where people run a distance of 42.195 kilometers: _____

13 _____ : to officially speak or take action for people in a group: _____

14 _____ : a large sports ground surrounded by rows of seats and usually other buildings: _____

15 _____ : a person who collects and reports news for newspapers, radio or television: _____

16 _____ : to tell someone that you are happy when something pleasant has happened to them: _____

보기			
marathon	stadium	far	author
reporter	training	toward	passion
give up	injury	athlete	realize
represent	remove	congratulate	accept

※ 다음 우리말과 일치하도록 빈칸에 알맞은 말을 쓰시오.

Listen & Speak 1 Listen

1. **B:** _____ was she _____ _____ become a great _____?
   G: She _____ 3 kilometers _____ _____.
2. **G:** How was he _____ to become a _____ player?
   B: He was _____, but he _____ _____ _____ shots a lot.
3. **B:** _____ was she _____ to _____ English so _____?
   G: She _____ English by _____ many Hollywood movies.
4. **G:** _____ was he able to _____ a famous _____?
   B: He _____ _____ with people in _____.

Listen & Speak 1-A

1. **B:** _____ was Thomas Edison _____ to invent so many things?
   G: Many people _____ that he _____ things on his _____ _____, but that's not _____.
   B: Oh, _____?
   G: Yes. _____ he invented something, he _____ many times.
   B: Maybe that's _____ so many people _____ him.
2. **G:** _____ was Hyeon Chung able to be one of the _____ four _____ in the tennis _____?
   B: He _____ do it _____ _____ years of hard _____.
   G: I see. When did he start _____ _____?
   B: He _____ _____ _____ tennis when he was _____.

Listen & Speak 2 Listen

1. **B:** _____ you _____ of the _____ of the singing _____?
   G: No, I _____. Who _____?
   B: The _____ is Vintop, who wrote all of his _____ songs.
2. **G:** _____ you _____ of Mia, the _____ _____?
   B: Yes, I have. I heard that she _____ _____ to play.
3. **B:** Have you _____ about BTG, the _____ _____ _____ group?
   G: Yes, I have. I have _____ their video _____ _____ on the Internet.
4. **G:** Have you _____ of Jiho, the _____?
   B: No, I _____. What _____ _____ _____ does he _____?
   G: He usually _____ pictures _____ _____ artists.

1. **B:** 어떻게 그녀는 훌륭한 달리기 선수가 될 수 있었니?
   G: 그녀는 매일 3킬로미터를 달렸어.
2. **G:** 어떻게 그는 농구 선수가 될 수 있었니?
   B: 그는 작았지만 3점 슛을 많이 연습했어.
3. **B:** 어떻게 그녀는 영어를 잘할 수 있었니?
   G: 그는 많은 할리우드 영화를 보면서 영어를 배웠어.
4. **G:** 어떻게 그는 유명한 기자가 될 수 있었니?
   B: 그는 대중 앞에서 사람들과 말하는 것을 연습했어.

1. **B:** 어떻게 토머스 에디슨은 그렇게 많은 것들을 발명할 수 있었을까?
   G: 많은 사람들은 그가 그것들을 첫 시도에 발명했다고 생각하지만 그것은 사실이 아니야.
   B: 오, 진짜?
   G: 응. 그는 무언가를 발명할 때마다 여러 번 실험했어.
   B: 아마 그것이 그렇게 많은 사람들이 그를 존경하는 이유일 거야.
2. **G:** 정현이 어떻게 테니스 경기에서 마지막 네 선수 중 한 명이 될 수 있었을까?
   B: 그는 혹독한 훈련을 몇 년 거친 뒤에야 그것을 할 수 있었어.
   G: 그렇구나. 그는 언제 테니스 치는 것을 시작했니?
   B: 그는 일곱 살 때 테니스 치는 것을 시작했어.

1. **B:** 노래 대회 우승자에 대해 들어 본 적 있니?
   G: 아니, 못 들어 봤어. 누가 이겼어?
   B: 우승자는 빈탑인데, 그는 자신의 모든 노래를 작곡했어.
2. **G:** 미아라는 기타 연주자에 대해 들어 본 적 있니?
   B: 응, 들어 봤어. 나는 그녀가 연주를 독학했다고 들었어.
3. **B:** BTG라는 세계적으로 유명한 댄스 그룹에 대해 들어 본 적 있니?
   G: 응, 들어 봤어. 나는 인터넷에서 그들의 영상을 여러 번 본 적이 있어.
4. **G:** 지호라는 사진작가에 대해 들어 본 적 있니?
   B: 아니, 못 들어 봤어. 그는 어떤 종류의 사진을 찍니?
   G: 그는 보통 거리 예술가들의 사진을 찍어.

Listen & Speak 2-A

1. **B:** _____ you _____ about the _____ club, Edutoon?

   G: Yes, I have. Are you _____ _____ _____ _____?

   B: Yes, I _____ _____ _____ a famous cartoon writer, so I want to _____ that club.

   G: Oh, I didn't _____ that you're _____ in _____ cartoons.

2. **G:** _____ you _____ of D.I.Y.?

   B: No, _____ is D.I.Y.?

   G: D.I.Y. _____ for 'do-it-yourself.' I'm really _____ it. Right now, I'm _____ a _____ _____.

   B: _____ are you going to make _____ you _____ that?

   G: When I'm _____ with the _____ case, I'm _____ _____ my own _____.

Real-Life Zone

G: _____ you _____ _____ Eui Hyun Sin, the _____?

B: No. _____ is _____?

G: He's a Paralympian _____. He _____ the first gold _____ for Korea in the 2018 Winter Paralympics.

B: Wow! That's _____.

G: He _____ in a car _____ in his _____ _____ and _____ his legs.

B: How was he _____ _____ _____ a skier?

G: After his _____, he tried _____ different sports to _____ better. Then he became _____ interested _____ _____.

B: _____ is not easy. Not many people _____ _____ at skiing.

G: That's _____ he's so _____.

Wrap Up

B: Sora, have you _____ about the _____ last night?

G: Yes, I _____ that there _____ a big fire in a building _____. Was anybody _____?

B: No, _____ man _____ ten people who _____ in the building.

G: Oh, really? _____ was he _____ _____ _____ so many people?

B: He _____ on _____ _____ to _____ people to _____ the building.

G: Wow, that's _____!

1. **B:** 에듀툰이라는 만화 동아리에 대해 들어 본 적 있니?

   G: 응, 있어. 만화 그리는 것에 관심이 있니?

   B: 나는 유명한 만화 작가가 되고 싶어서 그 동아리에 가입하고 싶어.

   G: 오, 나는 네가 만화 그리기에 관심이 있는 줄 몰랐어.

2. **G:** D.I.Y에 대해 들어 본 적 있니?

   B: 아니, D.I.Y가 뭐야?

   G: D.I.Y는 '너 스스로 해라'를 의미해. 나는 그것에 푹 빠졌어. 지금 나는 필통을 만들고 있어.

   B: 그것을 완성하고 나면 무엇을 만들 거니?

   G: 필통을 완성하면, 나는 내 책상을 만들 계획이야.

G: 신의현이라는 스키 선수에 대해 들어 본 적 있니?

B: 아니, 그가 누구야?

G: 그는 페럴림픽의 스키 선수야. 그는 2018 동계 페럴림픽에서 한국의 첫 금메달을 땄어.

B: 와! 훌륭하다.

G: 그는 20대 초반에 차 사고를 당하고 다리를 다쳤어.

B: 어떻게 그가 스키 선수가 될 수 있었니?

G: 사고 후에 그는 회복하기 위해 여러 가지 운동들을 시도했어. 그때 그는 특히 스키 타는 것에 관심을 가지게 됐어.

B: 스키를 타는 것은 쉽지 않잖아. 스키를 잘 타는 사람들은 많지 않아.

G: 그것이 그가 그렇게 존경받는 이유야.

B: 소라야, 지난밤 화재에 대해 들었니?

G: 응, 이 근처 건물에서 큰 화재가 있었다고 들었어. 다친 사람이 있어?

B: 아니, 한 남자가 건물 안에 있던 열 명의 사람들을 구했어.

G: 오, 진짜? 어떻게 그는 그 많은 사람들을 구할 수 있었니?

B: 그는 사람들에게 건물을 떠나라고 말하기 위해서 모든 문을 두드렸어.

G: 와, 정말 놀랍구나!

※ 다음 우리말에 맞도록 대화를 영어로 쓰시오.

Listen & Speak 1 Listen

1. B: _____
   G: _____

2. G: _____
   B: _____

3. B: _____
   G: _____

4. G: _____
   B: _____

Listen & Speak 1-A

1. B: _____
   G: _____
   B: _____
   G: _____
   B: _____

2. G: _____
   B: _____
   G: _____
   B: _____

Listen & Speak 2 Listen

1. B: _____
   G: _____
   B: _____

2. G: _____
   B: _____

3. B: _____
   G: _____

4. G: _____
   B: _____
   G: _____

해석

1. B: 어떻게 그녀는 훌륭한 달리기 선수가 될 수 있었니?
   G: 그녀는 매일 3킬로미터를 달렸어.
2. G: 어떻게 그는 농구 선수가 될 수 있었니?
   B: 그는 작았지만 3점 슛을 많이 연습했어.
3. B: 어떻게 그녀는 영어를 잘할 수 있었니?
   G: 그는 많은 할리우드 영화를 보면서 영어를 배웠어.
4. G: 어떻게 그는 유명한 기자가 될 수 있었니?
   B: 그는 대중 앞에서 사람들과 말하는 것을 연습했어.

1. B: 어떻게 토머스 에디슨은 그렇게 많은 것들을 발명할 수 있었을까?
   G: 많은 사람들은 그가 그것들을 첫 시도에 발명했다고 생각하지만 그것은 사실이 아니야.
   B: 오, 진짜?
   G: 응. 그는 무언가를 발명할 때마다 여러 번 실험했어.
   B: 아마 그것이 그렇게 많은 사람들이 그를 존경하는 이유일 거야.
2. G: 정현이 어떻게 테니스 경기에서 마지막 네 선수 중 한 명이 될 수 있었을까?
   B: 그는 혹독한 훈련을 몇 년 거친 뒤에야 그것을 할 수 있었어.
   G: 그렇구나. 그는 언제 테니스 치는 것을 시작했니?
   B: 그는 일곱 살 때 테니스 치는 것을 시작했어.

1. B: 노래 대회 우승자에 대해 들어 본 적 있니?
   G: 아니, 못 들어 봤어. 누가 이겼어?
   B: 우승자는 빈탑인데, 그는 자신의 모든 노래를 작곡했어.
2. G: 미아라는 기타 연주자에 대해 들어 본 적 있니?
   B: 응, 들어 봤어. 나는 그녀가 연주를 독학했다고 들었어.
3. B: BTG라는 세계적으로 유명한 댄스 그룹에 대해 들어 본 적 있니?
   G: 응, 들어 봤어. 나는 인터넷에서 그들의 영상을 여러 번 본 적이 있어.
4. G: 지호라는 사진작가에 대해 들어 본 적 있니?
   B: 아니, 못 들어 봤어. 그는 어떤 종류의 사진을 찍니?
   G: 그는 보통 거리 예술가들의 사진을 찍어.

Listen & Speak 2-A

1. B: _____
   G: _____
   B: _____
   G: _____
2. G: _____
   B: _____
   G: _____
   _____
   B: _____
   G: _____

Real-Life Zone

G: _____
B: _____
G: _____
_____
B: _____
G: _____
B: _____
G: _____
_____
B: _____
G: _____

Wrap Up

B: _____
G: _____
B: _____
G: _____
B: _____
G: _____

1. B: 에듀툰이라는 만화 동아리에 대해 들어 본 적 있니?
   G: 응, 있어. 만화 그리는 것에 관심이 있니?
   B: 나는 유명한 만화 작가가 되고 싶어서 그 동아리에 가입하고 싶어.
   G: 오, 나는 네가 만화 그리기에 관심이 있는 줄 몰랐어.
2. G: D.I.Y에 대해 들어 본 적 있니?
   B: 아니, D.I.Y가 뭐야?
   G: D.I.Y는 '너 스스로 해라'를 의미해. 나는 그것에 푹 빠졌어. 지금 나는 필통을 만들고 있어.
   B: 그것을 완성하고 나면 무엇을 만들 거니?
   G: 필통을 완성하면, 나는 내 책상을 만들 계획이야.

G: 신의현이라는 스키 선수에 대해 들어 본 적 있니?
B: 아니, 그가 누구야?
G: 그는 페럴림픽의 스키 선수야. 그는 2018 동계 페럴림픽에서 한국의 첫 금메달을 땄어.
B: 와! 훌륭하다.
G: 그는 20대 초반에 차 사고를 당하고 다리를 다쳤어.
B: 어떻게 그가 스키 선수가 될 수 있었니?
G: 사고 후에 그는 회복하기 위해 여러 가지 운동들을 시도했어. 그때 그는 특히 스키 타는 것에 관심을 가지게 됐어.
B: 스키를 타는 것은 쉽지 않잖아. 스키를 잘 타는 사람들은 많지 않아.
G: 그것이 그가 그렇게 존경받는 이유야.

B: 소라야, 지난밤 화재에 대해 들었니?
G: 응, 이 근처 건물에서 큰 화재가 있었다고 들었어. 다친 사람이 있어?
B: 아니, 한 남자가 건물 안에 있던 열 명의 사람들을 구했어.
G: 오, 진짜? 어떻게 그는 그 많은 사람들을 구할 수 있었니?
B: 그는 사람들에게 건물을 떠나라고 말하기 위해서 모든 문을 두드렸어.
G: 와, 정말 놀랍구나!

※ 다음 우리말과 일치하도록 빈칸에 알맞은 것을 골라 쓰시오.

1 The _____ _____
A. Runner   B. Last

2 The last runner _____ the race _____ _____ an hour _____.
A. before   B. finished   C. than   D. more

3 "There will be _____ _____ runners _____," the _____ decided.
A. more   B. officials   C. coming   D. no

4 They _____ the tape at the finish line and started to _____ for the _____ _____ for the 1996 Atlanta Summer Olympics in the United States.
A. prepare   B. ceremony   C. removed   D. closing

5 Someone _____, "Look! _____ comes _____ _____!"
A. there   B. runner   C. shouted   D. another

6 A runner was just _____ the stadium, but there was _____ _____ _____ his legs.
A. something   B. with   C. entering   D. wrong

7 Still, he _____ _____ _____ the finish line.
A. going   B. kept   C. toward

8 The band and the _____ _____ _____ their _____ for the closing _____.
A. stopped   B. ceremony   C. volunteers   D. preparations

9 _____ _____ were _____ the _____.
A. runner   B. eyes   C. all   D. on

10 _____, the band started playing _____ _____, and the volunteers _____.
A. cheered   B. celebration   C. suddenly   D. music

11 "Go! Go! _____ _____ _____!"
A. for   B. it   C. go

12 Two volunteers _____ to the _____ _____ _____ a tape.
A. line   B. ran   C. with   D. finish

13 _____, the runner _____ _____ the tape and then _____ to the ground.
A. through   B. finally   C. fell   D. ran

14 _____ _____ _____ Abdul Baser Wasiqi.
A. name   B. his   C. was

15 He _____ _____ Afghanistan.
A. from   B. was

16 Reporters _____ _____ _____ Wasiqi and started _____ him questions.
A. to   B. came   C. asking   D. up

17 **Reporter:** What _____ _____ you?
A. to   B. happened

18 **Wasiqi:** I _____ my leg _____ a _____ _____.
A. practice   B. injured   C. run   D. during

1 마지막 주자

2 마지막 주자가 한 시간도 더 전에 경주를 끝냈다.

3 "더 들어오는 선수는 없을 겁니다."라고 경기 임원들은 결론을 내렸다.

4 그들은 결승선에서 테이프를 걷어내고 1996년 미국 애틀랜타 하계 올림픽의 폐막식을 준비하기 시작했다.

5 누군가가 외쳤다. "봐! 저기 또 다른 선수가 온다!"

6 한 선수가 경기장으로 막 들어오고 있었는데, 그의 다리에 이상이 있었다.

7 그러나 그는 계속 결승선을 향해 움직였다.

8 밴드와 자원봉사자들이 폐막식을 위한 준비를 멈추었다.

9 모든 눈들이 그 선수에게 머물렀다.

10 갑자기 밴드가 축하 음악을 연주하기 시작했고, 자원봉사자들이 환호했다.

11 "달려! 달려! 잘해라!"

12 두 명의 자원봉사자가 테이프를 가지고 결승선으로 달려갔다.

13 결국, 그 주자는 테이프를 통과해 달렸고, 바닥에 쓰러졌다.

14 그의 이름은 압둘 베사르 와시키였다.

15 그는 아프가니스탄 출신이었다.

16 기자들은 와시키에게 가서 그에게 질문을 하기 시작했다.

17 리포터: 당신에게 무슨 일이 있었나요?

18 와시키: 저는 연습 경기를 하던 중 다리를 다쳤습니다.

19 The injury _____ _____ during the race, but I couldn't _____ _____.

A. worse   B. up   C. got   D. give

20 **Reporter:** _____ _____?

A. not   B. why

21 You knew _____ you were too _____ _____ to _____ a medal.

A. far   B. win   C. that   D. behind

22 **Wasiqi:** I am the _____ _____ here _____ _____.

A. representing   B. only   C. Afghanistan   D. athlete

23 There was _____ _____ I could _____ _____.

A. give   B. way   C. no   D. up

24 **Reporter:** Afghanistan is still _____ _____, _____ _____?

A. war   B. it   C. isn't   D. at

25 **Wasiqi:** Yes, we _____ _____ at war _____ 16 years.

A. been   B. for   C. have

26 _____ _____ we were not _____ to send _____ to the Barcelona Olympics four years ago.

A. why   B. athletes   C. that's   D. able

27 I was _____ _____ my country _____ _____ when I could see no Afghan athletes in the opening ceremony.

A. back   B. for   C. sad   D. then

28 **Reporter:** _____ you _____ marathons _____?

A. running   B. then   C. were

29 **Wasiqi:** No. I _____ _____ _____ Barcelona.

A. running   B. started   C. after

30 I ran in _____ _____ _____.

A. of   B. lots   C. races

31 Finally I _____ _____ _____ in Germany.

A. a   B. won   C. marathon

32 _____ a _____, I was _____ _____ come to Atlanta.

A. to   B. able   C. result   D. as

33 **Reporter:** _____ do you _____ now?

A. feel   B. how

34 **Wasiqi:** I am _____ _____ and proud to be _____ Afghanistan.

A. myself   B. proud   C. from   D. of

35 For me and my country, it was important _____ _____ _____ _____.

A. to   B. up   C. give   D. not

36 I _____ _____ here _____ _____.

A. come   B. win   C. didn't   D. to

37 For me, it was _____ _____ be here and to _____ the _____.

A. to   B. race   C. finish   D. enough

---

19 경기 중에 제 상처는 점점 더 심각해졌지만, 저는 포기할 수 없었습니다.

20 리포터: 왜 포기할 수 없었죠?

21 당신은 메달을 얻기에 너무도 크게 뒤떨어져 있었다는 것을 알고 있었잖아요.

22 와시키: 저는 아프가니스탄을 대표하는 유일한 선수입니다.

23 제가 포기할 수 있는 방법은 없었습니다.

24 리포터: 아프가니스탄은 여전히 전쟁 중입니다. 맞나요?

25 와시키: 네, 우리나라는 16년째 전쟁 중입니다.

26 그것이 우리가 4년 전 바르셀로나 올림픽에 선수들을 보낼 수 없었던 이유입니다.

27 저는 개회식에서 아프가니스탄 선수를 볼 수 없었던 그 당시, 제 나라에 대해 매우 슬펐습니다.

28 리포터: 그 당시 마라톤을 뛰고 있었나요?

29 와시키: 아니요. 저는 바르셀로나 올림픽 이후에 달리기를 시작했습니다.

30 저는 많은 경주에서 뛰었어요.

31 마침내 독일 마라톤에서 우승했지요.

32 그 결과 애틀란타에 올 수 있었어요.

33 리포터: 지금은 기분이 어떠신가요?

34 와시키: 저는 제 자신이, 그리고 제가 아프가니스탄 출신인 것이 자랑스러워요.

35 저와 제 조국을 위해서는, 포기하지 않는 것이 중요했어요.

36 저는 이곳에 이기러 온 것이 아닙니다.

37 제가 여기에 있고 경주를 끝마친 것으로 충분합니다.

※ 다음 우리말과 일치하도록 빈칸에 알맞은 말을 쓰시오.

1 The _____ _____

2 The last runner _____ the race _____ _____ an hour before.

3 "There will be _____ _____ runners _____," the _____ decided.

4 They _____ the tape at the _____ _____ and started to _____ _____ the _____ _____ for the 1996 Atlanta Summer Olympics in the United States.

5 Someone _____, "Look! _____ _____ _____ runner!"

6 A runner was just entering the stadium, but there was _____ _____ _____ his legs.

7 _____, he _____ _____ _____ the finish line.

8 The band and the volunteers _____ _____ _____ for the _____ _____.

9 _____ _____ _____ _____ the runner.

10 _____, the band started playing _____ _____, and the _____ _____.

11 "Go! Go! _____ _____ _____!"

12 Two volunteers ran to the finish line _____ _____ _____.

13 _____, the runner _____ _____ the tape and then _____ _____ the ground.

14 _____ _____ was Abdul Baser Wasiqi.

15 He _____ _____ Afghanistan.

16 Reporters _____ _____ _____ Wasiqi and _____ _____ him questions.

17 **Reporter:** What _____ _____ you?

18 **Wasiqi:** I _____ my leg _____ _____ _____ _____.

1 마지막 주자

2 마지막 주자가 한 시간도 더 전에 경주를 끝냈다.

3 "더 들어오는 선수는 없을 겁니다."라고 경기 임원들은 결론을 내렸다.

4 그들은 결승선에서 테이프를 걷어내고 1996년 미국 애틀랜타 하계 올림픽의 폐막식을 준비하기 시작했다.

5 누군가가 외쳤다. "봐! 저기 또 다른 선수가 온다!"

6 한 선수가 경기장으로 막 들어오고 있었는데, 그의 다리에 이상이 있었다.

7 그러나 그는 계속 결승선을 향해 움직였다.

8 밴드와 자원봉사자들이 폐막식을 위한 준비를 멈추었다.

9 모든 눈들이 그 선수에게 머물렀다.

10 갑자기 밴드가 축하 음악을 연주하기 시작했고, 자원봉사자들이 환호했다.

11 "달려! 달려! 잘해라!"

12 두 명의 자원봉사자가 테이프를 가지고 결승선으로 달려갔다.

13 결국, 그 주자는 테이프를 통과해 달렸고, 바닥에 쓰러졌다.

14 그의 이름은 압둘 베사르 와시키였다.

15 그는 아프가니스탄 출신이었다.

16 기자들은 와시키에게 가서 그에게 질문을 하기 시작했다.

17 리포터: 당신에게 무슨 일이 있었나요?

18 와시키: 저는 연습 경기를 하던 중 다리를 다쳤습니다.

19 The injury _____ _____ _____ the race, but I couldn't _____ _____.

20 **Reporter:** _____ _____?

21 You knew that you were too _____ _____ to win a medal.

22 **Wasiqi:** I am the _____ _____ here _____ _____.

23 There was _____ _____ I could _____ _____.

24 **Reporter:** Afghanistan is still _____ _____, _____ _____?

25 **Wasiqi:** Yes, we _____ _____ at war _____ 16 years.

26 _____ _____ we were not _____ _____ send athletes to the Barcelona Olympics four years ago.

27 I _____ _____ _____ my country _____ _____ when I could see no Afghan athletes in the _____ _____.

28 **Reporter:** _____ you _____ marathons then?

29 **Wasiqi:** No. I _____ _____ after Barcelona.

30 I ran in _____ _____ _____.

31 Finally I _____ _____ _____ in Germany.

32 _____ _____ _____, I was able to come to Atlanta.

33 **Reporter:** _____ do you _____ now?

34 **Wasiqi:** I am _____ _____ and proud _____ _____ _____ Afghanistan.

35 For me and my country, it was important _____ _____ _____ _____.

36 I didn't come here _____ _____.

37 For me, _____ _____ _____ to be here and _____ _____ the race.

19 경기 중에 제 상처는 점점 더 심각해졌지만, 저는 포기할 수 없었습니다.

20 리포터: 왜 포기할 수 없었죠?

21 당신은 메달을 얻기에 너무도 크게 뒤떨어져 있었다는 것을 알고 있었잖아요.

22 와시키: 저는 아프가니스탄을 대표하는 유일한 선수입니다.

23 제가 포기할 수 있는 방법은 없었습니다.

24 리포터: 아프가니스탄은 여전히 전쟁 중입니다. 맞나요?

25 와시키: 네, 우리나라는 16년째 전쟁 중입니다.

26 그것이 우리가 4년 전 바르셀로나 올림픽에 선수들을 보낼 수 없었던 이유입니다.

27 저는 개회식에서 아프가니스탄 선수를 볼 수 없었던 그 당시, 제 나라에 대해 매우 슬펐습니다.

28 리포터: 그 당시 마라톤을 뛰고 있었나요?

29 와시키: 아니요. 저는 바르셀로나 올림픽 이후에 달리기를 시작했습니다.

30 저는 많은 경주에서 뛰었어요.

31 마침내 독일 마라톤에서 우승했지요.

32 그 결과 애틀랜타에 올 수 있었어요.

33 리포터: 지금은 기분이 어떠신가요?

34 와시키: 저는 제 자신이, 그리고 제가 아프가니스탄 출신인 것이 자랑스러워요.

35 저와 제 조국을 위해서는, 포기하지 않는 것이 중요했어요.

36 저는 이곳에 이기러 온 것이 아닙니다.

37 제가 여기에 있고 경주를 끝마친 것으로 충분합니다.

※ 다음 문장을 우리말로 쓰시오.

1 The Last Runner

➡ _____

2 The last runner finished the race more than an hour before.

➡ _____

3 "There will be no more runners coming," the officials decided.

➡ _____

4 They removed the tape at the finish line and started to prepare for the closing ceremony for the 1996 Atlanta Summer Olympics in the United States.

➡ _____

5 Someone shouted, "Look! There comes another runner!"

➡ _____

6 A runner was just entering the stadium, but there was something wrong with his legs.

➡ _____

7 Still, he kept going toward the finish line.

➡ _____

8 The band and the volunteers stopped their preparations for the closing ceremony.

➡ _____

9 All eyes were on the runner.

➡ _____

10 Suddenly, the band started playing celebration music, and the volunteers cheered.

➡ _____

11 "Go! Go! Go for it!"

➡ _____

12 Two volunteers ran to the finish line with a tape.

➡ _____

13 Finally, the runner ran through the tape and then fell to the ground.

➡ _____

14 His name was Abdul Baser Wasiqi.

➡ _____

15 He was from Afghanistan.

➡ _____

16 Reporters came up to Wasiqi and started asking him questions.

➡ _____

17 Reporter: What happened to you?

➡ _____

18 Wasiqi: I injured my leg during a practice run.

➡ _____

19 The injury got worse during the race, but I couldn't give up.

➡ _____

20 Reporter: Why not?

➡ _____

21 You knew that you were too far behind to win a medal.

➡ _____

22 Wasiqi: I am the only athlete here representing Afghanistan.

➡ _____

23 There was no way I could give up.

➡ _____

24 Reporter: Afghanistan is still at war, isn't it?

➡ _____

25 Wasiqi: Yes, we have been at war for 16 years.

➡ _____

26 That's why we were not able to send athletes to the Barcelona Olympics four years ago.

➡ _____

27 I was sad for my country back then when I could see no Afghan athletes in the opening ceremony.

➡ _____

28 Reporter: Were you running marathons then?

➡ _____

29 Wasiqi: No. I started running after Barcelona.

➡ _____

30 I ran in lots of races.

➡ _____

31 Finally I won a marathon in Germany.

➡ _____

32 As a result, I was able to come to Atlanta.

➡ _____

33 Reporter: How do you feel now?

➡ _____

34 Wasiqi: I am proud of myself and proud to be from Afghanistan.

➡ _____

35 For me and my country, it was important not to give up.

➡ _____

36 I didn't come here to win.

➡ _____

37 For me, it was enough to be here and to finish the race.

➡ _____

※ 다음 괄호 안의 단어들을 우리말에 맞도록 바르게 배열하시오.

1 (Last / The / Runner)
➡ _____

2 (last / the / finished / runner / race / the / than / more / an / before. / hour)
➡ _____

3 (will / "there / no / be / runners / more / coming," / the / decided. / officials)
➡ _____

4 (removed / they / tape / the / at / finish / the / line / and / to / started / for / prepare / the / ceremony / closing / the / for / Atlanta / 1996 / Olympics / Summer / the / in / States. / United)
➡ _____

5 (shouted, / someone / "look! / comes / there / runner!" / another)
➡ _____

6 (runner / a / just / was / the / entering / stadium, / there / but / something / was / with / wrong / legs. / his)
➡ _____

7 (he / still, / kept / toward / going / finish / the / line.)
➡ _____

8 (band / the / and / volunteers / the / their / stopped / preparations / the / for / ceremony. / closing)
➡ _____

9 (eyes / all / on / were / runner. / the)
➡ _____

10 (the / suddenly, / band / playing / started / music, / celebration / and / volunteers / the / cheered.)
➡ _____

11 ("go! / go / go! / it!" / for)
➡ _____

12 (volunteers / two / to / ran / finish / the / with / line / tape. / a)
➡ _____

13 (the / finally, / runner / through / ran / tape / the / and / fell / then / to / ground. / the)
➡ _____

14 (name / his / was / Baser / Abdul / Wasiqi.)
➡ _____

15 (was / he / Afghanistan. / from)
➡ _____

16 (came / reporters / to / up / and / Wasiqi / asking / started / questions. / him)
➡ _____

17 (Reporter: / happened / what / you? / to)
➡ _____

18 (Wasiqi: / injured / I / leg / my / a / during / run. / practice.)
➡ _____

1 마지막 주자

2 마지막 주자가 한 시간도 더 전에 경주를 끝냈다.

3 "더 들어오는 선수는 없을 겁니다."라고 경기 임원들은 결론을 내렸다.

4 그들은 결승선에서 테이프를 걷어내고 1996년 미국 애틀랜타 하계 올림픽의 폐막식을 준비하기 시작했다.

5 누군가가 외쳤다. "봐! 저기 또 다른 선수가 온다!"

6 한 선수가 경기장으로 막 들어오고 있었는데, 그의 다리에 이상이 있었다.

7 그러나 그는 계속 결승선을 향해 움직였다.

8 밴드와 자원봉사자들이 폐막식을 위한 준비를 멈추었다.

9 모든 눈들이 그 선수에게 머물렀다.

10 갑자기 밴드가 축하 음악을 연주하기 시작했고, 자원봉사자들이 환호했다.

11 "달려! 달려! 잘해라!"

12 두 명의 자원봉사자가 테이프를 가지고 결승선으로 달려갔다.

13 결국, 그 주자는 테이프를 통과해 달렸고, 바닥에 쓰러졌다.

14 그의 이름은 압둘 베사르 와시키였다.

15 그는 아프가니스탄 출신이었다.

16 기자들은 와시키에게 가서 그에게 질문을 하기 시작했다.

17 리포터: 당신에게 무슨 일이 있었나요?

18 와시키: 저는 연습 경기를 하던 중 다리를 다쳤습니다.

19 (injury / the / worse / got / the / during / race, / I / but / give / couldn't / up.)

➡ _____

20 (Reporter: / not? / why)

➡ _____

21 (knew / you / that / were / you / far / too / behind / win / to / medal. / a)

➡ _____

22 (Wasiqi: / am / I / the / athlete / only / here / Afghanistan. / representing)

➡ _____

23 (was / there / way / no / could / I / up. / give)

➡ _____

24 (Reporter: / is / Afghanistan / at / still / war, / it? / isn't)

➡ _____

25 (Wasiqi: / we / yes, / been / have / war / at / 16 / years. / for)

➡ _____

26 (why / that's / were / we / able / not / send / to / athletes / the / to / Olympics / Barcelona / four / ago. / years)

➡ _____

27 (was / I / sad / my / for / back / country / then / I / when / see / could / Afghan / no / athletes / the / in / ceremony. / opening)

➡ _____

28 (Reporter: / you / were / marathons / running / then?)

➡ _____

29 (Wasiqi: / no. // started / I / after / running / Barcelona.)

➡ _____

30 (ran / I / lots / in / races. / of)

➡ _____

31 (I / finally / won / marathon / a / Germany. / in)

➡ _____

32 (a / as / result, / was / I / to / able / to / come / Atlanta.)

➡ _____

33 (Reporter: / do / how / feel / you / now?)

➡ _____

34 (Wasiqi: / am / I / of / proud / and / myself / to / proud / be / Afghanistan. / from)

➡ _____

35 (me / for / and / country, / my / was / it / not / important / to / up. / give)

➡ _____

36 (didn't / I / here / come / win. / to)

➡ _____

37 (me, / for / was / it / to / enough / be / and / here / to / the / finish / race.)

➡ _____

19 경기 중에 제 상처는 점점 더 심각해졌지만, 저는 포기할 수 없었습니다.

20 리포터: 왜 포기할 수 없었죠?

21 당신은 메달을 얻기에 너무도 크게 뒤떨어져 있었다는 것을 알고 있었잖아요.

22 와시키: 저는 아프가니스탄을 대표하는 유일한 선수입니다.

23 제가 포기할 수 있는 방법은 없었습니다.

24 리포터: 아프가니스탄은 여전히 전쟁 중입니다, 맞나요?

25 와시키: 네, 우리나라는 16년째 전쟁 중입니다.

26 그것이 우리가 4년 전 바르셀로나 올림픽에 선수들을 보낼 수 없었던 이유입니다.

27 저는 개회식에서 아프가니스탄 선수를 볼 수 없었던 그 당시, 제 나라에 대해 매우 슬펐습니다.

28 리포터: 그 당시 마라톤을 뛰고 있었나요?

29 와시키: 아니요. 저는 바르셀로나 올림픽 이후에 달리기를 시작했습니다.

30 저는 많은 경주에서 뛰었어요.

31 마침내 독일 마라톤에서 우승했지요.

32 그 결과 애틀랜타에 올 수 있었어요.

33 리포터: 지금은 기분이 어떠신가요?

34 와시키: 저는 제 자신이, 그리고 제가 아프가니스탄 출신인 것이 자랑스러워요.

35 저와 제 조국을 위해서는, 포기하지 않는 것이 중요했어요.

36 저는 이곳에 이기러 온 것이 아닙니다.

37 제가 여기에 있고 경주를 끝마친 것으로 충분합니다.

※ 다음 우리말을 영어로 쓰시오.

1 마지막 주자

➡ _____

2 마지막 주자가 한 시간도 더 전에 경주를 끝냈다.

➡ _____

3 "더 들어오는 선수는 없을 겁니다."라고 경기 임원들은 결론을 내렸다.

➡ _____

4 그들은 결승선에서 테이프를 걷어내고 1996년 미국 애틀랜타 하계 올림픽의 폐막식을 준비하기 시작했다.

➡ _____

_____

5 누군가가 외쳤다. "봐! 저기 또 다른 선수가 온다!"

➡ _____

6 한 선수가 경기장으로 막 들어오고 있었는데, 그의 다리에 이상이 있었다.

➡ _____

7 그러나 그는 계속 결승선을 향해 움직였다.

➡ _____

8 밴드와 자원봉사자들이 폐막식을 위한 준비를 멈추었다.

➡ _____

9 모든 눈들이 그 선수에게 머물렀다.

➡ _____

10 갑자기 밴드가 축하 음악을 연주하기 시작했고, 자원봉사자들이 환호했다.

➡ _____

11 "달려! 달려! 잘해라!"

➡ _____

12 두 명의 자원봉사자가 테이프를 가지고 결승선으로 달려갔다.

➡ _____

13 결국, 그 주자는 테이프를 통과해 달렸고, 바닥에 쓰러졌다.

➡ _____

14 그의 이름은 압둘 베사르 와시키였다.

➡ _____

15 그는 아프가니스탄 출신이었다.

➡ _____

16 기자들은 와시키에게 가서 그에게 질문을 하기 시작했다.

➡ _____

17 리포터: 당신에게 무슨 일이 있었나요?

➡ _____

18 와시키: 저는 연습 경기를 하던 중 다리를 다쳤습니다.

➡ _____

19 경기 중에 제 상처는 점점 더 심각해졌지만, 저는 포기할 수 없었습니다.

➡ _____

20 리포터: 왜 포기할 수 없었죠?

➡ _____

21 당신은 메달을 얻기에 너무도 크게 뒤떨어져 있었다는 것을 알고 있었잖아요.

➡ _____

22 와시키: 저는 아프가니스탄을 대표하는 유일한 선수입니다.

➡ _____

23 제가 포기할 수 있는 방법은 없었습니다.

➡ _____

24 리포터: 아프가니스탄은 여전히 전쟁 중입니다, 맞나요?

➡ _____

25 와시키: 네, 우리나라는 16년째 전쟁 중입니다.

➡ _____

26 그것이 우리가 4년 전 바르셀로나 올림픽에 선수들을 보낼 수 없었던 이유입니다.

➡ _____

27 저는 개회식에서 아프가니스탄 선수를 볼 수 없었던 그 당시, 제 나라에 대해 매우 슬펐습니다.

➡ _____

28 리포터: 그 당시 마라톤을 뛰고 있었나요?

➡ _____

29 와시키: 아니요. 저는 바르셀로나 올림픽 이후에 달리기를 시작했습니다.

➡ _____

30 저는 많은 경주에서 뛰었어요.

➡ _____

31 마침내 독일 마라톤에서 우승했지요.

➡ _____

32 그 결과 애틀랜타에 올 수 있었어요.

➡ _____

33 리포터: 지금은 기분이 어떠신가요?

➡ _____

34 와시키: 저는 제 자신이, 그리고 제가 아프가니스탄 출신인 것이 자랑스러워요.

➡ _____

35 저와 제 조국을 위해서는, 포기하지 않는 것이 중요했어요.

➡ _____

36 저는 이곳에 이기러 온 것이 아닙니다.

➡ _____

37 제가 여기에 있고 경주를 끝마친 것으로 충분합니다.

➡ _____

※ 다음 우리말과 일치하도록 빈칸에 알맞은 말을 쓰시오.

Communication Task

1. A: _____ you _____ _____ Jain Kim?

2. B: Yes, I have. She's _____ _____ _____ _____.

3. A: How _____ she _____ _____ _____ a famous rock climber?

4. B: She trained hard _____ _____ _____ _____.

Language in Use B

1. Last night, I _____ _____ _____ for 8 o'lock _____ _____ _____ _____ _____ school today.

2. _____ it is _____ _____ _____ _____ my school, _____ is important _____ _____ _____ the bus.

3. _____ _____ _____, I quickly _____ the house and _____ _____ the bus stop.

4. _____, there _____ _____.

5. _____, I _____ _____ today was Saturday.

6. _____ _____ _____, not to _____ it _____ again, I will always check _____ _____ _____ _____.

Writing Workshop Step 3

1. I _____ _____ _____ _____ _____ _____ the Singing Contest

2. I _____ _____ the school _____ _____.

3. I love singing, and _____ _____ I _____ _____ _____ _____.

4. _____, I am _____ _____ _____ _____ _____ many people.

5. _____ _____ _____ _____ during the contest, I will _____ my class first.

※ **다음 우리말을 영어로 쓰시오.**

Communication Task

1. A: 너는 김자인에 대하여 들어본 적이 있니?
➡ _____

2. B: 그래. 그녀는 유명한 암벽 등반가야.
➡ _____

3. A: 어떻게 그녀가 유명한 암벽 등반가가 될 수 있었지?
➡ _____

4. B: 그녀는 5년 동안 매일 열심히 훈련했어.
➡ _____

Language in Use B

1. 어젯밤에 나는 오늘 학교에 늦지 않으려고 시계를 8시에 맞춰 놓았다.
➡ _____

2. 학교까지는 길이 멀기 때문에, 버스를 놓치지 않는 것이 중요하다.
➡ _____

3. 아침도 먹지 않고 나는 빠르게 집을 떠나 버스 정거장으로 갔다.
➡ _____

4. 놀랍게도 아무도 없었다.
➡ _____

5. 그때, 나는 오늘이 토요일임을 기억했다.
➡ _____

6. 이제부터 그런 일이 다시 일어나지 않도록, 나는 항상 무슨 요일인지 확인하겠다.
➡ _____

Writing Workshop Step 3

1. 나는 노래 대회에서 이기려는 목표를 가지고 있다
➡ _____

2. 나는 학교 노래 대회에서 이기고 싶다.
➡ _____

3. 나는 노래 부르는 것을 좋아하고 목소리가 좋다고 생각한다.
➡ _____

4. 그러나, 나는 너무 수줍어서 많은 사람들 앞에서 노래를 부를 수 없다.
➡ _____

5. 대회 도중에 불안해하지 않기 위해서 먼저 학급 친구들 앞에서 노래 부르기를 연습할 것이다.
➡ _____

※ 다음 영어를 우리말로 쓰시오.

01	avoid	_____
02	counselor	_____
03	recently	_____
04	prove	_____
05	relax	_____
06	experiment	_____
07	still	_____
08	popular	_____
09	vocabulary	_____
10	latest	_____
11	management	_____
12	afraid	_____
13	final	_____
14	matter	_____
15	hurt	_____
16	match	_____
17	upset	_____
18	part	_____
19	protein	_____
20	helpful	_____
21	disagree	_____

22	sneakers	_____
23	misunderstand	_____
24	strict	_____
25	teenager	_____
26	decide	_____
27	hate	_____
28	worry	_____
29	mistake	_____
30	number	_____
31	speech contest	_____
32	P.E. teacher	_____
33	advise	_____
34	project	_____
35	in style	_____
36	for now	_____
37	ask somebody out	_____
38	without -ing	_____
39	focus on	_____
40	end up -ing	_____
41	for a long time	_____
42	have a hard time -ing	_____
43	not ~ anymore	_____

※ 다음 우리말을 영어로 쓰시오.

01 기분이 상한	
02 카운슬러, 상담역	
03 결정하다	
04 시합	
05 실험	
06 엄격한	
07 피하다	
08 문제	
09 인기 있는	
10 증명하다, 입증하다	
11 매우 싫어하다	
12 웅변대회	
13 오해하다	
14 아직도	
15 동의하지 않다	
16 단백질	
17 도움이 되는	
18 운동화	
19 결승, 기말고사; 마지막의	
20 어휘	
21 최신의	

22 관리	
23 부분, 배역, 역할	
24 다치다	
25 과제	
26 충고하다	
27 체육 교사	
28 번호를 매기다	
29 쉬다	
30 실수	
31 청소년	
32 걱정; 걱정하다	
33 최근에	
34 시도하다	
35 더 이상 ~가 아닌	
36 유행하는, 유행되는	
37 집중하다	
38 당분간은, 현재로는	
39 결국 ~하게 되다	
40 오랫동안	
41 ~의 역할을 하다	
42 ~하는 데 어려움이 있다	
43 ~에 준비가 되다	

※ 다음 영영풀이에 알맞은 단어를 <보기>에서 골라 쓴 후, 우리말 뜻을 쓰시오.

1 _____ : not long ago: _____

2 _____ : most recent and newest: _____

3 _____ : soft sided sports shoes: _____

4 _____ : to prevent something bad from happening: _____

5 _____ : to dislike something strongly: _____

6 _____ : words that are used in a language: _____

7 _____ : to have a different opinion: _____

8 _____ : the state or condition of worrying about something: _____

9 _____ : liked or enjoyed by a large number of people: _____

10 _____ : something that you do wrong without wanting to: _____

11 _____ : to show that something is true: _____

12 _____ : a person who is between the ages of 13 and 19: _____

13 _____ : to have same opinion as someone about a topic: _____

14 _____ : someone whose job it is to provide help and advice to people with problems:

_____

15 _____ : a scientific test that is done in order to study what happens and to gain

new knowledge: _____

16 _____ : to spend time resting or doing something enjoyable especially after you

have been doing work: _____

보기

prove	mistake	avoid	latest
relax	experiment	worry	hate
popular	teenager	recently	vocabulary
counselor	agree	disagree	sneakers

※ 다음 우리말과 일치하도록 빈칸에 알맞은 말을 쓰시오.

Listen & Speak 1 A Listen

1. **B:** I think _____ _____ music _____ you _____.
   G: I _____.

2. **G:** I think _____ history _____ _____ is _____.
   B: I agree. I _____ a lot _____ them.

3. **G:** Our school _____ is going to be a _____ of _____.
   B: I agree.

4. **B:** Our P.E. _____ is too _____. _____ you _____?
   G: No, I _____ agree. I don't think he's too _____.

Listen & Speak 1 A

1. **G:** Mom _____ me I could _____ the computer _____ _____ _____ _____ a _____. She thinks that's _____ time.
   M: I _____ _____ her.
   G: Sometimes, when _____ my homework, I _____ to use it _____ _____ _____ _____.
   M: Hmm. Then maybe we should all _____ and _____ about it.
   G: Thanks _____ your _____, Dad.

2. **B:** I _____ talked _____ the science _____ with Jinho and Mina.
   G: Has your team _____ _____ you will _____?
   B: No, _____ yet. Jinho wants to _____ a science museum, but Mina _____ _____ do an _____.
   G: Who do you _____ _____, Jinho or Mina?
   B: I agree _____ Mina _____ I think the _____ would be more _____.

Listen & Speak 2 A Listen

1. **B:** I _____ a big soccer _____ tomorrow. I'm _____.
   G: _____. I'm _____ you'll _____ very well.

2. **G:** I'm _____ about tomorrow's _____ _____.
   B: I'm _____ you'll _____ fine. Don't _____.

3. **G:** I'm _____ about making _____ at my new _____.
   M: _____ worry. I'm _____ you'll _____ a lot of _____ there.

해석

1. **B:** 나는 음악을 듣는 것이 긴장을 푸는 데 도움이 된다고 생각해.
   G: 나도 동의해.
2. **G:** 나는 역사 만화책을 읽는 것이 도움이 된다고 생각해.
   B: 나도 동의해. 나는 그것들로부터 많은 것을 배워.
3. **G:** 우리 학교 축제는 아주 재미있을 거야.
   B: 나도 동의해.
4. **B:** 우리 체육 선생님은 너무 엄격하셔. 너도 동의하지 않니?
   G: 응, 난 동의하지 않아. 나는 그가 너무 엄격하다고 생각하지 않아.

1. **G:** 엄마는 제가 하루에 한 시간만 컴퓨터를 사용할 수 있다고 말씀하셨어요. 그녀는 그게 충분한 시간이라고 생각하세요.
   M: 나도 그녀의 말에 동의한다.
   G: 숙제를 할 때 그것을 오래 사용할 필요가 있어요.
   M: 음. 그러면 아마 우리는 다 같이 모여 그것에 대해 이야기를 해야 할 것 같구나.
   G: 이해해 줘서 고마워요. 아빠.
2. **B:** 나는 진호랑 미나랑 과학 프로젝트에 대해 방금 이야기했어.
   G: 너희 팀은 무엇을 할지 결정했니?
   B: 아니, 아직. 진호는 과학 박물관을 방문하고 싶어하지만, 미나는 실험을 하고 싶어해.
   G: 너는 진호나 미나 중에 누구에게 동의해?
   B: 나는 실험이 더 흥미로울 거라고 생각해서 미나의 말에 동의해.

1. **B:** 내일 큰 축구 경기가 있어. 긴장돼.
   G: 걱정하지 마. 난 네가 아주 잘 경기할 거라고 확신해.
2. **G:** 내일 있을 말하기 대회 때문에 긴장돼.
   B: 난 네가 잘할 거라고 확신해. 걱정하지 마.
3. **G:** 새 학교에서 친구를 사귀는 게 걱정돼요.
   M: 걱정하지 마. 난 네가 그곳에서 많은 친구들을 사귈 거라고 확신해.

Listen & Speak 2 A

1. **B:** You look _____. Is _____ _____?
   G: Yes, my sister is _____ _____ me.
   B: _____? What did you _____?
   G: I _____ _____ _____ her shirts _____ asking.
   B: Tell her you're _____. I'm sure she'll _____.

2. **B:** I'm _____ a hard time _____ new English words.
   G: I _____ the same problem, so I _____ my English _____ _____ _____.
   B: _____ did he say?
   G: He _____ me to _____ an English _____ app. It has helped me a lot. I'm _____ it would _____ _____ you, too.

Real-Life Zone

B: The team _____ for English class is _____ a lot of time.
G: I _____. I have a problem. _____ _____ _____ the _____ on our team isn't _____ his _____.
B: _____ not good. Everybody on the _____ has to do their job.
G: I _____, but I don't _____ _____ _____ _____ _____ him _____ do his part.
B: Maybe he _____ know how to _____ _____ or doesn't _____ his _____.
G: Then _____ should I _____?
B: Talk _____ him. Ask him _____ he's not _____ his part. _____ tell him _____ help him _____ he _____.
G: Okay. I'll _____ that.
B: I'm _____ he'll do _____ _____ you _____ to him. Good luck _____ your _____.
G: Thanks.

Wrap Up

G: What's the _____, Dongha? You _____ _____.
B: I'm not _____ for the _____. I sit at my _____ to _____ but end _____ doing _____ _____.
G: Well, time _____ is not _____.
B: I _____. What _____ I do?
G: _____ the things you _____ to do. _____ write _____ how _____ time _____ _____ _____ each one.
B: Thank you, Emily. I'll _____ your idea.
G: I'm sure _____ will be _____ for you. Good _____ your finals.

---

1. **B:** 걱정스러워 보여. 무슨 일 있니?
   G: 응, 우리 언니가 나한테 화가 났어.
   B: 왜? 무엇을 했니?
   G: 내가 묻지도 않고 언니의 셔츠 중에 하나를 입었어.
   B: 그녀에게 미안하다고 말해. 나는 그녀가 이해해 줄 거라고 확신해.

2. **B:** 나는 새로운 영어 단어를 배우는 데 어려움을 겪고 있어.
   G: 나도 같은 문제가 있어서 영어 선생님께 조언을 구했어.
   B: 그가 뭐라고 하셨어?
   G: 그는 나에게 영어 어휘 앱을 사용하라고 조언해 주셨어. 그것은 나에게 큰 도움이 됐어. 나는 그것이 너에게도 효과가 있을 거라고 확신해.

B: 영어 수업의 팀 프로젝트는 시간이 많이 걸려.
G: 나도 동의해. 나 문제가 있어. 우리 팀의 한 사람이 자기 역할을 다하지 않아.
B: 좋지 않네. 팀의 모든 사람들은 자신들의 일을 해야 해.
G: 알아. 하지만 어떻게 그가 그의 역할을 하게 할지 모르겠어.
B: 어쩌면 그는 시작하는 법을 모르거나 자기 역할을 좋아하지 않을 수도 있어.
G: 그러면 나는 무엇을 해야 할까?
B: 그에게 말해. 그에게 왜 자신의 역할을 안 하는지 물어봐. 그러고 나서 원한다면 네가 도와주겠다고 말해.
G: 그래. 한번 해 볼게.
B: 나는 네가 말하고 나면 그가 더 잘할 거라고 확신해. 네 프로젝트가 잘 되길 바랄게.
G: 고마워.

G: 동하야, 무슨 일이야? 걱정스러워 보여.
B: 기말고사 준비가 안 됐어. 나는 공부하기 위해 책상에 앉지만 결국 다른 것을 하게 돼.
G: 음, 시간 관리가 쉽지 않지.
B: 나도 동의해. 내가 어떻게 해야 할까?
G: 해야 할 일에 번호를 매겨. 그러고 나서 각 항목을 끝내는 데 필요한 시간을 적어 봐.
B: 고마워, 에밀리. 네 방안을 한번 해 볼게.
G: 나는 그것이 너에게 도움이 될 거라고 확신해. 기말고사 잘 보길 바랄게.

※ 다음 우리말에 맞도록 대화를 영어로 쓰시오.

Listen & Speak 1 A Listen

1. B: _____
   G: _____
2. G: _____
   B: _____
3. G: _____
   B: _____
4. B: _____
   G: _____

Listen & Speak 1 A

1. G: _____
   _____
   M: _____
   G: _____
   M: _____
   G: _____
2. B: _____
   G: _____
   B: _____
   _____
   G: _____
   B: _____

Listen & Speak 2 A Listen

1. B: _____
   G: _____
2. G: _____
   B: _____
3. G: _____
   M: _____

해석

1. B: 나는 음악을 듣는 것이 긴장을 푸는 데 도움이 된다고 생각해.
   G: 나도 동의해.
2. G: 나는 역사 만화책을 읽는 것이 도움이 된다고 생각해.
   B: 나도 동의해. 나는 그것들로부터 많은 것을 배워.
3. G: 우리 학교 축제는 아주 재미있을 거야.
   B: 나도 동의해.
4. B: 우리 체육 선생님은 너무 엄격하셔. 너도 동의하지 않니?
   G: 응, 난 동의하지 않아. 나는 그가 너무 엄격하다고 생각하지 않아.

1. G: 엄마는 제가 하루에 한 시간만 컴퓨터를 사용할 수 있다고 말씀하셨어요. 그녀는 그게 충분한 시간이라고 생각하세요.
   M: 나도 그녀의 말에 동의한단다.
   G: 숙제를 할 때 그것을 오래 사용할 필요가 있어요.
   M: 음. 그러면 아마 우리는 다 같이 모여 그것에 대해 이야기를 해야 할 것 같구나.
   G: 이해해 줘서 고마워요. 아빠.
2. B: 나는 진호랑 미나랑 과학 프로젝트에 대해 방금 이야기했어.
   G: 너희 팀은 무엇을 할지 결정했니?
   B: 아니, 아직. 진호는 과학 박물관을 방문하고 싶어하지만, 미나는 실험을 하고 싶어해.
   G: 너는 진호나 미나 중에 누구에게 동의해?
   B: 나는 실험이 더 흥미로울 거라고 생각해서 미나의 말에 동의해.

1. B: 내일 큰 축구 경기가 있어. 긴장돼.
   G: 걱정하지 마. 난 네가 아주 잘 경기할 거라고 확신해.
2. G: 내일 있을 말하기 대회 때문에 긴장돼.
   B: 난 네가 잘할 거라고 확신해. 걱정하지 마.
3. G: 새 학교에서 친구를 사귀는 게 걱정돼요.
   M: 걱정하지 마. 난 네가 그곳에서 많은 친구들을 사귈 거라고 확신해.

Listen & Speak 2 A

1. B: _____

   G: _____

   B: _____

   G: _____

   B: _____

2. B: _____

   G: _____

   B: _____

   G: _____

Real-Life Zone

B: _____

G: _____
  _____

B: _____

G: _____

B: _____

G: _____

B: _____

G: _____

B: _____

G: _____

Wrap Up

G: _____

B: _____
  _____

G: _____

B: _____

G: _____
  _____

B: _____

G: _____

1. B: 걱정스러워 보여. 무슨 일 있니?
   G: 응, 우리 언니가 나한테 화가 났어.
   B: 왜? 무엇을 했니?
   G: 내가 묻지도 않고 언니의 셔츠 중에 하나를 입었어.
   B: 그녀에게 미안하다고 말해. 나는 그녀가 이해해 줄 거라고 확신해.

2. B: 나는 새로운 영어 단어를 배우는 데 어려움을 겪고 있어.
   G: 나도 같은 문제가 있어서 영어 선생님께 조언을 구했어.
   B: 그가 뭐라고 하셨어?
   G: 그는 나에게 영어 어휘 앱을 사용하라고 조언해 주셨어. 그것은 나에게 큰 도움이 됐어. 나는 그것이 너에게도 효과가 있을 거라고 확신해.

B: 영어 수업의 팀 프로젝트는 시간이 많이 걸려.
G: 나도 동의해. 나 문제가 있어. 우리 팀의 한 사람이 자기 역할을 다하지 않아.
B: 좋지 않네. 팀의 모든 사람들은 자신들의 일을 해야 해.
G: 알아. 하지만 어떻게 그가 그의 역할을 하게 할지 모르겠어.
B: 어쩌면 그는 시작하는 법을 모르거나 자기 역할을 좋아하지 않을 수도 있어.
G: 그러면 나는 무엇을 해야 할까?
B: 그에게 말해. 그에게 왜 자신의 역할을 안 하는지 물어봐. 그러고 나서 원한다면 네가 도와주겠다고 말해.
G: 그래. 한번 해 볼게.
B: 나는 네가 말하고 나면 그가 더 잘할 거라고 확신해. 네 프로젝트가 잘 되길 바랄게.
G: 고마워.

G: 동하야, 무슨 일이야? 걱정스러워 보여.
B: 기말고사 준비가 안 됐어. 나는 공부하기 위해 책상에 앉지만 결국 다른 것을 하게 돼.
G: 음, 시간 관리가 쉽지 않지.
B: 나도 동의해. 내가 어떻게 해야 할까?
G: 해야 할 일에 번호를 매겨. 그러고 나서 각 항목을 끝내는 데 필요한 시간을 적어 봐.
B: 고마워, 에밀리. 네 방안을 한번 해 볼게.
G: 나는 그것이 너에게 도움이 될 거라고 확신해. 기말고사 잘 보길 바랄게.

※ 다음 우리말과 일치하도록 빈칸에 알맞은 것을 골라 쓰시오.

1 What _____ I _____ ?
A. Do   B. Should

2 _____ has _____ .
A. worries   B. everyone

3 _____ you have _____ you _____ about, what do you do?
A. worry   B. things   C. when

4 _____ are some _____ that three _____ worry _____ .
A. teenagers   B. here   C. about   D. things

5 Sohui thought Hayeon was her best friend, but now, Sohui feels that Hayeon _____ _____ and she _____ _____ her.
A. avoiding   B. has   C. is   D. changed

6 Sohui: (To her _____ sister) You know my friend Hayeon, _____ _____ ?
A. you   B. don't   C. older

7 Sister: Yeah. Why? _____ _____ her?
A. about   B. what

8 Sohui: I _____ she's _____ me.
A. avoiding   B. feel

9 When I see her at school, she _____ _____ and _____ _____ from me.
A. around   B. away   C. turns   D. walks

10 Sister: I'm _____ _____ _____ that.
A. to   B. hear   C. sorry

11 Do you have any idea _____ _____ _____ _____ ?
A. she   B. why   C. that   D. does

12 Sohui: No. I don't think I've _____ _____ _____ .
A. anything   B. done   C. wrong

13 It just _____ she _____ like me _____ .
A. anymore   B. like   C. feels   D. doesn't

14 Sister: Maybe you _____ just ask her _____ there is _____ .
A. if   B. wrong   C. something   D. should

15 Sohui: _____ I _____ . I _____ want to be friends _____ her.
A. still   B. maybe   C. with   D. should

16 Daeho, _____ that new things will make him more _____ , often wants new things _____ _____ his friends have them.
A. just   B. thinking   C. popular   D. because

17 Daeho: Seongjin, look _____ my _____ .
A. sneakers   B. at   C. new

18 _____ do you _____ ?
A. think   B. what

---

1 제가 어떻게 해야 할까요?

2 누구나 고민은 있습니다.

3 여러분은 걱정되는 것이 있을 때 무엇을 하나요?

4 여기 세 명의 청소년이 걱정하는 것들이 있습니다.

5 소희는 하연이가 그녀의 가장 친한 친구라고 생각했지만, 지금은 하연이가 변했고 그녀를 피한다고 느낍니다.

6 소희: (그녀의 언니에게) 내 친구 하연이 알지, 그렇지?

7 언니: 응. 왜? 그녀가 어떤데?

8 소희: 나는 그녀가 나를 피하고 있다고 느껴.

9 학교에서 내가 그녀를 볼 때 그녀는 돌아서서 나로부터 멀리 걸어가.

10 언니: 그거 참 안타깝구나.

11 너는 그녀가 왜 그렇게 하는지 아니?

12 소희: 아니. 나는 내가 잘못한 것이 있다고 생각하지 않아.

13 단지 그녀가 더 이상 나를 좋아하지 않는다고 느껴져.

14 언니: 혹시 모르니 뭔가 잘못된 것이 있는지 그녀에게 물어봐.

15 소희: 아마 그래야겠어. 나는 여전히 그녀와 친구로 지내고 싶거든.

16 대호는 새 물건이 그를 더 인기 있게 만들어 줄 것이라고 생각해서 단지 친구들이 그것을 가지고 있다는 이유로 종종 새 물건을 사기를 원합니다.

17 대호: 성진아, 내 새 운동화 봐.

18 어떠니?

19 **Seongjin:** They're nice, but _____ _____ just buy new sneakers a _____ _____ months ago?

    A. couple   B. you   C. of   D. didn't

20 **Daeho:** Yeah, but they're _____ _____ _____ _____.

    A. style   B. no   C. in   D. longer

21 I _____ _____ in these, _____?

    A. look   B. right   C. cooler

22 **Seongjin:** Daeho, _____ the _____ fashion doesn't make you _____ or more _____.

    A. latest   B. popular   C. wearing   D. cooler

23 People like you _____ _____ _____, not because of your _____.

    A. you're   B. clothes   C. you   D. because

24 **Daeho:** Yeah?

25 **Seongjin:** Listen, you're _____ _____ _____.

    A. guy   B. great   C. a

26 You don't _____ new sneakers _____ it.

    A. prove   B. need   C. to

27 _____, Minkyeong was _____ _____ by a boy in her _____.

    A. class   B. asked   C. recently   D. out

28 She wants to _____ no _____ does not want to _____ his _____.

    A. hurt   B. but   C. feelings   D. say

29 **Minkyeong:** I _____ your _____.

    A. advice   B. need

30 A boy in my class _____ _____ _____.

    A. me   B. asked   C. out

31 I like him, but _____ _____ I don't want to _____ _____ with him.

    A. now   B. out   C. for   D. go

32 I _____ _____ _____ _____ my studies.

    A. focus   B. need   C. on   D. to

33 What _____ I _____?

    A. do   B. should

34 **Counselor:** _____ _____ _____ tell him why you _____ go?

    A. don't   B. can't   C. why   D. you

35 **Minkyeong:** I'm _____ I might _____ his _____.

    A. hurt   B. afraid   C. feelings

36 **Counselor:** If you don't tell him soon, he will _____ your feelings, and you may _____ _____ _____ him even more.

    A. end   B. misunderstand   C. hurting   D. up

37 **Minkyeong:** _____ you're _____.

    A. right   B. maybe

38 _____ _____ the _____.

    A. advice   B. thanks   C. for

---

19 성진: 멋지다. 그런데 너 겨우 몇 달 전에 새 운동화 사지 않았니?

20 대호: 응, 하지만 그건 더 이상 유행이 아니야.

21 이걸 신으니까 더 멋져 보이지, 그렇지?

22 성진: 대호야, 최신 유행하는 것을 입는 것이 너를 더 멋지고 더 인기 있게 만들어 주지는 않아.

23 사람들은 네가 너이기 때문에 너를 좋아하는 것이지, 네 옷 때문이 아니야.

24 대호: 그래?

25 성진: 들어봐. 너는 멋진 사람이야.

26 그것을 증명하기 위해 새 운동화가 필요하지 않아.

27 최근에 민경이는 그녀의 반 남자아이에게 데이트 신청을 받았습니다.

28 그녀는 거절하고 싶지만 그의 감정을 상하게 하고 싶지는 않습니다.

29 민경: 저는 선생님의 조언이 필요해요.

30 같은 반 남자아이가 저에게 데이트 신청을 했어요.

31 저는 그를 좋아하지만 당분간은 그와 데이트하고 싶지 않아요.

32 저는 공부에 집중해야 해요.

33 제가 어떻게 해야 할까요?

34 상담 선생님: 왜 네가 데이트를 할 수 없는지 그에게 말하는 것은 어떨까?

35 민경: 제가 그의 감정을 상하게 할까 봐 걱정돼요.

36 상담 선생님: 네가 그에게 빨리 말하지 않으면, 그는 네 감정을 오해할 것이고, 너는 그를 더 아프게 할 수도 있단다.

37 민경: 선생님 말씀이 맞는 것 같아요.

38 조언 감사합니다.

※ 다음 우리말과 일치하도록 빈칸에 알맞은 말을 쓰시오.

1 _____ _____ I Do?

2 Everyone _____ _____.

3 When you have things you _____ about, _____ _____ _____ _____?

4 _____ _____ _____ that three teenagers _____ _____.

5 Sohui thought Hayeon was _____ _____ _____, but now, Sohui feels that Hayeon _____ _____ and she _____ _____ her.

6 Sohui: (To her _____ sister) You know my friend Hayeon, _____ _____?

7 Sister: Yeah. Why? _____ _____ her?

8 Sohui: _____ _____ she's _____ me.

9 When I see her at school, she _____ _____ and _____ _____ me.

10 Sister: I'm sorry _____ _____ _____.

11 Do you have any idea _____ _____ _____ _____?

12 Sohui: No. I don't think _____ _____ _____.

13 It just _____ _____ she _____ like me _____.

14 Sister: _____ you _____ just ask her _____ there is _____ _____.

15 Sohui: Maybe I should. I _____ want to be friends _____ her.

16 Daeho, _____ that new things will _____ him more _____, often wants new things _____ _____ his friends have them.

17 Daeho: Seongjin, _____ _____ my _____ _____.

18 _____ do you _____?

1 제가 어떻게 해야 할까요?

2 누구나 고민은 있습니다.

3 여러분은 걱정되는 것이 있을 때 무엇을 하나요?

4 여기 세 명의 청소년이 걱정하는 것들이 있습니다.

5 소희는 하연이가 그녀의 가장 친한 친구라고 생각했지만, 지금은 하연이가 변했고 그녀를 피한다고 느낍니다.

6 소희: (그녀의 언니에게) 내 친구 하연이 알지, 그렇지?

7 언니: 응. 왜? 그녀가 어떤데?

8 소희: 나는 그녀가 나를 피하고 있다고 느껴.

9 학교에서 내가 그녀를 볼 때 그녀는 돌아서서 나로부터 멀리 걸어가.

10 언니: 그거 참 안타깝구나.

11 너는 그녀가 왜 그렇게 하는지 아니?

12 소희: 아니. 나는 내가 잘못한 것이 있다고 생각하지 않아.

13 단지 그녀가 더 이상 나를 좋아하지 않는다고 느껴져.

14 언니: 혹시 모르니 뭔가 잘못된 것이 있는지 그녀에게 물어봐.

15 소희: 아마 그래야겠어. 나는 여전히 그녀와 친구로 지내고 싶거든.

16 대호는 새 물건이 그를 더 인기 있게 만들어 줄 것이라고 생각해서 단지 친구들이 그것을 가지고 있다는 이유로 종종 새 물건을 사기를 원합니다.

17 대호: 성진아, 내 새 운동화 봐.

18 어떠니?

19 Seongjin: They're nice, but _____ _____ just buy new sneakers a _____ _____ _____ _____ ?

20 Daeho: Yeah, but they're _____ _____ _____ _____ .

21 I look _____ _____ _____ , right?

22 Seongjin: Daeho, _____ the _____ _____ doesn't make you _____ or _____ _____ .

23 People like you _____ _____ _____ , not _____ _____ your clothes.

24 Daeho: Yeah?

25 Seongjin: Listen, you're _____ _____ _____ _____ .

26 You don't need new sneakers _____ _____ _____ .

27 Recently, Minkyeong _____ _____ _____ by a boy in her class.

28 She wants to say no but does not want _____ _____ _____ _____ .

29 Minkyeong: I _____ your _____ .

30 A boy in my class _____ _____ _____ .

31 I like him, but _____ _____ I don't want to _____ _____ _____ him.

32 I need to _____ _____ my _____ .

33 What _____ I do?

34 Counselor: _____ _____ _____ tell him why you _____ _____ ?

35 Minkyeong: _____ _____ _____ I _____ _____ his feelings.

36 Counselor: _____ _____ _____ _____ _____ him soon, he will _____ your feelings, and you may _____ _____ _____ him even more.

37 Minkyeong: Maybe _____ _____ .

38 _____ _____ the _____ .

19 성진: 멋지다. 그런데 너 겨우 몇 달 전에 새 운동화 사지 않았니?

20 대호: 응, 하지만 그건 더 이상 유행이 아니야.

21 이걸 신으니까 더 멋져 보이지. 그렇지?

22 성진: 대호야. 최신 유행하는 것을 입는 것이 너를 더 멋지고 더 인기 있게 만들어 주지는 않아.

23 사람들은 네가 너이기 때문에 너를 좋아하는 것이지. 네 옷 때문이 아니야.

24 대호: 그래?

25 성진: 들어봐. 너는 멋진 사람이야.

26 그것을 증명하기 위해 새 운동화가 필요하지 않아.

27 최근에 민경이는 그녀의 반 남자아이에게 데이트 신청을 받았습니다.

28 그녀는 거절하고 싶지만 그의 감정을 상하게 하고 싶지는 않습니다.

29 민경: 저는 선생님의 조언이 필요해요.

30 같은 반 남자아이가 저에게 데이트 신청을 했어요.

31 저는 그를 좋아하지만 당분간은 그와 데이트하고 싶지 않아요.

32 저는 공부에 집중해야 해요.

33 제가 어떻게 해야 할까요?

34 상담 선생님: 왜 네가 데이트를 할 수 없는지 그에게 말하는 것은 어떨까?

35 민경: 제가 그의 감정을 상하게 할까 봐 걱정돼요.

36 상담 선생님: 네가 그에게 빨리 말하지 않으면. 그는 네 감정을 오해할 것이고, 너는 그를 더 아프게 할 수도 있단다.

37 민경: 선생님 말씀이 맞는 것 같아요.

38 조언 감사합니다.

※ 다음 문장을 우리말로 쓰시오.

1 ▶ What Should I Do?

➡ _____

2 ▶ Everyone has worries.

➡ _____

3 ▶ When you have things you worry about, what do you do?

➡ _____

4 ▶ Here are some things that three teenagers worry about.

➡ _____

5 ▶ Sohui thought Hayeon was her best friend, but now, Sohui feels that Hayeon has changed and she is avoiding her.

➡ _____

6 ▶ Sohui: (To her older sister) You know my friend Hayeon, don't you?

➡ _____

7 ▶ Sister: Yeah. Why? What about her?

➡ _____

8 ▶ Sohui: I feel she's avoiding me.

➡ _____

9 ▶ When I see her at school, she turns around and walks away from me.

➡ _____

10 ▶ Sister: I'm sorry to hear that.

➡ _____

11 ▶ Do you have any idea why she does that?

➡ _____

12 ▶ Sohui: No. I don't think I've done anything wrong.

➡ _____

13 ▶ It just feels like she doesn't like me anymore.

➡ _____

14 ▶ Sister: Maybe you should just ask her if there is something wrong.

➡ _____

15 ▶ Sohui: Maybe I should. I still want to be friends with her.

➡ _____

16 ▶ Daeho, thinking that new things will make him more popular, often wants new things just because his friends have them.

➡ _____

➡ _____

17 ▶ Daeho: Seongjin, look at my new sneakers.

➡ _____

18 ▶ What do you think?

➡ _____

19 Seongjin: They're nice, but didn't you just buy new sneakers a couple of months ago?

➡ _____

20 Daeho: Yeah, but they're no longer in style.

➡ _____

21 I look cooler in these, right?

➡ _____

22 Seongjin: Daeho, wearing the latest fashion doesn't make you cooler or more popular.

➡ _____

23 People like you because you're you, not because of your clothes.

➡ _____

24 Daeho: Yeah?

➡ _____

25 Seongjin: Listen, you're a great guy.

➡ _____

26 You don't need new sneakers to prove it.

➡ _____

27 Recently, Minkyeong was asked out by a boy in her class.

➡ _____

28 She wants to say no but does not want to hurt his feelings.

➡ _____

29 Minkyeong: I need your advice.

➡ _____

30 A boy in my class asked me out.

➡ _____

31 I like him, but for now I don't want to go out with him.

➡ _____

32 I need to focus on my studies.

➡ _____

33 What should I do?

➡ _____

34 Counselor: Why don't you tell him why you can't go?

➡ _____

35 Minkyeong: I'm afraid I might hurt his feelings.

➡ _____

36 Counselor: If you don't tell him soon, he will misunderstand your feelings, and you may end up hurting him even more.

➡ _____

37 Minkyeong: Maybe you're right.

➡ _____

38 Thanks for the advice.

➡ _____

※ 다음 괄호 안의 단어들을 우리말에 맞도록 바르게 배열하시오.

1 (Should / What / Do? / I)
➡ _____

2 (has / everyone / worries.)
➡ _____

3 (you / when / things / have / worry / you / about, / do / what / do? / you)
➡ _____

4 (are / here / things / some / three / that / teenagers / about. / worry)
➡ _____

5 (thought / Sohui / was / Hayeon / best / her / friend, / now, / but / feels / Sohui / that / has / Hayeon / changed / she / and / is / her. / avoiding)
➡ _____
_____

6 (Sohui: / her / (to / sister) / older // know / you / friend / my / Hayeon, / you? / don't)
➡ _____

7 (Sister: / yeah. // why? // about / her? / what)
➡ _____

8 (Sohui: / feel / I / avoiding / she's / me.)
➡ _____

9 (I / when / her / see / school, / at / turns / she / and / around / walks / from / away / me.)
➡ _____

10 (Sister: / sorry / I'm / hear / to / that.)
➡ _____

11 (you / do / have / idea / any / she / why / that? / does)
➡ _____

12 (Sohui: / no. // don't / I / I've / think / anything / done / wrong.)
➡ _____

13 (just / it / like / feels / doesn't / she / like / anymore. / me)
➡ _____

14 (Sister: / you / maybe / just / should / her / ask / there / if / something / is / wrong.)
➡ _____

15 (Sohui: / I / maybe / should. // still / I / to / want / friends / be / her. / with)
➡ _____

1 제가 어떻게 해야 할까요?

2 누구나 고민은 있습니다.

3 여러분은 걱정되는 것이 있을 때 무엇을 하나요?

4 여기 세 명의 청소년이 걱정하는 것들이 있습니다.

5 소희는 하연이가 그녀의 가장 친한 친구라고 생각했지만, 지금은 하연이가 변했고 그녀를 피한다고 느낍니다.

6 소희: (그녀의 언니에게) 내 친구 하연이 알지, 그렇지?

7 언니: 응. 왜? 그녀가 어떤데?

8 소희: 나는 그녀가 나를 피하고 있다고 느껴.

9 학교에서 내가 그녀를 볼 때 그녀는 돌아서서 나로부터 멀리 걸어가.

10 언니: 그거 참 안타깝구나.

11 너는 그녀가 왜 그렇게 하는지 아니?

12 소희: 아니. 나는 내가 잘못한 것이 있다고 생각하지 않아.

13 단지 그녀가 더 이상 나를 좋아하지 않는다고 느껴져.

14 언니: 혹시 모르니 뭔가 잘못된 것이 있는지 그녀에게 물어봐.

15 소희: 아마 그래야겠어. 나는 여전히 그녀와 친구로 지내고 싶거든.

16 (thinking / Daeho, / new / that / will / things / him / make / popular, / more / wants / often / things / new / because / just / friends / his / them. / have)

➡ _____

_____

17 (Daeho: / look / Seongjin, / my / at / sneakers. / new)

➡ _____

18 (do / what / think? / you)

➡ _____

19 (Seongjin: / nice, / they're / didn't / but / just / you / new / buy / a / sneakers / couple / months / of / ago?)

➡ _____

_____

20 (Daeho: / but / yeah, / they're / longer / no / stlye. / in)

➡ _____

21 (look / I / cooler / these, / in / right?)

➡ _____

22 (Seongjin: / wearing / Daeho, / the / fashion / latest / make / doesn't / cooler / you / more / or / popular.)

➡ _____

_____

23 (like / people / you / you're / because / you, / because / not / of / clothes. / your)

➡ _____

_____

24 (Yeah? / Daeho:)

➡ _____

25 (Seongjin: / you're / listen / guy. / great / a)

➡ _____

26 (don't / you / new / need / to / sneakers / it. / prove)

➡ _____

27 (Minkyeong / recently, / asked / was / by / out / boy / a / in / class. / her)

➡ _____

28 (wants / she / say / to / but / no / not / does / to / want / his / hurt / feelings.)

➡ _____

_____

29 (Minkyeong: / need / I / advice. / your)

➡ _____

16 대호는 새 물건이 그를 더 인기 있게 만들어 줄 것이라고 생각해서 단지 친구들이 그것을 가지고 있다는 이유로 종종 새 물건을 사기를 원합니다.

17 대호: 성진아, 내 새 운동화 봐.

18 어떠니?

19 성진: 멋지다. 그런데 너 겨우 몇 달 전에 새 운동화 사지 않았니?

20 대호: 응, 하지만 그건 더 이상 유행이 아니야.

21 이걸 신으니까 더 멋져 보이지, 그렇지?

22 성진: 대호야. 최신 유행하는 것을 입는 것이 너를 더 멋지고 더 인기 있게 만들어 주지는 않아.

23 사람들은 네가 너이기 때문에 너를 좋아하는 것이지, 네 옷 때문이 아니야.

24 대호: 그래?

25 성진: 들어봐. 너는 멋진 사람이야.

26 그것을 증명하기 위해 새 운동화가 필요하지 않아.

27 최근에 민경이는 그녀의 반 남자아이에게 데이트 신청을 받았습니다.

28 그녀는 거절하고 싶지만 그의 감정을 상하게 하고 싶지는 않습니다.

29 민경: 저는 선생님의 조언이 필요해요.

30 (boy / a / my / in / asked / class / out. / me)

➡ _____

31 (like / I / him, / for / but / I / now / want / don't / to / go / with / out / him.)

➡ _____

32 (need / I / focus / to / on / studies. / my)

➡ _____

33 (should / what / do? / I)

➡ _____

34 (Counselor: / don't / why / tell / you / why / him / can't / you / go?)

➡ _____

35 (Minkyeong: / afraid / I'm / might / I / his / hurt / feelings.)

➡ _____

36 (Counselor: / you / if / tell / don't / soon, / him / will / he / misunderstand / feelings, / your / and / may / you / up / end / him / hurting / more. / even)

➡ _____

➡ _____

37 (Minkyeong: / you're / maybe / right.)

➡ _____

38 (for / thanks / advice. / the)

➡ _____

---

30 같은 반 남자아이가 저에게 데이트 신청을 했어요.

31 저는 그를 좋아하지만 당분간은 그와 데이트하고 싶지 않아요.

32 저는 공부에 집중해야 해요.

33 제가 어떻게 해야 할까요?

34 상담 선생님: 왜 네가 데이트를 할 수 없는지 그에게 말하는 것은 어떨까?

35 민경: 제가 그의 감정을 상하게 할까 봐 걱정돼요.

36 상담 선생님: 네가 그에게 빨리 말하지 않으면, 그는 네 감정을 오해할 것이고, 너는 그를 더 아프게 할 수도 있단다.

37 민경: 선생님 말씀이 맞는 것 같아요.

38 조언 감사합니다.

※ 다음 우리말을 영어로 쓰시오.

1 제가 어떻게 해야 할까요?
➡ _____

2 누구나 고민은 있습니다.
➡ _____

3 여러분은 걱정되는 것이 있을 때 무엇을 하나요?
➡ _____

4 여기 세 명의 청소년이 걱정하는 것들이 있습니다.
➡ _____

5 소희는 하연이가 그녀의 가장 친한 친구라고 생각했지만, 지금은 하연이가 변했고 그녀를 피한다고 느낍니다.
➡ _____

6 소희: (그녀의 언니에게) 내 친구 하연이 알지, 그렇지?
➡ _____

7 언니: 응. 왜? 그녀가 어떤데?
➡ _____

8 소희: 나는 그녀가 나를 피하고 있다고 느껴.
➡ _____

9 학교에서 내가 그녀를 볼 때 그녀는 돌아서서 나로부터 멀리 걸어가.
➡ _____

10 언니: 그거 참 안타깝구나.
➡ _____

11 너는 그녀가 왜 그렇게 하는지 아니?
➡ _____

12 소희: 아니. 나는 내가 잘못한 것이 있다고 생각하지 않아.
➡ _____

13 단지 그녀가 더 이상 나를 좋아하지 않는다고 느껴져.
➡ _____

14 언니: 혹시 모르니 뭔가 잘못된 것이 있는지 그녀에게 물어봐.
➡ _____

15 소희: 아마 그래야겠어. 나는 여전히 그녀와 친구로 지내고 싶거든.
➡ _____

16 대호는 새 물건이 그를 더 인기 있게 만들어 줄 것이라고 생각해서 단지 친구들이 그것을 가지고 있다는 이유로 종종 새 물건을 사기를 원합니다.
➡ _____

17 대호: 성진아, 내 새 운동화 봐.
➡ _____

18 어떠니?
➡ _____

19 성진: 멋지다. 그런데 너 겨우 몇 달 전에 새 운동화 사지 않았니?

➡ _____

20 대호: 응, 하지만 그건 더 이상 유행이 아니야.

➡ _____

21 이걸 신으니까 더 멋져 보이지, 그렇지?

➡ _____

22 성진: 대호야, 최신 유행하는 것을 입는 것이 너를 더 멋지고 더 인기 있게 만들어 주지는 않아.

➡ _____

23 사람들은 네가 너이기 때문에 너를 좋아하는 것이지, 네 옷 때문이 아니야.

➡ _____

24 대호: 그래?

➡ _____

25 성진: 들어봐. 너는 멋진 사람이야.

➡ _____

26 그것을 증명하기 위해 새 운동화가 필요하지 않아.

➡ _____

27 최근에 민경이는 그녀의 반 남자아이에게 데이트 신청을 받았습니다.

➡ _____

28 그녀는 거절하고 싶지만 그의 감정을 상하게 하고 싶지는 않습니다.

➡ _____

29 민경: 저는 선생님의 조언이 필요해요.

➡ _____

30 같은 반 남자아이가 저에게 데이트 신청을 했어요.

➡ _____

31 저는 그를 좋아하지만 당분간은 그와 데이트하고 싶지 않아요.

➡ _____

32 저는 공부에 집중해야 해요.

➡ _____

33 제가 어떻게 해야 할까요?

➡ _____

34 상담 선생님: 왜 네가 데이트를 할 수 없는지 그에게 말하는 것은 어떨까?

➡ _____

35 민경: 제가 그의 감정을 상하게 할까 봐 걱정돼요

➡ _____

36 상담 선생님: 네가 그에게 빨리 말하지 않으면, 그는 네 감정을 오해할 것이고, 너는 그를 더 아프게 할 수도 있단다.

➡ _____

➡ _____

37 민경: 선생님 말씀이 맞는 것 같아요.

➡ _____

38 조언 감사합니다.

➡ _____

※ 다음 우리말과 일치하도록 빈칸에 알맞은 말을 쓰시오.

Communication Task

1. A: _____ _____ school _____ _____ _____ in the morning.

2. B: I _____ _____ you. We can _____ _____ _____ school starts _____ .

3. A: I think school _____ _____ _____ in the morning.

4. B: I _____ _____ _____ you. School _____ _____ _____ if it starts later.

Writing Workshop

Hena's World

1. I want to _____ _____ . I do not feel good _____ _____ in the group.

2. I'd _____ _____ _____ _____ I can _____ _____ .

tallboy1201

3. I heard you _____ _____ if you _____ _____ .

4. I _____ you eat _____ _____ _____ , milk, and beans.

5. These foods, _____ _____ _____ _____ and _____ , can _____ you _____ _____ .

6. _____ , you should sleep _____ _____ _____ _____ every night.

7. I hope these tips _____ _____ _____ _____ you.

After You Read B

1. I _____ _____ my best friend _____ _____ .

2. _____ _____ _____ ask her if there is _____ _____ ?

3. I need _____ _____ . They'll _____ me _____ .

4. People like you _____ _____ , not _____ _____ _____ .

5. How can I say _____ _____ _____ _____ ?

6. _____ _____ you tell him _____ _____ _____ _____ ?

1. A: 나는 학교가 아침에 더 늦게 시작해야 한다고 생각해.
2. B: 나도 네 말에 동의해. 학교가 늦게 시작하면 우리는 더 많이 잠을 잘 수 있어.
3. A: 나는 학교가 아침에 더 늦게 시작해야 한다고 생각해.
4. B: 나는 동의하지 않아. 학교가 늦게 시작하면 더 늦게 끝날 거야.

Hena의 세계
1. 나는 키가 더 크고 싶어. 나는 그룹에서 키가 가장 작아서 기분이 안 좋아.
2. 나는 내가 키가 더 클 수 있는 방법을 알고 싶어.
tallboy1201
3. 나는 네가 키가 더 클 수 있는지 궁금해한다고 들었어.
4. 나는 네가 달걀, 우유, 콩 같은 음식을 먹을 것을 제안해.
5. 이 음식들은 많은 단백질과 칼슘을 갖고 있어서 네가 키가 더 크는 것을 도와줄 수 있어.
6. 또한 너는 매일 밤 적어도 8시간을 자야 해.
7. 이 조언들이 네게 도움이 되기를 바라.

1. 내 가장 친한 친구가 나를 피하고 있다고 느껴.
2. 뭔가 잘못된 것이 있는지 그녀에게 물어보는 게 어때?
3. 나는 새 옷이 필요해. 그것들은 나를 더 인기 있게 만들어 줄 거야.
4. 사람들은 네가 너이기 때문에 너를 좋아하는 것이지, 네 옷 때문이 아니야.
5. 어떻게 그의 감정을 상하게 하지 않으면서 거절할 수 있을까?
6. 왜 네가 데이트를 할 수 없는지 그에게 말하는 것은 어떨까?

※ 다음 우리말을 영어로 쓰시오.

Communication Task

1. A: 나는 학교가 아침에 더 늦게 시작해야 한다고 생각해.
   ➡ _____

2. B: 나도 네 말에 동의해. 학교가 늦게 시작하면 우리는 더 많이 잠을 잘 수 있어.
   ➡ _____

3. A: 나는 학교가 아침에 더 늦게 시작해야 한다고 생각해.
   ➡ _____

4. B: 나는 동의하지 않아. 학교가 늦게 시작하면 더 늦게 끝날 거야.
   ➡ _____

Writing Workshop

Hena의 세계

1. 나는 키가 더 크고 싶어. 나는 그룹에서 가장 키가 작아서 기분이 안 좋아.
   ➡ _____

2. 내가 키가 더 클 수 있는 방법을 알고 싶어.
   ➡ _____

tallboy1201

3. 나는 네가 키가 더 클 수 있는지 궁금해한다고 들었어.
   ➡ _____

4. 나는 네가 달걀, 우유, 콩 같은 음식을 먹을 것을 제안해.
   ➡ _____

5. 이 음식들은 많은 단백질과 칼슘을 갖고 있어서 네가 키가 더 크는 것을 도와줄 수 있어.
   ➡ _____

6. 또한 너는 매일 밤 적어도 8시간을 자야 해.
   ➡ _____

7. 이 조언들이 네게 도움이 되기를 바라.
   ➡ _____

After You Read B

1. 내 가장 친한 친구가 나를 피하고 있다고 느껴.
   ➡ _____

2. 뭔가 잘못된 것이 있는지 그녀에게 물어보는 게 어때?
   ➡ _____

3. 나는 새 옷이 필요해. 그것들은 나를 더 인기 있게 만들어 줄 거야.
   ➡ _____

4. 사람들은 네가 너이기 때문에 너를 좋아하는 것이지, 네 옷 때문이 아니야.
   ➡ _____

5. 어떻게 그의 감정을 상하게 하지 않으면서 거절할 수 있을까?
   ➡ _____

6. 왜 네가 데이트를 할 수 없는지 그에게 말하는 것은 어떨까?
   ➡ _____

※ 다음 영어를 우리말로 쓰시오.

01 benefit _____

02 moreover _____

03 calming _____

04 nature-friendly _____

05 regret _____

06 produce _____

07 avoid _____

08 finally _____

09 blanket _____

10 flight _____

11 grade _____

12 regularly _____

13 brain _____

14 fortunately _____

15 calcium _____

16 journal _____

17 serotonin _____

18 wet _____

19 sunscreen _____

20 mood _____

21 properly _____

22 shine _____

23 protect _____

24 already _____

25 skin _____

26 weather _____

27 outdoors _____

28 peak _____

29 review _____

30 safely _____

31 direct _____

32 effect _____

33 bone _____

34 healthy _____

35 put on _____

36 keep ~ in mind _____

37 both A and B _____

38 full of _____

39 stay up _____

40 should have p.p. _____

41 put out _____

42 too ~ to ... _____

43 be good for _____

※ 다음 우리말을 영어로 쓰시오.

01 이미

02 흥미롭게도

03 이득; 이득을 보다

04 게다가

05 건강한

06 진정시키는

07 햇살

08 자연친화적인

09 야외에서

10 피부

11 피하다

12 항공편, 비행

13 이불, 담요

14 다행스럽게도

15 점검하다

16 걸다

17 복습하다

18 뇌

19 마침내

20 햇볕, 햇빛

21 효과

22 날씨

23 일지, 일기

24 뼈

25 기분, 감정

26 절정의, 최고조의

27 만들어 내다

28 후회하다

29 규칙적으로

30 역할

31 젖은

32 제대로

33 보호하다

34 안전하게

35 ~로 가득 찬

36 착용하다, 바르다

37 ~에 유익하다

38 제시간에

39 A와 B 둘 다

40 내놓다

41 깨어 있다

42 ~을 명심하다

43 인터넷 검색을 하다

※ 다음 영영풀이에 알맞은 단어를 <보기>에서 골라 쓴 후, 우리말 뜻을 쓰시오.

1 _____ : the highest point: _____

2 _____ : a temporary state of mind: _____

3 _____ : light and heat from the sun: _____

4 _____ : to take advantages from something: _____

5 _____ : to become higher or greater: _____

6 _____ : to study or look at something again: _____

7 _____ : the part assumed to be played by a person: _____

8 _____ : the outer layer of a person's or animal's body: _____

9 _____ : covered or touched with water or another liquid: _____

10 _____ : a large piece of cloth used as a covering for warmth: _____

11 _____ : to produce or reflect light: _____

12 _____ : at the same time every day, week, month, or year: _____

13 _____ : the organ inside the head that control movements and feelings: _____

14 _____ : the hard part of the body that forms a framework inside people or animals: _____

15 _____ : a book in which people regularly write about what has happened to them: _____

16 _____ : to make sure that someone or something is not harmed, injured, damaged, etc.: _____

보기			
journal	peak	brain	go up
shine	blanket	mood	benefit
protect	regularly	review	skin
role	bone	sunshine	wet

※ 다음 우리말과 일치하도록 빈칸에 알맞은 말을 쓰시오.

Listen & Speak 1 Listen

1. **G:** How _____ we _____ _____?
   B: _____, it's _____ _____ _____ a good _____.
2. **B:** _____ can we _____ _____ _____ good _____?
   G: It's _____ to _____ every day.
3. **G:** I _____ it's important to _____ a _____ after reading.
   B: I agree.
4. **B:** It's important _____ _____ _____ what you _____ your money _____.
   G: I _____ so, _____.

Listen & Speak 1 A

1. **B:** _____ did you _____ on the _____?
   G: I _____ tennis. I have _____ _____ _____ on the weekend _____ my health.
   B: Good for _____. It's _____ to _____ _____.
   G: _____. How _____ _____ tennis _____ me?
   B: Why _____?
2. **M:** John, you are _____ again.
   B: I'm sorry. I _____ the _____ _____.
   M: I _____ you need to _____ home a little _____.
   B: I think so, _____. Next time I _____ _____.
   M: It's important to _____ at school _____ _____.

Listen & Speak 2

1. **G:** Your bag is _____ small.
   B: Yes. I _____ _____ _____ a bigger _____.
2. **G:** Aren't you _____?
   B: Yes. I _____ _____ _____ a jacket.
3. **B:** We _____ our _____.
   G: Oh, no. We should _____ come _____.
4. **G:** _____ _____ my face. I _____ _____ _____ _____ some sunscreen.
   B: Yes. You're _____.

1. **G:** 우리는 어떻게 건강을 유지할 수 있을까?
   B: 음, 든든한 아침 식사를 하는 것이 중요해.
2. **B:** 좋은 점수를 받기 위해 우리는 무엇을 할 수 있을까?
   G: 매일 복습하는 것이 중요해.
3. **G:** 나는 독서 후에 일기를 쓰는 것이 중요하다고 생각해.
   B: 나도 동의해.
4. **B:** 네가 돈을 어디에 썼는지 적는 것은 중요해.
   G: 나도 그렇게 생각해.

1. **B:** 주말에 뭐 했니?
   G: 나는 테니스를 쳤어. 나는 건강을 위해 주말에 운동을 하기로 결정했어.
   B: 잘했어. 규칙적으로 운동하는 것은 중요해.
   G: 맞아. 나와 테니스 치는 것은 어때?
   B: 왜 안 되겠어?
2. **M:** 존, 또 지각이구나!
   B: 죄송해요. 버스를 잘못 탔어요.
   M: 나는 네가 집에서 좀 더 빨리 출발할 필요가 있다고 생각한단.
   B: 저도 그렇게 생각해요. 다음번에는 늦지 않을 게요.
   M: 학교에 제시간에 오는 것은 중요하단다.

1. **G:** 네 가방은 정말 작아.
   B: 응. 난 더 큰 것을 가져왔어야 했어.
2. **G:** 춥지 않니?
   B: 응. 나는 재킷을 입었어야 했어.
3. **B:** 우리 비행기를 놓쳤어.
   G: 오, 안 돼. 우리는 더 빨리 왔어야 했어.
4. **G:** 내 얼굴 좀 봐. 나는 자외선 차단제를 발랐어야 했어.
   B: 그래. 네 말이 맞아.

Listen & Speak 2 A

1. **B:** Mina, _____ was the _____?

   G: I didn't _____ it. It _____ _____.

   B: _____ was bad _____ it?

   G: I already _____ the _____. I shouldn't _____ read about it _____ _____ it.

   B: Oh, I'm _____ you didn't _____ it.

2. **B:** We _____ have 30 _____ to go _____ we reach the _____ of the mountain. Let's _____ _____ over there _____ have a _____.

   G: Oh, I _____ only water. I should have _____ some snacks.

   B: That's _____. I _____ a lot. We can _____.

   G: I'll _____ it in _____ to bring _____ snacks next _____.

Real-Life Zone

G: Ben, you _____ full of _____ today!

B: Do I? Maybe that's _____ I finally _____ a good night's sleep _____ night.

G: Why? Don't you _____ get _____ _____?

B: No, I _____ it's really _____ to get a good _____ sleep, but I _____ _____ _____ late _____ the Internet or _____ _____ my _____.

G: That _____ _____ to _____ too.

B: _____ I do that, I _____ it the next _____ and say, "I should _____ gone to bed _____ last night."

G: How was yesterday _____?

B: Well, yesterday afternoon I _____ the mountain with my _____. I was really _____ when I got _____. I went to _____ right _____ I _____ _____ _____.

G: _____ activities _____ a great _____ _____ _____ you _____ a good night's sleep.

Wrap Up 1

W: Oh, your _____ is _____ from the rain! I _____ _____ _____ the weather.

B: Did you _____ it?

W: No. I just _____ it _____ in the _____ this morning.

B: _____ didn't you _____ it?

W: Hanging a _____ in the sun is a nature-friendly _____ to _____ the blanket _____.

B: Oh, I didn't _____ that. I'll _____ that.

W: And it's also _____ to _____ to do it _____.

※ 다음 우리말에 맞도록 대화를 영어로 쓰시오.

Listen & Speak 1 Listen

1. G: _____
   B: _____

2. B: _____
   G: _____

3. G: _____
   B: _____

4. B: _____
   G: _____

Listen & Speak 1 A

1. B: _____
   G: _____
   B: _____
   G: _____
   B: _____

2. M: _____
   B: _____
   M: _____
   B: _____
   M: _____

Listen & Speak 2

1. G: _____
   B: _____

2. G: _____
   B: _____

3. B: _____
   G: _____

4. G: _____
   B: _____

해석

1. G: 우리는 어떻게 건강을 유지할 수 있을까?
   B: 음, 든든한 아침 식사를 하는 것이 중요해.
2. B: 좋은 점수를 받기 위해 우리는 무엇을 할 수 있을까?
   G: 매일 복습하는 것이 중요해.
3. G: 나는 독서 후에 일기를 쓰는 것이 중요하다고 생각해.
   B: 나도 동의해.
4. B: 네가 돈을 어디에 썼는지 적는 것은 중요해.
   G: 나도 그렇게 생각해.

1. B: 주말에 뭐 했니?
   G: 나는 테니스를 쳤어. 나는 건강을 위해 주말에 운동을 하기로 결정했어.
   B: 잘했어. 규칙적으로 운동하는 것은 중요해.
   G: 맞아. 나와 테니스 치는 것은 어때?
   B: 왜 안 되겠어?
2. M: 존, 또 지각이구나!
   B: 죄송해요. 버스를 잘못 탔어요.
   M: 나는 네가 집에서 좀 더 빨리 출발할 필요가 있다고 생각한단다.
   B: 저도 그렇게 생각해요. 다음번에는 늦지 않을 게요.
   M: 학교에 제시간에 오는 것은 중요하단다.

1. G: 네 가방은 정말 작아.
   B: 응. 난 더 큰 것을 가져왔어야 했어.
2. G: 춥지 않니?
   B: 응. 나는 재킷을 입었어야 했어.
3. B: 우리 비행기를 놓쳤어.
   G: 오, 안 돼. 우리는 더 빨리 왔어야 했어.
4. G: 내 얼굴 좀 봐. 나는 자외선 차단제를 발랐어야 했어.
   B: 그래. 네 말이 맞아.

Listen & Speak 2 A

1. B: _____
   G: _____
   B: _____
   G: _____
   B: _____
2. B: _____
   _____
   G: _____
   B: _____
   G: _____

Real-Life Zone

G: _____
B: _____
G: _____
B: _____
_____
G: _____
B: _____
_____
G: _____
B: _____
_____
G: _____

Wrap Up 1

W: _____
B: _____
W: _____
B: _____
W: _____
B: _____
W: _____

1. B: 미나야, 영화 어땠니?
   G: 나는 그것을 즐기지 못했어. 지루했어.
   B: 무엇이 별로였니?
   G: 나는 이미 결말을 알고 있었어. 보기 전에 그것에 대해 읽지 말았어야 했는데.
   B: 오, 네가 좋아하지 않다니 유감이야.
2. B: 우리는 산 정상에 도착하기까지 아직 30분은 더 가야 해. 저기서 앉아서 간식 먹고 가자.
   G: 오, 난 물만 가져왔어. 간식을 가져왔어야 했는데.
   B: 괜찮아. 내가 많이 가져왔어. 우리는 같이 먹을 수 있어.
   G: 다음번에는 간식을 가져올 것을 명심할게.

G: 벤, 너 오늘 기운 차 보여!
B: 내가 그래? 그건 아마 내가 지난밤 마침내 잠을 잘 잤기 때문일 거야.
G: 왜? 평소에 충분한 잠을 자지 못하니?
B: 응, 잠을 잘 자는 것이 정말 중요하다는 것은 알지만 나는 언제나 인터넷 검색을 하거나 휴대폰을 가지고 놀면서 늦게까지 깨어 있어.
G: 그건 나에게도 가끔 일어나는 일이야.
B: 그러고 난 뒤에, 나는 다음 날 아침 후회하고 "지난밤에 더 일찍 잠들었어야 했는데."라고 말해.
G: 어제는 어떻게 달랐니?
B: 음, 어제 오후에 나는 아빠와 등산을 했어. 집에 왔을 때 나는 매우 피곤했어. 나는 침대에 가자마자 바로 잠들었어.
G: 야외 활동은 네가 잠을 잘 자도록 돕는 훌륭한 방법이구나.

W: 오, 네 이불이 비에 젖었어! 내가 날씨를 확인했어야 했는데.
B: 그것을 빨았어요?
W: 아니. 오늘 아침에 그냥 햇볕에 널어놓았어.
B: 왜 빨지 않았어요?
W: 햇볕에 이불을 널어놓는 것은 이불을 깨끗하게 유지하는 친환경적인 방법이야.
B: 오, 저는 그것을 몰랐어요. 기억해 둘게요.
W: 그리고 정기적으로 그렇게 하는 것을 기억하는 것 또한 중요해.

※ 다음 우리말과 일치하도록 빈칸에 알맞은 것을 골라 쓰시오.

1   _____ the _____
A. Sunshine   B. Enjoy

2   How _____ time do you _____ every day _____ _____ the sun?
A. out   B. much   C. in   D. spend

3   _____ _____, right?
A. much   B. not

4   Most people are _____ _____ at school or at work to _____ much time _____.
A. outdoors   B. busy   C. spend   D. too

5   _____, the sun _____ an important _____ in your _____.
A. role   B. plays   C. health   D. however

6   It _____ you _____ _____.
A. stay   B. helps   C. healthy

7   Everyone _____ _____ when the sun _____.
A. happier   B. feels   C. shines

8   This is _____ of serotonin, the _____ _____ _____.
A. hormone   B. because   C. body's   D. happy

9   The _____ sun you get, the more "happy _____" the _____ _____.
A. brain   B. hormone   C. more   D. produces

10 _____ your serotonin level _____ _____, you feel happier and _____.
A. up   B. stronger   C. goes   D. when

11 This helps you _____ _____ _____.
A. stress   B. fight   C. everyday

12 Serotonin also has a _____ _____, helping you focus better on _____ you are _____.
A. effect   B. what   C. calming   D. doing

13 _____, serotonin helps you get a good _____ _____ because it helps the brain _____ a sleep hormone.
A. sleep   B. moreover   C. produce   D. night's

14 Sunshine does _____ _____ make you _____ and sleep _____.
A. just   B. better   C. not   D. feel

1 햇빛을 즐기세요

2 여러분은 매일 햇빛 속에서 얼마나 많은 시간을 보내나요?

3 많지 않죠, 그렇죠?

4 대부분의 사람들은 학교와 직장에서 너무 바빠서 많은 시간을 야외에서 보내지 못합니다.

5 그러나 햇빛은 여러분의 건강에 중요한 역할을 합니다.

6 그것은 여러분이 건강을 유지하는 데 도움을 줍니다.

7 모든 사람들은 해가 비칠 때 더 행복하게 느낍니다.

8 이것은 몸의 행복 호르몬인 세로토닌 때문입니다.

9 여러분이 햇빛을 쬘수록 뇌는 행복 호르몬을 더 만들어 냅니다.

10 여러분의 세로토닌 수치가 높아지면, 여러분은 더 행복하고 더 건강하게 느낍니다.

11 이것은 여러분이 매일의 스트레스를 이겨 내는 데 도움을 줍니다.

12 세로토닌은 또한 진정 효과가 있고, 여러분이 하는 일에 더 잘 집중할 수 있도록 도와줍니다.

13 게다가, 세로토닌은 뇌가 수면 호르몬을 생성하도록 도와주기 때문에 여러분이 숙면을 취하도록 해 줍니다.

14 햇빛은 단지 여러분이 더 기분 좋게 느끼고 잠을 더 잘 자게 하는 것만은 아닙니다.

15 It _____ helps _____ _____ _____.

    A. strong   B. also   C. bones   D. build

16 _____ you all know, it is calcium that _____ strong _____ and _____.

    A. bones   B. as   C. teeth   D. builds

17 However, _____ the _____ to _____ calcium _____, it needs vitamin D.

    A. properly   B. body   C. use   D. for

18 Interestingly, the skin _____ vitamin D _____ _____ on it.

    A. shines   B. creates   C. sunlight   D. when

19 The _____ way to make strong _____ is to _____ and enjoy the sun.

    A. outside   B. easiest   C. go   D. bones

20 _____ you can _____, sunshine has many _____, but how can you enjoy its benefits _____?

    A. benefits   B. safely   C. as   D. see

21 Fortunately, getting _____ _____ on your _____ for 10 to 20 minutes a day is enough to _____ from it.

    A. direct   B. benefit   C. sunlight   D. skin

22 Try to go out into the sun between _____ or during lunch _____ and get _____ on your _____ and hands.

    A. arms   B. sunshine   C. breaks   D. classes

23 A _____ in the sun, for just a _____ _____ every day, is good for both your _____ and your body.

    A. few   B. mind   C. walk   D. minutes

24 However, avoid the sun during _____ summer hours, between 11 and 3, and use sunscreen to _____ your _____ and _____.

    A. protect   B. neck   C. peak   D. face

25 Enjoy the sun _____ and see how a _____ sunshine can make a world of _____ in your health and your _____.

    A. difference   B. little   C. safely   D. mood

---

15 그것은 또한 튼튼한 뼈를 만드는 것을 돕습니다.

16 여러분 모두가 알다시피, 튼튼한 뼈와 치아를 만드는 것은 칼슘입니다.

17 그러나 몸이 칼슘을 적절하게 사용하기 위해서는 비타민 D가 필요합니다.

18 흥미롭게도, 피부는 햇빛이 피부에 비칠 때 비타민 D를 만들어 냅니다.

19 튼튼한 뼈를 만드는 가장 쉬운 방법은 밖으로 나가서 햇빛을 즐기는 겁니다.

20 보시다시피, 햇빛은 많은 이점이 있지만, 어떻게 그것의 이점을 안전하게 즐길 수 있을까요?

21 다행히도, 하루에 10분에서 20분 동안 피부에 직사광선을 쪼이는 것은 햇빛으로부터 이점을 얻는 데 충분합니다.

22 수업 시간 사이나 점심시간에 햇빛을 쪼려 밖으로 나가서 팔과 손에 햇빛을 쪼여 보세요.

23 매일 단 몇 분 동안 햇살을 쪼이며 걷는 것은 여러분의 마음과 몸 모두에 좋습니다.

24 그러나 여름 절정 시간인 11시에서 3시 사이에는 햇빛을 피하고, 얼굴과 목을 보호하기 위해 자외선 차단제를 사용하세요.

25 태양을 안전하게 즐기고 적은 양의 햇빛이 여러분의 건강과 기분에 얼마나 큰 차이를 만들어 내는지 보세요.

※ 다음 우리말과 일치하도록 빈칸에 알맞은 말을 쓰시오.

1 _____ the _____

2 How much time do you _____ every day _____ _____ _____ _____ ?

3 _____ _____ , right?

4 Most people are _____ _____ at school or _____ _____ _____ _____ much time _____ .

5 _____ , the sun _____ _____ _____ _____ in your health.

6 It _____ you _____ _____ .

7 Everyone _____ _____ when the sun _____ .

8 This is _____ _____ serotonin, _____ _____ _____ .

9 _____ _____ _____ you get, _____ _____ " _____ _____ " the brain _____ .

10 When your serotonin level _____ _____ , you _____ _____ and _____ .

11 This _____ you _____ _____ _____ .

12 Serotonin also has a _____ _____ , helping you _____ better on _____ _____ _____ _____ .

13 _____ , serotonin helps you get _____ _____ _____ because it _____ the brain _____ a sleep hormone.

14 Sunshine does _____ _____ make you feel and _____ .

1 햇빛을 즐기세요

2 여러분은 매일 햇빛 속에서 얼마나 많은 시간을 보내나요?

3 많지 않죠, 그렇죠?

4 대부분의 사람들은 학교와 직장에서 너무 바빠서 많은 시간을 야외에서 보내지 못합니다.

5 그러나 햇빛은 여러분의 건강에 중요한 역할을 합니다.

6 그것은 여러분이 건강을 유지하는 데 도움을 줍니다.

7 모든 사람들은 해가 비칠 때 더 행복하게 느낍니다.

8 이것은 몸의 행복 호르몬인 세로토닌 때문입니다.

9 여러분이 햇빛을 쬘수록 뇌는 행복 호르몬을 더 만들어 냅니다.

10 여러분의 세로토닌 수치가 높아지면, 여러분은 더 행복하고 더 건강하게 느낍니다.

11 이것은 여러분이 매일의 스트레스를 이겨 내는 데 도움을 줍니다.

12 세로토닌은 또한 진정 효과가 있고, 여러분이 하는 일에 더 잘 집중할 수 있도록 도와줍니다.

13 게다가, 세로토닌은 뇌가 수면 호르몬을 생성하도록 도와주기 때문에 여러분이 숙면을 취하도록 해 줍니다.

14 햇빛은 단지 여러분이 더 기분 좋게 느끼고 잠을 더 잘 자게 하는 것만은 아닙니다.

15 It _____ helps _____ _____ _____.

16 _____ _____ _____ _____, it is calcium that builds strong _____ and _____.

17 However, _____ _____ _____ _____ calcium _____, it needs vitamin D.

18 _____, the skin _____ vitamin D _____ _____ on it.

19 _____ _____ _____ to make strong bones is _____ _____ _____ and enjoy the sun.

20 _____ _____ _____ _____, sunshine has many benefits, but how can you _____ _____ _____ _____?

21 Fortunately, _____ _____ _____ on your skin for 10 to 20 minutes a day is enough _____ _____ _____ _____.

22 _____ _____ _____ _____ _____ the sun _____ classes or _____ lunch breaks and _____ _____ your arms and hands.

23 A walk in the sun, _____ _____ _____ _____ _____ _____, is good for _____ your mind _____ your body.

24 However, _____ the sun during _____ summer hours, between 11 and 3, and use sunscreen _____ _____ _____ _____ _____ _____.

25 Enjoy the sun safely and see how _____ _____ can _____ _____ in your _____ and your _____.

※ 다음 문장을 우리말로 쓰시오.

1 ▶ Enjoy the Sunshine

➡ _____

2 ▶ How much time do you spend every day out in the sun?

➡ _____

3 ▶ Not much, right?

➡ _____

4 ▶ Most people are too busy at school or at work to spend much time outdoors.

➡ _____

5 ▶ However, the sun plays an important role in your health.

➡ _____

6 ▶ It helps you stay healthy.

➡ _____

7 ▶ Everyone feels happier when the sun shines.

➡ _____

8 ▶ This is because of serotonin, the body's happy hormone.

➡ _____

9 ▶ The more sun you get, the more "happy hormone" the brain produces.

➡ _____

10 ▶ When your serotonin level goes up, you feel happier and stronger.

➡ _____

11 ▶ This helps you fight everyday stress.

➡ _____

12 ▶ Serotonin also has a calming effect, helping you focus better on what you are doing.

➡ _____

13 ▶ Moreover, serotonin helps you get a good night's sleep because it helps the brain produce a sleep hormone.

➡ _____

14 Sunshine does not just make you feel and sleep better.

➡ _____

15 It also helps build strong bones.

➡ _____

16 As you all know, it is calcium that builds strong bones and teeth.

➡ _____

17 However, for the body to use calcium properly, it needs vitamin D.

➡ _____

18 Interestingly, the skin creates vitamin D when sunlight shines on it.

➡ _____

19 The easiest way to make strong bones is to go outside and enjoy the sun.

➡ _____

20 As you can see, sunshine has many benefits, but how can you enjoy its benefits safely?

➡ _____

21 Fortunately, getting direct sunlight on your skin for 10 to 20 minutes a day is enough to benefit from it.

➡ _____

22 Try to go out into the sun between classes or during lunch breaks and get sunshine on your arms and hands.

➡ _____

23 A walk in the sun, for just a few minutes every day, is good for both your mind and your body.

➡ _____

24 However, avoid the sun during peak summer hours, between 11 and 3, and use sunscreen to protect your face and neck.

➡ _____

25 Enjoy the sun safely and see how a little sunshine can make a world of difference in your health and your mood.

➡ _____

※ 다음 괄호 안의 단어들을 우리말에 맞도록 바르게 배열하시오.

1 (the / Enjoy / Sunshine)
➡ _____

2 (much / how / time / you / do / every / spend / out / day / in / sun? / the)
➡ _____

3 (much, / not / right?)
➡ _____

4 (people / most / too / are / at / busy / or / school / at / to / work / much / spend / outdoors. / time)
➡ _____
_____

5 (the / however, / sun / an / plays / role / important / your / in / health.)
➡ _____

6 (helps / it / you / healthy. / stay)
➡ _____

7 (feels / everyone / when / happier / the / shines. / sun)
➡ _____

8 (is / this / of / because / serotonin, / body's / the / hormone. / happy)
➡ _____

9 (more / the / you / sun / get, / more / the / hormone" / "happy / the / produces. / brain)
➡ _____

10 (your / when / level / serotonin / up, / goes / feel / you / stronger. / and / happier)
➡ _____

11 (helps / this / fight / you / stress. / everyday)
➡ _____

12 (also / serotonin / a / has / effect, / calming / you / helping / better / focus / what / on / are / you / doing.)
➡ _____
_____

13 (serotonin / moreover, / you / helps / a / get / night's / good / because / sleep / helps / it / brain / the / a / produce / hormone. / sleep)
➡ _____
_____

14 (does / sunshine / just / not / you / make / feel / and / better. / sleep)
➡ _____

1 햇빛을 즐기세요

2 여러분은 매일 햇빛 속에서 얼마나 많은 시간을 보내나요?

3 많지 않죠, 그렇죠?

4 대부분의 사람들은 학교와 직장에서 너무 바빠서 많은 시간을 야외에서 보내지 못합니다.

5 그러나 햇빛은 여러분의 건강에 중요한 역할을 합니다.

6 그것은 여러분이 건강을 유지하는 데 도움을 줍니다.

7 모든 사람들은 해가 비칠 때 더 행복하게 느낍니다.

8 이것은 몸의 행복 호르몬인 세로토닌 때문입니다.

9 여러분이 햇빛을 쬘수록 뇌는 행복 호르몬을 더 만들어 냅니다.

10 여러분의 세로토닌 수치가 높아지면, 여러분은 더 행복하고 더 건강하게 느낍니다.

11 이것은 여러분이 매일의 스트레스를 이겨 내는 데 도움을 줍니다.

12 세로토닌은 또한 진정 효과가 있고, 여러분이 하는 일에 더 잘 집중할 수 있도록 도와줍니다.

13 게다가, 세로토닌은 뇌가 수면 호르몬을 생성하도록 도와주기 때문에 여러분이 숙면을 취하도록 해 줍니다.

14 햇빛은 단지 여러분이 더 기분 좋게 느끼고 잠을 더 잘 자게 하는 것만은 아닙니다.

15 (also / it / build / helps / bones. / strong)

➡ _____

16 (you / as / know, / all / is / it / that / calcium / strong / builds / teeth. / and / bones)

➡ _____

17 (for / however, / body / the / use / to / properly, / calcium / it / vitamin / needs / D.)

➡ _____

18 (the / interestingly, / skin / vitamin / creates / when / D / sunlight / on / shines / it.)

➡ _____

19 (easiest / the / to / way / strong / make / is / bones / go / to / and / outside / the / enjoy / sun. / the)

➡ _____

_____

20 (you / as / see, / can / has / sunshine / benefits, / many / how / but / you / can / its / enjoy / safely? / benefits)

➡ _____

_____

21 (getting / fortunately, / sunlight / direct / your / on / for / skin / to / 10 / minutes / 20 / day / a / enough / is / benefit / to / it. / from)

➡ _____

_____

22 (to / try / out / go / into / sun / the / classes / between / or / lunch / during / breaks / and / sunshine / get / your / on / arms / hands. / and)

➡ _____

_____

23 (walk / a / in / sun, / the / just / for / a / minutes / few / day, / every / good / is / both / for / mind / your / and / body. / your)

➡ _____

_____

24 (avoid / however, / sun / the / peak / during / hours, / summer / between / 3, / and / 11 / use / and / to / sunscreen / protect / face / your / fance / neck. / and)

➡ _____

_____

25 (the / enjoy / sun / and / safely / see / a / how / little / can / sunshine / a / make / world / difference / of / your / in / health / and / mood. / your)

➡ _____

_____

---

15 그것은 또한 튼튼한 뼈를 만드는 것을 돕습니다.

16 여러분 모두가 알다시피, 튼튼한 뼈와 치아를 만드는 것은 칼슘입니다.

17 그러나 몸이 칼슘을 적절하게 사용하기 위해서는 비타민 D가 필요합니다.

18 흥미롭게도, 피부는 햇빛이 피부에 비칠 때 비타민 D를 만들어 냅니다.

19 튼튼한 뼈를 만드는 가장 쉬운 방법은 밖으로 나가서 햇빛을 즐기는 겁니다.

20 보시다시피, 햇빛은 많은 이점이 있지만, 어떻게 그것의 이점을 안전하게 즐길 수 있을까요?

21 다행히도, 하루에 10분에서 20분 동안 피부에 직사광선을 쪼이는 것은 햇빛으로부터 이점을 얻는 데 충분합니다.

22 수업 시간 사이나 점심시간에 햇빛을 쬐러 밖으로 나가서 팔과 손에 햇빛을 쬐어 보세요.

23 매일 단 몇 분 동안 햇살을 쬐며 걷는 것은 여러분의 마음과 몸 모두에 좋습니다.

24 그러나 여름 절정 시간인 11시에서 3시 사이에는 햇빛을 피하고, 얼굴과 목을 보호하기 위해 자외선 차단제를 사용하세요.

25 태양을 안전하게 즐기고 적은 양의 햇빛이 여러분의 건강과 기분에 얼마나 큰 차이를 만들어 내는지 보세요.

※ 다음 우리말을 영어로 쓰시오.

1 햇빛을 즐기세요

➡ _____

2 여러분은 매일 햇빛 속에서 얼마나 많은 시간을 보내나요?

➡ _____

3 많지 않죠, 그렇죠?

➡ _____

4 대부분의 사람들은 학교와 직장에서 너무 바빠서 많은 시간을 야외에서 보내지 못합니다.

➡ _____

5 그러나 햇빛은 여러분의 건강에 중요한 역할을 합니다.

➡ _____

6 그것은 여러분이 건강을 유지하는 데 도움을 줍니다.

➡ _____

7 모든 사람들은 해가 비칠 때 더 행복하게 느낍니다.

➡ _____

8 이것은 몸의 행복 호르몬인 세로토닌 때문입니다.

➡ _____

9 여러분이 햇빛을 쬘수록 뇌는 행복 호르몬을 더 만들어 냅니다.

➡ _____

10 여러분의 세로토닌 수치가 높아지면, 여러분은 더 행복하고 더 건강하게 느낍니다.

➡ _____

11 이것은 여러분이 매일의 스트레스를 이겨 내는 데 도움을 줍니다.

➡ _____

12 세로토닌은 또한 진정 효과가 있고, 여러분이 하는 일에 더 잘 집중할 수 있도록 도와줍니다.

➡ _____

13 게다가, 세로토닌은 뇌가 수면 호르몬을 생성하도록 도와주기 때문에 여러분이 숙면을 취하도록 해 줍니다.

➡ _____

_____

14 햇빛은 단지 여러분이 더 기분 좋게 느끼고 잠을 더 잘 자게 하는 것만은 아닙니다.

➡ _____

15 그것은 또한 튼튼한 뼈를 만드는 것을 돕습니다.

➡ _____

16 여러분 모두가 알다시피, 튼튼한 뼈와 치아를 만드는 것은 칼슘입니다.

➡ _____

17 그러나 몸이 칼슘을 적절하게 사용하기 위해서는 비타민 D가 필요합니다.

➡ _____

18 흥미롭게도, 피부는 햇빛이 피부에 비칠 때 비타민 D를 만들어 냅니다.

➡ _____

19 튼튼한 뼈를 만드는 가장 쉬운 방법은 밖으로 나가서 햇빛을 즐기는 겁니다.

➡ _____

20 보시다시피, 햇빛은 많은 이점이 있지만, 어떻게 그것의 이점을 안전하게 즐길 수 있을까요?

➡ _____

21 다행히도, 하루에 10분에서 20분 동안 피부에 직사광선을 쪼이는 것은 햇빛으로부터 이점을 얻는 데 충분합니다.

➡ _____

_____

22 수업 시간 사이나 점심시간에 햇빛을 쬐러 밖으로 나가서 팔과 손에 햇빛을 쬐어 보세요.

➡ _____

_____

23 매일 단 몇 분 동안 햇살을 쬐며 걷는 것은 여러분의 마음과 몸 모두에 좋습니다.

➡ _____

24 그러나 여름 절정 시간인 11시에서 3시 사이에는 햇빛을 피하고, 얼굴과 목을 보호하기 위해 자외선 차단제를 사용하세요.

➡ _____

_____

25 태양을 안전하게 즐기고 적은 양의 햇빛이 여러분의 건강과 기분에 얼마나 큰 차이를 만들어 내는지 보세요.

➡ _____

_____

※ 다음 우리말과 일치하도록 빈칸에 알맞은 말을 쓰시오.

Communication Task

1. A: I think _____ _____ _____ _____ every day. Do you _____ _____ _____?

2. B: _____, I _____. But I'll _____.

3. A: _____.

1. A: 나는 매일 운동하는 것이 중요하다고 생각해. 너는 매일 운동하니?
2. B: 아니, 하지만 노력할 거야.
3. A: 알았어.

After You Read A

1. The _____ of _____

2. Sunshine _____ you _____ _____ stress and _____ _____.

3. Sunshine _____ _____ _____ _____ _____ _____ _____ you are doing.

4. If you _____ _____ _____, you _____ _____ _____ _____ at night.

5. _____ the _____ _____ _____ _____ _____, your skin produces vitamin D, _____ _____ _____ for strong bones.

1. 햇빛의 좋은 점
2. 햇빛은 여러분이 스트레스를 다루고 더 행복하게 느끼도록 돕는다.
3. 햇빛은 여러분이 하는 일에 더 잘 집중할 수 있도록 도와준다.
4. 햇빛을 충분히 쬐면 밤에 잠을 더 잘 잘 것이다.
5. 해가 여러분의 피부에 비칠 때, 여러분의 피부는 비타민 D를 만드는데, 그것은 튼튼한 뼈를 만드는 데 필요하다.

Writing Workshop

1. _____ Comes _____!

2. _____ your hands _____ _____ _____. You _____ _____ _____ _____ _____ easily _____ you wash your hands well.

3. Get _____ _____ for 10 to 20 minutes _____ _____.

4. _____ _____ sunlight you get, the _____ and _____ _____ _____.

5. _____ is a good breakfast _____ helps the _____ _____ _____.

6. _____ you eat a good breakfast, you can _____ _____ _____ _____ _____ and _____ things _____.

1. 건강이 먼저야!
2. 외출 후에는 손을 씻어라. 손을 잘 씻으면 쉽게 감기에 걸리지 않을 것이다.
3. 매일 직사광선을 10~20분간 받아라.
4. 햇빛을 더 많이 받을수록 더 행복하고 더 강하게 느낄 것이다.
5. 두뇌가 적절히 작동하도록 돕는 것은 좋은 아침식사이다.
6. 좋은 아침을 먹으면, 일에 분명히 집중하고 더 잘 기억할 수 있다.

※ 다음 우리말을 영어로 쓰시오.

Communication Task

1. A: 나는 매일 운동하는 것이 중요하다고 생각해. 너는 매일 운동하니?
   ➡ _____

2. B: 아니, 하지만 노력할 거야.
   ➡ _____

3. A: 좋아.
   ➡ _____

After You Read A

1. 햇빛의 좋은 점
   ➡ _____

2. 햇빛은 여러분이 스트레스를 다루고 더 행복하게 느끼도록 돕는다.
   ➡ _____

3. 햇빛은 여러분이 하는 일에 더 잘 집중할 수 있도록 도와준다.
   ➡ _____

4. 햇빛을 충분히 쬐면 밤에 잠을 더 잘 잘 것이다.
   ➡ _____

5. 해가 여러분의 피부에 비칠 때, 여러분의 피부는 비타민 D를 만드는데, 그것은 튼튼한 뼈를 만드는 데 필요하다.
   ➡ _____

Writing Workshop

1. 건강이 먼저야!
   ➡ _____

2. 외출 후에는 손을 씻어라. 손을 잘 씻으면 쉽게 감기에 걸리지 않을 것이다.
   ➡ _____

3. 매일 직사광선을 10~20분간 받아라.
   ➡ _____

4. 햇빛을 더 많이 받을수록 더 행복하고 강하게 느낄 것이다.
   ➡ _____

5. 두뇌가 적절히 작동하도록 돕는 것은 좋은 아침식사이다.
   ➡ _____

6. 좋은 아침을 먹으면, 일에 분명히 집중하고 더 잘 기억할 수 있다.
   ➡ _____

※ 다음 영어를 우리말로 쓰시오.

01	accident	
02	overuse	
03	although	
04	path	
05	uncomfortable	
06	peel	
07	regularly	
08	overwork	
09	earthquake	
10	cause	
11	electricity	
12	overeat	
13	pack	
14	explode	
15	feed	
16	oxygen	
17	garlic	
18	lightning	
19	location	
20	memory	
21	avoid	

22	overflow	
23	mosquito	
24	nature-friendly	
25	occasion	
26	prepare	
27	protect	
28	entrance	
29	sunscreen	
30	apply	
31	attention	
32	flooding	
33	fit	
34	safety	
35	use up	
36	pass out	
37	hang out	
38	keep away	
39	put up	
40	by -ing	
41	keep ~ in mind	
42	put on	
43	do one's best	

※ 다음 우리말을 영어로 쓰시오.

01	불편한		22	평평한	
02	사고		23	주의, 집중	
03	흘러넘치다, 범람하다		24	홍수, 범람	
04	마늘		25	걸다, 매달다	
05	~에 맞다		26	자연 친화적인	
06	모기		27	흘리다	
07	(과일 또는 채소의) 껍질		28	(특정한) 때, 경우	
08	비록 ~이긴 하지만		29	(짐을) 꾸리다	
09	(크림 등을) 바르다		30	준비하다, 대비하다	
10	번개		31	문지르다, 비비다	
11	규칙적으로		32	(세게) 치다	
12	(출)입구, 문		33	전기	
13	장소		34	피하다	
14	폭발하다		35	~을 바르다	
15	과식하다		36	~을 다 써버리다	
16	지진		37	~을 명심하다	
17	과로하다, 혹사하다		38	어울리다	
18	보호하다		39	~을 접근하지 못하게 하다	
19	산소		40	안 자다, 깨어 있다	
20	안전, 안전성		41	~ 대신에	
21	남용하다, 너무 많이 사용하다		42	의식을 잃다, 기절하다	
			43	최선을 다하다	

※ 다음 영영풀이에 알맞은 단어를 <보기>에서 골라 쓴 후, 우리말 뜻을 쓰시오.

1 _____ : something that you remember: _____

2 _____ : to give food to someone or something: _____

3 _____ : a sudden, violent shaking of the earth's surface: _____

4 _____ : the skin of a fruit: _____

5 _____ : the bright flashes of light that you see in the sky during a storm:

   _____

6 _____ : to hit someone or something hard or with force: _____

7 _____ : to press and move your hands or an object over a surface: _____

8 _____ : a door, gate, passage, etc. used for entering a room, building, or place:

   _____

9 _____ : a place where something happens or exists; the position of something:

   _____

10 _____ : a situation in which water from a river or from rain covers large areas of

   land: _____

11 _____ : to put something into a bag, suitcase, etc., so that you can take it with

   you: _____

12 _____ : to burst, or to make something burst, loudly and violently, causing

   damage: _____

13 _____ : to put or spread something such as paint, cream, etc. onto a surface:

   _____

14 _____ : a small flying insect that bites the skin of people and animals and sucks

   their blood: _____

15 _____ : a cream that you can rub onto your skin to stop it from being burned by

   the sun: _____

16 _____ : a vegetable of the onion family with a very strong taste and smell, used

   in cooking to give flavor to food: _____

보기

pack	location	rub	entrance
garlic	mosquito	feed	earthquake
flooding	explode	strike	lightning
apply	sunscreen	memory	peel

※ 다음 우리말과 일치하도록 빈칸에 알맞은 말을 쓰시오.

Listen & Speak 1 Listen

1. **B:** We _____ _____ _____ _____ for bees.
   G: Oh, there are bees. Run!

2. **G:** Can we go _____ _____? It _____ _____.
   B: No. We have to _____ _____ if we want _____ _____ _____ the top.

3. **B:** Oh, the _____ are _____.
   G: Then we _____ _____ _____ _____ the stairs slowly.

4. **G:** _____ _____ some more. I want to reach the _____ of the mountain.
   B: First we _____ _____ _____ the weather. Oh, it says it's _____ _____ _____. We _____ _____ _____.

Listen & Speak 1 A

1. **G:** Mom, can I _____ _____ this afternoon?
   W: Sure. _____ _____ _____ put on sunscreen before you _____ _____.
   G: But it's _____ today. Do I _____ _____ _____ _____ sunscreen?
   W: Yes, you have to _____ sunscreen _____ _____.
   G: Okay. Then I'll _____ some _____ now.

2. **B:** Let's _____ _____.
   G: I'm sorry, I can't. I have to _____ _____ _____ _____ _____.
   B: Oh, what's _____?
   G: I don't know, but my _____ _____.

Listen & Speak 2 Listen

1. **M:** _____ run. You _____ _____ _____.
   B: Okay, I _____ _____.

2. **B:** Jumping _____ cold water _____ _____ _____ _____ can _____ _____ _____.
   G: Oh, okay. I will _____ _____.

3. **G:** Mom, I want _____ _____ here.
   W: Okay, but first you should check _____ _____ _____. It may be _____ _____ you think.

4. **B:** Can I swim _____ _____ _____ _____?
   G: Swimming _____ a full stomach can be _____.

1. **B:** 우리는 벌들을 조심해야만 해.
   G: 오, 벌들이다. 뛰어!
2. **G:** 이쪽으로 갈 수 있을까? 좋아 보여.
   B: 아니. 정상에 가기를 원한다면 우리는 똑바로 가야 해.
3. **B:** 오, 계단이 젖었어.
   G: 그러면 우리는 계단을 천천히 내려가야 해.
4. **G:** 조금 더 올라가 보자. 나는 산 정상에 닿고 싶어.
   B: 우리는 먼저 날씨를 확인해야 해. 오, 비가 내릴 예정이래. 우리는 내려가야 해.

1. **G:** 엄마, 오후에 밖에서 놀아도 될까요?
   W: 물론이지. 나가기 전에 선크림 바르는 것을 잊지 말아라.
   G: 그렇지만 오늘은 흐려요. 선크림을 발라야 하나요?
   W: 그럼, 매일 선크림을 발라야 한단다.
   G: 알겠어요. 그러면 지금 바를게요.
2. **B:** 볼링 치러 가자.
   G: 미안해. 갈 수 없어. 병원에 가야 하거든.
   B: 오, 무슨 문제 있니?
   G: 몰라, 하지만 배가 아파.

1. **M:** 뛰지 마. 넘어질 수도 있단다.
   B: 알겠어요, 뛰지 않을게요.
2. **B:** 준비 운동을 하지 않고 차가운 물로 뛰어드는 것은 위험할 수 있어.
   G: 오, 알았어. 준비 운동할게.
3. **G:** 엄마, 여기에서 수영하고 싶어요.
   W: 그래, 하지만 우선 물이 얼마나 깊은지 확인해야 한단다. 네가 생각하는 것보다 물이 깊을 수 있어.
4. **B:** 먹고 난 후에 바로 수영해도 될까?
   G: 배가 부른 채로 수영하는 것은 불편할 수 있어.

Listen & Speak 2 A

1. **M:** Flooding _____ _____ big problems. However, you may not know _____ _____ _____ when it happens. There are several things you _____ _____ _____. First, you _____ _____ _____ _____ the water and the electricity. Second, _____ water and food when you leave the house. _____, you have to move to a high and _____ _____ and _____ _____ _____ the weather report.

2. **B:** Mina, are you _____ _____ _____?
   G: No, not _____. I _____ _____ check _____ I _____ _____ the gas.
   B: If we don't leave now, we _____ _____ _____ the concert _____ _____.
   G: Okay, but I _____ _____ _____ the gas first. It will only take a _____.

Real-Life Zone

B: Uncle John, _____ _____ my new bike. _____ do you _____?
M: It's really nice. Where _____ you _____?
B: To the park _____ _____ a friend.
M: Where's your helmet?
B: I _____ _____ _____. It's just a _____ _____.
M: _____ _____ your helmet. You may _____ _____.
B: But I see a _____ of people _____ bikes _____ helmets.
M: You _____ _____ _____ a helmet. It _____ your head in an accident.
B: Okay. I'll get my dad's helmet.
M: No. You _____ _____ _____ a helmet that _____ you. If _____, it cannot protect your head.
B: I guess I'll _____ _____ _____ one for myself.

Wrap Up

B: Here _____ the bus!
G: Oh, but first I have to _____ _____ my tea.
B: _____ _____ you just take it with you? I'm _____ _____ it will be okay if you are _____.
G: No. If the bus stops _____, I _____ _____ it.
B: Okay, then I can just _____ _____ you _____ your drink. I'm sure _____ _____ will come soon.
G: Thanks.

---

1. **M:** 홍수는 큰 문제들을 일으킬 수 있습니다. 그러나, 당신은 홍수가 발생할 때 무엇을 해야 하는지 모를 수도 있습니다. 당신이 해야 하는 몇 가지 것들이 있습니다. 첫째, 수도와 전기를 꺼야 합니다. 둘째, 집을 떠날 때 물과 음식을 꾸려야 합니다. 마지막으로, 높고 안전한 곳으로 이동하여 일기 예보를 계속 들어야 합니다.

2. **B:** 미나야, 떠날 준비됐니?
   G: 아니, 아직. 가스를 껐는지 확인해야 해.
   B: 만약 우리가 지금 떠나지 않으면, 제 시간에 콘서트에 도착하지 못할 수도 있어.
   G: 알았어. 하지만 나는 우선 가스를 확인해야 해. 잠깐이면 될 거야.

B: 존 삼촌. 제 새로운 자전거 좀 보세요. 어떻게 생각하세요?
M: 아주 멋지구나. 어디를 가고 있니?
B: 친구 만나러 공원에요.
M: 네 헬멧이 어디 있니?
B: 저는 헬멧이 없어요. 그냥 잠깐 타는 거예요.
M: 헬멧을 쓰렴. 다칠 수 있단다.
B: 하지만 저는 헬멧 없이 자전거를 타는 많은 사람들을 봐요.
M: 너는 헬멧을 써야만 한단다. 그것은 사고가 났을 때 네 머리를 보호해 줘.
B: 알았어요. 아빠의 헬멧을 가져올게요.
M: 아니. 너는 네게 맞는 헬멧을 써야 해. 그렇지 않으면 그것은 네 머리를 보호해 줄 수 없어.
B: 저를 위한 헬멧을 사야겠어요.

B: 버스가 온다!
G: 오, 그렇지만 나는 우선 차 마시는 것을 끝내야 해.
B: 그냥 그것을 가지고 타는 것은 어때? 네가 조심한다면 괜찮을 거라고 확신해.
G: 아니, 만약 버스가 갑자기 멈춘다면, 나는 차를 흘릴 수도 있어.
B: 알았어, 그러면 난 네가 음료를 다 마실 때까지 기다릴 수 있어. 곧 다른 버스가 올 것이라고 확신해.
G: 고마워.

※ 다음 우리말에 맞도록 대화를 영어로 쓰시오.

Listen & Speak 1 Listen

1. B: _____
   G: _____

2. G: _____
   B: _____

3. B: _____
   G: _____

4. G: _____
   B: _____

Listen & Speak 1 A

1. G: _____
   W: _____
   G: _____
   W: _____
   G: _____

2. B: _____
   G: _____
   B: _____
   G: _____

Listen & Speak 2 Listen

1. M: _____
   B: _____

2. B: _____
   G: _____

3. G: _____
   W: _____

4. B: _____
   G: _____

해석

1. B: 우리는 벌들을 조심해야만 해.
   G: 오, 벌들이다. 뛰어!
2. G: 이쪽으로 갈 수 있을까? 좋아 보여.
   B: 아니. 정상에 가기를 원한다면 우리는 똑바로 가야 해.
3. B: 오, 계단이 젖었어.
   G: 그러면 우리는 계단을 천천히 내려가야 해.
4. G: 조금 더 올라가 보자. 나는 산 정상에 닿고 싶어.
   B: 우리는 먼저 날씨를 확인해야 해. 오, 비가 내릴 예정이래. 우리는 내려가야 해.

1. G: 엄마, 오후에 밖에서 놀아도 될까요?
   W: 물론이지. 나가기 전에 선크림 바르는 것을 잊지 말아라.
   G: 그렇지만 오늘은 흐려요. 선크림을 발라야 하나요?
   W: 그럼, 매일 선크림을 발라야 한단다.
   G: 알겠어요. 그러면 지금 바를게요.

2. B: 볼링 치러 가자.
   G: 미안해. 갈 수 없어. 병원에 가야 하거든.
   B: 오, 무슨 문제 있니?
   G: 몰라, 하지만 배가 아파.

1. M: 뛰지 마. 넘어질 수도 있단다.
   B: 알겠어요, 뛰지 않을게요.
2. B: 준비 운동을 하지 않고 차가운 물로 뛰어드는 것은 위험할 수 있어.
   G: 오, 알았어. 준비 운동할게.
3. G: 엄마, 여기에서 수영하고 싶어요.
   W: 그래, 하지만 우선 물이 얼마나 깊은지 확인해야 한단다. 네가 생각하는 것보다 물이 깊을 수 있어.
4. B: 먹고 난 후에 바로 수영해도 될까?
   G: 배가 부른 채로 수영하는 것은 불편할 수 있어.

Listen & Speak 2 A

1. M: _____
   _____
   _____
   _____
   _____

2. B: _____
   G: _____
   B: _____
   G: _____

Real-Life Zone

B: _____
M: _____
B: _____
M: _____
B: _____
M: _____
B: _____
M: _____
B: _____
M: _____
B: _____

Wrap Up

B: _____
G: _____
B: _____
   _____
G: _____
B: _____
   _____
G: _____

1. M: 홍수는 큰 문제들을 일으킬 수 있습니다. 그러나, 당신은 홍수가 발생할 때 무엇을 해야 하는지 모를 수도 있습니다. 당신이 해야 하는 몇 가지 것들이 있습니다. 첫째, 수도와 전기를 꺼야 합니다. 둘째, 집을 떠날 때 물과 음식을 꾸려야 합니다. 마지막으로, 높고 안전한 곳으로 이동하여 일기 예보를 계속 들어야 합니다.

2. B: 미나야, 떠날 준비됐니?
   G: 아니, 아직. 가스를 껐는지 확인해야 해.
   B: 만약 우리가 지금 떠나지 않으면, 제 시간에 콘서트에 도착하지 못할 수도 있어.
   G: 알았어. 하지만 나는 우선 가스를 확인해야 해. 잠깐이면 될 거야.

B: 존 삼촌. 제 새로운 자전거 좀 보세요. 어떻게 생각하세요?
M: 아주 멋지구나. 어디를 가고 있니?
B: 친구 만나러 공원에요.
M: 네 헬멧이 어디 있니?
B: 저는 헬멧이 없어요. 그냥 잠깐 타는 거예요.
M: 헬멧을 쓰렴. 다칠 수 있단다.
B: 하지만 저는 헬멧 없이 자전거를 타는 많은 사람들을 봐요.
M: 너는 헬멧을 써야만 한단다. 그것은 사고가 났을 때 네 머리를 보호해 줘.
B: 알았어요. 아빠의 헬멧을 가져올게요.
M: 아니. 너는 네게 맞는 헬멧을 써야 해. 그렇지 않으면 그것은 네 머리를 보호해 줄 수 없어.
B: 저를 위한 헬멧을 사야겠어요.

B: 버스가 온다!
G: 오, 그렇지만 나는 우선 차 마시는 것을 끝내야 해.
B: 그냥 그것을 가지고 타는 것은 어때? 네가 조심한다면 괜찮을 거라고 확신해.
G: 아니, 만약 버스가 갑자기 멈춘다면, 나는 차를 흘릴 수도 있어.
B: 알았어, 그러면 난 네가 음료를 다 마실 때까지 기다릴 수 있어. 곧 다른 버스가 올 것이라고 확신해.
G: 고마워.

※ 다음 우리말과 일치하도록 빈칸에 알맞은 것을 골라 쓰시오.

Safe Camping

1 Although camping trips can _____ sweet _____ for many people, they can also be _____ when bad things _____.

    A. memories   B. happen   C. occasions   D. create

2 If you _____ to go camping with family or friends this summer, you _____ to _____ several things in _____ for your safety.

    A. need   B. mind   C. keep   D. plan

3 _____ to Yumin's family _____ about their _____.

    A. talk   B. trip   C. camping   D. listen

4 They _____ to know _____ to do to _____ their camping trip _____ and fun.

    A. safe   B. what   C. make   D. seem

5 Yumin: Dad, _____ don't we _____ our tent over here _____ this river?

    A. by   B. put   C. why   D. up

6 Dad: I _____ _____ that's a good _____.

    A. idea   B. think   C. don't

7 If it _____ _____ rain, the river _____ _____.

    A. overflow   B. to   C. might   D. starts

8 Yumin: I know, _____ the _____ is _____.

    A. clear   B. but   C. sky

9 I _____ like the _____ of the _____!

    A. sound   B. really   C. water

10 Dad: The _____ can _____ quickly in the _____.

    A. change   B. weather   C. mountains

11 You _____ know _____ it _____ start to _____.

    A. might   B. never   C. rain   D. when

12 Yumin: Okay. _____ first! _____ find _____ place.

    A. another   B. let's   C. safety

13 When you _____ a tent, _____ a _____, sunny area.

    A. up   B. set   C. flat   D. choose

14 _____ places too _____ to big trees that might _____ _____ by lightning.

    A. struck   B. avoid   C. be   D. close

15 Hajun: Mom, I'm _____. What's _____ _____?

    A. hungry   B. lunch   C. for

16 Mom: I'm _____ _____.

    A. Samgyepsal   B. cooking

17 Hajun: Mom, that's not _____ for _____ of us. Can we cook _____ in a _____ pan?

    A. all   B. more   C. enough   D. bigger

안전한 캠핑

1 캠핑 여행이 많은 사람들에게 좋은 추억을 만들어 주기도 하지만, 나쁜 일이 일어나는 때가 될 수도 있습니다.

2 여러분이 이번 여름에 가족이나 친구들과 함께 캠핑을 하려고 계획하고 있다면, 여러분은 여러분의 안전을 위해서 몇 가지 사항을 명심해야 합니다.

3 유민이의 가족이 그들의 캠핑 여행에 대해 이야기하는 것을 들어 보세요.

4 그들은 그들의 캠핑 여행이 안전하고 재미있게 하기 위해 무엇을 해야 하는지 알고 있는 것 같습니다.

5 유민: 아빠, 이 강 근처 이쪽에 텐트를 치면 어때요?

6 아빠: 그건 좋은 생각 같지 않구나.

7 만약 비가 내리기 시작하면, 강이 범람할지도 몰라.

8 유민: 저도 알아요. 하지만 하늘이 맑잖아요.

9 저는 물소리를 정말 좋아한단 말이에요!

10 아빠: 산속의 날씨는 곧 바뀔 수 있어.

11 언제 비가 올지 절대 알 수 없는 일이지.

12 유민: 알겠어요. 안전이 우선이지요! 다른 곳을 찾아봐요.

13 텐트를 칠 때는 평평하고 햇볕이 잘 드는 장소를 고르세요.

14 번개를 맞을지도 모르는 키 큰 나무에 너무 가까운 장소는 피해야 합니다.

15 하준: 엄마, 저 배고파요. 점심이 뭐예요?

16 엄마: 삼겹살을 요리하고 있단다.

17 하준: 엄마, 그건 우리 모두가 먹기에 충분하지 않아요. 우리 더 큰 팬에 더 많이 요리하면 안 돼요?

18 Mom: I'm going to cook _____, but we _____ _____ use this small _____.

    A. to   B. have   C. more   D. pan

19 Hajun: _____ do we _____ to _____ a small pan?

    A. have   B. use   C. why

20 Mom: _____ the pan should _____ be bigger _____ the _____.

    A. burner   B. because   C. not   D. than

21 _____ you use a big pan, it _____ the heat _____ to the burner, and the gas can _____!

    A. sends   B. explode   C. back   D. if

22 Hajun: Oh, I _____ _____ _____.

    A. know   B. didn't   C. that

23 _____ is one more _____ about fire _____ you go camping.

    A. tip   B. here   C. when

24 _____ _____ a gas heater or burner _____ a tent.

    A. inside   B. use   C. never

25 Your tent may catch fire, or you might _____ out because the fire will _____ up the _____ in the tent _____ it burns.

    A. oxygen   B. as   C. use   D. pass

26 Yumin: _____! _____!

    A. mosquitoes   B. ouch

27 Mom: Oh, I _____ _____ tell you to _____ some _____ spray. Here.

    A. bug   B. to   C. apply   D. forgot

28 Yumin: _____, Mom. Oh, you _____ _____ _____?

    A. what   B. know   C. thanks

29 We can _____ orange peels _____ our skin _____ of _____ bug spray.

    A. on   B. applying   C. rub   D. instead

30 It is a nature-friendly _____ _____ mosquitoes _____.

    A. away   B. to   C. way   D. keep

31 Mom: _____ _____!

    A. interesting   B. that's

32 _____ can also _____ bugs _____.

    A. away   B. garlic   C. keep

33 You can place _____ of garlic at the _____ to the tent, and bugs will not _____ _____.

    A. entrance   B. inside   C. pieces   D. come

18 엄마: 더 굽긴 할 거야. 하지만 우리는 이 작은 팬을 써야 해.

19 하준: 왜 우리는 작은 팬을 써야 하죠?

20 엄마: 왜냐하면 팬이 버너보다 더 크면 안 되기 때문이야.

21 만약 큰 팬을 사용하면, 팬이 열을 버너로 다시 돌려보내서, 가스가 폭발할 수 있어!

22 하준: 오, 그것은 몰랐어요.

23 캠핑할 때 불을 사용하는 것에 대한 또 하나의 팁이 있습니다.

24 텐트 안에서 가스난로나 버너를 절대 쓰지 마세요.

25 여러분의 텐트에 불이 붙거나, 불이 타면서 텐트 내 산소를 다 써 버려서 여러분이 의식을 잃을 수도 있습니다.

26 유민: 앗! 모기!

27 엄마: 아, 벌레 퇴치 스프레이를 뿌리라고 네게 말하는 걸 잊었구나. 여기 있단다.

28 유민: 고마워요, 엄마. 아, 그거 아세요?

29 벌레 퇴치 스프레이를 뿌리는 것 대신에 오렌지 껍질을 피부에 문질러도 돼요.

30 모기가 접근하지 못하게 하는 자연 친화적인 방법이에요.

31 엄마: 그거 재미있구나!

32 마늘 또한 벌레가 접근하지 못하게 막을 수 있습니다.

33 마늘 조각을 텐트 입구에 놓아 두면, 벌레가 안으로 들어오지 않을 것입니다.

※ 다음 우리말과 일치하도록 빈칸에 알맞은 말을 쓰시오.

Safe Camping

1 _____ camping trips can _____ sweet _____ for many people, they can also be occasions _____ bad things _____.

2 If you _____ _____ _____ _____ with family or friends this summer, you _____ to keep several things _____ _____ for your _____.

3 Listen to Yumin's family _____ about their _____ _____.

4 They _____ to know _____ _____ _____ to make their camping trip _____ and fun.

5 Yumin: Dad, _____ _____ we _____ _____ our tent over here _____ this river?

6 Dad: I don't _____ that's a good _____.

7 If it _____ _____ rain, the river _____ _____.

8 Yumin: I know, _____ the sky is _____.

9 I really like the _____ of the water!

10 Dad: The _____ can _____ _____ in the mountains.

11 You _____ know _____ it _____ start _____.

12 Yumin: Okay. _____ first! _____ find _____ place.

13 When you _____ a tent, _____ a flat, sunny area.

14 _____ places too _____ to big trees that might _____ _____ _____ _____.

15 Hajun: Mom, I'm _____. What's _____ lunch?

16 Mom: I'm _____ Samgyepsal.

17 Hajun: Mom, that's not _____ for _____ of us. Can we cook _____ in a _____ _____?

안전한 캠핑

1 캠핑 여행이 많은 사람들에게 좋은 추억을 만들어 주기도 하지만, 나쁜 일이 일어나는 때가 될 수도 있습니다.

2 여러분이 이번 여름에 가족이나 친구들과 함께 캠핑을 하려고 계획하고 있다면, 여러분은 여러분의 안전을 위해서 몇 가지 사항을 명심해야 합니다.

3 유민이의 가족이 그들의 캠핑 여행에 대해 이야기하는 것을 들어 보세요.

4 그들은 그들의 캠핑 여행이 안전하고 재미있게 하기 위해 무엇을 해야 하는지 알고 있는 것 같습니다.

5 유민: 아빠, 이 강 근처 이쪽에 텐트를 치면 어때요?

6 아빠: 그건 좋은 생각 같지 않구나.

7 만약 비가 내리기 시작하면, 강이 범람할지도 몰라.

8 유민: 저도 알아요. 하지만 하늘이 맑잖아요.

9 저는 물소리를 정말 좋아한단 말이에요!

10 아빠: 산속의 날씨는 곧 바뀔 수 있어.

11 언제 비가 올지 절대 알 수 없는 일이지.

12 유민: 알겠어요. 안전이 우선이지요! 다른 곳을 찾아봐요.

13 텐트를 칠 때는 평평하고 햇볕이 잘 드는 장소를 고르세요.

14 번개를 맞을지도 모르는 키 큰 나무에 너무 가까운 장소는 피해야 합니다.

15 하준: 엄마, 저 배고파요. 점심이 뭐예요?

16 엄마: 삼겹살을 요리하고 있단다.

17 하준: 엄마, 그건 우리 모두가 먹기에 충분하지 않아요. 우리 더 큰 팬에 더 많이 요리하면 안 돼요?

18 Mom: I'm _____ _____ cook _____, but we _____ _____ _____ this small pan.

19 Hajun: _____ do we _____ _____ _____ a small pan?

20 Mom: _____ the pan _____ _____ be _____ _____ the burner.

21 _____ you use a big pan, it _____ the heat _____ to the burner, and the gas can _____!

22 Hajun: Oh, I didn't _____ that.

23 _____ is one more _____ about fire _____ you _____.

24 _____ use a gas heater or burner _____ a tent.

25 Your tent _____ _____ _____, _____ you might _____ out because the fire will _____ up the _____ in the tent as it _____.

26 Yumin: Ouch! _____!

27 Mom: Oh, I _____ _____ tell you _____ _____ some bug spray. Here.

28 Yumin: Thanks, Mom. Oh, you know _____?

29 We can _____ orange _____ our skin _____ _____ _____ bug spray.

30 It is a _____ _____ _____ _____ mosquitoes _____.

31 Mom: That's _____!

32 Garlic can also _____ bugs _____.

33 You can place _____ _____ _____ at the _____ to the tent, and bugs will not _____ _____.

18 엄마: 더 굽긴 할 거야. 하지만 우리는 이 작은 팬을 써야 해.

19 하준: 왜 우리는 작은 팬을 써야 하죠?

20 엄마: 왜냐하면 팬이 버너보다 더 크면 안 되기 때문이야.

21 만약 큰 팬을 사용하면, 팬이 열을 버너로 다시 돌려보내서, 가스가 폭발할 수 있어!

22 하준: 오, 그것은 몰랐어요.

23 캠핑할 때 불을 사용하는 것에 대한 또 하나의 팁이 있습니다.

24 텐트 안에서 가스난로나 버너를 절대 쓰지 마세요.

25 여러분의 텐트에 불이 붙거나, 불이 타면서 텐트 내 산소를 다 써 버려서 여러분이 의식을 잃을 수도 있습니다.

26 유민: 앗! 모기!

27 엄마: 아, 벌레 퇴치 스프레이를 뿌리라고 네게 말하는 걸 잊었구나. 여기 있단다.

28 유민: 고마워요, 엄마. 아, 그거 아세요?

29 벌레 퇴치 스프레이를 뿌리는 것 대신에 오렌지 껍질을 피부에 문질러도 돼요.

30 모기가 접근하지 못하게 하는 자연 친화적인 방법이에요.

31 엄마: 그거 재미있구나!

32 마늘 또한 벌레가 접근하지 못하게 막을 수 있습니다.

33 마늘 조각을 텐트 입구에 놓아 두면, 벌레가 안으로 들어오지 않을 것입니다.

※ 다음 문장을 우리말로 쓰시오.

Safe Camping

1 Although camping trips can create sweet memories for many people, they can also be occasions when bad things happen.

➡ _____

2 If you plan to go camping with family or friends this summer, you need to keep several things in mind for your safety.

➡ _____

➡ _____

3 Listen to Yumin's family talk about their camping trip.

➡ _____

4 They seem to know what to do to make their camping trip safe and fun.

➡ _____

5 Yumin: Dad, why don't we put up our tent over here by this river?

➡ _____

6 Dad: I don't think that's a good idea.

➡ _____

7 If it starts to rain, the river might overflow.

➡ _____

8 Yumin: I know, but the sky is clear.

➡ _____

9 I really like the sound of the water!

➡ _____

10 Dad: The weather can change quickly in the mountains.

➡ _____

11 You never know when it might start to rain.

➡ _____

12 Yumin: Okay. Safety first! Let's find another place.

➡ _____

13 When you set up a tent, choose a flat, sunny area.

➡ _____

14 Avoid places too close to big trees that might be struck by lightning.

➡ _____

15 Hajun: Mom, I'm hungry. What's for lunch?

➡ _____

16 Mom: I'm cooking Samgyepsal.

➡ _____

17 Hajun: Mom, that's not enough for all of us. Can we cook more in a bigger pan?

➡ _____

18 ▶ Mom: I'm going to cook more, but we have to use this small pan.

➡ _____

19 ▶ Hajun: Why do we have to use a small pan?

➡ _____

20 ▶ Mom: Because the pan should not be bigger than the burner.

➡ _____

21 ▶ If you use a big pan, it sends the heat back to the burner, and the gas can explode!

➡ _____

22 ▶ Hajun: Oh, I didn't know that.

➡ _____

23 ▶ Here is one more tip about fire when you go camping.

➡ _____

24 ▶ Never use a gas heater or burner inside a tent.

➡ _____

25 ▶ Your tent may catch fire, or you might pass out because the fire will use up the oxygen in the tent as it burns.

➡ _____

26 ▶ Yumin: Ouch! Mosquitoes!

➡ _____

27 ▶ Mom: Oh, I forgot to tell you to apply some bug spray. Here.

➡ _____

28 ▶ Yumin: Thanks, Mom. Oh, you know what?

➡ _____

29 ▶ We can rub orange peels on our skin instead of applying bug spray.

➡ _____

30 ▶ It is a nature-friendly way to keep mosquitoes away.

➡ _____

31 ▶ Mom: That's interesting!

➡ _____

32 ▶ Garlic can also keep bugs away.

➡ _____

33 ▶ You can place pieces of garlic at the entrance to the tent, and bugs will not come inside.

➡ _____

※ 다음 괄호 안의 단어들을 우리말에 맞도록 바르게 배열하시오.

1 (camping / although / trips / create / can / memories / sweet / many / for / people, / can / they / be / also / occasions / bad / when / things / happen.)
➡ _____

2 (you / if / to / plan / camping / go / family / with / or / this / friends / summer, / need / you / to / several / keep / things / mind / in / your / for / safety.)
➡ _____

3 (to / listen / family / Yumin's / about / talk / camping / their / trip.)
➡ _____

4 (seem / they / know / to / to / what / do / make / their / trip / camping / safe / fun. / and)
➡ _____

5 (Yumin: / why / dad, / don't / put / we / our / up / tent / here / over / by / river? / this)
➡ _____

6 (Dad: / don't / I / think / a / that's / good / idea.)
➡ _____

7 (it / if / to / starts / rain, / river / the / overflow. / might)
➡ _____

8 (Yumin: / know, / I / but / sky / the / clear. / is)
➡ _____

9 (really / I / the / like / of / sound / water! / the)
➡ _____

10 (Dad: / weather / the / change / can / in / quickly / mountains. / the)
➡ _____

11 (never / you / when / know / might / it / to / start / rain.)
➡ _____

12 (Yumin: / okay. // first! / safety // find / let's / another / place.)
➡ _____

13 (you / when / up / set / tent, / a / choose / flat, / a / area. / sunny)
➡ _____

14 (places / avoid / close / too / big / to / trees / might / that / struck / be / lightning. / by)
➡ _____

15 (Hajun: / I'm / mom, / hungry. // for / what's / lunch?)
➡ _____

16 (mom: / cooking / I'm / Samgyepsal.)
➡ _____

17 (Hajun: / mom, / not / that's / enough / all / for / us. / of // we / can / more / cook / a / in / pan? / bigger)
➡ _____

안전한 캠핑

1 캠핑 여행이 많은 사람들에게 좋은 추억을 만들어 주기도 하지만, 나쁜 일이 일어나는 때가 될 수도 있습니다.

2 여러분이 이번 여름에 가족이나 친구들과 함께 캠핑을 하려고 계획하고 있다면, 여러분은 여러분의 안전을 위해서 몇 가지 사항을 명심해야 합니다.

3 유민이의 가족이 그들의 캠핑 여행에 대해 이야기하는 것을 들어 보세요.

4 그들은 그들의 캠핑 여행이 안전하고 재미있게 하기 위해 무엇을 해야 하는지 알고 있는 것 같습니다.

5 유민: 아빠, 이 강 근처 이쪽에 텐트를 치면 어때요?

6 아빠: 그건 좋은 생각 같지 않구나.

7 만약 비가 내리기 시작하면, 강이 범람할지도 몰라.

8 유민: 저도 알아요. 하지만 하늘이 맑잖아요.

9 저는 물소리를 정말 좋아한단 말이에요!

10 아빠: 산속의 날씨는 곧 바뀔 수 있어.

11 언제 비가 올지 절대 알 수 없는 일이지.

12 유민: 알겠어요. 안전이 우선이지요! 다른 곳을 찾아봐요.

13 텐트를 칠 때는 평평하고 햇볕이 잘 드는 장소를 고르세요.

14 번개를 맞을지도 모르는 키 큰 나무에 너무 가까운 장소는 피해야 합니다.

15 하준: 엄마, 저 배고파요. 점심이 뭐예요?

16 엄마: 삼겹살을 요리하고 있단다.

17 하준: 엄마, 그건 우리 모두가 먹기에 충분하지 않아요. 우리 더 큰 팬에 더 많이 요리하면 안 돼요?

18 (Mom: / going / I'm / cook / to / more, / we / but / to / have / this / use / pan. / small)
➡ _____

19 (Hajun: / do / why / have / we / use / to / small / a / pan?)
➡ _____

20 (Mom: / the / because / pan / not / should / be / than / bigger / burner. / the)
➡ _____

21 (you / if / a / use / pan, / big / sends / it / heat / the / to / back / the / burner, / the / and / gas / explode! / can)
➡ _____

22 (Hajun: / I / oh, / know / didn't / that.)
➡ _____

23 (is / here / more / one / about / tip / when / fire / you / camping. / go)
➡ _____

24 (use / never / gas / a / heater / or / inside / burner / tent. / a)
➡ _____

25 (tent / your / catch / may / fire, / you / or / pass / might / out / the / because / fire / use / will / up / oxygen / the / in / tent / the / it / as / burns.)
➡ _____

26 (Yumin: / mosquitoes! / ouch!)
➡ _____

27 (Mom: / I / oh, / to / forgot / you / tell / apply / to / bug / some / spray. // here.)
➡ _____

28 (Yumin: / Mom. / thanks, // you / oh, / what? / know)
➡ _____

29 (can / we / orange / rub / peels / our / on / skin / of / instead / bug / applying / spray.)
➡ _____

30 (is / it / nature-friendly / a / to / way / mosquitoes / keep / away.)
➡ _____

31 (Mom: / interesting! / that's)
➡ _____

32 (can / garlic / keep / also / away. / bugs)
➡ _____

33 (can / you / pieces / place / garlic / of / the / at / entrance / the / to / tent, / and / will / bugs / come / not / inside.)
➡ _____

18 엄마: 더 굽긴 할 거야. 하지만 우리는 이 작은 팬을 써야 해.

19 하준: 왜 우리는 작은 팬을 써야 하죠?

20 엄마: 왜냐하면 팬이 버너보다 더 크면 안 되기 때문이야.

21 만약 큰 팬을 사용하면, 팬이 열을 버너로 다시 돌려보내서, 가스가 폭발할 수 있어!

22 하준: 오, 그것은 몰랐어요.

23 캠핑할 때 불을 사용하는 것에 대한 또 하나의 팁이 있습니다.

24 텐트 안에서 가스난로나 버너를 절대 쓰지 마세요.

25 여러분의 텐트에 불이 붙거나, 불이 타면서 텐트 내 산소를 다 써 버려서 여러분이 의식을 잃을 수도 있습니다.

26 유민: 앗! 모기!

27 엄마: 아, 벌레 퇴치 스프레이를 뿌리라고 네게 말하는 걸 잊었구나. 여기 있단다.

28 유민: 고마워요, 엄마. 아, 그거 아세요?

29 벌레 퇴치 스프레이를 뿌리는 것 대신에 오렌지 껍질을 피부에 문질러도 돼요.

30 모기가 접근하지 못하게 하는 자연 친화적인 방법이에요.

31 엄마: 그거 재미있구나!

32 마늘 또한 벌레가 접근하지 못하게 막을 수 있습니다.

33 마늘 조각을 텐트 입구에 놓아두면, 벌레가 안으로 들어오지 않을 것입니다.

※ 다음 우리말을 영어로 쓰시오.

Safe Camping

1 캠핑 여행이 많은 사람들에게 좋은 추억을 만들어 주기도 하지만, 나쁜 일이 일어나는 때가 될 수도 있습니다.

➡ _____

_____

2 여러분이 이번 여름에 가족이나 친구들과 함께 캠핑을 하려고 계획하고 있다면, 여러분은 여러분의 안전을 위해서 몇 가지 사항을 명심해야 합니다.

➡ _____

_____

3 유민이의 가족이 그들의 캠핑 여행에 대해 이야기하는 것을 들어 보세요.

➡ _____

4 그들은 그들의 캠핑 여행이 안전하고 재미있게 하기 위해 무엇을 해야 하는지 알고 있는 것 같습니다.

➡ _____

5 유민: 아빠, 이 강 근처 이쪽에 텐트를 치면 어때요?

➡ _____

6 아빠: 그건 좋은 생각 같지 않구나.

➡ _____

7 만약 비가 내리기 시작하면, 강이 범람할지도 몰라.

➡ _____

8 유민: 저도 알아요. 하지만 하늘이 맑잖아요.

➡ _____

9 저는 물소리를 정말 좋아한단 말이에요!

➡ _____

10 아빠: 산속의 날씨는 곧 바뀔 수 있어.

➡ _____

11 언제 비가 올지 절대 알 수 없는 일이지.

➡ _____

12 유민: 알겠어요. 안전이 우선이지요! 다른 곳을 찾아봐요.

➡ _____

13 텐트를 칠 때는 평평하고 햇볕이 잘 드는 장소를 고르세요.

14 번개를 맞을지도 모르는 키 큰 나무에 너무 가까운 장소는 피해야 합니다.

➡ _____

15 하준: 엄마, 저 배고파요. 점심이 뭐예요?

➡ _____

16 엄마: 삼겹살을 요리하고 있단다.

➡ _____

17 하준: 엄마, 그건 우리 모두가 먹기에 충분하지 않아요. 우리 더 큰 팬에 더 많이 요리하면 안 돼요?

➡ _____

18 엄마: 더 굽긴 할 거야. 하지만 우리는 이 작은 팬을 써야 해.

➡ _____

19 하준: 왜 우리는 작은 팬을 써야 하죠?

➡ _____

20 엄마: 왜냐하면 팬이 버너보다 더 크면 안 되기 때문이야.

➡ _____

21 만약 큰 팬을 사용하면, 팬이 열을 버너로 다시 돌려보내서, 가스가 폭발할 수 있어!

➡ _____

22 하준: 오, 그것은 몰랐어요.

➡ _____

23 캠핑할 때 불을 사용하는 것에 대한 또 하나의 팁이 있습니다.

➡ _____

24 텐트 안에서 가스난로나 버너를 절대 쓰지 마세요.

➡ _____

25 여러분의 텐트에 불이 붙거나, 불이 타면서 텐트 내 산소를 다 써 버려서 여러분이 의식을 잃을 수도 있습니다.

➡ _____

_____

26 유민: 앗! 모기!

➡ _____

27 엄마: 아, 벌레 퇴치 스프레이를 뿌리라고 네게 말하는 걸 잊었구나. 여기 있단다.

➡ _____

28 유민: 고마워요, 엄마. 아, 그거 아세요?

➡ _____

29 벌레 퇴치 스프레이를 뿌리는 것 대신에 오렌지 껍질을 피부에 문질러도 돼요.

➡ _____

30 모기가 접근하지 못하게 하는 자연 친화적인 방법이에요.

➡ _____

31 엄마: 그거 재미있구나!

➡ _____

32 마늘 또한 벌레가 접근하지 못하게 막을 수 있습니다.

➡ _____

33 마늘 조각을 텐트 입구에 놓아두면, 벌레가 안으로 들어오지 않을 것입니다.

➡ _____

※ 다음 우리말과 일치하도록 빈칸에 알맞은 말을 쓰시오.

Before You Read

1. _____ _____ Our Sky Camping Trip!

2. We _____ _____ many activities for _____ _____ _____.

3. _____ we always think about your safety first, we _____ _____ _____ _____ that may happen.

4. We _____ _____ _____ a comfortable stay _____ _____ a can of bug spray in each tent so you can _____ _____ _____.

5. We hope _____ _____ _____ _____ _____ of the trip!

1. 스카이 캠핑에 오신 것을 환영합니다!
2. 저희는 이틀간의 캠핑 여행을 위해 많은 활동들을 준비했습니다.
3. 저희는 항상 여러분의 안전을 우선으로 생각하기 때문에, 발생할 수 있는 나쁜 일에 대비하기 위해 최선을 다합니다.
4. 저희는 여러분이 모기에 물리는 것을 피할 수 있도록 각각의 텐트에 벌레 퇴치 스프레이를 한 통씩 비치해 둠으로써 여러분이 편안하게 머물도록 돕습니다.
5. 저희는 모든 분들이 여행의 좋은 추억을 집으로 가져가시기를 바랍니다.

Writing Workshop

1. _____ you would think that you _____ _____ _____ _____ _____, that is not true.

2. Then, what should you do _____ _____ _____?

3. There are _____ _____ you _____ _____ _____.

4. First, _____ _____ and keep informed _____ _____ _____.

5. It _____ _____ _____ _____ _____ to go outside, but something _____ _____ _____ you.

6. Second, _____ _____ the gas and the electricity.

7. Third, _____ _____ the table and _____ _____ _____ _____ _____ _____.

8. _____ is important _____ _____ your head.

9. Finally, if you are outside, try to get as _____ _____ _____ buildings, trees, and streetlights _____ _____.

10. _____ _____ these tips, you _____ _____ _____ from the earthquake.

1. 비록 여러분이 지진으로부터 자유롭다고 생각할 수 있지만, 사실은 그렇지 않습니다.
2. 그러면 지진이 발생하면 여러분은 무엇을 해야 할까요?
3. 여러분이 명심해야 할 것이 몇 가지 있습니다.
4. 첫째, 흔들림이 멈출 때까지 안에서 머물며 계속 정보를 받아야 합니다.
5. 밖으로 나가는 게 안전해 보이지만 무언가가 여러분에게 떨어질 수도 있습니다.
6. 둘째, 가스와 전기를 끄십시오.
7. 셋째, 테이블 아래로 들어가서 팔로 머리를 감싸세요.
8. 여러분의 머리를 보호하는 것이 중요합니다.
9. 만일 여러분이 밖에 있다면, 가능한 한 건물이나 나무, 가로등으로부터 멀리 떨어지세요.
10. 이 팁을 따름으로써 여러분은 지진으로부터 안전할 수 있습니다.

Wrap Up

1. My Camping _____ _____

2. _____: Yeongwol Date: _____ 12

3. Traveled _____: my family

4. I _____ to Yeongwol _____ my family _____ _____ 12.

5. _____ the trip, we _____ _____ and _____.

6. _____ I _____ _____ _____ _____ _____ rafting _____ _____, it was really fun and exciting.

7. I'll _____ _____ again _____ I _____ _____ _____ _____.

1. 나의 캠핑 여행 일기
2. 위치: 영월 날짜: 9월 12일
3. 함께 여행한 사람: 나의 가족
4. 나는 9월 12일에 나의 가족과 함께 영월에 갔다.
5. 여행 중에 우리는 급류 타기와 하이킹을 즐겼다.
6. 나는 처음에 급류 타기를 무서워했지만, 그것은 정말 재미있고 신났다.
7. 기회가 있다면 나는 다시 급류 타기를 하러 갈 것이다.

※ 다음 우리말을 영어로 쓰시오.

Before You Read

1. 스카이 캠핑에 오신 것을 환영합니다!
➡ _____

2. 저희는 이틀간의 캠핑 여행을 위해 많은 활동들을 준비했습니다.
➡ _____

3. 저희는 항상 여러분의 안전을 우선으로 생각하기 때문에, 발생할 수 있는 나쁜 일에 대비하기 위해 최선을 다합니다.
➡ _____

4. 저희는 여러분이 모기에 물리는 것을 피할 수 있도록 각각의 텐트에 벌레 퇴치 스프레이를 한 통씩 비치해 둠으로써 여러분이 편안하게 머물도록 돕습니다.
➡ _____

5. 저희는 모든 분들이 여행의 좋은 추억을 집으로 가져가시기를 바랍니다.
➡ _____

Writing Workshop

1. 비록 여러분이 지진으로부터 자유롭다고 생각할 수 있지만, 사실은 그렇지 않습니다.
➡ _____

2. 그러면 지진이 발생하면 여러분은 무엇을 해야 할까요?
➡ _____

3. 여러분이 명심해야 할 것이 몇 가지 있습니다.
➡ _____

4. 첫째, 흔들림이 멈출 때까지 안에서 머물며 계속 정보를 받아야 합니다.
➡ _____

5. 밖으로 나가는 게 안전해 보이지만 무언가가 여러분에게 떨어질 수도 있습니다.
➡ _____

6. 둘째, 가스와 전기를 끄십시오.
➡ _____

7. 셋째, 테이블 아래로 들어가서 팔로 머리를 감싸세요.
➡ _____

8. 여러분의 머리를 보호하는 것이 중요합니다.
➡ _____

9. 마지막으로, 만일 여러분이 밖에 있다면, 가능한 한 건물이나 나무, 가로등으로부터 멀리 떨어지세요.
➡ _____

10. 이 팁을 따름으로써 여러분은 지진으로부터 안전할 수 있습니다.
➡ _____

Wrap Up

1. 나의 캠핑 여행 일기
➡ _____

2. 위치: 영월 날짜: 9월 12일
➡ _____

3. 함께 여행한 사람: 나의 가족
➡ _____

4. 나는 9월 12일에 나의 가족과 함께 영월에 갔다.
➡ _____

5. 여행 중에 우리는 급류 타기와 하이킹을 즐겼다.
➡ _____

6. 나는 처음에 급류 타기를 무서워했지만, 그것은 정말 재미있고 신났다.
➡ _____

7. 기회가 있다면 나는 다시 급류 타기를 하러 갈 것이다.
➡ _____

※ 다음 영어를 우리말로 쓰시오.

01	pack	22	lose
02	reopen	23	demand
03	college	24	either
04	part	25	order
05	contract	26	sign
06	seriously	27	refuse
07	except	28	grade
08	decision	29	follow
09	eventually	30	attend
10	allow	31	care
11	exactly	32	realize
12	famous	33	imagine
13	gym	34	disappointed
14	happen	35	by -ing
15	principal	36	find out
16	improve	37	A as well as B
17	promise	38	pay attention to
18	life	39	carry out
19	lock	40	become used to -ing
20	accept	41	in addition to
21	actually	42	one after anther
		43	to make matters worse

※ 다음 우리말을 영어로 쓰시오.

01 서명하다 _____

02 받아들이다 _____

03 체육관 _____

04 일어나다, 발생하다 _____

05 참석하다 _____

06 대학 _____

07 결정, 판단 _____

08 향상하다, 향상시키다 _____

09 마음을 쓰다, 걱정하다 _____

10 (충고 · 지시 등을) 따르다 _____

11 (짐을) 싸다, 꾸리다 _____

12 계약서 _____

13 실망한, 낙담한 _____

14 미래 _____

15 교장 _____

16 심각하게 _____

17 지다, 패하다 _____

18 결정하다 _____

19 결국, 마침내 _____

20 정확히 _____

21 ~을 제외하고 _____

22 실제로, 정말로 _____

23 명령하다 _____

24 (부정문에서) 역시, 또한 _____

25 성적 _____

26 깨닫다, 알아차리다 _____

27 상상하다 _____

28 연습하다 _____

29 잠그다 _____

30 요구 _____

31 거절하다 _____

32 승리자 _____

33 허락하다 _____

34 다시 문을 열다,
다시 시작하다 _____

35 게다가, ~에 더하여 _____

36 B뿐만 아니라 A도 _____

37 이행하다 _____

38 조치를 취하다 _____

39 ~을 찾아보다 _____

40 ~에 유의하다,
~에 관심을 가지다 _____

41 잇따라서 _____

42 설상가상으로 _____

43 ~하는 데 익숙해지다 _____

※ 다음 영영풀이에 알맞은 단어를 <보기>에서 골라 쓴 후, 우리말 뜻을 쓰시오.

1 _____ : to write your name on something: _____

2 _____ : to achieve victory in a fight, contest, game, etc.: _____

3 _____ : to make something better: _____

4 _____ : the person in charge of a school or college: _____

5 _____ : a person who teaches and trains an athlete: _____

6 _____ : to use your authority to tell someone to do something: _____

7 _____ : a document on which the words of a contract are written: _____

8 _____ : to go to and be present at an event, meeting, etc.: _____

9 _____ : an extra amount of money that is given to an employee: _____

10 _____ : to say that you will not do something that someone has asked you to do:
_____

11 _____ : to put something into a bag, suitcase, etc., so that you can take it with
you: _____

12 _____ : a room or hall with equipment for doing physical exercise, for example
in a school: _____

13 _____ : a forceful statement in which you say that something must be done or
given to you: _____

14 _____ : a statement that tells you what is or is not allowed in a particular game,
situation, etc.: _____

15 _____ : to think of or create something that is not real in your mind: _____

16 _____ : a place where students can study for a degree after they have finished
high school: _____

rule	refuse	order	principal
bonus	gym	sign	win
pack	college	imagine	improve
demand	attend	contract	coach

※ 다음 우리말과 일치하도록 빈칸에 알맞은 것을 골라 쓰시오.

1 _____ _____ *Movie Trip.*
A. to   B. welcome

2 Today we're _____ _____ _____ about the movie *Coach Carter.*
A. to   B. going   C. talk

3 Can you _____ a basketball coach who doesn't _____ his players _____ _____?
A. to   B. imagine   C. practice   D. allow

4 That's _____ _____ Coach Carter _____.
A. what   B. exactly   C. does

5 This movie is about a coach who _____ more _____ his students _____ about _____ games.
A. about   B. cares   C. winning   D. than

6 The basketball team at Richmond High School in Richmond, California, was _____ one _____ season _____ _____.
A. having   B. another   C. after   D. losing

7 The players _____ _____ _____ _____ _____.
A. to   B. became   C. losing   D. used

8 _____ _____ matters _____, they had no plans for the future; they went to school _____ to play basketball, and they did not do that very well.
A. worse   B. make   C. to   D. only

9 Then they _____ a _____ _____, Kenny Carter.
A. coach   B. got   C. new

10 Coach Carter _____ _____ _____ _____.
A. change   B. wanted   C. things   D. to

11 He wanted to teach kids _____ _____ _____ basketball well and _____.
A. win   B. to   C. how   D. play

12 But _____ _____ that, he wanted to give the players a future _____ _____ them to college.
A. sending   B. than   C. by   D. more

13 _____ _____ _____ his plan, Coach Carter had the players sign a _____.
A. contract   B. carry   C. to   D. out

1 「영화 여행」에 오신 것을 환영합니다.

2 오늘 우리는 영화 「코치 카터」에 대해 이야기할 것입니다.

3 선수들이 연습하는 것을 허락하지 않는 농구 코치를 상상할 수 있나요?

4 그것이 바로 카터 코치가 한 것입니다.

5 이 영화는 경기에서 이기는 것보다 학생들을 더 걱정하는 코치에 대한 영화입니다.

6 캘리포니아 리치몬드 지역의 리치몬드 고등학교 농구 팀은 연속해서 경기에서 지고 있었습니다.

7 선수들도 지는 것에 익숙하게 되었습니다.

8 설상가상으로 그들은 미래에 대한 계획도 없었습니다. 즉, 그들은 단지 농구하기 위해 학교에 갔고, 그것마저도 잘하지 못했습니다.

9 그때 그들은 케니 카터라는 새로운 코치를 선임했습니다.

10 카터 코치는 몇 가지를 바꾸고자 했습니다.

11 그는 아이들에게 어떻게 농구를 잘하고 이기는지를 가르치기를 원했습니다.

12 그러나 그것보다도, 그는 그들을 대학에 보냄으로써 선수들에게 미래를 주기를 원했습니다.

13 그의 계획을 실행하기 위해서, 카터 코치는 선수들에게 계약서에 서명하게 했습니다.

14 They _____ to promise to study hard _____ _____ _____ playing basketball.

    A. in   B. had   C. to   D. addition

15 _____ _____, students did not take his idea for a _____ _____.

    A. seriously   B. first   C. contract   D. at

16 Carter: I'm going to _____ _____ _____ _____.

    A. a   B. give   C. contract   D. you

17 Cruz: "_____ all _____," "Get a C$^+$ or higher," "Don't _____ _____...."

    A. late   B. attend   C. be   D. classes

18 What are _____ _____ _____ about?

    A. these   B. all   C. rules

19 Do I get a _____ _____ for signing this _____?

    A. signing   B. bonus   C. contract

20 Carter: Yes. You will get a big bonus _____ you will become a _____ in the game of basketball as _____ as in the game of _____.

    A. well   B. because   C. life   D. winner

21 _____ hard work and a new game plan, the team began to win for the first time _____ _____ _____.

    A. in   B. with   C. years   D. many

22 _____ that _____ _____, they won game _____ game.

    A. on   B. from   C. after   D. point

23 _____, _____ Coach Carter, was _____.

    A. happy   B. except   C. everybody

24 The players did not _____ the "study" _____ _____ their _____.

    A. of   B. part   C. contract   D. do

25 _____ of them actually believed they could go to college, so they _____ _____ _____ to their grades.

    A. attention   B. little   C. paid   D. few

26 Carter _____ to _____ stronger _____.

    A. action   B. take   C. decided

27 He locked the gym and refused to _____ them play basketball _____ their grades _____, _____ promised in the contract.

    A. improved   B. let   C. as   D. until

---

14 그들은 농구를 하는 것뿐만 아니라 열심히 공부할 것도 약속해야만 했습니다.

15 처음에는 학생들이 계약서에 대한 그의 생각을 심각하게 받아들이지 않았습니다.

16 카터: 내가 너희들에게 계약서를 줄 것이다.

17 크루즈: "모든 수업에 출석하라." "C 플러스 또는 그 이상 받아라." "지각하지 말아라."

18 이 모든 규칙들은 무엇이죠?

19 제가 이 계약서에 사인하면 사이닝 보너스를 받나요?

20 카터: 그래. 너는 큰 보너스를 받게 될 거야. 왜냐하면 인생의 게임에서뿐 아니라 농구 경기에서도 승리자가 될 것이기 때문이지.

21 맹연습과 새로운 경기 전략으로 그 팀은 몇 년 만에 처음으로 이기기 시작했습니다.

22 그때 이후로 경기마다 이겼습니다.

23 카터 코치를 제외한 모든 이들이 행복했습니다.

24 선수들은 그들 계약의 '학습' 부분을 하지 않았습니다.

25 그들 중 정말 그들이 대학을 갈 수 있다고 믿는 사람들은 거의 없었습니다. 그래서 그들은 성적에는 거의 관심을 두지 않았습니다.

26 카터는 더 강력한 조치를 취하기로 결심했습니다.

27 그는 체육관 문을 잠그고 계약서에서 약속한 대로 그들의 성적이 좋아질 때까지 농구를 못하게 했습니다.

28 The _____ did _____ like _____.

    A. it   B. players   C. not

29 They told him _____ his _____ were _____ for him, _____ for them.

    A. just   B. not   C. that   D. actions

30 Worm: We're _____ _____ _____.

    A. team   B. basketball   C. the

31 _____ we see is you _____ TV, _____ _____.

    A. getting   B. all   C. famous   D. on

32 Carter: _____ you think so, go home and ask _____, "Do I want a _____ _____?"

    A. yourself   B. life   C. if   D. better

33 If the _____ is yes, I will do _____ in my power _____ _____ you.

    A. everything   B. help   C. answer   D. to

34 But you _____ _____ _____ your _____.

    A. part   B. have   C. do   D. to

35 The players' _____ did not _____ Carter's _____ _____.

    A. either   B. parents   C. decision   D. like

36 At the parents' _____, the principal _____ Carter _____ _____ the gym.

    A. reopen   B. demand   C. to   D. ordered

37 _____, Carter _____ _____ _____ Richmond High.

    A. leave   B. decided   C. disappointed   D. to

38 _____ he entered the gym _____ _____ his things, however, all of his players _____ there.

    A. pack   B. when   C. to   D. were

39 We want you to enjoy the movie, so we _____ tell you _____ _____ _____.

    A. happens   B. what   C. won't   D. next

40 _____ _____ for yourself _____ _____ the movie _Coach Carter_.

    A. watching   B. out   C. by   D. find

28 선수들은 그것을 좋아하지 않았습니다.

29 그들은 그에게 그의 행동들이 그들을 위한 것이 아닌 단지 카터 자신을 위한 것이라고 말했습니다.

30 웜: 우리는 농구 팀이에요.

31 우리가 보는 모든 것은 유명세를 타며 TV에 있는 당신이에요.

32 카터: 네가 그렇게 생각한다면, 집으로 가서 너 자신에게 물어봐. "나는 더 나은 삶을 원하는가?"

33 대답이 '맞다'라면, 나는 너를 돕기 위해 내 힘이 닿는 한 모든 것을 할 거야.

34 그러나 너는 네 역할을 해야만 해.

35 선수들의 부모들 역시 카터의 결정을 좋아하지 않았습니다.

36 부모들의 요구에 따라 교장은 카터에게 체육관을 다시 열도록 했습니다.

37 실망한 카터는 리치몬드 고등학교를 떠나기로 결심했습니다.

38 그가 짐을 싸기 위해 체육관으로 들어섰을 때, 그의 선수들 모두가 그곳에 있었습니다.

39 우리는 여러분이 이 영화를 즐기기 원합니다. 그래서 당신에게 다음에 무슨 일이 일어나는지 이야기하지 않을 것입니다.

40 영화 「코치 카터」를 보고 스스로 찾아보세요.

※ 다음 우리말과 일치하도록 빈칸에 알맞은 것을 골라 쓰시오.

1 _____ _____ *Movie Trip*.

2 Today we're _____ _____ _____ about the movie *Coach Carter*.

3 Can you _____ a basketball coach who _____ _____ his players _____ _____?

4 That's _____ _____ Coach Carter _____.

5 This movie is about a coach who _____ more _____ his students _____ _____ _____ _____ _____.

6 The basketball team at Richmond High School in Richmond, California, was having _____ losing season _____ _____.

7 The players _____ _____ _____ _____ _____.

8 _____ _____ matters _____, they _____ _____ _____ for the future; they went to school _____ _____ _____ basketball, and they did not do that very well.

9 Then they got a _____ _____, Kenny Carter.

10 Coach Carter _____ _____ _____ things.

11 He wanted to teach kids _____ _____ _____ basketball well and _____.

12 But _____ _____ that, he wanted to give the players a future _____ _____ them _____ _____.

13 _____ _____ _____ his plan, Coach Carter had the players _____ _____ _____.

---

1 「영화 여행」에 오신 것을 환영합니다.

2 오늘 우리는 영화 「코치 카터」에 대해 이야기할 것입니다.

3 선수들이 연습하는 것을 허락하지 않는 농구 코치를 상상할 수 있나요?

4 그것이 바로 카터 코치가 한 것입니다.

5 이 영화는 경기에서 이기는 것보다 학생들을 더 걱정하는 코치에 대한 영화입니다.

6 캘리포니아 리치몬드 지역의 리치몬드 고등학교 농구 팀은 연속해서 경기에서 지고 있었습니다.

7 선수들도 지는 것에 익숙하게 되었습니다.

8 설상가상으로 그들은 미래에 대한 계획도 없었습니다. 즉, 그들은 단지 농구하기 위해 학교에 갔고, 그것마저도 잘하지 못했습니다.

9 그때 그들은 케니 카터라는 새로운 코치를 선임했습니다.

10 카터 코치는 몇 가지를 바꾸고자 했습니다.

11 그는 아이들에게 어떻게 농구를 잘하고 이기는지를 가르치기를 원했습니다.

12 그러나 그것보다도, 그는 그들을 대학에 보냄으로써 선수들에게 미래를 주기를 원했습니다.

13 그의 계획을 실행하기 위해서, 카터 코치는 선수들에게 계약서에 서명하게 했습니다.

14 They _____ _____ _____ to study hard _____ _____
_____ _____ basketball.

15 _____ _____, students did not _____ _____ _____
for a contract _____.

16 Carter: I'm going to _____ _____ _____ _____.

17 Cruz: "_____ all _____," "Get a C⁺ or higher," "Don't
_____ _____...."

18 What are _____ _____ _____ about?

19 Do I get a _____ _____ for signing this _____?

20 Carter: Yes. You will get a big bonus _____ you will _____
_____ _____ in the game of basketball _____ _____
_____ in the game of life.

21 _____ hard work and a new game plan, the team _____
_____ _____ for the first time _____ _____ _____.

22 _____ that _____ _____, they won game _____ game.

23 Everybody, _____ Coach Carter, was happy.

24 The players did not do the "study" _____ _____ their
contract.

25 _____ _____ them actually believed they could go to
college, so they _____ _____ _____ _____ their grades.

26 Carter decided to _____ _____ _____.

27 He locked the gym and _____ _____ _____ them
_____ basketball _____ their grades _____, _____
promised in the contract.

14 그들은 농구를 하는 것뿐만 아니라 열심히 공부할 것도 약속해야만 했습니다.

15 처음에는 학생들이 계약서에 대한 그의 생각을 심각하게 받아들이지 않았습니다.

16 카터: 내가 너희들에게 계약서를 줄 것이다.

17 크루즈: "모든 수업에 출석하라," "C 플러스 또는 그 이상 받아라," "지각하지 말아라."

18 이 모든 규칙들은 무엇이죠?

19 제가 이 계약서에 사인하면 사이닝 보너스를 받나요?

20 카터: 그래. 너는 큰 보너스를 받게 될 거야. 왜냐하면 인생의 게임에서뿐 아니라 농구 경기에서도 승리자가 될 것이기 때문이지.

21 맹연습과 새로운 경기 전략으로 그 팀은 몇 년 만에 처음으로 이기기 시작했습니다.

22 그때 이후로 경기마다 이겼습니다.

23 카터 코치를 제외한 모든 이들이 행복했습니다.

24 선수들은 그들 계약의 '학습' 부분을 하지 않았습니다.

25 그들 중 정말 그들이 대학을 갈 수 있다고 믿는 사람들은 거의 없었습니다. 그래서 그들은 성적에는 거의 관심을 두지 않았습니다.

26 카터는 더 강력한 조치를 취하기로 결심했습니다.

27 그는 체육관 문을 잠그고 계약서에서 약속한 대로 그들의 성적이 좋아질 때까지 농구를 못하게 했습니다.

28 The players did not like _____.

29 They told him _____ his _____ were _____ for him, _____ for them.

30 Worm: We're the _____ _____.

31 _____ _____ _____ is you on TV, _____ _____.

32 Carter: _____ you think so, go home and ask _____, "Do I want a _____ _____?"

33 _____ the answer is yes, I will do _____ in my power _____ _____ you.

34 But you _____ _____ do your _____.

35 The players' parents did not like Carter's _____ _____.

36 At the parents' _____, the _____ _____ Carter _____ _____ the gym.

37 _____, Carter _____ _____ leave Richmond High.

38 _____ he entered the gym _____ _____ his things, _____, _____ _____ his players _____ there.

39 We want you to enjoy the movie, so we won't tell you _____ _____ _____.

40 _____ _____ for yourself _____ _____ the movie *Coach Carter*.

---

28 선수들은 그것을 좋아하지 않았습니다.

29 그들은 그에게 그의 행동들이 그들을 위한 것이 아닌 단지 카터 자신을 위한 것이라고 말했습니다.

30 웜: 우리는 농구 팀이에요.

31 우리가 보는 모든 것은 유명세를 타며 TV에 있는 당신이에요.

32 카터: 네가 그렇게 생각한다면, 집으로 가서 너 자신에게 물어봐. "나는 더 나은 삶을 원하는가?"

33 대답이 '맞다'라면, 나는 너를 돕기 위해 내 힘이 닿는 한 모든 것을 할 거야.

34 그러나 너는 네 역할을 해야만 해.

35 선수들의 부모들 역시 카터의 결정을 좋아하지 않았습니다.

36 부모들의 요구에 따라 교장은 카터에게 체육관을 다시 열도록 했습니다.

37 실망한 카터는 리치몬드 고등학교를 떠나기로 결심했습니다.

38 그가 짐을 싸기 위해 체육관으로 들어섰을 때, 그의 선수들 모두가 그곳에 있었습니다.

39 우리는 여러분이 이 영화를 즐기기 원합니다. 그래서 당신에게 다음에 무슨 일이 일어나는지 이야기하지 않을 것입니다.

40 영화 「코치 카터」를 보고 스스로 찾아보세요.

※ 다음 문장을 우리말로 쓰시오.

1 ▸ Welcome to *Movie Trip*.

➡ _____

2 ▸ Today we're going to talk about the movie *Coach Carter*.

➡ _____

3 ▸ Can you imagine a basketball coach who doesn't allow his players to practice?

➡ _____

4 ▸ That's exactly what Coach Carter does.

➡ _____

5 ▸ This movie is about a coach who cares more about his students than about winning games.

➡ _____

6 ▸ The basketball team at Richmond High School in Richmond, California, was having one losing season after another.

➡ _____

7 ▸ The players became used to losing.

➡ _____

8 ▸ To make matters worse, they had no plans for the future; they went to school only to play basketball, and they did not do that very well.

➡ _____

_____

9 ▸ Then they got a new coach, Kenny Carter.

➡ _____

10 ▸ Coach Carter wanted to change things.

➡ _____

11 ▸ He wanted to teach kids how to play basketball well and win.

➡ _____

12 ▸ But more than that, he wanted to give the players a future by sending them to college.

➡ _____

13 To carry out his plan, Coach Carter had the players sign a contract.

➡ _____

14 They had to promise to study hard in addition to playing basketball.

➡ _____

15 At first, students did not take his idea for a contract seriously.

➡ _____

16 Carter: I'm going to give you a contract.

➡ _____

17 Cruz: "Attend all classes," "Get a C⁺ or higher," "Don't be late…."

➡ _____

18 What are all these rules about?

➡ _____

19 Do I get a signing bonus for signing this contract?

➡ _____

20 Carter: Yes. You will get a big bonus because you will become a winner in the game of basketball as well as in the game of life.

➡ _____

21 With hard work and a new game plan, the team began to win for the first time in many years.

➡ _____

22 From that point on, they won game after game.

➡ _____

23 Everybody, except Coach Carter, was happy.

➡ _____

24 The players did not do the "study" part of their contract.

➡ _____

25 Few of them actually believed they could go to college, so they paid little attention to their grades.

➡ _____

26 Carter decided to take stronger action.

➡ _____

27 He locked the gym and refused to let them play basketball until their grades improved, as promised in the contract.

➡ _____

28 The players did not like it.

➡ _____

29 They told him that his actions were just for him, not for them.

➡ _____

30 Worm: We're the basketball team.

➡ _____

31 All we see is you on TV, getting famous.

➡ _____

32 Carter: If you think so, go home and ask yourself, "Do I want a better life?"

➡ _____

33 If the answer is yes, I will do everything in my power to help you.

➡ _____

34 But you have to do your part.

➡ _____

35 The players' parents did not like Carter's decision either.

➡ _____

36 At the parents' demand, the principal ordered Carter to reopen the gym.

➡ _____

37 Disappointed, Carter decided to leave Richmond High.

➡ _____

38 When he entered the gym to pack his things, however, all of his players were there.

➡ _____

39 We want you to enjoy the movie, so we won't tell you what happens next.

➡ _____

40 Find out for yourself by watching the movie *Coach Carter*.

➡ _____

※ 다음 괄호 안의 단어들을 우리말에 맞도록 바르게 배열하시오.

1 (to / welcome / *Trip.* / *Movie*)
➡ _____

2 (we're / today / to / going / about / talk / the / *Coach* / movie / *Carter.*)
➡ _____

3 (you / can / a / imagine / basketball / who / coach / doesn't / his / allow / players / practice? / to)
➡ _____

4 (exactly / that's / Coach / what / does. / Carter)
➡ _____

5 (movie / this / about / is / coach / a / who / more / cares / his / about / than / students / about / games. / winning)
➡ _____

6 (basketball / the / at / team / High / Richmond / in / School / Richmond, / was / California, / one / having / season / losing / another. / after)
➡ _____

7 (players / the / used / became / losing. / to)
➡ _____

8 (make / to / worse, / matters / had / they / plans / no / the / for / future: / went / they / school / to / to / only / basketball, / play / and / did / they / do / not / very / that / well.)
➡ _____

9 (they / then / a / got / coach, / new / Carter. / Kenny)
➡ _____

10 (Carter / Coach / to / wanted / things. / change)
➡ _____

11 (wanted / he / teach / to / how / kids / play / to / well / basketball / win. / and)
➡ _____

12 (more / but / that, / than / wanted / he / give / to / players / the / future / a / sending / by / them / college. / to)
➡ _____

13 (carry / to / his / out / plan, / Carter / Coach / the / had / players / a / sign / contract.)
➡ _____

1 「영화 여행」에 오신 것을 환영합니다.

2 오늘 우리는 영화 「코치 카터」에 대해 이야기할 것입니다.

3 선수들이 연습하는 것을 허락하지 않는 농구 코치를 상상할 수 있나요?

4 그것이 바로 카터 코치가 한 것입니다.

5 이 영화는 경기에서 이기는 것보다 학생들을 더 걱정하는 코치에 대한 영화입니다.

6 캘리포니아 리치몬드 지역의 리치몬드 고등학교 농구 팀은 연속해서 경기에서 지고 있었습니다.

7 선수들도 지는 것에 익숙하게 되었습니다.

8 설상가상으로 그들은 미래에 대한 계획도 없었습니다. 즉, 그들은 단지 농구하기 위해 학교에 갔고, 그것마저도 잘하지 못했습니다.

9 그때 그들은 케니 카터라는 새로운 코치를 선임했습니다.

10 카터 코치는 몇 가지를 바꾸고자 했습니다.

11 그는 아이들에게 어떻게 농구를 잘하고 이기는지를 가르치기를 원했습니다.

12 그러나 그것보다도, 그는 그들을 대학에 보냄으로써 선수들에게 미래를 주기를 원했습니다.

13 그의 계획을 실행하기 위해서, 카터 코치는 선수들에게 계약서에 서명하게 했습니다.

14 (had / they / promise / to / hard / to / study / in / to / addition / basketball. / playing)

➡ _____

15 (first, / at / students / not / did / his / take / idea / a / for / seriously. / contract)

➡ _____

16 (Carter: / going / I'm / give / to / a / you / contract.)

➡ _____

17 (Cruz: / all / "attend / classes," / a / "get / C⁺ / higher," / or / be / "don't / late…")

➡ _____

18 (are / what / these / all / about? / rules)

➡ _____

19 (I / do / a / get / bonus / singing / signing / for / contract? / this)

➡ _____

20 (Carter: / yes. // will / you / a / get / bonus / big / you / because / will / a / become / in / winner / the / game / basketball / well / as / as / the / in / game / the / life. / of)

➡ _____

_____

21 (hard / with / and / work / new / a / plan, / game / team / the / to / began / for / win / first / the / in / time / years. / many)

➡ _____

_____

22 (that / from / on, / point / won / they / after / game / game.)

➡ _____

23 (except / everybody, / Carter, / Coach / happy. / was)

➡ _____

24 (players / the / not / did / the / do / part / "study" / of / contract. / their)

➡ _____

25 (of / few / them / believed / actually / could / they / to / go / college, / they / so / little / paid / attention / their / to / grades.)

➡ _____

_____

26 (decided / Carter / take / to / action. / stronger)

➡ _____

27 (locked / he / gym / the / and / to / refused / let / play / them / basketball / their / until / improved, / grades / promised / as / the / contract. / in)

➡ _____

_____

14 그들은 농구를 하는 것뿐만 아니라 열심히 공부할 것도 약속해야만 했습니다.

15 처음에는 학생들이 계약서에 대한 그의 생각을 심각하게 받아들이지 않았습니다.

16 카터: 내가 너희들에게 계약서를 줄 것이다.

17 크루즈: "모든 수업에 출석하라," "C 플러스 또는 그 이상 받아라," "지각하지 말아라."

18 이 모든 규칙들은 무엇이죠?

19 제가 이 계약서에 사인하면 사이닝 보너스를 받나요?

20 카터: 그래. 너는 큰 보너스를 받게 될 거야. 왜냐하면 인생의 게임에서뿐 아니라 농구 경기에서도 승리자가 될 것이기 때문이지.

21 맹연습과 새로운 경기 전략으로 그 팀은 몇 년 만에 처음으로 이기기 시작했습니다.

22 그때 이후로 경기마다 이겼습니다.

23 카터 코치를 제외한 모든 이들이 행복했습니다.

24 선수들은 그들 계약의 '학습' 부분을 하지 않았습니다.

25 그들 중 정말 그들이 대학을 갈 수 있다고 믿는 사람들은 거의 없었습니다. 그래서 그들은 성적에는 거의 관심을 두지 않았습니다.

26 카터는 더 강력한 조치를 취하기로 결심했습니다.

27 그는 체육관 문을 잠그고 계약서에서 약속한 대로 그들의 성적이 좋아질 때까지 농구를 못하게 했습니다.

28 (players / the / not / did / it. / like)

➡ _____

29 (told / they / that / him / actions / his / just / were / him, / for / for / not / them.)

➡ _____

30 (Worm: / the / we're / team. / basketball)

➡ _____

31 (we / all / is / see / on / you / TV, / famous. / getting)

➡ _____

32 (Carter: / you / if / so, / think / home / go / and / yourself, / ask / I / "do / want / better / a / life?")

➡ _____

33 (the / if / is / answer / yes, / will / I / everything / do / my / in / power / help / you. / to)

➡ _____

34 (you / but / to / have / your / do / part.)

➡ _____

35 (players' / the / did / parents / like / not / decision / Carter's / either.)

➡ _____

36 (the / at / demand, / parents' / principal / the / Carter / ordered / reopen / to / gym. / the)

➡ _____

37 (Carter / disappointed, / decided / leave / to / High. / Richmond)

➡ _____

38 (he / when / the / entered / to / gym / pack / things, / his / all / however, / of / playes / his / there. / were)

➡ _____

39 (want / we / to / you / the / enjoy / movie, / we / so / tell / won't / you / happens / what / next.)

➡ _____

40 (out / find / yourself / for / watching / by / movie / the / Carter. / Coach)

➡ _____

28 선수들은 그것을 좋아하지 않았습니다.

29 그들은 그에게 그의 행동들이 그들을 위한 것이 아닌 단지 카터 자신을 위한 것이라고 말했습니다.

30 웜: 우리는 농구 팀이에요.

31 우리가 보는 모든 것은 유명세를 타며 TV에 있는 당신이에요.

32 카터: 네가 그렇게 생각한다면, 집으로 가서 너 자신에게 물어봐. "나는 더 나은 삶을 원하는가?"

33 대답이 '맞다'라면, 나는 너를 돕기 위해 내 힘이 닿는 한 모든 것을 할 거야.

34 그러나 너는 네 역할을 해야만 해.

35 선수들의 부모들 역시 카터의 결정을 좋아하지 않았습니다.

36 부모들의 요구에 따라 교장은 카터에게 체육관을 다시 열도록 했습니다.

37 실망한 카터는 리치몬드 고등학교를 떠나기로 결심했습니다.

38 그가 짐을 싸기 위해 체육관으로 들어섰을 때. 그의 선수들 모두가 그곳에 있었습니다.

39 우리는 여러분이 이 영화를 즐기기 원합니다. 그래서 당신에게 다음에 무슨 일이 일어나는지 이야기하지 않을 것입니다.

40 영화 「코치 카터」를 보고 스스로 찾아보세요.

※ 다음 우리말을 영어로 쓰시오.

1 「영화 여행」에 오신 것을 환영합니다.

➡ _____

2 오늘 우리는 영화 「코치 카터」에 대해 이야기할 것입니다.

➡ _____

3 선수들이 연습하는 것을 허락하지 않는 농구 코치를 상상할 수 있나요?

➡ _____

4 그것이 바로 카터 코치가 한 것입니다.

➡ _____

5 이 영화는 경기에서 이기는 것보다 학생들을 더 걱정하는 코치에 대한 영화입니다.

➡ _____

6 캘리포니아 리치몬드 지역의 리치몬드 고등학교 농구 팀은 연속해서 경기에서 지고 있었습니다.

➡ _____

_____

7 선수들도 지는 것에 익숙하게 되었습니다.

➡ _____

8 설상가상으로 그들은 미래에 대한 계획도 없었습니다. 즉, 그들은 단지 농구하기 위해 학교에 갔고, 그것마저도 잘하지 못했습니다.

➡ _____

_____

9 그때 그들은 케니 카터라는 새로운 코치를 선임했습니다.

➡ _____

10 카터 코치는 몇 가지를 바꾸고자 했습니다.

➡ _____

11 그는 아이들에게 어떻게 농구를 잘하고 이기는지를 가르치기를 원했습니다.

➡ _____

12 그러나 그것보다도, 그는 그들을 대학에 보냄으로써 선수들에게 미래를 주기를 원했습니다.

➡ _____

13 ▶ 그의 계획을 실행하기 위해서, 카터 코치는 선수들에게 계약서에 서명하게 했습니다.

➡ _____

14 ▶ 그들은 농구를 하는 것뿐만 아니라 열심히 공부할 것도 약속해야만 했습니다.

➡ _____

15 ▶ 처음에는 학생들이 계약서에 대한 그의 생각을 심각하게 받아들이지 않았습니다.

➡ _____

16 ▶ 카터: 내가 너희들에게 계약서를 줄 것이다.

➡ _____

17 ▶ 크루즈: "모든 수업에 출석하라," "C 플러스 또는 그 이상 받아라," "지각하지 말아라."

➡ _____

18 ▶ 이 모든 규칙들은 무엇이죠?

➡ _____

19 ▶ 제가 이 계약서에 사인하면 사이닝 보너스를 받나요?

➡ _____

20 ▶ 카터: 그래. 너는 큰 보너스를 받게 될 거야. 왜냐하면 인생의 게임에서뿐 아니라 농구 경기에서도 승리자가 될 것이기 때문이지.

➡ _____

_____

21 ▶ 맹연습과 새로운 경기 전략으로 그 팀은 몇 년 만에 처음으로 이기기 시작했습니다.

➡ _____

22 ▶ 그때 이후로 경기마다 이겼습니다.

➡ _____

23 ▶ 카터 코치를 제외한 모든 이들이 행복했습니다.

➡ _____

24 ▶ 선수들은 그들 계약의 '학습' 부분을 하지 않았습니다.

➡ _____

25 ▶ 그들 중 정말 그들이 대학을 갈 수 있다고 믿는 사람들은 거의 없었습니다. 그래서 그들은 성적에는 거의 관심을 두지 않았습니다.

➡ _____

_____

26 ▶ 카터는 더 강력한 조치를 취하기로 결심했습니다.

➡ _____

27 ▶ 그는 체육관 문을 잠그고 계약서에서 약속한 대로 그들의 성적이 좋아질 때까지 농구를 못하게 했습니다.

➡ _____

_____

28 선수들은 그것을 좋아하지 않았습니다.

➡ _____

29 그들은 그에게 그의 행동들이 그들을 위한 것이 아닌 단지 카터 자신을 위한 것이라고 말했습니다.

➡ _____

30 웜: 우리는 농구 팀이에요.

➡ _____

31 우리가 보는 모든 것은 유명세를 타며 TV에 있는 당신이에요.

➡ _____

32 카터: 네가 그렇게 생각한다면, 집으로 가서 너 자신에게 물어봐. "나는 더 나은 삶을 원하는가?"

➡ _____

33 대답이 '맞다'라면, 나는 너를 돕기 위해 내 힘이 닿는 한 모든 것을 할 거야.

➡ _____

34 그러나 너는 네 역할을 해야만 해.

➡ _____

35 선수들의 부모들 역시 카터의 결정을 좋아하지 않았습니다.

➡ _____

36 부모들의 요구에 따라 교장은 카터에게 체육관을 다시 열도록 했습니다.

➡ _____

37 실망한 카터는 리치몬드 고등학교를 떠나기로 결심했습니다.

➡ _____

38 그가 짐을 싸기 위해 체육관으로 들어섰을 때, 그의 선수들 모두가 그곳에 있었습니다.

➡ _____

39 우리는 여러분이 이 영화를 즐기기 원합니다. 그래서 당신에게 다음에 무슨 일이 일어나는지 이야기하지 않을 것입니다.

➡ _____

40 영화 「코치 카터」를 보고 스스로 찾아보세요.

➡ _____

영어 기출 문제집

1학기

정답 및 해설

시사 | 송미정

중 3

Passion for Life

시험대비 실력평가   p.08

01 (1) celebrate (2) inform   02 officials / ③
03 ⑤   04 ④   05 ④   06 ②

01 invite 초대하다 invitation 초대, celebrate 축하하다 celebration 축하, inform 정보를 주다 informatrion 정보

02 주어진 문장의 빈칸에 들어가기에 적절한 것은 officials(공무원, 경기 임원)이다. ① Kelly가 퀴즈쇼에서 우리 반/학교...을 대표했다. ② 마라톤을 달리는 것은 힘들다 ③ 이 구역은 임원 전용입니다. ④ 그는 아침/점심/행사 등을 준비한다. ⑤ 그 학생은 수학 시험에서 좋은 점수를 받았을 때 자신이 자랑스러웠다.

03 ⑤ "give up"은 "포기하다"의 뜻이다.

04 ① 졸업식 = graduation ceremony ② cheered 환호했다 ③ 마라톤 = marathon ④ 준비하고 있다 = are preparing ⑤ 제거하다 = remove

05 주어진 단어는 "저자"라는 뜻으로 "writer"에 해당한다.① competitor 경쟁자 ② athlete 운동선수 ③ creator 창조자 ④ writer 저자, 작가 ⑤ developer 개발자

06 be proud of = ~을 자랑스러워하다, one of ~ = ~ 중의 하나

서술형 시험대비   p.09

01 preparation   02 experimentation
03 get / get   04 why / Why
05 (e)nthusiasm
06 (1) good (2) done (3) up (4) result
07 (1) interested (2) give (3) public (4) toward

01 "세심한 시험 대비가 필수적이다." prepare 준비하다, preparation 준비

02 주어진 단어는 동사-명사의 관계이다. congratulate 축하하다, congratulation 축하, experiment 실험하다, experimentation 실험

03 • 그녀는 눈을 감고 그가 낫기를 빌었다. • 방치해 두면 문제가 더 악화될 수 있어요. get better 좋아지다, 낫다, get worse 악화되다

04 • 버스 편이 없다. 그래서 나는 보통 택시를 타는 거야. that's why = 그래서, 그런 이유로 • "우리 외식하자." "그거 좋지." Why not? = 왜 아니겠어?, 좋지.

05 그의 아버지는 축구를 향한 그의 열정을 알아챘다. passion 열정 = enthusiasm

06 (1) ~을 잘하다 = be good at (2) ~을 끝내다 = be done with (3) ~에게 다가가다 = come up to (4) 결과적으로 = as a result

07 (1) ~에 관심이 있다 = be interested in (2) 포기하다 = give up (3) 공개적으로, 사람들이 있는 데서 = in public (4) ~을 향해서 = toward

교과서   Conversation

핵심 Check   p.10~11

1 How was she able to speak English so well
2 ②

01 "어떻게 ~할 수 있게 되었는가?"는 의문사 how를 사용하여 "How was she/he able to ~?"라고 물어본다.

02 알고 있는지 묻는 말은 "Have you heard of ~?" 또는 "Have you been told about ~?"이다.

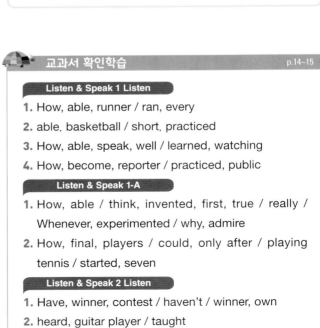

교과서 대화문 익히기

Check(√) True or False   p.12

1 T   2 F   3 T   4 F   5 T

교과서 확인학습   p.14~15

Listen & Speak 1 Listen

1. How, able, runner / ran, every
2. able, basketball / short, practiced
3. How, able, speak, well / learned, watching
4. How, become, reporter / practiced, public

Listen & Speak 1-A

1. How, able / think, invented, first, true / really / Whenever, experimented / why, admire
2. How, final, players / could, only after / playing tennis / started, seven

Listen & Speak 2 Listen

1. Have, winner, contest / haven't / winner, own
2. heard, guitar player / taught

3. heard, dance / watched, times

4. heard, photographer / haven't, pictures, take / takes, street

Listen & Speak 2-A

1. Have, heard, cartoon / interested, drawing cartoons / want to be, join / know, interested, drawing

2. heard / what / stands, into, making, case / What, after, finish / done, pencil, planning, desk

Real-Life Zone

Have, skier / Who, he / skier, medal / great / was, accident, twenties / become / accident, several, get, especially, skiing / Skiing, are good / why, respected

Wrap Up

heard, fire / heard, was, nearby, hurt / one, saved, were / How, save / knocked, tell, leave / amazing

---

시험대비 기본평가   p.16

01 ①   02 ④   03 ③

01 주어진 질문에 대한 답을 보았을 때 (A)는 방법을 묻는 How, (B)는 시간을 묻는 When이 적절하다.

02 "No, what is D.I.Y.?"라는 대답에 이어서 D.I.Y.가 무엇인지 설명해주는 것으로 보아 빈칸에는 D.I.Y.를 아는지 물어보는 질문인 "Have you heard of D.I.Y.?"가 적절하다.

03 (B) 다친 사람이 있느냐는 질문에 없다는 대답이 와야 하고 (C) 한 사람이 열 명을 구했다는 말에 어떻게 구할 수 있었는지를 묻고 (A) 사람들에게 건물을 떠나도록 모든 문을 두드렸다는 대답을 하는 순서가 자연스러운 배열이다.

시험대비 실력평가   p.17~18

01 ②   02 ①   03 ②   04 ③
05 ③   06 ①   07 ③   08 ④
09 ④   10 ⑤   11 ③

01 주어진 질문은 그녀가 어떻게 훌륭한 달리기 선수가 되었는지를 묻는 것으로 적절한 대답은 ②이다.

02 주어진 빈칸은 시간의 부사절을 나타내기 때문에 적절한 접속사는 Whenever이다.

03 소년은 Edison에 대하여 모르는 것은 아니다. 소년이 알고 있는 것 중에서 부족한 부분에 대하여 소녀가 정보를 제공하는 대화이다.

04 "Have you heard about ~?"은 알고 있는지 묻는 표현이다.

05 cartoon writer가 되고 싶어서 cartoon club에 관심이 있는

것은 the boy이다.

06 이어지는 대화에서 우승자를 소개하는 것으로 보아 질문은 우승자가 누구인지를 묻는 말일 것이다.

07 이어지는 대답을 보았을 때 (가)는 사람을 묻는 Who, (나)는 방법을 묻는 How가 적절하다.

08 스키에 관심을 가지게 된 것은 다른 운동을 시도한 이후의 일이기 때문에 (D)가 적절한 위치이다.

09 교통사고를 당하여 다리를 다친 후에 여러 가지 운동을 시도해보고 스키 선수가 된 과정은 소개되었지만 누가 그에게 스키 선수가 되라고 말했는지는 알 수 없다.

10 주어진 문장에 이어지는 대답의 내용을 보면 빈칸에는 화재에 관하여 들어보았는지를 묻는 ⑤가 적절하다.

11 빈칸에 들어가기에 적절한 말은 사람을 선행사로 하는 who/that이다. ① which/that ② which/that ③ who/that ④ why ⑤ where

서술형 시험대비   p.19

01 How was Thomas Edison able   02 why
03 ⓒ → that's not true
04 I heard that she taught herself to play.
05 I'm really into it   06 I'm done
07 (A) knocked   (B) leave

01 "어떻게 ~할 수 있었지?"에 해당하는 표현은 "How was+주어+able to ~?"이다.

02 결과를 유도하는 표현으로 "그것이 ~한 이유이다."에 해당하는 "That's why ~"가 되어야 한다.

03 소녀는 사람들이 Edison에 관하여 잘못 알고 있는 것을 설명하는 입장으로 사람들이 생각하고 있는 것은 사실이 아니라고 해야 자연스러운 연결이 된다.

04 "독학으로 ~을 배우다"는 "teach oneself to ~"이다.

05 "~에 대하여 관심을 가지다"는 'be into"이다.

06 "~을 끝내다"는 의미로 "be done with"가 적절하다.

07 "He knocked on every door to tell people to leave the building."을 보면 (A)는 "knocked", (B)는 "leave"가 적절하다는 것을 알 수 있다.

교과서 Grammar

핵심 Check   p.20~21

1 (1) too   (2) so   (3) old enough
2 (1) not to   (2) not to   (3) never to

01 ④　　　　02 ②, ⑤

03 (1) to wear　(2) to object　(3) come

04 (1) She was disappointed not to be chosen.

(2) It was so long ago that I can't remember.

(3) She was always too busy to listen.

(4) She was kind enough to buy us a meal.

01 too+형용사/부사+to부정사: 너무 ~해서 …할 수 없다[…하기에는 너무 ~하다] Is it too late to cancel my order?라고 쓰는 것이 적절하다.

02 to부정사의 부정은 to부정사 바로 앞에 'not'이나 'never'를 쓴다.

03 too … to부정사 = so … that+주어+can't[couldn't]+동사원형

04 (1) to부정사의 부정은 to부정사 바로 앞에 'not'이나 'never'를 쓴다. (2)~(4) too … to부정사 = so … that+주어+can't[couldn't]+동사원형: 너무 ~해서 …할 수 없다[…하기에는 너무 ~하다], enough to부정사 = so … that+주어+can[could]+동사원형: ~하기에 충분하다

01 ⑤　　　　02 ④　　　　03 ③

04 (1) to go　(2) too　(3) not to　(4) never to

05 ①, ②　　　　06 ④

07 (1) sailing → sail　(2) too → so

(3) enough believe → enough to believe

(4) to never → never to

(5) to pursue not → not to pursue

08 I am so shy that I can't sing in front of many people.

09 ③　　　　10 ②　　　　11 ⑤

12 (1) The cellphone was so expensive that I couldn't buy it.

(2) The ice is so thin that it can't bear your weight.

(3) The rope was so long that it can reach the ground.

(4) She is so healthy that she can travel.

13 ①　　　　14 ④

15 (1) too fast to avoid colliding　(2) not to cause

16 ⑤　　　　17 ②

18 My sister went to Japan to open a restaurant, not to study Japanese.

19 ③

01 'too … to ~'는 '…하기에는 너무 ~하다', '너무 ~해서 …할 수 없다'는 뜻이다.

02 ① Anne asked me not to wait for her. ② She studied hard not to fail the math exam. ③ The teacher warned us not to use our cell phone in class. ⑤ The doctor told me not to smoke.

03 '~할 만큼 충분히 …한'이란 의미의 'so … that 주어 can 동사원형'은 '… enough to부정사'와 같다

04 (1), (2) too … to ~': …하기에는 너무 ~하다, 너무 ~해서 …할 수 없다 (3), (4) to부정사의 부정은 to부정사 바로 앞에 'not'이나 'never'를 쓴다.

05 too … to부정사 = so … that+주어+can't[couldn't]+동사원형: 너무 ~해서 …할 수 없다[…하기에는 너무 ~하다]

06 to부정사의 부정은 not이나 never를 부정하고자 하는 to부정사의 to 앞에 붙인다.

07 (1) too+형용사/부사+to부정사: 너무 ~해서 …할 수 없다[…하기에는 너무 ~하다] (2) too … to부정사 = so … that+주어+can't[couldn't]+동사원형 (3) enough+to부정사: ~하기에 충분하다 (4), (5) to부정사의 부정은 to부정사 바로 앞에 'not'이나 'never'를 쓴다.

08 'too … to부정사'는 'so … that+주어+can't[couldn't]+동사원형'으로 바꾸어 쓸 수 있다.

09 to부정사의 부정은 not이나 never를 부정하고자 하는 to부정사의 to 앞에 붙인다.

10 too+형용사/부사+to부정사: 너무 ~해서 …할 수 없다[…하기에는 너무 ~하다]

11 'not to부정사'가 부사적 용법의 '목적'으로 쓰인 경우 'so as not to'나 'in order not to'로 바꿔 쓸 수 있다.

12 too … to부정사 = so … that+주어+can't[couldn't]+동사원형: 너무 ~해서 …할 수 없다[…하기에는 너무 ~하다], enough to부정사 = so … that+주어+can[could]+동사원형: ~하기에 충분하다 'too … to부정사'나 'enough to부정사'를 'so … that'을 이용하여 바꿔 쓸 때 문장의 주어나 목적어이기 때문에 생략되어 있던 to부정사의 목적어를 써 주어야 함에 주의한다.

13 to부정사의 부정은 not이나 never를 부정하고자 하는 to부정사의 to 앞에 붙인다.

14 too … to부정사: 너무 ~해서 …할 수 없다[…하기에는 너무 ~하다], to부정사의 부정은 not이나 never를 부정하고자 하는 to부정사의 to 앞에 붙인다.

15 (1) '너무 빨리 몰아서 충돌을 피할 수 없었다'라고 하는 것이 자연스러우므로 'too … to부정사'를 이용하고, avoid는 동명사를 목적어로 받으므로 colliding으로 써야 한다. (2) '사고를 일으키지 않도록'이라고 하는 것이 자연스러우므로 'not to cause'로 쓴다.

16 asked의 목적격 보어로 to부정사가 적절하며 to부정사의 부정은 not이나 never를 부정사 앞에 붙인다.

17 주어진 우리말을 10 단어로 쓰면 'My brother is too young

to eat food by himself.'이다.

18 to부정사의 부정은 not이나 never를 부정하고자 하는 to부정
사의 to 앞에 붙인다.

19 'too ... to부정사'는 'so ... that+주어+can't[couldn't]
+동사원형'으로 바꾸어 쓸 수 있다.

01 (1) This computer is so slow that I[we] can't surf
the web.

(2) Boris was so nervous that he couldn't give a
speech.

(3) The woman was so kind that she helped[could
help] the old lady.

(4) The cable is so long that it can reach the
socket.

(5) Your computer is so slow that I can't use it.

02 (1) This TV is too big to carry on my own.

(2) Susie was too slow to catch up with Mike.

(3) The bag is so small that I can't put the books
in it.

03 해석: (1) 나는 그에게 가라고 말하지 않았다.

(2) 나는 그에게 가지 말라고 말했다.

차이: (1)번 문장은 동사 tell을 부정하는 문장이고

(2)번 문장은 부정사 to go를 부정하는 문장이다.

04 (1) (a) The fried chicken is too spicy to eat.

(b) The fried chicken is so spicy that I can't eat
it

(2) (a) The questions are too difficult to answer.

(b) The questions are so difficult that I can't
answer them.

(3) (a) He is strong enough to lift a car.

(b) He is so strong that he can lift a car.

(4) (a) The print was clear enough to read.

(b) The print was so clear that I could read it.

05 not to use

06 (1) I run too slowly to finish the race within the
limited amount of time given.

(2) This coat is too big to fit you.

(3) The text is too long to read.

(4) The man is strong enough to move the rock.

(5) She is wise enough to make a good decision.

(6) The dress is beautiful enough for you to wear
at the party.

07 (1) not to make a noise   (2) not to run

08 (1) too young to   (2) too weak to

(3) good enough to   (4) smart enough

09 (1) Henry was so busy that he couldn't answer the
phone.

(2) The car is so old that I can't drive it.

(3) A boy under 15 is so young that he can't watch
the movie.

(4) The film was so interesting that I could watch
it again.

01 (1)~(5) too ... to부정사 = so... that+주어
+can't[couldn't]+동사원형, enough to부정사 = so ...
that+주어+can[could]+동사원형. (5) 'too ... to부정사'나
'enough to부정사'를 'so ... that'을 이용하여 바꿔 쓸 때 문장
의 주어나 목적어이기 때문에 생략되어 있던 to부정사의 목적어
를 써 주어야 함에 주의한다.

02 too ... to부정사 = so ... that+주어+can't[couldn't]+동사원
형: 너무 ~해서 …할 수 없다[…하기에는 너무 ~하다]

03 to부정사의 부정은 not이나 never를 to부정사 앞에 붙인다.

04 too ... to부정사 = so ... that+주어+can't[couldn't]+동사원
형, enough to부정사 = so ... that+주어+can[could]+동사
원형. 'too ... to부정사'나 'enough to부정사'를 'so ... that'을
이용하여 바꿔 쓸 때 문장의 주어나 목적어이기 때문에 생략되
어 있던 to부정사의 목적어를 써 주어야 함에 주의한다.

05 휴대폰을 사용하지 말라는 것이므로 'not to use'가 적절하다.
to부정사의 부정은 not이나 never를 to부정사 앞에 붙인다.

06 too ... to부정사 = so ... that+주어+can't[couldn't]+동사원형:
너무 ~해서 …할 수 없다[…하기에는 너무 ~하다], enough to부
정사 = so ... that+주어+can[could]+동사원형: ~하기에 충분하
다

07 각각의 목적격보어로 to부정사가 나와야 하는데 부정으로 써야
하므로 not을 to부정사 앞에 붙인다.

08 의미에 맞게 'too ... to부정사'나 'enough to부정사'를 이용한
다. not good enough to ~: ~할 자격[가치]이 없는

09 too ... to부정사 = so ... that+주어+can't[couldn't]+동사원
형, enough to부정사 = so ... that+주어+can[could]+동사
원형. 'too ... to부정사'나 'enough to부정사'를 'so ... that'을
이용하여 바꿔 쓸 때 문장의 주어나 목적어이기 때문에 생략되
어 있던 to부정사의 목적어를 써 주어야 함에 주의한다.

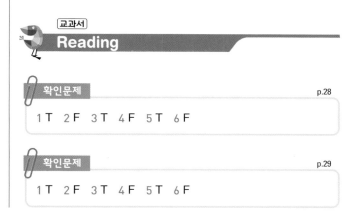

교과서
Reading

확인문제   p.28

1 T   2 F   3 T   4 F   5 T   6 F

확인문제   p.29

1 T   2 F   3 T   4 F   5 T   6 F

01 Last
02 more than
03 no more, coming
04 prepare for, closing ceremony
05 There comes another
06 something wrong
07 Still, kept going
08 stopped their preparations
09 All eyes were on
10 celebration musicm, cheered
11 Go for it
12 with a tape
13 Finally, ran through, fell to
14 His name
15 was from
16 came up to
17 happened to
18 during a practice run
19 got worse
20 Why not
21 far behind
22 representing Afghanistan
23 no way
24 at war, isn't it
25 have been
26 That's why
27 was sad for, back then
28 Were, running
29 started running
30 lots of
31 won a marathon
32 As a result
33 How
34 myself, to be from
35 not to give up
36 to win
37 it was enough

1 The Last Runner

2 The last runner finished the race more than an hour before.

3 "There will be no more runners coming," the officials decided.

4 They removed the tape at the finish line and started to prepare for the closing ceremony for the 1996 Atlanta Summer Olympics in the United States.

5 Someone shouted, "Look! There comes another runner!"

6 A runner was just entering the stadium, but there was something wrong with his legs.

7 Still, he kept going toward the finish line.

8 The band and the volunteers stopped their preparations for the closing ceremony.

9 All eyes were on the runner.

10 Suddenly, the band started playing celebration music, and the volunteers cheered.

11 "Go! Go! Go for it!"

12 Two volunteers ran to the finish line with a tape.

13 Finally, the runner ran through the tape and then fell to the ground.

14 His name was Abdul Baser Wasiqi.

15 He was from Afghanistan.

16 Reporters came up to Wasiqi and started asking him questions.

17 Reporter: What happened to you?

18 Wasiqi: I injured my leg during a practice run.

19 The injury got worse during the race, but I couldn't give up.

20 Reporter: Why not?

21 You knew that you were too far behind to win a medal.

22 Wasiqi: I am the onlya athlete here representing Afghanistan.

23 There was no way I could give up.

24 Reporter: Afghanistan is still at war, isn't it?

25 Wasiqi: Yes, we have been at war for 16 years.

26 That's why we were not able to send athletes to the Barcelona Olympics four years ago.

27 I was sad for my country back then when I could see no Afghan athletes in the opening ceremony.

28 Reporter: Were you running marathons then?

29 Wasiqi: No. I started running after Barcelona.

30 I ran in lots of races.

31 Finally I won a marathon in Germany.

32 As a result, I was able to come to Atlanta.

33 Reporter: How do you feel now?

34 Wasiqi: I am proud of myself and proud to be from Afghanistan.

35 For me and my country, it was important not to give up.

36 I didn't come here to win.

37 For me, it was enough to be here and to finish the race.

01 ④
02 who[that] are
03 Because the last runner finished the race more than an hour before.
04 ②, ⑤
05 because → why
06 the race → a practice run
  또는 Wasiqi injured his leg → The injury got worse
07 ②, ③
08 All of a sudden / All at once / On a sudden
09 ④
10 representing
11 of

01 ⓐ prepare for: ~을 준비하다, ⓑ for: ~을 위한

02 coming 앞에는 '관계대명사+be동사(who[that] are)'가 생략되었다.

03 마지막 주자가 한 시간도 더 전에 경주를 끝냈기 때문이다.

04 ⓐ와 ②, ⑤: happen to ~(<일·사건 등이> ~에게 일어나다, 생기다), ①, ③, ④: happen to+동사원형(우연히 ~하다)

05 '그것이 우리가 4년 전 바르셀로나 올림픽에 선수들을 보낼 수 없었던 이유'라고 해야 하므로, why로 고치는 것이 적절하다. That's why ~: 그래서 ~하게 된 것이다, why 뒤에는 어떤 행동의 결과가 되는 내용이 온다. That's because ~: 그것은 ~ 때문이다.

06 Wasiqi가 다리를 다친 것은 '연습 경기를 하던 중'이었고, 경기 중에 상처가 점점 더 심해졌다.

07 Wasiqi가 다리에 이상이 있는데도 계속 결승선을 향해 움직여 결국 테이프를 통과했다는 내용이므로 '감동적인' 분위기라고 하는 것이 적절하다. ②, ③: 감동적인, ① 수치스러운, 창피한, ④ 난처한, 쑥스러운, ⑤ 실망스러운, 기대에 못 미치는

08 Suddenly = All of a sudden, All at once, On a sudden: 갑자기

09 Wasiqi는 결승선의 테이프를 '통과해' 달린 다음에 바닥에 쓰러졌다.

10 앞의 명사 athlete를 수식하는 현재분사형이 적절하다.

11 ask는 간접목적어를 직접목적어 뒤로 보낼 때 of를 붙인다.

12 (B)와 ②, ⑤: 계속 용법, ①, ④: 경험 용법, ③: 완료 용법

13 (A) interviewee: 인터뷰 받는 사람, (B) Wasiqi는 심각한 상처에도 불구하고 '포기하지' 않고 마라톤을 완주함으로써 올림픽 정신을 보여주었다고 말할 수 있다.

14 to부정사의 부정은 to부정사 앞에 not을 쓰는 것이 적절하다.

15 ⓑ와 ②: 명사적 용법(진주어), It: 가주어, ② = To be present at the party was good enough. ①, ③, ④, ⑤: 부사적 용법

16 ⓐ와 ④: 그런데도, 그럼에도 불구하고(부사), ①, ⑤: 아직(도) (계속해서)(부사), ② (비교급을 강조하여) 훨씬[더욱](부사), ③ 가만히 있는, 고요한(형용사)

17 이 글은 'Wasiqi가 다리에 이상이 있는데도 불구하고 폐막식 준비를 하고 있을 정도로 뒤늦은 시간까지 계속 달려 결국 결승선 테이프를 통과했다'는 내용의 글이므로, 제목으로는 ①번 '마지막 그러나 가장 감명 깊은 주자'가 적절하다. ③ consideration: 배려, ⑤ alas: 아아(슬픔·유감을 나타내는 소리)

18 Wasiqi가 얼마나 오래 달렸는지는 대답할 수 없다. ① There was something wrong with his legs. ② No. ③ The band started playing celebration music, and the volunteers cheered. "Go! Go! Go for it!" ④ He fell to the ground.

19 앞의 내용의 결과가 나오고 있으므로 As a result가 적절하다. ③ 그럼에도 불구하고, ④ ~임에 비하여[반하여]

20 Wasiqi가 독일 마라톤에서 우승하기 전에 얼마나 많은 경주에서 뛰었는지는 대답할 수 없다. ① After the Barcelona Olympics. ③ He was proud of himself and proud to be from Afghanistan. ④ It was important not to give up. ⑤ No.

21 ⓐ preparation for: ~을 위한 준비, ⓑ through: ~을 통해, ~을 관통하여

22 '또 다른 선수'라고 해야 하므로 another로 고치는 것이 적절하다. the other: 둘 중 나머지 하나

23 All eyes were on ~: 모든 눈이 ~를 주시했다(~에게 머물렀다)

🦉 서술형 시험대비　　　p.38~39

01 (A) last　(B) removed　(C) closing

02 over

03 There will be no more runners coming

04 going　　　05 Go for it 또는 Way to go

06 to prepare → preparing

07 isn't it

08 you were so far behind that you couldn't win a medal

09 at war

10 (A) give up　(B) representing Afghanistan

11 At last, In the end, Eventually 중에서 쓰면 된다.

12 pride, pride

13 (A) many　(B) Germany

14 (A) giving up　(B) to win

01 (A) '마지막 주자'라고 해야 하므로 last가 적절하다. last: 마지막의, latest: 최근의, (B) 테이프를 '걷어냈다'고 해야 하므로 removed가 적절하다. install: 설치하다, (C) '폐막식'이라고 해야 하므로 closing이 적절하다.

02 more than = over: ~ 이상

03 no more: 더 이상 ~ 아닌

04 keep ~ing: 계속해서 ~하다

05 Go for it!: 자, 해봐!, 어서!, 힘내!, Way to go!: 잘한다, 잘해! = Come on! = Go! = Stick it out!, 우울해 보이는 사람에게 격려할 때: Cheer up!(힘내!)

06 stop+to부정사: ~하기 위하여 멈추다, stop+~ing: ~을 그만두다[멈추다]. '밴드와 자원봉사자들이 폐막식을 위한 준비를 멈

추었다'고 했기 때문에, 'stop+동명사'로 고치는 것이 적절하다.

07 be동사가 있으므로, be동사를 사용하여 부가의문문을 만드는 것이 적절하다.

08 too ~ to부정사 = so ~ that 주어 can't: 너무 ~해서 …할 수 없다

09 인터뷰 당시 아프가니스탄이 16년째 전쟁 중이라고 했으므로, 4년 전인 바르셀로나 올림픽 경기가 열리던 무렵에는 12년째 '전쟁 중'이었음을 알 수 있다. at war: 전쟁 중인

10 Wasiqi는 '아프가니스탄을 대표하는' 유일한 선수였기 때문에, 자신이 메달을 따는 것이 불가능하다는 것을 알았지만 '포기할 수' 없었다.

11 finally = at last = in the end = eventually: 마침내

12 be proud of = take pride in: ~을 자랑스러워하다, proud의 명사형인 pride를 쓰는 것이 적절하다.

13 Wasiqi가 달리기를 시작한 이후 그는 '많은' 경주에서 뛰었고, 마침내 '독일' 마라톤에서 우승했다. 그리고 그것이 그를 애틀랜타로 오게 이끌었다.

14 Wasiqi는 자기 자신, 그리고 자신이 아프가니스탄 선수인 것이 자랑스러웠다. 그와 그의 조국을 위해서는, '포기하지' 않는 것이 중요했다. 그는 애틀랜타에 '이기러' 온 것이 아니었고 그가 애틀랜타 올림픽에 참가하여 경주를 끝마친 것으로 충분했다. sufficient: 충분한

영역별 핵심문제
p.41~45

01 ③　　02 ⑤　　03 ①　　04 ③

05 Have you heard of the winner of the singing contest?

06 How was she able to speak English so well?

07 ③　　08 ⑤　　09 ③

10 Many people are good at skiing.
→ Not many people are good at skiing.

11 ①, ⑤　　12 ⑤　　13 ⑤　　14 ②

15 ⑤

16 I read a book quietly not to disturb my classmates.　　17 ③

18 They tried hard so as not to fail the entrance exam.　　19 ③

20 (1) We were too late to catch the last train.
(2) We were so late that we couldn't catch the last train.　　21 ④

22 The man was so tired that he couldn't play tennis.　　23 ④

24 (1) I was too tired to focus on the test.
(2) The presenter was too nervous to eat dinner.
(3) The evidence is detailed enough to support his argument.

25 The cellphone was so expensive that I couldn't buy it.

26 Afghanistan is still at war　　27 ⑤

28 racing　　29 ②　　30 ③

31 I am so shy that I can't sing in front of many people.

32 (1) 강점: 노래 부르는 것을 좋아하고 목소리가 좋다.
약점: 수줍어하고 불안해한다.
(2) 너무 수줍어해서 많은 사람들 앞에서 노래를 부를 수 없다.
(3) 콘테스트 도중에 불안해하지 않기 위해서 먼저 학급 친구들 앞에서 노래 부르기를 연습할 것이다.

01 come up to ~ = ~로 오다, 다가오다, give up = 포기하다

02 문장의 주어이기 때문에 동사 prepare의 명사형인 preparation이 적절하다.

03 "운동을 잘하는 사람"이라는 설명에 해당하는 단어는 "운동선수"이다.

04 "join"은 "가입하다, 합류하다"의 뜻이다.

05 "~에 대하여 들어 본 적 있니?"라는 의미로 상대가 아는지 물어보는 말은 "Have you heard of ~?"이다.

06 "어떻게 그녀가 ~할 수 있었니?"는 "How was she able to ~?"로 나타낸다.

07 앞에 나온 문장에서 새로운 것을 발명할 때마다 여러 번 실험을 하는 수고를 마다않았다는 내용이 사람들이 존경하는 이유이므로 "that's why"가 적절하다.

08 그는 20대 초반에 차 사고를 당했다 = He was in a car accident in his early twenties, 그는 다리를 다쳤다 He hurt his legs.

09 여러 가지 운동을 했지만 스키 선수가 된 것으로 보아 스키 타는 것에 관심을 가지게 된 것을 알 수 있다.

10 "Skiing is not easy."라고 한 후에 "Many people are good at skiing."이라고 한 것은 흐름에 일관성이 없다.

11 상대에게 알고 있는지를 묻는 말은 "Have you heard ~?", "Have you been told ~?", "Do you know ~?", "Are you aware of/that ~?" 등이다.

12 한 사람이 열 명을 어떻게 구했는지를 설명하는 말이 되도록 구체적인 방법을 소개한다. 모든 사람이 건물을 떠나도록 하기 위하여 문을 두드렸다고 하는 것이 적절하다.

13 화재가 났을 때 한 사람이 열 명을 구했다는 사실을 소개하는 대화로, 열 명을 구한 사람이 소방관이었다는 언급은 없다.

14 ②번은 '매우 느렸지만 이길 수 있었다'라는 의미이고 나머지는 모두 '너무 느려서 이길 수 없었다'라는 의미이다.

15 ① Some people told her not to become a professional. ② I read the newspaper every morning in order not to get behind the times. ③ The teacher asked us not

to make any sound during the class. ④ I hurried so as not to be late for the meeting.

16　to부정사의 부정은 not이나 never를 to부정사 앞에 붙인다.

17　too ... to부정사 = so ... that+주어+can't[couldn't]+동사원형: 너무 ~해서 …할 수 없다[…하기에는 너무 ~하다], enough to부정사 = so ... that+주어+can[could]+동사원형: ~하기에 충분하다 'too ... to부정사'나 'enough to부정사'를 'so ... that'을 이용하여 바꿔 쓸 때 문장의 주어나 목적어이기 때문에 생략되어 있던 to부정사의 목적어를 써 주어야 함에 주의한다.

18　so as to ~의 부정은 not을 to부정사 앞에 붙인다.

19　too ... to부정사 = so ... that+주어+can't[couldn't]+동사원형: 너무 ~해서 …할 수 없다[…하기에는 너무 ~하다]

20　too ... to부정사 = so ... that+주어+can't[couldn't]+동사원형: 너무 ~해서 …할 수 없다[…하기에는 너무 ~하다]

21　ask는 목적격 보어로 to부정사가 나오며 부정사의 부정은 not이나 never를 부정사 앞에 붙인다.

22　so ... that+주어+can't[couldn't]+동사원형: 너무 ~해서 …할 수 없다[…하기에는 너무 ~하다]

23　주어진 우리말을 영작하면 'The students promised not to make any noise again.'이다.

24　too ... to부정사 = so ... that+주어+can't[couldn't]+동사원형: 너무 ~해서 …할 수 없다[…하기에는 너무 ~하다], enough to부정사 = so ... that+주어+can[could]+동사원형: ~하기에 충분하다

25　too ... to부정사 = so ... that+주어+can't[couldn't]+동사원형: 너무 ~해서 …할 수 없다[…하기에는 너무 ~하다]. 'too ... to부정사'나 'enough to부정사'를 'so ... that'을 이용하여 바꿔 쓸 때 문장의 주어나 목적어이기 때문에 생략되어 있던 to부정사의 목적어를 써 주어야 함에 주의한다.

26　at war: 전쟁 중인

27　Wasiqi는 '4년 전 바르셀로나 올림픽의 개회식에서 아프가니스탄 선수를 볼 수 없어서' 슬펐다고 했다.

28　finish는 목적어로 동명사를 취하므로 racing으로 쓰는 것이 적절하다.

29　위 글은 '(신문·잡지의) 글, 기사'이다. ③ 전기, ④ 독후감, ⑤ (책·연극·영화 등에 대한) 논평[비평], 감상문

30　앞에 나오는 내용과 상반되는 내용이 뒤에 이어지므로 However가 가장 적절하다. ② 그러므로, ④ 즉[말하자면], ⑤ 게다가, 더욱이

31　too ~ to부정사 = so ~ that 주어 can't: 너무 ~해서 …할 수 없다

32　(1) Strength: love singing, good voice, Weakness: shy, nervous, (2) I am too shy to sing in front of many people. (3) Not to be nervous during the contest, I will practice singing in front of my class first.

---

01 (a)dmire　　02 ①　　03 ④　　04 ④
05 ③　　06 ④　　07 ⑤　　08 ④
09 ③　　10 ④　　11 ④　　12 ③
13 ①　　14 ②
15 (1) I'm so sick that I can't go out to eat.
　　(2) She is so old that she can do what she wants.
16 ①　　　　17 ④
18 Why couldn't you give up?
19 That's why we were not able to send athletes to the Barcelona Olympics four years ago.
20 ④　　　　21 me → myself　　　　22 ④
23 (A) kilometer　(B) given　(C) running
24 In order that I may not fall behind the other runners

01　주어진 단어는 유의어 관계이다. author 작가, writer 작가, admire 존경하다, respect 존경하다

02　이 그림은 무엇을 의미하고 있습니까? - represent 의미하다, 나타내다, 대표하다, reduce 줄이다, take 가지고 가다, realize 깨닫다

03　그녀는 틀림없이 자신이 아주 자랑스러울 것이다. be proud of = 자랑스러워하다 / 난 테니스를 별로 잘 치지는 못한다. be good at = 잘하다, 능숙하다

04　'① preparation 준비 ② removed 제거했다 ③ public 공적인 ④ famous 등의 형용사가 적절함. ⑤ officials 공무원

05　어떻게 될 수 있었는지를 묻는 말은 "How was he able to ~?"이다. "Could you tell me ~?"도 상대에게 궁금증을 물어보는 말이다.

06　(A) "~을 들어 본 적이 있니?"는 "Have you heard of ~?"이다. (B) "좋아지다, 회복하다"는 "get better"이다.

07　몇 가지 다른 운동을 시도한 것은 the boy가 아니라 Eui Hyun Sin이었다.

08　"be into"는 "~에 관심이 많다"는 뜻으로 "be interested in"에 해당한다.

09　D.I.Y.는 직접 만들어 보는 것을 나타낸다. D.I.Y.에 관심이 많다는 것은 직접 만드는 것을 좋아한다는 의미이므로 "buying"은 적절하지 않다. buying → making

10　소녀가 소년에게 D.I.Y.에 관하여 들어보았는지 묻는 것으로 보았을 때, 소녀는 D.I.Y.에 관하여 알고 있는 것을 알 수 있지만 어디에서 들었는지는 이 대화를 통해서 알 수 없다.

11　too ... to부정사 = so ... that+주어+can't[couldn't]+동사원형: 너무 ~해서 …할 수 없다[…하기에는 너무 ~하다]

12　위 글을 영어로 옮기면, 'The old man took a deep breath not to be upset.'이다.

13　주절의 시제가 과거이므로 that절에서도 과거형 couldn't로 쓰는 것이 적절하다.

14 ① Not to be nervous during the contest, I will practice singing in front of my class first. ③ The player practiced hard to be proud of himself, not to win a gold medal. ④ I was taught from the cradle never to cry. ⑤ For me and my country, it was important not to give up.

15 (1) too … to부정사 = so … that+주어+can't[couldn't]+동사원형: 너무 ~해서 …할 수 없다[…하기에는 너무 ~하다] (2) enough to부정사 = so … that+주어+can[could]+동사원형: ~하기에 충분하다

16 ⓐ with: [관계] ~에 관해서, ~에 대하여, ⓑ All eyes were on ~: 모든 눈이 ~를 주시했다(~에게 머물렀다)

17 Wasiqi가 다리에 이상이 있는데도 계속 결승선을 향해 움직여 결국 테이프를 통과해 달렸다는 것으로 보아, Wasiqi는 '의지가 강한' 성격이라고 하는 것이 적절하다. ① 관대한, ② 외향적인, 사교적인, ③ 수동적인, 소극적인, ⑤ 공격적인

18 Why not?은 '왜 포기할 수 없었죠?'라는 뜻이다.

19 why를 보충하면 된다.

20 '메달을 얻기에 너무도 크게 뒤떨어져 있었다는 것을 알고 있었지만 제가 포기할 수 있는 방법은 없었습니다.'라고 했으므로, 제목으로는 ④번 '내가 포기해야만 하는 것은 포기하는 것이다.'가 적절하다.

21 주어와 목적어가 같으므로 me를 재귀대명사로 고치는 것이 적절하다.

22 Wasiqi와 그의 조국을 위해서는, '포기하지 않는 것'이 중요했다.

23 (A) 단위명사가 형용사처럼 명사를 수식할 때는 단수로 써야 하므로 kilometer가 적절하다. (B) '주어진' 시간이라고 해야 하므로 given이 적절하다. (C) practice는 목적어로 동명사를 취하므로 running이 적절하다.

24 목적을 나타내는 부사적 용법의 to부정사는 in order that ~ may를 사용하여 고치는 것이 적절하다. 부정문의 경우, in order that ~ may not

---

서술형 실전문제   p.50~51

01 invented   02 Whenever

03 Maybe that's why so many people admire him.

04 (1) We are too busy to go out for a walk.
(2) Jin is so late that he can't take the 9 o'clock train.
(3) The apples are ripe enough to be picked.
(4) This stadium is so large that it can hold 1,000 people.
(5) Ellen exercises every day not to gain weight.
(6) The girl listened carefully in class not to miss a word.

---

05 (1) Andrew promised me never to be late for the meeting again.
(2) In order not to forget certain events with my dog, I always take pictures with her.
(3) I will practice running every morning so as not to fall behind the other runners.
(4) I was too busy to go to bed before midnight.
(5) No wonder my grade was too low for me to pass the exam.

06 There comes another runner!

07 (A) something wrong   (B) closing ceremony

08 run through

09 (A) during   (B) behind   (C) for

10 reason

---

01 Thomas Edison이 어떻게 많은 것을 발명할 수 있었는지를 묻는 질문에 대한 대답을 하는 문장이므로 빈칸에는 invented가 적절하다.

02 (B)는 "~할 때마다"의 뜻으로 부사절을 유도하는 접속사 "whenever"가 적절하다.

03 그것이 ~하는 이유이다 = that's why ~

04 (1), (2) too … to부정사 = so … that+주어+can't[couldn't]+동사원형: 너무 ~해서 …할 수 없다[…하기에는 너무 ~하다] (3), (4) enough to부정사 = so … that+주어+can[could]+동사원형: ~하기에 충분하다 (5), (6) to부정사의 부정은 not이나 never를 to부정사 앞에 붙인다.

05 (1)~(3) 부정사의 부정은 not이나 never를 to부정사 앞에 붙인다. 부사적 용법의 '목적'인 경우 to부정사 대신에 'so as to'나 'in order to'를 쓸 수 있는데 이 경우에도 to부정사의 to 앞에 붙인다. (4), (5) too … to부정사 = so … that+주어+can't[couldn't]+동사원형: 너무 ~해서 …할 수 없다[…하기에는 너무 ~하다]

06 부사 'there'를 강조하기 위해 문두로 이동시키면, 주어 'another runner'와 동사 'comes'를 도치시키는 것이 적절하다.

07 그의 다리에 '이상이 있었지만' Wasiqi는 경주를 포기하지 않고 너무나 오래 동안 계속 달려서 그가 경기장에 들어왔을 때 밴드와 자원봉사자들은 '폐막식'을 위한 준비를 하고 있었다.

08 Wasiqi가 그것을 '통과해 달릴 수' 있도록 테이프를 잡고 있기를 원했기 때문이다.

09 (A) 뒤에 기간을 나타내는 명사가 나오므로 during이 적절하다. while+주어+동사, (B) 메달을 타기에 너무도 멀리 '뒤떨어져' 있었다고 해야 하므로 behind가 적절하다. ahead: 앞에, (C) 뒤에 숫자가 나오므로 for가 적절하다. during+기간을 나타내는 명사, for+숫자

10 That's why = For that reason

|모범답안|

01 marathon, finished, closing, ran through, representing

02 (A) dangerous enough   (B) not to be

03 (A) 5 kilometer marathon
   (B) a lot of time to exercise
   (C) too slowly
   (D) within the limited amount of time given
   (E) running faster every morning

01 finish 끝내다, stadium 운동장, finally 마침내, fall to the ground 땅바닥에 쓰러지다

단원별 모의고사   p.53~56

01 transportation		02 ②	
03 (1) war (2) stadium (3) celebration (4) cheered			
04 ①	05 ②	06 before	
07 ③	08 ⑤	09 Not, good at	
10 ③	11 ②	12 ④	13 ⑤
14 ③	15 too difficult for me to solve		

16 (1) Sally wore warm clothes not to catch a cold.
   (2) People should stay quiet in public places not to disturb others.
   (3) Amy was too sick to play with her friends.

17 ③	18 preparations	19 ②
20 Afghan	21 ②	
22 (A) send athletes (B) opening		
23 running	24 officials	25 ⑤

01 두 단어의 관계는 동사-명사의 관계이다. invite 초대하다, invitation 초대, transport 수송하다, transportation 수송

02 영어 설명으로 "강렬한 정서나 감정"에 해당하는 단어는 "passion 열정"이다.

03 (1) at war 전쟁 중인 (2) stadium 경기장 (3) celebration 축하 행사 (4) cheer 환호하다

04 사람들 앞에서 노래 부르는 것은 쉬운 일이 아니었다. in public 사람들 앞에서, 공공연하게

05 "어떻게 ~할 수 있었니?"라는 의미로 정보를 묻는 표현은 "How was he/she able to ~?"이다.

06 "여러 해의 훈련 이후에야 그가 그것을 할 수 있었다."는 것은 "그가 그것을 하기 전에 여러 해의 훈련을 했다."는 의미이므로 빈칸에는 before가 적절하다.

07 ③ 주어진 대화에서 Hyeon Chung은 우승자가 아니라 "one of the final four players"(4강전에 출전한 선수)라고 했다.

08 주어진 문장은 사고를 겪은 후에 여러 가지 운동을 시도하고 나서 결국 스키에 관심을 가지게 되었다고 소개하는 문장으로 (E)에 들어가는 것이 자연스럽다.

09 "많은 사람이 ~하는 것은 아니다."는 "Not many people ~."이고 "잘하다, 능숙하다"는 "be good at"이다.

10 ① Eui Hyun Sin이 최초로 금메달을 딴 것인지는 알 수 없다. ② Eui Hyun Sin이 참가한 것은 2018년 Paralympics이다. ④ Eui Hyun Sin 여러 가지 운동을 시도한 후에 스키에 관심을 가지게 되었다. ⑤ Skiing은 쉽지 않기 때문에 많은 사람들이 그를 존경한다.

11 주어진 문장은 화재에서 다친 사람이 있는지 묻는 것으로 그에 대한 대답인 "No, one man saved ten people who were in the building." 앞 (B)가 적절한 위치이다.

12 ① Sora는 화재에 대해 알고 있었다. ② 소년은 아무도 다치지 않은 것을 알고 있었다. ③ 한 사람이 열 명을 구했다. ⑤ 건물에 있는 열 명을 구했다.

13 too ... to부정사 = so ... that+주어+can't[couldn't]+동사원형. 'too ... to부정사'나 'enough to부정사'를 'so ... that'을 이용하여 바꿔 쓸 때 문장의 주어나 목적어이기 때문에 생략되어 있던 to부정사의 목적어를 써 주어야 함에 주의한다.

14 to부정사의 부정은 not이나 never를 to부정사 앞에 붙이므로 I told him never to tell a lie again.이라고 쓰는 것이 적절하다.

15 too ... to부정사: 너무 ~해서 …할 수 없다[…하기에는 너무 ~하다]

16 (1), (2) to부정사의 부정은 not이나 never를 to부정사 앞에 붙인다. (3) too ... to부정사: 너무 ~해서 …할 수 없다[…하기에는 너무 ~하다]

17 ① The song is too difficult to sing. ② The question was easy enough to answer. ④ You must remember not to make a loud noise. ⑤ She is intelligent enough not to miss a trick.

18 소유격 다음에 prepare의 명사형으로 쓰는 것이 적절하고, 폐막식을 위한 준비가 여러 가지일 것이므로 복수형으로 쓰는 것이 적절하다.

19 위 글은 'Wasiqi가 다리에 이상이 있는데도 계속 결승선을 향해 달려 결국 테이프를 통과했다'는 내용의 글이므로, 주제로는 ②번 '고난에 결코 굴복하지 않는 진정한 스포츠 정신'이 적절하다. give in to: ~에 굴복하다, ⑤ exhausted: 기진맥진한, 진이 다 빠진, 탈진한

20 Afghan: 아프가니스탄(말, 사람)의

21 주어진 문장은 'Why couldn't you give up?'의 뜻으로 ②번 앞 문장의 마지막에서 Wasiqi가 한 말을 되묻는 말이므로 ②번이 적절하다.

22 그 당시 아프가니스탄은 전쟁 중이라서 바르셀로나 올림픽에 '선수들을 보낼 수' 없었고, 그래서 '개회식'에서 아프가니스탄을 대표하는 선수들이 없었기 때문이었다.

23 give up은 목적어로 동명사를 취하므로 running으로 쓰는 것이 적절하다.

24 official: (고위) 공무원[관리], 임원, 조직에서 지휘권을 가진 자리에 있는 사람

25 'Wasiqi가 얼마나 오래 달렸는지'는 알 수 없다. ① When most runners finished racing, and the officials started to prepare for the closing ceremony. ② Yes. ③ No. ④ For his country.

Teens' Worries

시험대비 실력평가
p.60

01 (1) (d)etest (2) (n)ervous   02 ④

03 ③   04 ⑤   05 ⑤   06 ②

01 주어진 보기의 단어는 유의어 관계이다. decide 결정하다, determine 결정하다, hate 몹시 싫어하다, detest 몹시 싫어하다, afraid 걱정하는, 불안한, nervous 불안한

02 주어진 문장의 빈칸에 들어가기에 적절한 것은 "proved"(입증했다)이다. (엘라는 판사에게 그녀가 돈을 훔치지 않았음을 입증했다.) ① 우리 견학에 대한 너의 의견에 동의해. agree ② 클레어가 메이슨에게 데이트를 신청했고, 그들은 영화를 보러 갔다. asked ③ 많은 사람들이 스미스 씨 의견에 동의하지 않았다. disagreed ④ 그는 자신이 실수하지 않았다는 것을 입증했다. (proved) ⑤ 두 아이는 서로 좋아/싫어했다. liked/hated

03 ① 대니얼은 치과에 가는 것을 두려워한다. ② 카운슬러가 나에게 잠을 더 자라고 조언했다. ③ 잭은 최신 모델의 차를 샀다. - latest 최신의 ④ 루카스는 너무 많은 실수를 해서 수학 시험에서 C를 받았다. ⑤ 라이언은 내가 한 말을 오해했다.

04 ① a couple of 두서너 개의, 몇 개의, 몇 사람의 ② end up 결국 ~하게 되다 ③ guy (비격식) 녀석, 남자 (informal) ④ hate 매우 싫어하다 ⑤ in style 유행하는, 유행되는

05 주어진 단어는 "결정하다"라는 뜻으로 "determine"에 해당한다.

06 열 셀 때까지 시작해야 해. get started 시작하다 / 당신이 하루 속히 완쾌되기를 바랍니다. get better 회복하다

서술형 시험대비
p.61

01 management   02 proof

03 for / for   04 out / out

05 (1) about (2) end (3) now (4) style

06 (1) taking (2) having (3) without (4) together

01 시간 관리를 배우는 것은 그들에게 중요한 기술이다. manage 관리하다 – management 관리

02 주어진 단어는 동사-명사의 관계이다. relax 쉬다, relaxation 휴식, prove 입증하다, proof 증거, 입증

03 • 그 집은 오랫동안 비어 있었다. for a long time 오래 동안 • 그 비행기는 이륙 준비가 되어 있다. be ready for ~할 준비가 되다

04 • 난 저녁 데이트 신청을 받았다. be asked out 데이트 신청을 받다 • 그녀는 방에서 나갔다. go out of ~에서 나가다

05 (1) be worried about ~ = ~에 대하여 걱정하다 (2) end up –ing = 결국 ~하게 되다 (3) for now = 당분간, 지금은 (4) in style = 유행하는

06 (1) 시간이 걸리다 = take time (2) ~하는 데 어려움을 겪다 have a hard time -ing (3) without -ing = ~하지 않고 (4) get together = 모이다

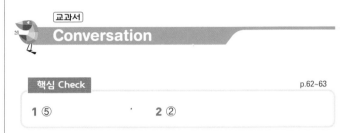

교과서 Conversation

핵심 Check
p.62~63

1 ⑤   2 ②

01 ⑤는 동의하는지 상대에게 묻는 말이고, 나머지는 모두 동의한다는 표현이다.

02 상대가 불안하다고 했으므로 안심시키는 표현이 적절하다.

교과서 대화문 익히기

Check(√) True or False
p.64

1 F 2 T 3 T 4 F

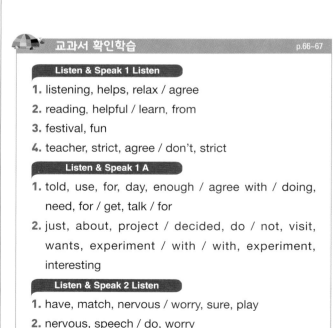

교과서 확인학습
p.66~67

Listen & Speak 1 Listen

1. listening, helps, relax / agree

2. reading, helpful / learn, from

3. festival, fun

4. teacher, strict, agree / don't, strict

Listen & Speak 1 A

1. told, use, for, day, enough / agree with / doing, need, for / get, talk / for

2. just, about, project / decided, do / not, visit, wants, experiment / with / with, experiment, interesting

Listen & Speak 2 Listen

1. have, match, nervous / worry, sure, play

2. nervous, speech / do, worry

3. worried, friends, school / sure, make, friends

1. worried, wrong / upset / Why, do / wore, without / sorry, understand

2. having, learning / had, asked, teacher / What / advised, use, vocabulary, sure

Real-Life Zone

project, taking / agree, One, people, doing / That's, team / know, know, get, to / doesn't, started, like, part / what, do / to, why, doing, Then, you'll, if, wants / try / sure, better, talk, project

Wrap Up

matter, look / ready, finals, desk, study, up, something / management, easy / agree, should / Number, have, Then, down, much, you, finish / try / that, with

---

시험대비 기본평가　　　　　　　　p.68

01 ①　　　　02 ④　　　　03 ⑤

01 소녀가 엄마의 의견에 대한 반대 의견이 있는 것으로 보아 빈칸에는 아빠가 앞에 나온 엄마의 의견에 동의하는 의미의 "I agree with her."가 되는 것이 자연스럽다.

02 "Tell her you're sorry."는 소녀의 걱정을 덜어주기 위한 말이다. 이어서 안심시키는 "I'm sure ~."가 들어가는 것이 적절하다.

03 앞의 질문에 대하여 (C) 아직 아니라고 대답한 이유로 진호와 미나가 서로 다른 것을 원한다고 말한다. (B) 서로 다른 의견에 대하여 누구에게 동의하는지 묻자 (A) 실험이 재미있을 것이기 때문에 미나에게 동의한다고 대답한다.

시험대비 실력평가　　　　　　　　p.69~70

01 ①　　02 ⑤　　03 ②　　04 ②
05 ③　　06 ③　　07 agree　　08 ③
09 ③　　10 ③　　11 ⑤　　12 ⑤

01 역사 만화책을 읽는 것이 유익하다는 말에 동의한다고 하였으므로 그것에 대한 장점을 언급한 ①이 적절하다.

02 "I had the same problem."이라는 대답이 이어지는 것으로 보아 그 앞에는 문제에 대한 언급이 있었음을 알 수 있다.

03 소녀는 소년과 같은 문제가 있었지만 영어 선생님의 도움으로 어휘 앱을 통해서 문제를 해결하고 있으므로 현재 어려움을 가지고 있다는 ②는 대화의 내용과 일치하지 않는다.

04 상대에게 무슨 문제가 있는지 묻는 것으로 보아 걱정스러워 보이

거나 불안해 보이는 상황임을 알 수 있다.

05 주어진 문장은 상대의 문제를 해결하기 위한 조언으로 구체적인 방법이 제시되고 있는 문장에 이어서 (C)에 들어가는 것이 가장 적절하다.

06 이 대화에서 동하는 시간 관리를 하지 못해서 기말고사 대비를 제대로 못한 상황이고, Emily가 어떻게 시간 관리를 할지 조언을 해주고 있다. 시간 관리가 왜 중요한지에 대한 언급은 없다.

07 "어떤 주제에 대하여 다른 사람과 같은 의견을 가지다"는 "agree 동의하다"에 해당한다.

08 (A) ~에게 …하도록 하다 = get + 목적어 + to부정사, (B) 시작하다 = get started

09 ③ 소녀가 문제를 겪고 있는 것은 자기 조별과제에 속한 한 사람이 맡은 역할을 하지 않는 것이다.

10 (가) "Is something wrong?"이라고 하는 것으로 보아 걱정스럽거나 불안스러워 보이는 상황이 적절하다. (B) 언니가 화난 이유로 무엇을 했는지 묻는 말로 What이 적절하다.

11 전치사 without의 목적어로 동명사 without가 적절하다.

12 "I'm sure ~"는 자신이 확신한다는 의미로 상대가 잘할 거니까 걱정하지 말라는 의미로 안심시키려는 의도라고 할 수 있다.

서술형 시험대비　　　　　　　　p.71

01 I'm sure you'll play very well.　　02 agree
03 I'm having a hard time learning new English words.
04 vocabulary　　　　　　05 against → for
06 job
07 I'm sure he'll do better after you talk to him.

01 상대가 불안해 할 때 안심을 시키려는 의도로 "~을 확신하다."라고 할 때는 "I'm sure ~."라고 한다.

02 주어진 대화에서 두 사람은 체육 선생님이 엄격하신지에 대한 서로 다른 의견을 가지고 있기 때문에 서로 동의하는지를 묻고, 대답하는 agree가 적절하다.

03 "~하는 데 어려움을 겪다"는 "have a hard time -ing"이다.

04 "어떤 언어에서 사용되는 단어"는 "vocabulary 어휘"이다.

05 "work against"는 "불리하게 되다"는 뜻으로 도움을 주기위한 앱에 대한 설명으로 적절하지 않다. "work for 효과가 있다"가 되어야 한다.

06 "자신이 맡은 일을 하다"는 의미로 "do one's part = do one's job"이다.

07 "~할 것이라고 확신하다"는 "I'm sure 주어+동사"이다. "그가 더 잘할 것이다 = he'll do better", "네가 그와 이야기한 이후로 = after you talk to him"

핵심 Check
p.72~73

1 (1) watching　(2) Listening

2 (1) if[whether]　(2) if[whether]　(3) whether

시험대비 기본평가
p.74

01 ①

02 (1) walking　(2) Not knowing　(3) if　(4) whether

03 ⑤

04 (1) Looking at me, she smiled brightly.

(2) While walking home from work, I found this great bakery.

(3) We need to find out if the rumor is true.

01 접속사 없이 '주어+동사'가 이어지고 있으므로 빈칸에는 '접속사+주어+동사'의 역할을 할 수 있는 현재분사로(그가 나를 보는 능동이므로) 분사구문이 되어야 한다.

02 (1) 접속사가 없으므로 '접속사+주어+동사'의 역할을 할 수 있는 walking이 적절하다. (2) 분사구문의 부정은 분사 앞에 'not'이나 'never'를 쓴다. (3) '내가 그 퍼즐을 풀 수 있다는 것을 물었다'는 말은 어색하다. 사실의 여부를 확인하거나 불확실함을 나타내는 if가 적절하다. (4) 바로 뒤에 'or not'이 이어지고 있으므로 whether가 적절하다.

03 know의 목적어가 나와야 하는데 '~인지 (아닌지)'라는 의미로 명사절을 이끄는 접속사 if가 적절하다.

04 (1) looking을 '접속사+주어+동사'의 역할을 하는 분사로 하여 알맞게 배열한다. (2) 분사구문의 뜻을 명확히 하기 위해 접속사 while을 생략하지 않고 남겨둔 경우이다. (3) '~인지 (아닌지)'라는 의미의 접속사로 어떠한 사실의 여부를 확인하거나 불확실함을 나타낼 때 쓰이는 if를 이용한다.

시험대비 실력평가
p.75~77

01 ③　　02 ④　　03 ①

04 (1) if　(2) whether　(3) whether　(4) Neglecting

(5) talking　(6) Not getting

05 ⑤　　06 ③　　07 ①　　08 ⑤

09 Being　10 ②　　11 ②

12 (1) I was　(2) he was　　13 ④

14 (1) We don't know if Mark will succeed.

(2) Whether I believe you or not is not important now.

(3) Riding a bike, he always wears his helmet.

(4) Not feeling good about it, he wrote a letter to her.

(5) Disappointed with the result, she walked out of her room.

15 ⑤　　　　　　16 ②, ③

17 She advises Sohui to ask Hayeon if[whether] there is something wrong.

01 Mike was standing outside the house, waiting for her.

02 '~인지 (아닌지)'라는 의미의 접속사 if[whether]를 쓰는 것이 적절하다. I just wanted to know if[whether] everything was all right.

03 첫 번째 빈칸에는 '~인지 (아닌지)'라는 의미의 접속사 if나 whether가 적절하다. 두 번째 빈칸에는 접속사가 없으므로 '접속사+주어+동사'의 역할을 할 수 있는 Finishing이 적절하다.

04 (1) 내용상 '~인지 (아닌지)'라는 의미의 접속사 if가 적절하다. (2) 내용상 '~인지 (아닌지)'라는 의미의 접속사 whether가 적절하다. (3) 뒤에 or not이 바로 이어서 나오고 있으므로 whether가 적절하다. (4) 접속사가 없으므로 '접속사+주어+동사'의 역할을 할 수 있는 분사구문으로 써야 한다. (5) 분사구문의 뜻을 명확히 하기 위해 접속사 when을 생략하지 않고 남겨둔 경우이다. (6) 분사구문의 부정은 분사 앞에 'not'이나 'never'를 쓴다.

05 '접속사+주어+동사'의 부사절을 분사구문으로 바꾸어 쓸 수 있다. 이때, 분사구문의 뜻을 명확히 하기 위해 접속사를 생략하지 않기도 하지만 주어를 생략하지는 않는다.

06 (A) 내용상 '~인지 (아닌지)'라는 의미가 자연스러우므로 if나 whether가 적절하고, (B) 바로 뒤에 or not이 나오므로 Whether가 적절하다.

07 ⓐ 접속사가 없으므로 thinking으로 분사구문을 만들어야 한다. 분사구문이 문장의 중간에 삽입된 형태이다.

08 동사의 목적어로 쓰인 명사절을 이끄는 접속사 if는 whether로 바꿔 쓸 수 있다.

09 'Because I was lonely, I decided to make some friends.'라고 한 문장으로 쓸 수 있고, 이것을 분사구문으로 바꾸면 빈칸에는 'Because I was'를 현재분사 Being으로 고쳐야 한다.

10 '~인지 (아닌지)'라는 의미의 명사절을 이끄는 if나 whether가 적절하며 if는 바로 뒤에 or not을 붙여 쓰지 않는다. Justine이 영어 시험에서 좋은 점수를 받았는지를 묻는 것이므로 asks는 현재로, got은 과거로 나타낸다.

11 주어진 문장과 ②번은 '조건'을 나타낸다. ① 시간 ③ 이유, ④ 동시동작, ⑤ 양보

12 부사절에서 주어가 주절의 주어와 같을 때 '주어+be동사'를 생략할 수 있으며 이것은 분사구문으로 고쳤을 때 being을 생략하고 접속사를 남겨둔 것과 같다.

13 '~인지 (아닌지)'라는 의미의 명사절을 이끄는 if는 바로 뒤에 'or not'을 붙여 쓰지 않는다.

14 (1) if가 know의 목적어로 쓰인 명사절을 이끌고 있는데 명사절에서는 미래시제를 현재시제로 쓸 수 없으므로 succeeds를 'will succeed'로 고치는 것이 적절하다. (2) If가 이끄는 명사절이 주어 역할을 할 수 없으므로 Whether로 고치는 것이 적절하다. (3) 자전거를 타는 '능동'이므로 Ridden을 Riding으로 고치는 것이 적절하다. (4) 분사구문의 부정은 분사 앞에 'not'이나 'never'를 쓴다. (5) Being이 생략된 분사구문으로 '실망시키는' 것이 아니라 '실망한' 것이므로 Disappointing을 Disappointed로 고쳐야 한다. 감정동사의 과거분사임에 유의한다.

15 'As[Because] he wanted to get good grades, he decided to study hard.'를 분사구문으로 바꾼 것이므로 'As[Because] he wanted' 대신에 'Wanting'으로 쓰는 것이 적절하다.

16 ② if는 전치사의 목적어로 쓰인 명사절을 이끌지 못한다. if 대신에 whether로 써야 한다. ③ if는 to부정사와 함께 쓰지 않는다. if 대신에 whether로 써야 한다.

17 if[whether] 뒤에 오는 절은 의문사가 없는 간접의문문으로 'if[whether]+주어+동사'의 어순으로 쓴다.

서술형 시험대비
p.78~79

01 (1) Being so upset, he went out without saying anything.
(2) Cancelling the order, you will lose your money.
(3) Being tired of a lot of homework, I won't give up.
(4) Not feeling good, I stayed in bed all morning.
(5) It being fine, I will start tomorrow.

02 (1) He couldn't tell if she was laughing or crying.
(2) I'm not sure if he explained everything about your compensation.

03 (1) Taking this train, you'll get to Busan at 1 p.m.
(2) Being busy, Amy is always willing to help me.
(3) I wonder if he lives near here.
(4) I am not sure if he still remembers me.

04 (1) Whether he will continue to be successful in future is open to doubt.
(2) Some friends asked me whether or not I had an accident.
(3) I was debating in my mind whether to go or not.

05 (1) if[whether] she can make friends
(2) if[whether] he can play
(3) whether she can do

06 (1) Doing check-in   (2) having a talk
(3) Coming out

07 (1) Being sick, he stayed home all day long.
As he was sick, he stayed home all day long.

(2) Don't look at your phone, walking on the street.
Don't look at your phone when[as] you walk on the street.
(3) Can I ask if[whether] you have the ticket?
(4) I wonder if[whether] he can pass the exam.

08 (1) Written in haste, this book has a lot of mistakes.
(2) There being no train left, he had to stay at a hotel.

01 '접속사+주어+동사'로 이루어진 부사절의 주어가 주절의 주어와 일치할 때 접속사와 주어를 생략하고 동사를 분사(동사원형+-ing)로 만든다. (1) '이유', (2) '조건' (3) '양보' (4) 분사구문의 부정은 분사 앞에 'not'이나 'never'를 쓴다. (5) 주절의 주어와 부사절의 주어가 다르므로 주어를 생략하면 안 된다. (독립분사구문)

02 '~인지 (아닌지)'라는 의미의 접속사로 쓰이는 if를 이용한다. if 뒤에 오는 절은 의문사가 없는 간접의문문으로 'if+주어+동사'의 어순으로 쓴다.

03 (1), (2) 현재분사가 분사구문을 이끌도록 한다. (3), (4) if가 명사절을 이끌도록 한다.

04 (1) 문두에서 주어절을 이끄는 역할을 하고 있으므로 If를 Whether로 고치는 것이 적절하다. (2) 바로 뒤에 or not이 나오고 있으므로 if를 whether로 고치는 것이 적절하다. (3) whether 다음에는 to부정사를 쓸 수 있지만 if는 쓸 수 없으므로 if를 whether로 고치는 것이 적절하다.

05 (1), (2) 명사절을 이끄는 if나 whether를 이용한다. (3) 전치사 about의 목적어이므로 whether를 이용한다.

06 (1) = When he did '시간' (2) = as she had '동시동작' (3) = when he came '시간'의 분사구문을 이용한다.

07 (1), (2) '접속사+주어+동사'로 이루어진 부사절의 주어가 주절의 주어와 일치할 때 접속사와 주어를 생략하고 동사를 분사(동사원형+-ing)로 만들어서 분사구문으로 바꿔 쓴다. (3), (4) '~인지 (아닌지)'라는 의미의 접속사로 쓰이는 if[whether]를 이용한다. 뒤에 오는 절은 의문사가 없는 간접의문문으로 'if+주어+동사'의 어순으로 쓴다.

08 (1) 책이 '쓰여지는' '수동'의 의미가 되어야 하므로 Writing을 Written으로 고쳐 써야 한다. (2) 부사절과 주절의 주어가 다를 때는 부사절의 주어를 생략하지 않는다. (독립분사구문)

교과서
Reading

확인문제
p.80

1 T   2 F   3 T   4 F   5 T   6 F

1 T   2 F   3 T   4 F   5 T   6 F

교과서 확인학습 A   p.82~83

01 Should
02 has
03 what do you do
04 Here are some things
05 her best friend, has changed, is avoiding
06 don't you
07 What about
08 I feel
09 turns around, walks away from
10 to hear that
11 why she does that
12 I've done anything wrong
13 feels like
14 should, if, something wrong
15 still, with
16 thinking, just because
17 new sneakers
18 What
19 didn't you, couple of
20 in style
21 in these
22 wearing, cooler, more popular
23 because you're you
25 a great guy
26 to prove it
27 was asked out
28 to hurt his feelings
29 advice
30 asked me out
31 for now, go out with
32 focus on
33 should
34 Why don't you
35 I'm afraid
36 If you don't tell, end up hurting
37 you're right
38 Thanks for

교과서 확인학습 B   p.84~85

1 What Should I Do?

2 Everyone has worries.

3 When you have things you worry about, what do you do?

4 Here are some things that three teenagers worry about.

5 Sohui thought Hayeon was her best friend, but now, Sohui feels that Hayeon has changed and she is avoiding her.

6 Sohui: (To her older sister) You know my friend Hayeon, don't you?

7 Sister: Yeah. Why? What about her?

8 Sohui: I feel she's avoiding me.

9 When I see her at school, she turns around and walks away from me.

10 Sister: I'm sorry to hear that.

11 Do you have any idea why she does that?

12 Sohui: No. I don't think I've done anything wrong.

13 It just feels like she doesn't like me anymore.

14 Sister: Maybe you should just ask her if there is something wrong.

15 Sohui: Maybe I should. I still want to be friends with her.

16 Daeho, thinking that new things will make him more popular, often wants new things just because his friends have them.

17 Daeho: Seongjin, look at my new sneakers.

18 What do you think?

19 Seongjin: They're nice, but didn't you just buy new sneakers a couple of months ago?

20 Daeho: Yeah, but they're no longer in style.

21 I look cooler in these, right?

22 Seongjin: Daeho, wearing the latest fashion doesn't make you cooler or more popular.

23 People like you because you're you, not because of your clothes.

24 Daeho: Yeah?

25 Seongjin: Listen, you're a great guy.

26 You don't need new sneakers to prove it.

27 Recently, Minkyeong was asked out by a boy in her class.

28 She wants to say no but does not want to hurt his feelings.

29 Minkyeong: I need your advice.

30 A boy in my class asked me out.

31 I like him, but for now I don't want to go out with him.

32 I need to focus on my studies.

33 What should I do?

34 Counselor: Why don't you tell him why you can't go?

35 Minkyeong: I'm afraid I might hurt his feelings.

36 Counselor: If you don't tell him soon, he will misunderstand your feelings, and you may end up hurting him even more.

37 Minkyeong: Maybe you're right.

38 Thanks for the advice.

시험대비 실력평가   p.86~89

01 in
02 ②, ⑤
03 you're a great guy
04 How[What] about
05 ③
06 about
07 ④
08 ⑤
09 ③
10 ②
11 new sneakers
12 ④
13 ④

14 Recently, a boy in Minkyeong's[her] class asked Minkyeong out.

01 ⓐ in style 유행하는, 유행되는, ⓑ in: ~을 착용한[입은/쓴]

02 (A)와 ②, ⑤: 현재분사, ①, ③, ④: 동명사

03 '네가 멋진 사람이라는 것'을 가리킨다.

04 Why don't you 동사원형 ~?= How[What] about ~ing?: ~하는 게 어때?

05 이 글은 '민경이가 데이트 신청을 받았지만 당분간은 공부에 집중하기 위해 상대방의 감정을 상하게 하지 않으면서 거절하려고 조언을 구하는' 내용의 글이므로, 제목으로는 ③번 '미안해요! 당분간은 저는 공부에 집중해야 해요!'가 적절하다.

06 worry about: ~에 대해 걱정하다

07 ④ 여기 세 명의 청소년이 걱정하는 것들이 있다고 했으므로, 뒤에 올 내용으로는 '세 명의 청소년의 걱정들'이 가장 적절하다. ⑤ routine: (판에 박힌) 일상

08 ①~④: 소희, ⑤: 하연

09 ⓐ와 ③: 원인, ① 결과, ② 판단의 근거, ④ 형용사 수식 ⑤ 목적

10 ② 학교에서 소희가 하연이를 볼 때, '하연이'가 돌아서서 '소희'로부터 멀리 걸어간다.

11 대호가 몇 달 전에 샀던 '새 운동화'를 가리킨다.

12 ④ trendy: 유행을 따르는(형용사), 유행을 따르는 사람(명사), 대호는 새 물건이 그를 더 인기 있게 만들어 줄 것이라고 생각해서 단지 친구들이 그것을 가지고 있다는 이유로 종종 새 물건을 사기를 원하는 사람이라고 했으므로, '유행을 따르는'이 적절하다. ① 구식의, ② 사람들과 어울리기 좋아하는, ③ 얌전한, 수수한, ⑤ 유행에 뒤떨어진

13 ⓐ for now: 우선은, 현재로는, 당분간은, ⓑ focus on: ~에 주력하다, 초점을 맞추다.

14 ask somebody out: ~에게 데이트를 신청하다

15 (B)와 ②: 훨씬(비교급을 강조) ①, ④: (예상 밖이나 놀라운 일을 나타내어) …도[조차] ③ 평평한, 반반한(형용사) ⑤ 균등한, 동일한(형용사)

16 '새 물건들'을 가리킨다.

17 these가 new sneakers를 가리키므로 '신을 신으면'이라는 의미의 착용을 나타내는 전치사 in이 적절하다.

18 'of'를 보충하면 된다.

19 주어진 문장의 that에 주목한다. ④번 앞 문장의 내용을 받고 있으므로 ④번이 적절하다.

20 ⓐ와 ①, ④: 현재완료(결과 용법), 현재완료의 결과 용법은 과거에 행해진 어떤 행동의 결과가 현재까지 영향을 미칠 때 쓴다. ②, ⑤: 계속 용법, ③ 경험 용법

21 이 글은 '친구가 변했다고 느끼는 동생에게, 뭔가 잘못된 것이

있는지 그녀에게 물어보라고 언니가 충고해 주자, 아마 그래야 될 것 같다고 동생이 대답하는' 내용이므로, 제목으로는 ④번 '너는 변했어. 뭔가 잘못된 것이 있는지 궁금해'가 적절하다. ① I mean it.: 진심입니다. ② That's enough.: 이제 됐다!, 그쯤 해둬! ③ Every dog has his day.: 쥐구멍에도 볕들 날 있다. ⑤ ignore: 무시하다

🐺 서술형 시험대비　　　　　　　　p.90~91

01 hurting　　　　　　02 Unless you

03 (A) out　(B) hurting his feelings

04 as[because] he thinks that new things will make him more popular

05 because your clothes → because of your clothes

06 (A) his friends　(B) in style

07 (A) What　(B) latest　(C) clothes

08 (my) new sneakers　　　09 No, he doesn't.

10 why she does that

11 thinks → doesn't think, something → anything

12 (A) has changed　(B) is avoiding　(C) wrong

01 end up ~ing: 결국 ~하게 되다

02 If ~ not = Unless

03 민경이의 반 남자아이가 그녀에게 데이트 신청을 했지만, 그녀는 그의 감정을 상하게 하지 않으면서 거절하기를 원한다. turned ~ down: ~을 거절하다

04 '이유'를 나타내는 분사구문이므로, 접속사 as 또는 because를 사용하여 고치는 것이 적절하다.

05 'because+주어와 동사로 이루어진 절', 'because of+명사(구)'이므로, because of your clothes로 고치는 것이 적절하다.

06 대호는 단지 '친구들'이 그것을 가지고 있다는 이유로 종종 새 물건을 사기를 원하고, 몇 달 전에 산 운동화가 더 이상 '유행이' 아니라는 생각 때문에 다시 새 운동화를 샀다.

07 (A) 'think'의 목적어를 써야 하므로 What이 적절하다. (B) '최신' 유행이라고 해야 하므로 latest가 적절하다. last: 맨 마지막의, latest: 최근의[최신의], (C) 네 '옷'이라고 해야 하므로 clothes가 적절하다. cloths: 옷감들, 직물들, clothes: 옷, 의복

08 '(내) 새 운동화'를 가리킨다.

09 성진이는 '최신 유행하는 것을 입는 것이 대호를 더 멋지고 더 인기 있게 만들어 주지는 않는다.'고 생각한다.

10 간접의문문(의문사+주어+동사)의 순서로 쓰는 것이 적절하다.

11 소희는 자신이 잘못한 것이 있다고 생각하지 않는다. 부정문에서 something을 anything으로 고치는 것이 적절하다.

12 소희의 고민: 나의 가장 친한 친구 하연이가 '변했고' 나를 '피한다'고 느낀다. 조언: 뭔가 '잘못된' 것이 있는지 그녀에게 물어보는 게 어때?

01 ⑤   02 ①   03 ③   04 ②

05 when doing my homework, I need to use it for a long time

06 I'm sure you'll make a lot of friends there.

07 ③   08 ④   09 ⑤

10 ⓓ: Ask him why he's not doing his part.

11 (A) for   (B) up   (C) for   12 ⑤   13 ②

14 ②   15 ①   16 ⑤

17 if[whether] she would give up

18 (1) As she listened to music

    (2) because[as] he was

19 ③   20 ⓔ, ⓖ   21 ④   22 ③

23 ②

24 I feel she's avoiding me. When I see her at school, she turns around and walks away from me.

25 ②, ③, ⑤ / ①, ④   26 ⑤   27 ③

28 ②   29 ②, ⑤

30 Because for now she needs to focus on her studies.

31 (A) grow taller   (B) shortest

32 as[because] they have lots of protein and calcium

33 (1) 달걀, 우유, 그리고 콩과 같은 음식을 먹어야 한다.

    (2) 매일 밤 적어도 8시간을 자야 한다.

---

01 친구들이 가지고 있기 때문에 자신도 가지고 싶어 하는 것은 사람들에게 잘 보이기 위한 것으로 popular가 적절하다.

02 "문제가 있는 사람에게 도움이나 조언을 제공하는 직업을 가진 사람"은 "counselor 카운슬러, 상담역"이다.

03 ask A for help = A에게 도움을 요청하다, be ready for ~ = ~에 준비가 되다

04 주어진 문장과 ②의 문장에서 part는 "역할, 배역"이고, 나머지는 문장에서는 "부분"이라는 뜻이다.

05 "숙제할 때"는 "when I do my homework"이지만 "분사구문으로 'when doing my homework"라고 할 수 있다.

06 "나는 확신한다."는 "I'm sure ~"이다.

07 상대의 말에 동의하는 표현은 "I agree.", "Same here.", "You can say that again.", "So do I.", "Me, too." 등이다.

08 "팀의 모든 사람들"은 "Everybody on the team"이고 단수 취급해야 한다.

09 이어서 소년이 어떻게 대응을 해야 할지를 설명하는 것으로 보아 문제를 해결하기 위하여 무엇을 할지 묻는 말이 적절하다.

10 자기 역할을 하지 않는 구성원에게 왜 그 역할을 하지 않는지 물어보고 해결책을 찾는 것으로 "why he's not doing his part."가 적절하다.

11 (A) be ready for ~: ~에 준비가 되다 (B) end up -ing : 결국 ~하게 되다 (C) be helpful for ~: ~에게 도움이 되다

12 each는 단수명사와 함께 사용하므로 "each+단수명사"가 되어야 한다.

13 동하는 시험 공부를 하려고 책상에 앉지만 공부를 하지 않고 결국 다른 일을 하게 된다고 했으므로 책상에 앉지 않는다는 ②는 글의 내용과 일치하지 않는다.

14 주어진 문장은 '시간'을 나타내는 분사구문으로 볼 수 있으며, 시간이나 조건의 부사절에서는 미래시제를 현재시제로 나타내는 것에 주의한다.

15 동사의 목적어로 쓰인 명사절을 이끄는 접속사 if는 whether로 바꿔 쓸 수 있다.

16 출세한 것이 거만해진 것보다 앞서는 시제이므로 'Having made'로 고쳐야 한다. *make a name for oneself: 유명해지다 *arrogant: 거만[오만]한

17 명사절을 이끄는 접속사 if나 whether를 이용하고 주절이 과거 시제이므로 will을 would로 써야 하는 것에 유의한다.

18 (1) '동시동작' (2) '이유'의 분사구문으로 보는 것이 적절하다.

19 ③의 if는 명사절을 이끄는 접속사로 '~인지 아닌지'라는 의미이며, 나머지는 모두 조건의 부사절을 이끄는 접속사로 '만약 ~라면'의 의미로 쓰였다.

20 ⓐ ate → eating ⓑ Knowing not → Not knowing ⓒ Seeing → Seen ⓓ Being → It being ⓕ that → if[whether]

21 '접속사+주어+동사'로 이루어진 부사절의 주어가 주절의 주어와 일치할 때 접속사와 주어를 생략하고 동사를 분사(동사원형+-ing)로 만든다.

22 Many people wonder if he will resign before the election. if절이 부사절로 쓰일 때는 미래시제 대신에 현재시제가 쓰이지만 명사절로 쓰였으므로 미래로 나타내야 한다.

23 ② Not having enough money, I cannot buy the smartphone. = Because I don't have enough money, I cannot buy the smartphone.

24 바로 앞 대화에서 소희가 말한 내용들을 가리킨다.

25 ⓑ, ②, ③, ⑤: …하는대로[…하는 것처럼](접속사), ② 어느 누구도 그녀(가 그랬던 것)처럼 블루스를 부르지는 못해. ③ 그것은 내가 의도한 대로 되지 않았다. ⑤ 내가 전에 말한 대로, 네가 와서 지내는 건 언제나 환영이야. ⓒ, ①, ④: ~을 좋아하다 (동사)

26 ⑤ 하연이가 더 이상 자기를 좋아하지 않는다고 소희가 느끼고 있는 것일 뿐이고, 사실 그런지는 아직 모르는 것이므로, 대답할 수 없다. ① Because she feels Hayeon is avoiding her. ② Yes. ③ No. ④ She advises Sohui to ask Hayeon if there is something wrong.

27 주어진 문장의 they에 주목한다. ③번 앞 문장의 new

sneakers를 받고 있으므로 ③번이 적절하다.

28 대호는 새 물건이 그를 더 인기 있게 만들어 줄 것이라고 생각해서 종종 새 물건을 사기를 원하지만, 성진이는 사람들이 대호를 좋아하는 것이 그가 최신 유행하는 것을 입어서가 아니라 그가 그이기 때문이라고 말해준다. 그러므로 제목으로는 ②번 '새 물건들이 정말 너를 더 인기 있게 만들어 줄 수 있을까?'가 적절하다.

29 ②와 ⑤ thoughtful = considerate: 배려심 있는, 사려 깊은, 민경이의 반 남자아이가 그녀에게 데이트 신청을 했지만, 그녀는 그의 감정을 상하게 하지 않으면서 거절하기를 원한다는 것으로 보아, 민경이는 '배려심 있는', '사려 깊은' 성격이라고 하는 것이 적절하다. ① 이기적인, ③ 외향적인, 사교적인, ④ 말하기를 좋아하는, 수다스러운

30 당분간은 공부에 집중해야 하기 때문이다.

31 (A) Hena는 '키가 더 크기를' 원한다. (B) 그녀는 그룹에서 '키가 제일 작아서 기분이 좋지 않다.

32 '이유'를 나타내는 분사구문이므로, 접속사 as 또는 because를 사용하여 고치는 것이 적절하다.

33 (1) I suggest you eat foods like eggs, milk, and beans.
(2) You should sleep at least eight hours every night.

단원별 예상문제
p.99~103

01 (p)roject   02 ⑤   03 ④   04 ④
05 ③   06 ④   07 ①   08 ④
09 ⑤   10 ④   11 ②   12 ③
13 (1) My concern is whether or not they are alive.
(2) I'll check if he will see this painting.
(3) Winning the game, Ben is very happy.
(4) Properly conducted, this business is not a public danger.
14 ①
15 (1) Feeling tired, he took a warm bath.
(2) I make delicious food, dreaming to be a cook.
(3) It being raining, 75 people were waiting for her.
16 if[whether] Minji was[will be] late   17 ④
18 no more[longer]   19 ①, ④, ⑤
20 ③   21 out of → in   22 ③
23 (A) he's he   (B) his clothes
24 Why don't you tell him why you can't go?
25 won't → don't   26 ②   27 ②, ⑤
28 ②, ⑤

01 주어진 단어는 유의어 관계이다. strict 엄격한, rigid 엄격한, project 과제, task 과제

02 그는 너무 소심해서 그녀에게 데이트 신청을 못한다. / ask+사람+out = 데이트 신청을 하다

---

03 네 치마는 요즘 유행하고 있는 거야. in style 유행하고 있는 / 어젯밤 결국 뭐 했어? end up -ing 결국 ~하다

04 ① 그녀가 지갑을 찰칵 하고 닫았다. snap 찰칵하는 소리를 내며 움직이는 것 ② 그는 낡은 청바지에 운동화를 신고 있었다. sneakers 운동화 ③ 그들은 자녀들에게 항상 아주 엄격했다. strict 엄격한 ④ 그의 실수는 경험이 부족해서 발생한 것이었다. mistake 실수 ⑤ 여기 세 명의 청소년이 걱정하는 것들이 있습니다. teenager 청소년

05 상대가 걱정스러워 보인다고 했으므로 안부를 묻거나 걱정을 표현하는 것이 적절하다. ③은 주로 긍정적인 상황에서 "무슨 일이니?"하고 물어보는 표현이다.

06 (A) 화가 났다고 했으므로 그 이유로 "물어보지도 않고 = without asking"이 되어야 한다. (B) 안심시키는 말로 "그녀가 이해할 거라고 확신해. = I'm sure she'll understand."가 적절하다.

07 걱정이 있어서 우울해 보이는 것은 소녀이므로 ①은 대화의 내용과 일치하지 않는다.

08 상대의 말에 동의한다는 의미로 "You can say that again. 네 말이 맞아.가 적절하다. "So do I."는 앞에 말한 내용이 말하는 사람 자신에 관한 것이고 일반동사를 사용할 때 동의의 의미로 쓸 수 있다.

09 시험 준비가 되지 않아서 걱정하는 친구에게 도움이 될 만한 충고를 하고 그것이 유익할 것이라고 말하는 것이 자연스럽다. ⑤ I'm sure that will be helpful for you.

10 동하는 공부하려고 책상에 앉지만 딴 짓을 하게 된다고 해서 그 문제를 해결할 방법을 Emily가 알려주는 대화이다. 이 대화를 읽고 언제 동하가 책상에 앉을지는 알 수 없다.

11 decide의 목적어로 쓰인 명사절은 간접의문문으로 "의문사+주어+동사"의 어순이 되도록 해야 한다.

12 ① 대화에 나오는 소녀는 같은 팀이 아니다. ② 소녀는 대화 속에 나오는 실험과는 관계없다. ④ 진호와 미나가 원하는 것은 다르다. ⑤ 진호가 물어볼지는 알 수 없다.

13 (1) whether 다음에 'or not'을 붙여 쓸 수 있지만 if는 'or not'을 붙여 쓰지 않는다. (2) if가 이끄는 절이 명사절이므로 미래는 미래시제로 나타내야 한다. (3) 접속사가 없으므로 Win을 Winning으로 바꾸어 분사구문으로 만든다. (4) 분사구문이 주어와 수동의 관계이므로 being이 생략된 과거분사 conducted로 시작하는 문장으로 바꾼다.

14 '~인지 (아닌지)'라는 의미의 명사절을 이끄는 if나 whether가 적절하다.

15 (1) '접속사+주어+동사'로 이루어진 부사절의 주어가 주절의 주어와 일치할 때 접속사와 주어를 생략하고 동사를 분사(동사원형+-ing)로 만든다. (2) 의미에 맞게 'with a dream'을 dreaming으로 고쳐 분사구문으로 쓴다. (3) 부사절의 주어가 주절의 주어와 일치하지 않으므로 접속사와 주어를 생략하면 안 된다.

16 명사절을 이끄는 접속사 if나 whether를 이용하여 'if[whether]+주어+동사'의 어순으로 쓴다.

17 ① These foods, having lots of protein and calcium, can help you grow taller. ② Mason listened to the music, taking a shower. ③ When serving in the army, he felt a strong tie with his colleagues. ⑤ Being disappointed, I kept writing and now I'm a writer.
colleague: 동료

18 not ~ anymore = no more = no longer

19 ⓑ와 ①, ④, ⑤: 명사절을 이끄는 접속사(…인지 아닌지), ②, ③: (조건을 나타내어) (만약) …이라면

20 ③ 속상한, 마음이 상한, '소희는 가장 친한 친구라고 생각했던 하연이가 변했고 자기를 피한다고 느끼고 있으므로 '속상한' 심경이라고 하는 것이 적절하다. ① 부끄러운, ② 안도하는, 다행으로 여기는, ④ 겁먹은, 무서워하는, ⑤ 지루한

21 '그건 더 이상 유행이 아니야'라고 해야 하므로, out of style을 in style로 고치는 것이 적절하다. out of style: 유행이 지난, in style 유행하는, 유행되는

22 ⓑ와 ③, ④: 동명사, ①, ②, ⑤: 현재분사

23 성진이는 사람들이 '그가 그이기(대호가 대호이기)' 때문에 대호를 좋아하는 것이지, '그의 옷' 때문이 아니라고 생각한다.

24 Why don't you 동사원형 ~?: ~하는 게 어때?

25 조건절에서는 현재시제가 미래시제를 대신하기 때문에, won't를 don't로 고치는 것이 적절하다.

26 민경이는 그를 '좋아하지만' 당분간은 공부에 집중해야 하기 때문에 그와 데이트하고 싶지 않다고 했다.

27 '~인지 아닌지'라는 뜻을 나타내는 접속사 if나 whether가 적절하다.?

28 swimming, jumping rope, or playing basketball을 예로 들고 있다. ② play tug-of-war: 줄다리기를 하다

서술형 실전문제 p.104~105

01 has 　　　　　　02 get
03 Ask him why he's not doing his part.
04 (1) Because[As, Since] I was interested in soccer, I joined a soccer club.
　　(2) Emily opened her birthday present, as she smiled happily.
　　(3) Hearing about the accident, she was shocked.
　　(4) It being cold tomorrow, I won't go there.
05 (1) He can't decide whether to buy it.
　　(2) I don't know if she will come tomorrow.
　　(3) Jane watched a baseball game on TV, having dinner.
　　(4) Putting eggs on the bread, Yena made the sandwiches more delicious.

06 don't you
07 학교에서 소희가 그녀(하연이)를 보면 그녀가 돌아서서 소희로부터 멀리 걸어가는 것
08 (A) worried　 (B) advises
09 a couple of months ago
10 needs → doesn't need
11 (A) new　 (B) more popular　 (C) because of (D) because

01 "~해야 한다"의 의무를 나타내는 표현이 되어야 한다. 주어 Everyone은 단수 취급하기 때문에 "has to"가 되어야 한다.
02 (B)는 "…에게 ~하도록 하다"의 의미로 사역의 의미가 있지만 목적격보어로 to부정사가 쓰였기 때문에 get이 들어가는 것이 적절하다.
03 "왜 ~하는지 물어봐."는 "Ask him why ~."이다.
04 (1) 의미상 '이유'를 나타내는 분사구문이다. (2) 의미상 '동시동작'을 나타내는 분사구문이다. 이때의 접속사는 보통 as를 쓴다. (3) 의미상 '시간'을 나타내는 분사구문으로 바꾼다. (4) 의미상 '조건'을 나타내는 분사구문으로 바꾼다. 이때 주절의 주어와 다르므로 주어를 생략하면 안 된다.
05 (1) whether 다음에는 to부정사를 쓸 수 있지만 if는 to부정사와 함께 쓰이지 않는다. (2) if가 이끄는 절이 명사절이므로 미래는 미래시제로 나타내야 한다. (3) 접속사가 없으므로 had를 having으로 바꾸어 분사구문으로 만든다. (4) 접속사가 없으므로 Put을 Putting으로 바꾸어 분사구문으로 만든다.
06 일반동사가 있는 긍정문이므로, don't를 사용하여 부가의문문을 만드는 것이 적절하다.
07 'When I see her at school, she turns around and walks away from me'를 가리킨다.
08 소희가 그녀의 가장 친한 친구인 하연이가 변해서 그녀를 피한다고 '걱정'하자, 그녀의 언니가 뭔가 잘못된 것이 있는지 하연이에게 물어보라고 '충고한다.'
09 a couple of: 둘의, 두서너 개의, 몇 개의, 몇 사람의
10 성진이는 대호가 멋진 사람이라는 것을 증명하기 위해 새 운동화가 '필요하지 않다'고 말한다.
11 대호의 고민: 나는 '새' 옷이 필요하다. 그것들은 나를 '더 인기 있게' 만들어 줄 것이다. 조언: 사람들은 네 옷 '때문'이 아니라 네가 너이기 '때문에' 너를 좋아하는 것이다.

창의사고력 서술형 문제 p.106

|모범답안|
01 (1) if[whether] listening to music helps you relax
　　(2) if[whether] reading history comic books is helpful
　　(3) if[whether] our P.E. teacher is too strict

        (4) if[whether] our school festival will be a lot of
            fun
    02 (A) grow taller   (B) being the shortest
        (C) eggs, milk, and beans   (D) eight hours

단원별 모의고사
p.107~110

01 (d)isagree   02 ④
03 (1) agree   (2) avoid   (3) relax   (4) worry
04 ①   05 ③   06 ④   07 ②
08 ③   09 ④   10 ③
11 (1) Hearing the news, he dropped down on the
       floor from shock.
   (2) After talking to my dad, I felt much better.
   (3) I am not sure if[whether] you remember me.
   (4) Leaving the house, you should check if you
       turned off the stove.

01 두 단어의 관계는 반의어 관계이다. avoid 피하다, face 마주하
   다, agree 동의하다, disagree 동의하지 않다

02 영어 설명의 "13세에서 19세 사이에 있는 사람"에 해당하는 단
   어는 "teenager 십대"이다.

03 (1) 난 전적으로 네 말에 동의해. (agree) (2) 나는 교통 혼잡
   시간을 피하기 위해 일찍 출발했다. avoid 피하다 (3) 그냥 느
   긋하게 영화를 즐겨. relax 느긋하게 쉬다 (4) 시험에 대해서는
   걱정하지 말고 그저 최선을 다해. worry 걱정하다

04 너는 그 문제를 풀기 어려울 것이다. "~하는 것이 어렵다, ~
   하는 데 어려움을 겪다" = have difficulty/a hard time/
   trouble/a difficult time -ing

05 앞에 나온 문제가 되는 상황에 대한 언급으로 "그것은 좋지 않
   아."에 해당하는 ③이 적절하다.

06 주어진 문장은 자신의 역할을 하고 있지 않은 구성원의 문제를 해
   결하기 위한 과정으로 그 방법을 알려주는 내용인 (D)에 들어가
   는 것이 적절하다.

07 ① 소년은 과제에 시간이 많이 걸린다고 했다. ③ 소녀가 자신의
   역할을 좋아하는지에 대해서는 언급하지 않았다. ④ 어떻게 시작
   할지 모르는 것은 다른 구성원일 것이다. ⑤ 소년의 조언을 듣고
   소녀가 물어볼 내용이다.

08 "공부를 하려고 책상에 앉지만 결국 다른 것을 하게 된다."는 의
   미로 "end up –ing"가 되는 것이 자연스럽다.

09 "write down"에 이어지는 "how much ~"는 간접의문문으로
   "의문사+주어+동사"의 순서가 되어야 한다. do를 빼고 "how
   much time you need ~"가 되어야 적절하다.

10 Emily가 동하에게 시간 관리하는 방법을 알려주는 것으로 보아
   Emily는 시간 관리하는 방법을 알고 있다고 하는 것이 적절하
   다.

11 (1) '접속사+주어+동사'로 이루어진 부사절의 주어가 주절의
   주어와 일치할 때 접속사와 주어를 생략하고 동사를 분사(동사
   원형+-ing)로 만든다. (2) 분사구문의 뜻을 명확히 하기 위해
   접속사를 생략하지 않기도 한다. (3) '~인지 (아닌지)'라는 의미
   의 명사절을 이끄는 접속사 if[whether]를 이용한다. (4) 글자
   수에 맞추려면 부사절을 분사구문으로 영작해야 한다.

Healthy Living, a Happy Life

시험대비 실력평가 p.114

01 ⑤	02 ④	03 ③
04 (1) dry (2) irregular	05 ④	06 ⑤

01 주어진 단어는 "이점"이라는 뜻으로 "advantage 이점, 장점"에 해당한다. ① 영향 ② 호의 ③ 즐거움 ④ 사건 ⑤ 이점

02 사회 연결망 사이트들의 긍정적 효과와 부정적 효과가 무엇입니까? - effects 효과 / ① 오늘 아침에 네 앞으로 편지가 한 통 왔어. - arrived ② 그는 모든 신체 접촉을 피하는 경향이 있다. - avoid ③ 그는 팔뼈에 금이 갔다. - bone ④ 그 약은 부작용이 좀 있다. - effects ⑤ 뼈를 튼튼하게 하려면 칼슘이 필요하다. - calcium

03 내 얼굴을 봐. 자외선 차단제를 발랐어야 했는데. put on 바르다 / 나는 오늘 아침에 담요를 햇빛에 내놓았다. put ~ out ~을 내놓다

04 주어진 보기의 단어는 반의어 관계이다. avoid 피하다, face 마주하다, wet 젖은, dry 마른, regular 규칙적인, irregular 불규칙적인

05 ④ 이 스테이크는 직화로 요리되었다. direct (열기나 빛이) 직접 닿는

06 ① 다행스럽게도, 그 태풍은 우리 마을에 오기 전에 약해졌다. fortunately 다행스럽게도 ② 추울 때 목도리를 하는 것이 큰 차이를 만들 것이다. make a world of difference 큰 차이를 만들다 ③ 이 책은 나쁜 기분에서 벗어나는 방법에 대해 말한다. mood 기분, 감정 ④ 아이들은 야외에서 노는 것을 즐긴다. outdoors 야외에서 ⑤ 전기 사용이 절정인 시간이 언제인가요? peak 절정의, 최고조의

서술형 시험대비 p.115

01 for / for 02 on / on 03 (p)roperly
04 arrival 05 indirect
06 (1) produces (2) properly (3) role (4) skin
07 (1) sunlight (2) journal (3) grade (4) mind

01 • 햇빛을 쬐며 걷는 것은 여러분의 마음과 몸 모두에 좋습니다. be good for ~에 좋다 • 나는 건강을 위하여 주말에 운동을 하기로 결심했다. for ~을 위하여

02 • 학교에 제시간에 도착하는 것은 중요하다. on time 제시간에 • 세로토닌은 네가 하는 일에 더 잘 집중하도록 도와준다. focus on 집중하다

03 전 사실 파티에 어울리게 옷을 입지 않았어요. – suitably 적절하게 = properly

04 기차가 연착된 것을 사과드립니다. arrive 도착하다 arrival 도착, late arrival 연착

05 주어진 단어는 반의어 관계이다. healthy 건강한, unhealthy 건강하지 못한, direct 직접적인, indirect 간접적인

06 (1) 이 공장은 자동차 부품을 만든다. produce 만들어 내다 (2) 시간 관리를 제대로 하는 것이 성공의 열쇠이다. properly 제대로 (3) Sue는 우리 모둠에서 중요한 역할을 맡고 있다. role 역할 (4) 나는 건조한 피부를 위해 얼굴 크림을 사야 한다. skin 피부

07 (1) 햇살 = sunlight (2) 일기를 쓰다 = keep a journal (3) 학점, 점수, 등급 = grade (4) 명심하다, 유의하다 = keep in mind

Conversation

핵심 Check p.116~117

1 ④	2 ⑤

01 ④는 "또한, 역시"에 해당하는 표현을 사용한 것으로 보아, 동의하는지를 나타내는 표현이고 나머지는 전달하고자 하는 내용을 강조하는 표현이다.

02 춥지 않느냐고 물어보는 말에 대하여 춥다는 대답을 하는 것으로 보아 재킷을 입지 않은 것에 대한 후회의 의미를 담은 ⑤가 가장 적절하다.

교과서 대화문 익히기

Check(√) True or False p.118

1 F 2 T 3 F 4 F

교과서 확인학습 p.120~121

Listen & Speak 1 Listen

1. can, stay / Well, important, breakfast
2. What, do, grades / important
3. think, write, journal

4. write down, spend, on / think

1. What, do, weekend / played, decided, exercise, for / you, important, regularly / Right, about, with

2. late / took, bus / think, leave, earlier / too, won't / arrive, on

Listen & Speak 2

1. too / should, brought, one

2. cold / have

3. missed / have, earlier

4. Look, should, put on / right

Listen & Speak 2 A

1. how, movie / enjoy, was / What, about / knew, have, before / sorry, like

2. still, minutes, before, top, down, and, snack / brought, brought / okay, share / keep, mind, some, time

Real-Life Zone

look, energy / because, got, last / usually, enough / know, important, night's, always, up, surfing, playing, phone / sometimes, me / After, regret, morning, have, earlier / different / climbed, dad, tired, home, sleep, after / Outdoor, are, way, get

Wrap Up 1

blanket, wet, checked / wash / put, sun / Why, wash / blanket, way, keep, clean / know, remember / important, remember, regularly

---

시험대비 기본평가
p.122

01 ①   02 ⑤   03 ④

01 소년이 규칙적으로 운동하는 것이 중요하다고 한 말과 빈칸 뒤에 이어지는 대답이 "Why not?"이라고 하는 것으로 보아 함께 테니스를 치자는 제안이 있었다고 생각할 수 있다.

02 또 다시 지각했다고 야단치는 것에 대하여 미안하다는 말에 이어서 버스를 잘못 타서 지각하게 되었다는 이유를 덧붙이는 것이 자연스럽다.

03 영화를 즐기지 못했다는 말에 (C) 무엇이 나빠서 영화를 즐기지 못했는지 이유를 묻자 (A) 이미 결말을 알았기 때문이라고 대답하고, 그것에 대해 읽어본 것을 후회한다. (B) 상대의 말에 공감하는 의미로 유감을 표시한다.

시험대비 실력평가
p.123~124

01 ③   02 ④   03 ②   04 ③
05 ④   06 ③   07 ①   08 ④

---

09 ⑤   10 I should have brought some snacks.
11 ①   12 ③

01 "too"가 나타내는 것은 앞에 나온 말에 대한 동의의 의미라고 볼 수 있기 때문에, 앞에서 강조하는 의미에 동의하는 말에 해당하는 ③이 적절하다.

02 "It's important to exercise regularly"가 앞의 빈칸에 나온 말에 대한 반응이기 때문에 운동에 대한 언급이 있는 ④가 적절하다.

03 앞에 나온 내용을 보면 소녀가 테니스를 친 것은 주말이기 때문에 "weekday 평일"이라고 할 수는 없다.

04 밤에 늦게 잔 것을 후회한다는 것으로 보아 빈칸에는 밤에 잠을 자지 않고 깨어 있는 것을 나타내는 ③이 적절하다.

05 주어진 문장은 산에 다녀온 이후의 상황을 나타내는 것이기 때문에 (D)가 적절한 곳이다.

06 Ben은 밤늦게 인터넷 서핑을 하면서 보낸 것을 후회하기 때문에 인터넷 서핑을 밤늦게까지 계속하지는 않을 것이다.

07 이어지는 대화를 보았을 때 소녀는 결말을 알고 있어서 영화가 지루했다는 것을 알 수 있으므로 ①이 적절하다.

08 대화의 흐름상 앞에 있었던 일에 대한 유감의 내용이 되어야 하기 때문에 ⓓ"I shouldn't have read about it before seeing it."이 옳다.

09 미나가 본 영화에 대하여 두 사람이 이야기하고 있다. 영화에 대한 미나의 반응은 있지만 소년이 영화를 좋아하는지 싫어하는지는 알 수 없다.

10 간식을 가져오지 않은 것에 대한 후회를 나타내야 하므로 should bring을 should have brought로 고쳐야 한다.

11 (B) 한 사람이 가지고 온 것을 함께 먹는 것은 share에 해당한다. (C) "명심하다, 염두에 두다"는 "keep in mind"이다.

12 두 사람이 등산 중에 휴식을 취하려는 상황에서 소녀가 간식을 가지고 오지 않았다고 하니까 소년이 자기가 많이 가지고 와서 나눠먹을 수 있다고 하는 것으로 보아 간식이 충분하지 않다는 것은 본문의 내용과 일치하지 않는다.

서술형 시험대비
p.125

01 I should have worn a jacket.

02 (B) – (C) – (A)   03 exercise

04 It's important to exercise regularly.

05 playing

06 I shouldn't have read about it before seeing it.

07 I'm sorry   08 good → bad

01 춥지 않은지 묻는 말에 춥다고 하는 것으로 보아 재킷을 입지 않은 것을 후회하는 의미의 "should have+과거분사" 형태가 들어가야 한다.

02 어젯밤 잠을 못 잤다는 말에 (B) 이유를 묻자 (C) TV로 영화를 봤다고 말하고, (A) 그것에 대해 유감을 나타내는 말을 한다.

03 "자신을 더 강하고 건강하게 만들기 위해서 신체 활동을 하다"에 해당하는 단어는 "exercise 운동하다"이다.

04 강조하는 의미의 "~하는 것이 중요하다"는 "It's important to ~"이다.

05 권유나 제안의 표현은 "How about -ing?"이다.

06 유감을 나타내는 의미의 "should have+과거분사"를 써야 한다. before 다음에는 적절한 주어로 쓰일 말이 없으므로 seeing을 쓰도록 한다.

07 내용상 상대의 후회에 대한 유감을 나타내는 "I am sorry"가 적절하다.

08 소녀가 영화를 즐기지 못했다고 했으므로 무엇이 좋지 않았는지 묻는 "What was bad about it?"이 적절하다.

Grammar

핵심 Check   p.126~127

1 (1) longer (2) less
2 (1) that (2) It (3) whom

시험대비 기본평가   p.128

01 ④   **02** ③   **03** ②

04 (1) It is you that I love.
(2) It is calcium that builds strong bones and teeth.
(3) The more I exercise, the stronger I get.
(4) The more, the better.

01 'It ~ that 강조 구문'은 'It is/was ~ that ...'의 형태로, 강조하고자 하는 부분을 'It is/was'와 that 사이에 넣고, 나머지 부분을 that 뒤에 써서 주어, 목적어인 명사, 부사(구/절) 등을 강조한다. 공통으로 that이 들어가는 것이 적절하다.

02 the 비교급+주어+동사 ~, the 비교급+주어+동사 …: ~하면 할수록 더 …하다

03 It was John who[that] loved her. 강조되는 어구가 사람일 때는 that 대신에 who를 쓸 수 있다.

04 (1), (2) 'It is/was 강조어(구) that ...'의 형태로 특정 부분을 강조하여 나타낼 때 사용한다. (3), (4) 'the 비교급+주어+동사 ~, the 비교급+주어+동사 …'의 형태로 '~하면 할수록 더 …하다'라는 뜻이며, 점점 더해지거나 덜해지는 것을 표현할 때 사용한다.

시험대비 실력평가   p.129~131

01 ②   **02** ①   **03** ④   **04** ⑤
05 ③, ⑤   **06** ③   **07** ④   **08** ②
09 ①   **10** ①, ④

11 (1) The higher I went up, the fresher the air was.
(2) The more you walk, the more tired you will get.

12 ②

13 (1) This red dress looks the prettier of the two.
(2) The more water we use, the drier our well will become.
(3) The more stress I get, the more emotional I become.

14 ⑤   **15** ③

16 (1) why → that   (2) who → that[which]
(3) July 26 → on July 26

17 (1) The spicier, the more
(2) The more, the more   (3) when   (4) where
(5) whom

18 ②   **19** ①

01 the 비교급+주어+동사 ~, the 비교급+주어+동사 …: ~할수록 더 …하다 The hotter it gets, the harder it is to work.

02 ② which → that[who] ③ where → that[when] ④ 두 개의 much → more ⑤ wise → wiser

03 'the 비교급+주어+동사 ~, the 비교급+주어+동사 …: ~할수록 …하다' 구문은 'As+주어+동사+비교급 ~, 주어+동사+비교급 …'으로 바꿔 쓸 수 있다.

04 'It ~ that ...' 강조구문에서 강조하는 대상이 사람일 경우 that 대신에 관계대명사 who로 바꿔 쓸 수 있다.

05 the 비교급+주어+동사 ~, the 비교급+주어+동사 … = As+주어+동사+비교급 ~, 주어+동사+비교급 …: ~할수록 …하다

06 'an apple'을 강조하므로 which나 that을 써야 한다.

07 the 비교급+주어+동사 ~, the 비교급+주어+동사 …: ~할수록 …하다

08 <보기>와 ②번은 강조 용법의 that이다. ① 지시부사 ③ 지시대명사 ④ 접속사 ⑤ 지시형용사

09 the 비교급+주어+동사 ~, the 비교급+주어+동사 …: ~할수록 …하다

10 'It ~ that …' 강조구문에서 강조하는 대상이 사물일 경우 that 대신에 관계대명사 which로 바꿔 쓸 수 있다.

11 the 비교급+주어+동사 ~, the 비교급+주어+동사 … = As+주어+동사+비교급 ~, 주어+동사+비교급 …: ~할수록 …하다
(2) '많이 걸으면 피곤해질 것이다.'라는 의미이므로 비교급을 이용하여 바꿔 쓰면, '더 많이 걸을수록 더 피곤해질 것이다.'라고 쓸 수 있다.

12 ②번은 'It: 가주어, that절: 진주어'이고 나머지는 모두 It ~

that 강조 용법으로 쓰였다.

13 (1) 비교급에는 the를 사용하지 않는 것이 원칙이지만 문장 속에 'of the two'와 같이 비교의 대상이 명확히 둘인 경우 'the+비교급'으로 쓴다. (2), (3) the 비교급+주어+동사 ~, the 비교급+주어+동사 …: ~할수록 …하다

14 ① That → It ②, ③ 'It ~ that …' 강조구문에서 형용사나 동사는 강조할 수 없다. ④ make → makes

15 ① ugly → uglier ② more safe → safer ④ good and good → better and better ⑤ nicer → the nicer

16 (1) why를 that으로 고치는 것이 적절하다. (2) 강조되는 것이 'a good breakfast'이므로 who를 that[which]로 고치는 것이 적절하다. (3) 태어난 날(부사구)을 강조하는 것이므로 전치사 on을 붙여야 한다.

17 (1), (2) the 비교급+주어+동사 ~, the 비교급+주어+동사 …: ~할수록 …하다 (3), (4) 강조하는 대상이 시간 또는 장소의 부사(구/절)일 경우, when(시간) 또는 where(장소)로 바꿔 쓸 수 있다. (5) 강조하는 대상이 사람으로 목적격이므로 that 대신에 whom으로 바꿔 쓸 수 있다.

18 'the movie'를 강조하는 것이므로 'It was the movie that[which] …'가 적절하다.

19 the gloomier로 쓰는 것이 적절하다.

서술형 시험대비 p.132~133

01 (1) The higher a bird flies, the farther it can see.
　(2) The more they have, the more they want.

02 (1) The more stress I get, the more emotional I become.
　(2) Ryan thinks the more slowly he eats, the fuller he gets.
　(3) The younger you are, the easier it is to learn.
　(4) This country is the better of the two.
　(5) It was Hamin that[who] played basketball with Eric last Saturday.
　(6) It is on Saturdays that[when] there are lots of weddings.
　(7) It was in Hangang Park that[where] Ms. Jones was at 2 p.m. last Saturday.
　(8) It was Amy's house that[which] James visited last Friday.

03 (1) It was Jenny's family that[who] went to the beach last summer.
　(2) It was to the beach that[where] Jenny's family went last summer.
　(3) It was last summer that[when] Jenny's family went to the beach.

04 (1) The more I like her, the more I miss her.
　(2) The earlier you leave, the earlier you will arrive there.
　(3) The harder you study for the exam, the better you will do.
　(4) The more careful you are, the fewer mistakes you will make.

05 (1) It was Anna who bought the dress on the Internet last Sunday.
　(2) Anna did buy the dress on the Internet last Sunday.
　(3) It was the dress which Anna bought on the Internet last Sunday.
　(4) It was on the Internet where Anna bought the dress last Sunday.
　(5) It was last Sunday when Anna bought the dress on the Internet.

06 (1) the healthier you will feel
　(2) the harder doing outdoor activities is
　(3) the more dangerous you will be

07 (1) The more you study, the smarter you will become.
　(2) The less money you spend, the more money you will have in your account.
　(3) It was five years ago that[when] Mr. Smith moved to our apartment.
　(4) It was at the Italian restaurant that[where] I learned this recipe.
　(5) It was his book that[which] Jack lost at the market.

---

01 the 비교급+주어+동사 ~, the 비교급+주어+동사 …: ~할수록 …하다

02 (1)~(3) the 비교급+주어+동사 ~, the 비교급+주어+동사 …: ~할수록 …하다 (4) 비교급에는 the를 사용하지 않는 것이 원칙이지만 문장 속에 'of the two'와 같이 비교의 대상이 명확히 둘인 경우 'the+비교급'으로 쓴다. (5) 강조하는 것이 'Hamin'이므로 that이나 who를 쓰는 것이 적절하다. (6) 강조하는 것이 'on Saturdays'이므로 that이나 when을 쓰는 것이 적절하다. (7) which 다음에 완전한 절이 나오므로 Hangang Park를 강조하는 것으로 볼 수 없다. 'in Hangang Park'를 강조하는 것으로 that이나 where를 쓰는 것이 적절하다. (8) 강조하는 것이 'Amy's house'이므로 that이나 which를 쓰는 것이 적절하다..

03 It was와 that 사이에 강조하고자 하는 부분을 넣고, that 대신에 사람이면 who, 장소일 경우 where, 시간이면 when을 쓸 수도 있다.

04 (1) '많이 좋아하면, 많이 그리워할 것이다.'를 비교급을 이용하

25

여 '더 많이 좋아할수록 더 그리워할 것이다.'라고 쓸 수 있다. (2) '일찍 출발하면, 일찍 도착할 것이다.'를 비교급을 이용하여 '더 일찍 출발할수록 더 일찍 도착할 것이다.'라고 쓸 수 있다. (3), (4) the 비교급+주어+동사 ~, the 비교급+주어+동사 … = As+주어+동사+비교급 ~, 주어+동사+비교급 …: ~할수록 …하다

05 과거시제이므로 강조하고자 하는 부분을 It was와 that 사이에 넣고, 나머지 부분을 that 뒤에 쓴다. 이때 that을 사용하지 말라고 하였으므로 that 대신에 사람이면 who, 사물이면 which, 장소일 경우 where, 시간일 경우 when을 사용한다. 또한 'It is[was] ~ that …' 구문은 동사를 강조할 수 없으므로 동사는 동사 앞에 did를 사용하여 강조한다.

06 the 비교급+주어+동사 ~, the 비교급+주어+동사 …: ~할수록 …하다

07 (1), (2) the 비교급+주어+동사 ~, the 비교급+주어+동사 …: ~할수록 …하다 (3)~(5) 강조하고자 하는 부분을 It was와 that 사이에 넣고, 나머지 부분을 that 뒤에 쓴다. 이때 that 대신에 시간일 경우 when, 장소일 경우 where, 사물이면 which를 사용할 수 있다.

교과서
Reading

확인문제   p.134

| 1 T | 2 F | 3 T | 4 F | 5 T | 6 F |

확인문제   p.135

| 1 T | 2 F | 3 T | 4 F | 5 T | 6 F |

교과서 확인학습 A   p.136~137

01 Sunshine   02 out in the sun
03 Not much
04 too busy, to spend, outdoors
05 plays an important role   06 stay healthy
07 feels happier
08 the body's happy hormone
09 The more sun, the more, happy hormone
10 goes up   11 fight everyday stress
12 calming effect, what you are doing
13 Moreover, a good night's sleep
14 not just
15 also, build strong bones   16 As you all know
17 for the body to use

18 when sunlight shines   19 to go outside
20 As you can see, enjoy its benefits safely
21 getting direct sunlight, to benefit from it
22 Try to go out into, get sunshine on
23 for just a few minutes every day
24 to protect your face and neck
25 a little sunshine, make a world of difference

교과서 확인학습 B   p.138~139

1 Enjoy the Sunshine
2 How much time do you spend every day out in the sun?
3 Not much, right?
4 Most people are too busy at school or at work to spend much time outdoors.
5 However, the sun plays an important role in your health.
6 It helps you stay healthy.
7 Everyone feels happier when the sun shines.
8 This is because of serotonin, the body's happy hormone.
9 The more sun you get, the more "happy hormone" the brain produces.
10 When your serotonin level goes up, you feel happier and stronger.
11 This helps you fight everyday stress.
12 Serotonin also has a calming effect, helping you focus better on what you are doing.
13 Moreover, serotonin helps you get a good night's sleep because it helps the brain produce a sleep hormone.
14 Sunshine does not just make you feel and sleep better.
15 It also helps build strong bones.
16 As you all know, it is calcium that builds strong bones and teeth.
17 However, for the body to use calcium properly, it needs vitamin D.
18 Interestingly, the skin creates vitamin D when sunlight shines on it.
19 The easiest way to make strong bones is to go outside and enjoy the sun.
20 As you can see, sunshine has many benefits, but how can you enjoy its benefits safely?
21 Fortunately, getting direct sunlight on your skin for 10 to 20 minutes a day is enough to benefit from it.

22 Try to go out into the sun between classes or during lunch breaks and get sunshine on your arms and hands.

23 A walk in the sun, for just a few minutes every day, is good for both your mind and your body.

24 However, avoid the sun during peak summer hours, between 11 and 3, and use sunscreen to protect your face and neck.

25 Enjoy the sun safely and see how a little sunshine can make a world of difference in your health and your mood.

시험대비 실력평가　　　　　　　　p.140~143

01 ⑤　　　　　02 (A) Most　(B) outdoors　(C) healthy
03 part　　　　04 spend → can't spend　　　05 ②
06 sunscreen 또는 sunblock
07 it is calcium that builds strong bones and teeth
08 ③　　　　09 ⑤　　　　10 Vitamin D　11 ③
12 ④　　　　13 ④　　　　14 ①, ④
15 serotonin　　　　　　　16 ③
17 (A) serotonin　(B) sleep hormone
18 Sunshine helps build strong bones as well as makes you feel and sleep better.
19 ①, ④　　　　　　　　20 the body
21 As you can see　　　　22 ①
23 and it helps you focus better on what you are doing
24 ④

01 앞에 나오는 내용과 상반되는 내용이 뒤에 이어지므로 However가 가장 적절하다. ① 따라서, 그러므로, ② 게다가, 더욱이, ③ 예를 들면, ④ 다시 말해서

02 (A) '대부분의' 사람들이라고 해야 하므로 Most가 적절하다. almost: 거의, most: 대부분(의), (B) outdoor: 옥외[야외]의(형용사) [주로 명사 앞에만 씀], outdoors: 옥외[야외]에서(부사), (C) stay 뒤에 형용사 보어를 써야 하므로, healthy가 적절하다.

03 play a role = play a part: 역할을 맡다, 한몫을 하다

04 대부분의 사람들은 학교와 직장에서 너무 바빠서 많은 시간을 야외에서 '보내지 못한다.' spend를 can't spend로 고치는 것이 적절하다. too ~ to부정사 = so ~ that 주어 cannot ...(너무 ~해서 …할 수 없다), Almost all the people = Most people, outdoors = outside a building or in the open air

05 이 글은 '햇빛의 많은 이점을 안전하게 즐길 수 있는 방법을 소개하고 있는 글'이므로, 제목으로는 ②번 '햇빛의 많은 이점을

안전하게 즐길 수 있는 법'이 적절하다. ④ spare time: 자투리 시간, 여가 시간, ⑤ make a difference: 변화를 가져오다, 차이를 낳다, 영향을 주다, 중요하다

06 sunscreen = sunblock: 자외선 차단제, 특히 더운 날씨에 태양 광선으로부터 당신의 피부를 보호해 주는 크림

07 it ~ that 강조 구문: 강조하고자 하는 부분을 it과 that 사이에 쓰고, it 뒤에 오는 be동사는 문장의 시제에 맞춰 is나 was를 사용한다.

08 ⓑ와 ②, ⑤: 부사적 용법, ①, ④: 명사적 용법, ③: 형용사적 용법

09 이 글은 '칼슘은 튼튼한 뼈를 만들어 주는데, 그 칼슘을 몸이 적절하게 사용하기 위해서는 비타민 D가 필요하고 햇빛이 피부에 비칠 때 비타민 D를 만들어 내므로 튼튼한 뼈를 만드는 가장 쉬운 방법은 밖으로 나가서 햇빛을 즐기는 것'이라는 내용의 글이므로, 주제로는 ⑤번 '햇빛은 튼튼한 뼈를 만드는 가장 쉬운 방법이다'가 적절하다.

10 '비타민 D'가 필요하다.

11 ⓐ for+숫자: ~ 동안, ⓑ in the sun: 햇빛을 쬐며

12 주어진 문장의 However에 주목한다. ④번 앞 문장의 내용과 상반되는 내용이 뒤에 이어지므로 ④번이 적절하다.

13 ⓐ와 ④: (작업 중의) 휴식 (시간)(명사), lunch breaks: 점심 시간, ① 부수다(동사), ② (~ 사이의) 틈[구멍](명사), ③ (법·약속 등을) 어기다(동사), ⑤ (무엇을 갑자기) 중단시키다(동사)

14 ⓐ와 ①, ④: 현재분사, ②, ③, ⑤: 동명사

15 '세로토닌'을 가리킨다.

16 여러분의 세로토닌 수치가 '높아지면', 여러분은 더 행복하고 더 건강하게 느낀다.

17 '세로토닌' 덕분에 여러분은 숙면을 취할 수 있는데, 세로토닌이 뇌가 '수면 호르몬'을 생성하도록 도와주기 때문이다. get a good night's sleep = have a good night's sleep: 충분히 숙면을 취하다

18 본문에서는 ⓐ와 ⓑ가 각각의 문장이라서 접속사가 필요하지 않지만, 한 문장일 경우는 접속사를 써야 하므로, not just[only] A but also B = B as well as A(A 뿐만 아니라 B도) 구문을 사용하여 고치는 것이 적절하다.

19 ⓒ와 ②, ③, ⑤: 'It is[was] ~ that ...'의 형태의 강조 구문, ① so ~ that ...: 너무 ~해서 …하다(부사절을 이끄는 접속사), ④ 진주어를 이끄는 접속사

20 '몸'을 가리킨다.

21 as: ~한 것처럼, ~하다시피(접속사)

22 다행히도, 하루에 10분에서 20분 동안 피부에 직사광선을 쪼이는 것은 햇빛으로부터 이점을 얻는 데 충분하다고 했으므로, '햇빛의 이점들을 안전하게 즐길 수 있는 방법은 찾기 어렵다'는 말은 옳지 않다.

23 helping 이하는 분사구문으로 앞 절에 대한 추가 설명을 제공

한다.

24 이 글은 '세로토닌의 이로운 점들'에 관한 글이므로, 제목으로는 ④번 '세로토닌의 여러 가지 이로운 점들'이 적절하다. benefit: 이익; 편의, 이로움

서술형 시험대비 p.144~145

01 Most people are so busy at school or at work that they cannot spend much time outdoors.

02 the sun   03 (A) health   (B) healthy

04 As you get more sun, the brain produces more "happy hormone".

05 helping you focus better on what you are doing

06 (A) the brain   (B) happy hormone

07 (1) It[Sunshine] makes you feel better.
   (2) It[Sunshine] makes you sleep better.
   (3) It[Sunshine] helps build strong bones.

08 Therefore → However   09 the skin

10 (A) vitamin D   (B) sunlight   (C) enjoy the sun

11 does not make → does not just[only/merely/simply] make

12 (A) during   (B) protect   (C) a world of

13 10 to 20

01 too ~ to부정사: so ~ that 주어 cannot ...(너무 ~해서 …할 수 없다)

02 '해[햇빛]'를 가리킨다.

03 햇빛은 여러분이 '건강'을 유지하는 데 도움을 주며 여러분의 '건강'에 중요한 영향을 미친다(역할을 한다). play a role(part) in = have an effect on

04 the 비교급 ~, the 비교급 …: '~할수록 …하다', As를 이용하여 고칠 때는 the를 생략하고 비교급을 원래의 자리에 쓰는 것이 적절하다.

05 'on'을 보충하면 된다. focus on: ~에 주력하다, 초점을 맞추다

06 여러분이 햇살을 받을 때 '뇌'는 세로토닌을 만들어 내고, 세로토닌 수치에 비례하여 여러분은 더 행복하게 느낄 수 있다. 그래서 여러분은 세로토닌을 '행복 호르몬'이라고 부를 수 있다. be in the sun: 햇살을 받다

07 (1) 햇빛은 여러분이 더 기분 좋게 느끼게 해준다. (2) 햇빛은 여러분이 잠을 더 잘 자게 해 준다. (3) 햇빛은 튼튼한 뼈를 만드는 것을 돕는다.

08 튼튼한 뼈와 치아를 만드는 것은 칼슘'이지만', 몸이 칼슘을 적절하게 사용하기 위해서는 비타민 D가 필요하다고 하는 것이 적절하므로 'However'나 'But' 등으로 고치는 것이 적절하다.

09 '피부'를 가리킨다.

10 몸이 튼튼한 뼈를 만들어 주는 칼슘을 적절하게 사용하기 위해

서는 '비타민 D'가 필요하다. 피부는 '햇빛'이 피부에 비칠 때 비타민 D를 만들어 내므로, 튼튼한 뼈를 만드는 가장 쉬운 방법은 밖으로 나가서 '햇볕을 즐기는 것'이다.

11 '햇빛은 단지 여러분이 더 기분 좋게 느끼고 잠을 더 잘 자게 하는 것만은 아니다.'라고 해야 하므로 does not just[only/merely/simply] make로 고치는 것이 적절하다.

12 (A) '여름의 절정 시간 동안'이라고 해야 하므로 during이 적절하다. during+기간을 나타내는 명사, for+숫자, (B) 얼굴과 목을 '보호하기 위해'라고 해야 하므로 protect가 적절하다. prevent: 막다, 예방하다, protect: 보호하다, (C) '큰 차이'라고 해야 하므로 a world of가 적절하다. a world of: 산더미 같은, 막대한, a number of+복수명사: 많은

13 햇빛으로부터 이점을 얻으려면 하루에 '10분에서 20분' 동안 피부에 직사광선을 쪼이는 것이 필요하다.

영역별 핵심문제 p.147~151

01 ①   02 ④   03 ⑤   04 ④

05 It's important to arrive at school on time.

06 I shouldn't have read about it

07 ⑤   08 (A) boring   (B) like   09 ⑤

10 ③   11 ②   12 ⑤   13 ①

14 (1) It was Tina that[who] bought a camera at the shop yesterday.
   (2) Tina did buy a camera at the shop yesterday.
   (3) It was a camera that[which] Tina bought at the shop yesterday.
   (4) It was at the shop that[where] Tina bought a camera yesterday.
   (5) It was yesterday that[when] Tina bought a camera at the shop.

15 ③   16 ④

17 (1) The healthier, the healthier
   (2) the more, the sadder   (3) darker and darker
   (4) where   (5) which

18 It was, that[where]

19 ④   20 ⑤   21 ①, ②   22 ①

23 for 10 to 20 minutes a day

24 between   25 ②

26 As you get more sunlight, you feel happier and stronger.

27 wash your hands   28 ⑤

29 good breakfast

01 그것은 그녀 평생의 가장 어려운 결정이었다. be동사의 보어로 명사 decision이 적절하다.

02 "사람이나 동물 신체의 표피층"은 "피부 skin"를 가리킨다.

03 버스는 정확히 제시간에 왔다. 제시간에 = on time / 너는 이 추운 날씨에 코트를 입는 것이 낫다. 입다 = put on

04 건강을 유지하기 위해 뭘 하니? stay healthy = 건강을 유지하다, stay = ~한 상태를 유지하다

05 "~하는 것이 중요하다"는 "It's important to ~"이다.

06 "~하지 말았어야 했는데"의 의미로 유감이나 후회를 나타내는 표현은 "shouldn't[should not] have+과거분사"이다.

07 타야 할 비행기를 놓쳤기 때문에 일찍 오지 않은 것에 대한 유감을 나타내는 표현이 적절하다.

08 (A) 영화를 즐기지 못했다는 말에 이어지므로 영화에 대한 부정적인 단어가 적절하다. (B) 상대가 영화를 즐기지 못했다는 말에 대한 유감의 의미가 되는 단어가 적절하다.

09 영화를 보기 전에 읽지 말았어야 했다는 의미이다. 전치사 before 뒤에 오기 때문에 동명사 seeing이 되어야 한다.

10 위 대화에서 미나는 영화를 즐기지 못한 것은 미리 읽은 것 때문이라고 생각하면서 유감스럽게 생각하고 있다.

11 'It is[was] ~ that …' 강조구문에서 that 대신에 강조하는 것이 사람이면 who, 사물이면 which, 장소일 경우에는 where, 시간일 경우에는 when을 쓸 수 있다.

12 the 비교급+주어+동사 ~, the 비교급+주어+동사 …: ~할수록 …하다

13 ① of the two로 수식을 받는 경우 비교급이라도 the를 붙인다. ② The higher the top of a mountain, the better the view. ③ The more I got to know her, the more I liked her. ④ The angrier she got, the more loudly she yelled. ⑤ The older David gets, the wiser he becomes.

14 강조하고자 하는 부분을 It is[was]와 that 사이에 넣고, 나머지 부분을 that 뒤에 쓴다. that 대신에 강조하는 것이 사람이면 who, 사물이면 which, 장소일 경우에는 where, 시간일 경우에는 when을 쓸 수 있다. 하지만 'It is[was] ~ that …' 구문은 동사를 강조할 수는 없고 동사는 동사 앞에 do/does/did를 사용하여 강조한다.

15 ① It was my uncle that[who] bought this smartphone for me on my birthday. ② It is Brian that[who] broke the door. ④ It is the new car that my son wants to buy. ⑤ It was on the day that[when] I met her.

16 the 비교급+주어+동사 ~, the 비교급+주어+동사 …: ~할수록 …하다

17 (1), (2) the 비교급+주어+동사 ~, the 비교급+주어+동사 …: ~할수록 …하다 (3) '비교급 and 비교급'은 '점점 더 …하다'의 뜻이다. (4)~(5) 'It is[was] ~ that …' 구문에서 that 대신에 강조하는 것이 사람이면 who, 사물이나 동물이면 which, 시간이면 when, 장소이면 where를 쓸 수 있다.

18 'It is[was] ~ that …' 구문은 강조하고자 하는 부분을 It is[was]와 that 사이에 넣고, 나머지 부분을 that 뒤에 쓰며. 강

19 앞에 나오는 내용에 추가하는 내용이 뒤에 이어지므로 Moreover가 가장 적절하다. Moreover 게다가, 더욱이, ② 즉[말하자면], ③ 그러므로

조하는 것이 장소이면 that 대신에 where를 쓸 수 있다.

20 세로토닌은 뇌가 수면 호르몬을 생성하도록 도와주기 때문에 여러분이 숙면을 취하도록 해 준다고 했으므로, 세로토닌이 숙면과 아무 관계가 없다는 말은 옳지 않다. have nothing to do with: ~와는 전혀 관계가 없다

21 ⓐ와 ①, ②: 명사적 용법, ③, ⑤: 부사적 용법, ④: 형용사적 용법

22 이 글은 '칼슘은 튼튼한 뼈를 만들어 주는데, 그 칼슘을 몸이 적절하게 사용하기 위해서는 비타민 D가 필요하고, 햇빛이 피부에 비칠 때 비타민 D를 만들어 내므로, 튼튼한 뼈를 만드는 가장 쉬운 방법은 밖으로 나가서 햇빛을 즐기는 것'이라는 내용의 글이므로, 제목으로는 ①번 '햇빛을 즐기기, 튼튼한 뼈를 만드는 가장 쉬운 방법!'이 적절하다.

23 10 to 20 minutes: 10분에서 20분

24 between A and B: A와 B 사이에

25 ② '무슨 근거로 하루에 10분에서 20분 동안 피부에 직사광선을 쪼이는 것이 햇빛으로부터 이점을 얻는 데 충분한 것인지'는 대답할 수 없다. on what ground: 무슨 까닭으로, 무슨 근거로, ① Yes. ③ Between classes or during lunch breaks. ④ During peak summer hours, between 11 and 3. ⑤ By using sunscreen.

26 the 비교급 ~, the 비교급 …: '~할수록 …하다', As를 이용하여 고칠 때는 the를 생략하고 비교급을 원래의 자리에 쓰는 것이 적절하다.

27 외출한 다음에 '손을 잘 씻으면' 감기에 쉽게 걸리지 않을 것이다. catch[take, get, have] a cold: 감기에 걸리다

28 ⑤ 아침 식사를 잘하면 당신의 일에 더 잘 집중할 수 있고 사물들을 더 잘 기억할 수 있다.

29 '좋은 아침 식사'는 당신의 일에 더 잘 집중할 수 있고 사물들을 더 잘 기억할 수 있도록 도와준다.

단원별 예상문제
p.152~155

01 irregularly   02 ③   03 ④
04 ⑤   05 ③   06 ②   07 ①
08 ①   09 ⑤

10 (1) It is the whole thing that[which] we are pretty much unsure about.
(2) It was with her friends that[who, whom] she went to the movies last Sunday.
(3) It was yesterday that[when] a friend of mine bought a luxurious car.

11 ④　　　12 ③, ⑤

13 (1) The more careful we are, the fewer mistakes
　　　 we make.

　　(2) It is sunscreen that you should put on before
　　　 you go out.

14 ②

15 Everyone feels happier when the sun shines.

16 ③　　　17 ③　　　18 ④

19 safe → safely

20 (A) peak summer hours　　　21 ⑤

22 ③　　　23 sunscreen → umbrella　　24 ④

01 주어진 단어는 반의어 관계이다. wet 젖은, dry 건조한,
　　regularly 규칙적으로, irregularly 불규칙하게

02 태양을 안전하게 즐기고 적은 양의 햇빛이 여러분의 건강과 기
　　분에 얼마나 큰 차이를 만들어 내는지 보세요. / make a world
　　of difference 큰 차이를 만들다

03 나는 여가 시간이 있을 때 보통 인터넷 서핑을 한다. surf the
　　Internet 인터넷 서핑을 하다 / 햇빛은 여러분의 건강에 중요한
　　역할을 합니다. play an important role 중요한 역할을 하다

04 ① effect 효과 ② flight 항공편 ③ grade 성적 ④ journal
　　일기, 일지 ⑤ regret 후회하다

05 산꼭대기에 도달하다는 의미의 타동사로 쓰이는 것은 reach이
　　다.

06 "~했어야 했는데"는 "should have+과거분사"의 형태로 과거
　　에 하지 못한 일에 대한 유감이나 후회를 나타낸다.

07 두 사람은 산을 오르는 중이고 꼭대기까지는 30분 정도 남은 지
　　점에 도착했지만 지금까지 얼마나 시간이 걸렸는지는 알 수 없
　　다.

08 stay up late: 늦게까지 자지 않고 있다

09 일찍 잠자리에 들었어야 했다는 의미가 적절하므로 "should
　　have+과거분사"가 와야 한다.

10 강조하고자 하는 부분을 'It is[was]'와 that 사이에 넣고, 나머
　　지 부분을 that 뒤에 쓴다.

11 ④ The redder the apples are, the sweeter they taste.

12 ① The higher I went up, the foggier it became. ②
　　Of the two boys, Simon is the taller. ④ Buying new
　　furniture may prove too costly. 강조되는 부분에 형용사
　　나 동사는 사용할 수 없다. ⑥ He played basketball at the
　　playground. ⑦ last Friday를 강조하는 것이므로 that이나
　　when을 써야 한다.

13 (1) the 비교급+주어+동사 ~, the 비교급+주어+동사 …: ~할
　　수록 …하다 (2) 강조하고자 하는 부분을 'It is[was]'와 that
　　사이에 넣고, 나머지 부분을 that 뒤에 쓴다.

14 ②번 다음 문장의 This에 주목한다. 주어진 문장의 내용을 받고
　　있으므로 ②번이 적절하다.

15 앞 문장 전체를 가리킨다.

16 이 글은 '세로토닌의 이로운 점들'에 관한 글이므로, 주제
　　로는 ③번 '유익한 호르몬인 세로토닌의 역할'이 적절하다.
　　beneficial: 유익한, 이로운

17 ⓐ와 ③: ~한 것처럼, ~하다시피(접속사), 녹이 쇠를 좀먹듯이
　　근심은 마음을 좀먹는다. ① [보통 'as ~ as …'로 형용사·부사
　　앞에서] ~와 같은 정도로, ('as ~ as …'에서, 앞의 as가 지시부
　　사, 뒤의 as는 접속사), ② 때(접속사), ④ 이유(접속사), ⑤ [비
　　례] ~함에 따라, ~할수록(접속사)

18 몸이 '칼슘'을 적절하게 사용하기 위해서는 '비타민 D'가 필요하
　　다.

19 동사 enjoy를 수식하는 것이기 때문에, 부사로 고치는 것이 적
　　절하다.

20 '여름의 절정 시간'인 11시에서 3시 사이에는 햇빛을 피하는 것
　　이 좋다.

21 매일 '적은' 양의 햇빛이라도 쬐면 자신의 건강과 기분에 큰 차이
　　를 만들어 낼 수 있다.

22 위 글은 '일기 예보'이다. ① book report: 독후감, ② article:
　　(신문·잡지의) 글, 기사, ④ review: (책·연극·영화 등에 대한)
　　논평[비평], 감상문, ⑤ travel essay: 기행문

23 서울과 파리는 비가 예보되고 있기 때문에 '우산'을 가지고 가라
　　고 하는 것이 적절하다. sunscreen 자외선 차단제

24 뉴욕은 현재 날씨가 흐리다.

서술형 실전문제　　　　　　　　p.156~157

01 ④, How was yesterday different?

02 I finally got a good night's sleep last night

03 Outdoor

04 (1) I think the older Sue gets, the wiser she
　　　 becomes.

　　(2) The fewer the words, the better the prayer.

　　(3) It was in the library that he lent me the book
　　　 yesterday.

　　(4) It was last year that[when] my family traveled
　　　 to Busan.

　　(5) It was because she lost her mother that the girl
　　　 was confused.

05 It, she is waiting for in the rain

06 (A) up　　(B) calming　　(C) helping

07 (A) everyday stress　　(B) serotonin level

08 sunlight

09 see how a little sunshine can make a world of difference in your health and your mood

10 (A) many benefits   (B) safe   (C) sunscreen

02 "하룻밤을 잘 자다"는 "get a good night's sleep"이다.

03 앞에서 언급한 등산을 지칭하는 의미로 "Outdoor activities"가 되도록 해야 한다.

04 (1), (2) the 비교급+주어+동사 ~, the 비교급+주어+동사 …: ~할수록 …하다 (3) that 다음에 이어지는 절이 완전하므로 'the library'를 'in the library'로 고쳐야 한다. (4) last year를 강조하고 있으므로 that[when]을 써야 한다. (5) who 다음에 나오는 절이 완전하므로 who를 that으로 고쳐 'because she lost her mother'라는 부사절을 강조하는 문장으로 만들어야 한다.

05 빗속에서 버스를 기다리고 있는 그림이므로 'It is'와 that 사이에 the bus를 넣어 강조한다. be동사가 주어졌으므로 'is waiting for'로 현재진행형으로 쓴다.

06 (A) 세로토닌 수치가 '높아지면' 더 행복하고 더 건강하게 느끼는 것이므로 up이 적절하다. (B) '진정시키는' 효과라고 해야 하므로 calming이 적절하다. (C) and it helps나 분사구문으로 써야 하므로 helping이 적절하다.

07 여러분이 '매일의 스트레스'를 이겨낼 필요가 있다면 여러분의 '세로토닌 수치'를 높이는 편이 낫겠다. 왜냐하면 그것이 여러분을 더 행복하고 더 건강하게 느끼도록 도와줄 수 있기 때문이다. may as well ~: ~하는 편이 낫다

08 '햇빛'을 가리킨다.

09 see의 목적어로 간접의문문(의문사+주어+동사) 순서로 쓰는 것이 적절하다.

10 여러분은 여름의 절정 시간인 11시에서 3시 사이에는 햇빛을 피하고 얼굴과 목을 보호하기 위해 '자외선 차단제'를 사용하면서, 하루에 10분에서 20분 동안 피부에 직사광선을 쪼임으로써 그것의 '많은 이점'을 '안전하게' 즐길 수 있다.

창의사고력 서술형 문제 p.158

|모범답안|

01 1. stress, happier   2. focus   3. sleep
   4. vitamin D, bones

02 (1) It is Paul that[who] is having breakfast.
   (2) It was Susan that[who] prepared breakfast.
   (3) It is ham and egg that[which] Paul is having.
   (4) It is in the kitchen that[where] they are.

03 (A) after going out   (B) wash your hands
   (C) direct sunlight   (D) 10 to 20 minutes
   (E) a good breakfast

01 deal with 처리하다, 해결하다 focus on 집중하다

02 강조하고자 하는 부분을 'It is[was]'와 that 사이에 넣고, 나머지 부분을 that 뒤에 쓴다.

단원별 모의고사 p.159~162

01 unhealthy   02 ③   03 ⑤
04 (1) mood   (2) outdoors   (3) peak   (4) properly
05 ②   06 ④   07 ③   08 ①
09 ②   10 ⑤
11 (1) I become richer, I am happier
   (2) the magnet is bigger, it is stronger
   (3) you practice more, your English speaking skills are better
12 (1) It is your smartphone that[which] you should put away.
   (2) It was not until I came to Korea that[when] I learned Hangeul.
   (3) It was for dessert that Jina had a chocolate cake.
   (4) It is Minji and Jian that[who] want to join the art club.
13 ④   14 ②, ④, ⑥, ⑦
15 (1) The longer I boil the soup, the better it tastes.
   (2) The better the weather is, the better I feel.
   (3) It was at school that[where] Layla met Jinho.
   (4) It is her father that[who/whom] Ella respects the most.
16 ②
17 The more sun you get, the more "happy hormone" the brain produces.
18 (When your serotonin level goes up,) you feel happier and stronger.
19 ①, ②, ④   20 ③   21 ②
22 Benefits   23 ③

01 두 단어의 관계는 반의어 관계이다. wide 넓은, narrow 좁은, healthy 건강한, unhealthy 건강하지 못한

02 "자신들에게 일어난 일을 규칙적으로 기록하는 책"은 "journal 일지, 일기"이다.

03 라일라는 외출 전에 항상 자외선 차단제를 바른다. / sunscreen 자외선 차단제 apply 바르다

04 (1) 그는 늘 기분이 안 좋다. (mood 기분) (2) 비 때문에 그들은 야외에서 식사를 하지 못했다. (outdoors 야외에서) (3) 호텔들이 성수기에는 항상 만원이 된다. (peak 최고조의) (4) 텔

레비전이 제대로 작동이 안 된다. (properly 제대로, 적절하게)

05 앞에서 담요가 비에 젖었다는 것으로 볼 때 날씨에 관해서 주의를 기울이지 않은 것에 대한 유감의 의미가 적절하다.

06 주어진 문장은 상대가 알려주는 새로운 사실에 대한 응답이므로 자연친화적인 방법에 대한 설명 다음인 (D)에 들어가는 것이 적절하다.

07 "Did you wash it?"이라는 질문에 No라고 대답하는 것으로 보아 여자는 담요를 빨지 않았다.

08 "you look full of energy today"에 대한 대답이기 때문에 잠을 잘 잤다는 내용이 적절하다. 밤에 잠을 잘 자는 것을 나타내는 표현이 "get a good night's sleep"이다.

09 ② 접속사 or로 이어지는 동사 "play"는 surfing과 병렬 관계에 있기 때문에 playing이 되어야 한다.

10 Ben이 등산을 다녀온 뒤에 잠을 잘 잤다는 말은 있지만, 어떤 야외 활동을 좋아하는지에 대한 언급은 없다.

11 'the 비교급, the 비교급' 구문은 'As+주어+동사+비교급 ~, 주어+동사+비교급 …'으로 바꿔 쓸 수 있다.

12 강조하고자 하는 부분을 시제에 맞춰 'It is[was]'와 that 사이에 넣고, 나머지 부분을 that 뒤에 쓴다. 이때 that 대신에 사람이면 who, 사물이면 which, 장소일 경우 where, 시간일 경우 when을 쓸 수 있다.

13 the 비교급+주어+동사 ~, the 비교급+주어+동사 …: ~할수록 …하다 bitter는 형용사로 '맛이 쓴, 격렬한'의 뜻이며 비교급은 'more bitter'이다.

14 ② The faster you go, the earlier you will reach your grandma's house. ④ It was the window that John broke. ⑥, ⑦ 'It ~ that …' 강조 구문은 동사나 양태부사를 강조하는 데 쓰이지 않는다.

15 (1), (2) the 비교급+주어+동사 ~, the 비교급+주어+동사 …: ~할수록 …하다 (3), (4) 강조하고자 하는 부분을 시제에 맞춰 'It is[was]'와 that 사이에 넣고, 나머지 부분을 that 뒤에 쓴다. 이때 that 대신에 사람이면 who, 사물이면 which, 장소일 경우 where, 시간일 경우 when을 쓸 수 있다.

16 선행사를 포함하는 관계대명사 'what'을 쓰는 것이 적절하다.

17 the 비교급 ~, the 비교급 …: ~할수록 …하다

18 '(여러분의 세로토닌 수치가 높아지면,) 여러분은 더 행복하고 더 건강하게 느끼는 것'을 가리킨다.

19 ⓐ와 ①, ②, ④: 동명사, ① get ahead of: [경쟁자 따위]를 앞지르다, 능가하다, ③, ⑤: 현재분사

20 이 글은 '햇빛의 많은 이점을 안전하게 즐길 수 있는 방법을 소개하고 있는 글'이므로, 주제로는 ③번 '햇빛의 많은 이점을 안전하게 즐길 수 있는 방법'이 적절하다.

21 하루에 10분에서 20분 동안 피부에 직사광선을 쪼이는 것은 햇빛으로부터 이점을 얻는 데 '충분하다.'

22 benefits: 혜택들, 이득들, 좋은 점들, 여러분이 어떤 것으로부터 얻는 도움이 되는 것들 또는 어떤 것의 결과로 나오는 이점들, helps: 도움이 되는[요긴한] 것들

23 햇빛을 충분히 쬐면 밤에 잠을 '더 잘 잘 것이다.'

Safety First

01 exit   02 ⑤   03 put up   04 ②

05 ②   06 ③

07 (1) overeat   (2) exploded   (3) attention

01 주어진 관계는 반의어 관계이다. 젖은 : 마른 = 입구 : 출구

02 '강물이나 빗물이 넓은 땅을 덮고 있는 상황'을 가리키는 말은 flooding(홍수, 범람)이다.

03 put up: 설치하다, 세우다

04 place는 명사로는 '(경주•대회에서 입상권에 드는) 등위'를 의미하지만, 동사로는 '놓다, 두다'를 의미한다.

05 ②번 문장에서 apply는 '(크림 등을) 바르다'를 의미한다.

06 pass out: 의식을 잃다, 기절하다 / use up: ～을 다 써버리다

01 irregularly

02 (1) earthquake   (2) memory   (3) lightning

03 (1) apply   (2) safety   (3) overflow   (4) entrance

04 Keep in mind what I told you.

05 rub

06 (1) keep away   (2) passed out   (3) put on

     (4) instead of

01 주어진 관계는 반의어 관계이다. 규칙적으로 : 불규칙적으로

02 (1) 지구 표면의 갑작스럽고 격렬한 흔들림: 지진 (2) 기억하고 있는 것: 기억 (3) 폭풍우가 몰아칠 때 여러분이 하늘에서 보는 밝은 빛: 번개

03 (1) 우리는 밖에 나가기 전에 자외선 차단제를 피부에 발라야 한다. (2) 우리는 다른 어떤 것보다 안전을 우선시해야 한다. (3) 비가 많이 오기 때문에 그 강은 범람할 수 있다. (4) 많은 사람들이 야구 경기장 입구에서 기다리고 있었다.

04 keep in mind: ～을 명심하다

05 손이나 물체를 어떤 표면 위로 누르고 움직이다 / rub: 비비다, 문지르다

06 (1) keep away: ～을 접근하지 못하게 하다 (2) pass out: 기절하다 (3) put on: ～을 바르다 (4) instead of: ～ 대신에

교과서 Conversation

1 have to

2 we have to walk down the stairs slowly

3 can[may] be uncomfortable

4 (C) → (B) → (A)

교과서 대화문 익히기

1 F   2 T   3 F   4 T

교과서 확인학습

Listen & Speak 1 Listen

1. have to watch out

2. looks nice / to get to

3. wet / have to walk down

4. Let's climb, top / have to check, going to rain, should

Listen & Speak 1 A

1. play outside / Don't forget to / cloudy, have to put on / wear, every day / put, on

2. go bowling / go see a doctor / wrong / hurts

Listen & Speak 2 Listen

1. may fall / won't run

2. into, without warming up

3. to swim / how deep the water is, deeper than

4. right / with, uncomfortable

Listen & Speak 2 A

1. can cause, what to do, have to do, have to turn off, pack, Finally, safe place, keep listening to

2. ready to / yet, if, turned off / may not get to, in time / have to check

Real-Life Zone

look at, What, think / are, going / to meet / one, short ride / Put on, yourself / riding, without / have to wear, protects / fits, not / have to buy

Wrap Up

finish drinking / Why don't, sure that / suddenly, may spill / wait for, another bus

시험대비 기본평가　p.174

01 ③　　　　02 (B) → (D) → (A) → (C)　　03 ②

04 we may not get to the concert in time

01 have to는 '~해야 한다'는 의미로 의무를 나타내는 표현이다.

02 (B) 제안 → (D) 거절 → (A) 증상 묻기 → (C) 증상 말하기

03 if: ~인지 아닌지

04 may not: ~하지 못할 수도 있다, get to: ~에 도착하다, in time: 제 시간에, 늦지 않게

시험대비 실력평가　p.175~176

01 ④　　　02 Put on　　03 ②, ④, ⑤　　04 ⑤

05 ③　　　06 Do I have to put on sunscreen?

07 some sunscreen　　　08 ①

09 spill　　　10 ③　　　11 ②

12 Why don't we

13 I have to go see a doctor.

14 Because her stomach hurts.

01 주어진 문장의 It은 a helmet을 가리키므로 ④가 적절하다.

02 put on: ~을 쓰다

03 '~해야 한다'는 의미의 should, need to, have to 등이 들어가야 한다.

04 소년이 헬멧을 언제 살 것인지는 알 수 없다.

05 밖에 나가기 전에 선크림을 바르라는 당부의 말이 적절하다. Don't forget to+동사원형 ~.: ~할 것을 잊지 마라.

06 Do I have to ~?: 제가 ~해야 하나요?, put on: ~을 바르다, sunscreen: 선크림

07 some은 부정대명사로 some sunscreen을 가리킨다.

08 may는 '~할 수도 있다'는 의미로 추측을 나타낸다.

09 대개 실수로 용기의 가장자리로 어떤 것이 넘치거나 흐르거나 나오게 하다: spill(흘리다, 엎지르다, 쏟다)

10 소녀는 차를 다 마시고 버스를 탈 것이다.

11 식사 후 배부른 상태에서 수영하는 것이 편하다는 대답은 어색하다.

12 Let's ~.(~합시다)는 제안을 나타내는 표현으로 Why don't we ~?, How[What] about -ing? 등으로 바꿔 쓸 수 있다.

13 go see a doctor: 병원에 가다

14 소녀는 배가 아프기 때문에 병원에 가야 한다.

서술형 시험대비　p.177

01 (A) → (D) → (B) → (C)

02 I have to finish drinking my tea

03 (A) if　(B) stops　(C) another

04 wait, drinks　　　05 (A) To　(B) on

06 You have to wear a helmet that fits you.

07 a helmet

01 (A) 떠날 준비를 했는지 묻자 → (D) 아직 준비가 안 되었다고 대답한다. → (B) 콘서트에 늦을까봐 걱정하자 → (C) 알겠다고 답하는 순서가 적절하다.

02 have to: ~해야 한다, finish+동명사: ~하는 것을 끝내다

03 (A) if: ~인지 아닌지 (B) 조건을 나타내는 if절에서는 미래시제 대신 현재시제를 쓴다. (C) another+단수명사

04 소년은 소녀가 그녀의 차를 다 마실 때까지 기다릴 수 있다고 했다.

05 (A) To: ~에, ~로 (B) put on: ~을 쓰다, ~을 입다

06 have to: ~해야 한다, a helmet that fits you: 너에게 맞는 헬멧

07 one은 부정대명사로 앞에 나온 a helmet을 가리킨다.

Grammar

핵심 Check　p.178~179

1 (1) although　(2) eats

2 (1) It seems that you dance very well.

(2) It seems that Sara likes you.

(3) It seems that you are angry.

시험대비 기본평가　p.180

01 (1) Besides → Although[Even though, Though]

(2) is → be

(3) enjoying → enjoy

(4) to → that

02 Even though I have a lot to do, I am doing nothing. / I am doing nothing even though I have a lot to do.

03 ③

04 (1) Even though this cup is beautiful, it has a crack on the side. / This cup has a crack on the side even though it is beautiful.

(2) Rose seemed to have gone to bed late. / It seemed that Rose had gone to bed late.

(3) Alex seems to be depressed these days. / It seems that Alex is depressed these days.

01 (1) 종속절과 주절이 서로 대조적인 의미를 나타내므로 Besides가 아니라 Although가 적절하다. (2), (3) 'seem to 부정사' 구문. (4) seem to부정사 = It seems that 주어 동사

02 부사절 접속사 even though를 활용하여 연결한다.

03 'seem to부정사'이므로 ③이 적절하다.

04 (1) Even though 주어 동사, 주어 동사: 비록 ~하더라도 …하다 (2), (3) seem+to부정사 = seem that 주어 동사: ~인 것처럼 보이다

01 Despite → Although[Though]　　　　02 ⑤

03 (1) He seems to be lonely. / It seems that he is lonely.

　(2) She seems to be happy. / It seems that she is happy.

　(3) Sally seems to be in a hurry. / It seems that Sally is in a hurry.

　(4) It seemed that the computer didn't work at all.

04 ③　　　　05 ①　　　　06 ①　　　　07 ①

08 (1) Although there was a loud noise, the baby did not wake up.

　(2) Although he disliked movies, he went to the movies with his girlfriend to please her.

09 ④　　　　10 (1) to be　(2) that　　　　11 ③

12 (1) she is three years old / she can read and write

　(2) they haven't won any games this season / they're fantastic

　(3) you put on two or three jumpers / You're still going to be cold

13 ①　　　　14 ①, ②　　　　15 ③　　　　16 ①, ③

17 (1) rich, not 또는 him, he　(2) have

　(3) have　(4) despite 또는 day

01 문제에서 Despite 뒤에 주어와 동사가 나와 있으므로 접속사가 필요하다는 것을 알 수 있다. 그러므로 Despite 대신 Although[Though]가 적절하다.

02 'seem to부정사' 구문을 'It seems/seemed that' 구문으로 바꾼 것이다. 각 빈칸에 that이 들어가는 것이 적절하다. • Jay는 대답을 알고 있는 것처럼 보인다. • 그는 곧 떠날 것처럼 보인다.

03 seem to부정사 = It seems/seemed 주어 동사

04 ① 아빠는 화나 보이신다. ② 그들은 곧 돌아올 것처럼 보인다. ③ Kidson은 그녀의 헤어스타일을 맘에 들어 하지 않는 것 같다. seem → seem to ④ 그는 아무런 계획이 없는 것 같다. ⑤ 그녀는 가족을 그리워하고 있는 것 같다.

05 그는 아주 바빴던 것처럼 보인다. 'It seems[seemed] that 주어 과거동사'는 '주어 seem(s/ed) to have been'으로 바꿔 쓸 수 있다.

06 그는 90세인데도 정신적인 기능이 아직 약화되지 않았다. 빈칸 뒤에 절이 있고, 이어서 주절이 나왔으므로 빈칸에는 접속사가 들어가야 한다. 종속절과 주절이 의미상 대조를 이루므로 although가 적절하다.

07 • 뛰어가도 너는 여전히 늦을 거야. • 이상하게 들릴지 모르겠지만, 나는 게임이 끝나서 기뻤다. 단독으로 또는 even과 함께 양보의 뜻으로 쓰이는 접속사는 though이다.

08 'although 주어 동사, 주어 동사' 구문으로 쓰는 것이 적절하다.

09 ④ It seemed that they had known what to do to make their camping trip safe. 완료부정사가 나왔으므로 주절의 시제보다 하나 앞선 시제가 되어야 한다.

10 ' 주어 seem(s/ed) to부정사' 또는 'It seems[seemed] that 주어+동사'의 형태로 쓴다.

11 '주어 seem(s/ed) to부정사'의 형태로 쓰며 주어가 Harry and Catherine으로 복수이므로 seem이 적절하다.

12 (1) 비록 그녀는 3살이지만 읽고 쓸 줄 안다. (2) 나는 그들이 이번 시즌에 어떤 경기도 이기지 못했음에도 불구하고 그들이 환상적이라고 생각한다. (3) 너는 점퍼를 두세 벌 입어도 여전히 추울 거다.

13 그는 정직한 사람처럼 보인다. 'seem to부정사' 구문으로 be가 적절하다.

14 Although 주어+동사 ~, 주어+동사. / Though 주어+동사, 주어+동사 ~: 비록 ~하지만 …한다.

15 • 그녀는 모든 것에 대해 걱정하는 것처럼 보인다. • Kevin은 그의 새 학교를 마음에 들어 하는 것 같아 보인다. • 아이들은 배고파 보였다.

16 ① 그 재킷은 숨겨진 주머니가 있는 것 같다. It seems that the jacket has a hidden pocket.이 적절하다. ② 너 열나는 것 같아. ③ 나는 열쇠 꾸러미를 잘 못 들고 나온 것 같다. It seems that I picked up the wrong set of keys.가 적절하다. ④ 너는 이런 소문에 대해 많이 알고 있는 것 같다. ⑤ 그는 이 제안에 동의하는 것 같지 않다.

17 어법에 맞게 배열하면, (1) Even though he is rich, I will not marry him. 또는 I will not marry him even though he is rich. (2) I seem to have a cold. (3) I seem to have forgotten something. (4) They enjoyed their day at the zoo, despite the bad weather. 또는 Despite the bad weather, they enjoyed their day at the zoo.

01 (1) seem to cry all the time / seems that they cry all the time

　(2) seems to get along with bad guys / seems that she gets along with bad guys

　(3) didn't seem to enjoy the movie

35

(4) seemed that nothing could stop the team this year

(5) seemed that she was disappointed

02 (1) He seems to be ill. / It seems that he is ill.

(2) They seem to know everything. / It seems that they know everything.

(3) It seems that he was not there.

(4) It seems that he was poisoned.

03 Although cars crashed(또는 Altough there was a car crash), no lives were lost.

04 seem to enjoy themselves

05 (1) seems to be

(2) seem to have

(3) seem to know

(4) seem to have

06 (1) It seems that

(2) It seems that

07 (1) It seems that she was angry last night.

(2) He seems to have fallen in love with the girl.

08 seems to be cold

09 (1) Although it rained, they played soccer outside. 또는 They played soccer outside although it rained.

(2) Although my younger brother ate food, he was still hungry. 또는 My younger brother was still hungry although he ate food.

(3) Although I didn't sleep much last night, I'm not tired. 또는 I'm not tired although I didn't sleep much last night.

(4) Although she was busy, she would never ask for help. 또는 She would never ask for help although she was busy.

10 Though, don't like, agree, agree, though, don't like

01 '~인 것처럼 보인다.'는 '주어 seem(s/ed) to부정사' 또는 'It seems(ed) that 주어 동사'이다.

02 '~인 것처럼 보인다'는 '주어 seem(s/ed) to부정사' 또는 'It seems(ed) that 주어 동사'이다.

03 although가 이끄는 부사절과 주절이 서로 상반된 내용이다.

04 주어+seem+to부정사

05 to부정사를 활용한 '~인 것처럼 보인다.'는 '주어 seem to부정사'로 쓴다.

06 주어와 동사가 있는 절이 나와 있으므로 'It seems(ed) that 주어 동사'로 쓴다.

07 (1) 어젯밤 그녀는 매우 화가 났던 것처럼 보인다. (2) 그는 그녀와 사랑에 빠졌던 것처럼 보인다.

08 날씨가 매우 추워 보인다.

09 Although+주어+동사 ~, 주어+동사: 비록 ~이지만 …하다.

10 Though가 이끄는 부사절과 주절의 내용은 서로 상반된다.

Reading

확인문제   p.186

1 F   2 T   3 T   4 F   5 T

확인문제   p.187

1 T   2 F   3 T   4 T   5 F   6 T

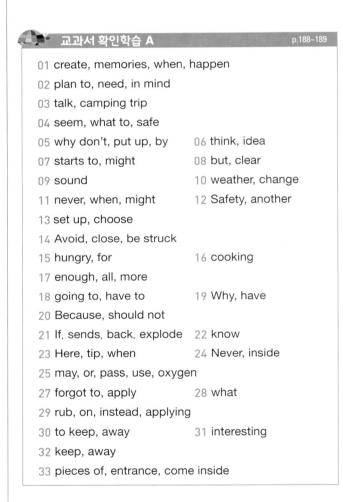

교과서 확인학습 A   p.188~189

01 create, memories, when, happen

02 plan to, need, in mind

03 talk, camping trip

04 seem, what to, safe

05 why don't, put up, by   06 think, idea

07 starts to, might   08 but, clear

09 sound   10 weather, change

11 never, when, might   12 Safety, another

13 set up, choose

14 Avoid, close, be struck

15 hungry, for   16 cooking

17 enough, all, more

18 going to, have to   19 Why, have

20 Because, should not

21 If, sends, back, explode   22 know

23 Here, tip, when   24 Never, inside

25 may, or, pass, use, oxygen

27 forgot to, apply   28 what

29 rub, on, instead, applying

30 to keep, away   31 interesting

32 keep, away

33 pieces of, entrance, come inside

교과서 확인학습 B   p.190~191

1 Although camping trips can create sweet memories for many people, they can also be occasions when bad things happen.

2 If you plan to go camping with family or friends

this summer, you need to keep several things in mind for your safety.

3 Listen to Yumin's family talk about their camping trip.

4 They seem to know what to do to make their camping trip safe and fun.

5 Yumin: Dad, why don't we put up our tent over here by this river?

6 Dad: I don't think that's a good idea.

7 If it starts to rain, the river might overflow.

8 Yumin: I know, but the sky is clear.

9 I really like the sound of the water!

10 Dad: The weather can change quickly in the mountains.

11 You never know when it might start to rain.

12 Yumin: Okay. Safety first! Let's find another place.

13 When you set up a tent, choose a flat, sunny area.

14 Avoid places too close to big trees that might be struck by lightning.

15 Hajun: Mom, I'm hungry. What's for lunch?

16 Mom: I'm cooking Samgyepsal.

17 Hajun: Mom, that's not enough for all of us. Can we cook more in a bigger pan?

18 Mom: I'm going to cook more, but we have to use this small pan.

19 Hajun: Why do we have to use a small pan?

20 Mom: Because the pan should not be bigger than the burner.

21 If you use a big pan, it sends the heat back to the burner, and the gas can explode!

22 Hajun: Oh, I didn't know that.

23 Here is one more tip about fire when you go camping.

24 Never use a gas heater or burner inside a tent.

25 Your tent may catch fire, or you might pass out because the fire will use up the oxygen in the tent as it burns.

26 Yumin: Ouch! Mosquitoes!

27 Mom: Oh, I forgot to tell you to apply some bug spray. Here.

28 Yumin: Thanks, Mom. Oh, you know what?

29 We can rub orange peels on our skin instead of applying bug spray.

30 It is a nature-friendly way to keep mosquitoes away.

31 Mom: That's interesting!

32 Garlic can also keep bugs away.

33 You can place pieces of garlic at the entrance to the tent, and bugs will not come inside.

01 ④	02 in	03 ④	04 ④
05 이쪽 강 옆에 텐트를 치는 것		06 ③	07 ②
08 explode	09 ①	10 ①	
11 camping	12 ②, ④	13 up	14 to tell
15 ④	16 ②	17 ②	
18 텐트 입구에 놓을 수 있다.		19 ④	20 ①
21 safety	22 they should do		23 ⑤
24 ②	25 ④	26 ④	

01 선행사가 occasions이므로 관계부사 when이 적절하다.

02 keep ~ in mind: ~을 명심하다

03 유민의 가족이 자주 캠핑을 가는지는 알 수 없다.

04 주어진 문장은 산에서는 날씨가 급격히 변할 수 있다는 뜻이므로 언제 비가 올지도 모른다는 문장 앞에 와야 한다.

05 that은 지시대명사로 앞에 나온 문장의 내용을 받을 수 있다.

06 강 옆은 비가 올지 몰라 위험하다는 내용이므로 '안전이 우선이다!'라는 문장이 가장 적절하다.

07 enough for ~: ~에게 충분한

08 어떤 것이 요란하게 그리고 맹렬한 기세로 터져 종종 손실이나 부상을 입히는 것은 '폭발하다(explode)'이다.

09 접속사 앞뒤의 문장이 상반되는 내용이므로 (A)는 but이 적절하다. (B)는 문맥상 작은 팬이 적절하고, (C)는 조건을 나타내는 접속사가 적절하다.

10 하준이가 왜 배가 고픈지는 알 수 없다.

11 go camping: 캠핑하러 가다

12 ⓑ, ①, ③, ⑤는 추측을 나타내고, ②, ④는 허가를 나타낸다.

13 use up: ~을 다 써버리다

14 '~할 것을 잊다'는 'forget+to부정사'가 알맞다.

15 '그거 알아요?, 있잖아요.'라고 상대방이 모르는 새로운 주제를 꺼낼 때에는 You know what?의 표현을 쓴다.

16 ⓐ, ② 형용사적 용법 ①, ⑤ 명사적 용법 ③, ④ 부사적 용법

17 유민이의 엄마가 벌레 퇴치 스프레이를 뿌렸는지는 알 수 없다.

19 빈칸 (A)와 ①, ②, ③, ⑤번에는 although가 적절하다. ④번에는 조건의 접속사 if가 알맞다.

20 keep ~ in mind: ~을 명심하다

21 safe의 명사형으로 고쳐야 한다.

22 '의문사+to부정사'는 '의문사+주어+should+동사원형'으로 바꿔 쓸 수 있다.

23 ⑤ 유민이의 가족은 안전하고 재미있는 캠핑을 할 수 있는 법을 아는 것 같다고 위 글에서 언급되었다.

24 주어진 문장은 상대방의 의견에 반대하는 내용이므로 강가에 텐트를 치자는 문장의 대답인 ②에 와야 한다.

25 ⓓ other 뒤에는 복수명사가 오므로 another로 고쳐야 한다.

26 ④ 산에서 왜 날씨가 갑자기 변하는 지는 알 수 없다.

01 hungry
02 I'm going to cook more, but we have to use this small pan.
03 Because
04 버너보다 더 큰 팬을 사용하면 팬이 버너로 열을 도로 보내서 가스가 폭발할 수 있는 것
05 Here is one more tip about fire when you go camping.
06 catch   07 of
08 벌레 퇴치 스프레이를 뿌리는 대신에 오렌지 껍질을 피부에 문지르는 것
09 She forgot to tell Yumin to apply some bug spray.
10 memories
11 in which   12 seems that, know
13 유민이의 가족은 캠핑 여행을 안전하고 재미있게 하는 방법을 아는 것처럼 보인다.

01 얼마 동안 먹지 않아서 위에 불편하거나 고통스러운 느낌이 있어서 음식을 먹기를 원하는: hungry(배가 고픈)
02 be going to와 have to, 그리고 much의 비교급 more를 이용한다.
03 이유를 나타내는 접속사 Because가 알맞다.
04 that은 지시대명사로 앞에 나온 문장을 받을 수 있다.
05 조언이 하나 더: one more tip
06 catch fire: 불이 붙다
07 instead of ~ing: ~하는 대신에 pieces of garlic: 몇 조각의 마늘
08 That은 지시대명사로 앞 문장의 내용을 받는다.
09 유민이의 어머니는 유민에게 벌레 퇴치 스프레이를 뿌리라고 말하는 것을 잊었다.
10 과거로부터 기억하는 어떤 것: memory(추억)
11 관계부사 when을 '전치사+관계대명사 which'로 바꿔 쓴다. 선행사가 occasions이므로 전치사는 in을 쓴다.
12 'seem to부정사'는 'It seems that ~' 구문으로 바꿔 쓸 수 있다.

01 ④   02 garlic   03 keep
04 (1) out   (2) up   (3) away   (4) on
05 (1) overuse   (2) overwork   (3) overeat
06 Remember 07 ⑤   08 wear
09 a helmet   10 ⑤   11 ⑤   12 ④
13 (1) The tickets seemed to have got lost.
    (2) Although[Though] the sun was shining, it wasn't very warm.

(3) The children always seem to be hungry.
(4) Although[Though] he's nearly 80, he is still very active.
14 ①   15 I don't mind even if she doesn't come.
16 Although the kitchen is small, it is well designed. 또는 Although small, the kitchen is well designed.
17 (1) didn't love him, though
    (2) is coming to stay next week although
18 he is very young / he acts like an old man
19 seems to be happy / seems to be sad
20 (1) millionaire, lives in
    (2) went out, was raining
21 despite   22 let's   23 ②, ④   24 ②
25 비가 내리기 시작하면 강이 범람할 위험이 있기 때문이다.
26 여러분이 지진으로부터 자유롭다고 생각하는 것
27 ③   28 ③   29 ②
30 Location   31 ①   32 exciting   33 ⑤

01 폭탄이 폭발하는 소리를 들었을 때 나는 경찰에게 전화를 걸었다. explode: 폭발하다
02 강한 맛을 내기 위해 요리에 사용되는 작은 양파 같은 식물에 해당하는 단어는 garlic(마늘)이다.
03 keep ~ in mind: ~을 명심하다 / 케이트, 이 교훈을 명심하라. keep 동사ing: ~을 계속하다, 반복하다 / 그녀가 그에게 설거지하라고 말해서 그는 계속해서 TV를 볼 수 없었다.
04 (1) hang out: 어울려 놀다 / 난 방과 후에 친구들이랑 자주 어울려 논다. (2) use up: ~을 다 써 버리다 / 불이 타면서 텐트 내 산소를 다 써 버릴 것입니다. (3) keep away from: ~에게서 떨어져 있다 / 그는 Billy에게 자신의 딸에게 접근하지 말라고 경고했다. (4) put on: ~을 바르다 / 밖에 나가기 전에, 선크림을 바르는 것을 잊지 마세요.
05 (1) overuse: 너무 많이 사용하다 / 컴퓨터를 너무 많이 사용하는 것은 좋지 않다. (2) overwork oneself: 과로하다 / 건강에 유념하시고, 너무 과로하지 마세요. (3) overeat: 과식하다 / 아침을 거르면 점심에 과식하기 쉽다.
06 Don't forget to+동사원형 ~.은 Remember to+동사원형 ~.으로 바꿔 쓸 수 있다.
07 ⑤를 제외한 나머지는 의무를 나타내는 표현이다. ⑤ 제가 선크림을 발라도 될까요?
08 wear: ~을 바르다
09 one은 부정대명사로 앞에 나온 'a+단수명사'를 받는다.
10 주어진 문장의 If not은 If you don't wear a helmet that fits you를 대신하는 말이므로 ⑤가 적절하다.
11 for의 목적어가 주어 자신이므로 재귀대명사를 쓴다.
12 소년이 자전거를 타다가 다쳤다는 내용은 언급되지 않았다.
13 (1), (3) 주어 seem to부정사 (2) 주어와 동사가 이어지므

로 Despite를 Although[Though]로 고쳐야 한다. (4) 부사절과 주절의 내용이 상반되므로 Because가 아니라 Although[Though]가 적절하다.

14 ① 그는 비록 경험은 가장 적지만 가장 훌륭한 선생님이다. ② 그녀는 여유가 될 때에도 절대 택시를 타지 않았다. even → even though ③ 나는 슬프지만 그들 앞에서 울 수는 없지. Because → Even though ④ 그건 거저 줘도 싫다. Even → Even if ⑤ 비록 갈 수 있다 하더라도 난 안 갈 것이다. if → even if

15 '그녀가 오지 않더라도'라는 가정이 들어가기 때문에 even if가 사용된 문장이다.

16 although가 이끄는 부사절과 주절의 내용은 상반된 의미를 갖는다.

17 although, though가 이끄는 부사절과 주절의 내용은 상반된 의미를 갖는다.

18 although가 쓰인 문장은 부사절과 주절 간 상반된 의미의 내용이 온다.

19 거북은 경기에 이겨서 행복해 보인다. 토끼는 경기에 져서 슬퍼 보인다.

20 although와 even though는 '~임에도 불구하고'라는 뜻으로 부사절과 주절 간에 상반된 내용이 온다.

21 despite는 전치사이므로 뒤에 명사나 대명사가 오고 although는 '주어+동사'가 온다.

22 Why don't we ~?는 제안을 나타내는 말로 Let's ~로 시작하는 표현으로 바꿔 쓸 수 있다.

23 ⓑ, ①, ③, ⑤는 추측을 나타내고, ②, ④는 허가를 나타낸다.

24 ② 유민이의 아빠는 위험하다고 유민이의 의견에 반대한다.

26 that은 지시대명사로 앞 문장의 내용을 받는다.

27 문맥상 '흔들림이 멈출 때까지'이므로 until이 알맞다.

28 문맥상 가스와 전기를 끄라고 해야 하므로 turn on을 turn off로 고쳐야 한다.

29 ② 흔들림이 멈출 때까지 집안에 머물고, 또 밖으로 나갈 때는 무엇인가 떨어질지도 모르므로 주의하라고 언급되었다.

30 어떤 것이 일어나거나 위치하는 장소: location(장소, 위치)

31 문맥상 '처음에는 급류 타기가 무서웠다'이므로 at first가 알맞다.

32 사물이 사람을 흥미진진하게 하는 것이므로 현재분사형의 형용사가 알맞다.

33 ⑤ 기회가 있다면 다시 가겠다고 하였다.

단원별 예상문제
p.204~207

01 shallow 02 (1) up (2) keep
03 overflow 04 ③
05 (1) try (2) stay (3) put (4) close
06 ④ 07 ⑤ 08 ①

09 drinking 10 ③
11 I'm sure that another bus will come soon.
12 (F)looding 13 ③
14 There are several things you have to do.
15 (1) Although (2) Despite (3) Although
   (4) Although (5) Despite (6) Despite
16 Although Jamin studied hard, he didn't do well on the test.
17 ①
18 (1) He seems to know the test result.
   (2) It seems that they are satisfied with the test result.
   (3) It seems that everyone is looking at my face.
   (4) Suji seems to have breakfast every day.
19 ② 20 (A) more (B) bigger
21 버너보다 더 큰 팬을 사용하면 팬이 열을 버너로 다시 보내어 가스가 폭발하는 것
22 ④ 23 ③ 24 ③
25 an earthquake 26 you can

01 주어진 단어는 반의어 관계이다. 안전 : 위험, 깊은 : 얕은

02 (1) use up: ~을 다 써버리다, put up: ~을 설치하다 (2) keep in mind: ~을 명심하다, keep ~ away from: ~을 멀리 두다

03 어떤 것의 언저리나 꼭대기 너머로 흐르다: overflow: 넘쳐흐르다, 범람하다

04 (A) instead of: ~ 대신에 (B) although: ~임에도 불구하고, 비록 ~이지만 / Despite와 In spite of는 전치사이므로 뒤에 명사나 동명사가 올 수 있다.

05 (1) try to 동사원형: ~하려고 애쓰다 (2) stay up late: 늦게까지 자지 않고 있다 (3) put on: ~을 바르다 (4) close to: ~에 가까운

06 flooding: 홍수

07 turn off: [가스·라디오·텔레비전을] 끄다

08 get to: ~에 도착하다

09 finish는 동명사를 목적어로 취한다.

10 차를 가지고 버스를 탔을 때 주의하면 괜찮을 거라고 확신한다는 내용이 적절하므로 careful(주의 깊은)이 알맞다.

11 I'm sure that ~.은 '나는 ~라고 확신해.'라는 의미이다. another+단수명사

12 위 글은 홍수가 발생했을 때의 행동 요령에 관한 글이다.

13 unpack → pack / 집을 떠날 때 물과 음식을 꾸려야 한다는 내용이 적절하다. unpack: (짐을) 풀다

14 There are ~. ~들이 있다, have to: ~해야 한다

39

15 although와 despite는 모두 '~임에도 불구하고'라는 의미를 가지지만, although는 부사절 접속사로 뒤에 '주어+동사'가 이어지고 despite는 전치사로 뒤에 명사가 이어진다. (1) 나는 열심히 공부했지만 시험에 떨어졌다. (2) 나쁜 날씨에도 불구하고, 우리는 소풍을 가기로 했던 계획을 이행하기로 결정했다 .(3) Jay는 일찍 일어났지만 평소보다 집에서 늦게 출발했다. (4) Jay는 우산을 가지고 왔지만, 여전히 비를 맞았다. (5) 우리의 염려에도 불구하고 모든 것이 잘 해결됐다. (6) 그의 울부 짖음에도 불구하고 아무도 그를 도우러 오지 않았다.

16 Although 주어 동사, 주어 동사

17 ① 비록 비싸더라도 난 그것을 사고 말 거야. although로 이끌리는 부사절과 주절 간에는 상반된 내용이 나오므로 '그것을 사고 말 것이다'와 상반되는 '못사는 상황의 내용'이 나오는 것이 적절하므로 cheap을 expensive로 고치는 것이 적절하다. ② 시험은 비록 떨어졌지만 포기하지 않을 거야 ③ 더운 날씨인데도 코트를 입고 있구나. ④ 비록 그는 모든 것을 잃었지만 난 여전히 그를 사랑합니다. ⑤ 불경기에도 불구하고 수요가 늘고 있다.

18 '~인 것처럼 보인다'는 '주어 seem(s/ed) that 주어 동사' 또는 'It seems(ed) that 주어 동사'로 나타낸다.

19 음식이 우리 모두에게 충분하지 않다는 말 다음인 ②에 와야 한다.

20 각각 much와 big의 비교급이 와야 한다.

21 that은 지시대명사로 앞에 나온 문장의 내용을 받는다.

22 ④ 하준의 엄마는 더 요리할 것이라고 말했다.

23 (A) although: 비록 ~이지만 (B) but: 그러나

24 문맥상 지진으로부터 '안전할' 수 있다가 자연스럽다.

25 it은 인칭대명사로 앞에 나온 단수명사를 받는다.

26 'as ~ as possible'은 'as ~ as 주어+can'으로 바꿔 쓸 수 있다.

01 Put on

02 I see a lot of people riding bikes without helmets

03 He is going to the park to meet a friend.

04 Because it protects our head in an accident.

05 (1) It seems that they love each other. / They seem to love each other.

(2) It seems that they loved each other. / They seem to have loved each other.

(3) It seems that Reina raises a cat at home. / Reina seems to raise a cat at home.

(4) It seems that Reina raised a cat at home. Reina seems to have raised a cat at home.

06 (1) Although, has a headache / has a headache although

(2) seem to prepare / seems that they prepare

07 During   08 up

09 I will never forget how much fun we had.

10 They baked potatoes.   11 to tell

12 applying   13 entrance

01 어떤 것을 옷, 장식 또는 보호로써 몸에 지니고 있다: put on(입다, 쓰다, 신다)

02 see+목적어+목적격보어: ~가 …하는 것을 보다

03 소년은 친구를 만나러 공원에 가고 있다.

04 사고가 났을 때 머리를 보호해 주기 때문이다.

05 (1)과 (3)은 문장 내에서 시제의 차이가 없으므로 '주어 seem(s/ed) to부정사' 또는 'It seems that 주어 동사'로 쓴다. (2)와 (4)는 문장 내에서 시제의 차이가 있으므로 완료부정사를 써야 한다.

06 (1) 그는 어젯밤 잘 잤지만 머리가 아프다. (2) 그들은 음식을 준비하는 것처럼 보인다.

07 기간을 나타내는 특정한 명사가 오므로 during이 알맞다. while 뒤에는 주어와 동사를 포함하는 부사절이 온다.

08 stay up: 깨어 있다

09 how much fun we had: 우리가 얼마나 즐겁게 지냈는지

11 forget+~ing: ~한 것을 잊다(과거의 일) forget+to부정사: ~할 것을 잊다(미래의 일)

12 전치사의 목적어이므로 동명사형이 되어야 한다.

13 어떤 장소로 들어가는 길, 예를 들면 문이나 정문: entrance(출입구)

|모범답안|

01 what I like about the product / They are very comfortable, so I wear them often / what I don't like about the product / The color of the shoes is white, so they get dirty easily / satisfied with / four stars

02 (2) → (1) → (4) → (6) → (5) → (7) → (3) → (8)

01 put   02 overuse   03 peel   04 ③

05 (C) – (B) – (D) – (A)   06 (c)ause

07 listening

08 첫째, 수도와 전기를 꺼야 한다. 둘째, 집을 떠날 때 물과 음식을 꾸려야 한다. 마지막으로, 높고 안전한 곳으로

이동하여 일기 예보를 계속 들어야 한다.

09 ④　　　　　10 ①

11 (1) seem to　(2) seems to

(3) Although 또는 Even though

(4) Although 또는 Even though

12 Even if he gets accepted to Harvard, he won't be able to afford the tuition. / You should always exercise even if it's only 10 minutes a day. / Even if the government survives this crisis, they still face big problems. / He's going to buy the farm even if the government raises the price.

13 ④

14 Even though he was born in America, he is a Korean son.

15 tried to, to have been

16 ②　　　　　17 ①　　　　　18 sunny

19 Because they might be struck by lightning.

20 ③　　　　　21 of　　　　　22 ②

23 벌레 퇴치 스프레이를 뿌리는 대신에 오렌지 껍질을 피부에 문지르는 것

24 ①　　　　　25 ③　　　　　26 ④

01 put up: 설치하다, put A on ~: ~에 A를 바르다

02 '어떤 것을 너무 많이 또는 자주 사용하다'는 'overuse (남용하다, 너무 많이 사용하다)'가 적절하다. 약을 남용하지 않도록 해라.

03 '과일의 껍질'은 peel이 적절하다. 나는 바나나 껍질을 밟고 미끄러졌다.

04 ① flat: 평평한 ② pan: 냄비 ③ overflow: 흘러넘치다, 범람하다 ④ memory: 기억, 추억 ⑤ avoid: 피하다

05 밖에 나가 놀아도 되는지 묻자 - (C) 허락하며 선크림을 바를 것을 당부한다. (B) 선크림을 발라야만 하는지 묻자 - (D) 매일 발라야 한다고 대답한다. - (A) 알겠다며 선크림을 바르겠다는 순서가 적절하다.

06 어떤 것이 발생하거나 존재하게 하다: cause(야기하다)

07 keep -ing: 계속해서 ~하다

09 • 걸어가야 한다 해도 나는 거기에 갈 것이다. • 비록 그는 나에게 거짓말을 했지만 난 그를 믿어.

10 미국에 살고 있지만 영어를 말하는 데에 어려움을 겪고 있다. even though는 부사절과 주절 간의 내용이 서로 상반되므로 주절의 '영어를 말하는 데 어려움을 겪고 있다'는 내용과 반대 의미를 지니려면 live가 적절하다.

11 (1), (2) '~인 것 같다', '~처럼 보인다'는 'seem to'를 사용한다. (3), (4) '비록 ~이지만'은 although[though] 또는 even though 등을 쓴다.

12 • 하버드에서 그를 받아주더라도, 그는 수업료를 감당하지 못할 것이다. • 하루에 10분이라도 넌 운동해야 한다. • 정부가 간신히 위기를 넘기더라도 그들은 여전히 수 많은 문제에 직면해 있다. • 정부가 가격을 올리더라도 그는 농장을 살 것이다.

13 ④ '주어+동사'가 이어지므로 Despite를 Although 또는 Even though로 바꿔야 한다.

14 부사절의 내용은 '태어났지만'이고 주절은 '대한민국의 아들이다'이므로 even though를 사용하여 '미국에서 태어났지만'을 쓰고, 주절에는 '그는 대한민국의 아들이다'를 쓴다.

15 엄마는 다림질을 시도했지만 잘 되지 않았다. 다리미는 고장 난 것처럼 보인다. 시제가 앞서므로 완료부정사를 이용한다.

16 ② make의 목적보어이므로 형용사 safe가 적절하다.

17 (A) '무엇을 해야 할지'이므로 what to do가 알맞다. (B) '우리 ~하는 게 어때요?'이므로 Why don't we ~?가 알맞다.

18 sun의 형용사형은 sunny이다.

19 큰 나무들은 번개를 맞을지도 모르므로 피하라고 하였다.

20 주어진 문장은 '아, 그거 아세요?'의 뜻으로 새로운 사실을 언급할 때 흔히 쓰이므로 ③에 와야 한다.

21 instead of: ~하는 대신에 pieces of garlic: 마늘 몇 조각

22 ⓐ, ② 형용사적 용법 ①, ④ 명사적 용법 ③, ⑤ 부사적 용법

23 that은 지시대명사로 앞에 나온 문장의 내용을 받는다.

24 ① '이틀간의 캠핑 여행'이란 뜻으로 two-day가 camping trip을 수식하는 것이므로 단수형인 two-day가 적절하다.

25 (A)와 ③의 may는 '~일지도 모르다'의 뜻으로 약한 추측을 나타낸다.

26 so (that) 주어+can ~: ~하기 위해서

Coach Carter

교과서 Reading

확인문제   p.218

1 T   2 F   3 T   4 F   5 T   6 F

확인문제   p.219

1 T   2 F   3 F   4 T   5 T

확인문제   p.220

1 T   2 T   3 F   4 F   5 F

교과서 확인학습 A   p.221~223

01 Welcome to
02 going to talk
03 imagine, allow, to practice
04 what, does
05 cares, about, about winning games
06 one, after another
07 became used to losing
08 To make, worse, only to play
09 new coach
10 to change
11 how to play
12 more than, by sending
13 To carry out, contract
14 had to, in addition to
15 At first, seriously
16 give you a contract
17 Attend, be late
18 all these rules
19 signing bonus
20 because, as well as
21 With, in many years
22 From, point on, after
23 except
24 part of
25 Few of, paid little attention to
26 take, action
27 let, play, until, improved, as
28 it
29 that, just, not
30 basketball team
31 All we see
32 If, yourself, better life
33 to help
34 have to
35 either
36 demand, ordered, to reopen

37 Disappointed, decided to
38 When, to pack, were
39 what happens next
40 Find out, by watching

교과서 확인학습 B   p.224~226

1 Welcome to *Movie Trip*.
2 Today we're going to talk about the movie *Coach Carter*.
3 Can you imagine a basketball coach who doesn't allow his players to practice?
4 That's exactly what Coach Carter does.
5 This movie is about a coach who cares more about his students than about winning games.
6 The basketball team at Richmond High School in Richmond, California, was having one losing season after another.
7 The players became used to losing.
8 To make matters worse, they had no plans for the future; they went to school only to play basketball, and they did not do that very well.
9 Then they got a new coach, Kenny Carter.
10 Coach Carter wanted to change things.
11 He wanted to teach kids how to play basketball well and win.
12 But more than that, he wanted to give the players a future by sending them to college.
13 To carry out his plan, Coach Carter had the players sign a contract.
14 They had to promise to study hard in addition to playing basketball.
15 At first, students did not take his idea for a contract seriously.
16 Carter: I'm going to give you a contract.
17 Cruz: "Attend all classes," "Get a C⁺ or higher," "Don't be late…."
18 What are all these rules about?
19 Do I get a signing bonus for signing this contract?
20 Carter: Yes. You will get a big bonus because you will become a winner in the game of basketball as well as in the game of life.
21 With hard work and a new game plan, the team began to win for the first time in many years.
22 From that point on, they won game after game.
23 Everybody, except Coach Carter, was happy.
24 The players did not do the "study" part of their contract.

25 Few of them actually believed they could go to college, so they paid little attention to their grades.

26 Carter decided to take stronger action.

27 He locked the gym and refused to let them play basketball until their grades improved, as promised in the contract.

28 The players did not like it.

29 They told him that his actions were just for him, not for them.

30 Worm: We're the basketball team.

31 All we see is you on TV, getting famous.

32 Carter: If you think so, go home and ask yourself, "Do I want a better life?"

33 If the answer is yes, I will do everything in my power to help you.

34 But you have to do your part.

35 The players' parents did not like Carter's decision either.

36 At the parents' demand, the principal ordered Carter to reopen the gym.

37 Disappointed, Carter decided to leave Richmond High.

38 When he entered the gym to pack his things, however, all of his players were there.

39 We want you to enjoy the movie, so we won't tell you what happens next.

40 Find out for yourself by watching the movie *Coach Carter*.

서술형 실전문제
p.227~229

01 unlock

02 (1) for the first time (2) carry out (3) take action
　(4) one after another

03 (1) sign (2) contract (3) except

04 (1) improve (2) attend (3) order (4) pack

05 (1) when (2) to wash (3) too

06 (1) Mr. Brown let his son go to the party.
　(2) The project manager had us meet at 9 a.m.
　(3) They made me repeat the whole story.
　(4) She helped me to complete this assignment.

07 (1) What I want to do for the community is to pick up trash.
　(2) I liked what Yuna gave to me last month.
　(3) Did you enjoy what we saw at the movie theater last night?

08 He has experience as well as knowledge.

09 ⓐ out ⓑ to　　10 seriously

11 what　　12 winning

13 To make matters worse

14 그들은 농구를 별로 잘하지 못했다

15 how

16 (1) 아이들에게 농구를 잘해서 이기는 법을 가르치기를 원했다.
　(2) 아이들을 대학에 보내서 그들에게 미래를 주기를 원했다.

17 after　　18 little

19 Because the players did not do the "study" part of their contract.

20 Carter는 체육관을 잠그고 선수들의 성적이 향상될 때까지 농구를 못하게 했다.

01 주어진 관계는 반의어 관계이다. lock: 잠그다 : unlock: 열다

02 (1) for the first time: 처음으로 (2) carry out: 이행하다 (3) take action: 조치를 취하다 (4) one after another: 잇따라서

03 (1) sign: 서명하다 (2) contract: 계약서 (3) except: ~을 제외하고

04 (1) 어떤 것을 더 나아지게 하다: improve(향상시키다) (2) 행사, 모임 등에 참석하다: attend(참석하다) (3) 권위를 사용하여 누군가에게 어떤 일을 하라고 시키다: order(명령하다) (4) 어떤 것을 가져갈 수 있도록 가방, 여행 가방 등에 넣다: pack((짐을) 꾸리다)

05 (1) '너는 언제 이곳에 다시 올지 아니?'의 뜻이므로 when이 알맞다. (2) order는 목적보어로 to부정사를 취한다. (3) too ... to ~: 너무 …해서 ~하지 못하다

06 (1) let+목적어+원형부사(go) (2) have+목적어+원형부사(meet) (3) make+목적어+원형부사(repeat) (4) help+목적어+to부정사[원형부사](to complete) 등에 유의하여 영작한다.

07 what은 선행사를 포함한 관계대명사로 '~하는 것'으로 해석하며, the thing(s) which[that]를 나타낸다.

08 not only A but also B = B as well as A: A뿐만 아니라 B도. B에 강조의 초점이 맞춰져 있다.

09 carry out: ~을 실행하다 in addition to: ~ 외에도

10 동사 take를 수식하는 부사형으로 고친다.

11 선행사를 포함하는 관계대명사 what이 알맞다.

12 전치사의 목적어이므로 동명사 winning이 알맞다.

13 to make matters worse: 설상가상으로

14 do that은 앞에 언급된 play basketball을 받는다.

15 how to play basketball well: 농구를 어떻게 하면 잘하는지

16 위 글의 마지막 두 문장의 내용을 쓰면 된다.

17 win game after game: 경기를 연달아 이기다

43

18 '주의를 거의 기울이지 않았다'는 부정의 의미이므로 little이 알맞다. a little은 긍정의 의미이다.

p.230~234

단원별 예상문제

01 (1) exactly (2) lock (3) college (4) coach
   (5) imagine
02 ④   03 ④   04 refusal   05 ③
06 (1) carry (2) make (3) pay (4) take
07 demand   08 ③   09 ②   10 ④
11 (1) I will wait here until you come back.
   (2) He spoke clearly so (that) we might hear him
       well.
   (3) I want to know if[whether] she can sleep in this
       noisy place.
   (4) He has not been practicing dancing since last
       Friday.
   (5) She felt too hungry to keep walking.
   (6) He danced so well that he won (the) first
       prize.
12 ④   13 ③
14 (1) I should do (2) I should[could] open
   (3) he should[can] get
15 ③   16 losing   17 play basketball
18 ②   19 ①   20 Attend at → Attend
21 rules   22 ④   23 ④
24 From that point on, they won game after game.
25 ③
26 Carter 코치가 체육관에 자물쇠를 채우고 선수들의 성적이
   향상될 때까지 농구 경기를 하도록 허락하지 않은 것
27 ②   28 getting
29 우리가 보는 것은 오직 유명해져서 TV에 나오는 당신을
   보는 것
30 ④   31 decision   32 Disappointed
33 (A) to reopen   (B) entered   (C) yourself
34 ④

01 (1) exactly: 정확히 (2) lock: 잠그다 (3) college: 대학 (4) coach (스포츠 팀의) 코치 (5) imagine: 상상하다
02 계약의 내용을 적은 서류를 의미하는 단어는 'contract(계약서)'이다.
03 except: ~을 제외하고
04 주어진 단어는 동사와 명사의 관계이다. refuse는 뒤에 -al을 붙여 명사형을 만든다. decide: 결정하다 decision: 결정, refuse: 거절하다 refusal: 거절
05 order: 명령하다, 주문하다
06 (1) carry out: 이행하다 (2) to make matters worse: 설

상가상으로 (3) pay attention to: ~에 주의를 기울이다 (4) take action: 조치를 취하다
07 어떤 것을 해야 한다거나 또는 받아야 한다는 강력한 주장을 의미하는 단어는 'demand(요구)'이다.
08 ③ That he says의 선행사가 없으므로 That을 선행사를 포함하는 관계대명사 What으로 고쳐야 한다.
09 ② make는 사역동사이므로 원형부정사를 목적보어로 취한다.
10 ① what → that[which] ② That → What ③ what → that[which] ⑤ that → what
11 (1) until이 이끄는 부사절에서는 미래의 일이라도 현재형을 쓴다. (2) 목적을 나타내는 so that 주어+may[can] ~ 구문에서 구어체에서는 that을 생략할 수 있다. (3) 명사절을 이끄는 접속사 if[whether]를 이용한다. (4) 현재완료진행의 부정문을 이용한다. (5) 'so ~ that 주어 can't ⋯ = too ~ to ⋯: 너무 ~해서 ⋯할 수 없다' 구문을 이용한다. (6) 'so ~ that ... 구문을 이용한다.
12 have 대신에 get을 쓸 수 있다. have는 사역동사이므로 원형부정사를 목적보어로 취하지만, get은 to부정사를 목적보어로 취한다.
13 let 대신에 allow를 쓸 수 있다. let은 사역동사이므로 원형부정사를 목적보어로 취하지만, allow는 to부정사를 목적보어로 취한다.
14 '의문사+to부정사'는 '의문사+주어+should[can] ~'으로 바꿔 쓸 수 있다.
15 hear는 지각동사이므로 원형부정사를 목적보어로 취한다. allow는 to부정사를 목적보어로 취한다.
16 become used to ~ing: ~하는 데 익숙해지다
17 do that은 앞에 언급된 play basketball을 받는다.
18 문맥상 '아이들에게 어떻게 하면 농구를 잘하고 이기는지 가르쳐 주고 싶었다'라고 하는 것이 적절하다.
19 ① 왜 그 농구팀이 연달아 경기에 졌는지는 위 글의 내용으로 보아 알 수 없다.
20 attend는 타동사이므로 목적어 앞에 전치사가 필요없다.
21 당신에게 어떤 것은 할 수 있고 어떤 것은 할 수 없다고 말해 주는 지시들: rules(규칙, 원칙)
22 문맥상 이유를 나타내는 접속사가 알맞다.
23 let은 사역동사이므로 목적보어로 원형부정사를 취한다.
24 '경기를 연달아 이겼다'의 뜻으로 전치사 after에 연결되어 관용적으로 쓰일 때는 부정관사 a를 붙이지 않는다.
25 문맥상 결과를 나타내는 접속사가 알맞다.
26 it은 인칭대명사로 앞에 나온 문장을 받는다.
27 ② Carter를 제외한 모든 사람이 행복해 했다고 언급되었다.
28 '유명해지면서'의 뜻으로 능동의 의미를 나타내므로 현재분사형이 알맞다.
29 so는 지시대명사로 앞에 나온 내용을 받는다.

30 ©, ④ 부사적 용법 ①, ⑤ 형용사적 용법 ②, ③ 명사적 용법

31 decide의 명사형이 와야 한다.

32 분사구문으로 수동의 의미이므로 과거분사로 고쳐야 한다.

33 (A) order는 to부정사를 목적보어로 취한다. (B) enter가 '~에 들어가다'의 뜻일 때는 전치사 없이 목적어를 취한다. (C) 전치사 for의 목적어가 주어 자신이므로 재귀대명사를 취한다.

34 선수들이 Carter가 리치몬드 고등학교를 떠나는 것을 환영했는지는 알 수 없다.

교과서 파헤치기

Lesson 1

01 운동선수	02 축하하다, 기념하다	
03 ~할 때마다	04 시합	05 존경하다
06 결정하다	07 유명한	08 일어나다
09 열정	10 부상을 입히다	11 사고
12 대표하다	13 대중	14 깨닫다
15 존중하다	16 부상	17 받다
18 다치다	19 거짓말	20 연습
21 갑자기	22 부근의; 부근에	
23 관료, 공무원, 경기 임원		24 식, 의식
25 개발자	26 특별히	27 훈련
28 실험하다	29 준비	30 작가
31 환호성을 지르다, 환호하다		32 제거하다
33 외치다	34 ~쪽으로, ~을 향하여	
35 ~에 관심이 많다	36 포기하다	37 독학하다
38 ~을 자랑스러워하다		39 결과적으로
40 ~을 끝내다	41 나타내다, 상징하다	
42 ~에 다가가다	43 멀리 뒤처진	

01 realize	02 competition	03 decide
04 practice	05 developer	06 remove
07 hurt	08 accident	09 ceremony
10 represent	11 cheer	12 finish line
13 admire/respect		14 injury
15 athlete	16 author	17 injure
18 celebration	19 experiment	20 public
21 happen	22 nearby	23 knock
24 suddenly	25 toward	26 official
27 passion	28 accept	29 preparation
30 whenever	31 prepare	32 especially
33 winner	34 training	35 stand for
36 give up	37 far behind	38 be into
39 be done with	40 come up to	41 teach oneself
42 as a result	43 be proud of	

1 author, 작가　2 far, 멀리　3 accept, 받다
4 athlete, 운동선수　5 passion, 열정　6 realize, 깨닫다
7 remove, 없애다　8 toward, ~을 향해서
9 give up, 포기하다　10 injury, 부상　11 training, 훈련
12 marathon, 마라톤　13 represent, 대표하다
14 stadium, 경기장　15 reporter, 리포트, 기자
16 congratulate, 축하하다

Listen & Speak 1 Listen

1. How, able to, runner / ran, every day
2. able, basketball / short, practiced shooting three-point
3. How, able, speak, well / learned, watching
4. How, become, reporter / practiced speaking, public

Listen & Speak 1-A

1. How, able / think, invented, first try, true / really / Whenever, experimented / why, admire
2. How, final, players, competition / could, only after, training / playing tennis / started to play, seven

Listen & Speak 2 Listen

1. Have, heard, winner, contest / haven't, won / winner, own
2. Have, heard, guitar player / taught herself
3. heard, world famous dance / watched, many times
4. heard, photographer / haven't, kind of pictures, take / takes, of street

Listen & Speak 2-A

1. Have, heard, cartoon / interested in drawing cartoons / want to be, join / know, interested, drawing
2. Have, heard / what / stands, into, making, pencil case / What, after, finish / done, pencil, planning to make, desk

Real-Life Zone

Have, heard of, skier / Who, he / skier, won, medal / great / was, accident, early twenties, hurt / able to become / accident, several, get, especially, in skiing / Skiing, are good / why, respected

Wrap Up

heard, fire / heard, was, nearby, hurt / one, saved, were / How, able to save / knocked, every door, tell, leave / amazing

Listen & Speak 1 Listen

1. B: How was she able to become a great runner?

G: She ran 3 kilometers every day.

2. G: How was he able to become a basketball player?

B: He was short, but he practiced shooting three-point shots a lot.

3. B: How was she able to speak English so well?

G: She learned English by watching many Hollywood movies.

4. G: How was he able to become a famous reporter?

B: He practiced speaking with people in public.

Listen & Speak 1-A

1. B: How was Thomas Edison able to invent so many things?

G: Many people think that he invented things on his first try, but that's not true.

B: Oh, really?

G: Yes. Whenever he invented something, he experimented many times.

B: Maybe that's why so many people admire him.

2. G: How was Hyeon Chung able to be one of the final four players in the tennis competition?

B: He could do it only after years of hard training.

G: I see. When did he start playing tennis?

B: He started to play tennis when he was seven.

Listen & Speak 2 Listen

1. B: Have you heard of the winner of the singing contest?

G: No, I haven't. Who won?

B: The winner is Vintop, who wrote all of his own songs.

2. G: Have you heard of Mia, the guitar player?

B: Yes, I have. I heard that she taught herself to play.

3. B: Have you heard about BTG, the world famous dance group?

G: Yes, I have. I have watched their video many times on the Internet.

4. G: Have you heard of Jiho, the photographer?

B: No, I haven't. What kind of pictures does he take?

G: He usually takes pictures of street artists.

Listen & Speak 2-A

1. B: Have you heard about the cartoon club, Edutoon?

G: Yes, I have. Are you interested in drawing cartoons?

B: Yes, I want to be a famous cartoon writer, so I want to join that club.

G: Oh, I didn't know that you're interested in drawing cartoons.

2. G: Have you heard of D.I.Y.?

B: No, what is D.I.Y.?

G: D.I.Y. stands for 'do-it-yourself.' I'm really into it. Right now, I'm making a pencil case.

B: What are you going to make after you finish that?

G: When I'm done with the pencil case, I'm planning to make my own desk.

Real-Life Zone

G: Have you heard of Eui Hyun Sin, the skier?

B: No. Who is he?

G: He's a Paralympian skier. He won the first gold medal for Korea in the 2018 Winter Paralympics.

B: Wow! That's great.

G: He was in a car accident in his early twenties and hurt his legs.

B: How was he able to become a skier?

G: After his accident, he tried several different sports to get better. Then he became especially interested in skiing.

B: Skiing is not easy. Not many people are good at skiing.

G: That's why he's so respected.

Wrap Up

B: Sora, have you heard about the fire last night?

G: Yes, I heard that there was a big fire in a building nearby. Was anybody hurt?

B: No, one man saved ten people who were in the building.

G: Oh, really? How was he able to save so many people?

B: He knocked on every door to tell people to leave the building.

G: Wow, that's amazing!

01 Last Runner

02 finished, more than, before

03 no more, coming, officials

04 removed, prepare, closing ceremony

05 shouted, There, another runner

06 entering, something wrong with

07 kept going toward
08 volunteers stopped, preparations, ceremony
09 All eyes, on, runner
10 Suddenly, celebration music, cheered
11 Go for it
12 ran, finish line with
13 Finally, ran through, fell
14 His name was
15 was from
16 came up to, asking
17 happened to
18 injured, during, practice run
19 got worse, give up
20 Why not
21 that, far behind, win
22 only athlete, representing Afghanistan
23 no way, give up
24 at war, isn't it
25 have been, for
26 That's why, able, athletes
27 sad for, back then
28 Were, running, then
29 started running after
30 lots of races
31 won a marathon
32 As, result, able to
33 How, feel
34 proud of myself, from
35 not to give up
36 didn't come, to win
37 enough to, finish, race

26 That's why, able to
27 was sad for, back then, opening ceremony
28 Were, running
29 started running
30 lots of races
31 won a marathon
32 As a result
33 How, feel
34 proud of myself, to be from
35 not to give up
36 to win
37 it was enough, to finish

본문 TEST Step 2   p.11~12

01 Last Runner
02 finished, more than
03 no more, coming, officials
04 removed, finish line, prepare for, closing ceremony
05 shouted, There comes another
06 something wrong with
07 Still, kept going toward
08 stopped their preparations, closing ceremony
09 All eyes were on
10 Suddenly, celebration music, volunteers cheered
11 Go for it
12 with a tape
13 Finally, ran through, fell to
14 His name
15 was from
16 came up to, started asking
17 happened to
18 injured, during a practice run
19 got worse during, give up
20 Why not
21 far behind
22 only athlete, representing Afghanistan
23 no way, give up
24 at war, isn't it
25 have been, for

본문 TEST Step 3   p.13~14

1 마지막 주자
2 마지막 주자가 한 시간도 더 전에 경주를 끝냈다.
3 "더 들어오는 선수는 없을 겁니다."라고 경기 임원들은 결론을 내렸다.
4 그들은 결승선에서 테이프를 걷어내고 1996년 미국 애틀랜타 하계 올림픽의 폐막식을 준비하기 시작했다.
5 누군가가 외쳤다. "봐! 저기 또 다른 선수가 온다!"
6 한 선수가 경기장으로 막 들어오고 있었는데, 그의 다리에 이상이 있었다.
7 그러나 그는 계속 결승선을 향해 움직였다.
8 밴드와 자원봉사자들이 폐막식을 위한 준비를 멈추었다.
9 모든 눈들이 그 선수에게 머물렀다.
10 갑자기 밴드가 축하 음악을 연주하기 시작했고, 자원봉사자들이 환호했다.
11 "달려! 달려! 잘해라!"
12 두 명의 자원봉사자가 테이프를 가지고 결승선으로 달려갔다.
13 결국, 그 주자는 테이프를 통과해 달렸고, 바닥에 쓰러졌다.
14 그의 이름은 압둘 베사르 와시키였다.
15 그는 아프가니스탄 출신이었다.
16 기자들은 와시키에게 가서 그에게 질문을 하기 시작했다.
17 리포터: 당신에게 무슨 일이 있었나요?
18 와시키: 저는 연습 경기를 하던 중 다리를 다쳤습니다.
19 경기 중에 제 상처는 점점 더 심각해졌지만, 저는 포기할 수 없었습니다.
20 리포터: 왜 포기할 수 없었죠?
21 당신은 메달을 얻기에 너무도 크게 뒤떨어져 있었다는 것을 알고 있었잖아요.
22 와시키: 저는 아프가니스탄을 대표하는 유일한 선수입니다.
23 제가 포기할 수 있는 방법은 없었습니다.
24 리포터: 아프가니스탄은 여전히 전쟁 중입니다. 맞죠?
25 와시키: 네, 우리나라는 16년째 전쟁 중입니다.
26 그것이 우리가 4년 전 바르셀로나 올림픽에 선수들을 보낼 수 없었던 이유입니다.
27 저는 개회식에서 아프가니스탄 선수를 볼 수 없었던 그 당시, 제 나라에 대해 매우 슬펐습니다.
28 리포터: 그 당시 마라톤을 뛰고 있었나요?

29 와시키: 아니요. 저는 바르셀로나 올림픽 이후에 달리기를 시작했습니다.

30 저는 많은 경주에서 뛰었어요.

31 마침내 독일 마라톤에서 우승했지요.

32 그 결과 애틀랜타에 올 수 있었어요.

33 리포터: 지금은 기분이 어떠신가요?

34 와시키: 저는 제 자신이, 그리고 제가 아프가니스탄 출신인 것이 자랑스러워요.

35 저와 제 조국을 위해서는, 포기하지 않는 것이 중요했어요.

36 저는 이곳에 이기러 온 것이 아닙니다.

37 제가 여기에 있고 경주를 끝마친 것으로 충분합니다.

본문 TEST Step 4-Step 5   p.15~18

1 The Last Runner

2 The last runner finished the race more than an hour before.

3 "There will be no more runners coming," the officials decided.

4 They removed the tape at the finish line and started to prepare for the closing ceremony for the 1996 Atlanta Summer Olympics in the United States.

5 Someone shouted, "Look! There comes another runner!"

6 A runner was just entering the stadium, but there was something wrong with his legs.

7 Still, he kept going toward the finish line.

8 The band and the volunteers stopped their preparations for the closing ceremony.

9 All eyes were on the runner.

10 Suddenly, the band started playing celebration music, and the volunteers cheered.

11 "Go! Go! Go for it!"

12 Two volunteers ran to the finish line with a tape.

13 Finally, the runner ran through the tape and then fell to the ground.

14 His name was Abdul Baser Wasiqi.

15 He was from Afghanistan.

16 Reporters came up to Wasiqi and started asking him questions.

17 Reporter: What happened to you?

18 Wasiqi: I injured my leg during a practice run.

19 The injury got worse during the race, but I couldn't give up.

20 Reporter: Why not?

21 You knew that you were too far behind to win a medal.

22 Wasiqi: I am the onlya athlete here representing Afghanistan.

23 There was no way I could give up.

24 Reporter: Afghanistan is still at war, isn't it?

25 Wasiqi: Yes, we have been at war for 16 years.

26 That's why we were not able to send athletes to the Barcelona Olympics four years ago.

27 I was sad for my country back then when I could see no Afghan athletes in the opening ceremony.

28 Reporter: Were you running marathons then?

29 Wasiqi: No. I started running after Barcelona.

30 I ran in lots of races.

31 Finally I won a marathon in Germany.

32 As a result, I was able to come to Atlanta.

33 Reporter: How do you feel now?

34 Wasiqi: I am proud of myself and proud to be from Afghanistan.

35 For me and my country, it was important not to give up.

36 I didn't come here to win.

37 For me, it was enough to be here and to finish the race.

구석구석지문 TEST Step 1   p.19

Communication Task

1. Have, heard of

2. a famous rock climber

3. was, able to become

4. for five hours every day

Language in Use B

1. set my clock, not to be late for

2. Because, a long way to, it, not to miss

3. Without having breakfast, left, went to

4. Surprisingly, was nobody

5. Then, remembered that

6. From now on, let, happen, what day it is

Writing Workshop Step 3

1. Have a Goal to Win

2. want to win, singing contest

3. I think, have a good voice

4. However, too shy to sing in front of

5. Not to be nervous, practice singing in front of

Communication Task

1. A: Have you heard of Jain Kim?
2. B: Yes, I have. She's a famous rock climber.
3. A: How was she able to become a famous rock climber?
4. B: She trained hard for five hours every day.

Language in Use B

1. Last night, I set my clock for 8 o'lock not to be late for school today.
2. Because it is a long way to my school, it is important not to miss the bus.
3. Without having breakfast, I quickly left the house and went to the bus stop.
4. Surprisingly, there was nobody.
5. Then, I remembered that today was Saturday.
6. From now on, not to let it happen again, I will always check what day it is.

Writing Workshop Step 3

1. I Have a Goal to Win the Singing Contest
2. I want to win the school singing contest.
3. I love singing, and I think I have a good voice.
4. However, I am too shy to sing in front of many people.
5. Not to be nervous during the contest, I will practice singing in front of my class first.

01 피하다	02 카운슬러, 상담역	03 최근에
04 증명하다, 입증하다		05 쉬다
06 실험	07 아직도	08 인기 있는
09 어휘	10 최신의	11 관리
12 걱정하는, 불안한	13 결승, 기말고사; 마지막의	
14 문제	15 다치다	16 시합
17 기분이 상한	18 부분, 배역, 역할	19 단백질
20 도움이 되는	21 동의하지 않다	22 운동화
23 오해하다	24 엄격한	25 청소년
26 결정하다	27 매우 싫어하다	28 걱정; 걱정하다
29 실수	30 번호를 매기다	31 웅변대회
32 체육 교사	33 충고하다	34 과제
35 유행하는, 유행되는		
36 당분간은, 현재로는		
37 ~에게 데이트를 신청하다		
38 ~하지 않고, ~ 없이		39 집중하다
40 결국 ~하게 되다 41 오랫동안		
42 ~하는 데 어려움이 있다		43 더 이상 ~가 아닌

01 upset	02 counselor	03 decide
04 match	05 experiment	06 strict
07 avoid	08 matter	09 popular
10 prove	11 hate	
12 speech contest		13 misunderstand
14 still	15 disagree	16 protein
17 helpful	18 sneakers	19 final
20 vocabulary	21 latest	22 management
23 part	24 hurt	25 project
26 advise	27 P.E. teacher	28 number
29 relax	30 mistake	31 teenager
32 worry	33 recently	34 try
35 not ~ anymore	36 in style	37 focus on
38 for now	39 end up -ing	40 for a long time
41 do one's part		
42 have a hard time -ing		43 be ready for

1 recently, 최근에 2 latest, 최신의 3 sneakers, 운동화

4 avoid, 피하다 5 hate, 매우 싫어하다

6 vocabulary, 어휘 7 disagree, 동의하지 않다

8 worry, 걱정 9 popular, 인기 있는 10 mistake, 실수

11 prove, 증명하다, 입증하다 12 teenager, 청소년

13 agree, 동의하다 14 counselor, 카운슬러, 상담역

15 experiment, 실험 16 relax, 쉬다

Listen & Speak 1 Listen

1. listening to, helps, relax / agree

2. reading, comic books, helpful / learn, from

3. festival, lot, fun

4. teacher, strict, Don't, agree / don't, strict

Listen & Speak 1 A

1. told, use, for only one hour, day, enough / agree with / doing, need, for a long time / get together, talk / for, understanding

2. just, about, project / decided what, do / not, visit, wants to, experiment / agree with / with, because, experiment, interesting

Listen & Speak 2 Listen

1. have, match, nervous / Don't worry, sure, play

2. nervous, speech contest / sure, do, worry

3. worried, friends, school / Don't, sure, make, friends

Listen & Speak 2 A

1. worried, something wrong / upset with / Why, do / wore one of, without / sorry, understand

2. having, learning / had, asked, teacher for advice / What / advised, use, vocabulary, sure, work for

Real-Life Zone

project, taking / agree, One of, people, doing, part / That's, team / know, know how to get, to / doesn't, get started, like, part / what, do / to, why, doing, Then, you'll, if, wants / try / sure, better after, talk, with, project

Wrap Up

matter, look worried / ready, finals, desk, study, up, something else / management, easy / agree, should / Number, have, Then, down, much, you need to finish / try / that, helpful, luck with

Listen & Speak 1 Listen

1. B: I think listening to music helps you relax.
   G: I agree.

2. G: I think reading history comic books is helpful.
   B: I agree. I learn a lot from them.

3. G: Our school festival is going to be a lot of fun.
   B: I agree.

4. B: Our P.E. teacher is too strict. Don't you agree?
   G: No, I don't agree. I don't think he's too strict.

Listen & Speak 1 A

1. G: Mom told me I could use the computer for only one hour a day. She thinks that's enough time.
   M: I agree with her.
   G: Sometimes, when doing my homework, I need to use it for a long time.
   M: Hmm. Then maybe we should all get together and talk about it.
   G: Thanks for your understanding, Dad.

2. B: I just talked about the science project with Jinho and Mina.
   G: Has your team decided what you will do?
   B: No, not yet. Jinho wants to visit a science museum, but Mina wants to do an experiment.
   G: Who do you agree with, Jinho or Mina?
   B: I agree with Mina because I think the experiment would be more interesting.

Listen & Speak 2 Listen

1. B: I have a big soccer match tomorrow. I'm nervous.
   G: Don't worry. I'm sure you'll play very well.

2. G: I'm nervous about tomorrow's speech contest.
   B: I'm sure you'll do fine. Don't worry.

3. G: I'm worried about making friends at my new school.
   M: Don't worry. I'm sure you'll make a lot of friends there.

Listen & Speak 2 A

1. B: You look worried. Is something wrong?
   G: Yes, my sister is upset with me.
   B: Why? What did you do?
   G: I wore one of her shirts without asking.
   B: Tell her you're sorry. I'm sure she'll understand.

2. B: I'm having a hard time learning new English words.
   G: I had the same problem, so I asked my English teacher for advice.
   B: What did he say?
   G: He advised me to use an English vocabulary

app. It has helped me a lot. I'm sure it would work for you, too.

Real-Life Zone

B: The team project for English class is taking a lot of time.

G: I agree. I have a problem. One of the people on our team isn't doing his part.

B: That's not good. Everybody on the team has to do their job.

G: I know, but I don't know how to get him to do his part.

B: Maybe he doesn't know how to get started or doesn't like his part.

G: Then what should I do?

B: Talk to him. Ask him why he's not doing his part. Then tell him you'll help him if he wants.

G: Okay. I'll try that.

B: I'm sure he'll do better after you talk to him. Good luck with your project.

G: Thanks.

Wrap Up

G: What's the matter, Dongha? You look worried.

B: I'm not ready for the finals. I sit at my desk to study but end up doing something else.

G: Well, time management is not easy.

B: I agree. What should I do?

G: Number the things you have to do. Then write down how much time you need to finish each one.

B: Thank you, Emily. I'll try your idea.

G: I'm sure that will be helpful for you. Good luck with your finals.

본문 TEST Step 1　　　　　　　　　　p.28~29

01 Should, Do　　　　02 Everyone, worries

03 When, things, worry

04 Here, things, teenagers. about

05 has changed, is avoiding　06 older, don't you

07 What about　　　　08 feel, avoiding

09 turns around, walks away

10 sorry to hear　　　11 why she does that

12 done anything wrong

13 feels like, doesn't, anymore

14 should, if, something wrong

15 Maybe, should, still, with

16 thinking, popular, just because

17 at, new sneakers　　18 What, think

---

19 didn't you, couple of　20 no longer in style

21 look cooler, right

22 wearing, latest, cooler, popular

23 because you're you, clothes

25 a great guy　　　　26 need, to prove

27 Recently, asked out, class

28 say, but, hurt, feelings　29 need, advice

30 asked me out　　　31 for now, go out

32 need to focus on　　33 should, do

34 Why don't you, can't　35 afraid, hurt, feelings

36 misunderstand, end up hurting

37 Maybe, right　　　38 Thanks for, advice

본문 TEST Step 2　　　　　　　　　　p.30~31

01 What Should　　　　02 has worries

03 worry, what do you do

04 Here are some things, worry about

05 her best friend, has changed, is avoiding

06 older, don't you　　07 What about

08 I feel, avoiding

09 turns around, walks away from

10 to hear that　　　11 why she does that

12 I've done anything wrong

13 feels like, doesn't, anymore

14 Maybe, should, if, something wrong

15 still, with

16 thinking, make, popular, just because

17 look at, new sneakers　18 What, think

19 didn't you, couple of months ago

20 no longer in style　　21 cooler in these

22 wearing, latest fashion, cooler, more popular

23 because you're you, because of

25 a great guy　　　　26 to prove it

27 was asked out　　　28 to hurt his feelings

29 need, advice　　　30 asked me out

31 for now, go out with　32 focus on, studies

33 should

34 Why don't you, can't go　35 I'm afraid, might hurt

36 If you don't tell, misunderstand, end up hurting

37 you're right　　　38 Thanks for, advice

본문 TEST Step 3　　　　　　　　　　p.32~33

1 제가 어떻게 해야 할까요?

2 누구나 고민은 있습니다.

3 여러분은 걱정되는 것이 있을 때 무엇을 하나요?

4 여기 세 명의 청소년이 걱정하는 것들이 있습니다.

5 소희는 하연이가 그녀의 가장 친한 친구라고 생각했지만,

지금은 하연이가 변했고 그녀를 피한다고 느낍니다.

6 소희: (그녀의 언니에게) 내 친구 하연이 알지, 그렇지?

7 언니: 응. 왜? 그녀가 어떤데?

8 소희: 나는 그녀가 나를 피하고 있다고 느껴.

9 학교에서 내가 그녀를 볼 때 그녀는 돌아서서 나로부터 멀리 걸어가.

10 언니: 그거 참 안타깝구나.

11 너는 그녀가 왜 그렇게 하는지 아니?

12 소희: 아니. 나는 내가 잘못한 것이 있다고 생각하지 않아.

13 단지 그녀가 더 이상 나를 좋아하지 않는다고 느껴져.

14 언니: 혹시 모르니 뭔가 잘못된 것이 있는지 그녀에게 물어봐.

15 소희: 아마 그래야겠어. 나는 여전히 그녀와 친구로 지내고 싶거든.

16 대호는 새 물건이 그를 더 인기 있게 만들어 줄 것이라고 생각해서 단지 친구들이 그것을 가지고 있다는 이유로 종종 새 물건을 사기를 원합니다.

17 대호: 성진아, 내 새 운동화 봐.

18 어떠니?

19 성진: 멋지다. 그런데 너 겨우 몇 달 전에 새 운동화 사지 않았니?

20 대호: 응, 하지만 그건 더 이상 유행이 아니야.

21 이걸 신으니까 더 멋져 보이지, 그렇지?

22 성진: 대호야. 최신 유행하는 것을 입는 것이 너를 더 멋지고 더 인기 있게 만들어 주지는 않아.

23 사람들은 네가 너이기 때문에 너를 좋아하는 것이지, 네 옷 때문이 아니야.

24 대호: 그래?

25 성진: 들어봐. 너는 멋진 사람이야.

26 그것을 증명하기 위해 새 운동화가 필요하지 않아.

27 최근에 민경이는 그녀의 반 남자아이에게 데이트 신청을 받았습니다.

28 그녀는 거절하고 싶지만 그의 감정을 상하게 하고 싶지는 않습니다.

29 민경: 저는 선생님의 조언이 필요해요.

30 같은 반 남자아이가 저에게 데이트 신청을 했어요.

31 저는 그를 좋아하지만 당분간은 그와 데이트하고 싶지 않아요.

32 저는 공부에 집중해야 해요.

33 제가 어떻게 해야 할까요?

34 상담 선생님: 왜 네가 데이트를 할 수 없는지 그에게 말하는 것은 어떨까?

35 민경: 제가 그의 감정을 상하게 할까 봐 걱정돼요.

36 상담 선생님: 네가 그에게 빨리 말하지 않으면, 그는 네 감정을 오해할 것이고, 너는 그를 더 아프게 할 수도 있단다.

37 민경: 선생님 말씀이 맞는 것 같아요.

38 조언 감사합니다.

1 What Should I Do?

2 Everyone has worries.

3 When you have things you worry about, what do you do?

4 Here are some things that three teenagers worry about.

5 Sohui thought Hayeon was her best friend, but now, Sohui feels that Hayeon has changed and she is avoiding her.

6 Sohui: (To her older sister) You know my friend Hayeon, don't you?

7 Sister: Yeah. Why? What about her?

8 Sohui: I feel she's avoiding me.

9 When I see her at school, she turns around and walks away from me.

10 Sister: I'm sorry to hear that.

11 Do you have any idea why she does that?

12 Sohui: No. I don't think I've done anything wrong.

13 It just feels like she doesn't like me anymore.

14 Sister: Maybe you should just ask her if there is something wrong.

15 Sohui: Maybe I should. I still want to be friends with her.

16 Daeho, thinking that new things will make him more popular, often wants new things just because his friends have them.

17 Daeho: Seongjin, look at my new sneakers.

18 What do you think?

19 Seongjin: They're nice, but didn't you just buy new sneakers a couple of months ago?

20 Daeho: Yeah, but they're no longer in style.

21 I look cooler in these, right?

22 Seongjin: Daeho, wearing the latest fashion doesn't make you cooler or more popular.

23 People like you because you're you, not because of your clothes.

24 Daeho: Yeah?

25 Seongjin: Listen, you're a great guy.

26 You don't need new sneakers to prove it.

27 Recently, Minkyeong was asked out by a boy in her class.

28 She wants to say no but does not want to hurt his feelings.

29 Minkyeong: I need your advice.

30 A boy in my class asked me out.

31 I like him, but for now I don't want to go out with him.

32 I need to focus on my studies.

53

33 What should I do?

34 Counselor: Why don't you tell him why you can't go?

35 Minkyeong: I'm afraid I might hurt his feelings.

36 Counselor: If you don't tell him soon, he will misunderstand your feelings, and you may end up hurting him even more.

37 Minkyeong: Maybe you're right.

38 Thanks for the advice.

구석구석지문 TEST Step 1

Communication Task

1. I think, should start later
2. agree with, get more sleep, if, later
3. should start later
4. don't agree with, will finish later

Writing Workshop

1. grow taller, being the shortest
2. like to know how, get taller
3. are wondering, can get taller
4. suggest, foods like eggs
5. having lots of protein, calcium, help, grow taller
6. Also, at least eight hours
7. will be helpful to

After You Read B

1. fell like, avoids me
2. Why don't you, anything wrong
3. new clothes, make, more popular
4. because you're you, because of your clothes
5. no without hurting his feelings
6. Why don't, why you can't go

구석구석지문 TEST Step 2

Communication Task

1. A: I think school should start later in the morning.
2. B: I agree with you. We can get more sleep if school starts later.
3. A: I think school should start later in the morning.
4. B: I don't agree with you. School will finish later if it starts later.

Writing Workshop

1. I want to grow taller. I do not feel good being the shortest in the group.
2. I'd like to know how I can get taller.
3. I heard you are wondering if you can get taller.

4. I suggest you eat foods like eggs, milk, and beans.

5. These foods, having lots of protein and calcium, can help you grow taller.

6. Also, you should sleep at least eight hours every night.

7. I hope these tips will be helpful to you.

After You Read B

1. I fell like my best friend avoids me.
2. Why don't you ask her if there is anything wrong?
3. I need new clothes. They'll make me more popular.
4. People like you because you're you, not because of your clothes.
5. How can I say no without hurting his feelings?
6. Why don't you tell him why you can't go?

16 protect, 보호하다

단어 TEST Step 1   p.41

01 이득; 이득을 보다   02 게다가   03 진정시키는

04 자연친화적인   05 후회하다   06 만들어 내다

07 피하다   08 마침내   09 이불, 담요

10 항공편, 비행   11 성적   12 규칙적으로

13 뇌   14 다행스럽게도   15 칼슘

16 일지, 일기   17 세로토닌   18 젖은

19 자외선 차단제   20 기분, 감정   21 제대로

22 빛나다   23 보호하다   24 이미

25 피부   26 날씨   27 야외에서

28 절정의, 최고조의; 절정, 최고조   29 복습하다

30 안전하게   31 직접적인, (열기나 빛이) 직접 닿는

32 효과   33 뼈   34 건강한

35 착용하다, 바르다

36 ~을 명심하다   37 A와 B 둘 다   38 ~로 가득 찬

39 깨어 있다   40 ~했어야 했는데   41 내놓다

42 너무 ~해서 …할 수 없다   43 ~에 유익하다

단어 TEST Step 2   p.42

01 already   02 interestingly   03 benefit

04 moreover   05 healthy   06 calming

07 sunlight   08 nature-friendly   09 outdoors

10 skin   11 avoid   12 flight

13 blanket   14 fortunately   15 check

16 hang   17 review   18 brain

19 finally   20 sunshine   21 effect

22 weather   23 journal   24 bone

25 mood   26 peak   27 produce

28 regret   29 regularly   30 role

31 wet   32 properly   33 protect

34 safely   35 full of   36 put on

37 be good for   38 on time   39 both A and B

40 put out   41 stay up   42 keep ~ in mind

43 surf the Internet

단어 TEST Step 3   p.43

1 peak, 절정, 최고조   2 mood, 기분, 감정

3 sunshine, 햇빛   4 benefit, 이득을 보다

5 go up, 올라가다   6 review, 복습하다   7 role, 역할

8 skin, 피부   9 wet, 젖은   10 blanket, 이불, 담요

11 shine, 빛나다   12 regularly, 규칙적으로

13 brain, 뇌   14 bone, 뼈   15 journal, 일지, 일기

대화문 TEST Step 1   p.44~45

Listen & Speak 1 Listen

1. can, stay healthy / Well, important to eat, breakfast
2. What, do to get, grades / important, review
3. think, write, journal
4. to write down, spend, on / think, too

Listen & Speak 1 A

1. What, do, weekend / played, decided to exercise, for / you, important, exercise regularly / Right, about playing, with / not
2. late / took, wrong bus / think, leave, earlier / too, won't be late / arrive, on time

Listen & Speak 2

1. too / should have brought, one
2. cold / should have worn
3. missed, flight / have, earlier
4. Look at, should have put on / right

Listen & Speak 2 A

1. how, movie / enjoy, was boring / What, about / knew, ending, have, before seeing / sorry, like
2. still, minutes, before, top, sit down, and, snack / brought, brought / okay, brought, share / keep, mind, some, time

Real-Life Zone

look, energy / because, got, last / usually, enough sleep / know, important, night's, always stay up, surfing, playing, with, phone / sometimes happens, me / After, regret, morning, have, earlier / different / climbed, dad, tired, home, sleep, after, went to bed / Outdoor, are, way to help, get

Wrap Up 1

blanket, wet, should have checked / wash / put, out, sun / Why, wash / blanket, way, keep, clean / know, remember / important, remember, regularly

대화문 TEST Step 2   p.46~47

Listen & Speak 1 Listen

1. G: How can we stay healthy?

   B: Well, it's important to eat a good breakfast.

2. B: What can we do to get good grades?

   G: It's important to review every day.

3. B: I think it's important to write a journal after reading.

   G: I agree.

4. B: It's important to write down what you spend your money on.

G: I think so, too.

1. B: What did you do on the weekend?

G: I played tennis. I have decided to exercise on the weekend for my health.

B: Good for you. It's important to exercise regularly.

G: Right. How about playing tennis with me?

B: Why not?

2. M: John, you are late again.

B: I'm sorry. I took the wrong bus.

M: I think you need to leave home a little earlier.

B: I think so, too. Next time I won't be late.

M: It's important to arrive at school on time.

1. G: Your bag is too small.

B: Yes. I should have brought a bigger one.

2. G: Aren't you cold?

B: Yes. I should have worn a jacket.

3. B: We missed our flight.

G: Oh, no. We should have come earlier.

4. G: Look at my face. I should have put on some sunscreen.

B: Yes. You're right.

1. B: Mina, how was the movie?

G: I didn't enjoy it. It was boring.

B: What was bad about it?

G: I already knew the ending. I shouldn't have read about it before seeing it.

B: Oh, I'm sorry you didn't like it.

2. B: We still have 30 minutes to go before we reach the top of the mountain. Let's sit down over there and have a snack.

G: Oh, I brought only water. I should have brought some snacks.

B: That's okay. I brought a lot. We can share.

G: I'll keep it in mind to bring some snacks next time.

G: Ben, you look full of energy today!

B: Do I? Maybe that's because I finally got a good night's sleep last night.

G: Why? Don't you usually get enough sleep?

B: No, I know it's really important to get a good night's sleep, but I always stay up late surfing the Internet or playing with my phone.

G: That sometimes happens to me too.

B: After I do that, I regret it the next morning and say, "I should have gone to bed earlier last night."

G: How was yesterday different?

B: Well, yesterday afternoon I climbed the mountain with my dad. I was really tired when I got home. I went to sleep right after I went to bed.

G: Outdoor activities are a great way to help you get a good night's sleep.

W: Oh, your blanket is wet from the rain! I should have checked the weather.

B: Did you wash it?

W: No. I just put it out in the sun this morning.

B: Why didn't you wash it?

W: Hanging a blanket in the sun is a nature-friendly way to keep the blanket clean.

B: Oh, I didn't know that. I'll remember that.

W: And it's also important to remember to do it regularly.

01 Enjoy, Sunshine
02 much, spend, out in
03 Not much
04 too busy, spend, outdoors
05 However, plays, role, health
06 helps, stay healthy
07 feels happier, shines
08 because, body's happy hormone
09 more, hormone, brain produces
10 When, goes up, stronger
11 fight everyday stress
12 calming effect, what, doing
13 Moreover, night's sleep, produce
14 not just, feel, better
15 also, build strong bones
16 As, builds, bones, teeth
17 for, body, use, properly
18 creates, when sunlight shines
19 easiest, bones, go outside
20 As, see, benefits safely
21 direct sunlight, skin, benefit
22 classes, breaks, sunshine, arms
23 walk, few minutes, mind
24 peak, protect, face, neck
25 safely, little, difference, mood

01 Enjoy, Sunshine

02 spend, out in the sun

03 Not much

04 too busy, at work to spend, outdoors

05 However, plays an important role

06 helps, stay healthy   07 feels happier, shines

08 because of, the body's happy hormone

09 The more sun, the more, happy hormone, produces

10 goes up, feel happier, stronger

11 helps, fight everyday stress

12 calming effect, focus, what you are doing

13 Moreover, a good night's sleep, helps, produce

14 not just, sleep better

15 also, build strong bones

16 As you all know, bones, teeth

17 for the body to use, properly

18 Interestingly, creates, when sunlight shines

19 The easiest way, to go outside

20 As you can see, enjoy its benefits safely

21 getting direct sunlight, to benefit from it

22 Try to go out into, between, during, get sunshine
on

23 for just a few minutes every day, both, and

24 avoid, peak, to protect your face and neck

25 a little sunshine, make a world of difference,
health, mood

1 햇빛을 즐기세요

2 여러분은 매일 햇빛 속에서 얼마나 많은 시간을 보내나요?

3 많지 않죠, 그렇죠?

4 대부분의 사람들은 학교와 직장에서 너무 바빠서 많은 시간을
야외에서 보내지 못합니다.

5 그러나 햇빛은 여러분의 건강에 중요한 역할을 합니다.

6 그것은 여러분이 건강을 유지하는 데 도움을 줍니다.

7 모든 사람들은 해가 비칠 때 더 행복하게 느낍니다.

8 이것은 몸의 행복 호르몬인 세로토닌 때문입니다.

9 여러분이 햇빛을 쬘수록 뇌는 행복 호르몬을 더 만들어 냅니다.

10 여러분의 세로토닌 수치가 높아지면, 여러분은 더 행복하고 더
건강하게 느낍니다.

11 이것은 여러분이 매일의 스트레스를 이겨 내는 데 도움을
줍니다.

12 세로토닌은 또한 진정 효과가 있고, 여러분이 하는 일에 더 잘
집중할 수 있도록 도와줍니다.

13 게다가, 세로토닌은 뇌가 수면 호르몬을 생성하도록 도와주기
때문에 여러분이 숙면을 취하도록 해 줍니다.

14 햇빛은 단지 여러분이 더 기분 좋게 느끼고 잠을 더 잘 자게
하는 것만은 아닙니다.

15 그것은 또한 튼튼한 뼈를 만드는 것을 돕습니다.

16 여러분 모두가 알다시피, 튼튼한 뼈와 치아를 만드는 것은
칼슘입니다.

17 그러나 몸이 칼슘을 적절하게 사용하기 위해서는 비타민 D가
필요합니다.

18 흥미롭게도, 피부는 햇빛이 피부에 비칠 때 비타민 D를 만들어
냅니다.

19 튼튼한 뼈를 만드는 가장 쉬운 방법은 밖으로 나가서 햇빛을
즐기는 겁니다.

20 보시다시피, 햇빛은 많은 이점이 있지만, 어떻게 그것의 이점을
안전하게 즐길 수 있을까요?

21 다행히도, 하루에 10분에서 20분 동안 피부에 직사광선을
쏘이는 것은 햇빛으로부터 이점을 얻는 데 충분합니다.

22 수업 시간 사이나 점심시간에 햇빛을 쬐러 밖으로 나가서 팔과
손에 햇빛을 쬐어 보세요.

23 매일 단 몇 분 동안 햇살을 쬐며 걷는 것은 여러분의 마음과 몸
모두에 좋습니다.

24 그러나 여름 절정 시간인 11시에서 3시 사이에는 햇빛을
피하고, 얼굴과 목을 보호하기 위해 자외선 차단제를
사용하세요.

25 태양을 안전하게 즐기고 적은 양의 햇빛이 여러분의 건강과
기분에 얼마나 큰 차이를 만들어 내는지 보세요.

1 Enjoy the Sunshine

2 How much time do you spend every day out in
the sun?

3 Not much, right?

4 Most people are too busy at school or at work to
spend much time outdoors.

5 However, the sun plays an important role in your
health.

6 It helps you stay healthy.

7 Everyone feels happier when the sun shines.

8 This is because of serotonin, the body's happy
hormone.

9 The more sun you get, the more "happy hormone"
the brain produces.

10 When your serotonin level goes up, you feel
happier and stronger.

11 This helps you fight everyday stress.

12 Serotonin also has a calming effect, helping you
focus better on what you are doing.

13 Moreover, serotonin helps you get a good night's
sleep because it helps the brain produce a sleep

hormone.

14 Sunshine does not just make you feel and sleep better.

15 It also helps build strong bones.

16 As you all know, it is calcium that builds strong bones and teeth.

17 However, for the body to use calcium properly, it needs vitamin D.

18 Interestingly, the skin creates vitamin D when sunlight shines on it.

19 The easiest way to make strong bones is to go outside and enjoy the sun.

20 As you can see, sunshine has many benefits, but how can you enjoy its benefits safely?

21 Fortunately, getting direct sunlight on your skin for 10 to 20 minutes a day is enough to benefit from it.

22 Try to go out into the sun between classes or during lunch breaks and get sunshine on your arms and hands.

23 A walk in the sun, for just a few minutes every day, is good for both your mind and your body.

24 However, avoid the sun during peak summer hours, between 11 and 3, and use sunscreen to protect your face and neck.

25 Enjoy the sun safely and see how a little sunshine can make a world of difference in your health and your mood.

구석구석지문 TEST Step 1 p.58

Communication Task

1. it's important to exercise, exercise every day

2. No, don't, try

3. Okay

After You Read A

1. Benefits, Sunshine

2. helps, deal with, feel happier

3. helps you focus better on what

4. get enough sunshine, will sleep better

5. When, sun shines on your skin, which is needed

Writing Workshop

1. Health, First

2. Wash, after going out, will not catch a cold, if

3. direct sunlight, every day

4. The more, that, happier, stonger you feel

5. It, that, brain work properly

6. When, focus more clearly on your work, remember, better

구석구석지문 TEST Step 2 p.59

Communication Task

1. A: I think it's important to exercise every day. Do you exercise every day?

2. B: No, I don't. But I'll try.

3. A: Okay.

After You Read A

1. The Benefits of Sunshine

2. Sunshine helps you deal with stress and feel happier.

3. Sunshine helps you focus better on what you are doing.

4. If you get enough sunshine, you will sleep better at night.

5. When the sun shines on your skin, your skin produces vitamin D, which is needed for strong bones.

Writing Workshop

1. Health Comes First!

2. Wash your hands after going out. You will not catch a cold easily if you wash your hands well.

3. Get direct sunlight for 10 to 20 minutes every day.

4. The more sunlight you get, the happier and stonger you feel.

5. It is a good breakfast that helps the brain work properly.

6. When you eat a good breakfast, you can focus more clearly on your work and remember things better.

단어 TEST Step 1   p.60

01 사고	02 남용하다, 너무 많이 사용하다
03 비록 ~이긴 하지만	04 길, 통로
05 불편한	06 (과일 또는 채소의) 껍질
07 규칙적으로	08 과로하다, 혹사하다
09 지진	10 ~을 야기하다 11 전기
12 과식하다	13 (짐을) 꾸리다 14 폭발하다
15 먹이를 주다	16 산소 17 마늘
18 번개	19 장소 20 기억, 추억
21 피하다	22 흘러넘치다, 범람하다
23 모기	24 자연 친화적인 25 (특정한) 때, 경우
26 준비하다, 대비하다	27 보호하다
28 (출)입구, 문	29 자외선 차단제, 선크림
30 (크림 등을) 바르다 31 주의, 집중	
32 홍수, 범람 33 ~에 맞다	34 안전, 안전성
35 ~을 다 써버리다 36 의식을 잃다, 기절하다	
37 어울리다	38 ~을 접근하지 못하게 하다
39 설치하다, 세우다 40 ~함으로써	41 ~을 명심하다
42 ~을 바르다 43 최선을 다하다	

단어 TEST Step 2   p.61

01 uncomfortable		02 accident
03 overflow	04 garlic	05 fit
06 mosquito	07 peel	08 although
09 apply	10 lightning	11 regularly
12 entrance	13 location	14 explode
15 overeat	16 earthquake	17 overwork
18 protect	19 oxygen	20 safety
21 overuse	22 flat	23 attention
24 flooding	25 hang	26 nature-friendly
27 spill	28 occasion	29 pack
30 prepare	31 rub	32 strike
33 electricity	34 avoid	35 put on
36 use up	37 keep ~ in mind	
38 hang out	39 keep away	40 stay up
41 instead of	42 pass out	43 do one's best

단어 TEST Step 3   p.62

1 memory, 기억, 추억   2 feed, 먹이를 주다

3 earthquake, 지진   4 peel, (과일 또는 채소의) 껍질

5 lightning, 번개   6 strike, (세게) 치다

7 rub, 문지르다, 비비다   8 entrance, (출)입구, 문

9 location, 장소   10 flooding, 홍수, 범람

11 pack, (짐을) 꾸리다   12 explode, 폭발하다

13 apply, (크림 등을) 바르다   14 mosquito, 모기

15 sunscreen, 자외선 차단제, 선크림   16 garlic, 마늘

대화문 TEST Step 1   p.63~64

Listen & Speak 1 Listen

1. have to watch out

2. this way, looks nice / go straight, to get to

3. stairs, wet / have to walk down

4. Let's climb, top / have to check, going to rain, should go down

Listen & Speak 1 A

1. play outside / Don't forget to, go out / cloudy, have to put on / wear, every day / put, on

2. go bowling / go see a doctor / wrong / stomach hurts

Listen & Speak 2 Listen

1. Don't, may fall / won't run

2. into, without warming up, be dangerous

3. to swim / how deep the water is, deeper than

4. right after eating / with, uncomfortable

Listen & Speak 2 A

1. can cause, what to do, have to do, have to turn off, pack, Finally, safe place, keep listening to

2. ready to leave / yet, have to, if, turned off / may not get to, in time / have to check, minute

Real-Life Zone

look at, What, think / are, going / to meet / don't have one, short ride / Put on, hurt yourself / lot, riding, without / have to wear, protects / have to wear, fits, not / have to buy

Wrap Up

comes / finish drinking / Why don't, sure that / careful / suddenly, may spill / wait for, to finish, another bus

대화문 TEST Step 2   p.65~66

Listen & Speak 1 Listen

1. B: We have to watch out for bees.

   G: Oh, there are bees. Run!

2. G: Can we go this way? It looks nice.

   B: No. We have to go straight if we want to get to the top.

3. B: Oh, the stairs are wet.

G: Then we have to walk down the stairs slowly.

4. G: Let's climb some more. I want to reach the top of the mountain.

B: First we have to check the weather. Oh, it says it's going to rain. We should go down.

1. G: Mom, can I play outside this afternoon?

W: Sure. Don't forget to put on sunscreen before you go out.

G: But it's cloudy today. Do I have to put on sunscreen?

W: Yes, you have to wear sunscreen every day.

G: Okay. Then I'll put some on now.

2. B: Let's go bowling.

G: I'm sorry, I can't. I have to go see a doctor.

B: Oh, what's wrong?

G: I don't know, but my stomach hurts.

1. M: Don't run. You may fall.

B: Okay, I won't run.

2. B: Jumping into cold water without warming up can be dangerous.

G: Oh, okay. I will warm up.

3. G: Mom, I want to swim here.

W: Okay, but first you should check how deep the water is. It may be deeper than you think.

4. B: Can I swim right after eating?

G: Swimming with a full stomach can be uncomfortable.

1. M: Flooding can cause big problems. However, you may not know what to do when it happens. There are several things you have to do. First, you have to turn off the water and the electricity. Second, pack water and food when you leave the house. Finally, you have to move to a high and safe place and keep listening to the weather report.

2. B: Mina, are you ready to leave?

G: No, not yet. I have to check if I turned off the gas.

B: If we don't leave now, we may not get to the concert in time.

G: Okay, but I have to check the gas first. It will only take a minute.

B: Uncle John, look at my new bike. What do you think?

M: It's really nice. Where are you going?

B: To the park to meet a friend.

M: Where's your helmet?

B: I don't have one. It's just a short ride.

M: Put on your helmet. You may hurt yourself.

B: But I see a lot of people riding bikes without helmets.

M: You have to wear a helmet. It protects your head in an accident.

B: Okay. I'll get my dad's helmet.

M: No. You have to wear a helmet that fits you. If not, it cannot protect your head.

B: I guess I'll have to buy one for myself.

B: Here comes the bus!

G: Oh, but first I have to finish drinking my tea.

B: Why don't you just take it with you? I'm sure that it will be okay if you are careful.

G: No. If the bus stops suddenly, I may spill it.

B: Okay, then I can just wait for you to finish your drink. I'm sure another bus will come soon.

G: Thanks.

---

01 create, memories, occasions, happen

02 plan, need, keep, mind

03 Listen, talk, camping trip

04 seem, what, make, safe

05 why, put up, by   06 don't think, idea

07 starts to, might overflow   08 but, sky, clear

09 really, sound, water

10 weather, change, mountains

11 never, when, might, rain

12 Safety, Let's, another   13 set up, choose, flat

14 Avoid, close, be struck

15 hungry, for lunch

16 cooking Samgyepsal

17 enough, all, more, bigger

18 more, going to, pan   19 Why, have, use

20 Because, not, than, burner

21 If, sends, back, explode   22 didn't know that

23 Here, tip, when   24 Never use, inside

25 pass, use, oxygen, as   26 Ouch! Mosquitoes

27 forgot to, apply, bug   28 Thanks, know what

29 rub, on, instead, applying

30 way to keep, away   31 That's interesting

---

32 Garlic, keep, away

33 pieces, entrance, come inside

01 Although, create, memories, when, happen

02 plan to go camping, need, in mind, safety

03 talk, camping trip

04 seem, what to do, safe

05 why don't, put up, by   06 think, idea

07 starts to, might overflow   08 but, clear

09 sound

10 weather, change quickly

11 never, when, might, to rain

12 Safety, Let's, another   13 set up, choose

14 Avoid, close, be struck by lightning

15 hungry, for   16 cooking

17 enough, all, more, bigger pan

18 going to, more, have to use

19 Why, have to use

20 Because, should not, bigger than

21 If, sends, back, explode   22 know

23 Here, tip, when, go camping

24 Never, inside

25 may catch fire, or, pass, use, oxygen, burns

26 Mosquitoes   27 forgot to, to apply

28 what

29 rub, peels on, instead of applying

30 nature-friendly way to keep, away

31 interesting   32 keep, away

33 pieces of garlic, entrance, come inside

1 캠핑 여행이 많은 사람들에게 좋은 추억을 만들어 주기도 하지만, 나쁜 일이 일어나는 때가 될 수도 있습니다.

2 여러분이 이번 여름에 가족이나 친구들과 함께 캠핑을 하려고 계획하고 있다면, 여러분은 여러분의 안전을 위해서 몇 가지 사항을 명심해야 합니다.

3 유민이의 가족이 그들의 캠핑 여행에 대해 이야기하는 것을 들어 보세요.

4 그들은 그들의 캠핑 여행이 안전하고 재미있게 하기 위해 무엇을 해야 하는지 알고 있는 것 같습니다.

5 유민: 아빠, 이 강 근처 이쪽에 텐트를 치면 어때요?

6 아빠: 그건 좋은 생각 같지 않구나.

7 만약 비가 내리기 시작하면, 강이 범람할지도 몰라.

8 유민: 저도 알아요. 하지만 하늘이 맑잖아요.

9 저는 물소리를 정말 좋아한단 말이에요!

10 아빠: 산속의 날씨는 곧 바뀔 수 있어.

11 언제 비가 올지 절대 알 수 없는 일이지.

12 유민: 알겠어요. 안전이 우선이지요! 다른 곳을 찾아봐요.

13 텐트를 칠 때는 평평하고 햇볕이 잘 드는 장소를 고르세요.

14 번개를 맞을지도 모르는 키 큰 나무에 너무 가까운 장소는 피해야 합니다.

15 하준: 엄마, 저 배고파요. 점심이 뭐예요?

16 엄마: 삼겹살을 요리하고 있단다.

17 하준: 엄마, 그건 우리 모두가 먹기에 충분하지 않아요. 우리 더 큰 팬에 더 많이 요리하면 안 돼요?

18 엄마: 더 굽긴 할 거야. 하지만 우리는 이 작은 팬을 써야 해.

19 하준: 왜 우리는 작은 팬을 써야 하죠?

20 엄마: 왜냐하면 팬이 버너보다 더 크면 안 되기 때문이야.

21 만약 큰 팬을 사용하면, 팬이 열을 버너로 다시 돌려보내서, 가스가 폭발할 수 있어!

22 하준: 오, 그것은 몰랐어요.

23 캠핑할 때 불을 사용하는 것에 대한 또 하나의 팁이 있습니다.

24 텐트 안에서 가스난로나 버너를 절대 쓰지 마세요.

25 여러분의 텐트에 불이 붙거나, 불이 타면서 텐트 내 산소를 다 써 버려서 여러분이 의식을 잃을 수도 있습니다.

26 유민: 앗! 모기!

27 엄마: 아, 벌레 퇴치 스프레이를 뿌리라고 네게 말하는 걸 잊었구나. 여기 있단다.

28 유민: 고마워요, 엄마. 아, 그거 아세요?

29 벌레 퇴치 스프레이를 뿌리는 것 대신에 오렌지 껍질을 피부에 문질러도 돼요.

30 모기가 접근하지 못하게 하는 자연 친화적인 방법이에요.

31 엄마: 그거 재미있구나!

32 마늘 또한 벌레가 접근하지 못하게 막을 수 있습니다.

33 마늘 조각을 텐트 입구에 놓아두면, 벌레가 안으로 들어오지 않을 것입니다.

1 Although camping trips can create sweet memories for many people, they can also be occasions when bad things happen.

2 If you plan to go camping with family or friends this summer, you need to keep several things in mind for your safety.

3 Listen to Yumin's family talk about their camping trip.

4 They seem to know what to do to make their camping trip safe and fun.

5 Yumin: Dad, why don't we put up our tent over here by this river?

6 Dad: I don't think that's a good idea.

7 If it starts to rain, the river might overflow.

8 Yumin: I know, but the sky is clear.

9 I really like the sound of the water!

10 Dad: The weather can change quickly in the mountains.

11 You never know when it might start to rain.

12 Yumin: Okay. Safety first! Let's find another place.

13 When you set up a tent, choose a flat, sunny area.

14 Avoid places too close to big trees that might be struck by lightning.

15 Hajun: Mom, I'm hungry. What's for lunch?

16 Mom: I'm cooking Samgyepsal.

17 Hajun: Mom, that's not enough for all of us. Can we cook more in a bigger pan?

18 Mom: I'm going to cook more, but we have to use this small pan.

19 Hajun: Why do we have to use a small pan?

20 Mom: Because the pan should not be bigger than the burner.

21 If you use a big pan, it sends the heat back to the burner, and the gas can explode!

22 Hajun: Oh, I didn't know that.

23 Here is one more tip about fire when you go camping.

24 Never use a gas heater or burner inside a tent.

25 Your tent may catch fire, or you might pass out because the fire will use up the oxygen in the tent as it burns.

26 Yumin: Ouch! Mosquitoes!

27 Mom: Oh, I forgot to tell you to apply some bug spray. Here.

28 Yumin: Thanks, Mom. Oh, you know what?

29 We can rub orange peels on our skin instead of applying bug spray.

30 It is a nature–friendly way to keep mosquitoes away.

31 Mom: That's interesting!

32 Garlic can also keep bugs away.

33 You can place pieces of garlic at the entrance to the tent, and bugs will not come inside.

Before You Read

1. Welcome to

2. have prepared, the two-day camping trip

3. Because, do our best to prepare for anything bad

4. help people have, by placing, avoid getting bitten

by mosquitoes

5. everyone tales home good memories

Writing Workshop

1. Although, are free from an earthquake

2. when it strikes

3. several things, need to keep in mind

4. stay inside, until the shaking stops

5. seems to be safe, might fall on

6. turn off

7. get under, cover your head with your arms

8. It, to protect

9. far away from, as possible

10. By following, can be safe

Wrap Up

1. Trip Diary

2. Location, September

3. with

4. went, with, on September

5. During, enjoyed rafting, hiking

6. Although, was afraid of doing, at first

7. go rafting, if, have a chance

Before You Read

1. Welcome to Our Sky Camping Trip!

2. We have prepared many activities for the two-day camping trip.

3. Because we always think about your safety first, we do our best to prepare for anything bad that may happen.

4. We help people have a comfortable stay by placing a can of bug spray in each tent so you can avoid getting bitten by mosquitoes.

5. We hope everyone tales home good memories of the trip!

Writing Workshop

1. Although you would think that you are free from an earthquake, that is not true.

2. Then, what should you do when it strikes?

3. There are several things you need to keep in mind.

4. First, stay inside and keep informed until the shaking stops.

5. It seems to be safe to go outside, but something might fall on you.

6. Second, turn off the gas and the electricity.

7. Third, get under the table and cover your head with your arms.

8. It is important to protect your head.

9. Finally, if you are outside, try to get as far away from buildings, trees, and streetlights as possible.

10. By following these tips, you can be safe from the earthquake.

Wrap Up

1. My Camping Trip Diary

2. Location: Yeongwol Date: September 12

3. Traveled with: my family

4. I went to Yeongwol with my family on September 12.

5. During the trip, we enjoyed rafting and hiking.

6. Although I was afraid of doing rafting at first, it was really fun and exciting.

7. I'll go rafting again if I have a chance.

Lesson S

단어 TEST Step 1   p.79

01 (짐을) 싸다, 꾸리다

02 다시 문을 열다, 다시 시작하다   03 대학

04 역할, 부분   05 계약, 계약서   06 심각하게

07 ~을 제외하고   08 결정, 판단   09 결국, 마침내

10 허락하다   11 정확히   12 유명한

13 체육관   14 일어나다, 발생하다

15 교장   16 향상하다, 향상시키다

17 약속하다   18 인생, 삶   19 잠그다

20 받아들이다   21 실제로, 정말로

22 지다, 패하다   23 요구

24 (부정문에서) 역시, 또한   25 명령하다

26 서명하다   27 거절하다   28 성적

29 (충고·지시 등을) 따르다   30 참석하다

31 마음을 쓰다, 걱정하다

32 깨닫다, 알아차리다   33 상상하다

34 실망한, 낙담한   35 ~함으로써   36 ~을 찾아보다

37 B뿐만 아니라 A도

38 ~에 유의하다, ~에 관심을 갖다

39 이행하다, 수행하다   40 ~하는 데 익숙해지다

41 게다가, ~에 더하여   42 잇따라서

43 설상가상으로

단어 TEST Step 2   p.80

01 sign   02 accept   03 gym

04 happen   05 attend   06 college

07 decision   08 improve   09 care

10 follow   11 pack   12 contract

13 disappointed   14 future   15 principal

16 seriously   17 lose   18 decide

19 eventually   20 exactly   21 except

22 actually   23 order   24 either

25 grade   26 realize   27 imagine

28 practice   29 lock   30 demand

31 refuse   32 winner   33 allow

34 reopen   35 in addition to   36 A as well as B

37 carry out   38 take action   39 find out

40 pay attention to

41 one after another

42 to make matters worse

43 become used to -ing

1 sign, 서명하다   2 win, 이기다   3 improve, 향상시키다
4 principal, 교장   5 coach, (스포츠 팀의) 코치
6 order, 명령하다   7 contract, 계약서   8 attend, 참석하다
9 bonus, 상여금, 보너스   10 refuse, 거절하다
11 pack, (짐을) 꾸리다   12 gym, 체육관
13 demand, 요구   14 rule, 규칙   15 imagine, 상상하다
16 college, 대학

01 Welcome to   02 going to talk
03 imagine, allow, to practice   04 exactly what, does
05 cares, about, than, winning
06 having, losing, after another
07 became used to losing
08 To make, worse, only   09 get, new coach
10 wanted to change things   11 how to play, win
12 more than, by sending
13 To carry out, contract
14 had, in addition to
15 At first, contract seriously
16 give you a contract
17 Attend, classes, be late   18 all these rules
19 signing bonus, contract
20 because, winner, well, life   21 With, in many years
22 From, point on, after
23 Everybody, except, happy
24 do, part of, contract
25 Few, paid little attention
26 decided, take, action
27 let, until, improved, as   28 players, not, it
29 that, actions, just, not
30 the basketball team
31 All, on, getting famous
32 If, yourself, better life
33 answer, everything, to help
34 have to do, part
35 parents, like, decision either
36 demand, ordered, to reopen
37 Disappointed, decided to leave
38 When, to pack, were
39 won't, what happens next
40 Find out, by watching

01 Welcome to   02 going to talk
03 imagine, doesn't allow, to practice
04 exactly what, does
05 cares, about, than about winning games
06 one, after another
07 became used to losing
08 To make, worse, had no plans, only to play
09 new coach   10 wanted to change
11 how to play, win
12 more than, by sending, to college
13 To carry out, sign a contract
14 had to promise, in addition to playing
15 At first, take his idea, seriously
16 give you a contract
17 Attend, classes, be late   18 all these rules
19 signing bonus, contract
20 because, become a winner, as well as
21 With, began to win, in many years
22 From, point on, after   23 except
24 part of
25 Few of, paid little attention to
26 take stronger action
27 refused to let, play, until, improved, as
28 it
29 that, actions, just, not
30 basketball team
31 All we see, getting famous
32 If, yourself, better life
33 If, everything, to help
34 have to, part   35 decision either
36 demand, principal ordered, to reopen
37 Disappointed, decided to
38 When, to pack, however, all of, were
39 what happens next
40 Find out, by watching

1 「영화 여행」에 오신 것을 환영합니다.
2 오늘 우리는 영화 「코치 카터」에 대해 이야기할 것입니다.
3 선수들이 연습하는 것을 허락하지 않는 농구 코치를 상상할 수 있나요?
4 그것이 바로 카터 코치가 한 것입니다.
5 이 영화는 경기에서 이기는 것보다 학생들을 더 걱정하는 코치에 대한 영화입니다.
6 캘리포니아 리치몬드 지역의 리치몬드 고등학교 농구 팀은 연속해서 경기에서 지고 있었습니다.

7 선수들도 지는 것에 익숙하게 되었습니다.

8 설상가상으로 그들은 미래에 대한 계획도 없었습니다. 즉, 그들은 단지 농구하기 위해 학교에 갔고, 그것마저도 잘하지 못했습니다.

9 그때 그들은 케니 카터라는 새로운 코치를 선임했습니다.

10 카터 코치는 몇 가지를 바꾸고자 했습니다.

11 그는 아이들에게 어떻게 농구를 잘하고 이기는지를 가르치기를 원했습니다.

12 그러나 그것보다도, 그는 그들을 대학에 보냄으로써 선수들에게 미래를 주기를 원했습니다.

13 그의 계획을 실행하기 위해서, 카터 코치는 선수들에게 계약서에 서명하게 했습니다.

14 그들은 농구를 하는 것뿐만 아니라 열심히 공부할 것도 약속해야만 했습니다.

15 처음에는 학생들이 계약서에 대한 그의 생각을 심각하게 받아들이지 않았습니다.

16 카터: 내가 너희들에게 계약서를 줄 것이다.

17 크루즈: "모든 수업에 출석하라," "C 플러스 또는 그 이상 받아라," "지각하지 말아라."

18 이 모든 규칙들은 무엇이죠?

19 제가 이 계약서에 사인하면 사이닝 보너스를 받나요?

20 카터: 그래. 너는 큰 보너스를 받게 될 거야. 왜냐하면 인생의 게임에서뿐 아니라 농구 경기에 서도 승리자가 될 것이기 때문이지.

21 맹연습과 새로운 경기 전략으로 그 팀은 몇 년 만에 처음으로 이기기 시작했습니다.

22 그때 이후로 경기마다 이겼습니다.

23 카터 코치를 제외한 모든 이들이 행복했습니다.

24 선수들은 그들 계약의 '학습' 부분을 하지 않았습니다.

25 그들 중 정말 그들이 대학을 갈 수 있다고 믿는 사람들은 거의 없었습니다. 그래서 그들은 성적에는 거의 관심을 두지 않았습니다.

26 카터는 더 강력한 조치를 취하기로 결심했습니다.

27 그는 체육관 문을 잠그고 계약서에서 약속한 대로 그들의 성적이 좋아질 때까지 농구를 못하게 했습니다.

28 선수들은 그것을 좋아하지 않았습니다.

29 그들은 그에게 그의 행동들이 그들을 위한 것이 아닌 단지 카터 자신을 위한 것이라고 말했습니다.

30 웜: 우리는 농구 팀이에요.

31 우리가 보는 모든 것은 유명세를 타며 TV에 있는 당신이에요.

32 카터: 네가 그렇게 생각한다면, 집으로 가서 너 자신에게 물어봐. "나는 더 나은 삶을 원하는가?"

33 대답이 '맞다'라면, 나는 너를 돕기 위해 내 힘이 닿는 한 모든 것을 할 거야.

34 그러나 너는 네 역할을 해야만 해.

35 선수들의 부모들 역시 카터의 결정을 좋아하지 않았습니다.

36 부모들의 요구에 따라 교장은 카터에게 체육관을 다시 열도록 했습니다.

37 실망한 카터는 리치몬드 고등학교를 떠나기로 결심했습니다.

38 그가 짐을 싸기 위해 체육관으로 들어섰을 때, 그의 선수들 모두가 그곳에 있었습니다.

39 우리는 여러분이 이 영화를 즐기기 원합니다. 그래서 당신에게 다음에 무슨 일이 일어나는지 이야기하지 않을 것입니다.

40 영화 「코치 카터」를 보고 스스로 찾아보세요.

1 Welcome to *Movie Trip*.

2 Today we're going to talk about the movie *Coach Carter*.

3 Can you imagine a basketball coach who doesn't allow his players to practice?

4 That's exactly what Coach Carter does.

5 This movie is about a coach who cares more about his students than about winning games.

6 The basketball team at Richmond High School in Richmond, California, was having one losing season after another.

7 The players became used to losing.

8 To make matters worse, they had no plans for the future; they went to school only to play basketball, and they did not do that very well.

9 Then they got a new coach, Kenny Carter.

10 Coach Carter wanted to change things.

11 He wanted to teach kids how to play basketball well and win.

12 But more than that, he wanted to give the players a future by sending them to college.

13 To carry out his plan, Coach Carter had the players sign a contract.

14 They had to promise to study hard in addition to playing basketball.

15 At first, students did not take his idea for a contract seriously.

16 Carter: I'm going to give you a contract.

17 Cruz: "Attend all classes," "Get a C⁺ or higher," "Don't be late…."

18 What are all these rules about?

19 Do I get a signing bonus for signing this contract?

20 Carter: Yes. You will get a big bonus because you will become a winner in the game of basketball as well as in the game of life.

21 With hard work and a new game plan, the team began to win for the first time in many years.

22 From that point on, they won game after game.

23 Everybody, except Coach Carter, was happy.

24 The players did not do the "study" part of their contract.

25 Few of them actually believed they could go to college, so they paid little attention to their grades.

26 Carter decided to take stronger action.

27 He locked the gym and refused to let them play basketball until their grades improved, as promised in the contract.

28 The players did not like it.

29 They told him that his actions were just for him, not for them.

30 Worm: We're the basketball team.

31 All we see is you on TV, getting famous.

32 Carter: If you think so, go home and ask yourself, "Do I want a better life?"

33 If the answer is yes, I will do everything in my power to help you.

34 But you have to do your part.

35 The players' parents did not like Carter's decision either.

36 At the parents' demand, the principal ordered Carter to reopen the gym.

37 Disappointed, Carter decided to leave Richmond High.

38 When he entered the gym to pack his things, however, all of his players were there.

39 We want you to enjoy the movie, so we won't tell you what happens next.

40 Find out for yourself by watching the movie *Coach Carter.*

MEMO

MEMO

3학년 영어 1학기 중간고사(1과) 1회

반		점수	
이름			

문항수 : 선택형(24문항) 서술형(2문항)　　　20 . . .

◎ 선택형 문항의 답안은 컴퓨터용 수정 싸인펜을 사용하여 OMR 답안지에 바르게 표기하시오.

◎ 서술형 문제는 답을 답안지에 반드시 검정 볼펜으로 쓰시오.

◎ 총 26문항 100점 만점입니다. 문항별 배점은 각 문항에 표시되어 있습니다.

1. 다음 영영 풀이가 설명하는 단어로 알맞은 것은?　(3점)

_____ : to take off something

① remove　　② accept　　③ injure
④ prepare　　⑤ represent

2. 다음 대화 후에 Tom이 가장 먼저 할 행동으로 알맞은 것은? (4점)

Tom: Have you heard about the cartoon club, Edutoon?

Jane: Yes, I have. Are you interested in drawing cartoons?

Tom: Yes, I want to be a famous cartoon writer, so I'll visit and join that club today.

Jane: Oh, I didn't know that you're interested in drawing cartoons.

① He will learn how to draw cartoons.
② He will take some cartoon lessons.
③ He will meet a famous cartoon writer.
④ He will read some cartoons with his friends.
⑤ He will join the cartoon club.

3. 다음 중 두 사람의 대화가 어색한 것은?　(3점)

① A: Have you heard of the cartoon club, Edutoon?
　B: My brother wants to be a famous webtoon writer.
② A: Brian said that he ran 3 kilometers every day.
　B: That is why he became a great runner.
③ A: What will you make after you complete the desk?
　B: I'm planning to make my own chair.
④ A: I heard she practiced dancing for 15 hours every day.
　B: Wow. I am very impressed by her great efforts.
⑤ A: How was Roy able to go to the final in the tennis competition?
　B: He could do it after years of hard training.

4. 다음 대화의 (A)~(C)에 들어갈 말로 가장 적절한 것은?　(4점)

A: Sora, have you (A)_____ about the fire last night?

B: Yes, I heard that there was a big fire in a building nearby. Was anybody hurt?

A: No, one man saved ten people who were in the building.

B: Oh, really? How was he (B)_____ to save so many people?

A: He knocked on every door to tell people (C)_____ the building.

B: Wow, that's amazing!

	(A)	(B)	(C)
①	heard	able	leave
②	heard	unable	to leave
③	heard	able	to leave
④	hear	unable	leave
⑤	hear	able	leave

[5~6] 다음 대화를 읽고 물음에 답하시오.

> G: Have you heard of Eui Hyun Sin, the skier?
>
> B: No. Who is he?
>
> G: He's a Paralympian skier. He won the first gold medal for Korea in the 2018 Winter Paralympics.
>
> B: Wow! That's great.
>
> G: He was in a car accident in his early twenties and hurt his legs.
>
> B: How was he able to become a skier?
>
> G: After his accident, he tried several different sports to get better. Then he became especially interested in skiing.
>
> B: Skiing is not easy. Not many people are good at skiing.
>
> G: That's _____ he's so respected.
>
> *G: Girl, B: Boy

5. 위 대화의 내용과 일치하지 <u>않는</u> 것은? (4점)

① 소년은 대화 이전에 Eui Hyun Sin에 대해 알지 못했다.
② Eui Hyun Sin은 금메달을 땄다.
③ Eui Hyun Sin은 20대에 자동차 사고를 당해 다리를 다쳤다.
④ Eui Hyun Sin은 여러 가지 종목의 운동 중 특히 스키에 관심을 가졌다.
⑤ 소년은 스키가 재활 치료에 적절하고 배우기 쉽다고 생각한다.

6. 위 대화의 내용과 어법을 고려할 때, 빈칸에 들어갈 말로 가장 적절한 것은? (3점)

① who ② why ③ when
④ which ⑤ where

7. 다음 대화의 빈칸에 들어갈 말로 가장 적절한 것은? (3점)

> B: Sora, have you heard about the fire last night?
>
> G: Yes, I heard that there was a big fire in a building nearby. Was anybody hurt?
>
> B: No, one man saved ten people who were in the building.
>
> G: Oh, really? _____
>
> B: He knocked on every door to tell people to leave the building.
>
> G: Wow, that's amazing!
>
> *G: Girl, B: Boy

① Have you heard of Mia, the guitar player?
② How was he able to save so many people?
③ How was he able to invent so many things?
④ How was he able to become a famous writer?
⑤ Have you heard of the winner of the singing contest?

8. 다음 주어진 문장을 〈보기〉와 같이 바꾸어 쓰시오. (5점)

┌ 보기 ┐
I am too tired to walk to school.
→ I am so tired that I can't walk to school.
└──────┘

I was too busy to go out for a walk.
→ _____

→ _____

[9~10] 다음 글을 읽고 물음에 답하시오.

Someone shouted. "Look! (A)There come another runner!" A runner was just entering the stadium, (B)but there was wrong something with his legs. (C)Still, he kept go toward the finish line. (D)The band and the volunteers stopped their preparations for the closing ceremony. (E)All eyes were on the runner.

9. 위 글의 (A)~(E) 중 어색한 문장을 <u>모두</u> 고른 것은? (4점)

① (A)
② (A), (B)
③ (A), (B), (C)
④ (A), (B), (E)
⑤ (C), (D), (E)

10. 위 글의 내용과 일치하지 <u>않는</u> 것은? (4점)

① 모든 눈들이 그 선수에게 머물렀다.
② 저기 또 다른 선수가 온다고 누군가가 외쳤다.
③ 그러나 그는 계속 결승선을 향해 움직였다.
④ 밴드와 자원 봉사자들이 폐막식을 위한 준비를 멈추었다.
⑤ 한 선수가 경기장으로 이미 들어왔는데, 그의 다리에 이상이 생겼다.

11. 다음 부가의문문 중 어색한 것은? (정답 2개) (4점)

① You came to school yesterday, <u>didn't you</u>?
② You don't eat fish, <u>do you</u>?
③ Andy won't be late, <u>will he</u>?
④ Amy is your sister, <u>isn't Amy</u>?
⑤ Your mom works at the bank, <u>didn't she</u>?

12. 다음 대화의 흐름에 맞게 <보기>의 문장을 가장 적절하게 배열한 것은? (4점)

After Wasiqi, the last runner, finished the race in 1996 Atlanta Summer Olympics, reporters came up to him and started to ask questions.

Reporter: What happened to you?
Wasiqi: _____
Reporter: _____
Wasiqi: _____
Reporter: _____
Wasiqi: For me, it was enough to be here and to finish the race. I am proud of myself and proud to be from Afghanistan.

┤ 보기 ├

(A) I think you already knew that you were too far behind to win a medal.
(B) That's why you could not give up and kept running.
(C) My leg was injured during a practice run. The injury got worse during the race, but I couldn't give up.
(D) Yes, but I am the only athlete here representing Afghanistan.

① (A)–(C)–(B)–(D)
② (B)–(A)–(D)–(C)
③ (C)–(A)–(D)–(B)
④ (C)–(B)–(A)–(D)
⑤ (D)–(B)–(A)–(C)

13. 다음 두 문장의 의미가 같도록 (A)와 (B)에 들어갈 말이 순서대로 짝지어진 것은? (4점)

> Tom spoke slowly enough for me to understand what he said.
> = Tom spoke (A)_____ slowly (B)_____ I could understand what he said.

① so – that　　② to – too　　③ too – to

④ that – so　　⑤ so – too

[14~17] 다음 글을 읽고 물음에 답하시오.

> Suddenly, the band started playing celebration music, and the volunteers cheered. "Go! Go! Go for it!"
> Two volunteers ran to the finish line with a tape.
> (A)_____, the runner ran through the tape and (B)_____ to the ground. His name was Abdul Baser Wasiqi. He was from Afghanistan. Reporters came up to Wasiqi and started asking him questions.
>
> **Reporter:** What happened to you?
> **Wasiqi:** I injured my leg (C)_____ a practice run. The injury got worse (D)_____ the race, but I couldn't give up.
> **Reporter:** Why not? You knew that you were too far (E)_____ to win a medal.
> **Wasiqi:** I'm the only athlete here representing Afghanistan. There was the reason I could not give up.
> **Reporter:** Afghanistan is still at war, isn't it?
> **Wasiqi:** Yes, we have been at war for 16 years. That's why we were not able to send athletes to the Barcelona Olympics four years ago.

14. 위 글 (A)에 들어갈 적당한 것은? (3점)

① So　　② Gladly　　③ However

④ Slowly　　⑤ Finally

15. 위 글 (B)에 들어갈 적당한 것은? (3점)

① lied　　② lay　　③ fell

④ felled　　⑤ fallen

16. 위 글 (C), (D)에 들어갈 적당한 것은? (4점)

① for　　② till　　③ during

④ when　　⑤ while

17. 위 글 (E)에 들어갈 적당한 것은? (4점)

① forward　　② behind　　③ below

④ above　　⑤ up

18. 다음 글의 빈칸에 들어갈 말로 가장 적절한 것은? (4점)

In a small village in Spain lives a boy whose name is Antoni Gaudí. For him, the world is Catalonia. Mountain peaks jag against the sky. Silvery olive trees sway in the breeze. The sea sparkles blue.

Little Gaudí often feels sick. His bones and joints ache. He can't always run and play with his sister and brother. But _____. With wide eyes, he observes the world. All around him is light, form, and the Great Book of Nature. He will read from it all his life.

Gaudí grows stronger. He makes friends with two boys. Together, they explore an ancient monastery. He dreams of rebuilding the ruins. After high school, Gaudí goes to Barcelona to be an architect.

① he is able to compete with his siblings

② he has to eat his favorite food to be healthy

③ he has time to look around the beautiful village

④ he notices that he has to stay at home all the time

⑤ he is planning to visit Barcelona to meet his parents

[19~20] 다음 글을 읽고 물음에 답하시오.

Reporters came up to Wasiqi and started asking him questions.

Reporter: What happened to you?

Wasiqi: I injured my leg during a practice run. ⓐThe injury get worse during the race, but I couldn't give up.

Reporter: Why not? ⓑYou knew that you were so far behind that you can win a medal.

Wasiqi: I am the only athlete here representing Afghanistan. There was no way I could give up.

Reporter: ⓒAfghanistan is still at war, doesn't it?

Wasiqi: Yes, we have been at war for 16 years. ⓓThat's why we were not able to send athletes to the Barcelona Olympics four years ago. I was sad for my country back then when I could see no Afghan athletes in the opening ceremony.

Reporter: Were you running marathons then?

Wasiqi: No. I started running after Barcelona. I ran in lots of races. Finally I won a marathon in Germany. As a result, I was able to come to Atlanta.

Reporter: How do you feel now?

Wasiqi: I am proud of myself and proud to be from Afghanistan. ⓔFor me and my country, it was important to not give up. I didn't come here to win. For me, it was enough to be here and to finish the race.

19. 위 글의 밑줄 친 ⓐ~ⓔ 중 올바른 문장은? (4점)

① ⓐ　　② ⓑ　　③ ⓒ　　④ ⓓ　　⑤ ⓔ

20. 위 글에서 아프가니스탄이 운동선수들을 바르셀로나 올림픽에 보내지 못한 이유를 찾아 우리말로 쓰시오. (4점)

정답: _____

① All eyes were focused on the medalist.
② People in the stadium paid attention to the runner.
③ The runner was healthy enough to enter the stadium.
④ Other Afghan athletes were waiting for him to arrive.
⑤ The officials were busy because of the opening ceremony.

21. 다음 글의 빈칸에 들어갈 말로 가장 적절한 것은? (4점)

The last runner finished the race more than an hour before. "There will be no more runners coming," the officials decided. They removed the tape at the finish line and started their preparations for the closing ceremony for the 1996 Atlanta Summer Olympics in the United States.

Someone shouted, "Look! There comes another runner!" A runner was just entering the stadium, but it seemed he had hurt his legs. Still, he kept going toward the finish line. The band and the volunteers stopped their preparations for the closing ceremony.

_____.

Suddenly, the band started playing celebration music, and the volunteers cheered. "Go! Go for it!" Two volunteers ran to the finish line with a tape. Finally, the runner ran through the tape and then fell to the ground. His name was Abdul Baser Wasiqi, who was the one and only player from Afghanistan.

[22~25] 다음 글을 읽고 물음에 답하시오.

The last runner finished the race more than an hour before. "There will be no more runners coming," the officials decided. They removed the tape at the finish line and started (A)to prepare for the closing ceremony for the 1996 Atlanta Summer Olympics in the United States.

Someone shouted, "Look! There comes another runner!" A runner was just entering the stadium, but there was something wrong with his legs. Still, he kept going toward the finish line. The band and the volunteers stopped their preparations for the closing ceremony. (B)_____.

Suddenly, the band started playing celebration music, and the volunteers cheered. "Go! Go! Go for it!" Two volunteers ran to the finish line with a tape. Finally, the runner ran through the tape and then fell to the ground. His name was Abdul Baser Wasiqi. He was from Afghanistan.

22. 위 글의 제목으로 가장 적절한 것은? (4점)

① Let's Be Smart
② My Bucket List
③ A Love of Parents
④ The School Club Activity Day
⑤ A Hero from Afghanistan

23. 위 글의 내용과 일치하지 않는 것은? (5점)

① This story happened in 1996.
② The officials waited more than an hour.
③ Wasiqi broke the tape at the finish line.
④ Wasiqi's injury kept him from finishing the race.
⑤ Volunteers cheered for Wasiqi to finish the race.

24. 위 글의 밑줄 친 (A)와 어법상 쓰임이 같은 것은? (4점)

① I study hard to pass the exam.
② There are many books to read.
③ She wants to become a lawyer.
④ I have a lot of homework to do.
⑤ I exercise every day to stay healthy.

25. 위 글의 빈칸 (B)에 들어갈 말로 가장 적절한 것은? (4점)

① The runner won the gold medal.
② All eyes were on the runner.
③ The runner decided to join the army.
④ The runner was too young to join the race.
⑤ The runner entered the stadium during the closing ceremony.

26. 다음 글의 밑줄 친 ⓐ~ⓔ 중, 어법상 어색한 것은? (4점)

If you are ⓐunderlined{interested} in skiing or Winter Olympics, you might have heard of Eui Hyun Sin, the skier. He is a cross-country skier and the South Korean Paralympic athlete ⓑwho won the first gold medal for Korea in the 2018 Winter Paralympics. He was a healthy man until his early twenties, but his life completely changed after a car accident. He hurt his legs from the accident and ⓒlost his two legs. However, he did not give up, ⓓtrying several different sports to get better. Then he found out his special interest in skiing. As you know, skiing is not easy and not many people are good at skiing. However, he overcame his hardship. His passion and patience are now highly ⓔrespecting.

① ⓐ   ② ⓑ   ③ ⓒ   ④ ⓓ   ⑤ ⓔ

◎ 선택형 문항의 답안은 컴퓨터용 수정 싸인펜을 사용하여 OMR 답안지에 바르게 표기하시오.

◎ 서술형 문제는 답을 답안지에 반드시 검정 볼펜으로 쓰시오.

◎ 총 23문항 100점 만점입니다. 문항별 배점은 각 문항에 표시되어 있습니다.

[충남 ○○중]

1. 다음 대화의 내용과 일치하는 것은? (4점)

Jane: Have you heard of Eui Hyun Sin, the skier?

Tom: No. Who is he?

Jane: He's a Paralympian skier. He won the first gold medal for Korea in the 2018 Winter Paralympics.

Tom: Wow! That's great.

Jane: He was in a car accident in his early twenties and hurt his legs.

Tom: How was he able to become a skier?

Jane: After his accident, he tried several different sports to get better. Then he became especially interested in skiing.

Tom: Skiing is not easy. Not many people are good at skiing.

Jane: That's why he's so respected.

① Most people can ski well.
② Eui Hyun Sin tried only one sport.
③ Eui Hyun Sin won a gold medal in 2018.
④ Both speakers knew well about Eui Hyun Sin.
⑤ Eui Hyun Sin was in car accident before his twenties.

[충남 ○○중]

2. 다음 중 대화의 흐름이 가장 자연스러운 것은? (4점)

① A: I don't know what kind of job I want.
　 B: Don't worry. I'm not sure you'll do well.
② A: I'm nervous about tomorrow's speech contest.
　 B: I'm sure you'll sing very well.
③ A: I have a big soccer match tomorrow. I'm nervous.
　 B: Don't worry. You can pass the exam.
④ A: I'm having a hard time learning new English words.
　 B: You can ask your math teacher for advice.
⑤ A: I'm worried about making friends at my new school.
　 B: I'm sure you will make a lot of friends.

[경기 ○○중]

3. 다음 중 어법상 옳은 문장은? (5점)

① No one is too old to learning.
② We agreed never to telling the secret.
③ It is next Sunday who we will go for a picnic.
④ The older Sue gets, a wiser she becomes.
⑤ The boy told a lie to his mom not to disappoint her.

[충남 ○○중]

4. 다음 우리말과 일치하도록 할 때 빈칸에 알맞은 것은? (4점)

우리는 그 가수를 볼 수 있는 기회를 놓치지 않기 위해서 콘서트 표를 미리 예약했다.
→ We booked the concert tickets in advance _____ the chance to see the singer.

① not to missing
② never miss
③ never missing
④ not to miss
⑤ to not miss

5. 다음 대화의 빈칸에 가장 알맞은 표현은? (4점)

> **G:** Have you heard of Eui Hyun Sin, the skier?
>
> **B:** No. Who is he?
>
> **G:** He's a Paralympian skier. He won the first gold medal for Korea in the 2018 Winter Paralympics.
>
> **B:** Wow! That's great.
>
> **G:** He was in a car accident in his early twenties and hurt his legs.
>
> **B:** How was he able to become a skier?
>
> **G:** After his accident, he tried several different sports to get better. Then he became especially interested in skiing.
>
> **B:** Skiing is not easy. Not many people are good at skiing.
>
> **G:** That's why he's so _____.

① respected　　② silent　　③ lonely
④ handsome　　⑤ weak

6. 다음 문장은 순서 없이 나열한 것이다. 자연스러운 대화가 되도록 ⓐ~ⓔ의 문장을 순서대로 배열할 때, 가장 마지막에 오게 되는 것은? (5점)

> ⓐ Have you heard of D.I.Y.?
>
> ⓑ D.I.Y. stands for 'do-it-yourself.' I'm really into it. Right now, I'm making a pencil case.
>
> ⓒ No, what is D.I.Y.?
>
> ⓓ When I'm done with the pencil case, I'm planning to make my own desk.
>
> ⓔ What are you going to make after you finish that?

① ⓐ　　② ⓑ　　③ ⓒ　　④ ⓓ　　⑤ ⓔ

7. 다음 문장을 올바르게 바꿔 쓴 것은? (3점)

> He was too young to drive a car.

① He was so young to drive a car.
② He was so young enough to drive a car.
③ He was so young that he could drive a car.
④ He was so young that he could not drive a car.
⑤ He was too young that he could drive a car.

8. 다음 주어진 의미에 맞도록 영작한 문장 중, 가장 적절한 것은? (4점)

① 배우기에 너무 나이 든 사람은 없다.
　→ No one is too old to learn.
② 나는 가장 위의 선반에 닿기엔 키가 너무 작다.
　→ I was tall to reach the top shelf.
③ 우리는 마지막 열차를 타기엔 너무 늦었다.
　→ We were to catch the last train too late.
④ 그 휴대 전화는 너무 비싸서 살 수 없다.
　→ The cellphone was not too expensive to buy.
⑤ 나의 남동생은 너무 어려서 그 공포 영화를 볼 수 없다.
　→ My brother was old enough to see that horror movie.

[9~10] 다음 글을 읽고 물음에 답하시오.

Reporters came up to Wasiqi and started asking him questions.

R: What happened to you?

(A) Why not? You knew that you were too far behind to win a medal.

(B) I am the only athlete here representing Afghanistan. There was no way I could give up.

(C) I injured my leg during a practice run. The injury got worse during the race, but I couldn't give up.

R: Afghanistan is still at war, isn't it?

W: Yes, we have been at war for 16 years. That's why we were not able to send athletes to the Barcelona Olympics four years ago. I was sad for my country back then when I could see no Afghan athletes in the opening ceremony.

R = Reporter W = Wasiqi

9. 위 글의 (A)~(C)의 순서로 가장 적절한 것은? (4점)

① (A)–(B)–(C) ② (A)–(C)–(B)
③ (B)–(A)–(C) ④ (C)–(A)–(B)
⑤ (C)–(B)–(A)

10. According to the passage, why couldn't Afghanistan send athletes to the Barcelona Olympics? (4점)

① 당시 전쟁 중이었다.
② 올림픽 참가 금지 국가였다.
③ 과학 기술 발전에 중점을 두었다.
④ 전쟁이 종료된 지 얼마 안 지나서이다.
⑤ 지난 대회에서 모든 종목의 선수들이 예선 탈락하였다.

11. 다음 대화의 내용과 일치하는 것은? (5점)

A: Have you heard of Eui Hyun Sin, the skier?

B: No. Who is he?

A: He's a Paralympian skier. He won the first gold medal for Korea in the 2018 Winter Paralympics.

B: Wow! That's great.

A: He was in a car accident in his early twenties and hurt his legs.

B: How was he able to become a skier?

A: After his accident, he tried several different sports to get better. Then he became especially interested in skiing.

B: Skiing is not easy. Not many people are good at skiing.

A: That's why he's so respected.

① Eui Hyun Sin teaches Paralympian skiers.
② Eui Hyun Sin hurt his leg in his early thirties.
③ Eui Hyun Sin tried several different sports to win the medal.
④ Eui Hyun Sin became interested in skiing although it was not easy.
⑤ Eui Hyun Sin didn't win any medals in the 2018 Winter Paralympics.

12. 다음 글에서 전체 흐름과 관계<u>없는</u> 문장은? (5점)

> I Have a Goal to Win the Singing Contest
> ⓐI want to win the school singing contest. ⓑ I love singing, and I think I have a good voice. ⓒHowever, I am too shy to sing in front of many people. ⓓI realize that I want to see a concert of my favorite band right in front of the stage. ⓔNot to be nervous during the contest, I will practice singing in front of my class first.

① ⓐ   ② ⓑ   ③ ⓒ   ④ ⓓ   ⑤ ⓔ

[13~14] 다음 글을 읽고 물음에 답하시오.

> The last runner finished the race more than an hour before. "There will be no more runners (A)[come / coming]," the officials decided. They removed the tape at the finish line and started to prepare for the closing ceremony for the 1996 Atlanta Summer Olympics in the United States.
> Someone shouted, "Look! There comes another runner!" A runner was just entering the stadium, but there was something wrong with his legs. Still, he kept (B)[going / to go] toward the finish line. The band and the volunteers stopped their preparations for the closing ceremony. All eyes were on the runner.
> Suddenly, the band started playing celebration music, and the volunteers cheered. "Go! Go! Go for it!" Two volunteers ran to the finish line with a tape. Finally, the runner ran through the tape and then (C)[falling / fell] to the ground. His name was Abdul Baser Wasiqi. He was from Afghanistan.

13. 위 글의 괄호 (A), (B), (C) 안에서 적절한 표현끼리 짝지은 것은? (4점)

	(A)	(B)	(C)
①	come	going	falling
②	come	going	fell
③	coming	to go	fell
④	coming	to go	falling
⑤	coming	going	fell

14. 위 글의 내용과 일치하지 <u>않는</u> 것은? (5점)

① Wasiqi ran through the tape at the finish line.
② Wasiqi entered the stadium during the closing ceremony.
③ Wasiqi's injury did not keep him from finishing the race.
④ There was something wrong with his legs when Wasiqi entered the stadium.
⑤ The officials started to prepare for the closing ceremony before Wasiqi finished the race.

15. 다음 글의 밑줄 친 ⓐ~ⓔ 중, 어법상 적절하지 <u>않은</u> 것은? (5점)

> Last night, I set my clock for 8 o'clock ⓐ<u>not to be</u> late for school today. Because it is a long way to my school, it is important ⓑ<u>not to miss</u> the bus. Without having breakfast, I quickly left the house and went to the bus stop. Surprisingly, ⓒ<u>there was</u> nobody. Then, I remembered ⓓ<u>that</u> today was Saturday. From now on, ⓔ<u>it happen not to let</u> again, I will always check what day it is.

① ⓐ   ② ⓑ   ③ ⓒ   ④ ⓓ   ⑤ ⓔ

16. 다음 대화의 Wasiqi의 심정으로 가장 적절한 것은? (5점)

R: Were you running marathons then?

W: No. I started running after Barcelona Olympics. I ran in lots of races. Finally I won a marathon in Germany. As a result, I was able to come to Atlanta.

R: How do you feel now?

W: I am proud of myself and proud to be from Afghanistan. For me and my country, it was important not to give up. I didn't come here to win. For me, it was enough to be here and to finish the race.

R = Reporter W = Wasiqi

---

① scared
② satisfied
③ annoyed
④ concerned
⑤ disappointed

[17~20] 다음 글을 읽고 물음에 답하시오.

The last runner finished the race ⓐmore than an hour before. "There will be no more runners coming," the officials decided. They removed the tape at the finish line and started to prepare for the closing ceremony for the 1996 Atlanta Summer Olympics in the United States.

Someone shouted, "Look! There ⓑcome another runner!" A runner was just entering the stadium, but there was something wrong with his legs. Still, he kept going toward the finish line. The band and the volunteers stopped their preparations for the closing ceremony. All eyes were on the runner.

Suddenly, the band started playing celebration music, and the volunteers cheered. "Go! Go! Go for it!" Two volunteers ran to the finish line with a tape.

Finally, the runner ran through the tape and then fell to the ground. His name was Abdul Baser Wasiqi. He was from Afghanistan.

Reporters came up to Wasiqi and started asking him questions.

Reporter: What happened to you?

Wasiqi: I injured my leg during a practice run. The injury got worse during the race, but I couldn't give up.

Reporter: Why not? You knew that you were ⓒtoo far behind to win a medal.

Wasiqi: I am the only athlete here representing Afghanistan. There was no way I could give up.

Reporter: Afghanistan is still at war, isn't it?

Wasiqi: Yes, we have been at war for 16 years. That's why we were not able to send athletes to the Barcelona Olympics four years ago. I was sad for my country ⓓback then when I could see no Afghan athletes in the opening ceremony.

Reporter: Were you running marathons then?

Wasiqi: No. I started running after Barcelona. I ran in lots of races. Finally I won a marathon in Germany. As a result, I was able to come to Atlanta.

Reporter: How do you feel now?

Wasiqi: I am proud of myself and proud to be from Afghanistan. For me and my country, it was important not to give up. I didn't come here to win. For me, it was ⓔenough to be here and to finish the race.

17. 위 글의 제목으로 알맞은 것은? (4점)

① The First Winner
② The First Game
③ The Last Dinner
④ The Last Runner
⑤ The Last Kingdom

18. 위 글의 ⓐ~ⓔ 중, 어법상 적절하지 <u>않은</u> 것은? (4점)

① ⓐ   ② ⓑ   ③ ⓒ   ④ ⓓ   ⑤ ⓔ

19. 다음은 위 글을 읽고 퀴즈를 푼 학생의 답안지이다. 학생의 답안 중, 맞는 것은 몇 개인가? (5점)

Quiz #1

Nam YooJung

1. Who removed the tape at the finish line?
   → The first runner removed the tape.
2. What was wrong with the runner entering the stadium?
   → He had something wrong with his legs.
3. When did Wasiqi injure his leg?
   → He injured his leg during a practice run.
4. Why couldn't Afghanistan send athletes to the Barcelona Olympics?
   → It has been at war for 6 years.
5. What was important for Wasiqi?
   → It was important not to give up.

---

① 1개   ② 2개   ③ 3개   ④ 4개   ⑤ 5개

20. 다음은 위 글에 등장하는 리포터가 인터뷰 후 작성한 신문기사의 내용이다. 글의 내용으로 볼 때 ⓐ~ⓔ 중, <u>어색한</u> 것은? (5점)

A Hero from Afghanistan

There was a marathon race at the end of ⓐ<u>the 1996 Atlanta Summer Olympics</u>. When most runners finished racing, and ⓑ<u>the officials started to prepare for the closing ceremony</u>, a runner entered the stadium. The runner finally ran through the tape and ⓒ<u>then fell to the ground</u>. His name was Abdul Baser Wasiqi, and ⓓ<u>he was the only athlete representing Afghanistan</u>. ⓔ<u>He gave up running the race for his country.</u>

---

① ⓐ   ② ⓑ   ③ ⓒ   ④ ⓓ   ⑤ ⓔ

[21~23] 다음 글을 읽고 물음에 답하시오.

Reporters ⓐ<u>came up to</u> Wasiqi and started (A) <u>asking</u> him questions.

Reporter: What happened to you?

Wasiqi: I injured my leg during a practice run. The injury ⓑ<u>got worse</u> during the race, but I couldn't give up.

Reporter: Why not? You knew that you were too far behind to win a medal.

Wasiqi: I'm the only athlete here representing Afghanistan. There was no way I could ⓒ<u>give up</u>.

Reporter: Afghanistan is still ⓓ<u>at war</u>, isn't it?

Wasiqi: Yes, we have been at war for 16 years. That's why we ⓔ<u>were not able to send</u>

---

athletes to the Barcelona Olympics four years ago. I was sad for my country back then when I could see no Afghan athletes in the opening ceremony.

21. 위 글의 밑줄 친 ⓐ~ⓔ 중 의미가 어색한 것은?　　　(4점)

① ⓐ – ~에게 다가왔다
② ⓑ – 더 심해졌다
③ ⓒ – 승리하다
④ ⓓ – 전쟁 중인
⑤ ⓔ – ~할 수 없었다

22. 위 글의 밑줄 친 (A)와 바꿔 쓸 수 있는 것은?　　　(4점)

① ask　　　　② to ask
③ to be asked　　④ to be asking
⑤ to have asked

23. 위 글을 읽고, 다음 질문에 가장 알맞은 대답을 고르면?　(4점)

Q: Why couldn't Afghanistan send athletes to the Barcelona Olympics?

① Because reporters didn't interview Wasiqi.
② Because Wasiqi injured his leg during a practice run.
③ Because Afghanistan has been at war for 16 years.
④ Because there were no athletes from Afghanistan in the Barcelona Olympics.
⑤ Because Afghanistan took part in the Barcelona Olympics four years ago.

3학년 영어 1학기 중간고사(2과) 1회

| 반 | | 점수 | |
| 이름 | | | |

문항수 : 선택형(23문항) 서술형(1문항)   20 . . .

◎ 선택형 문항의 답안은 컴퓨터용 수정 싸인펜을 사용하여 OMR 답안지에 바르게 표기하시오.
◎ 서술형 문제는 답을 답안지에 반드시 검정 볼펜으로 쓰시오.
◎ 총 24문항 100점 만점입니다. 문항별 배점은 각 문항에 표시되어 있습니다.

1. 다음 빈칸에 공통으로 들어갈 말로 가장 적절한 것은?   (4점)

> <가>
>
> **B:** I have a big soccer match tomorrow. I'm nervous.
> **G:** Don't worry. ＿＿＿＿＿＿ you'll play very well.
>
> <나>
>
> **G:** I'm worried about making friends at my new school.
> **M:** Don't worry. ＿＿＿＿＿＿ you'll make friends there.

① I agree   ② I'm sure
③ I was sure   ④ I'm not sure
⑤ I don't agree

2. Which one is NOT a natural conversation?   (4점)

① A: How was he able to become a famous reporter?
  B: He practiced speaking with people in public.

② A: Have you heard of Mia, the guitar player?
  B: Yes, I have.

③ A: I think listening to music helps you relax.
  B: I agree with you.

④ A: I'm worried about making friends at my new school.
  B: Don't worry. I'm sure you'll not make a lot of friends there.

⑤ A: I think it's important to eat a good breakfast.
  B: I think so, too.

[3~4] 다음 대화를 읽고 물음에 답하시오.

> **A:** The team project for English class is taking a lot of time.
> **B:** I agree. I have a problem. ⓐUnderlined One of the people on our team isn't doing his part.
> **A:** That's not good. Everybody on the team has to do their job.
> **B:** ⓑI don't know, but I know how to get him to do his part-time job.
> **A:** Maybe he doesn't know how to get started or doesn't like his part.
> **B:** Then what should I do?
> **A:** Talk to him. ⓒAsk him why he's not doing his part. Then tell him you'll help him if he wants.
> **B:** Okay. I'll try that.
> **A:** ⓓI'm sure he'll do better after you talk to him. ⓔGood luck with your project.

3. 위 대화의 내용상 어색한 문장은?   (4점)

① ⓐ   ② ⓑ   ③ ⓒ   ④ ⓓ   ⑤ ⓔ

4. 위 대화의 내용과 일치하지 않는 것은? (4점)

① 영어 수업의 팀 과제는 시간이 적게 소모된다.

② 팀원 중 한 명이 적극적으로 참여하지 않는다.

③ 팀 과제에서 자기 역할을 하지 않는 것은 좋지 않다.

④ 자신의 역할을 하지 않는 팀원은 어떻게 시작해야 하는지 모를 수도 있다.

⑤ 자신의 역할을 하지 않는 팀원에게 그 이유를 물어보기로 했다.

[5~7] 다음 대화를 읽고 물음에 답하시오.

(A)

B: The team project for English class is taking a lot of time.

G: I agree. I have a problem. One of the people on our team isn't doing his part.

B: That's not good. Everybody on the team has to do their job.

G: I know, but I don't know how to get him to do this part.

B: Maybe he doesn't know how to get started or doesn't like his part.

G: Then what should I do?

B: Talk to him. Ask him why he's not doing his part. Then tell him you'll help him if he wants.

G: Okay. I'll try that.

B: I'm sure he'll do better after you talk to him. Good luck with your project.

G: Thanks.

↓

(B)

G: Taemin, can I talk with you about our _____ for a while?

B: Sure. What is it?

G: I don't think you've started on _____ yet. Are you having any problems doing it?

B: Actually, I don't know _____. My part is really difficult to me.

G: I see. If you want, I can _____.

B: That would be great. Can you go with me to the library and _____ find information?

B: Sure.

5. 위 대화 (A)의 주제로 가장 알맞은 것은? (4점)

① 팀원들과 잘 지내는 방법

② 팀으로 일하는 것의 장점들

③ 팀 프로젝트에 대한 소녀의 고민

④ 팀 프로젝트에 대한 소녀의 의무

⑤ 팀 프로젝트가 잘 진행된다는 자랑

6. 위 대화 (A)의 내용과 일치하지 않는 것은? (3점)

① 영어 수업을 위한 팀 프로젝트는 많은 시간이 필요하다.

② 소녀의 팀 프로젝트 수행에 문제가 있다.

③ 소녀는 팀원들 중 한 명에게 그의 일을 하라고 이야기할 수 있는 방법을 알고 싶어 한다.

④ 소녀는 팀원들 중 한 명에게 왜 그의 역할을 하지 않는지 물어볼 예정이다.

⑤ 소녀의 팀원들은 합심하여 영어 수업의 과제를 잘 수행하고 있다.

7. 위 대화 (B)는 소녀가 (A)에서 언급한 팀원인 Taemin과 대화하는 내용이다. (A)의 내용을 참고하여 (B)의 빈칸에 넣어 대화를 완성할 때, 어디에도 들어갈 수 <u>없는</u> 것은? (5점)

① help me
② my part
③ help you
④ team project
⑤ how to get started

8. 다음 말에 대한 대답으로 가장 알맞은 것은? (4점)

> I think reading history comic books is helpful.

① I agree. I don't think they're helpful.
② I agree. Reading books is not helpful.
③ I agree. I learn a lot from them.
④ I don't agree. I think they're helpful.
⑤ I disagree. Reading history books is helpful.

9. 다음 대화의 흐름에 맞게 〈보기〉의 문장을 가장 적절하게 배열한 것은? (5점)

> B: I just talked about the science team project with Jinho and Mina.
> G: _____
> B: _____
> G: _____
> B: _____
> G: Then you should persuade Jinho to do an experiment.

┌ 보기 ┐
(A) I agree with Mina because I think the experiment would be more interesting.
(B) Has your team decided what to do?
(C) Who do you agree with, Jinho or Mina?
(D) No, not yet. Jinho wants to visit a science museum, but Mina wants to do an experiment.

① (A)–(B)–(D)–(C) ② (A)–(D)–(B)–(C)
③ (B)–(C)–(A)–(D) ④ (B)–(D)–(C)–(A)
⑤ (C)–(D)–(B)–(A)

10. 다음 대화의 빈칸에 들어갈 알맞은 표현은? (4점)

> B: Our P.E. teacher is too strict. Don't you agree?
> A: _____ I don't think he's too strict.

① Yes, I do. ② Yes, I am.
③ No, I don't. ④ No, I am not.
⑤ Thanks a lot.

11. 다음 능동태의 문장을 수동태로 바꿀 때 올바른 것은? (4점)

① She made me a pretty doll.
　→ I was made a pretty doll by her.
② I saw him enter the room.
　→ He was seen enter the room by me.
③ They think that the movie is touching.
　→ The movie is thought that is touching.
④ The kids were painting the walls.
　→ The walls were been painted by the kids.
⑤ They elected him chairman.
　→ He was elected chairman (by them).

12. 다음 괄호 안의 표현을 이용하여 주어진 문장을 〈보기〉와 같이 바꾸어 쓰시오. (6점)

┌─ 보기 ┤
_____, Minji walked into the classroom. (listen to music)
　→ Listening to music, Minji walked into the classroom.

(1) _____, I just stayed home. (have a bad cold)
(2) _____, he started talking to Hana. (stand by the tree)

(1) _____
(2) _____

Everyone ⓐhas worries. When you have things you worry about, what do you do? Here are some things ⓑthat three teenagers worry about.

Sohui thought Hayeon was her best friend, but now, Sohui feels that Hayeon ⓒhas changed and she is avoiding her.

Sohui: (To her older sister) You know my friend Hayeon, don't you?

Sister: Yeah. Why? What about her?

Sohui: I feel she's avoiding me. When I see her at school, she turns around and walks away from me.

Sister: I'm sorry to hear that. Do you have any idea why she does that?

Sohui: No. I don't think I've done ⓓanything wrong. It just feels like she doesn't like me Ⓐanymore.

Sister: Maybe you should just ask her if there is ⓔwrong something.

Sohui: Maybe I should. I still want to be friends with her.

13. 위 글의 밑줄 친 ⓐ~ⓔ 중 어법상 어색한 것은? (4점)

① ⓐ　　② ⓑ　　③ ⓒ　　④ ⓓ　　⑤ ⓔ

14. 밑줄 친 Ⓐ와 바꿔 쓸 수 있는 것은? (4점)

① the more　　② any longer
③ any long　　④ some longer
⑤ some long

[충남 ○○중]

15. 위 글의 내용과 일치하는 것은? (4점)

① 소희는 하연이가 그녀의 가장 친한 친구라고 생각하지 않았다.

② 소희는 하연이가 요새 그녀를 피한다고 느끼지 않는다.

③ 소희는 자신이 하연이에게 잘못한 게 많다고 생각한다.

④ 소희의 언니는 소희에게 뭔가 잘못된 것이 있을 수 있으니 하연이에게 물어보는 게 좋을 것 같다고 충고하였다.

⑤ 소희는 이젠 하연이와 친구로 지내고 싶어하지 않는다.

[경기 ○○중]

16. 다음 글의 밑줄 친 ⓐ~ⓔ 중, 어법상 옳은 것은? (5점)

One day, Jane got a call from her friend. "Can you walk my dog? I can't go out right now!" It was a very busy day for Jane, too. ⓐ<u>She had to be prepared an important presentation for the next day.</u> Before thinking, however, she found herself saying yes. "Oh, sure. Why not?"

After hanging up the phone, ⓑ<u>she realized there was wrong something.</u> "What about my presentation? Why can't I say no to people?" After some serious thought, ⓒ<u>Jane realized she had said yes because she wanted her friends to accept her.</u> She thought she might lose her friend if she said no. "I can't live like this for the rest of my life, but how can I fix it?" she kept thinking. ⓓ<u>An idea was struck her and she called her friend.</u> "I'm sorry. I am very busy so I won't be able to go to your place to pick the dog today. ⓔ<u>If you come to my place and drop the dog, I will be able to walk them later.</u> Can you do that?" Her friend said "yes, that would be fine."

[17~20] 다음 글을 읽고 물음에 답하시오.

Recently, Minkyeong was (A)_____ out by a boy in her class. She wants to say no but does not want to hurt his feelings.

Minkyeong: I need your advice. A boy in my class ⓐ<u>asked me out</u>. I like him, but for now I don't want to go out with him. I need ⓑ<u>to focus</u> on my studies. What should I do?

Counselor: Why don't you tell him ⓒ<u>why can't you go</u>?

Minkyeong: I'm afraid _____.

Counselor: If you ⓓ<u>don't tell</u> him soon, he will misunderstand your feelings, and you may end up (B)_____ him ⓔ<u>even more</u>.

Minkyeong: Maybe you're right. Thanks for the advice.

[충남 ○○중]

17. 위 글의 빈칸 (A)와 (B)에 들어갈 적당한 것은? (4점)

	(A)	(B)
①	ask	hurting
②	asked	hurt
③	asking	hurting
④	asked	hurting
⑤	asked	hurts

18. 위 글의 빈칸에 들어갈 적당한 것은? (4점)

① she might say yes
② she could get bad grades
③ he might have a girlfriend
④ I might hurt his feelings
⑤ he could understand my feelings

19. 위 글의 밑줄 친 부분 중, 어법상 어색한 것은? (4점)

① ⓐ ② ⓑ ③ ⓒ ④ ⓓ ⑤ ⓔ

20. 위 글의 내용과 일치하는 것은? (4점)

① Minkyeong went out with a boy recently.
② Minkyeong likes the boy, so she wants to go out with him.
③ Minkyeong asked the counselor how to ask a boy out.
④ The counselor advised to tell him as late as possible.
⑤ Minkyeong thinks that she could not focus on her studies if she goes out with the boy.

21. 다음 밑줄 친 (a)~(e) 중, 어법상 틀린 것은? (4점)

> Daeho, (a)thinking that new things will make him more popular, often wants new things just because his friends have (b)them.
>
> **Daeho:** Seongjin, look at my new sneakers. What do you think?
>
> **Seongjin:** They're nice, but didn't you buy new sneakers a couple of months ago?
>
> **Daeho:** Yeah, but they're (c)no longer in style. I look cooler in these, right?
>
> **Seongjin:** Daeho, wearing the latest fashion (d)doesn't make you cooler or more popular. People like you (e)because of you're you, not because of your clothes.
>
> **Daeho:** Yeah?
>
> **Seongjin:** Listen, you're a great guy. You don't need new sneakers to prove it.

① (a) ② (b) ③ (c) ④ (d) ⑤ (e)

[22~23] 다음 글을 읽고 물음에 답하시오.

> Sohui thought Hayeon was her best friend, but now, Sohui feels that Hayeon ⓐhas changed and she is avoiding her.
>
> **Sohui:** (To her older sister) You know my friend Hayeon, ⓑdon't you?
>
> **Sister:** Yeah. Why? What about her?
>
> **Sohui:** I feel she's avoiding me. When I see her at school, she turns around and walks away from me.

Sister: I'm sorry to hear that. Do you have any idea ⓒwhy she does that?

Sohui: No. I don't think I've done anything wrong. It just feels like she doesn't like me anymore.

Sister: Maybe you should just ask her ⓓif there is wrong something.

Sohui: Maybe I should. I still want to be friends with her.

Daeho, (A)as he thinks that new things will make him more popular, often wants new things just because his friends have them.

Daeho: Seongjin, look at my new sneakers. What do you think?

Seongjin: They're nice, but didn't you buy new sneakers a couple of months ago?

Daeho: Yeah, but they're no longer in style. I look cooler in these, right?

Seongjin: Daeho, wearing the latest fashion doesn't make you cooler or more popular.

[인천 ○○중]

22. 위 글의 밑줄 친 ⓐ~ⓓ 중, 어법상 옳은 것을 있는 대로 고른 것은? (4점)

① ⓐ, ⓑ
② ⓑ, ⓒ
③ ⓑ, ⓓ
④ ⓐ, ⓑ, ⓒ
⑤ ⓑ, ⓒ, ⓓ

[경북 ○○중]

23. 위 글의 (A)를 분사구문으로 바르게 바꾼 것은? (4점)

① thought that new things will make him more popular

② thinking that new things will make him more popular

③ he thought that new things will make him more popular

④ as thinking that new things will make him more popular

⑤ he is thinking that new things will make him more popular

[세종 ○○중]

24. 다음 밑줄 친 (a)~(e) 중에서 문맥상 낱말의 쓰임이 적절하지 않은 것은? (4점)

Recently, Minkyeong was asked (a)out by a boy in her class. She wants to say no but does not want to hurt his feelings.

Minkyeong: I need your (b)advice. A boy in my class asked me out. I like him, but for now I don't want to go out with him. I need to (c)focus on my studies. What should I do?

Counselor: Why don't you tell him (d)why you can't go?

Minkyeong: I'm afraid I might hurt his feelings.

Counselor: If you don't tell him soon, he will (e)understand your feelings, and you may end up hurting him even more.

Minkyeong: Maybe you're right. Thanks for the advice.

① (a)　　② (b)　　③ (c)　　④ (d)　　⑤ (e)

◎ 선택형 문항의 답안은 컴퓨터용 수정 싸인펜을 사용하여 OMR 답안지에 바르게 표기하시오.
◎ 서술형 문제는 답을 답안지에 반드시 검정 볼펜으로 쓰시오.
◎ 총 27문항 100점 만점입니다. 문항별 배점은 각 문항에 표시되어 있습니다.

[울산 ○○중]

1. 다음 대화 중 어색한 것은? (3점)

① A: I think reading history comic books is helpful.
   B: I think so, too. I learn a lot from them.
② A: You look worried. Is something wrong?
   B: Yes, my sister is upset with me. I wore one of her shirts without asking.
③ A: I'm nervous about tomorrow's speech contest.
   B: I'm sure you'll do fine. Don't worry.
④ A: Our P.E. teacher is too strict. Don't you agree?
   B: Yes, I agree. I don't think he's too strict.
⑤ A: I'm having a hard time learning new English words.
   B: I had the same problem, so I asked my English teacher for advice.

[경기 ○○중]

2. 다음 대화에서 앞으로 John이 할 일로 가장 적절한 것은? (4점)

John: Mom told me that I could use the computer for only one hour a day. She thinks that's enough time.
Dad: I agree with her.
John: Sometimes, when doing my homework, I need to use it for a long time.
Dad: Hmm. Then maybe we should all get together and talk about it.
John: Thanks for your understanding. I'll do as you said.

① He will check if his computer works well.
② He will play a computer game with his father.
③ He will do his homework instead of talking with his mom.
④ He will discuss the time of using a computer with his parents.
⑤ He will promise his mom not to use a computer when doing his homework.

[경기 ○○중]

3. 다음 대화에서 Emma의 고민으로 가장 적절한 것은? (4점)

Hajun: The team project for English class is taking a lot of time.
Emma: I agree. I have a problem. One of the people on our team isn't doing his part.
Hajun: That's not good. Everybody on the team has to do their job.
Emma: I know, but I don't know how to get him to do his part.
Hajun: Maybe he doesn't know how to get started or doesn't like his part.
Emma: Then what should I do?
Hajun: Talk to him. Ask him why he's not doing his part. Then tell him you'll help him if he wants.
Emma: Okay. I'll try that.
Hajun: I'm sure he'll do better after you talk to him. Good luck with your project.
Emma: Thanks.

① 자신의 역할을 다하지 않는 팀원
② 맡은 일을 하기 싫어하는 팀원의 불만
③ 프로젝트 주제를 바꾸고 싶어 하는 팀원
④ 너무 어려운 팀 프로젝트 주제와 짧은 기한
⑤ 다른 팀과 비교되는 프로젝트 준비 과정 및 결과물

[울산 ○○중]

Tom: The team project for English class is taking a lot of time.

Jane: I agree. I have a problem. One of the people on our team isn't doing his part.

Tom: That's not good. Everybody on the team has to do their job.

Jane: I know, but I don't know how to get him to do his part.

Tom: Maybe he doesn't know how to get started or doesn't like his part.

Jane: (A)그러면 어떻게 하면 좋을까?

Tom: Talk to him. Ask him why he's not doing his part. Then tell him you'll help him if he wants.

Jane: Okay. I'll try that.

Tom: I'm sure he'll do better after you talk to him. Good luck with your project.

Jane: Thanks.

6. 다음 대화의 흐름에 맞게 'agree'를 이용하여 빈칸에 들어갈 문장을 완성하시오. (4점)

A: I just talked about the science project with Jinho and Mina.

B: Has your team decided what you will do?

A: No, not yet. Jinho wants to visit a science museum, but Mina wants to do an experiment.

B: _____,
Jinho or Mina?

A: I agree with Mina because I think the experiment would be more interesting.

정답: _____

[경기 ○○중]

4. 위 대화의 내용과 일치하는 것은? (4점)

① Tom은 영어 수업을 어려워하고 있다.

② Jane은 조별 과제를 수행하는 데 문제가 있다.

③ Jane의 조원들은 대부분 과제를 포기하고 있다.

④ Jane은 Tom에게 과제에 대한 조언을 해주고 있다.

⑤ Tom은 과제를 모두 마치고 Jane을 도와주고 있다.

[경기 ○○중]

5. 위 대화의 (A)를 바르게 영작한 것은? (3점)

① Then what I should do?

② Then what should I do?

③ What should I have to do?

④ How we should do something?

⑤ Then what are you have to do?

[충남 ○○중]

7. 다음 중 대화가 어색한 것은? (3점)

① A: I think listening to music helps you relax.
   B: I agree. I like listening to music.

② A: I think reading history comic books is helpful.
   B: I agree. I learn a lot from them.

③ A: Our school festival is going to be a lot of fun.
   B: I agree.

④ A: Our P.E. teacher is too strict. Don't you agree?
   B: No, I don't agree. I think he's too strict.

⑤ A: English homework is taking a lot of time.
   B: I agree. It's really difficult.

8. 주어진 문장 다음에 이어지는 문장의 순서로 가장 적절한 것은?

(4점)

> G: You look worried. Is something wrong?
>
> B: _____
>
> G: _____
>
> B: _____
>
> G: _____
>
> *G: Girl, B: Boy

> (A) Why? What did you do?
> (B) Yes, my sister is upset with me.
> (C) I wore one of her shirts without asking.
> (D) Tell her you're sorry. I'm sure she'll understand.

① (B)–(A)–(C)–(D)　② (B)–(C)–(D)–(A)
③ (B)–(C)–(A)–(D)　④ (D)–(A)–(B)–(C)
⑤ (D)–(B)–(C)–(A)

9. 두 문장의 의미가 같도록 빈칸에 알맞은 말을 넣으면? (3점)

> Because I don't have enough money, I cannot buy the smartphone.
> = _____ having enough money, I cannot buy the smartphone.

① Because　② Not　③ No
④ Don't　⑤ As

10. 다음 문장의 밑줄 친 부분과 의미가 같은 것은? (4점)

> <u>When she heard about the accident</u>, she was shocked.

① Heard about the accident
② Hearing about the accident
③ She hearing about the accident
④ When she hear about the accident
⑤ When she hearing about the accident

11. What is the reason Jane's sister is upset? (4점)

> Tom: You look worried. Is something wrong?
> Jane: Yes, my sister is upset with me.
> Tom: Why? What did you do?
> Jane: I wore one of her shirts without asking.
> Tom: Tell her you're sorry. I'm sure she'll understand.

① Jane told her sister she's sorry.
② Jane didn't understand what was wrong.
③ Jane didn't lend her shirts to her sister.
④ Jane didn't understand why her sister is upset.
⑤ Jane wore her sister's clothes without permission.

12. 다음 밑줄 친 'if'의 쓰임이 나머지와 넷과 다른 것은? (4점)

① I doubt <u>if</u> she will like my present.
② I'm wondering <u>if</u> you could help me.
③ I am not sure <u>if</u> he still remembers me.
④ I don't know <u>if</u> he will follow my advice.
⑤ I will tell you everything <u>if</u> you keep the secret.

13. 다음 밑줄 친 'if'의 쓰임이 나머지 넷과 <u>다른</u> 것은? (4점)

① I wonder <u>if</u> he can pass the exam.

② Please check <u>if</u> everything is correct.

③ Mr. Brown asked me <u>if</u> I knew the answer.

④ We will not go on a picnic <u>if</u> it rains tomorrow.

⑤ I am not sure <u>if</u> she will like my present.

[14~16] 다음 글을 읽고 물음에 답하시오.

> Recently, Minkyeong was asked out by a boy in her class. She wants to ⓐ<u>say no</u> but does not want to hurt his feelings.
>
> **Minkyeong:** I need your advice. A boy in my class ⓑ<u>asked me out</u>. I like him, but for now I don't want to ⓒ<u>go out with</u> him. I need to ⓓ<u>focus on</u> my studies. What should I do?
>
> **Counselor:** Why don't you tell him why you can't go?
>
> **Minkyeong:** I'm afraid I might hurt his feelings.
>
> **Counselor:** If you don't tell him soon, he will misunderstand your feelings, and you may ⓔ<u>end up</u> hurting him Ⓐ<u>even</u> more.
>
> **Minkyeong:** Maybe you're right. Thanks for the advice.

14. 위 글의 밑줄 친 ⓐ~ⓔ 중 의미가 <u>틀린</u> 것은? (4점)

① ⓐ – 거절하다

② ⓑ – 나에게 물어보았다

③ ⓒ – ~와 데이트를 하다

④ ⓓ – 집중하다

⑤ ⓔ – 결국 ~하게 되다

15. 위 글의 밑줄 친 Ⓐ와 바꿔 쓸 수 <u>없는</u> 것은? (3점)

① still   ② far   ③ very

④ a lot   ⑤ much

16. 위 글을 읽고, 다음 질문에 가장 알맞은 대답을 고르시오. (4점)

> Q: Why does Minkyeong want to say no to the boy?

① Because she needs to focus on her studies for now.

② Because she needs his advice about her studies.

③ Because she wants to go out with him for now.

④ Because she does not want to hurt his feelings.

⑤ Because she needs to tell him why she can't go out with him.

[17~18] 다음 글을 읽고 물음에 답하시오.

> Sohui thought Hayeon was her best friend, but now, Sohui feels that Hayeon has changed and she is avoiding (a)<u>her</u>.
>
> **Sohui:** (To her older sister) You know my friend Hayeon, don't you?
>
> **Sister:** Yeah. Why? What about (b)<u>her</u>?
>
> **Sohui:** I feel she's avoiding me. When I see her at school, (c)<u>she</u> turns around and walks away from me.
>
> **Sister:** Do you have any idea why she does that?
>
> **Sohui:** No. I don't think I've done anything

wrong. It just feels like (d)she doesn't like me anymore.

Sister: Maybe you should just ask (e)her if there is something wrong.

Sohui: Maybe I should. I still want to be friends with her.

[경기 ○○중]

17. 위 글의 밑줄 친 (a)~(e) 중에서 가리키는 대상이 나머지 넷과 <u>다른</u> 것은? (4점)

① (a)　　② (b)　　③ (c)　　④ (d)　　⑤ (e)

[경기 ○○중]

18. 위 글의 주제로 가장 적절한 것은? (4점)

① the ways to be a good friend
② Sohui and her sister's school life
③ the relationship with friends and siblings
④ Sohui's happy memory with her friend
⑤ the worries of Sohui and advice from her sister

[19~23] 다음 글을 읽고 물음에 답하시오.

Everyone has worries. When you have things you worry about, what do you do? Here are some things that three teenagers worry about.

(A)
Sohui thought Hayeon was her best friend, but now, Sohui feels that Hayeon has changed and she is avoiding her.

Sohui: (To her older sister) You know my friend Hayeon, don't you?

Sister: Yeah. Why? What about her?

Sohui: I feel she's avoiding me. When I see her at school, she turns around and walks

away from me.

Sister: I'm sorry to hear that. Do you have any idea why she does that?

Sohui: No. I don't think I've done anything wrong. It just feels like she doesn't like me anymore.

Sister: Maybe you should just ask her if there is something wrong.

Sohui: Maybe I should. I still want to be friends with her.

(B)
ⓐThinking that new things will make him more popular, Daeho often wants new things just because his friends have them.

Daeho: Seongjin, look at my new sneakers. What do you think?

Seongjin: They're nice, but didn't you just buy new sneakers a couple of months ago?

Daeho: Yeah, but they're no longer in style. I look cooler in these, right?

Seongjin: Daeho, wearing the latest fashion doesn't make you cooler or more popular. People like you because you're you, not because of your clothes.

Daeho: Yeah?

Seongjin: Listen, you're a great guy. You don't need new sneakers to prove it.

(C)
Recently, Minkyeong was asked out by a boy in her class. She wants to say no but does not want to hurt his feelings.

Minkyeong: I need your advice. A boy in my class asked me out. I like him, but for now I don't want to go out with him. I need to focus on my studies. What should I do?

Counselor: Why don't you tell him why you can't go?

Minkyeong: I'm afraid I might hurt his feelings.

Counselor: If you don't tell him soon, he will misunderstand your feelings, and you may end up hurting him even more.

Minkyeong: Maybe you're right. Thanks for the advice.

[양천구 ○○중]

19. 위 글 (A)의 내용에 대한 의견으로 옳지 <u>않은</u> 것은? (3점)

① 근오: 소희는 하연이가 자신을 피한다고 생각해.
② 수홍: 소희는 하연이와 친한 사이였다고 생각했어.
③ 주완: 언니는 하연이와 사이좋게 지내라고 충고했어.
④ 준희: 소희는 하연이에게 잘못한 게 있다고 생각하지 않아.
⑤ 민재: 소희는 계속해서 하연이와 친구로 지내는 것을 원해.

[양천구 ○○중]

20. 위 글 (B)의 밑줄 친 ⓐ와 의미가 같은 것은? (4점)

① As he thinks that new things will make him more popular
② If he thinks that new things will make him more popular
③ That he thinks that new things will make him more popular
④ But he thinks that new things will not make him more popular
⑤ Though he thinks that new things will not make him more popular

[양천구 ○○중]

21. 위 글의 (A)와 (C)에 나타난 소희와 민경의 공통된 심경으로 알맞은 것은? (4점)

① glad   ② angry   ③ worried
④ happy   ⑤ pleased

[양천구 ○○중]

22. 위 글 (C)를 읽고 답할 수 <u>없는</u> 질문은? (4점)

① What is Minkyeong worried about?
② Who recently asked Minkyeong out?
③ Who does Minkyeong ask for advice?
④ Why does Minkyeong want to say "No" to a boy?
⑤ What subject does Minkyeong want to study harder?

[양천구 ○○중]

23. 위 글 (A)와 (C)의 주제로 가장 알맞은 것은? (3점)

① 십대들을 지도하는 것에 대한 어려움
② 십대들의 적성과 진로에 대한 고민들
③ 십대들이 좋아하는 패션에 대한 고민들
④ 십대들이 가지고 있는 다양한 고민들
⑤ 십대들이 가지고 있는 친구나 가족과의 갈등에 대한 고민

[양천구 ○○중]

24. 다음 두 문장의 의미가 같도록 할 때 빈칸에 알맞은 것을 쓰시오. (4점)

As he didn't know what to do, he asked for my advice.
→ _____, he asked for my advice.

→ _____

[25~27] 다음 대화를 읽고 물음에 답하시오.

27. 위 대화의 내용과 일치하지 <u>않는</u> 것은?　　　(4점)

① 하연이는 소희의 친구다.

② 소희는 하연이에게 용서를 빌고 싶어 한다.

③ 소희는 하연이의 행동이 변했다고 느낀다.

④ 소희의 언니가 소희에게 충고를 해주고 있다.

⑤ 소희는 하연이와 계속 친구로 지내고 싶어한다.

Sohui: (To her older sister) You know my friend Hayeon, don't you?

Sister: Yeah. Why? What about her?

Sohui: I feel she's (A)_____ me. (B)_____ I see her at school, she turns around and walks away from me.

Sister: I'm sorry to hear that. Do you have any idea (C)_____ she does that?

Sohui: No, I don't think I've done anything wrong. It just feels like doesn't like me anymore.

Sister: Maybe you should ask her if there is something wrong.

Sohui: Maybe I should still want to be friends with her.

---

25. 위 대화의 빈칸 (A)에 들어갈 말로 적당한 것은?　　(3점)

① preparing　　　② giving

③ following　　　④ avoiding

⑤ calling

---

26. 위 대화의 빈칸 (B), (C)에 들어갈 말로 적당한 것은?　　(4점)

① When – why

② Where – why

③ What – where

④ What – which

⑤ When – where

◎ 선택형 문항의 답안은 컴퓨터용 수정 싸인펜을 사용하여 OMR 답안지에 바르게 표기하시오.

◎ 서술형 문제는 답을 답안지에 반드시 검정 볼펜으로 쓰시오.

◎ 총 27문항 100점 만점입니다. 문항별 배점은 각 문항에 표시되어 있습니다.

[경기 ○○중]

1. 다음 빈칸에 공통으로 들어갈 말로 가장 적절한 것은? (4점)

• The children were playing in the warm spring _____.

• Without enough _____, our bodies would become less healthy.

① benefit
② hormone
③ sunshine
④ climate
⑤ sunscreen

[대전 ○○중]

2. 다음 대화의 흐름이 자연스럽지 <u>않은</u> 것은? (3점)

① A: Aren't you cold?
　B: Yes. I should have worn a jacket.

② A: We missed our flight.
　B: Oh, no. We should have come earlier.

③ A: Your bag is too small.
　B: Yes. I should have brought a smaller one.

④ A: I got good grades in all subjects except English.
　B: You should have studied English harder.

⑤ A: Look at my face. I should have put on some sunscreen.
　B: Yes. You're right.

[울산 ○○중]

3. 다음 대화의 내용과 일치하는 것은? (4점)

A: We still have 30 minutes to go before we reach the top of the mountain. Let's sit down over there and have a snack.

B: Oh, I brought only water. I should have brought some snacks.

A: That's okay. I brought a lot. We can share.

B: I'll keep it in mind to bring some snacks next time.

① 산 정상에 도착하려면 아직 30분이 남았다.
② 30분 전에 간식을 먹고 출발하였다.
③ B는 간식을 나누어 준 것을 후회하였다.
④ A는 간식으로 생수를 준비하였다.
⑤ B는 A에게 간식 챙겨 올 것을 충고하였다.

[울산 ○○중]

4. 다음 대화의 내용과 일치하는 것은? (4점)

G: Ben, you look full of energy today!

B: Do I? Maybe that's because I finally got a good night's sleep last night.

G: Why? Don't you usually get enough sleep?

B: No, I know it's really important to get a good night's sleep, but I always stay up late surfing the Internet or playing with my phone.

G: That sometimes happens to me too.

B: After I do that, I regret it the next morning and say, "I should have gone to bed earlier last night."

G: How was yesterday different?

B: Well, yesterday afternoon I climbed the mountain with my dad. I was really tired when I got home. I went to sleep right after I went to bed.

G: Outdoor activities are a great way to help you get a good night's sleep.

① Ben looks tired today.

② Ben usually goes to bed early.

③ Ben didn't sleep well last night.

④ The girl climbed the mountain with her dad yesterday.

⑤ The girl thinks that outdoor activities are a good way to help us get a good night's sleep.

5. 위 대화의 괄호 (A), (B), (C) 안에 들어갈 말로 바르게 짝지어진 것은? (4점)

(A) — (B) — (C)

① up — happens — should have gone

② up — is happened — shouldn't have gone

③ up — happens — shouldn't have gone

④ down — is happened — shouldn't have gone

⑤ down — happens — should have gone

[5~6] 다음 대화를 읽고 물음에 답하시오.

G: Ben, you look full of energy today!

B: Do I? Maybe that's because I finally got a good night's sleep last night.

G: Why? Don't you usually get enough sleep?

B: No, I know it's really important to get a good night's sleep, but I always stay (A)[up / down] late surfing the Internet or playing with my phone.

G: That sometimes (B)[happens / is happened] to me too.

B: After I do that, I regret ⓐit the next morning and say, "I (C)[should have gone / shouldn't have gone] to bed earlier last night."

G: How was yesterday different?

B: Well, yesterday afternoon I climbed the mountain with my dad. I was really tired when I got home. I went to sleep right after I went to bed.

G: Outdoor activities are a great way to help you get a good night's sleep.

*G: Girl, B: Boy

6. 위 대화의 밑줄 친 ⓐ가 가리키는 것으로 가장 적절한 것은? (4점)

① 지난 밤 숙면을 취한 것

② 어제 오후에 아버지와 산행을 간 것

③ 숙면을 취하는 것이 중요하다고 여기는 것

④ 밤 늦게까지 인터넷 서핑을 하거나 휴대전화를 가지고 논 것

⑤ 밤 늦게까지 게임과 채팅을 하며 노느라 피곤하여 일찍 잠든 것

7. 다음 밑줄 친 두 개의 ⑺that이 다음 대화에서 의미하는 바로 가장 적절한 것은? (4점)

> G: Ben, you look full of energy today!
> B: Do I? Maybe that's because I finally got a good night's sleep last night.
> G: Why? Don't you usually get enough sleep?
> B: No, I know it's really important to get a good night's sleep, but I always stay up late surfing the Internet or playing with my phone.
> G: ⑺That sometimes happens to me too.
> B: After I do ⑺that, I regret it the next morning and say, "I should have gone to bed earlier last night."
> G: How was yesterday different?
> B: Well, yesterday afternoon I climbed the mountain with my dad. I was really tired when I got home. I went to sleep right after I went to bed.
> G: Outdoor activities are a great way to help you get a good night's sleep.

① 숙면을 취하는 것
② 아버지와 함께 등산하는 것
③ 일찍 자는 것
④ 인터넷 검색을 하거나 휴대폰을 가지고 놀면서 늦게까지 깨어 있는 것
⑤ 다양한 실외 활동에 적극적으로 참여하여 사회성과 체력을 기르는 것

8. 다음 대화의 빈칸에 알맞은 것은? (4점)

> G: Don't you usually get enough sleep?
> B: No, I know it's really important to get a good night's sleep, but I always stay up late surfing the Internet or playing with my phone.
> G: That sometimes happens to me too.
> B: After I do that, I regret it the next morning and say, "I _____ to bed earlier last night."

① had to
② should have
③ should have go
④ should have went
⑤ should have gone

9. 다음 주어진 문장의 특정 부분을 강조하는 구문을 만든 것 중, 그 의미나 어법이 적절하지 않은 것은? (4점)

> Hamin played soccer with Eric last Saturday.

① It was Hamin that played soccer with Eric last Saturday.
② It was played that Hamin soccer with Eric last Saturday.
③ It was soccer that Hamin played with Eric last Saturday.
④ It was with Eric that Hamin played soccer last Saturday.
⑤ It was last Saturday that Hamin played soccer with Eric.

10. 다음 중 어법상 <u>어색한</u> 것은? (4점)

① It was at the station that Layla met Jinho.

② It was his book who Jack lost at the market.

③ It is Minji and Jian who want to join the art club.

④ It was last year when my family traveled to Busan.

⑤ It was James that went to Amy's birthday party last Friday.

11. 다음 두 문장의 의미가 같도록 ⓐ와 ⓑ에 들어갈 말이 순서대로 짝 지어진 것은? (3점)

> As you laugh more, you get more beautiful.
> = (_____ⓐ_____) you laugh, (_____ⓑ_____) beautiful you get.

① The more – the more

② The more – the much

③ The much – the much

④ The many – the more

⑤ The more – the many

12. 다음 중 어법상 옳은 문장은? (5점)

① The longer I boil the soup, better it tastes.

② The fast you go, the earlier you will reach your grandma's house.

③ The more I heard about Mason, the much sympathetic I felt for him.

④ Less money you spend, the more money you will have in your account.

⑤ The more careful we are, the fewer mistakes we make.

How much time do you spend every day out in the sun? Not much, right? Most people are too busy, at school or at work to spend much time outdoors. (A)_____, the sun plays an important role in your health. It helps you stay healthy.

Everyone feels happier when the sun shines. This is because of serotonin, the body's happy hormone, The more sun you get, the more "happy hormone" the brain produces. When your serotonin level goes up, you feel happier and stronger. This helps you fight everyday stress. Serotonin also has a calming effect, helping you focus better on what you are doing. Moreover, serotonin helps you get a good night's sleep because it helps the brain produce a sleep hormone.

Sunshine does not just make you feel and sleep better. It also helps build strong bones. As you all know, it is calcium that builds strong bones and teeth. However, for the body to use calcium properly, it needs vitamin D. Interestingly, the skin creates vitamin D when sunlight shines on it. The easiest way to make strong bones is to go outside and enjoy the sun.

13. 빈칸 (A)에 들어갈 말로 알맞은 것은? (4점)

① Finally

② However

③ Therefore

④ In addition

⑤ In other words

14. 위 글에 언급된 세로토닌과 관련이 없는 설명은? (3점)

① 진정 효과가 있다.

② 뼈와 이를 튼튼하게 해준다.

③ 행복 호르몬이라고도 불린다.

④ 숙면을 할 수 있도록 도와준다.

⑤ 스트레스와 싸울 수 있도록 도와준다.

16. 위 글의 내용과 일치하지 않는 것은? (4점)

① 햇빛은 많은 장점이 있다.

② 매일 단 몇 분 동안이라도 햇빛을 쬐며 걷는 것은 당신의 몸과 마음에 좋다.

③ 여름의 절정 시간인 11시에서 3시 사이에는 햇빛을 피하는 것이 좋다.

④ 직사광선을 많이 쪼이는 것은 항상 당신의 몸에 좋다.

⑤ 자외선 차단제를 사용하여 당신의 얼굴과 목을 보호할 수 있다.

[15~16] 다음 글을 읽고 물음에 답하시오.

As you can see, sunshine has many benefits, but how can you enjoy its benefits safely? Fortunately, getting direct sunlight on your skin for 10 to 20 minutes a day is enough to benefit from ⓐit. Try to go out into the sun between classes or during lunch breaks and get sunshine on your arms and hands. A walk in the sun, for just a few minutes every day, is good for both your mind and your body. However, avoid the sun during peak summer hours, between 11 and 3, and use sunscreen to protect your face and neck. Enjoy the sun safely and see how a little sunshine can make a world of difference in your health and your mood.

[17~19] 다음 글을 읽고 물음에 답하시오.

(A)_____ does not just make you feel and sleep better. It also helps build strong bones. As you all know, it is calcium that builds strong bones and teeth. However, for the body to use calcium properly, it needs vitamin D. Interestingly, the skin creates vitamin D when sunlight shines on (B)it. The easiest way to make strong bones is to go outside and enjoy the sun.

17. 위 글의 흐름상 빈칸 (A)에 가장 알맞은 것은? (3점)

① Bone　　② Sunshine　　③ Calcium

④ Vitamin　　⑤ Tooth

15. 위 글의 내용상, ⓐit이 가리키는 것으로 가장 적절한 것은? (3점)

① benefit　　　　② sunshine

③ a world　　　　④ your skin

⑤ lunch break

18. 위 글의 밑줄 친 (B)가 의미하는 것은? (4점)

① a strong bone　　② the body

③ the skin　　　　④ sunlight

⑤ the sun

19. 위 글의 내용과 일치하지 <u>않는</u> 것은?　　　　　(4점)

① Sunshine helps build strong bones.

② Calcium builds strong bones and teeth.

③ The body needs vitamin D to use calcium properly.

④ The skin creates vitamin D when we sleep.

⑤ We need to go outside and enjoy the sun to make strong bones.

20. 다음 글의 빈칸에 알맞은 것은?　　　　　(3점)

Good morning. Welcome to the Weather Report. I'm Hana Kim. Here's today's weather for three cities in different parts of the world. The sun is shining and it's warm in Seoul. In the afternoon, there may be a shower. In New York, the rain stopped early this morning. It's clear now. In Paris, it'll be windy today. If you're in ＿＿＿＿＿＿, take your umbrella. Have a wonderful day.

① Seoul　　　　② Paris

③ New York　　　④ Seoul and Paris

⑤ Paris and New York

21. 다음 글의 흐름으로 보아, 빈칸에 들어갈 말로 가장 적절한 것은?　　　　　(3점)

Do you want to be healthy? I started mountain biking last month for my health. Mountain biking helps you stay healthy and can change your mood. ＿＿＿＿＿＿＿. It was my dad that advised me to do mountain biking. Thank you, Dad!

① The older my dad gets, the wiser he becomes.

② The harder you study, the better you will do.

③ The longer you ride a bike, the more tired you feel.

④ The more you ride a mountain bike, the more you will enjoy it.

⑤ The older I get, the more I realize that money is more important than time.

[22~24] 다음 글을 읽고 물음에 답하시오.

ⓐ As you can see, sunshine has many benefits, but how can you enjoy its benefits safely? ⓑ Fortunately, getting direct sunlight on your skin for 10 to 20 minutes a day is enough to benefit from Ⓐ<u>it</u>. ⓒ Try to go out into the sun between classes or during lunch breaks and get sunshine on your arms and hands. ⓓ A walk in the sun, for just a few minutes every day, is good for both your mind and your body. ⓔ Enjoy the sun safely and see how a little sunshine can make a world of difference in your health and your mood.

22. 위 글의 ⓐ~ⓔ 중, 글의 흐름상 아래 문장이 들어가기에 가장 알맞은 곳은? (4점)

> However, avoid the sun during peak summer hours, between 11 and 3, and use sunscreen to protect your face and neck.

① ⓐ   ② ⓑ   ③ ⓒ   ④ ⓓ   ⑤ ⓔ

23. 위 글의 밑줄 친 Ⓐ의 "it"이 의미하는 것은? (3점)

① benefit   ② skin   ③ sunshine
④ class   ⑤ world

24. 위 글의 내용과 일치하지 <u>않는</u> 것은? (4점)

① Sunshine has many benefits.
② Try to go out into the sun between classes or during lunch breaks.
③ Get sunshine on your arms and hands.
④ A walk in the sun, for just a few minutes every day, isn't good for both your mind and your body.
⑤ A little sunshine can make a world of difference in your health and your mood.

[25~26] 다음 글을 읽고 물음에 답하시오.

> Wash your hands after going out, using the toilet, touching or eating food, and using smartphones. It will ⓐ<u>remove</u> germs and harmful bacteria from our hands, ⓑ<u>prevent</u> the spread of diseases, and keep your environment safe, fresh, and clean.
> It is a good breakfast that helps the brain work ⓒ<u>properly</u>. When you eat a good breakfast, it improves your energy levels so that you can focus ⓓ<u>less</u> clearly on your task and remember things better.
> It is your smartphone that you should put away for your health. ⓔ<u>Staring</u> at your smartphone too much can cause back pain and eye problems. Give yourself a short break from time to time and stretch your body regularly.

25. 위 글의 제목으로 가장 적절한 것은? (4점)

① Tips for Healthier Life
② Negative Effect of Technology
③ Habits of Highly Effective People
④ Importance of Exercise in Daily Lives
⑤ Reasons Why People Should Eat Breakfast

26. 위 글의 밑줄 친 ⓐ~ⓔ 중, 문맥상 낱말의 쓰임이 적절하지 <u>않은</u> 것은? (4점)

① ⓐ   ② ⓑ   ③ ⓒ   ④ ⓓ   ⑤ ⓔ

27. 강조 용법으로 쓰인 문장이 <u>아닌</u> 것은? (3점)

① It is true that she is honest.
② It is Tom that I teach math.
③ It was a window that I broke yesterday.
④ It was on the street that I ran into Bob.
⑤ It was she that used this machine at first.

◎ 선택형 문항의 답안은 컴퓨터용 수정 싸인펜을 사용하여 OMR 답안지에 바르게 표기하시오.

◎ 서술형 문제는 답을 답안지에 반드시 검정 볼펜으로 쓰시오.

◎ 총 27문항 100점 만점입니다. 문항별 배점은 각 문항에 표시되어 있습니다.

[경기 ○○중]

1. 다음 밑줄 친 write a journal의 의미로 가장 적절한 것은?　　　(3점)

> Girl: I think it's important to write a journal after reading.
>
> Boy: I agree.

① 일지를 쓰다　　　② 운동을 하다
③ 여행을 가다　　　④ 취재를 하다
⑤ 명상을 하다

[경기 ○○중]

2. 다음 대화의 내용과 일치하지 않는 것은?　　　(3점)

> M: John, you are late again.
> B: I'm sorry. I took the wrong bus.
> M: I think you need to leave home a little earlier.
> B: I think so, too. Next time I won't be late.
> M: It's important to arrive at school on time.

① John은 이전에 늦은 적이 있다.
② M은 버스를 잘못 탔다.
③ M은 John이 집에서 좀 더 일찍 출발할 필요가 있다고 생각한다.
④ John은 다음에 늦지 않겠다고 다짐한다.
⑤ M은 학교에 제시간에 도착하는 것을 중요하게 생각한다.

[대전 ○○중]

3. 다음 대화의 밑줄 친 (A)의 의미로 가장 적절한 것은?　　　(4점)

> G: Ben, you look full of energy today!
> B: Do I? Maybe that's because I finally got a good night's sleep last night.
> G: Why? Don't you usually get enough sleep?
> B: No, I always stay up late surfing the Internet or playing with my phone.
> G: That sometimes happens to me too.
> B: After I do that, I regret (A)it the next morning and say, "I should have gone to bed earlier last night."
> G: How was yesterday different?
> B: Well, yesterday afternoon I climbed the mountain with my dad. I was really tired when I got home. I went to sleep right after I went to bed.
>
> G = Grace, B = Ben

① 등교 시간에 늦은 것
② 숙면의 중요성을 알게 된 것
③ 어제 오후에 아버지와 등산을 한 것
④ 등산 후 침대에 가자마자 바로 잠든 것
⑤ 휴대폰을 가지고 놀면서 늦게까지 깨어 있는 것

[대전 ○○중]

4. Why does the girl play tennis?　　　(4점)

> B: What did you do on the weekend?
> G: I played tennis. I have decided to exercise on the weekend for my health.
> B: Good for you. It's important to exercise regularly.
> G: Right. How about playing tennis with me?
> B: Why not?
>
> B = Boy, G = Girl

① To keep herself healthy
② To pass the time with friends
③ To relax and get some fresh air
④ To enjoy the sun and go outside
⑤ To reduce stress in her daily life

6. 다음 빈칸에 공통으로 들어갈 말은? (3점)

> 1. G: Your bag is too small.
>   B: Yes. I _____ brought a bigger one.
> 2. G: Aren't you cold?
>   B: Yes. I _____ worn a jacket.
> 3. B: We missed our flight.
>   G: Oh, no. We _____ come earlier.

① should give   ② should eat
③ should go   ④ should have
⑤ should be

5. 다음 빈칸 (A), (B)에 들어갈 말로 가장 적절한 것은? (4점)

> <가>
> B: What did you do on the weekend?
> G: I played tennis. I have decided to exercise on the weekend for my health.
> B: Good for you. It's ___(A)___ to exercise regularly.
> G: Right.
>
> <나>
> B: Mina, how was the movie?
> G: I didn't enjoy it. It was boring.
> B: What was bad about it?
> G: I already knew the ending. I ___(B)___ about it before seeing it.
> B: Oh, I'm sorry you didn't like it.

	(A)	(B)
①	important	should have read
②	important	shouldn't have read
③	important	must have read
④	unnecessary	should have read
⑤	unnecessary	shouldn't have read

7. 다음 대화의 내용과 일치하는 것은? (4점)

> Anna: John, you are late again.
> John: I'm sorry. I took the wrong bus.
> Anna: I think you need to leave home a little earlier.
> John: I think so, too. Next time I won't be late.
> Anna: It's important to arrive at school on time.

① John은 지각을 처음 했다.
② John은 택시를 잘못 탔다.
③ Anna는 John이 집에서 좀 더 빨리 출발할 필요가 있다고 생각한다.
④ John은 Anna의 조언에 동의하지 않는다.
⑤ Anna는 John이 반드시 제시간에 학교에 올 필요는 없다고 생각한다.

8. 다음 〈보기〉의 문장을 영어로 가장 바르게 옳긴 것은? (3점)

┌ 보기 ┐
지민이로부터 초대장을 받은 사람은 바로 브라이언이었다.
└────────┘

① It was Brian which got an invitation card from Jimin.
② It was Jimin that got Brian from an invitation card.
③ It was Brian that got an invitation card from Jimin.
④ It was Jimin which got an invitation card from Brian.
⑤ It was Brian that got Jimin from an invitation card.

9. What does the girl regret? (4점)

┌────────────────────┐
B: How was the movie?
G: I didn't enjoy it. It was boring.
B: What was bad about it?
G: I already knew the ending. I shouldn't have read about it before seeing it.
B: Oh, I'm sorry you didn't like it.

B = Boy, G = Girl
└────────────────────┘

① Taking the wrong bus
② Choosing a sad movie
③ Going to the movies alone
④ Visiting a science museum with her family
⑤ Reading about the movie before seeing it

10. 다음 〈보기〉의 문장을 영어로 가장 바르게 옳긴 것은? (4점)

┌ 보기 ┐
우리는 더 주의할수록 실수를 더 적게 한다.
└────────┘

① The careful we are, the mistakes we make.
② The careful we are, the few mistakes we make.
③ The carefuler we are, the few mistakes we make.
④ The more careful we are, the less mistakes we make.
⑤ The more careful we are, the fewer mistakes we make.

11. 다음 중 강조 용법으로 쓰인 문장이 <u>아닌</u> 것은? (3점)

① It was at school that Linda met Tim.
② It is true that exercise is good for your health.
③ It was his book that Jack lost at the market.
④ It is Minji and Jian who want to join the festival.
⑤ It was last year when my family traveled to Busan.

12. 다음 〈보기〉의 문장을 영어로 가장 바르게 옳긴 것은? (4점)

┌ 보기 ┐
David는 더 나이를 먹을수록, 더 현명해진다.
└────────┘

① The older David got, the wiser he became.
② The older David gets, the wiser he became.
③ The older David gets, the wiser he becomes.
④ The more old David gets, the wiser he becomes.
⑤ The more old David gets, the more wise he becomes.

13. 다음 밑줄 친 부분을 강조하는 문장으로 바르게 고친 것은? (4점)

Eric lent me a book in the library yesterday.

① It was Eric that lent me a book in the library yesterday.

② It was me that Eric lent a book in the library yesterday.

③ It was a book that Eric lent me in the library yesterday.

④ It was in the library that Eric lent me a book yesterday.

⑤ It was yesterday that Eric lent me a book in the library.

[14~16] 다음 글을 읽고 물음에 답하시오.

As you can see, sunshine has many benefits, but how can you enjoy its benefits safely? Fortunately, getting direct sunlight on your skin for 10 to 20 minutes a day is enough to benefit from it. Try to go out into the sun between classes or during lunch breaks and get sunshine on your arms and hands. A walk in the sun, for just a few minutes every day, is good for both your mind and your body. (A) However, avoid the sun during peak summer hours, between 11 and 3. (B) It is the time when the sun is usually strongest and if you stay for a long time, you may suffer skin damage. (C) Therefore, it is better to avoid it during that time. (D) Also, you should use sunscreen, and wear hats, sunglasses, or clothes to protect your face and neck from it.

(E) Staying in shade can be another good way to protect yourself from the harmful effects on sunlight. Keeping these tips, enjoy the sun safely and see how a little sunshine can make a world of difference in your health and your mood.

14. 위 글의 흐름으로 보아, (A)~(E) 중 주어진 문장이 들어가기에 가장 적절한 곳은? (4점)

This damage is because the sun's ultraviolet light can kill skin cells, which may cause skin cancer in the end.　　*ultraviolet light: 자외선

① (A)　　② (B)　　③ (C)　　④ (D)　　⑤ (E)

15. 위 글의 내용을 바르게 이해한 것은? (4점)

① 잠깐이라도 직접적으로 햇빛을 쬐는 것은 몸에 좋지 않아.

② 자외선은 우리 몸에 흡수될 때 긍정적인 영향을 미치는구나.

③ 오후 3시와 5시 사이의 햇빛은 피부를 손상시킬 위험이 있어.

④ 강한 햇빛을 피하기 위해 선크림을 바르거나 그늘에 있는 것은 도움이 돼.

⑤ 햇빛의 긍정적인 효과를 보려면 반드시 하루에 30분 이상 햇빛을 쬐어야 해.

16. 위 글의 주제로 가장 적절한 것은? (4점)

① 햇빛을 안전하게 즐기는 방법을 알고 실천할 필요가 있다.
② 햇빛이 우리 몸에 제공하는 다양한 이점들을 더 연구할 필요가 있다.
③ 햇빛의 유해한 물질을 막는 다양한 제품들이 개발될 필요가 있다.
④ 현대인의 바쁜 일상에서 햇빛의 이점을 즐길 수 있는 업무 환경이 보장되어야 한다.
⑤ 일상에서 다양한 방법으로 햇빛을 즐길 수 있는 야외 활동과 운동이 소개될 필요가 있다.

17. 다음 글에 드러난 'I'의 심경으로 가장 적절한 것은? (3점)

Do you want to be healthy? I started mountain biking last month for my health. Mountain biking helps you stay healthy and can change your mood. The more you ride a mountain bike, the more you will enjoy it. It was my dad that suggested I do mountain biking. Thank you, Dad!

① uneasy   ② gloomy
③ satistied   ④ frustrated
⑤ indifferent

[18~20] 다음 글을 읽고 물음에 답하시오.

Everyone feels happier when the sun shines. This is because of serotonin, ⓐthe body's happy hormone. The more sun you get, the more ⓑ"happy hormone" the brain produces. When your ⓒserotonin level goes up, you feel happier and stronger. This helps you fight everyday stress. Serotonin also has a calming effect, helping you focus better on what you are doing. Moreover, serotonin helps you get a good night's sleep because ⓓit helps the brain produce a sleep hormone.

(A)Sunshine does not just make you feel and sleep better. It also helps build strong bones. As you all know, it is calcium that builds strong bones and teeth. However, for the body to use calcium properly, ⓔit needs vitamin D. Interestingly, the skin creates vitamin D when sunlight shines on it. The easiest way to make strong bones is to go outside and enjoy the sun.

18. 위 글의 밑줄 친 ⓐ~ⓔ 중에서 지칭하는 것이 다른 하나는?(4점)

① ⓐ   ② ⓑ   ③ ⓒ   ④ ⓓ   ⑤ ⓔ

19. 위 글의 밑줄 친 (A)를 가장 올바르게 해석한 것은? (4점)

① 햇살은 단지 당신이 잠을 잘 자도록 만들 뿐이다.
② 햇살은 당신이 잠들었을 때 더 기분 좋게 만든다.
③ 햇살은 단지 당신이 더 기분 좋게 그리고 더 잘 자게 만드는 것만이 아니다.
④ 햇살은 당신을 더 기분 좋게 그리고 더 잠을 잘 자게 만들지 않는다.
⑤ 햇살은 단지 당신이 더 기분 좋게 그리고 더 잘 자게 만드는 것 밖에는 하지 않는다.

20. 위 글의 내용과 일치하지 않는 것은? (4점)

① 햇빛을 더 많이 쬐면 더 많은 행복 호르몬을 뇌가 생성한다.

② 세로토닌 수치가 올라갈수록 더 행복하고 강해짐을 느낀다.

③ 세로토닌은 뇌가 잠을 자게 하는 호르몬을 만들도록 도와서 수면에 도움이 된다.

④ 세로토닌은 강한 뼈와 이를 만드는 데 도움을 준다.

⑤ 피부에 햇빛을 쬐면 피부가 비타민 D를 만들어 낸다.

[21~22] 다음 글을 읽고 물음에 답하시오.

As you can see, sunshine has many ⓐbenefits, but how can you enjoy its benefits safely? Fortunately, getting ⓑdirect sunlight on your skin for 10 to 20 minutes a day is enough to benefit from (A)it. Try to go out into the sun ⓒbetween classes or during lunch breaks and get sunshine on your arms and hands. ⓓA walk in the sun, for just a few minutes every day, is good for both your mind and your body. However, avoid the sun during ⓔpeak summer hours, between 11 and 3, and use sunscreen to protect your face and neck. Enjoy the sun safely and see how a little sunshine can make a world of difference in your health and your mood.

21. 위 글의 밑줄 친 ⓐ~ⓔ를 우리말로 옮길 때 문맥상 의미가 잘못된 것은? (4점)

① 이점   ② 직사광선

③ 교실과 교실 사이   ④ 산책

⑤ 절정

22. 위 글의 밑줄 친 (A)it이 가리키는 것은? (3점)

① sunshine   ② body   ③ skin

④ health   ⑤ sunscreen

[23~25] 다음 글을 읽고 물음에 답하시오.

ⓐHow much time do you spend every day out in the sun? Not much, right? Most people are too busy at school or at work to spend much time outdoors. ⓑHowever, the sun plays an important role in your health. It helps you stay healthy.

Everyone feels happier when the sun shines. This is because of serotonin, the body's happy hormone. ⓒThe more sun you get, the less "happy hormone" the brain produces. ⓓWhen your serotonin level goes up, you feel happier and stronger. This helps you fight everyday stress. ⓔSerotonin also has a calming effect, helping you focus better on what you are doing. ⒶMoreover, serotonin helps you get a good night's sleep because (Ⓑ).

23. 위 글의 밑줄 친 ⓐ~ⓔ 중 글의 흐름상 어색한 것은? (4점)

① ⓐ   ② ⓑ   ③ ⓒ   ④ ⓓ   ⑤ ⓔ

24. 위 글의 밑줄 친 Ⓐ와 바꿔 쓸 수 있는 것은? (3점)

① But   ② However

③ And   ④ Furthermore

⑤ Therefore

25. 위 글의 빈칸 ⑧에 들어갈 말로 가장 적절한 것은? (4점)

① it helps keep the brain healthy
② it helps our serotonin level go down
③ it helps people feel happier and stronger
④ it helps the brain produces sleep hormone
⑤ it helps people get stressed out in their daily lives

26. 위 글의 내용과 가장 일치하지 <u>않는</u> 것은? (4점)

① 햇빛은 많은 장점이 있다.
② 한여름에는 12시에 햇빛을 쬐는 것이 좋다.
③ 햇빛은 신체와 정신 건강 모두에 좋다.
④ 쉬는 시간이나 점심시간에 밖에 나가 팔이나 손에 햇빛을 쬐는 것은 도움이 된다.
⑤ 한여름에는 자외선 차단제를 바르는 것이 햇빛으로부터 얼굴과 목을 보호할 수 있다.

[26~27] 다음 글을 읽고 물음에 답하시오.

As you can see, sunshine has many benefits, but how can you enjoy its benefits safely? (A)[Fortunately / Fortunate], getting direct sunlight on your skin for 10 to 20 minutes a day is enough to benefit from it. Try to go out into the sun between classes or during lunch breaks and get sunshine on your arms and hands. A walk in the sun, for just a few minutes every day, is good for (B)[either / both] your mind and your body. However, (C)[avoiding / avoid] the sun during peak summer hours, between 11 and 3, and use sunscreen to protect your face and neck. Enjoy the sun safely and see how a little sunshine can (D)[take / make] a world of difference in your health and your mood.

27. 위 글의 괄호 (A)~(D)에 들어갈 적절한 표현끼리 짝지은 것은? (4점)

	(A)	(B)	(C)	(D)
①	Fortunately	both	avoiding	make
②	Fortunately	either	avoiding	take
③	Fortunate	both	avoiding	make
④	Fortunate	either	avoid	take
⑤	Fortunately	both	avoid	make

◎ 선택형 문항의 답안은 컴퓨터용 수정 싸인펜을 사용하여 OMR 답안지에 바르게 표기하시오.

◎ 서술형 문제는 답을 답안지에 반드시 검정 볼펜으로 쓰시오.

◎ 총 25문항 100점 만점입니다. 문항별 배점은 각 문항에 표시되어 있습니다.

[전북 ○○중]

1. 다음 우리말 뜻이 <u>어색한</u> 것은?　(4점)

① overeat: 과식하다

② overwork: 과로하다

③ overpay: 초과 지급하다

④ overact: 과장된 연기를 하다

⑤ overestimate: 과소평가하다

[대전 ○○중]

2. 다음 대화의 내용과 일치하는 것은?　(4점)

B: Uncle John, look at my new bike. What do you think?

M: It's really nice. Where are you going?

B: To the park to meet a friend.

M: Where's your helmet?

B: I don't have one. It's just a short ride.

M: Put on your helmet. You may hurt yourself.

B: But I see a lot of people riding bikes without helmets.

M: You have to wear a helmet. It protects your head in an accident.

B: Okay. I'll get my dad's helmet.

M: No. You have to wear a helmet that fits you. If not, it cannot protect your head.

B: I guess I'll have to buy one for myself.

B = Boy, M = Uncle John

① 삼촌은 새로운 자전거를 샀다.

② 소년은 자신의 헬멧을 가지고 있다.

③ 삼촌은 친구를 만나러 공원에 가는 길이다.

④ 소년은 삼촌에게 안전을 위해 헬멧 착용을 권한다.

⑤ 헬멧을 쓰지 않고 자전거를 타는 사람이 많다.

[경기 ○○중]

3. 여자의 마지막 말에 대한 남자의 응답으로 가장 적절한 것은? (4점)

Man: You should not feed the animals.

Woman: Why?

Man: _____

① The animals can be safe.

② The animals may get sick.

③ The animals can be hunted.

④ The animals may be hungry.

⑤ The animals may not like to sleep.

[경기 ○○중]

4. 다음 대화의 내용과 일치하지 <u>않는</u> 것은?　(5점)

B: Mina, are you ready to leave?

G: No, not yet. I have to check if I turned off the gas.

B: If we don't leave now, we may not get to the concert in time.

G: Okay, but I have to check the gas first. It will only take a minute.

(G: girl, B: boy)

① Mina isn't sure if she turned off the gas.

② Mina wants to check the gas first before they leave.

③ They are going to go to a concert.

④ The boy thinks that they may be late if they don't leave now.

⑤ They have to stop by a gas station to check their car.

[5~7] 다음 대화를 읽고 물음에 답하시오.

B: Uncle John, look at my new bike. What do you think?

M: It's really nice. Where are you going?

(A)

B: I don't have one. It's just a short ride.

M: Put on your helmet. You may hurt yourself.

(B)

B: Okay. I'll get my dad's helmet.

M: No. You have to wear a helmet that fits you. If not, it cannot protect your head.

(C)

B: To the park to meet a friend.

M: Where's your helmet?

(D)

B: But I see a lot of people riding bikes without helmets.

M: You have to wear a helmet. It protects your head in an accident.

B: I guess I'll have to buy one for myself.

(B: boy, M: man)

[경기 ○○중]

5. 위 대화가 자연스러운 대화가 되도록 (A)~(D)를 적절하게 배열한 것은? (5점)

① (A)–(B)–(D)–(C)   ② (A)–(D)–(B)–(C)
③ (B)–(D)–(A)–(C)   ④ (C)–(A)–(D)–(B)
⑤ (C)–(D)–(A)–(B)

[경기 ○○중]

6. 위 대화의 내용과 일치하도록 빈칸 (A), (B)에 알맞은 것은? (4점)

Q: What does the boy's uncle tell him to do when riding a bike?

A: The boy's uncle advises him (A)_____ a helmet because it helps him (B)_____ his head in an accident.

(A)	(B)
① wear	hurt
② worn	to hurting
③ to wear	to not hurt
④ to wear	not to hurt
⑤ to have worn	not to be hurt

[경기 ○○중]

7. 위 대화의 안전 수칙으로 가장 적절한 것은? (3점)

① Check your bike regularly.

② Put on a helmet which fits you.

③ Drink water often on a hot day.

④ Wear gloves before riding a bike.

⑤ Tightly hold a bicycle handle with your hands.

8. 다음 대화의 빈칸 (A)에 들어갈 적절한 것은?　　　(3점)

> G: Mom, can I play outside this afternoon?
>
> W: Sure. (A)_____
>   before you go out.
>
> G: But it's sunny today. Do I have to take it?
>
> W: Yes, you do. The weather can change easily in rainy season.
>
> G: Okay. Then I'll take it now.
>
> (G: girl, W: woman)

① Never check the weather
② Forget to put on sunscreen
③ Call your friends to play with
④ Don't forget to take the umbrella
⑤ Walk down the wet stairs slowly

[9~10] 다음 글을 읽고 물음에 답하시오.

> (A)_____ camping trips can create sweet memories for many people, they can also be occasions when bad things happen. If you plan to go camping with family or friends this summer, you need to keep several things in mind for your safety.
>
> Listen to Yumin's family talk about their camping trip. (B)They seem to know what to do to make their camping trip safe and fun.

9. 위 글의 빈칸 (A)에 가장 적절한 것은?　　　(4점)

① As　　　　　　② Although
③ Unless　　　　④ While
⑤ Because

10. 위 글의 밑줄 친 (B)와 의미가 같은 것은?　　　(4점)

① They know what to do to make their camping trip safe and fun.

② It seems that they know what to do to make their camping trip safe and fun.

③ They seem that they know what to do to make their camping trip safe and fun.

④ It knows that they seem what to do to make their camping trip safe and fun.

⑤ It seems that they seem to know what to do to make their camping trip safe and fun.

11. 다음 두 문장이 같은 뜻이 되도록 빈칸에 알맞은 말을 쓰시오.

　　　(5점)

> He seemed to be very tired.
> = It seemed _____.

정답: _____

- 45 -

12. 다음 글에서 전체 흐름과 관계가 없는 문장은? (4점)

Although you would think that you are free from an earthquake, that is not true. Then, what should you do when it strikes? There are several things you need to keep in mind. ⓐFirst, when you are inside, stay inside and keep informed until the shaking stops. ⓑIt seems to be safe to go outside, but something might fall on you. ⓒAlso, turn off the gas and the electricity because they can cause a gas leak and an explosion and fire may happen. ⓓElectricity has a lot of benefits in our daily lives and you should learn how to use it wisely to save the energy. ⓔIn addition, to protect your head, get under the table and cover your head with your arms. Finally, instead of using the elevator, use the stairs. By following these tips, you can be safe from earthquakes.

① ⓐ   ② ⓑ   ③ ⓒ   ④ ⓓ   ⑤ ⓔ

13. 다음 문장 중 어법상 적절한 것은? (5점)

① Despite the rain, we played outside.

② Big trees might be strike by lightning.

③ Jason finished the race even though injuring.

④ This is the best novel who I have read until now.

⑤ The grades what he got this year were better than those from last year.

[14~16] 다음 글을 읽고 물음에 답하시오.

Although camping trips can create sweet memories for many people, they can also be occasions when bad things happen. If you plan to go ⓐcamping with family or friends this summer, you need to keep several things in mind for your safety.

Listen to Yumin's family ⓑto talk about their camping trip. They seem to know what ⓒto do to make their camping trip safe and fun.

Yumin: Dad, why don't we ⓓput up our tent over here by this river?

Dad: I don't think that's a good idea. If it starts to rain, the river might overflow.

Yumin: I know, but the sky is clear. I really like the sound of the water!

Dad: (A)_____ You never know when it might start to rain.

Yumin: Okay. Safety first! Let's find another place.

When you set up a tent, choose a flat, sunny area. Avoid places too close to big trees that might be ⓔstruck by lightning.

14. 위 글의 밑줄 친 ⓐ~ⓔ 중 어법상 어색한 것은? (4점)

① ⓐ   ② ⓑ   ③ ⓒ   ④ ⓓ   ⑤ ⓔ

15. 위 글의 흐름상 빈칸 (A)에 가장 알맞은 말은?   (4점)

① The weather can be always fine in the mountains.

② The weather isn't important in the mountains.

③ The weather doesn't change quickly in the mountains.

④ The weather can change slowly in the mountains.

⑤ The weather can change quickly in the mountains.

16. 위 글을 읽고, 다음 질문에 알맞은 대답을 고르면?   (4점)

> Q: What is the best place for setting up a tent?

① A flat, sunny area

② Near the river or sea

③ A wet place

④ Beside big trees

⑤ The place that can hear the sound of the water

17. 다음 〈보기〉의 문장과 같은 의미가 되도록 바꾼 것으로 적절한 것은?   (4점)

┌ 보기 ┐
Although I see him every day, I've never talked to him.
└─────┘

① Even though I see him every day, I've never talked to him.

② Because I see him every day, I've never talked to him.

③ Before I see him every day, I've never talked to him.

④ When I see him every day, I've never talked to him.

⑤ Though I see him every day, I've talked to him.

[18~19] 다음 글을 읽고 물음에 답하시오.

Although camping trips can create sweet memories for many people, they can also be occasions when bad things happen. If you plan to go camping with family or friends this summer, you need to keep several things in mind for your ⓐsafety.

Listen to Yumin's family talk about their camping trip. They seem to know what to do to make their camping trip ⓑsafe and fun.

Yumin: Dad, why don't we put up our tent over here by this river?

Dad: I don't think that's a good idea. If it starts to rain, the river might overflow.

- 47 -

Yumin: I know, but the sky is ⓒcloudy. I really like the sound of the water!

Dad: The weather can change ⓓslowly in the mountains. You never know when it might start to rain.

Yumin: Okay. Safety first! Let's find another place.

When you set up a tent, choose a flat, sunny area. ⓔAvoid places too close to big trees that might be struck by lightning.

[경기 ○○중]

18. 위 글의 밑줄 친 ⓐ~ⓔ 중, 내용상 흐름에 맞지 <u>않는</u> 것을 있는 대로 고른 것은? (5점)

① ⓐ, ⓑ
② ⓑ, ⓒ
③ ⓒ, ⓓ
④ ⓐ, ⓒ, ⓔ
⑤ ⓑ, ⓓ, ⓔ

[경기 ○○중]

19. 위 글의 내용과 일치하는 것은? (3점)

① 캠핑은 즐거운 경험보다 나쁜 경험을 더 많이 준다.
② Yumin의 가족은 방금 여름 캠핑을 다녀왔다.
③ Yumin의 가족은 강 옆에 텐트를 설치하려고 하고 있다.
④ 텐트를 설치하는 장소는 햇빛을 막아 주는 큰 나무 밑이 좋다.
⑤ Yumin의 아버지는 비가 올 때, 강이 범람할지 모른다고 생각한다.

[대전 ○○중]

20. 다음 문장을 바르게 영작한 것은? (4점)

> 나는 영어를 잘하지 못하지만, 영어 공부하는 것을 좋아한다.

① I'm good at English, although I love studying it.
② Although I'm good at English, I love studying it.
③ Although I'm not good at English, I love studying it.
④ Even though I'm good at English, but I love studying English.
⑤ Even though I'm not good at English, I don't like studying English.

[충남 ○○중]

21. 다음 두 문장의 의미가 같도록 바꿔 쓸 때 어법상 <u>어색한</u> 것은? (4점)

① It seemed that he was very tired.
   = He seemed to be very tired.
② It seems that she worries about everything.
   = She seems to worry about everything.
③ Kevin seems to like his new school.
   = It seems that Kevin like his new school.
④ The children seemed to be hungry.
   = It seemed that the children were hungry.
⑤ Mr. Kim seems to have been handsome.
   = It seems that Mr. Kim was handsome.

Hajun: Mom, I'm hungry. ⓐWhat's for lunch?

Mom: I'm cooking Samgyeopsal.

Hajun: Mom, (A)_____.
　　　Can we cook more in a bigger pan?

Mom: I'm going to cook more, but we have to use this small pan.

Hajun: Why do we have to use a small pan?

Mom: Because the pan should not be bigger than the burner. If you use a big pan, it ⓑsends the heat back to the burner, and the gas can explode!

Hajun: Oh, I didn't know that.

Here is one more tip about fire when you go camping. Never use a gas heater or burner inside a tent. Your tent may ⓒcatch fire, or you might ⓓpass out because the fire will ⓔuse up the oxygen in the tent as it burns.

[경기 ○○중]

22 위 글의 빈칸 (A)에 알맞은 문장을, 주어진 단어를 이용하여 알맞게 영작한 것은? (3점)

that / enough / not / be / all of us / for

① that is for enough not all of us
② that is not enough for all of us
③ enough is not for that all of us
④ enough is all of us not that for
⑤ all of us are that not enough for

[경기 ○○중]

23. 위 글의 밑줄 친 ⓐ~ⓔ의 의미로 적절하지 <u>않은</u> 것은? (4점)

① ⓐ: 점심이 뭐예요?　② ⓑ: 열을 뒤로 보내다
③ ⓒ: 불이 붙다　④ ⓓ: 의식을 잃다
⑤ ⓔ: 이용하다

[경기 ○○중]

24. 위 글의 위험 상황을 대비해 안전 요원이 할 말로 가장 적절한 것은? (4점)

① Choose a bigger pan than the burner to cook more.

② Never use gas when you cook something.

③ Use a gas heater or burner inside a tent if you are cold.

④ Make sure that the pan you use is smaller than the burner.

⑤ Use up the oxygen in the tent when your tent may catch fire.

[대전 ○○중]

25. 다음 행동 요령이 필요한 재난 상황으로 가장 적절한 것은? (4점)

This can cause big problems. However, you may not know what to do when it happens. There are several things you have to do. First, you have to turn off the water and the electricity. Second, pack water and food when you leave the house. Finally, you have to move to a high and safe place and keep listening to the weather report.

① Volcano eruption　② Lightning
③ Flooding　④ Earthquake
⑤ Electric shock

◎ 선택형 문항의 답안은 컴퓨터용 수정 싸인펜을 사용하여 OMR 답안지에 바르게 표기하시오.
◎ 서술형 문제는 답을 답안지에 반드시 검정 볼펜으로 쓰시오.
◎ 총 25문항 100점 만점입니다. 문항별 배점은 각 문항에 표시되어 있습니다.

[경기 ○○중]

1. 다음 대화의 빈칸에 공통으로 들어갈 말로 적절한 것은?   (3점)

B: Mina, are you ready to leave?
G: No, not yet. I _____ check if I turned off the gas.
B: If we don't leave now, we may not get to the concert in time.
G: Okay, but I _____ check the gas first. It will only take a minute.

① can   ② may   ③ might
④ have to   ⑤ was going to

[경기 ○○중]

2. 다음 대화의 빈칸에 들어갈 말로 적절하지 않은 것은?   (3점)

B: Let's go bowling.
G: I'm sorry. I can't. I have to go see a doctor.
B: Oh, _____
G: I don't know, but my stomach hurts.

① what's wrong?
② are you sick?
③ what's the matter?
④ what is your dream?
⑤ is there something wrong?

[경기 ○○중]

3. 다음 대화의 내용과 일치하지 않는 것은?   (4점)

Ben: Uncle John, look at my new bike. What do you think?
Uncle: It's really nice. Where are you going?
Ben: To the park to meet a friend.
Uncle: Where's your helmet?
Ben: I don't have one. It's just a short ride.
Uncle: Put on your helmet. You may hurt yourself.
Ben: But I see a lot of people riding bikes without helmets.
Uncle: You have to wear a helmet. It protects your head in an accident.
Ben: Okay. I'll get my dad's helmet.
Uncle: No. You have to wear a helmet that fits you. If not, it cannot protect your head.
Ben: I guess I'll have to buy one for myself.

① Ben은 새로운 자전거를 샀다.
② Ben은 친구를 만나러 공원에 가고 있다.
③ Ben의 아버지는 헬멧을 가지고 있다.
④ 삼촌은 헬멧의 중요성을 강조한다.
⑤ Ben은 헬멧을 사지 않을 것이다.

[대전 ○○중]

4. 엄마가 딸에게 당부하는 것으로 적절한 것은?   (4점)

G: Mom, can I play outside this afternoon?
M: Sure. Don't forget to put on sunscreen before you go out.
G: But it's cloudy today. Do I have to put on sunscreen?
M: Yes, you have to wear sunscreen every day.

① 선크림을 가지고 다녀야 한다.
② 화창한 날에만 선크림을 발라야 한다.
③ 날씨와 상관없이 매일 선크림을 발라야 한다.
④ 선크림은 피부에 좋지 않아 바를 필요가 없다.
⑤ 구름이 낀 날에는 선크림을 바를 필요가 없다.

[5~6] 다음 대화를 읽고 물음에 답하시오.

> B: Uncle John, look at my new bike. What do you think?
> M: It's really nice. (A)_____ are you going?
> B: To the park to meet a friend.
> M: (A)_____ is your helmet?
> B: I don't have one. It's just a ⓐshort ride.
> M: Put on your helmet. You may hurt yourself.
> B: But I see a lot of people riding bikes ⓑunderline{without} helmets.
> M: You ⓒhave to wear a helmet. It protects your head in an accident.
> B: Okay. I'll get my dad's helmet.
> M: No. You have to wear a helmet that ⓓfits you. If not, it cannot protect your head.
> B: I guess I'll have to buy one for ⓔyourself.

[경기 ○○중]

5. 위 대화에서 밑줄 친 표현의 쓰임이 어색한 것은? (5점)

① ⓐ   ② ⓑ   ③ ⓒ   ④ ⓓ   ⑤ ⓔ

[충남 ○○중]

6. 위 대화의 빈칸 (A)에 공통으로 들어갈 알맞은 표현은? (4점)

① Why   ② Who   ③ What
④ When   ⑤ Where

[경기 ○○중]

7. 다음 대화의 내용으로 보아 버너를 사용할 때 유의 사항을 가장 잘 설명하는 안내문을 고른 것은? (5점)

> Hajun: Mom, I'm hungry. What's for lunch?
> Mom: I'm cooking Samgyeopsal.
> Hajun: Mom, that's not enough for all of us. Can we cook more in a bigger pan?
> Mom: I'm going to cook more, but we have to use this small pan.
> Hajun: Why do we have to use a small pan?
> Mom: Because the pan should not be bigger than the burner. If you use a big pan, it sends the heat back to the burner, and the gas can explode!
> Hajun: Oh, I didn't know that.

① 버너보다 큰 팬은 사용하지 마십시오. 열이 버너로 되돌아 갈 수 있으므로 매우 위험합니다.
② 버너 밑면이 뜨거우니 사용시 불에 약한 장판이나 융단 등을 깔고 사용하지 마십시오. (특히 종이류, 돗자리류, 전기 장판류 등을 절대 깔고 사용하지 마십시오.)
③ 불꽃이 부탄가스 용기 쪽으로 가지 않게 각별히 주의하십시오. (가스 용기가 과열로 인해 폭발 위험이 있습니다.)
④ 의류를 말리는 데 사용하지 마십시오. (의류에 불이 붙어 화재 위험이 있습니다.)
⑤ 인화물질이 있는 곳에서는 사용하지 마십시오. (화재의 원인이 됩니다.)

8. 다음 중 어떤 상황에 관한 행동 요령인지 알맞은 것은? (4점)

There are several things you have to do. First, you have to turn off the water and the electricity. Second, pack water and food when you leave the house. Finally, you have to move to a high and safe place and keep listening to the weather report.

① Flooding
② Electric shock
③ Traffic accident
④ Earthquake
⑤ Snowstorm

[9~10] 다음 글을 읽고 물음에 답하시오.

Yumin: Ouch! Mosquitoes in our camp!

Mom: Oh, I forgot (A)_____ you to apply some bug spray. Here.

Yumin: Thanks, Mom. Oh, you know what? We can rub orange peels on our skin (B)_____ applying bug spray. It is a nature-friendly way to keep mosquitoes away.

Mom: That's interesting!

Garlic can also keep bugs away. You can place pieces of garlic at the entrance to the tent, and bugs will not come inside.

9. 위 글의 빈칸 (A), (B)에 알맞은 것은? (4점)

	(A)	(B)
①	telling	despite of
②	to tell	despite of
③	to tell	instead of
④	to telling	instead of
⑤	to be told	in order to

10. 위 글의 내용과 일치하지 않는 것은? (4점)

① Yumin knows a nature-friendly way to keep mosquitoes away.
② Mom didn't tell Yumin to apply some bug spray.
③ There are mosquitoes around the camping site.
④ Orange peels are used for keeping mosquitoes away.
⑤ Placing pieces of garlic at the gate of the tent isn't a useful way to keep bugs away.

11. 다음 글의 흐름상 어색한 것은? (4점)

Flooding can cause big problems. ⓐ However, you may not know what to do when it happens. There are several things you have to do. ⓑFirst, you have to turn off the water and the electricity. ⓒSecond, pack water and food when you leave the house to move to a safe place. ⓓIt seems to be safe to stay in your house, but your friend will help release your stress. ⓔFinally, you have to move to a high and safe place and keep listening to the weather report. By following these tips, you can be safe from the flooding.

① ⓐ　　② ⓑ　　③ ⓒ　　④ ⓓ　　⑤ ⓔ

12. 다음 〈보기〉의 문장과 같은 의미로 바꿔 쓴 것으로 적절한 것은?

(4점)

┌─ 보기 ├─

She seems to miss her family.

① It seems to miss her family.

② It seems that misses her family.

③ It seems to she misses her family.

④ It seems as she misses her family.

⑤ It seems that she misses her family.

13. 다음 문장의 빈칸에 들어갈 말로 알맞은 것은? (3점)

_____ we tried our best to win the game, we lost in the end.

① While   ② When   ③ Since

④ Until   ⑤ Although

[14~15] 다음 글을 읽고 물음에 답하시오.

H: Mom, I'm hungry. What's for lunch?

M: I'm cooking Samgyeopsal.

H: Mom, that's not enough for all of us. Can we cook more in a bigger pan?

M: I'm going to cook more, but we have to use this small pan.

H: Why do we have to use a small pan?

M: Because the pan should not be bigger than the burner. If you use a big pan, it sends the heat back to the burner, and the gas can explode!

H: Oh, I didn't know that.

Here is one more tip about fire when you go camping. Never use a gas heater or burner inside a tent because your tent may catch fire. And also, you might pass out. It's because the fire will use up the oxygen in the tent as it burns.

H = Hajun, M = Mom

14. 위 글의 내용과 일치하는 것은? (5점)

① 엄마는 불고기를 요리하고 있다.

② 모든 가족이 함께 고기를 굽고 있다.

③ 하준이는 음식이 충분하다고 생각한다.

④ 텐트 안에서 가스 버너를 사용하면 기절할 수 있다.

⑤ 가스 버너가 팬보다 크면 가스 폭발의 위험이 있다.

15. What does Hajun suggest that his mom do? (4점)

① They should have lunch earlier.
② She should cook Samgyeopsal inside the tent.
③ She should use a bigger burner.
④ They should eat other food for lunch.
⑤ She should cook more Samgyeopsal in a bigger pan.

17. 홍수 발생 시 행동 요령에 관한 다음 글의 내용과 일치하는 것은? (4점)

Flooding can cause big problems. However, you may not know what to do when it happens. There are several things you have to do. First, you have to turn off the water and the electricity. Second, pack water and food when you leave the house. Finally, you have to move to a high and safe place and keep listening to the weather report.

① 홍수는 큰 문제를 일으키지는 않는다.
② 모든 사람들은 홍수 대비책을 알고 있다.
③ 수도와 전기를 차단할 필요는 없다.
④ 집을 떠날 때는 물과 음식을 챙겨야 한다.
⑤ 안전하고 낮은 지대로 이동해야 한다.

16. 다음 글의 밑줄 친 부분 중 흐름상 자연스럽지 않은 것은? (4점)

We have prepared many activities for the two-day camping trip. Because we always think about your ⓐsafety first, we do our best to prepare for anything ⓑbad that may happen. We help people have ⓒuncomfortable stay by placing a can of bug spray in each tent so you can avoid getting ⓓbitten by mosquitoes. We hope everyone takes home good ⓔmemories of the trip.

① ⓐ   ② ⓑ   ③ ⓒ   ④ ⓓ   ⑤ ⓔ

18. 다음 문장의 밑줄 친 부분과 바꿔 쓸 수 있는 것은? (3점)

Although we tried our best to win the game, we lost in the end.

① Why   ② When
③ Until   ④ Even though
⑤ Since

Y: Dad, why don't we put up our tent over here by this river?

D: I don't think that's a good idea. If it starts to rain, the river might overflow.

Y: I know, but the sky is clear. I really like the sound of the water!

D: The weather can change quickly in the mountains. You never know when it might start to rain.

Y: Okay. Safety first! Let's find another place.

When you set up a tent, choose a flat, sunny area. Avoid places too close to big trees that might be struck by lightning.

Y = Yumin, D = Dad

[대전 ○○중]

19. 위 글을 읽고 다음 질문에 대답할 수 없는 것은? (4점)

① What is the weather like now?

② What is the name of the place they stayed?

③ Where is a good place for setting up a tent?

④ Why does Yumin want to put up their tent by the river?

⑤ What is the reason Yumin's father doesn't want to put up their tent by the river?

[대전 ○○중]

20. 위 글의 뒤에 바로 이어질 행동으로 가장 적절한 것은? (4점)

① They will play some games.

② They will have lunch together.

③ They will find another place to set up their tent.

④ They will check whether the river overflows or not.

⑤ They will listen to the sound of the water by the river.

[전북 ○○중]

21. 다음 글의 빈칸 (A), (B)에 들어갈 말이 차례대로 바르게 연결된 것은? (4점)

Here is one more tip about fire when you go camping. Never use a gas heater or burner inside a tent. Your tent may catch fire, or you might pass (A)_____ because the fire will use (B)_____ the oxygen in the tent as it burns.

(A) – (B)	(A) – (B)
① in – up	② out – up
③ in – out	④ up – out
⑤ out – in	

[대전 ○○중]

22. 다음 각 질문에 대한 대답을 〈보기〉에서 골라 순서대로 나열한 것은? (5점)

1. M: Don't run. You may fall.

   B: _____

2. B: Jumping into cold water without warming up can be dangerous.

   G: _____

3. G: Mom, I want to swim here.

   W: _____

4. B: Can I swim right after eating?

   G: _____

┤ 보기 ├

(A) Okay, but first you should check how deep the water is. It may be deeper than you think.

(B) Oh, okay. I will warm up.

(C) Okay, I won't run.

(D) Swimming with a full stomach can be uncomfortable.

① (A)–(B)–(C)–(D) ② (B)–(C)–(A)–(D)
③ (B)–(A)–(C)–(D) ④ (C)–(B)–(D)–(A)
⑤ (C)–(B)–(A)–(D)

[경기 ○○중]

23. 위 글의 밑줄 친 ⓐ∼ⓔ 중에서 어법상 <u>어색한</u> 것은?　(4점)

① ⓐ　　② ⓑ　　③ ⓒ　　④ ⓓ　　⑤ ⓔ

[23~25] 다음 글을 읽고 물음에 답하시오.

> Yumin: Dad, why don't we ⓐ<u>put up</u> our tent over here by this river?
>
> Dad: I don't think that's a good idea. If it ⓑ<u>starts</u> to rain, the river might overflow.
>
> Yumin: I know, but the sky is clear. I really like the sound of the water!
>
> Dad: The weather can ⓒ<u>change</u> quickly in the mountains. You never know when it might start to rain.
>
> Yumin: Okay. (A) _____ Let's find another place.
>
> When you set up a tent, choose a flat, sunny area. Avoid places too close to big trees that might be struck by lightning.
>
> Yumin: Ouch! Mosquitoes!
>
> Mom: Oh, I forgot to tell you ⓓ<u>apply</u> some bug spray. Here.
>
> Yumin: Thanks, Mom. Oh, you know what? We can rub orange peels on our skin instead of ⓔ<u>applying</u> bug spray. It is a nature-friendly way to keep mosquitoes away.
>
> Mom: That's interesting!
>
> Garlic can also keep bugs away. You can place pieces of garlic at the entrance to the tent, and bugs will not come inside.

[경기 ○○중]

24. 위 글의 내용과 일치하는 것은?　(4점)

① 산에서는 날씨가 급격히 변하기 때문에 비가 올 것을 예측할 수 없다.

② 산에서 텐트를 칠 때는 커다란 나무 밑에 치는 것이 좋다.

③ 오렌지 껍데기를 피부에 바르면 피부에 좋지 않다.

④ 오렌지 껍데기를 피부에 바르는 것은 자연을 파괴하는 방법이다.

⑤ 마늘을 텐트 앞에 두는 것은 벌레가 더 많이 생기도록 한다.

[울산 ○○중]

25. 위 글의 흐름상 빈칸 (A)에 들어갈 말로 가장 적절한 것은?　(4점)

① I don't care!　　② Safety first!

③ Money first!　　④ Help yourself!

⑤ Enjoy this moment!

정답 및 해설

Lesson 1 (중간) 1회

01 ①	02 ⑤	03 ①	04 ③
05 ⑤	06 ②	07 ②	
08 I was so busy that I couldn't go out for a walk.			
09 ③	10 ⑤	11 ④, ⑤	12 ③
13 ①	14 ⑤	15 ⑤	16 ③
17 ②	18 ③	19 ④	
20 아프카니스탄이 전쟁 중이어서			
21 ②	22 ⑤	23 ④	24 ③
25 ②	26 ⑤		

01 '무언가를 벗다[벗기다]'를 뜻하는 단어는 'remove(제거하다)' 이다

02 'I'll visit and join that club today.'라고 했다.

03 만화 동아리인 Edutoon에 대해 들어 보았는지 묻고 있는데 형이 웹툰 작가가 되고 싶어한다는 답은 어색하다.

04 (A) 완료형은 'have+과거분사'이므로 heard (B) 구할 수 있었던 것이므로 able (C) tell의 목적격 보어로 to leave가 적절하다.

05 '소년은 스키가 재활 치료에 적절하고 배우기 쉽다고 생각한다.'라는 언급은 없다.

06 앞에서 'Skiing is not easy. Not many people are good at skiing.'이라고 했으므로 그것이 존경받는 '이유'라는 것이 적절하다.

07 뒤에서 'He knocked on every door to tell people to leave the building.'이라고 했으므로 방법을 묻는 ②번이 적절하다.

08 'too+형용사/부사(+for+의미상의 주어)+to부정사'는 'so+형용사/부사+that+주어+can't ~'으로 쓸 수 있다.

09 (A) comes (B) something wrong (C) kept going

10 'A runner was just entering the stadium, but there was something wrong with his legs.'라고 했으므로 들어와서 이상이 생긴 것이 아니다.

11 ④ isn't she? ⑤ doesn't she?

12 (C)에서 다쳤지만 포기할 수 없었다 (A) 메달을 받을 수 없다는 것을 알았다 (D)에서 그렇지만 아프가니스탄을 대표해서 여기 온 것이다 (B) 그게 포기하지 못하고 달린 이유라고 알게 되는 순서가 적절하다.

13 '형용사/부사+enough for+의미상의 주어+to부정사'는 'so+형용사/부사+that+주어+can ~'으로 쓸 수 있다.

14 finally: 결국, 마침내

15 '바닥에 쓰러졌다'고 하는 것이 적절하므로 fell(fall의 과거형)을 쓴다.

16 '~ 동안'을 뜻하는 'during'이 적절하다. for는 보통 뒤에 숫자를 동반한 기간이 온다.

17 뒤쳐진 것이므로 behind가 적절하다.

18 뒤에서 'With wide eyes, he observes the world. All around him is light, form, and the Great Book of Nature.'라고 했으므로 ③번이 적절하다.

19 ⓐ get → got ⓑ can win → couldn't win ⓒ doesn't → isn't ⓔ to not give up → not to give up

20 'we have been at war for 16 years. That's why we were not able to send athletes to the Barcelona Olympics four years ago.'라고 했다.

21 폐막식 준비 중에 들어오는 선수가 있어서 준비를 멈춘 상황이므로 ②번이 적절하다.

22 다리를 다치고도 올림픽에서 마라톤을 끝까지 완주한 아프간 출신 선수에 대한 글이다.

23 와시키는 부상을 당했지만 경주를 끝냈다.

24 (A)와 ③: 명사적 용법 ①, ⑤: 부사적 용법 ②, ④: 형용사적 용법

25 폐막식 준비 중에 들어오는 선수가 있어서 준비를 멈춘 상황이므로 ②번이 적절하다.

26 'His passion and patience'가 주어이므로 ⓔ는 respected가 적절하다.

Lesson 1 (중간) 2회

01 ③	02 ⑤	03 ⑤	04 ④
05 ①	06 ④	07 ④	08 ①
09 ④	10 ①	11 ④	12 ④
13 ⑤	14 ②	15 ⑤	16 ②
17 ④	18 ②	19 ③	20 ⑤
21 ③	22 ②	23 ③	

01 'He won the first gold medal for Korea in the 2018 Winter Paralympics.'라고 했다.

02 친구 사귀는 것에 대해 걱정하는 사람에게 많은 친구를 사귈 거라고 응하고 있다.

03 ① to learn ② to tell ③ who → that ④ the wiser

04 부정사의 부정은 'not[never] to+동사원형'의 형태이다.

05 앞에서 'Skiing is not easy. Not many people are good at skiing.'라고 했으므로 'respected'가 적절하다.

06 ⓐ에서 'D.I.Y.'에 대해 들어 봤는지 묻자 ⓒ에서 아니라며 무엇인지 묻고 ⓑ에서 설명하며 요즘 필통을 만들고 있다고 답하자 ⓔ에서 그 다음에는 무엇을 만들지 묻고 ⓓ에서 책상을 만들

거라고 답하는 순서이다.

07 'too+형용사/부사(+for+의미상의 주어)+to부정사'는 'so+형용사/부사+that+주어+can't ~'로 쓸 수 있다.

08 ② I am too short to reach the top shelf. ③ We are too late to catch the last train. ④ The cellphone was too expensive to buy. ⑤ My brother is too young to see that horror movie.

09 무슨 일인지 묻자 (C)에서 다쳤지만 포기할 수 없었다고 답하고 (A)에서 메달을 받을 수 없다는 것을 알았다고 생각한다고 하자 (B)에서 아프가니스탄을 대표해서 여기 온 유일한 선수라 포기할 수 없었다고 답하는 순서가 적절하다.

10 'Yes, we have been at war for 16 years. That's why we were not able to send athletes to the Barcelona Olympics four years ago.'라고 했다.

11 'Then he became especially interested in skiing.'이라고 했고 'Skiing is not easy. Not many people are good at skiing.'이라고 했다.

12 노래 대회에서 우승하고 싶은데 수줍어서 많은 사람 앞에서 노래를 못하니 반에서 먼저 노래 연습을 하겠다는 글에서 좋아하는 밴드의 콘서트를 보고 싶다는 ⓓ는 어색하다.

13 (A) runners를 수식하는 coming (B) keep ~ing: 계속 ~하다 (C) ran과 병렬로 fell이 적절하다.

14 폐막식을 준비하고 있는 동안에 경기장으로 들어왔다.

15 ⓔ는 not to let it happen이 적절하다.

16 'I am proud of myself and proud to be from Afghanistan. I didn't come here to win. For me, it was enough to be here and to finish the race.'에서 ②번이 적절함을 알 수 있다.

17 다친 다리로 마라톤을 마지막까지 완주하여 마지막으로 들어온 선수에 대한 글이므로 ④번이 적절하다.

18 ⓑ는 another runner가 주어이므로 comes가 되어야 한다.

19 1. X 2. O 3. O 4. X 5. O

20 Wasiqi는 끝까지 포기하지 않고 완주했다.

21 ⓒ give up: 포기하다

22 동사 start는 to부정사와 동명사를 목적어로 쓸 수 있다.

23 'Yes, we have been at war for 16 years. That's why we were not able to send athletes to the Barcelona Olympics four years ago.'라고 했다.

Lesson 2 (중간)

01 ②	02 ④	03 ②	04 ①
05 ③	06 ⑤	07 ②	08 ③
09 ④	10 ③	11 ⑤	
12 (1) Having a bad cold			
(2) Standing by the tree			
13 ⑤	14 ②	15 ④	16 ③
17 ④	18 ④	19 ③	20 ⑤
21 ⑤	22 ④	23 ②	24 ⑤

01 'Don't worry. I'm sure ~'는 안심시키는 표현이다.

02 새로운 친구 사귀는 것에 대해 걱정하자 걱정하지 말라며 많은 친구를 못 사귈 거라고 하는 것은 어색하다.

03 ⓑ의 'I don't know, but I know'는 'I know, but I don't know'가 되어야 한다.

04 'The team project for English class is taking a lot of time.'이라고 했다.

05 'One of the people on our team isn't doing his part.'라며 'what should I do?'라고 했다.

06 'One of the people on our team isn't doing his part.'라고 했다.

07 순서대로 team project, your part, how to get started, help you, help me이다.

08 ③번을 제외한 나머지는 앞과 뒤의 호응이 일치하지 않는다.

09 진호와 미나와 말했다고 하자 (B)에서 팀에서 할 일을 결정했는지 묻고 (D)에서 아니라며 두 사람의 의견이 다른 것을 말하고 (C)에서 누구 의견에 동의하는지 묻고 (A)에서 미나에게 동의한다고 하자 그럼 진호를 설득시키라고 하는 순서가 적절하다.

10 엄격하다면서 동의하는지 묻자 빈칸 뒤에서 'I don't think he's too strict.'라고 했으므로 ③번이 적절하다.

11 ① A pretty doll was made for me by her. ② He was seen to enter the room by me. ③ The movie is thought to be touching by them. ④ The walls were being painted by the kids.

12 분사구문은 주절과 종속절의 주어가 같을 때, 종속절의 접속사와 주어를 삭제하고 동사를 현재분사로 바꾸는 것이다. 이때 being은 생략 가능하다. (1) As I have → Having (2) While he was standing → (Being) Standing

13 '-thing'으로 끝나는 부정대명사는 형용사가 뒤에서 수식하므로 ⓔ는 something wrong이 되어야 한다.

14 anymore는 '더 이상'이라는 뜻으로 any longer로 바꿔 쓸 수 있다.

15 'Maybe you should just ask her if there is something wrong.'이라고 했다.

16 ⓐ She had to be prepared for an important presentation for the next day. ⓑ she realized there was something wrong ⓓ An idea struck her and she called her friend. ⓔ If you come to my place and drop the dog, I will be able to walk it later.

17 (A) 수동태이므로 asked (B) end up -ing: 결국 ~하게 되다

18 'She wants to say no but does not want to hurt his feelings.'라고 했으므로 ④번이 적절하다.

19 간접의문문이므로 ⓒ는 why you can't go가 되어야 한다.

20 'I like him, but for now I don't want to go out with him. I need to focus on my studies.'라고 했다.

21 뒤에 절이 이어지므로 (e)의 because of는 because로 고쳐야 한다.

22 ⓓ if there is something wrong

23 분사구문은 주절과 종속절의 주어가 같을 때, 종속절의 접속사와 주어를 삭제하고 동사를 현재분사로 바꾸는 것이므로 as he를 삭제하고 thinks를 thinking으로 고친다.

24 '그가 네 감정을 오해해서 그를 더 아프게 할 수도 있다.'라고 하는 것이 자연스러우므로 (e)의 understand를 misunderstand로 고치는 것이 적절하다.

Lesson 2 (중간)

01 ④	02 ④	03 ①	04 ②
05 ②	06 Who[Whom] do you agree with		
07 ④	08 ①	09 ②	10 ②
11 ⑤	12 ⑤	13 ④	14 ②
15 ③	16 ①	17 ①	18 ⑤
19 ③	20 ①	21 ③	22 ⑤
23 ④	24 Not knowing what to do		
25 ④	26 ①	27 ②	

01 동의를 구하자 동의한다고 하고 반대되는 의견을 말하고 있으므로 어색하다.

02 'Then maybe we should all get together and talk about it.'이라고 했으므로 ④번이 적절하다.

03 Emma는 'One of the people on our team isn't doing his part.'라고 했다.

04 Jane은 'One of the people on our team isn't doing his part.'라고 했다.

05 그러면: then 어떻게 하면 좋을까?: What should I do? do의 목적어가 있어야 하므로 what을 써야 함에 주의한다.

06 뒤에서 'I agree with Mina'라고 답하고 있으므로 '누구와 동의하는지' 묻는 것이 적절하다.

07 ④번은 앞과 뒤의 호응이 적절하지 않다.

08 무슨 일인지 묻자 (B)에서 동생이 화났다고 하고 (A)에서 무엇을 했는지 묻고 (C)에서 물어보지도 않고 그녀의 옷을 입었다고 답하고 (D)에서 미안하다고 하면 이해해 줄 거라고 하는 순서가 적절하다.

09 분사구문의 부정은 not이나 never를 분사 앞에 쓴다.

10 'When she heard about the accident'에서 접속사와 주어를 지우고 동사를 현재분사로 만든다.

11 'I wore one of her shirts without asking.'이라고 했다.

12 ⑤번은 조건절을 이끄는 접속사이지만 나머지는 명사절을 이끄는 접속사이다.

13 ④번은 조건절을 이끄는 접속사이지만 나머지는 명사절을 이끄는 접속사이다.

14 asked me out: 나에게 데이트 신청을 했다

15 비교급을 강조하는 것으로 very는 쓸 수 없다.

16 'I need to focus on my studies.'라고 했다.

17 (a)는 Sohui이고 나머지는 모두 Hayeon이다.

18 Sohui가 걱정이 있어서 언니와 상의하는 글이다.

19 'Maybe you should just ask her if there is something wrong.'이라고 했다.

20 '이유'를 나타내는 분사구문이다.

21 소희와 민경이 모두 걱정거리를 상담하고 있다.

22 민경이가 무슨 과목을 더 열심히 공부하고 싶어하는지는 알 수 없다.

23 십대들이 가지고 있는 다양한 걱정거리에 대한 글이다.

24 접속사와 주어를 삭제한 후 knowing을 쓰고 그 앞에 not을 쓴다.

25 뒤에서 'When I see her at school, she turns around and walks away from me.'라고 했으므로 avoiding이 적절하다.

26 (B) '~할 때'를 의미하는 When, (C) 이유를 나타내는 why

27 소희가 하연이에게 용서를 빌고 싶어 한다는 언급은 없다.

Lesson 3 (기말)

01 ③	02 ③	03 ①	04 ⑤
05 ①	06 ④	07 ④	08 ⑤
09 ②	10 ②	11 ①	12 ⑤
13 ②	14 ②	15 ②	16 ④
17 ②	18 ③	19 ④	20 ①
21 ④	22 ⑤	23 ③	24 ④
25 ①	26 ④	27 ①	

01 문맥상 'sunshine(햇빛)'이 적절하다.

02 가방이 너무 작다고 하는데 더 작은 가방을 갖고 왔어야 했다고 하는 것은 어색하다.

03 'We still have 30 minutes to go before we reach the top of the mountain.'이라고 했다.

04 'Outdoor activities are a great way to help you get a good night's sleep.'이라고 했다.

05 (A) stay up: (평상시보다 더 늦게까지) 안 자다[깨어 있다] (B) happen은 자동사이므로 수동태로 쓰이지 않는다. (C) 'should have+과거분사'는 '~했어야 했다'라는 의미로 과거의 사실에 대한 안타까움이나 후회를 나타낸다. 문맥상 should have gone이 적절하다.

06 후회하는 내용으로 ④번이 적절하다.

07 앞에서 말한 'stay up late surfing the Internet or playing with my phone'을 가리킨다.

08 'should have+과거분사'는 '~했어야 했다'라는 의미로 과거의 사실에 대한 안타까움이나 후회를 나타낸다. 문맥상 should have gone이 적절하다.

09 'It was'와 'that' 사이에 강조하고자 하는 것을 쓰고 나머지는 that 뒤에 쓰면 된다. 이 구문은 동사를 강조할 수는 없다.

10 'It was ~ that' 강조구문에서 that 대신에 강조하는 것이 사람이면 who, 사물이면 which, 시간이면 when, 장소면 where를 쓸 수 있다. ②에서 who를 that[which]으로 고쳐야 한다.

11 'the 비교급+주어+동사 ~, the 비교급+주어+동사 …'는 '~할수록 …하다'라는 뜻으로 'As+주어+동사 ~, 주어+동사 …'로 바꿔 쓸 수 있다.

12 ① better → the better ② The fast → The faster ③ the much → the more ④ Less → The less

13 상반되는 말이 이어지므로 However가 적절하다.

14 뼈와 이를 튼튼하게 해 주는 것은 칼슘이다.

15 ⓐit은 앞에 나온 sunshine을 가리킨다.

16 'However, avoid the sun during peak summer hours, between 11 and 3, and use sunscreen to protect your face and neck.'라고 했다.

17 햇빛이 우리 건강에 미치는 영향에 대한 글이므로 Sunshine이 적절하다.

18 밑줄 친 (B)는 앞에 나온 the skin을 가리킨다.

19 'the skin creates vitamin D when sunlight shines on it'이라고 했다.

20 'The sun is shining and it's warm in Seoul. In the afternoon, there may be a shower.'라고 했다. shower: 소나기

21 mountain biking에 관한 글이므로 'the 비교급+주어+동사 ~, the 비교급+주어+동사 …' 구문을 이용하여 mountain biking을 언급하고 있는 ④번이 적절하다.

22 주어진 문장의 However로 ⓔ 앞의 내용과 상반되므로 ⓔ가 적절하다.

23 ⓐ의 "it"은 sunshine을 의미한다.

24 'A walk in the sun, for just a few minutes every day, is good for both your mind and your body.'라고 했다.

25 손 씻기, 아침 먹기, 스마트폰 멀리하기 등을 통해 건강을 증진시킬 수 있다는 글이므로 ①번이 적절하다.

26 앞에서 'it improves your energy levels'라고 했으므로 ⓓ의 less를 more로 고치는 것이 적절하다.

27 ①번은 '가주어-진주어' 구문이다.

Lesson 3 (기말)

01 ①	02 ②	03 ⑤	04 ①
05 ②	06 ④	07 ③	08 ③
09 ⑤	10 ⑤	11 ②	12 ③
13 ③	14 ③	15 ④	16 ①
17 ③	18 ⑤	19 ③	20 ④
21 ③	22 ①	23 ③	24 ④
25 ④	26 ②	27 ⑤	

01 write a journal: 일지를 쓰다 journal: 일지, 일기

02 John이 'I'm sorry. I took the wrong bus.'라고 했다.

03 후회하는 내용으로는 ⑤번이 적절하다.

04 'I have decided to exercise on the weekend for my health.'라고 했다.

05 (A) 정기적으로 운동하는 것은 중요하다. (B) 읽지 말았어야 했다고 후회하는 것이 적절하다.

06 'should have+과거분사'는 '~했어야 했다'라는 의미로 과거의 사실에 대한 안타까움이나 후회를 나타낸다.

07 Anna는 'I think you need to leave home a little earlier.'라고 했다.

08 'It was'와 'that' 사이에 강조하고자 하는 것을 쓰고 나머지는 that 뒤에 쓰면 된다. 강조 전의 문장은 'Brian got an invitation card from Jimin.'이다.

09 소녀는 그 영화에 대해 읽지 말았어야 했다고 후회한다.

10 'the 비교급+주어+동사 ~, the 비교급+주어+동사 …'는 '더 ~할수록 더 …하다'라는 뜻이다.

11 'It was ~ that' 강조구문에서 that 대신에 강조하는 것이 사람이면 who, 사물이면 which, 시간이면 when, 장소면 where를 쓸 수 있다. ②번은 '가주어-진주어' 구문이다.

12 'the 비교급+주어+동사 ~, the 비교급+주어+동사 …'는 '~할수록 …하다'라는 뜻이다.

13 'It was'와 'that' 사이에 강조하고자 하는 것을 쓰고 나머지는 that 뒤에 쓰면 된다.

14 주어진 문장의 This damage가 가리키는 것이 (C) 앞의 skin damage이므로 (C)가 적절하다.

15 'Also, you should use sunscreen, and ~ to protect your face and neck from it. Staying in shade can be another good way to protect yourself from the harmful effects on sunlight.'라고 했다.

16 'sunshine has many benefits, but how can you enjoy its benefits safely?'에서 답을 찾을 수 있다.

17 'The more you ride a mountain bike, the more you will enjoy it.'과 'Thank you, Dad!' 등에서 ③번이 적절함을 알 수 있다. uneasy: 불안한 gloomy: 울적한, 침울한 frustrated: 좌절감을 느끼는 indifferent: 무관심한

18 ⓔ는 the body를 가리키고, 나머지는 모두 serotonin을 가리킨다.

19 다음 문장의 also와 함께 'not just[only] A (but) also B' 구문을 이룬다.

20 세로토닌이 아니라 햇빛이 강한 뼈와 이를 만드는 데 도움을 준다.

21 between classes: 수업 시간 사이

22 (A)의 it은 앞에 나온 sunshine을 가리킨다.

23 ⓒ는 'The more sun you get, the more "happy hormone" the brain produces.'가 되어야 한다.

24 Moreover = Furthermore: 더욱이

25 '숙면을 취하도록 해 준다'고 한 이유에 해당하는 것으로 ④번이 적절하다.

26 However, avoid the sun during peak summer hours, between 11 and 3, and use sunscreen to protect your face and neck.'이라고 했다.

27 (A) 문장 전체를 수식하는 부사 Fortunately (B) both A and B: A와 B 둘 다 (C) 명령문이므로 avoid (D) make a world of difference: 큰 차이를 만들다

Lesson 4 (기말)

01 ⑤	02 ⑤	03 ②	04 ⑤
05 ④	06 ④	07 ②	08 ④
09 ②	10 ②		
11 that he was very tired			
12 ④	13 ①	14 ②	15 ⑤
16 ①	17 ①	18 ③	19 ⑤
20 ③	21 ③	22 ②	23 ⑤
24 ④	25 ③		

01 overestimate: 과대평가하다

02 'But I see a lot of people riding bikes without helmets.'라고 했다.

03 동물들에게 먹이를 주지 말라고 하자 이유를 물었으므로 그에 적절한 답은 ②번이다.

04 주유소에 들려야 한다는 언급은 없다. gas station: 주유소

05 어디로 가느냐는 질문에 이어 (C)에서 공원으로 간다는 답에 이어 헬멧을 묻고 (A)에서 없다고 답하고 헬멧을 써야 한다고 하자 (D)에서 많은 사람들이 안 쓴다고 하자 써야만 한다고 하고 (B)에서 아빠 것을 쓰겠다고 하자 맞는 것을 써야 한다고 하고 하나 사야겠다는 말로 이어지는 것이 자연스럽다.

06 (A) advises의 목적격 보어로 to부정사(내용상 능동) (B) helps의 목적격 보어로 동사원형이나 to부정사(내용상 능동)가 적절하며 to부정사의 부정은 to부정사 앞에 not을 붙인다.

07 자신에게 맞는 헬멧을 써야 한다는 내용이다.

08 'The weather can change easily in rainy season.'이라고 했으므로 ④번이 적절하다.

09 뒤에 절이 이어지며 주절의 내용과 상반되므로 'although'가 적절하다.

10 'seem to'는 'It seems that ~'으로 바꿔 쓸 수 있다. 이때 'that'절의 시제는 주절의 시제와 일치시킨다.

11 'seem to'는 'It seems that ~'으로 바꿔 쓸 수 있다. 이때 'that'절의 시제는 주절의 시제와 일치시킨다.

12 지진 발생시의 행동 요령을 쓴 글에서 전기가 유용하며 에너지를 절약해야 한다는 ⓓ는 어색하다.

13 ② strike → struck ③ even though → despite ④ who → that ⑤ what → that[which]

14 지각동사 Listen to의 목적격 보어로 ⓑ는 동사원형 talk가 되어야 한다.

15 뒤에서 'You never know when it might start to rain.'이라고 했으므로 ⑤번이 적절하다.

16 'When you set up a tent, choose a flat, sunny area. Avoid places too close to big trees that might be struck by lightning.'이라고 했다.

17 'although'는 '비록 ~이긴 하지만, ~에도 불구하고'를 뜻하는 접속사로 부사절을 이끌며 비슷한 접속사로는 'even though'와 'though'가 있다.

18 ⓒ cloudy → clear ⓓ slowly → quickly

19 'I don't think that's a good idea. If it starts to rain, the river might overflow.'라고 했다.

20 'although'는 '비록 ~이긴 하지만, ~에도 불구하고'를 뜻하는 접속사로 부사절을 이끌며 'although+주어+동사'의 순서로 쓴다.

21 'seems to'를 'It seems that ~'으로 바꿔 쓸 때 'that'절의 시제는 주절의 시제와 일치시켜야 하므로 ③번은 'It seems that Kevin likes his new school.'로 likes로 써야 한다.

22 'that'을 주어로 쓰고 'is not enough'로 서술한 후 'for all of us'를 쓴다.

23 use up: ~을 다 써 버리다

24 버너보다 큰 팬을 쓰면 안 된다는 내용이 적절하다.

25 물과 전기를 끄고 물과 음식을 싸서 높고 안전한 곳으로 가라고 했으므로 'Flooding(홍수)'이 적절하다.

Lesson 4 (기말)

01 ④	02 ④	03 ⑤	04 ③
05 ⑤	06 ⑤	07 ①	08 ①
09 ③	10 ⑤	11 ④	12 ⑤
13 ⑤	14 ④	15 ⑤	16 ③
17 ④	18 ④	19 ②	20 ③
21 ②	22 ⑤	23 ④	24 ①
25 ②			

01 '~해야만 한다'라는 의미의 '의무'를 나타내는 have to가 적절하다.

02 I don't know, but my stomach hurts.'라는 대답으로 보아 '무엇이 문제인지 묻는 질문'이 적절하다. ④번은 꿈이 무엇인지 묻고 있다.

03 Ben은 'I guess I'll have to buy one for myself.'라고 했다.

04 엄마가 'Yes, you have to wear sunscreen every day.'라고 했다.

05 주어와 같은 대상이며, 주어가 I이므로 myself가 적절하다.

06 'To the park'라는 대답으로 보아 '장소'를 물었음을 알 수 있다.

07 'Because the pan should not be bigger than the burner. If you use a big pan, it sends the heat back to the burner, and the gas can explode!'라고 했다.

08 물과 전기를 끄고 물과 음식을 싸서 높고 안전한 곳으로 가라고 했으므로 'Flooding(홍수)'이 적절하다.

09 (A) forget+to부정사: 미래의 일, forget+동명사: 과거의 일 (B) instead of: ~ 대신에

10 'Garlic can also keep bugs away. You can place pieces of garlic at the entrance to the tent, and bugs will not come inside.'라고 했다.

11 홍수 때 취할 행동 요령을 설명하는 글에서 집에 머물라는 ⓓ는 어색하다.

12 'seem to'는 'It seems that ~'으로 바꿔 쓸 수 있다. 이때 'that'절의 시제는 주절의 시제와 일치시킨다.

13 뒤에 절이 이어지며 주절의 내용과 상반되므로 'although'가 적절하다.

14 'Never use a gas heater or burner inside a tent because your tent may catch fire. And also, you might pass

15 'Can we cook more in a bigger pan?'이라고 했다.

16 벌레 퇴치 스프레이를 두었다고 했고 좋은 추억을 가지고 가라고 한 것으로 보아 ⓒ는 comfortable이 적절하다.

17 'Second, pack water and food when you leave the house.'라고 했다.

18 'although' 대신 'even though'나 'though'를 쓸 수 있다.

19 그들이 머물고 있는 장소 이름은 알 수 없다.

20 글의 마지막 부분에서 'Let's find another place.'라고 했다.

21 (A) pass out: 의식을 잃다, 기절하다 (B) use up: ~을 다 써 버리다

22 1. 'Don't run.': (C) 2. 'warming up': (B) 3. 'swim': (A) 4. 'right after eating': (D)

23 tell의 목적격 보어이므로 ⓓ는 to apply가 되어야 한다.

24 'The weather can change quickly in the mountains. You never know when it might start to rain.'이라고 했다.

25 아빠의 말을 듣고 'Let's find another place.'라고 했으므로 ②번이 적절하다.